THE
WELL-TRAINED
MIND

ALSO BY SUSAN WISE BAUER

The Well-Educated Mind: A Guide to the Classical Education You Never Had,
revised and expanded ed. (W. W. Norton, 2015)

*The Story of Western Science: From the Writings of Aristotle
to the Big Bang Theory*
(W. W. Norton, 2015)

The History of the World Series
(W. W. Norton)
The History of the Ancient World (2007)
The History of the Medieval World (2010)
The History of the Renaissance World (2013)

*The Art of the Public Grovel:
Sexual Sin and Public Confession in America*
(Princeton University Press, 2008)

The Story of the World: History for the Classical Child
(Peace Hill Press)
Volume I: Ancient Times, rev. ed. (2006)
Volume II: The Middle Ages, rev. ed. (2007)
Volume III: Early Modern Times (2003)
Volume IV: The Modern World (2004)

The Writing With Ease Series
(Peace Hill Press, 2008–2010)

The Writing With Skill Series
(Peace Hill Press, 2012–2013)

ALSO BY JESSIE WISE

First Language Lessons for the Well-Trained Mind Series
(Peace Hill Press, 2002–2008)

The Ordinary Parent's Guide to Teaching Reading
(Peace Hill Press, 2004)

THE
WELL-TRAINED
MIND

A Guide to Classical Education at Home

Fourth Edition

SUSAN WISE BAUER

JESSIE WISE

W. W. Norton & Company
Independent Publishers Since 1923
New York   London

For information about permission to reproduce selections from this book,
write to Permissions, W. W. Norton & Company, Inc.,
500 Fifth Avenue, New York, NY 10110

For information about special discounts for bulk purchases, please contact
W. W. Norton Special Sales at specialsales@wwnorton.com or 800-233-4830

Manufacturing by LSC Harrisonburg
Production manager: Julia Druskin

Library of Congress Cataloging-in-Publication Data

Names: Bauer, Susan Wise, author. | Wise, Jessie, author.
Title: The well-trained mind : a guide to classical education at home / Susan Wise
Bauer, Jessie Wise.
Description: Fourth edition. | New York : W. W. Norton & Company, [2016] |
Includes bibliographical references and index.
Identifiers: LCCN 2016021472 | ISBN 9780393253627 (hardcover)
Subjects: LCSH: Classical education—United States—Handbooks, manuals, etc. |
Home schooling—United States—Handbooks, manuals, etc. | Education, Humanis-
tic—United States—Handbooks, manuals, etc. | Education—Parent participation—
United States—Handbooks, manuals, etc.
Classification: LCC LC40 .B39 2016 | DDC 373.241—dc23 LC record available at
https://lccn.loc.gov/2016021472

W. W. Norton & Company, Inc.
500 Fifth Avenue, New York, N.Y. 10110
www.wwnorton.com

W. W. Norton & Company Ltd.
15 Carlisle Street, London W1D 3BS

4 5 6 7 8 9 0

For Christopher, Daniel, and Emily,
for Ben, Lauren, and Siobhan,
for Dot, Linus, and Newton,
and for Brooke

CONTENTS

PROLOGUE: THE STORY OF A CLASSICAL
HOME EDUCATION

PART I. THE GRAMMAR STAGE: KINDERGARTEN THROUGH FOURTH GRADE

PART II. THE LOGIC STAGE: FIFTH GRADE THROUGH EIGHTH GRADE

PART III. THE RHETORIC STAGE:
NINTH GRADE THROUGH TWELFTH GRADE

PART IV. COMING HOME:
HOW TO EDUCATE YOUR CHILD AT HOME

ACKNOWLEDGMENTS

I am grateful to Amelia and Luther Morecock—Meme and Uncle Luther—for adopting me, teaching me to read before I went to school, and requiring me to be diligent. The credit for any academic or professional success I have enjoyed begins with them. My introduction to phonics materials came from a York, Maine, first-grade teacher in whose class *every* child learned to read. She showed me her systematic phonics program and told me how to order it, with the result that I taught my children how to read and started down the path to home education. I am immensely thankful that, when I took my "misfit" children to the Henrico Mental Clinic in Henrico, Virginia, I met a perceptive and encouraging psychologist, Jeffrey C. Fracher. Dr. Fracher told me to teach my children at home, an idea that had never occurred to me. I'm grateful to my children, Bob, Deborah, and Susan, for learning with me and for continuing to study and learn as adults. Working with Susan on this book has been a challenging, rewarding task. When she was a child, I nudged her beyond her intellectual comfort zone, and she is now continually doing the same for me. Finally, my husband of over fifty years, Jay, has been in the midst of all of this since our college years. He has encouraged and supported me at every turn.

—*Jessie Wise*

In the fifteen-plus years since the first edition of *The Well-Trained Mind* came out, our list of debts has grown exponentially. I owe my thanks to:

The wonderful folks at W. W. Norton who have stood by this project since its first appearance in 1999: our original (and still my) editor, Starling Lawrence, who first took an interest in the book and continues to champion it, and the team members who've worked with us over the years. Some are still at Norton and some have moved on, but we owe you all: Patricia Chui, Carol Flechner, Dosier Hammond, Bill Rusin, Jenn Chan, Golda Rademacher, Deidre Dolan, Jeannie Luciano, Drake McFeely, Ryan Harrington, Don Rifkin, and the sales reps who continue to work so ably on our behalf. Richard Henshaw, who has represented this book in all its incarnations. The present and past employees of Peace Hill Press who have supported this book and all of its spin-off projects: Kim Norton, John Hamman, Mollie Bauer, Mel Moore, Justin Moore, Jackie Violet, Sarah Park, Sara Buffington, Charlie Park, and Peter Buffington. My executive assistant, Pattie Worth, who keeps my life from falling apart while I'm writing, revising, speaking, and traveling. Madelaine Wheeler, Diane Wheeler, Sherrill Fink, and Christopher Bauer, all of whom did valiant duty in checking prices, details, and publication information. All of the home-schooling parents who have so generously shared their experiences and expertise with us over the years, including Diane Wheeler, Beth Ferguson, Peggy Ahern, Diane Montgomery, Beth Galvez, Traci Winyard, and Heather Quintero. The members of the Well-Trained Mind message boards, who have broadened our horizons, expanded our understanding, challenged our interpretations, and put up with our technological experimenting for over a decade. And finally, my family: Bob and Heather Wise, who looked out for Peace Hill Press during a difficult and busy time; Deborah Wise, now joining us in the project of classical education with her own daughter; my mother and father, Jay and Jessie Wise; my husband, Peter; and, most of all, my kids. Christopher, Ben, Daniel, and Emily: thank you for bearing with the home education project even when it led us in strange and unexpected directions. I'm proud of you all.

—*Susan Wise Bauer*

WHAT
THE WELL-TRAINED MIND
DOES: AN OVERVIEW

If you're fortunate, you live in a school system filled with excellent, well-paid teachers who are dedicated to developing your child's skills in reading, writing, mathematics, history, and science. The teachers at the elementary school have small classes—no more than ten students—and can give each student plenty of attention. The elementary school sits next to a middle school that is safe (no drugs, guns, or knives). The middle-school teachers train their students in logic, critical thinking, and advanced writing, and plenty of one-on-one instruction is offered, especially in writing. And in the distance (not too far away) is a high school that steers older students through world history, the classics of literature, the techniques of advanced writing, high-level mathematics and science, debate, art history, and music appreciation (not to mention vocational and technical training, résumé preparation, and job-hunting skills).

This book is for the rest of us.

After a combined total of over forty years in education—Jessie as an elementary and middle-school teacher and administrator in both public and private schools, Susan as student, graduate student, and college teacher—we have come to one simple conclusion: if you want your child to have an excellent education, you need to take charge of it yourself. You don't have to reform your entire school system. All you have to do is teach your own child.

Never mind educational rhetoric about the years of specialized training necessary for teachers. Forget everything you've heard about the need for classes in child development and educational psychology. These things are indeed necessary for the teacher faced with thirty squirming first graders or twenty-five turned-off adolescents. But you have an entirely different task: the education of your own child, one-on-one.

You probably feel that you don't have the skills to teach your child at home. You aren't alone; every home-schooling parent has felt this way (see Chapter 1). But we have consulted with scores of parents—some college-educated, some without high-school diplomas—who have successfully guided their children's education. At conferences and seminars, we've met hundreds more. Home-education magazines overflow with stories of parent-taught teens who excel at reading, writing, science, and math.

All you need to teach your child at home is dedication, some basic knowledge about how children learn, guidance in teaching the particular skills of each academic subject, and lots of books, CDs, posters, kits, and other resources. This book will provide you with everything except the dedication.

The Well-Trained Mind is a parent's guide to a do-it-yourself, academically rigorous, comprehensive education—a *classical* education.

What is classical education?

It is language-intensive—not image-focused. It demands that students use and understand words, spoken and written, rather than communicating primarily through images.

It is history-intensive, providing students with a comprehensive view of human endeavor from the beginning until now.

It trains the mind to analyze and draw conclusions.

It both requires and develops self-discipline—the ability to tackle a difficult task that doesn't promise an immediate reward, for the sake of future gain.

It produces literate, curious, intelligent students who have a wide range of interests and the ability to follow up on them.

The Well-Trained Mind is a handbook on how to prepare your child to read, write, calculate, think, and *understand.* In the Prologue, we'll outline what a classical education is and tell you about our own experience with classical education and with various forms of school at home.

Part I tells you how to lay the foundations of academic excellence, from kindergarten through fourth grade. Part II outlines a program that will train the maturing mind of a middle-school child (grades 5 through 8). Part III covers high-school skills. Even if you're starting with an older child, though, consider reading through the earlier sections so that you understand the basic principles of classical education. Each section includes a grade-by-grade summary so that you can see at a glance what each school year should include.

The progression of learning that we describe in Parts I–III is a model—an ideal. Every ideal has to shift (often, in unexpected ways) when it comes into contact with real human beings. Make sure to read Chapter 37, which deals briefly with learning difficulties and points you toward additional resources.

Part IV is dedicated to the issues surrounding full-time home education—getting started, socialization, grade and record keeping, standardized testing, college applications, athletics, and other home-schooling matters.

You may decide to remove your child from school; you may decide to leave her in regular classes. Either way, this book will give you the tools you need to teach her at home or to supplement and reinforce what she's learning in the classroom. We have heard from parents all over the world who are choosing to "afterschool" their children—to work with them individually in the evenings and on weekends and over summers, either to remediate or enrich their classroom educations. If you want to keep your child in school but do additional work in grammar or math, you can use the curricula and methods we suggest in the evenings or during breaks. If your child wants to go above and beyond what she's learning in history or science, she can pursue on her own time the at-home programs we outline.

A word about resources. We find huge lists of resources overwhelming. When Susan had four children at home, she didn't want to sort through an extensive list of recommended books to find the best second-grade guide to ancient Egypt—she just wanted two or three of the best choices. For this reason, we've sorted through available resources and listed our top picks. There are many books, programs, and resources that are compatible with the goals of classical education, and we have made no effort to list them all here. The resources that appear in this book are those that combine academic excellence, ease of use for the parent, clarity, and (when possible) affordability. Other excellent programs may not be listed because they duplicate material in a program we've listed; because they seem unnecessarily complicated, especially for beginners; because they have grown hard to find; or because they are (in our opinion) overpriced. But you can substitute with confidence wherever needed.

Many of our recommendations have changed from edition to edition. In some cases, books and programs have simply gone out of print, forcing us to find new titles to replace them. But in many cases, new curricula have been developed that (in our opinion) supersede our earlier recommendations.

Finally, please visit www.welltrainedmind.com, where we've provided additional resource pages: curricula for kids who don't fit the traditional progression described in these pages—because they have leapt ahead, are dealing with learning challenges, or simply process information differently; a continuously updated list of popular apps, web-based learning games, and online enrichment activities; alternative curricula that we found too complicated, expensive, specialized, or quirky to recommend in these pages, but which have enthusiastic support among many veteran home schoolers. And at www.forums.welltrainedmind.com, you can join thousands of home-schooling parents who are discussing learning challenges, sharing their curricula discoveries, swapping teaching tips, and much, much more.

PRACTICAL CONSIDERATIONS: USING *THE WELL-TRAINED MIND* WITHOUT LOSING YOUR OWN

This is a very big book. *The Well-Trained Mind* provides information on teaching all the subjects in the classical curriculum for all twelve grades—literature, writing, grammar, history, science, math, Latin, modern languages, art, music, debate, and more.

It's a rare parent who will follow this program exactly. The freedom to tailor an academic program to your child's particular interests and needs, strengths and struggles, is one of home education's greatest advantages. We've explained the general philosophy that governs each part of the curriculum, but our specific schedules, texts, and programs are just *illustrations* of how to put this philosophy into practice. We think the texts and programs we've settled on are the best available, but you should always feel free to substitute, to pick and choose and adapt.

For example, in Chapter 17 we recommend that middle-grade history students spend time outlining their history reading, and we demonstrate this process by quoting from the *Kingfisher History Encyclopedia,* one of our recommended texts. But you can accomplish the same goal using other good world history texts. And although we recommend that students use standard outline form (I, II, III; A, B, C; 1, 2, 3; etc.), our *purpose* is to teach students to distinguish between organizing ideas ("topics"), supporting statements, and additional details—to teach them familiarity with the structure of a well-written piece. So if the student has learned elsewhere how to do a spider diagram or a flow chart and those methods fit the student's way of thinking better (and still reveal the underlying design of an essay), you can substitute one of them for the traditional outline.

You can follow one part of the program, but not another. If, for example, you've found a math curriculum that works well for your sixth grader, you can use the language resources we suggest without feeling as though you've got to convert to the math books we like. If your high-school student already has a literature list he's reading his way through, you can still use our writing and grammar suggestions without adopting our reading list.

No student will do *all* the work we suggest—especially in the early grades, when learning to read, write, and understand arithmetic may take most of the child's study time. In the classical tradition, reading, writing, grammar, and mathematics are the center of the curriculum. History and science become more and more important as the child matures. Foreign languages, music, art, and electives have to follow these foundational curricula areas. And many students have extracurricular activities (soccer, swimming, music lessons, serious hobbies, clubs, skills courses such as accounting or typing) that may bump art appreciation or French (or even Latin) from your schedule.

After you read through Parts I, II, and III, you should have a good grasp of the principles that guide a classical education. As you put them into effect, take seriously our constant direction toward texts and curricula that are systematic and rigorous. Remember that a child *must* have a thorough grounding in the basic skills of grammar, spelling, writing, and arithmetic before he can proceed to more complex analytical work (more on this in Part I). But when you teach your child at home, *you* make the final decision on which books you'll use and how much time you'll spend on schoolwork. Our suggestions are simply that: suggestions, meant to guide you as you plan your child's education at home.

SUPPLEMENTING YOUR
CHILD'S EDUCATION:
THE WELL-TRAINED MIND
AND FULL-TIME SCHOOL

Not everyone who uses this book will want to join the ranks of full-time home schoolers. Although much in this book (and most of the information in Part IV) will be useful to parents who are educating their children completely at home, the information on teaching each subject and the resource lists that follow each chapter will help you supplement the education of a child who's already in school.

Every involved parent is a home educator. If you're checking your child's compositions, talking him through his history homework, or drilling him in math, you're already teaching him. In this case, you're acting as a teacher's aide—helping to teach and reinforce material that has already been presented in the classroom.

You may find, though, that you want to move beyond this role and take on the job of organizing and presenting new material yourself. Your child may need extra tutoring and practice in a subject in order to master it. Or he may be so interested in a subject that he wants to go beyond the pre-scribed curriculum.

Either way, we suggest that you read Chapters 1 and 2, which explain our basic theory of classical education, and the chapters that deal with each stage of the mind's development: Chapter 3, "The Parrot Years"; Chapter 13, "The Argumentative Child"; and Chapter 25, "Speaking Your Mind." These will give you an overview of the process of learning, no mat-ter what age your child is.

Encourage your child toward absorption in grades 1 through 4, critical thought in grades 5 through 8, and expression in grades 9 through 12. She must have good, phonics-based reading skills. Use one of the phonics pro-grams that we recommend to teach beginning reading skills; make sure she does plenty of extra reading in the early grades; and use the logic resources and primary source recommendations in Part II to help her think critically about middle-grade history, science, and math. In the high-school years, examine our rhetoric resources to improve your student's writing skills. Writing is a difficult skill to teach in a group setting, and most students need extra practice and individual attention to write well.

If you want to encourage your child to go beyond the classroom, use the information we present, and adapt it to his school schedule. For exam-ple, in Chapter 16, "Recognizing the Patterns," we describe a science pro-gram for fifth through eighth grade that requires the student to complete experiments, write reports, and sketch diagrams. You can use the science resources we recommend and key the child's study to what he's learning in the classroom. If he's studying fifth-grade biology and wants to know more, use our biology resource sections to provide your child with supple-mentary learning.

You can also use these chapters to guide a course of summer study. But bear in mind that a twelve-week summer course can't cover all the mate-rial listed in these chapters, which are designed to provide a school year's worth of study at home.

If you want to make sure that your child masters a skill area that's giving her trouble, you can use the books and programs we describe as systematic and drill-oriented. You shouldn't try to key these to classroom work, since each skill builds on what has already been taught. Instead, devote an appropriate amount of time to pursuing the additional study as an extracurricular activity.

If you're particularly unhappy with the way one subject is being taught, consider asking your school system whether your child can study that particular material with a tutor. Many schools will allow this as long as the child shows steady progress. You can then substitute one of the programs we outline, either acting as tutor yourself or hiring someone to work one-on-one with your child (see Chapters 44 and 45 for information on approaching your local school and finding reliable tutors). It sometimes happens that an excellent teacher and a bright student are unable to connect in the classroom because their learning styles conflict. And many children need one-on-one instruction in order to do their best work.

For we let our young men and women go out unarmed in a day when armor was never so necessary. By teaching them to read, we have left them at the mercy of the printed word. By the invention of the film and the radio, we have made certain that no aversion to reading shall secure them from the incessant battery of words, words, words. They do not know what the words mean; they do not know how to ward them off or blunt their edge or fling them back; they are a prey to words in their emotions instead of being the masters of them in their intellects. . . . We have lost the tools of learning, and in their absence can only make a botched and piecemeal job of it.

—Dorothy L. Sayers, "The Lost Tools of Learning"

THE
WELL-TRAINED
MIND

PROLOGUE

THE STORY OF
A CLASSICAL
HOME EDUCATION

1

UNCHARTED
TERRITORY: JESSIE

The first day I taught my three children at home, I cleaned up the playroom and set up three desks. I hung an American flag at the front of the room and led them in the Pledge of Allegiance. I was shaking with nervousness.

It was 1973, and my husband, Jay, and I had just done something radical. We had removed our children from school.

I was terrified, which was ridiculous. After all, I was a state-certified teacher. I'd taught public school for six years; I'd taken postgraduate courses in education from Tulane University, the College of William and Mary, and the University of Virginia. One year, I'd managed thirty-eight second graders from dawn till dusk—no lunch break, no recess break, and no teacher's aide.

Yet I was completely intimidated by those three little children, certain that I couldn't do an adequate job of teaching them myself. All my teacher education had brainwashed me. I was convinced that parents couldn't possibly teach their own children—certainly not at home. It had to be done in an institutional setting, run by professionals, with their resources and specialized training and expertise.

Unfortunately, the professionals had let us down.

I wasn't a stranger to failures in the system. The last year I taught public school, I had in my sixth-grade class two sixteen-year-old boys who had not yet learned to read. I'd never even heard of home schooling, but I remember thinking: If I ever have a child, he will know how to read before he goes to school. I will not have my son sitting in sixth grade, unable to read.

So when my oldest child turned four, I said to him one day, "Bob, would you rather take a nap, or would you like to learn how to read?" He chose reading (not surprisingly), and I started him on the old-fashioned phonics I'd been taught when I was a child. I'd lie down with him on his little bed after lunch and work on his letters (since I also had a two-year-old and a thirteen-month-old, I was always glad to lie down). We practiced vowels and consonants, and sounded out new words that year. We called it "doing kindergarten." By the time my middle child was three, she wanted in. "My do kindergarten, too," she'd say, and I would boost her up and let her repeat the sounds after me.

I was proud of myself. I was preparing my children for school. Kindergarten, when it came, was uneventful and purely social. Bob loved to play at school. At home, I went on reading to him and teaching him his language and number skills.

But when Bob reached first grade, he didn't fit in. He already knew the material, and he was bored. The school—a well-regarded private school—was cooperative and moved him into second grade. He was bored there, too. The class was working on early reading skills, and we'd already done that. The second graders didn't like him because he was a little upstart invading their turf. The administration moved him back to first grade, but now the first graders were hostile. He was a big shot who'd been thought worthy of second grade, and they wouldn't play with him. They were jealous because he was well prepared.

So here he was, in first grade, already feeling that doing well in school made him unpopular. He started to change. He had been an excited, exuberant, curious child. Now he was a behavior problem. He stopped doing well in school. His papers had always been meticulously done, but suddenly his writing became sloppy. The teacher complained to us that Bob was always questioning her in class. And the bus ride to school was horrendous: the older kids made the younger ones sit on the floor, stole their lunches, and dirtied their clothes so they'd get demerits from the teachers at school. Every day, Bob got off the school bus with a handful of bad papers, and he was either fighting mad or crying.

At this point, Jay and I realized that we were spending most of our time with this child trying to undo what was happening to him when he was at school. And we were afraid that our second child, Susan, would go through the same metamorphosis. Susan had just started kindergarten, and the teacher was already protesting to us that she would be a social misfit because she wanted to read during free time instead of playing. We were experiencing firsthand the terrific leveling pressure applied in so many schools: the effort to smooth out the bumps by bringing well-prepared kids down to the level of the rest.

This still happens in some schools. Not long ago, the best private preschool in our area agreed to stop teaching four-year-olds beginning reading skills. Kindergarten teachers in the local public schools had complained that the children turned out by this preschool were bored in kindergarten because they already knew the material. The schools demanded that the preschool quit turning out such well-prepared five-year-olds so that all the kindergartners would start at the same level of ignorance. I was appalled when the preschool buckled and went back to teaching colors and "social skills."

Back in 1973, no one told me to stop teaching phonics to my preschoolers. And we didn't know what to do with these academic misfits I had managed to produce. So we took our two school-age children to a psychologist in the local mental-health system. He tested both of them, and I found out what my careful preparation for kindergarten had done: Bob, the second grader, was reading on a seventh-grade level; Susan, the kindergartner, was reading fifth-grade material. The psychologist called us into his office afterward. "Listen," he said, "if you keep those children in school, they are going to become nonlearners. They're bored to death. You've got a teacher's certificate. Why don't you take them out of school and teach them yourself?"

This had never occurred to us. After all, education was the domain of schools . . . and these were *our* children! We didn't know anyone else who was home-schooling. The whole idea was odd and radical, and we weren't sure it was even legal; Virginia law was fuzzy on this point.

But we had no other choice. The local public school was a terrible environment socially, and test scores ranked our county at the bottom of the state year after year. The private school had been our solution. So, quaking in my boots, I set up the desks and the American flag and started to teach my children at home. I worried the whole time. I worried that my children weren't going to get into college. I worried that the school system was going to come and take them away from us for neglect and truancy. I worried that their social development would suffer.

Those worries didn't come true. Bob, my early reader, went on to excel in math and sciences. He studied computer science at the College of William and Mary, earned his master's degree from the University of Virginia, and went into a high-profile career in technology; he's worked with innovative start-ups in Seattle and has also held executive positions with HP and Samsung. Susan went to college at seventeen as a National Merit finalist, and then completed three graduate degrees, ending up with her Ph.D. in American Studies. She taught literature and writing at William and Mary for a number of years, has a thriving career as a writer, and also runs her own publishing company. Deborah graduated from the University College at the University of Maryland; she achieved certification as a forensics evidence technician, and then became a Maryland police officer. After an on-the-job injury, she retrained as a paralegal and joined a Baltimore law firm.

As I look back on the education I gave these children, I can see that it follows a pattern that has mostly disappeared from public education. To begin with, I filled their heads with facts when they were small. I taught them to read early and kept books everywhere in the house; we had books for presents and rewards, and I was known at the local public library as "the lady with the laundry basket" because I took my children in every week and filled a laundry basket with their books. On each library visit, I had them check out the following books: one science book, one history book, one art or music appreciation book, one practical book (a craft, hobby, or "how-to"), a biography or autobiography, a classic novel (or an adaptation suited to age), an imaginative storybook, a book of poetry. They were allowed to choose the titles, but I asked them to follow this pattern. And they were also allowed to check out other books on any topic they pleased.

Furthermore, I made them memorize. They could recite multiplication tables, lists of linking verbs, dates, presidents, and Latin declensions.

As their thought processes matured, I taught them how to fit knowledge into logical structures. I spent a lot of time in one-on-one discussion and interaction. We learned spelling rules, mathematics, and basic logic; we followed an unfashionably strict grammar book and diagrammed sentences of increasing complexity; we kept science notebooks and time lines so that we could organize their growing knowledge of facts into logical and chronological order. I taught them how to organize a paragraph, an essay, a research paper. We studied Latin grammar, took music lessons, carried out science experiments (including one memorable dissection of a cow's eyeball, acquired from a farmer neighbor). They learned how to follow custom-made schedules, balancing academics and personal interests like music, programming, and creative writing. And they continued to read.

As they moved into high school, I spent more time working on skills in writing and self-expression. They wrote critical essays and research papers, studied the principles of rhetoric, read widely—and, most importantly, began to develop their own special interests. Bob spent much of his study time learning to program on his brand-new computer. Susan had a bent for words; she wrote two novels, researched early British history and literature, and taught herself Welsh and Gaelic (certainly nothing I would have come up with). Deborah studied art and also became an accomplished violinist.

I didn't know until later that I had followed the pattern of classical education called the trivium. I did know that what I was doing worked.

Susan will write about the trivium in the next chapter; it's the classical theory of education, which organizes learning around the maturing capacity of the child's mind. It no longer exists in public education. *I* didn't learn by this method when I was educated in the county public schools back in the 1940s and '50s. But I was raised by elderly relatives who had been taught by classical methods popular before the turn of the century. Meme, as I called her, had only finished eighth grade in a one-room schoolhouse, and Uncle Luther hadn't even gone that far. But by eighth grade, Meme had learned Latin and algebra, and Uncle Luther had learned advanced practical mathematics and how to think and write. They taught me to read before I ever went to school. The first-grade teacher was our neighbor, and when she heard that Meme was drilling me in phonics, she made a special trip over to warn us that I'd be ruined for life if Meme used such an out-dated method. Meme was undaunted, and when I did enter school I was put straight into second grade because of the skills I'd already acquired.

When I came home from school in the evenings, Meme and Uncle Luther sat me down and made me learn. Meme would point at the lists in the books—multiplication tables, parts of speech—and say, "Memorize those."

"But the teacher said we don't have to memorize them," I protested. "We just have to be able to use them."

"I don't care what the teacher says," Meme insisted. "These are things you have to know."

I had been trained to be obedient and disciplined, so I memorized the lists, even though memorization was difficult for me. I learned my algebra and grammar. I went on to college and a professional position; I was the only girl in my high-school class to graduate from college. When I had children of my own, I used Meme's method and found that the three-part process of memorization, logical organization, and clear expression put them far above their peers.

In the middle of this century, Dorothy Sayers, author and creator of Lord Peter Wimsey, told an audience at Oxford University that education had given up on the trivium and was now running on what she called the "educational capital." We no longer teach our children the process of memorization, organization, and expression—the *tools* by which the mind learns. The leftover remnants of those methods have carried us through several decades of schooling without catastrophe; I made it through public school at the top of my class because my guardians taught me from *what they had learned*. But sooner or later, the capital gets used up. My own children were faced with teachers who brought them down to the level of the class; teachers who thought it was more important to teach social skills than academic subjects; textbooks that had abandoned grammatical rules and mathematical logic in favor of scattershot, incidental learning. They were surrounded by peers who considered anyone good at learning to be a geek. They spent seven hours every day sitting in desks, standing in lines, riding buses, and doing repetitive seatwork so that their classmates could learn what they already knew.

I wanted something better for them. As I've watched home education develop over the last decades, I've become convinced that any dedicated parent can do what I did. My own education didn't stretch to Latin or Gaelic or calculus or computer science or art or violin, but my children learned all of these things. With the help of resources and support groups now in place throughout the country—and with the principles we'll give you in this book—you can provide your child with a classical education at home, even if you've never glanced at Latin or logic.

You can do what my guardians did and, on your own time, teach your child the basic skills she may not be learning at school. Your young student may need particular help in math, science, reading, or writing. Even the best and most diligent teacher (I speak from experience) is often prevented from giving necessary individual attention by the growing size of her class. If you use the resources we've collected in this book and invest in some one-on-one time with your child, you will be capable of educating him.

When I taught school, I was convinced that parents couldn't teach their own children. But forty years later, I can look back and say: The experiment was a success. I was the best teacher my children could possibly have had *because* I was their parent.

I happened to have a teacher's certificate. But during my years of home schooling, I learned more academic material, more about how to manage individual relationships with children, and more about how to teach than I did in any of my teacher-education courses. Teacher-education courses gave me a great deal of good information on how to manage large groups of children. I needed that in schools, but a parent doesn't need it to teach at home.

I happened to have a college degree. But in the forty years since I first became involved with the home-education movement, I've seen parents who only finished high school lead their children successfully through twelfth grade, and I've watched those children thrive in college.

You shouldn't be afraid to take your child out of school, if necessary. This is a radical step for most parents; it means a change in schedule, in priorities, in lifestyle. And apart from academic concerns, many parents ask, "What about my child's social development? Doesn't he need peers?" Children need friends. Children do *not* need to be surrounded by large groups of peers who inevitably follow the strongest personality in the crowd. The question for any parent is: Do I want my child to be like his peers? Or do I want my child to rise above them?

Finally, if you're accustomed to sending your child to school every morning and allowing the professionals to worry about what he learns and how he learns it, the idea of supervising an entire education may overwhelm you. I sympathize. When I started, I was convinced I could never do it. But if you feel your child is being shortchanged in school, we can give you a plan to fix that. In this book, not only will we introduce you to the trivium method, but we'll give you resources to carry it out and a plan for the entire twelve years of school.

I discovered that home education has a great advantage I knew nothing about when I started. Home education teaches children to *learn* and eventually to teach themselves. By the time my children were twelve or so, I did less and less actual teaching. I supervised; I discussed content with them; I held them accountable; I graded; I bought books and organized coursework and found tutors for their advanced courses. But by early high school, they had been trained in the methods of learning. From this point, they began the process of educating themselves, with some help from tutors and correspondence courses. As adults, they continue to educate themselves, to widen their intellectual horizons. Certainly, this should be the first goal of education.

2

✽

A PERSONAL LOOK AT
CLASSICAL EDUCATION:
SUSAN

I loved going to school at home. As a high-school student, I would get up
in the morning, practice the piano for two hours, do my math and grammar lessons, finish off my science, and then devote the rest of my school
day to my favorite subjects—history, ancient languages, and writing. Once
a week, we all piled into the car and drove around to music lessons, math
tutoring sessions, library visits, college classes. On weekends, we went to
athletic meets—my brother's bicycle races, the horse shows my sister and
I trained for and rode in.

But I was nervous when I went away to college. Although I'd done well
on standardized exams, I'd never really sat in a regular classroom, facing
inflexible deadlines. I was used to taking tests from my mother.

I shouldn't have worried. I tested out of thirty hours' worth of college
courses; by my second semester, I was taking 400-level courses. I had a
host of strange skills: I could diagram sentences; I could read Latin; I knew

enough logic to tell whether an assertion was true or faulty. And I was surrounded by eighteen-year-olds who couldn't write, didn't want to read, and couldn't reason.

I worked in the Peer Tutoring Center for two years, tutoring English composition and Greek grammar. I found myself teaching fifth-grade grammar to college students. My peers came in because they were getting failing grades in composition; I discovered that they couldn't tell the difference between fragments and run-on sentences. Students of Greek came in because they were having trouble translating; they couldn't identify nouns and verbs or tell me what the difference was.

This college was small and nonexclusive, but the problem is universal. Ten years later, I taught my first semester of university classes at the College of William and Mary in Virginia. William and Mary, which still holds to the model of classical education, *is* selective about admissions. The students in my literature classes had high grades, high test scores, lots of extracurricular credits. I had sixty students my first year and taught two sections of Major British Writers, Eighteenth and Nineteenth Centuries: Jonathan Swift to Arthur Conan Doyle in one fell swoop.

I spent the beginning of the semester teaching remedial English to these freshmen. My first hint of trouble came when I assigned Wordsworth's "Ode: Intimations of Immortality" and gave a reading quiz. As I collected the test, I saw that Wordsworth's title had been thoroughly mangled: "Intemmitions," "Intimmations," "Inntemisions."

"Didn't any of you learn phonetic spelling?" I asked. Most of them shook their heads. Well, I already knew that phonics tends to be unfashionable, so I decided to be merciful. After all, I thought, they can always run a spell checker on their papers. I told them to write a four- to six-page paper comparing two of the poems we'd covered or comparing one of the poems to a modern work—no footnotes necessary, no research into scholarly articles required. Almost at once, the e-mail started to flood into my electronic mailbox:

Professor Bauer, I never wrote a paper on a poem before and I don't know where to start.

Professor Bauer, I want to write on "The Rime of the Ancient Mariner," but I don't think I can say enough about it to fill up four pages.

("The Rime of the Ancient Mariner" has enough metaphor and philosophy in it to provide material for a doctoral thesis.)

> While thinking about my paper topic, I have realized that I have no clue as to what I should write on.

> Professor Bauer, I'm completely lost, I only have dillusions of correct paper topics.

The papers, when finally turned in, contained a few gems, but the majority were badly written, illogical, and full of grammatical errors. And, with a few exceptions, my privately educated students struggled right along with the public-school graduates. They labored to put a thesis into words. They sweated and complained and groaned, trying to prove it. And they didn't know whether they'd proved it or not when they got to the end of their paper.

I spent a great deal of time talking to these freshmen and sophomores in my office. They were bright, lively, energetic, interesting kids. They had ideas and passions and philosophical insights and social concerns and creative aspirations. But they'd been done a great disservice. Their schools gave them few tools; their minds were filled with the raw materials needed for success, but they had to dig with their hands.

I was ahead of them when I was their age—not because of superior mental abilities, but because I'd been equipped with a closetful of mental tools. My mother taught us the way she'd been taught at home. Our education was language-centered, not image-centered; we read and listened and wrote, but we rarely watched. She spent the early years of school giving us facts, systematically laying the foundation for advanced study. She taught us to think through arguments, and *then* she taught us how to express ourselves.

This is the classical pattern of the trivium, the three-part process of training the mind.

The first years of schooling are called the "grammar stage"—not because you spend four years doing English, but because these are the years in which the building blocks for all other learning are laid, just as grammar is the foundation for language. In the elementary-school years—grades 1 through 4—the mind is ready to absorb information. Since children at this age actually find memorization fun, during this period education involves not primarily self-expression and self-discovery, but rather the learning of facts and training in basic thinking skills: rules of phonics and spelling and how to use them, rules of grammar and understanding good sentence structure, poems, the vocabulary of foreign languages, the stories of history and literature, descriptions of plants and animals and the human body, how numbers work and the basics of mathematical thinking—the list goes on.

Somewhere around fourth or fifth grade, children begin to think more analytically. Middle-school students are less interested in finding out facts than in asking, "Why?" The second phase of the classical education, the "logic stage," is a time when the child begins to pay attention to cause and effect, to the relationships among different fields of knowledge, to the way facts fit together into a logical framework.

A student is ready for the logic stage when the capacity for abstract thought begins to mature. During these years, the student begins the study of algebra and applies mathematical reasoning to real-life situations. She studies the rules of logic, and begins to apply logic to all academic subjects. The logic of writing, for example, includes paragraph construction and support of a thesis; the logic of reading involves the criticism and analysis of texts, not simple absorption of information; the logic of history demands that the student find out why the War of 1812 was fought, rather than simply reading its story; the logic of science requires the child to learn and apply the scientific method.

The final phase of a classical education, the "rhetoric stage," builds on the first two. At this point, the high-school student learns to write and speak with force and originality. The student of rhetoric applies the rules of logic learned in middle school to the foundational information learned in the early grades and expresses her conclusions in clear, forceful, elegant language. The student also begins to specialize in whatever branch of knowledge attracts her; these are the years for art camps, college courses, foreign travel, apprenticeships, and other forms of specialized training.

A classical education is more than just a pattern of learning, though. First, it is *language-focused:* learning is accomplished primarily through words, written and spoken, rather than mostly through images (pictures, videos, and television). Why is this important? Language learning and image learning require very different habits of thought. Language requires the mind to work harder; in reading, the brain is forced to translate a symbol (words on the page) into a concept. Images, such as those on videos and television, allow the mind to be passive. In front of a video screen, the brain can "sit back" and relax; faced with the written page, the mind is required to roll its sleeves up and get to work.

Second, a classical education follows a specific three-part pattern: the mind must be first supplied with facts and images, then given the logical tools for organization of those facts and images, and finally equipped to express conclusions.

Third, classical education strives for *mastery* in the skill areas, but *discovery and exploration* in the content areas. Skill areas are those parts of the curriculum that give the student tools for learning: grammar, phonics and spelling, the mechanics of sentence and paragraph construction, mathematical operations (from addition to complex equations), basic concepts in science. Skills are developed in a prescribed sequence, each step building on the one before; addition and subtraction come before multiplication and division, comma use is mastered before compound-complex sentences are addressed. Workbooks and textbooks are valuable for building skill areas.

Content areas are literature, history, the sciences, mathematical thinking and understanding, written composition, art, music—fields of study that are open-ended and that can't be "mastered." Students will never learn all of history or science or read all of the great books. In these content areas, there is room for students to choose their own direction, to develop a deep and narrow expertise or a broader, wider knowledge, to tailor their study to their interests. When possible, we steer away from textbooks in the content areas, and toward collections of "living books"—books written by single authors, exploring particular issues and ideas.

Fourth, to the classical mind, all knowledge is interrelated. Astronomy, for example, isn't studied in isolation; it's learned along with the history of scientific discovery, which leads into the church's relationship to science and from there to the intricacies of medieval church history. The reading of the *Odyssey* allows the student to consider Greek history, the nature of heroism, the development of the epic, and humankind's understanding of the divine. This is easier said than done. The world is full of knowledge, and finding the links between fields of study can be a mind-twisting task. A classical education meets this challenge by taking history as its organizing outline—beginning with the ancients and progressing forward to the moderns in history, literature, art, and music—and by connecting the history of scientific discoveries to the study of scientific principles whenever possible.

We suggest that the twelve years of education consist of three repetitions of the same four-year pattern: the ancients (5000 B.C.–A.D. 400), the medieval period through the early Renaissance (400–1600), the late Renaissance through early modern times (1600–1850), and modern times (1850–present). The child studies these four time periods at varying levels—simple for grades 1 through 4, more difficult in grades 5 through 8 (when the student begins to read original sources), and taking an even more complex approach in grades 9 through 12, when the student works through these time periods using original sources (from Homer to Hitler) and also has the opportunity to pursue a particular interest (music, dance, technology, medicine, biology, creative writing) in depth.

This four-year pattern isn't set in stone. We've seen parents use three-year sequences, six-year sequences, and take a year out for concentrated national or state history study. The principle, not the exact time frame, is what matters: Move forward chronologically, and organize the bulk of your history by time period, rather than by individual country. The traditional American method of studying history by region (United States, Europe, Asia, etc.) does nothing to help students draw connections between events, vital to critical thinking about history. (We'll expand on this in the chapters about history that follow.)

Literature is linked to history studies. The student who is working on ancient history will read Greek and Roman mythology, the tales of the *Iliad* and *Odyssey*, early medieval writings, Chinese and Japanese fairy tales, and (for the older student) the classical texts of Plato, Herodotus, Virgil, Aristotle. She'll read *Beowulf*, Dante, Chaucer, Shakespeare the following year, when she's studying medieval and early Renaissance history. When the eighteenth and nineteenth centuries are studied, she starts with Swift (*Gulliver's Travels*) and ends with Dickens; finally, she reads modern literature as she is studying modern history.

The sciences should be studied in a way that does not isolate them from the humanities (and vice versa); science is a human pursuit, and students must understand both its development and its current state. In earlier editions of *The Well-Trained Mind,* we suggested that the sciences be studied in a four-year pattern that roughly corresponds to the periods of scientific discovery: biology, classification, and the human body (subjects known to the Ancients); earth science and basic astronomy (which flowered during the early Renaissance); chemistry (which came into its own during the early modern period); and basic physics and computer science (very modern subjects).

The Study of Science

Name of period	Years covered	Scientific subjects	Studied during grades . . .
Ancients	5000 B.C.–A.D. 400	Biology Classification Human body	1, 5, 9
Medieval–early Renaissance	400–1600	Earth science Astronomy	2, 6, 10
Late Renaissance– early modern	1600–1850	Chemistry	3, 7, 11
Modern	1850–present	Physics Computer science	4, 8, 12

This pattern has proved helpful to many families, but others—particularly those with a primary focus on STEM subjects (science, technology, engineering, and mathematics)—have found the yearlong focus on a single field awkward. In the chapters on science that follow, we'll offer several different ways to put classical methods to use in the study of science. All of them maintain the pattern that is so central to classical education: exploration in the early years, critical thinking and analysis in the middle grades, specialization and self-expression in the high-school years. No matter what topics they study (or in what order), young scientists will spend their grammar-stage years observing the world around them as you nurture their curiosity and sense of wonder; logic-stage students will learn to really *grasp* the central concepts of science, through a combination of reading, demonstration, and experimentation; high-school students will begin to truly understand scientific inquiry, the techniques of science, and the development of scientific theories over time.

The classical pattern lends coherence to the study of history, science, and literature—subjects that are too often fragmented and confusing. The pattern widens and deepens as the student matures and learns. For example, a first grader listens to you read the story of the *Iliad* from one of the picture-book versions available at any public library. (My experience has been that first graders think the *Iliad* is a blast, especially when Achilles starts hauling Hector's body around the walls of Troy.) Four years later, the fifth grader reads one of the popular middle-grade adaptations—Olivia Coolidge's *The Trojan War* or Roger L. Green's *The Tale of Troy*. Four more years go by, and the ninth grader—faced with Homer's *Iliad* itself—plunges right in, undaunted. She already knows the story. What's to be scared of?

In the chapters that follow, we'll show you how to follow this pattern for each subject, list the resources you'll need, and tell you where to find these resources.

Classical education is, above all, systematic—in direct contrast to the scattered, unorganized nature of so much secondary education. Rigorous, systematic study has two purposes. Rigorous study develops virtue in the student: the ability to act in accordance to what one knows to be right. Virtuous men or women can force themselves to do what they know is right, even when it runs against their inclinations. Classical education continually asks a student to focus not on what is immediately pleasurable (another half hour of TV or computer game, for example) but on the steps needed to reach a future goal—mastery of vital academic skills.

Systematic study allows the student to join what Mortimer J. Adler calls the "Great Conversation": the ongoing conversation of great minds down through the ages. Much modern education is so eclectic that the student has little opportunity to make connections between past events and the flood of current information. "The beauty of the classical curriculum," writes classical schoolmaster David Hicks, "is that it dwells on one problem, one author, or one epoch long enough to allow even the youngest student a chance to exercise his mind in a scholarly way: to make connections and to trace developments, lines of reasoning, patterns of action, recurring symbolisms, plots, and motifs."[1]

My mother struggled hard to give us the benefits of a classical education. She began to teach us at home in a day when few materials existed for home-educating parents; she had to create her own curriculum. We're going to lay out a whole plan of study for you—not just theory, but resources and textbooks and curricula.

It's still hard work. We don't deny it. We'll give you a clear view of the demands and requirements of this academic project. But a classical education is worth every drop of sweat—I can testify to that. I am constantly grateful to my mother for my education. It gave me an immeasurable head start, the independence to innovate and work on my own, confidence in my ability to compete in the job market, and the mental tools to build a satisfying career. And now that I have grown children of my own—children who were educated in this same classical tradition—I see those advantages working for them as well.

---

[1] David Hicks, *Norms and Nobility: A Treatise on Education* (New York: Praeger, 1981), p. 133.

PART I

THE GRAMMAR STAGE

Kindergarten through Fourth Grade

3

THE PARROT YEARS

So far (except, of course, for the Latin), our curriculum contains nothing that departs very far from common practice. The difference will be felt rather in the attitude of the teachers, who must look upon all these activities less as "subjects" in themselves than as a gathering-together of material for use in the next part of the *Trivium*.

—Dorothy Sayers, "The Lost Tools of Learning"

Houses rest on foundations. Journalists gather all the facts before writing their stories; scientists accumulate data before forming theories; violinists and dancers and defensive tackles rely on muscle memory, stored in their bodies by hours of drill.

A classical education requires a student to collect, understand, memorize, and categorize information. Although this process continues through all twelve grades, the first four grades are the most intensive for fact collecting.

This isn't necessarily a fashionable approach to early education. Much classroom time and energy has been spent in an effort to give children every possible opportunity to express what's inside them. There's nothing wrong with self-expression, but when self-expression pushes the accumulation of knowledge offstage, something's out of balance.

Young children are described as sponges because they soak up knowledge. But there's another side to the metaphor. Squeeze a dry sponge, and nothing comes out. First the sponge has to be filled. Language teacher Ruth Beechick writes, "Our society is so obsessed with creativity that people want children to be creative before they have any knowledge or skill to be creative with."[1] Your job, during the elementary years, is to supply the knowledge and skills that will allow your child to overflow with creativity as his mind matures.

That doesn't mean that your first grader has to learn about complex subjects in depth or that you're going to force him to memorize long lists of details. In the first four years of learning, you'll be filling your child's mind and imagination with as many pictures, stories, and facts as you can. Your goal is to supply mental pegs on which later information can be hung. Think of an experience most adults have had. You read about a minor movie star, and suddenly you see his name everywhere. You learn a new vocabulary word and instantly notice it sprinkled through all sorts of different texts. You happen across the name of a tiny, obscure foreign country and in the next few days you notice a dozen news items about it.

You might remark to your spouse, "What a coincidence!" Usually, though, that information has surrounded you all along. The movie star's name, the new word, the foreign country were already in the magazines and newspapers at the checkout line, but because the information was unfamiliar to you, your eyes passed over it without recognition. Once the information entered your memory, you recognized it and began to accumulate more and more details.

This is what you'll be doing with your elementary-school child. You might read a book about the planet Mars to your second grader. If it's the first time she's heard about Mars, she probably won't grasp all the information you're giving her. But she may hear on the news that night the most recent information from the Mars space probe, and suddenly something that would have passed by her clicks in her mind. You'll tell her, in history, about the Roman god Mars, the father of Romulus and Remus, and she'll hang this detail on the peg you provided when you read that book about the planets. When she runs across the word *martial* and asks what

---

[1] Ruth Beechick, *A Strong Start in Language: Grades K–3* (Pollock Pines, CA: Arrow Press, 1993), p. 6.

it means, you can tell her that it means *warlike* and comes from the name Mars, god of war—and the information will stick.

The whole structure of the trivium recognizes that there is an ideal time and place for each part of learning: memorization, argumentation, and self- expression. The elementary years are ideal for soaking up knowledge.

A classical education assumes that knowledge of the world, past and present, takes priority over self-expression. Intensive study of facts equips the student for fluent and articulate self-expression later on. Too close a focus on self-expression at an early age can actually cripple a child later on; a student who has always been encouraged to look inside himself may not develop a frame of reference, a sense of how his ideas measure up against the thoughts and beliefs of others.

So the key to the first stage of the trivium is content, content, content. In history, science, literature, and, to a lesser extent, art and music, the child should be accumulating masses of information: stories of people and wars; names of rivers, cities, mountains, and oceans; scientific names, properties of matter, classifications; plots, characters, and descriptions. The young writer should be memorizing the nuts and bolts of language— parts of speech, parts of a sentence, vocabulary roots. The young mathematician should be preparing for higher math by mastering the basic math facts and developing an understanding of arithmetical operations.

NOW OR NEVER

Why are the first four grades a particularly fruitful time to concentrate on content?

This is the first time your child will encounter Egyptian embalming rites or the atmosphere of Venus; this is the first time he will understand what light is made of or why Americans rebelled against the British. He will never get a second chance to read *The Lion, the Witch, and the Wardrobe*, or hear *The Hobbit* read aloud for the first time. Seize this early excitement. Let the child delve deep. Let him read, read, read. Don't force him to stop and reflect on it yet. Don't make him decide what he likes and doesn't like about ancient Rome; let him wallow in gladiators and chariot races. He wants to find out how things work, how ancient people lived, where Mount

Vesuvius is located, and what Pompeii looked like covered with volcanic ash. This thirst for sheer accumulation won't ever die completely, but it is more easily satisfied later on. And the wonder of that first encounter with a strange civilization will never come again.

The immature mind is more suited to absorption than argument. For most children, the critical and logical faculties simply don't develop until later on. The typical second grader will take great joy in singing the latest television commercials to you word for word but will stare at you slack-jawed if you ask her why the advertiser wants her to buy the product or what the merits of the product are or whether it's reasonably priced. There is nothing wrong with a child accumulating information that she doesn't yet understand. It all goes into the storehouse for use later on.

Susan recalls that somewhere around second grade she learned to chant the entire list of helping verbs. The uses of a helping verb weren't clear to her until much later on. But she finds that list popping into her mind whenever she's checking her own writing for grammatical errors or learning a foreign language.

Finally, there's the enjoyment factor. Children *like* lists at this age. They like rattling off rote information, even if they don't understand it. They enjoy the accomplishment, the look on the face of an adult when they trot out their stored knowledge, and the sounds of the syllables rolling off their tongues. As adults, we may tend to "protect" our children from memory work because *we* find it difficult and tedious. But most young children enjoy repetition and delight in the familiarity of memorized words. How many times have you read *Green Eggs and Ham* to a four-year-old who already knows the entire book by heart?

HOW TO TEACH THE POLL-PARROT STAGE

As your child's teacher, you'll serve as a source of information. In the early grades, you'll be telling your child stories, reading to him from history and science books, teaching him math facts. And you'll expect him to be able to repeat back to you the stories and facts he's heard. This process—which we'll outline in detail for each area of the curriculum—will train him to grasp facts and express them in his own words.

Don't make K–4 students dig for information. Fill their minds and imaginations with images and concepts, pictures and stories. Spread knowledge out in front of them, and let them feast.

As you go through this section, keep two important principles in mind.

First, the goal of grammar-stage instruction is *not* to restrict your child ("No, you can't think critically about that yet! Go memorize!"), but rather to protect her love of learning. Children mature out of the grammar stage and into the logic stage (see Chapter 13) at different times. A young student who is already thinking abstractly and critically can be encouraged to do so—but a child who is still firmly in the grammar stage will be frustrated and discouraged by curricula that ask her to speculate, predict, analyze, or carry out other tasks that require more mental maturity than she possesses. Children who cry, sulk, or grow angry when faced with schoolwork are probably being asked to work at a developmental level that they haven't reached. They should be allowed to continue with the grammar-level work described in this section until the earth has gone around the sun a little bit longer; maturity can't be rushed.

Second, children mature unevenly. Some second graders may already be ready for abstract mathematical concepts, but not prepared to think critically about literature until fifth grade or even later. Other third graders may be eager to analyze and dissect literature (a logic-stage skill), but are still years away from algebraic thinking—or vice versa. When a child leaps ahead into logic-stage thinking in one or more areas, we tend to use the word "gifted, " which is not entirely accurate. What has actually happened is a faster maturing process. Give your children the time and space to mature, in each subject area, from grammar into logic-stage thinking.

PRIORITIES

Schools struggle to make time for all the subjects students need and want—grammar, writing, reading, math, history, science, art, music, religion, typing, test preparation, and so forth.

Part of the school dilemma results from an over-focus on testing results; home educators are free from that pressure, so you won't have to decide between test prep and expository writing. But home schoolers also struggle with the mass of material that *could* be covered. There are so many good history books, science experiments, works of classic literature, engaging math resources, piano pieces, art techniques. How do you pick and choose?

In the elementary grades, we suggest that you prioritize reading, writing, grammar, and math. History and science are important. But if you don't do much biology in first grade, it doesn't matter: your child's going to get to biology at least two more times before he goes to college. If you skimp on reading or writing, though, you're likely to hamper your child's educational progress. History and science are reading-dependent. A child who reads and writes well will pick up surprising amounts of history and science as he browses. A child who has difficulty reading and writing will struggle with every subject.

In first grade especially, the child's mind is busy with new skills. You spend an immense amount of time in one-on-one tutoring. Language skills and math will take up most of that time. If you do history and science two or three times a week, that's fine. If you don't start music, the sky won't fall. If you don't do art until much later, nothing drastic will happen. Don't feel that you must teach every subject in depth.

Remember, classical education teaches a child *how* to learn. The child who knows how to learn will grow into a well-rounded—and well-equipped—adult . . . even if he didn't finish his first-grade science book.

4

UNLOCKING THE DOORS:
THE PRESCHOOL YEARS

Very soon after I went to live with Mr. and Mrs. Auld, she very kindly
commenced to teach me the A, B, C. After I had learned this, she
assisted me in learning to spell words of three or four letters. . . . I had
no regular teacher [but] . . . the first step had been taken. Mistress, in
teaching me the alphabet, had given me the inch, and no precaution
could prevent me from taking the ell. The plan which I adopted, and
the one by which I was most successful, was that of making friends of
all the little white boys whom I met in the street. As many of these as
I could, I converted into teachers. With their kindly aid, obtained at
different times and in different places, I finally succeeded in learning
to read.

—Frederick Douglass, *Narrative of the Life of Frederick Douglass,*
an American Slave, Written by Himself

SUBJECT: **Preparation for reading, writing, and math, birth–age 5**
TIME REQUIRED: **Start with 10 minutes a day for each subject, gradu-**
ally increasing to about 30 minutes a day by age 5

When you educate your child at home, you don't have to draw a line
between parenting and teaching. Teaching—preparing the child for
the twelve formal years of classical education—begins at birth.

PRESCHOOL: BIRTH TO THREE

The best early teaching you can give your child is to immerse her in language from birth.

Reading

Turn off the television—half an hour per day is plenty for any child under five. Talk, talk, talk—adult talk, not baby talk. Talk in complete sentences. Talk to her while you're walking in the park, while you're riding in the car, while you're fixing dinner. Tell her what you're doing while you're doing it. ("Now I'm going to send a fax. I put the paper in facedown and punch in the telephone number of the fax machine I'm calling . . . and then the paper starts to feed through like this." "I spilled flour on the floor. I'm going to get out the vacuum cleaner and plug it in. I think I'll use this brush—it's the furniture brush, but the flour's down in the cracks, so it should work better than the floor brush.") This sort of constant chatter lays a verbal foundation in your child's mind. She's learning that words are used to plan, to think, to explain; she's figuring out how the English language organizes words into phrases, clauses, and complete sentences. We have found that children from silent families ("We never really talk much during the day," one mother told us) struggle to read.

Read, read, read. Start reading chunky books to your baby in her crib. Give her sturdy books that she can look at alone. (A torn book or two is a small price to pay for literacy.) Read picture books, pointing at the words with your finger. Read the same books over and over; repetition builds literacy (even as it slowly drives you insane). Read longer books without pictures while she sits on your lap or plays on the floor or cuts and pastes and colors. Invest in a toddler-safe MP3 player and load it with audio versions of preschool books. Record yourself reading, along with the child's comments, so that she can listen to you reading, singing, talking, telling stories, and reciting poems while she plays in her crib.

After you read to your toddler, ask her questions about the story. What did the gingerbread boy do when the old woman tried to eat him? When the dogs got to the top of the tree at the end of *Go, Dog, Go*, what did they find? What happened after Bananas Gorilla stole all the bananas? If she doesn't know, answer the question yourself in a complete sentence and encourage her to repeat it after you.

As soon as your child begins to talk (which will be early if she's this immersed in language), teach her the alphabet. Sing the alphabet song whenever you change her diaper (often). Stencil alphabet letters, both capital letters and lowercase letters, to the wall, or put up a chart. Read alphabet rhymes and alphabet books.

When she knows the names of the letters, tell her that each letter has a sound, just as each animal makes a sound—"Pigs say *oink*"; "Dogs say *woof*"; and "B says *b, b, b* as in *baby*." Start with the sounds of the consonants (that's everything except *a, e, i, o,* and *u*). Tell her that *b* is the sound at the beginning of *bat, ball,* and *Ben;* say, "*T, t, tickle*" and "*M, m, mommy*" and "*C, c, cat*."

Then tell her that the vowels (*a, e, i, o, u*) are named *A, E, I, O,* and *U*. Sing, "Old McDonald had a farm, A, E, I, O, U." Then teach her that each vowel has a sound, just as each animal makes a sound—"*A* as in *at*," "*E* as in *egg*," "*I* as in *igloo*," "*O* as in *octopus*," and "*U* as in *umbrella*." These are the *short sounds* of the vowels, the only vowel sounds you should teach at first. All of this is *prereading*.

Prereading preparation works. Susan was reading on a fifth-grade level in kindergarten. Her son Christopher was checking out fourth- and fifth-grade books halfway through his first year of school at home. We've seen these results duplicated by many other home schoolers. If you create a language-rich home, limit TV and videos, and then teach systematic phonics, you can produce readers.

Writing

Very young children (under two) will pick up a pencil and imitate scribbling. Teach a child from the beginning to hold the pencil correctly. Draw lots of circles and loops *in a counterclockwise direction*. Most printed letters use counterclockwise circles; although many children naturally want to draw circles clockwise, this habit will make cursive handwriting difficult later on. Make snowmen, Slinkies, smoke from a train, car wheels, and so forth counterclockwise.

Let the child practice making letters without using a regular pencil. A young child lacks fine-motor maturity, but she can form letters and numbers by writing in rice or sand with her finger. Or, if she wants to use a writing tool, she can use chalk on a big chalkboard or a crayon or pencil on large sheets of paper. Regular-diameter short pencils are often easier for small fingers to handle than fat "preschool" pencils. Teach your three-year-old basic dot-to-dot skills by drawing your own dot-to-dot picture (a house, a smiley face) using four or five big dots, then guiding the child's crayon from dot to dot so that she can see the picture emerge. Continual drawing and making counterclockwise circles will prepare the preschooler for kindergarten writing.

Math

Start to make your child "mathematically literate" in the toddler years. Just as you read to the toddler, surrounding him with language until he understood that printed words on a page carried meaning, now you need to expose him to mathematical processes and language continually. Only then will he understand that mathematical symbols carry meaning.

Bring numbers into everyday life as often as possible. Start with counting: fingers, toes, eyes, and ears; toys and treasures; rocks and sticks. Play hide-and-seek, counting to five and then to ten, fifteen, or twenty together. Count by twos, fives, and tens before shouting, "Coming, ready or not!" Play spaceship in cardboard boxes, and count backward for take-off. Read number books together. Once the child is comfortable counting, you can start working on simple math sums—usually during the K–4 and K–5 years.

General Preschool Learning

In addition to teaching your child prereading and beginning math skills, you can prepare her for kindergarten work by using the preschool enrichment materials listed in the Resources section. One caution: it's easy to over-buy and over-schedule preschool. Don't push an unwilling toddler into cutting and pasting or other activities; lots of informal learning and active play are the most valuable preparation for the school years.

KINDERGARTEN YEARS: FOUR AND FIVE

We have mixed feelings about formal kindergarten programs for four- and five-year-olds. A kindergarten program that combines beginning reading and writing with lots of artwork and active play can be productive. But it's a rare five-year-old who's ready to do very much paper-and-pencil work at a desk, and a six-year-old who hasn't done a formal kindergarten program can easily begin first-grade work.

"I can always tell the children who've been to kindergarten from the ones who haven't," a first-grade teacher told Susan.

"Are they that much further ahead?" Susan asked.

"No," she said, "but they already know how to stand in line."

Kindergarten *does* teach five-year-olds to stand in line, to wait to go to the bathroom, to raise their hand when they want to ask a question, and to walk through a cafeteria without spilling their food. But if you're teaching your child at home, these aren't the survival skills she has to have right away.

Kindergarten for four–year-olds accomplishes even less. Most four-year-olds have microscopic attention spans, immature hand-eye coordination, and a bad case of the wiggles. And normal four-year-olds differ widely in their maturity levels: one might be ready to read but be completely disinterested in writing; another might enjoy drawing and handwork but show no desire to read; a third might like to play endless games of Uno™ but reject anything having to do with letters and words.

We feel that there's little point in following a formal, academic K–4 or K–5 curriculum at home. Rather, the first four or five years of a child's life should be spent in informal teaching—preparing the child for first-grade work. In about thirty minutes per day, plus informal teaching as you go about your family life, you can easily teach your child beginning reading, writing, and math concepts, all without workbooks or teacher's manuals.

If you're already teaching an older child at home, your four-year-old may beg to "do school" as well. At the end of the chapter, we'll recommend several reading and math programs that will keep a kindergartner occupied at one end of the table while her big sister does second-grade math at the other end. But try not to think of these curricula as schoolwork, or you may find yourself pushing a reluctant preschooler to "just finish that page" when her attention span has long since expired.

Rather, you should aim to teach reading and math in the same way that you taught the child to speak, to tie her shoes, to dress, to clean up after herself—by demonstrating the basic skills yourself, practicing them for a few minutes each day, and talking about them as you go through the routines of life. ("There are four of us. How many spoons should you put on the table so that we can each have one?" "Can you get me the can that says *Tomato* on it? You'll recognize the *T* that says *t, t, tomato*.")

You can use charts, CDs, games, workbooks, and stickers if you want to. But you don't need them.

Reading

A classical education relies heavily on the written word. As a parent-educator, your number one goal should be to have your child well on the path to fluent reading when he starts first-grade work.

Here's the good news: For children who are on a normal developmental path, reading is a straightforward skill—and learning to teach it is simple. You don't have to be an expert in phonemic awareness and decoding skills in order to teach your child to read.[1]

Frederick Douglass, as well as Abraham Lincoln, Benjamin Franklin, and thousands of eighteenth-century pioneer children, learned to read with the alphabet and a few good books. Douglass learned his ABCs from an adult and obtained the rest of his reading competency skills from street urchins. I [Jessie] learned to read from a set of alphabet blocks. Between the ages of four and six, most children who have been read to since toddlerhood and who are not suffering from a learning disorder (see "When Learning Doesn't Improve" on pages 711–714) can learn to read. And any

---

[1] However, don't be surprised if you are discouraged by some professional educators. I (Jessie) was verbally accosted decades ago when I went to a reading professor to find readers for Susan. He demanded, "*What* do you think you are doing, teaching your child to read yourself?" I was so intimidated that I never went back to him for help. In contrast, a first-grade teacher who was successfully teaching *all* her first graders to read directed me to the phonics material she was using so that I could get it for myself. Alas, the material has now been revised beyond recognition.

reasonably literate adult (which includes anyone who can read this book) can serve as tutor for basic phonics skills.[2]

You should continue to immerse four- and five-year-olds in language, just as you've been doing since birth. Read with them in the "real world": billboards, store names, bumper stickers, cereal boxes in the grocery store, banners at the gas station.

Get them audiobooks—not the fifteen-minute children's tapes with all the bells and whistles designed to keep children occupied, but real books read in their entirety without sound effects. Most public libraries have shelves of books on CD in the children's section. Children can listen to and enjoy books that are far, far above their vocabulary level; in one year, Susan's three-year-old and five-year-old listened to all of Kipling's *Just So Stories*, the original *Jungle Book*, all of Edith Nesbit's books, *The Chronicles of Narnia*, Barrie's densely written *Peter Pan*, E. B. White's *Charlotte's Web* and *The Trumpet of the Swan*, Frances Hodgson Burnett's *A Little Princess*, the unabridged *Christmas Carol* by Dickens. Audiobooks stock a child's mind with the sounds of thousands of words. When children start sounding out words later on, they'll progress much more quickly if they recognize the words.

Read yourself. Turn off the TV and read a book, do a crossword puzzle, buy the *New York Times*.

Keep on reading together. Start to ask slightly more complex questions about the stories. "What was Wilbur afraid of in *Charlotte's Web*?" "Did Fern's mother worry when Fern told her that the animals were talking to her?"

By the age of four, the average child should know her alphabet and the sounds that each letter makes. Continue to work on letter names and sounds. Lowercase magnetic refrigerator letters are a good way to do this. You can give the child a *d* magnet and say, *"D, d, d, dog"*; you can say, "Mary, go get me the letter that says *t, t, t*," and Mary will go over to the refrigerator and decide which letter makes that sound.

Sometime around age four or five, most children are ready to start reading. Sit down with a simple primer that teaches phonics—the sounds that letters make when they're combined together into words. The primer should contain clear step-by-step instructions on how to teach reading

---

[2] See pages 271–275 for a brief discussion of the phonics–whole language debate.

from the very beginning stages, starting with letter sounds and moving systematically through blending sounds into reading real words and sentences. Your goal is to get the child reading quickly and confidently; handwriting and spelling can be delayed until she has enough fine motor coordination to write without frustration.

Progress systematically through the primer. Go slowly, with plenty of repetition; reread the lessons until your child is completely comfortable with the sounds and their combination into words. Do this for five minutes to start with; work up to ten or fifteen minutes per session.

At some other time during the day, sit down with the child and a "real book," and let her read it. At the end of this chapter, you'll find a list of books that can be read with relative ease, even by a child who's only learned consonants and one or two vowel sounds. (The lowest levels use only the *a* vowel sound, so you can start on a "real book" right after the first few lessons!) Don't forget that you've already done your drill. Give the child a good chance to sound words out, but if she gets stuck, sound it out for her and move on. If you get to a word that uses a rule she hasn't used yet, simply tell her what the rule is and keep going.

CHILD: Ann went to the steps and went—(*Sticks on the word "down."*)
YOU: That says "down." *O* and *w* together say "ow." *D-ow-n.*
CHILD:—down.

If you don't know the rule yourself, tell the child the word and move on. (Look the rule up later.)

Although *The Ordinary Parent's Guide to Teaching Reading* is our first choice because it is a thorough phonics program that provides clear and explicit instruction for the parent, you can follow this process with any systematic phonics program.

In beginning reading instruction, it is best to stay with supplementary readers that are strictly phonetic (see suggested "Beginning Readers" in the Resources at the end of this chapter). But as your child becomes more confident in his ability to sound out words, he will want to read easy books that contain "sight" words that don't follow phonetic rules (and that he will need to recognize on "sight"). Such words used frequently in beginning story books include: *are, build, busy, buy, come, do, does, done, eye, father, gone, have, love, mother, of, oh, one, there, they, to, two, was, were, where, you.*

Could, should, and *would,* although phonetic, appear in many early readers before they are taught in systematic programs, and may be treated as sight words. Make flash cards for these words and teach them a few at a time as you see them occur in your child's books. Do not teach these in isolation! Wait until they occur in the beginning readers. Reading is best taught in the context of meaningful content. And you don't want your beginning reader to memorize whole words as a habit, rather than sounding out the phonetic elements in each word.

Start with five minutes of drill and five minutes of reading in an easy book every day. Work up to fifteen minutes of each. Don't ask, "Do you want to do your reading now?" (They always say no.) Plan it as matter-of-factly as you would plan tooth brushing and bed making. You'll be astounded at the speed with which children begin to sound out words on their own.

The advantage of this method is that you're not limited in what you read with the child; if you sound out words that are beyond the child's "drill level," together the two of you can read practically anything in the "easy reading" or "beginning reader" section of the library. And you'll often find that your child has already absorbed a rule by the time you get to it in the primer. If you say enough times, while reading, "The *e* on the end makes the *a* say its name—that's the difference between *hat* and *hate,*" your little reader will greet that rule when you arrive at it with a shrug and "I already knew that."

And that's it.

Don't you need songs, drills, exercises, workbooks, and charts? We don't think so, for a whole host of reasons.

In the first place, lots of people who teach a four- or five-year-old to read also have a toddler or newborn. (Susan had both when her oldest son was five.) Sorting through charts and songs and trying to follow a program with lots of aids make teaching more complicated than it needs to be. With our method, all you need is a primer and lots of books.

Second, all those reinforcements and aids create extra mental steps for the learner. If you're teaching a child to sing the song "*A* is for apple, *b* is for bear, . . . ," you're teaching her to see an *a*, think "apple," and then think the sound of short *a*. If you have a flash card with a *b* and a picture of a bird on it, the picture—not the letter—becomes a signal to the child to say the *b* sound. The child goes through an extra step in associating the sound with the letter. Instead of looking at a *b* and forming the *b* sound, the mental process becomes "B . . . bird . . . *b*." This is slow, and in many cases the child stays slow because he becomes dependent on the clue. Without the clue, he has no idea how to "break" the code of the word. There's an easier way. Just point to the *a* and say "A, *a*, *a*" (that's the short *a* sound as in *at*); point to the *b* and say, "B, *b*, *b*." Even two- and three-year-olds love this game, and they learn these associations much faster than you might expect.

Third, most reinforcements—even though they may be advertised and produced for a home-education setting—were originally designed for a classroom of children. A teacher teaching a whole group of students to read can't sit down with each one and teach him or her to pronounce each letter correctly whenever he or she sees it on the page. That's an intensive, one-on-one process. The teacher has to resort to the second-best method: reinforcing the correct sound through secondary aids in a nonreading context. You don't have to do that.

Fourth, you're not teaching your four- or five-year-old the exhaustive elements of the English language. Beginning in first grade, your child will receive a more thorough grounding in the rules of spelling, which are simply phonics rules applied to writing. (We'll recommend resources for doing this in Chapter 5.) During the K–4 and K–5 years, your goal is simply to get the child reading as quickly and fluently as possible. A kindergartner doesn't need to be able to list from memory all the different ways a long-*e* sound can be spelled; he just needs to be able to pronounce *meal, field,* and *teeth* when he sees them.

And finally, workbook-centered reading programs demand a fair amount of fine muscle coordination from young children. Kindergartners vary widely in the amount of pencil work that they're prepared to do; boys in particular mature more slowly when it comes to handwriting. Tying reading instruction to assignments that require handwriting can retard reading progress, since many five-year-olds are capable of reading far ahead of what they're able to write. Children with slower muscle development can grow frustrated with reading, when in fact they're perfectly ready to read; they're just not ready to write. Separating the act of reading from physical writing assignments allows them to progress forward at a natural, enjoyable rate.

If you prefer a workbook approach and have a coordinated preschooler who doesn't have trouble with writing skills, or if you have a younger child who's anxious to do workbooks in imitation of an older sibling, you might consider investing in one of the more pencil-centered resources listed at the end of this chapter.

But be very sensitive to signs of hand fatigue, and treat the workbook pages as games rather than assignments; none of them have to be "finished," and you can skip anything that seems too laborious.

What if my child isn't ready to read? If you've read to your preschooler since she could stare at a page, you can start this process at age four and take a couple of years to go through it. Or you can start at age five and do it in less time. Second and third children, who've watched older brothers and sisters learn to read, are likely to want to start sooner. If your four-year-old asks you for a reading lesson, oblige her. I [Jessie] taught Susan to read at three because every time I sat down with her five-year-old brother to do a phonics lesson, she wanted to be included.

Reading readiness (like everything else in this chapter) isn't complicated. A child is ready to learn to read when she collects her stuffed animals and a picture book and tells them a story; or when she picks up a book, sits on the sofa, and pretends she's reading to you; or when she constantly asks you, "What does this say?" All of these activities show that she understands that printed words carry a message.

Most five-year-olds are capable of learning to read, which doesn't mean that they'll want to do it. A child who squirms, complains, and protests every time you produce the primer isn't necessarily demonstrating "reading unreadiness." She's simply being five. It's a rare child who wants to do something unfamiliar that involves work; as a matter of fact, we've yet to meet a five-year-old who could be convinced to set her eyes on long-range goals.[3] If the child doesn't want to learn to read, tell her that you're going to do five minutes per day anyway.

[3] I (Jessie) am not impressed by "child-led" education (waiting until the child brings you a book and begs for a reading lesson) for the same reasons that I didn't let my elementary-school children eat exactly what they want: young children do not usually realize that real food is not only better for them than Twinkies, but actually more satisfying in the long run. A typical learning-to-read-at-home dialogue might sound like this:

PARENT: Don't you want to learn to read? If you work on these lists of rules for a year, you can read books to yourself!

CHILD: (*Eyeing twenty pages of rules and reasoning that the parent reads books to her anytime she wants anyway.*) I don't like it.

The beginning stage, when you're teaching the child to sound out three-letter words for the first time, is the most difficult. Persist until you can start the child on the earliest readers listed at the end of this chapter. Most children will swell up with pride over being able to read a "whole book all alone." Once they've started putting sentences together, they'll tell you they don't need to do the drill anymore; they just want to read. That's a good sign, but insist on the ten minutes of drill every day until you've covered all the rules in the phonics primer. Use common sense, though. If you've started on three-letter words, doing a faithful ten minutes per day for three or four weeks, and the child shows no comprehension, she hasn't made the connection between print and sounds yet. Drop it for a month or two, and then come back to it.

When to Get Help

A five-year-old who isn't catching on to phonetic reading is still in the normal range.

As we'll discuss in the next chapter, if your child remains mystified by phonetic principles into the first-grade year, professional evaluation might be called for. But at age five, you can feel comfortable waiting for a little more maturity. If the child is willing to sit with you for ten minutes per day to sound out three-letter words, keep on working on this basic skill. If she resists, give the drill a rest and play more alphabet games, and then try again in six or eight weeks.

However, there are a couple of signposts that might indicate an earlier need for intervention. Preschool and kindergarten children who are normally compliant and enjoy other "schoolish" activities, but who throw tantrums or

---

PARENT: But you haven't even tried yet.
CHILD: But I don't like it anyway.

This exchange ought to sound familiar to anyone who's served a child a new food:

PARENT: These are fresh strawberries. You'll love them.
CHILD: (Eyeing the strawberries.) I don't like them.
PARENT: But you've never eaten a strawberry.
CHILD: I don't like them anyway.

The reasonable response is: Eat one every time I serve them, and you'll learn to like them. Reading is no different.

weep when faced with reading, are signaling that something is wrong. Speech delay (by age three, a child should be using phrases longer than two words on a regular basis; by four, complete sentences; your pediatrician can provide you with the standard benchmarks) can point to hearing or processing problems. Lack of interest in reading combined with physical signs such as inability to hold a crayon, catch a ball, or do up buttons can signal a developmental difficulty. Inability to recognize the alphabet by age five is a warning sign.

In these cases, get both eyesight and hearing evaluated first. If the physical findings are normal, consider an evaluation by a qualified therapist. (See Chapter 37 for more on this.)

Writing

Many phonics programs insist that you combine writing with reading. In other words, teach the child the consonants and the sound of *a*, but don't go on to the next step until the child is able both to read and write *sat, cat, fat, bat*.

As we've said above, this tends to frustrate very young readers. Remember, you want the child to read quickly, easily, and early. Many children are ready to read long before they have the muscular coordination to write. Why delay reading until the muscles of the hand and eye catch up? So do your reading and writing drills separately during your child's fourth and fifth years.

When the child is able to hold the pencil comfortably and has some control over it, then move on to formal writing instruction. Get a beginning writing workbook along with plenty of lined writing paper, sized for preschool and kindergarten writers (see pages 51–53).

Your writing workbook should teach a style of printing that transitions easily into cursive writing. In traditional ball-and-stick writing, the student continually lifts her hand—if she writes a small *d*, for example, she draws a circle, picks up her pencil, and then connects a line to the circle. Then, when she starts to do traditional cursive instruction (usually halfway through second grade), she has to learn an entirely new set of strokes, just as her muscle memory is becoming solid. Instead, look for a *continuous stroke* method, in which letters are written in one motion; this makes for an easier transition into cursive. Italic writing is an alternative style that also avoids an abrupt change during second grade. See the Resources list at the end of this chapter for curricula that meet these standards.

Teach only one letter (always do a capital and small letter together) or one number at a time until you've gone through the entire alphabet and the numbers 1 through 10. You can either follow the suggested workbook sequence or teach the letters in the order presented in your phonics primer. The writing workbooks have arrows and numbers to show the exact way that letters should be written: the circle for a small *a* is always drawn counterclockwise; the straight edge of a capital *D* is always drawn first, with the curve of the letter drawn second. *This is important!* Make sure you teach the child to write each letter properly, and for the first few months supervise her carefully so that she doesn't fall into bad habits.

When you've worked through the entire alphabet, let the child begin to copy words that you write out for her—family names are a good place to start. Eventually, ask her to copy very short sentences: "I love you." "Ben is smart!" "Do you like to write?" In this way, the five-year-old not only practices writing, but begins to learn the conventions of written language: capitals for names and the beginnings of sentences, spaces between words, periods and exclamation points. You'll continue on with copywork more systematically in first grade, and then progress to dictation, where the child will write without a model in front of her. But for now, write out the sentences for her to copy, and let her refer to your models as often as needed. Ten minutes per day, three to five times per week, is sufficient. Frequency and consistency bring quicker results than prolonged sessions.

A word about cursive writing. A great debate is on about *when* to introduce cursive penmanship. Some educators say that children should begin with cursive and skip manuscript printing; others recommend beginning cursive anywhere between first and fourth grade. We have always chosen to teach printing until the child is writing quickly and well, and then begin cursive penmanship, usually in the middle of second grade. This seems easier for most children, as long as a complete change in stroke style is not required; many beginning writers have a great need to form letters that look something like the letters they see in books, and cursive writing frustrates them.

We would not teach typing until fourth grade. Although students will probably type the majority of their written work in the middle- and high-school years, during the early years they are still learning the differences between letters and associating letters (and letter combinations) with sounds. When a student prints an *a* and a *t*, her hand makes very different motions; this helps her brain to continue to distinguish between the two letters and the two very different sounds that they make. In typing, each letter is produced with essentially the same finger motion. So take handwriting seriously in the early years. Once language skills are firmly established, typing can take its place as a useful tool for the budding writer.

Math

Now that the child can count, continue to do "daily" math by adding and subtracting in the context of everyday family life. Setting the table is a great math exercise: ask your child to figure out how many plates, knives, forks, and spoons are necessary. Add and subtract in the grocery store ("Look, Mike. I'm picking up four tomatoes and then one more tomato—that makes five!"). Cook together—recipes are full of fractions and measures. When you cut a sandwich in half or quarters, say, "Look, I cut this in half!" or "I cut this into fourths!"

Play games that use numbers. Uno™ is a classic—it teaches both number and color matching. Simple card games such as Battle and Go Fish require children to remember which numbers are higher and which are lower.

Practice writing numbers using pencil and paper, chalk and chalkboard, crayons and poster paper, fingers and sand. Big numbers are fun and easy—don't insist that preschoolers and kindergartners write their numbers neatly on lined paper.

Do lots of addition and subtraction with manipulatives (beans, buttons, pencils, chocolate chips). Play with math manipulatives: Cuisenaire Rods, counting bears, fraction circles. Practice counting to one hundred by twos, fives, and tens. Learn about money, tell time, and name geometric figures—circles, squares, triangles, rectangles.

Your public library should have a colorful selection of kindergarten-level math books—easy problems worked out with photographed objects. Get a book every week, and read through it with your child.

If you do this, your child will be ready for first-grade math. Susan's children had no difficulty going directly into a first-grade math curriculum without first completing a formal kindergarten math program. As in reading, though, younger children may enjoy having a math program to work on along with an older brother or sister; many kindergarten math programs are fun and full of manipulatives.

Again, think of a kindergarten math program as a game, not as an academic pursuit. If the child gets tired after five or ten minutes, don't force her to finish the lesson.

Science Learning

If you'd like to do kindergarten science projects with your preschooler, use the elementary activity guides listed in our Resources section; they offer clear instructions and experiments that use common household items. You can supplement beginning reading, writing, and math by doing a science experiment once or twice a week. More formal science study isn't necessary at this stage.

General Learning

Kindergarten students may enjoy cutting, pasting, coloring, and game playing. If you need some assistance coming up with related projects, consult the activity guides we've listed under General Learning in the Resources below.

RESOURCES

Most books can be obtained from any bookseller or library; most curricula can be bought directly from the publisher or from a major home-school supplier such as Rainbow Resource Center. Contact information for publishers and suppliers can be found at www.welltrainedmind.com. If availability is limited, we have noted it. Where indicated, resources are listed in chronological order (the order you'll want to use them in). Books in series are listed together. Remember that additional curricula choices and more can be found at www.welltrainedmind.com. Prices change constantly, but we have included 2016 pricing to give an idea of affordability.

Reading Skills: Phonics Primers

Hiskes, Dolores G. *Phonics Pathways.* 10th ed. Indianapolis, IN: Jossey-Bass, 2011.

$32.95. This phonics primer covers all the letter sounds and combinations needed for fluent reading. Sample pages can be viewed at the author's website, Dorbooks.

Wise, Jessie. *The Ordinary Parent's Guide to Teaching Reading.* Charles City, VA: Well-Trained Mind Press, 2004.

$29.95. A scripted phonics primer that supplies full parent support; all you have to do is read the instructor dialogue out loud. Flash cards and an audio companion are also available. Sample pages can be viewed at the publisher's website.

Reading Skills: Additional Practice

Explode the Code. Cambridge, MA: Educators Publishing Service, 2003.

Order from EPS. Each workbook drills a particular phonetic sound; the introductory books (A, B, and C) teach the letters. The "½" books provide additional practice. The student books are $9.40 each. If you find an answer key is necessary, they are available for each book and are priced at $9.35.

Get Ready for the Code Book A. Consonant sounds *b, f, k, m, r, t.*

Get Set for the Code Book B. Consonant sounds *d, h, j, n, p, s.*

Go for the Code Book C. Consonant sounds *c, g, l, q, v, w, y, z, x.*

Book 1. Consonants, short vowels.

Book 1 ½.

Book 2. Blends.

Book 2 ½.

Book 3. Beginning long vowels, consonant digraphs, diphthongs.

Book 3 ½.

Book 4. Compound words, common endings, syllables.

Book 4 ½.

Book 5. Word families, three-letter blends.

Book 5 ½.

Book 6. Vowels plus *r*, diphthongs.

Book 6 ½.

Book 7. Soft *c* and *g*, silent consonants, *ph.*

Book 8. Suffixes and irregular endings.

Hiskes, Dolores G. *Reading Pathways: Simple Exercises to Improve Reading Fluency.* 5th ed. Indianapolis, IN: Jossey-Bass, 2007.

$24.95. Exercises build from single words to phrases to short sentences and from short to multisyllabic words, using a pyramid layout that improves eye movement. Sample pages can be viewed at the author's website, Dorbooks.

Beginning Readers

Animal Friends. Pensacola, FL: A Beka Book, various dates.
$9.35. Order from A Beka Book. A set of eight full-color booklets, phonetically progressing from three-letter words to words with long vowel sounds.

The Emergent Reader series. Lyme, NH: Flyleaf Publishing, various dates.
$8.50 each, or order the entire 41-book series for $162. Available directly from the publisher (and at some local libraries). Samples and a complete listing of titles can be found on the publisher's website. These colorful readers progress from two- and three-letter words ("vowel consonant" and "consonant vowel consonant") in the first seven books, to short- and long-vowel words with consonant blends in books 8–14, compound words in books 15–21, multisyllabic and long-vowel words in books 22–28, and words with endings and variant vowels sounds in books 29–41. Some sight words are also used (e.g., see the short-vowel readers).

Books 1–7
I Am Sam
Cam and Sam
Ann Can
C and K
Can You See 3?
Pam Likes to Nap
Can I See Tom?
Books 8–14
We Can't Stop!
Dot and Dan
Dot Likes to Dig
To the Top
On a Log
Hal Likes Hats
Fran Can Flip

Books 15–21

   Ted Can Do Tricks

   My Wagon Is Red

   The Sunset Pond

   Jen's Best Gift Ever

   We Can Get Fit

   This and That

   Scamp Gets a Bath

Books 22–28

   It Is Halloween!

   Fred and Max in the Sandbox

   Will Is Up at Bat

   I Like Soccer

   I Can Mix Colors

   Vivid

   Meg and Jim's Sled Trip

Books 29–41

   A Cricket Sings

   Stink Bug

   Grandma Dot

   Fun in Winter, Spring, Summer, Fall

   Just a Box

   Am I Lucky?

   Hints of Fall

   I Like Spectrums

   I Sang a Song to Spring

   Balls

   Insects

   Dogs

   I Can Plant a Seed

Little Books 1–12. Pensacola, FL: A Beka Book, various dates. $10.80. Order from A Beka Book. Twelve small storybooks that begin with only short vowel words and progress through blends, words, and simple sentences. Includes pages to color.

Maslen, Bobby Lyn. Bob Books series, illus. John R. Maslen. New York: Scholastic, 2006.

The sets contain 8–10 small paperbacks inside each box. These are the first books your child will be able to read alone; children love them because they can start on the Bob Books after only a few weeks of phonics lessons. The experience of reading an entire book independently right at the beginning of the learning process provides young readers with immense encouragement. *Highly recommended.* Most libraries carry them; but the books are in high demand, and you may have trouble getting them (and keeping them for more than a couple of weeks). If you plan to teach more than one child how to read, they're worth buying because older children can help younger siblings sound them out.

Bob Books, Set 1: Beginning Readers. $10.25.

Bob Books, Set 2: Advancing Beginners. $9.60.

Bob Books, Set 3: Word Families. $10.90.

Bob Books, Set 4: Complex Words. $14.16.

Bob Books, Set 5: Long Vowels. $13.71.

Bob Books: Rhyming Words. $13.59. Short-vowel stories told in rhyme; can follow Set 1 for additional practice.

Bob Books: Sight Words, Kindergarten. $9.48. The thirty most common sight words; use any time after Set 1.

Beginning Story Books: "Easy Readers"

The "Easy Reader" category is confusing because most of these books are fun and engaging, but not geared to phonetic instruction. They have just a few words on the page, but beginning readers cannot read some of these books unless they have memorized whole words. If there are many sight words or words the child has not yet encountered in his phonics instruction, read these books *to* the child, pointing to the pictures and asking the child to sound out only those words that you know he is ready to decode.

These are just a few of the multiple titles available, but starting with these will lead you to many more.

Brown, Margaret Wise. *Big Red Barn.* New York: HarperFestival, 1995.

———. *I Like Bugs.* New York: Random House, 1999.

Eastman, P. D. *Are You My Mother?* New York: Random House, 2010.

————. *The Best Nest.* New York: Random House, 2010.

————. *Go, Dog, Go.* New York: Beginner Books, 1961.

————. *Sam and the Firefly.* New York: Random House, 2010.

————. *Snow.* New York: Beginner Books, 1962.

Geisel, Theodore Seuss (Dr. Seuss). *The Cat in the Hat.* New York: Random House, 2013.

————. *Dr. Seuss's A.B.C.* New York: Random House, 1996.

————. *The Foot Book.* New York: Random House, 1968.

————. *Green Eggs and Ham.* New York: Random House, 2013.

————. *Hop On Pop.* New York: Random House, 1963.

————. *One Fish, Two Fish, Red Fish, Blue Fish.* New York: Random House, 1960.

————. *There's a Wocket in My Pocket.* New York: Random House, 1974.

Gustafson, Scott. *Alphabet Soup: A Feast of Letters.* Shelton, CT: Greenwich Workshop Press, 1994.

Hoff, Syd. *Danny and the Dinosaur.* New York: HarperCollins, 2008.

————. *Oliver.* 2000.

Lobel, Arnold. *Frog and Toad Storybook Treasury.* New York: HarperCollins, 2013.

————. *Grasshopper on the Road.* 1986.

————. *Mouse Soup.* 1983.

————. *Owl at Home.* 2012.

————. *Small Pig.* 1988.

Lopshire, Robert. *Put Me in the Zoo.* New York: Random House, 2011.

Minarik, Elsie. *A Kiss for Little Bear.* New York: HarperTrophy, 2003.

————. *Little Bear.* 2003.

————. *Little Bear's Friend.* 2003.

————. *Little Bear's Visit.* 1979.

Penguin Young Readers. New York: Penguin.
  Level 1 series.
    Andrews, Alexa. *At the Beach.* 2013.
    ————. *Cat Days.* 2012.
    ————. *On a Farm.* 2013.
    Blevins, Wiley. *Max Has a Fish.* 2012.
    ————. *A New Friend.* 2013.
    Ingalls, Ann. *Ice Cream Soup.* 2013.
  Level 2 series.
    Abramson, Jill, and Jane O'Connor. *Puppy Parade.* 2013.
    Herman, Gail. *Lucky Goes to School.* 2001.
    ————. *What a Hungry Puppy!* 1993.
    Holub, Joan. *The Pizza That We Made.* 2001.
    Masurel, Claire. *That Bad, Bad Cat!* 2002.
    Moffat, Judith. *Who Stole the Cookies?* 1996.
    Thomas, Shelley Moore. *Good Night, Good Knight.* 2002.
  Level 3 series.
    Aboff, Marcie. *The Giant Jellybean Jar.* 2004.
    Clarke, Ginjer L. *Fake Out! Animals That Play Tricks.* 2007.
    Dussling, Jennifer. *Pink Snow and Other Weird Weather.* 1998.
    Holub, Joan. *Why Do Cats Meow?* 2001.
    ————. *Why Do Dogs Bark?* 2001.
    Kramer, Sydelle. *Wagon Train.* 1997.
    Thomas, Shelley Moore. *Get Well, Good Knight.* 2004.
    ————. *Happy Birthday, Good Knight.* 2014.

Rylant, Cynthia. *Henry and Mudge: The First Book.* New York: Simon & Schuster, 1996.

————. *Henry and Mudge and Annie's Good Move.* 2000.

————. *Henry and Mudge and the Forever Sea.* 1989.

————. *Henry and Mudge and the Happy Cat.* 1990.

————. *Henry and Mudge and the Long Weekend.* 1992.

———. *Henry and Mudge and the Wild Goose Chase.* 2003.

———. *Henry and Mudge in Puddle Trouble.* 1987.

Thomas, Patricia. *"Stand Back," Said the Elephant, "I'm Going to Sneeze,"* illus. Wallace Tripp. New York: Lothrop, Lee & Shepard, 1990.
This rhyming story contains many vowel combinations that look different but sound the same (for example, *bear, fair, declare* all in a row).

Wiseman, B. *Morris the Moose.* New York: HarperCollins, 1991.

Writing

Olsen, Jan Z. *Handwriting Without Tears* program. Cabin John, MD: Handwriting Without Tears.
An alternative handwriting program for children who are very challenged in the area of muscular coordination. This program emphasizes using short pencils of the standard diameter rather than fat preschool pencils, since the shorter pencils are easier for children to manipulate. The program also has the child do manipulative work before he actually writes. When he does begin to copy letters, instead of writing a whole line of letters (as most penmanship books suggest), he writes fewer letters at a time but concentrates on writing them as perfectly as possible. Each lesson involves fifteen minutes of penmanship time: ten minutes of instruction and five minutes of carefully supervised practice. The student does less work than in traditional penmanship books, but what he does is as perfect as he can make it. The workbooks have many model letters per line, so the child doesn't write a line of one letter, consistently getting worse and worse as he goes (children tend to copy the last letter *they* made, rather than looking back at the correct model). Although this program offers many excellent insights for teaching writing, it isn't our first recommendation because the script itself is not as attractive as the Zaner-Bloser script (below); the focus is on legibility rather than beauty. However, a child who is struggling will benefit greatly from this program. Sample pages can be viewed at the publisher's website.
The books below are listed in progressive order.
Letters and Numbers for Me (K). $9.50.

Kindergarten Teacher's Guide. $10.50. Provides an overview of the program and tips on teaching.

My Printing Book (First grade). $9.50.

1st Grade Printing Teacher's Guide. $10.50.

Printing Power (Second grade). $9.50.

2nd Grade Printing Teacher's Guide. $10.50.

Notebook Paper. Designed specifically to go along with the skills taught in this program.

Wide (K–1). 100 sheets. $3.75.

Wide (K–1). 500 sheets. $11.75.

Regular (2–3). 100 sheets. $3.75.

Regular (2–3). 500 sheets. $11.75.

Zaner-Bloser Handwriting series. Columbus, OH: Zaner-Bloser, 2008.

Our favorite resources for teaching writing are from Zaner-Bloser, which publishes colorful learn-to-write workbooks using the "continuous-stroke" alphabet. In traditional ball-and-stick writing, the student continually lifts her hand—if she writes a small *d*, for example, she draws a circle, picks up her pencil, and then connects a line to the circle. In the continuous-stroke alphabet, the letter is written in one motion. This simplifies writing and makes for an easier transition into cursive. Also, some capital letters in the cursive alphabet have been simplified so that they look more like the printed versions. Start with *Grade K Student Book* and let the child progress at her own rate. The manuscript lines become smaller with each book. The books don't give a lot of practice space, so you'll want to order some extra writing paper. The teacher editions are not necessary. Sample pages can be viewed at the publisher's website.

Zaner-Bloser Handwriting. $11.49 each.

Grade K Student Book.

Grade 1 Student Book.

Zaner-Bloser Handwriting Paper. $10.99 per ream.

Order these packs of writing paper for extra handwriting practice from Zaner-Bloser. One ream per year is plenty. The ruled lines on these sheets narrow each year. A child who is having difficulty with handwriting will sometimes improve if you move to a paper with narrower lines.

Grade K paper (¾" wide).

Grade 1 paper (⅝" wide).
Grade 2 paper (½" wide).

Mathematics: Guides

Although we don't think you need a formal math curriculum for preschool and kindergarten, these guides can provide you with a pattern for developing mathematical literacy.

Kumon. *Are You Ready for Kindergarten? Math Skills*. Teaneck, NJ: Kumon Publishing, 2010.
$6.95. Pre-K skills in counting and shape recognition, with simple workbook activities (drawing lines, circling shapes).

Snow, Kate. *Preschool Math at Home: Simple Activities to Build the Best Possible Foundation for Your Child*. Charles City, VA: Well-Trained Mind Press, 2016.
$19.99. Fun games and simple activities that build mathematical awareness, along with clear explanations for the parent of the concepts behind the play. No writing required.

Williams, Robert A., Debra Cunningham, and Joy Lubawy. *Preschool Math*. Beltsville, MD: Gryphon House, 2005.
$19.95. Written for preschool teachers but accessible to any parent, this guide gives principles for hands-on math teaching and suggests numerous activities that can be done with common household objects. Not as "pick up and go" as the Snow or Kumon guides, but excellent for creating greater math awareness.

Mathematics: Manipulatives

Cuisenaire Rods Introductory Set. Order from Hand2Mind.
$9.25. An individual set of seventy-four Cuisenaire® Rods along with a brief guide on their use.

Fraction Circles. Order from Didax Educational Resources.
$6.95. Nine plastic circles divided into halves, quarters, eighths, etc.

Geosolids. Order from Hand2Mind.
$13. A set of nineteen wooden geometric solids, from cubes to ellipsoids.

Jumbo Sorting & Counting Bears. Order from Lakeshore Learning Materials.

$29.99. Twenty-seven bears in three sizes and three colors, plus a storage jar.

Kumon Flash Cards: Write and Wipe! Teaneck, NJ: Kumon Publishing.

$9.95. Each set contains thirty-two hard, laminated flash cards and a dry erase pen. Students learn numbers and shapes through tracing and dot-to-dot exercises.

Easy Telling Time
Numbers 1–30
Shapes

Wooden Pattern Blocks. Order from Didax Educational Resources.

$22.95. One of the most useful preschool manipulative sets; each 250-piece set of 1-cm-thick blocks contains 25 yellow hexagons, 25 orange squares, 50 green triangles, 50 red trapezoids, 50 blue parallelograms, and 50 tan rhombuses. Stack them, count them, make pictures with them, wallow in them.

Mathematics: Story Books

Check your local library or bookstore for these math story books and make them part of your reading routine. Once you start exploring, you'll find many more wonderful titles.

Allen, Nancy Kelly. *Once Upon a Dime: A Math Adventure*. Watertown, MA: Charlesbridge, 1999.

Anno, Mitsumasa. *Anno's Math Games*. New York: Putnam & Grosset, 1997.

———. *Anno's Mysterious Multiplying Jar*. New York: Penguin, 2008.

Axelrod, Amy. *Pigs Will Be Pigs: Fun with Math & Money*. New York: Aladdin, 1997.

Burns, Marilyn. *Greedy Triangle*. New York: Scholastic, 2008.

———. *Spaghetti and Meatballs for All: A Mathematical Story*. New York: Scholastic, 2008.

Jonas, Ann. *Splash!* New York: Mulberry Books, 1997.

Miranda, Anne. *Monster Math*. New York: Harcourt, 2002.

Mogard, Sue. *Gobble Up Math: Fun Activities to Complete and Eat for Kids in Grades K–3*. Huntington Beach, CA: Learning Works, 1994.

Murphy, Stuart J. *Divide and Ride*. New York: HarperCollins, 1997.

Myllar, Rolf. *How Big Is a Foot?* New York: Yearling, 1991.

Neuschwander, Cindy. *Sir Cumference and the First Round Table: A Math Adventure*. Watertown, MA: Charlesbridge, 2002. Also look for Sir Cumference's six additional adventures.

Pinczes, Elinor J. *One Hundred Hungry Ants*. Boston: Houghton Mifflin, 1999.

Schwartz, David M. *How Much Is a Million?* New York: HarperCollins, 2004.

Scieska, Jon, and Lane Smith. *Math Curse*. New York: Viking Children's Books, 2007.

Tang, Greg. *Math for All Seasons: Mind-Stretching Math Riddles*. New York: Scholastic, 2005.

Wright, Alexandra. *Alice in Pastaland: A Math Adventure*. Watertown, MA: Charlesbridge, 1997.

General Learning

Use any of these resources to round out your preschool and kindergarten experience. Remember to visit www.welltrainedmind.com for links to additional resources.

The Complete Book series. Greensboro, NC: Thinking Kids, 2015.
   $12.99 each. Phonic and math readiness, coloring activities, stickers, and more.
      The Complete Book of Grade PreK.
      The Complete Book of Grade K.

Kuffner, Trish. *The Toddler's Busy Book: 365 Creative Games and Activities to Keep Your 1½-to-3-Year-Old Busy.* Minnetonka, MN: Meadowbrook, 1999.

$9.95. Ideas for learning activities in art, music, active play, and much more.

Kumon. *Are You Ready for Kindergarten?* Teaneck, NJ: Kumon Publishing.

$6.95 for each workbook. Practice in fine motor skills for preschoolers.
Coloring Skills.
Pasting Skills.
Pencil Skills.
Scissor Skills.

Roux, Nicolette, et al. *99 Fine Motor Ideas for Ages 1–5.* CreateSpace, 2014.

$18.99. Written by ten mothers and teachers of young children, this guide offers dozens of creative and fun ways to develop fine motor coordination in toddlers and preschoolers.

Schiller, Pam, and Patt Phipps. *The Complete Daily Curriculum for Early Childhood: Over 1200 Easy Activities to Support Multiple Intelligences and Learning Styles,* 2nd ed. Beltsville, MD: Gryphon House, 2011.

$39.95. Designed for preschool and kindergarten teachers, this guide offers activities, games, and projects. Some of the games can only be done with a group, but most of the suggestions are easily adapted to a home environment. A good idea-generator.

Science Exploration

Citro, Asia. *The Curious Kid's Science Book: 100+ Creative Hands-On Activities for Ages 4–8.* Woodinville, WA: Innovative Press, 2015.

$21.95. A wonderful series of experiments and projects in natural and physical science. Some are too advanced for preschool and kindergarten-aged children, but there are a number of age-appropriate activities for the younger set.

The Little Hands series. Charlotte, VT: Williamson Publishing.

$14.99 each. (Some are now out of print, but easily found secondhand.) Colorful and engaging guides to science exploration, with projects, crafts, and clear explanations.

Castaldo, Nancy. *The Little Hands Nature Book: Earth, Sky, Critters & More.* 1997.

Hauser, Jill Frankel. *Science Play!* 2006.

Press, Judy. *Animal Habitats!* 2005.

————. *Sea Life Art & Activities.* 2003.

VanCleave, Janice. *Janice VanCleave's Big Book of Play and Find Out Science Projects.* New York: Jossey-Bass, 2007.

$19.95. Explorations in natural science, physical science, and the human body; all designed for parents and children to do at home.

Audiobooks

Many books are worth listening to—here are a few of our favorites. Many are available from your local library. Many different versions of these classics have been made; make sure you look for *unabridged* versions.

Barrie, J. M. *Peter Pan.*

Carroll, Lewis. *Alice in Wonderland.*

————. *Through the Looking-Glass and What Alice Found There.*

Kipling, Rudyard. *The Jungle Books,* I and II.

————. *Just So Stories.*

Lawson, Robert. *Rabbit Hill.*

Lewis, C. S. *The Chronicles of Narnia.*

The 7-volume CD box set from HarperFestival features wonderful performances by Derek Jacobi, Kenneth Branagh, Patrick Stewart, and other classically trained actors.

Macdonald, Betty. The Mrs. Piggle-Wiggle series.

If you can locate the John McDonough recordings, they are preferable to later versions.

MacDonald, George. *The Princess and Curdie.*

Milne, A. A. *Winnie-the-Pooh.*

Don't miss Peter Dennis's award-winning and unmatchable audio performances, sold as *The Complete Works of Winnie-the-Pooh*. Visit his website, poohcorner.com, for samples. Worth every penny.

Nesbit, Edith. *The Complete Book of Dragons.*

———. *The Railway Children.*

White, E. B. *Charlotte's Web.*

———. *Stuart Little.*

———. *The Trumpet of the Swan.*
Look for versions read by E. B. White himself, which are very pleasant listening.

Read-Aloud Books

We have too many favorites to list here. But a good guide to reading aloud is *The Read-Aloud Handbook,* 7th ed., by Jim Trelease (New York: Penguin Books, 2013). It contains hundreds of wonderful suggestions.

5

WORDS, WORDS, WORDS: SPELLING, GRAMMAR, READING, AND WRITING

> For their Studies, First they should begin with the chief and necessary rules of some good Grammar. . . . Next to make them expert in the usefullest points of Grammar, and withall to season them, and win them early to the love of vertue and true labour, ere any flattering seducement, or vain principle seize them wandering, some easie and delightful Book of Education would be read to them.
>
> —John Milton, "Of Education"

SUBJECT: **Spelling, grammar, reading, and writing**
TIME REQUIRED: **60–110 minutes per day (by fourth grade)**

Your goal, in grades 1 through 4, is to make the proper use of language second nature to your child. In the logic and rhetoric stages of classical education (grades 5 through 8 and 9 through 12, respectively), the student will need to use language to reason, argue, and express ideas. He can't do this as long as he's still struggling with the how-tos of written and verbal expression.

The first four years of formal classical education are called the grammar stage because the student spends them learning the conventions and basic facts—the "grammar"—of each academic subject. In a way, the grammar of language is the foundation on which all other subjects rest. Until a student reads without difficulty, he can't absorb the grammar of history, literature, or science; until a student writes with ease, he can't express his growing mastery of this material.

Acquiring the "grammar" of language involves practice in four separate disciplines: spelling (the "grammar" of individual words—how each one is put together), English grammar itself (the way those words fit together into sentences), reading (through which the student's mind will be filled with images, stories, and words), and writing (the way in which sentences are formed and assembled). Because language skills are the cornerstone of classical education, the student will spend more time on reading and writing than on any other task.

KEEPING IT ORGANIZED

When you act as your child's teacher, you need a way to organize and store all of the child's work. One way to do this is to keep three-ringed notebooks for each major subject: reading, writing, history, and science.[1] Soon you'll have a fat stack of books, each showing the student's growing comprehension of a subject. These notebooks will also be useful for evaluation at testing time (see Part IV for more on testing for home schoolers).

Begin the academic year with three-ringed notebooks, a three-hole punch, and lots of paper, both lined and plain. Also lay in a boxful of art supplies: glue, scissors, construction paper, colored pencils (good artist-quality ones like Sanford Prismacolor), stickers, and anything else that strikes the child's (or your) fancy. For elementary language arts, you'll want to make use of two of these notebooks. Label one "Literature" and the other "Writing."

You can also use accordion folders or file boxes to keep assignments organized. Notebooks, though, allow the student to flip quickly through his past work and appreciate how much he's produced.

---

[1] Spelling, grammar, and math programs tend to come with their own workbooks, so you won't need to keep additional notebooks for these subjects. For art and music, the elementary student does very little writing; but if you wish to keep drawings in a portfolio, you can do so (see Chapter 12).

GENERAL INSTRUCTIONS
FOR GRADES 1 THROUGH 4

In the early years of school, children vary so widely in their development that assigning a child to a particular "grade" can be extremely difficult. Normal children can begin first grade reading "first grade" books and writing comfortably, reading "third grade" books and writing reasonably well, or reading "sixth grade" books and hardly writing at all. For this reason, much of the material we recommend isn't divided into grades, but rather into levels. You should always spend as much time on one level as you need and progress on to the next level only when your child has mastered the first level, whether that comes before or after the "normal" age.

Adjust the time you spend on each subject so that you can concentrate on weaker areas. Your goal will be to bring the child up to fourth-grade level in each area—spelling, grammar, reading, and writing—by the end of fourth grade (ages 10 to 11).

Reading: Skills

In the elementary grades, reading has two parts: ongoing instruction in *how* to read and the actual reading of worthwhile books (which we'll discuss shortly; see pages 62–69). We'll call these "Reading: Skills" and "Reading: Literature." Try to make time for both during the week; while reading skills are essential, young students also need the chance to *use* them in reading actual, interesting books. (Otherwise they may lose interest in the whole project.)

If you're using one of the phonics primers listed in the last chapter, continue on with your daily practice sessions until you've completed the book or curriculum. If you haven't begun phonics instruction yet, go back and read Chapter 4 before continuing on.

Your spelling lessons (see below) will reinforce and strengthen those phonics skills; it isn't necessary to continue on with further direct phonics instruction once the primer is done. Instead, once the student is reading fluently, give the student at least three "reading periods" during the week, during which he will spend at least thirty minutes reading books of his own choice. (Chosen with your help, that is.)

As you help the student choose reading books, be aware that there are three levels at which beginners read.

1. Instructional level. The student is still working hard at the mechanics of reading—thinking about letter combinations and the sounds they represent and struggling to remember how words are actually pronounced. Most phonics instruction is done at "instructional level." It's very common for a student to read a difficult instructional-level sentence perfectly, and then have no idea what it said—he was concentrating on the sounds, not the meaning they convey. You shouldn't expect perfect comprehension from instructional level reading.

2. At-level reading. The student knows all of the letter combinations and words she'll encounter. Her phonics knowledge may not be automatic, but she's comfortable enough to focus on meaning. She will still encounter words she doesn't know, so you should be prepared to help as necessary. At-level reading tends to be slow and requires good concentration.

3. Below-level (or "fun") reading. These are books that use only the words and combinations that the student is completely comfortable with. Below-level reading is important: it allows students to *enjoy* reading (rather than work at it), and it improves reading speed.

Aim for the "reading periods" to include all three skills, each week. You can combine them into every reading period: begin with ten minutes or so of instructional reading (you'll want to ask the student to read out loud so that you can hear her word attack skills and pick up any errors), allow the student to read "at-level" books for another ten minutes, and then let her finish up with ten minutes or so of fun, easy reading. Or use one reading period for instructional reading, another for at-level reading, and a third for fun reading.

We have provided a brief list of classic beginner books to use for your reading sessions; you will find many more by browsing the library shelves.

Reading Skills: When It Doesn't Seem to Be Working

If you've been pursuing the reading primer approach described in Chapter 4, the student should be sounding out at *least* short vowel words and consonant blends within a few months of beginning the primer, and then should progress forward steadily (everyone's speed is different) without showing constant frustration.

What if that doesn't happen?

The approach we suggest is straightforward, simple, and effective for the majority of beginning readers, so start there. But there's a solid subset of students who need a different way to understand the written word. Another road to reading is the "Orton-Gillingham" method—an approach that is more complicated and involves much more prep time on the part of the parent/teacher, but which can open up the world of books in a whole new way for a significant number of children.

The Orton-Gillingham method doesn't just offer letters and sounds (auditory and visual learning). Instead, students are taught to understand written language through a "multisensory approach"—tracing in the air, tracing on paper, writing in sand, dictation, workbook exercises, and other techniques that bring kinesthetic and tactile instruction into the mix. Reading curricula based on the Orton-Gillingham method teach the student seventy-two different "phonograms" (letters and letter combinations that represent single sounds), making use of plenty of activities and constantly reviewing skills previously taught.

The Orton-Gillingham approach was originally developed for dyslexic students, but programs using the O-G principles can be helpful for any student who struggles with the primer approach. If your student is showing frustration and lack of progress with the primer, consider changing over to an O-G program. Be aware, however, that since the system was originally developed to be used as remedial instruction for older students, many O-G curricula tie reading and handwriting together in a way that can force very young learners—already frustrated with the reading process—to do far too much handwritten work, making the whole reading project even more fraught. Our recommendations for an age-appropriate curriculum are in the Resources list at the end of the chapter; you can find additional programs and parent reviews at welltrainedmind.com.

How do you know if you're dealing with actual dyslexia (defined by the National Institutes of Health as "a brain-based type of learning disability that specifically impairs a person's ability to read")?

If, by the end of first grade, your student is still struggling to understand how reading works, we would suggest professional evaluation—

particularly if this struggle is accompanied by an inability to grasp basic spelling principles, trouble following verbal directions, and lack of coordination. A neuropsychologist or other qualified specialist (see Chapter 37 for more) can tell you whether you're dealing with a learning disability or simply a slow-maturing reader—in which case you may just need to be patient. But in our opinion, it's better to rule out dyslexia early, rather than to lose months or years of learning time to frustration.

Reading: Literature

While the student is developing his basic reading skills, he should also begin his acquaintance with literature—stories that offer rich character development, fascinating settings, complex plots, and beauty of expression.

You won't be using a textbook for literature. We strongly feel that "reading texts" (books with snippets of stories and poems followed by comprehension exercises) turn reading into a chore. Books, even in the early grades, ought to be sources of delight and information, not exercises to be mastered. A good classical education instills a passion for books in the student. "Reading texts" mutilate real books by pulling sections out of context and presenting them as "assignments." Even worse are textbooks that provide selections designed especially for textbook use, which means that your child spends his time reading generic prose produced by textbook writers instead of stories written by masters.

During the first four years of education, you have two purposes: not only to get the child to read quickly, well, and habitually, but to fill his mind with stories of every kind—myths, legends, classic tales, biographies, great stories from history. Instead of a "literature curriculum," you'll use your library and the notebook labeled "Literature." Divide the notebook into two subsections: "My Books" and "Memory Work."

We suggest that literature follow the same pattern as history studies:

First grade	Ancients (5000 B.C.–A.D. 400)
Second grade	Medieval–early Renaissance (400–1600)
Third grade	Late Renaissance–early modern (1600–1850)
Fourth grade	Modern (1850–present)

See Chapter 7 for a full explanation of these divisions. (Once you've read Chapter 7, the following will make more sense.)

The principle is simple: try to give the child simplified versions of the original literature that he'll be reading in the higher grades or introduce him (through stories or biographies) to a writer he'll encounter later. Begin with twenty to thirty minutes of reading, three times per week, in first grade; you'll want to work up to forty-five minutes by fourth grade.

At the end of this chapter, you'll find a list of major authors for each period. Search in the children's section of the library for books about the lives of these writers and paraphrases of their works. We've supplied you with a list of some of our favorite resources: retellings of ancient myths, of the *Iliad* and *Odyssey*, of Shakespeare and Dickens. First graders who are working with the ancients can begin on the fairy tales of ancient China and Japan, stories of the Bible, myths of Rome and Greece, Aesop's fables, stories about the great Greeks and Romans, and simplified versions of Homer. Susan and her husband, Peter, spent six weeks reading through a lavishly illustrated child's version of the *Iliad* with their six- and four-year-olds. Since the children hadn't learned to be frightened of the classics, they were enthralled and eventually put on a puppet show with their stuffed animals: *The Fall of Troy*, starring a stuffed bear as Ajax.

Don't overlook audiobooks as a supplement to (not a replacement for) reading. Most fourth graders, for example, can't read Shakespeare independently but will listen to a dramatized version of *As You Like It* (or the *Odyssey*, or *Oliver Twist*, or to Robert Frost reading his own poetry). The biographies listed in the history resources can also be read. (You should find history and reading assignments overlapping quite a bit—this helps the student's comprehension, since history will be giving him the context that he needs to appreciate his literature studies. Generally, put imaginative literature—stories, myths, fairy tales, poems, novels—in the "My Books" section of the Literature notebook. Put factual books and biographies in the history notebook. See Chapter 7 for a full explanation.)

Don't limit the student's reading to works on a first- or second-grade level. He's already doing independent reading practice during his "reading periods," so you can feel free to read *to* him during literature study. In fact, students who are struggling can benefit the most from read-aloud literature sessions; listening to an exciting picture book read out loud is *fun*, and shows them that reading won't always be pure hard work. And some of the most enthralling works will remain above any young child's reading level. For example, we've recommended several interesting and beautifully illustrated versions of the *Odyssey* for first-grade reading. These books will be well beyond most first graders' reading ability. But try reading them aloud; first graders are fascinated by the adventures of Odysseus and will listen openmouthed.

The My Books section of the Literature notebook will become a record of the literature that the child has read and enjoyed or that you have read to him. Although you shouldn't make him report on every book, you should ask him at least once or twice a week to tell you, in two to four sentences, something about the plot of the book you have just read. Younger students will need you to ask them specific questions about the book: "What was the most exciting thing that happened in the book?" or "Who was your favorite character, and what did he do?" are two useful questions that help the child narrow in on the book's central theme. Some third and fourth graders will be able to answer the more general question "What was the book about?" while others will still need more guidance. In either case, help the child narrow the answer down to under five sentences. These oral answers are called *narrations*.

Learning how to identify one or two items about a book as *more* important than the rest is a vital first step in learning to write; a young writer will flounder as long as he cannot pick out one or two of the ideas in his mind as *central* to his composition. For first grade and second grade, you should write the narration down, have the child read it back to you, and then place it under My Reading. Most first graders will enjoy drawing crayon pictures to illustrate these narrations. You can also copy out favorite poems to file under My Reading, letting the child decorate the pages with stickers and glitter.

In third and fourth grade, students can begin to write down their own narrations. (See the "Writing" section on pages 72–79 for a fuller description of the elementary writing process.) Narration removes the need for "comprehension exercises." Instead of learning to complete fill-in-the-blank questions, the child uses all his mental faculties to understand, remember, and relate the main points of a story.

Every three or four weeks, the child should also memorize a poem and recite it to you. Memorization and recitation of poetry is an important part of the reading process; it exercises the child's memory, stores beautiful language in his mind, and gives him practice in speaking aloud (early preparation for the rhetoric stage). Aim for memorization of at least four to eight short poems during each school year. Pick poems that the child has read and enjoyed, either during his literature studies or his reading practice, or use one of the memorization resources we suggest in the Resources list. These poems don't have to be tied to the progression of literature from ancient to modern; let him memorize anything that he likes. Make a recording of either you or the child reading the poem, and allow him to listen to it over and over again. When he can recite the poem along with the recording, ask him to stand up and recite for you all by himself.

Many children don't like this—not because they can't memorize, but because they don't like to be watched while they recite. Let them practice in front of the mirror or in front of their stuffed animals. Then have them stand up and, with their hands and feet still, recite the poem in front of you. When they can do that, bring in an extra audience member: your spouse, a grandparent, a neighbor. You're now building public-speaking skills.

When a poem has been memorized and recited to your satisfaction, write it out (or have the child write it out, if his skills are up to the job) and place it in the Memory Work section of the Literature notebook along with the date of recitation. This will serve as a reward—visual proof of the child's accomplishment—as well as a reminder to review the memory work every few weeks.

You'll follow this basic pattern during second, third, and fourth grades as well. Second-grade students should spend at least thirty minutes, three days per week, reading literature from the Middle Ages and early Renaissance: simple tales from Chaucer and Shakespeare, written for children; books about Shakespeare's life; stories of King Arthur and the Knights of the Round Table. We've supplied a list at the end of this chapter. As in first grade, you can read aloud anything that's beyond the child's reading level. Continue making notebook pages once or twice a week and filing them under My Reading in the Literature notebook. By second grade, many children can dictate short narrations to you and then copy some of these narrations themselves. Continue to memorize poetry and any speeches that the child finds and likes in his reading. Aim to memorize eight to twelve pieces during the second-grade year. If possible, expand the audience to include grandparents and friends.

Your third grader will spend thirty to forty-five minutes per day reading writers from the late Renaissance–early modern period, which includes John Bunyan (the simplified *Pilgrim's Progress*) and Charles Dickens (abridged versions), along with the simpler poetry of Wordsworth and Blake. We provide a full list at the end of this chapter. By third grade, you should be encouraging the child to read all by himself; read to him only if you want him to read an original text instead of an abridgment (*A Christmas Carol* is a good book to read aloud in its entirety), or if he is still struggling with the mechanics of reading. Don't be afraid to assign the child abridged and simplified versions of the classics. In grades 5 through 8, he'll cycle through the ancient, medieval, Renaissance, and modern eras again. If he's already read *Great Expectations* in a simplified form, he'll know the basic outline of the plot and won't be intimidated by the original.

Continue to make notebook pages once or twice a week, summarizing the books the child is reading. By the end of third grade, your student may be able to narrate the plot back to you and write it down himself without the intermediate step of dictating and then copying. In short, he'll have gradually worked his way up to writing his own paragraphs.

Aim to memorize and recite twelve to fifteen poems and speeches during the third-grade year. Third-grade history, like third-grade reading, covers the years 1600 to 1850, a period during which great American documents and speeches (the preamble to the Constitution, the Declaration of Independence, and Patrick Henry's "Give Me Liberty" speech, among others) abound. Third grade isn't too early to memorize many of these foundational American works.

The fourth grader will read and make notebook pages for literature of the modern period, 1850 to the present. We've listed a few reading suggestions at the end of the chapter, but children vary widely in reading ability by fourth grade. Your best bet would be to consult with your local children's librarian. Also, don't neglect poetry; Carl Sandburg, T. S. Eliot, Walter de la Mare, and other great poets of the modern period wrote much that can be enjoyed by young children.

A fourth grader's written summary of a book should fill half a notebook page or a little more.

It is *not* necessary for your elementary student to be answering critical questions about the books he's reading, either for literature or in his other studies. While some young readers may enjoy talking about plot development and character motivation, most are still at the stage of absorbing—figuring out how stories work, encountering many different heroes and villains, hearing different kinds of language and dialogue. The elementary years are a time to fill the student's mind with as many different stories as possible. This will act as the raw material for critical thinking in literature, which begins in earnest during the middle grades. Asking students to criticize literature at too young an age can be counterproductive—it encourages them to draw conclusions too quickly, turns reading into laborious work, and has the potential to damage their budding love of books. There will be plenty of time to develop skills in literary analysis in the years to come.

Spelling

Spelling is the first step in writing. Before you can put a word on paper, you have to know what letters to use.

You can begin spelling once the student has learned all of the consonants and vowels and can sound out three-letter short vowel words; it's fine to wait until blends and long vowels have also been covered. The student must also be able to form his letters. He does *not* need to write with ease; many bright children (especially boys) take time to develop the fine motor skills associated with handwriting. It's perfectly acceptable to wait and begin spelling lessons in second grade; first grade is already a very busy year.

In the beginning, spelling is simply phonics in reverse. In the phonics primer, your child has already encountered basic spelling rules. For example, the reading rule "The silent *e* at the end of a word makes the vowel say its name" is also a spelling rule; it tells you that a word such as *late*, where *a* says its name, must have a silent *e* at the end. Now it's time for the child to start applying those rules of reading to words he wants to write. Elementary spelling, then, is a matter of transforming rules of reading into rules of writing.

So when you first begin spelling, you don't necessarily need to invest in an entirely separate spelling program. You can go back to the page in your phonics primer that first combined consonant and vowel sounds into words, review the rule with your student ("When you see the letters *s* and *h* side-by-side, you should say the sound /*sh*/, as in "Sh, sh, don't wake the baby!"), look together at the word list given (*ship, shop, shed, shut, shall, shack*), and then dictate the word list back to the student as spelling practice. Only dictate as many words as the student can comfortably write.

Unfortunately, English is not a completely phonetic language; students encounter numerous "sight words" as they learn to read, and the phonics primer will only get you so far. So most parents will want to invest in a separate spelling program.

In our Resources section, we've listed several different programs, from the simplest to the most time-consuming. You can substitute any of them for the primer approach at any point, or begin any of them at grade level after you finish going through the primer rules. Whichever resource you use, if you begin spelling in first grade, aim to spend just ten to fifteen minutes per day working on your spelling lesson. By second grade, you can expand this to twenty minutes. Try to avoid spending more than twenty minutes per day on spelling during the elementary grades; we don't think you should allow spelling to consume your language arts time.

Remember *not* to tie spelling instruction to reading (or to writing—more on this in the Writing section that follows). Some students are natural spellers; others need much more direct instruction; and a small subset will always struggle with correct spelling. A student who is ready to progress from copywork to dictation (see page 74), or from dictation to logic-stage writing, should be allowed to do so even if she is still working on second- or third-grade spelling; simply give her as much help as necessary while she writes, and correct her misspelled words without making a big fuss about it.

Spelling, grammar, reading, and writing are related skills, but they ask for different kinds of mastery. It's important to allow students to progress at a natural pace in each of the language arts areas without frustrating them by limiting their progress to the speed of their worst subject. For this reason, you won't find integrated language arts curricula that try to tackle all four subjects at once in our recommendations.

Grammar

You'll begin oral grammar lessons in first grade, transitioning slowly into lessons that require more physical handwriting.

In the elementary years, grammar involves learning the names of the parts of speech ("A noun is the name of a person, place, thing, or idea"), the proper relationships between these parts of speech ("Singular nouns take singular verbs"), and the mechanics of the English language (indenting paragraphs, using quotation marks, and so on).

Why bother with grammar in the early years?

Grammar and spelling are both supporting skills for *writing*, which we'll get to shortly. In many ways, writing is an unnatural code, invented by human beings long, long after they learned how to talk. Written language is *very* unlike spoken language; it has different rules and conventions. (If you doubt this, have a look at any transcript of an oral interview—spoken language that sounded literate and intelligent often becomes incoherent when it's put down on paper.)

The goal of grammar study is to make those rules and conventions second nature to the student, at a time when his brain is particularly open to language learning. If you teach a young writer the correct use of semicolons, the difference between a complete and incomplete sentence, and the proper way to use commas to divide a series of nouns, that knowledge will be something he pulls up as he does his copywork and dictation. By the time he's moving into independent composition, he won't have to stop and think about his punctuation or his syntax; correct form will have become automatic.

If, on the other hand, your fourth- or fifth-grade writer has to pause to consider mechanics as he writes, he'll be constantly brought to a halt. Every time he stops to think about form, he'll lose his train of thought and have to recapture it. Doing grammar early is one way to avoid reluctance in writing in the middle grades.

"Doing grammar early" doesn't mean hours of workbook time. In first and second grade, students simply cannot do very much handwriting work; hand muscles take time and slow, steady exercise to develop. Actual *writing* assignments will use up most of the student's writing energy. So grammar exercises should be done orally—either using an oral language text or adapting a traditional workbook-centered grammar program to oral use. (Read through the lesson with the student, have him repeat definitions after you until he has them memorized, and then do exercises by asking him to tell you the answers or point them out on the page.) Most traditional language arts programs require *far* too much physical handwriting from first- and second-grade students, so be sensitive to your child's physical limitations. If he says his hand feels like it's going to fall off, he means it. Give his hand a break.

In first grade, ten to fifteen minutes per day of grammar work is plenty; this can expand to twenty minutes in second grade, most of this done orally. Third graders can begin to do more workbook exercises, and by fourth grade, grammar study can expand to thirty minutes per day.

We have listed our favorite oral language and traditional grammar programs in the Resources. In most cases we suggest that you do *not* complete any writing element of the grammar program. In our experience, language arts programs tend to do *either* grammar *or* writing well; when they are folded in together, either the grammar suffers (it becomes nonsequential and confusing), or the writing is badly designed and rigid.

By the end of fourth grade, the child should know the proper names and usages of all the parts of speech, the rules of punctuation and capitalization, dictionary use, and proper sentence structure. Until these basic skills are mastered, he won't be able to exercise language with the mastery that the logic stage demands.

Writing

At the beginner level, writing is simply penmanship practice. As the child is able, work up from five to fifteen minutes per day, using a handwriting book, such as one from the Zaner-Bloser or Handwriting Without Tears series (see Chapter 4 for details). Traditionally, children transition into cursive writing in second grade. If you are using the Zaner-Bloser handwriting program recommended in Chapter 4, you'll begin the Zaner-Bloser *Grade 2C Student Book* around the beginning of the second-grade year; this book begins with practice of manuscript letters and then moves on to cursive handwriting. The Handwriting Without Tears program introduces cursive later (closer to third grade). Either way, until the child is comfortable with all cursive letters, she can continue to print her spelling and writing assignments. Make sure you order second-grade paper at the beginning of the second-grade year—the lines are slightly narrower than those on first-grade paper (see the ordering information on pages 103–104). Continue penmanship through at least the end of fourth grade.

What about actual *writing*?

Writing is a difficult skill because it requires the child to express content at the same time that she is learning the tools of expression. For this reason, early writing instruction should focus on developing those tools, rather than demanding a great deal of original content. In grades 1–4, students should progress from copywork to dictation, and from oral narration (retelling passages from history, science, or literature) to written narrations.

It's important to understand *why* you're focusing on copywork, dictation, and narration, rather than on writing essays and book reports. Writing is a process that involves two distinct mental steps. First, the writer puts an idea into words; then, she puts the words down on paper.

INARTICULATE IDEA ⟶ IDEA IN WORDS

IDEA IN WORDS ⟶ WORDS ON PAPER

Mature writers are able to do both steps without paying much attention to the fact that their brains are actually carrying out two different operations. But for the beginning writer, even a simple writing exercise ("Write down what you did this morning") requires the simultaneous performance of two new and difficult tasks. And so the student struggles—just as a baby who has barely learned to walk will struggle if you simultaneously ask her to perform some other task (such as rubbing her head). All of the baby's attention needs to go into moving her feet, until that action becomes automatic. If you ask her to walk and rub her head, she'll probably freeze in one place, swaying back and forth uncertainly—just like many new writers.

Some young students—those with a natural affinity for language arts—manage to grasp this process intuitively. But the majority need to be taught, explicitly, how to do both tasks. And because it is important not to teach students how to do two new and difficult things at the same time, pull the process apart. Teach students how to put ideas into words through practicing narration. Help them learn to put words down on paper through copywork and dictation. When they can perform both tasks with ease, they are ready to begin original writing.

This is the essence of good teaching in the classical tradition: breaking tasks down into their component elements and teaching students how to perform each element, before putting the elements back together.

The pianist practices first the right hand, and then the left hand, before putting the two together; the young writer practices putting ideas into words, and then putting words down on paper, before trying to do both simultaneously.

Let's start with the second part of the process—putting words down on paper. This is not a simple task. It requires physical labor, fine motor coordination, and an understanding of the rules that govern written presentation: capitalization, punctuation, spacing, letter formation. The beginning student doesn't even know yet how written language is supposed to look. Before she can put words down on paper, she must have some visual memory of what those words are supposed to look like. So, during first grade, she'll copy out sentences from good writers, practicing the look and feel of properly written language.

Once the student has become accustomed to reproducing, on her own paper, properly written sentences placed in front of her as a model, you'll take the model away. Now that her mind is stocked with mental images of properly written language, she needs to learn how to visualize a written sentence in her mind and then put it down on paper. From second grade on, rather than putting the written model in front of the student, you will dictate sentences to her. This will force her to bring her memory into play, to picture the sentence in her mind before writing it down. Eventually you'll be dictating two and three sentences at a time to a student, encouraging her to hold longer and longer chunks of text in her mind as she writes. Many students who struggle with writing put down sentences that are lacking in punctuation, capitalization, or spacing—a clue that they have never learned to picture written language in their minds. Others can tell you with great fluency exactly what they want to write; if you then say to them, "Great! Write that down!" they'll ask, "What did I just say?" Both are clues that students have not learned to visualize sentences and hold them in mind—both essential if the student is ever going to get words down on paper. Moving from copywork to dictation develops these skills.

At the same time, you will be working on the first part of the writing process—putting ideas into words—through practicing narration. Narration happens when the student takes something she's just read (or heard you read) and puts it into her own words.

This begins on a very simple level: You read to the student and ask her specific questions about what she's heard, such as "What was the most interesting thing in that story?" or "Who was that history lesson about?" You then require her to answer you in complete sentences. As the student grows more familiar with the process of narration, you can move on to more general questions such as "Summarize what we just read in your own words."

This allows the young student to practice the new and difficult skill of putting an idea into her own words without having to come up with original ideas first; because her narrations are always rooted in content that she's just read or heard, she can concentrate on the task of expressing herself with words.

She is also practicing this new skill without having to worry about the second part of the writing process: putting those words down on paper. As she narrates, you—the teacher—write the words down for her as she watches. She can simply concentrate on the task at hand, without worrying about the mechanical difficulties of wielding a pencil. (For students whose fine motor skills are still developing, this is essential; they cannot focus on narration if they're also contemplating how much their hand is going to hurt when they have to write the narration down.)

Around third grade, most students are ready to begin putting the two skills together. In third grade, students will begin to use part of their own narrations as dictation exercises. They will tell you the narration; you will write it down for them, and then dictate the first sentence back to them. Eventually they will learn that, in order to write, all they need to do is put an idea into words (something they've practiced extensively through narration), and then put those words down on paper (which they're accustomed to doing during dictation).

During the last two years of the elementary grades, concentrate on drawing the two skills together for the student. Some students will be able to bring the two steps together instinctively, without a struggle. But many need to be led through the process gradually, with plenty of practice, so that it can become second nature—and if they are not given this practice, they continue to struggle into middle school, high school, and beyond.

It is completely normal for students to work on this process through fourth grade. Students who catch on a little earlier should continue to practice their written narrations, but can move on to sentence and paragraph composition (see Resources, pages 106–107).

Does this process stifle creativity? No—it builds the skills the child needs in order to be truly creative. When a first grader copies a sentence from *Charlotte's Web*, she's learning spelling, mechanics (punctuation and so forth), basic grammar (subject-verb agreement, adjective use), and vocabulary from a master of English prose. She'll need all this information in order to write down the sentences she forms in her own head. Jack London learned to write by copying literature in the San Francisco Public Library; Benjamin Franklin learned to write by copying essays from *The Spectator*. The classical pupil learns to write by copying great writers.

If your first grader has a sudden desire to write a story, poem, or letter to a friend (or to Santa Claus), by all means put the copying away and help her do it. Put the stories and poems in the Writing notebook. If at all possible, photocopy the letter before you send it, and keep the copy. But the next day, get the copying work back out. You're laying the groundwork for dictation (second grade), which in turn will develop the skills needed for original writing (third and fourth grades . . . and the rest of the child's life).

Encourage any creative impulses. If the child does have a bent toward storytelling, you can follow the same pattern you're using for narration: write down the stories that the first grader tells and put them in the notebook; write down the stories that the second grader tells and have the child copy them in his own writing; help a third or fourth grader write his own stories and poems without a written model. But don't require the child to be creative during the grammar stage of education. She's still absorbing and taking in. If she's naturally creative, fine. If not, demanding creativity will only be counterproductive. In many cases, creativity will develop later, once the child is comfortable with writing skills. And some children may never become creative writers. That's fine; they'll still have the expository writing skills they need.

What programs should you use?

For parents who are not comfortable with language arts or just need a little more structure, we've recommended copywork and dictation resources at the end of this chapter, along with several good options for moving on to sentence and paragraph composition. But you don't necessarily need a "writing curriculum" to teach these skills. Copywork, dictation, and narration can be practiced as part of literature, history, and science. We've already recommended narration as part of literature studies (page 66), and you'll see us suggesting narrations in history and science as well.

Copywork and dictation can also be drawn from the student's work across the curriculum. You can pick sentences from good literature (E. B. White, C. S. Lewis, Lynn Reid Banks), from the child's history, or from science. Aim to work up from five-word sentences to longer and more complex sentences. Write these sentences out (in your best handwriting) on first-grade manuscript paper (see the ordering information on pages 103–104). Put the paper in front of the child and ask her to copy the sentence. At this stage, it's best to sit with the child and correct her when she begins to make a mistake. There is no point in allowing her to copy incorrectly. She should always use a pencil, so that she can erase and correct if necessary. Encourage her to compare her work frequently with the model. Praise her when she's finished! Put the copywork in the Writing notebook.

Once your child is copying sentences easily, move on to dictation (usually around second grade). The process is simple: Dictate a short sentence slowly to the child as she writes. Choose sentences from your phonics primer, history, science, or literature. If the child makes a mistake, stop her and have her write the word correctly. Give her all necessary help with punctuation and spelling. Make sure that she uses a pencil so she can erase and correct as she goes. Remind her of proper spacing as she writes. That's all there is to it.

At first, this will take a lot of time. Start with simple words in very short sentences, three or four words maximum ("The cat sat up"). You'll have to help the child sound the letters out, reminding her of her phonics (and telling her the answers if she's stuck). Don't frustrate her, especially at the beginning. "What letters make the *th* sound? *T* and *h*, remember? Now write a *t* and an *h*. Do you remember what letter comes at the end of the word *the*? You don't? It's an *e*. *The*. *Cat*. Do you remember what letters make a *k* sound? Does a *k* or a *c* come at the beginning of *cat*? Now what letter makes that middle sound?" The child who's spent first grade copying will already have a visual memory of common words. But during the transition from copying to dictation, you'll need to help her develop the skills of sounding out and writing down words without looking at a model. When she's finished writing, praise some aspect of the work.

Like any new skill, this is difficult at first. But do it for a brief time—three days per week. Ten to twenty minutes per day on a regular basis will result in a rapid improvement in writing skills.

When these short sentences become easy, progress to dictating sentences from literature—any ten- to fifteen-word sentence from the child's books. Susan likes E. B. White's books: *Charlotte's Web, Stuart Little,* and *The Trumpet of the Swan.* White's books are full of amusing sentences, and he's a wonderful stylist. C. S. Lewis's *Chronicles of Narnia* is another good source for dictation. Repeat dictation sentences as often as necessary, but always repeat the entire selection from the beginning and encourage the child to say it after you—don't dictate one word at a time (this does nothing to help develop the student's memory). Give all necessary help in punctuation and spelling.

By third grade, begin to encourage the child to do all formal work using cursive writing. Continue to practice penmanship. Require all work to be done neatly; don't be afraid to tell a third grader to recopy something that's carelessly done. Order third-grade paper for all writing exercises. Third graders should continue to do dictation exercises three times per week. Most third graders can now progress to complex sentences or two or three sentences at a time. Also in third grade, begin to use the student's own narrations from literature, science, and history for some of your dictation lessons.

By the fourth grade, the student should be able to write several sentences from dictation, inserting punctuation marks such as quotation marks and semicolons where appropriate. A typical fourth-grade dictation, repeated as often as the student needs to hear it, might be:

> The house was really a small castle. It seemed to be all towers; little towers with long pointed spires on them, sharp as needles. They looked like huge dunce's caps or sorcerer's caps. And they shone in the moonlight and their long shadows looked strange on the snow! Edmund began to be afraid of the house.[2]

The fourth grader who writes this from dictation is practicing spelling and punctuation (semicolons and exclamation points); he's learning vocabulary (What is a dunce cap?); and he's working on spelling (*sorcerer, moonlight, afraid*). Most of all, he's learning what a vivid, evocative description sounds like.

---

[2] C. S. Lewis, *The Lion, the Witch, and the Wardrobe* (New York: Macmillan, 1978), pp. 88–89.

Keep filing these dictation exercises or place them in a Writing notebook. This will allow your child to look back over his work and see how he's improved or what areas of punctuation and form continue to trip him up.

Fourth-grade students should also begin to write down their own narrations in literature, history, and science. Use fourth-grade paper for all work.

Writing: When It Doesn't Seem to Be Working

Children who are still struggling with simple copywork at the end of first grade, or who still have difficulty with one-sentence narrations by the end of second grade, should be evaluated by a professional—particularly if these difficulties are combined with very slow reading progress. Difficulty in writing can be a pointer to dyslexia; it can also be a sign of dysgraphia (a "transcription disability" that affects the student's ability to translate oral language into written language). Don't allow students to suffer through years of frustration before getting help!

See Chapter 37 for more.

OVERVIEW OF LANGUAGE WORK

First Grade

Reading: Skills	15–20 minutes per day of phonics work; introduce 30–minute periods of reading, 3 days per week. Reading at all three levels (instructional, at-level, below-level) each week.
Reading: Literature	20–30 minutes, 3 days per week, focusing on ancient myths and legends; make notebook pages (narrations) 1–2 times per week; memorize a poem every 3–6 weeks.
Spelling	10–15 minutes per day, 3–4 days per week.
Grammar	10–15 minutes per day, 3–4 days per week.
Writing	Penmanship 5–10 minutes per day; copy short sentences 2–3 days per week; do a total of three narrations per week from literature (above), history, and science.

Second Grade

Reading: Skills	Phonics until program is finished; 30–minute periods of reading, 3 days per week. Reading at all three levels (instructional, at-level, below-level) each week.
Reading: Literature	30 minutes, 3 days per week, focusing on stories of the Middle Ages; make notebook pages (narrations) 1–2 times per week; memorize a poem every 2–4 weeks.
Spelling	20 minutes per day, 3–4 days per week.
Grammar	20 minutes per day, 3–4 days per week.
Writing	Penmanship 10 minutes per day, introducing cursive script halfway through the year; dictation exercises 2–3 times per week; do a total of three narrations per week from literature (above), history, and science.

Third Grade

Reading: Skills	30–minute periods of reading, 3 days per week. Reading at all three levels (instructional, at-level, below-level) each week. (Phonics instruction continues until primer or program is finished.)
Reading: Literature	30–45 minutes, 3 days per week, focusing on literature of the late Renaissance and early modern eras; make notebook pages (narrations) 1–2 times per week; memorize a poem every 2–3 weeks.
Spelling	20 minutes per day, 3–4 days per week.
Grammar	20–30 minutes per day, 3–4 days per week.
Writing	Penmanship 10–15 minutes per day; dictation exercises 3 times per week; do a total of at least three narrations per week from literature (above), history, and science.

Fourth Grade

Reading: Skills	30–minute periods of reading, 3 days per week. Reading at all three levels (instructional, at-level,

	below-level) each week. (Phonics instruction continues until primer or program is finished.)
Reading: Literature	30–45 minutes, 3 days per week; make notebook pages (narrations) 1–2 times per week; memorize a poem every 2–3 weeks.
Spelling	20 minutes per day, 3–4 days per week.
Grammar	30 minutes per day, 3–4 days per week.
Writing	Penmanship 15 minutes per day; student should write his own narrations at least 3 times per week in literature (above), history, and science. May add work in sentence and paragraph construction if student is writing easily.

RESOURCES

Most books can be obtained from any bookseller or library; most curricula can be bought directly from the publisher or from a major home-school supplier such as Rainbow Resource Center. Contact information for publishers and suppliers can be found at www.welltrainedmind.com. If availability is limited, we have noted it. Where indicated, resources are listed in chronological order (the order you'll want to use them in). Books in series are listed together. Remember that additional curricula choices and more can be found at www.welltrainedmind.com. Prices change constantly, but we have included 2016 pricing to give an idea of affordability.

Reading: Skills

For phonics primers, see the Chapter 4 resource list on pages 44–45.

All About Reading. Eagle River, WI: All About Learning Press, 2011–2016. Order from the publisher.

We find this to be the most age-appropriate and parent-friendly Orton-Gillingham program on the market. Developed by dyslexia researcher Marie Rippel, *All About Reading* is a four-level series that uses the Orton-Gillingham system, but avoids handwritten assignments. The accompanying workbooks use flash cards, flip charts, cutting and pasting, and other nonwriting activities to reinforce phonics learning.

Each Teacher's Manual contains between forty-nine and sixty-three scripted lessons, with suggested dialogue and directions that are clear to nonspecialists. Lessons begin with a brief instructor preparation; plan to do these ahead of time; most should take only ten to fifteen minutes. Each lesson contains three to eight "mini-lessons"; do as many as your child can comfortably manage in a single sitting. For example, Lesson 26 of Level 1 (teaching the ending sounds *ff*, *ll*, and *ss*, and the sight words *said* and *I*) contains seven mini-lessons: Review, Blend Sounds with Letter Tiles, Complete Activity Sheets, Compass Points (a game), Practice Reading Words, Teach Two Sight Words, Practice Fluency. The previous lesson has only three mini-lessons: review, a short reading assignment for the student, and twenty minutes of reading out loud *to* the student. (If you decide to use *All About Reading*, the recommended "Read-Aloud Time" which is part of many lessons can be completed during your literature study.)

Each level of the series requires a Teacher's Manual, a Student Packet with a softcover workbook and various sets of cards, and a set of levelled hardcover readers. You will also need to buy one Interactive Kit (containing letter tiles, a "Phonogram Sounds" app, and other multisensory teaching aids) for the entire series. A 2 × 3-foot magnetic whiteboard is highly recommended but not mandatory.

All About Reading will take considerably more time and effort than our phonics primer approach, so you will need to adjust your other language arts areas: if you're spending forty-five minutes per day on *All About Reading* in first grade, you'll need to spend less time on reading sessions, literature, grammar, or writing. The redistribution of time is worthwhile, though; students who need the multisensory approach can be reading well by the end of fourth grade and ready to move on in all the language arts areas.

Samples of each level and placement tests are available on the publisher's website.

Reading Interactive Kit, $21.85.

  Level 1, $99.95.

   Level 1 Teacher's Manual

   Level 1 Student Packet

   Run, Bug, Run! A Collection of Short Stories

   The Runt Pig: A Collection of Short Stories

   Cobweb the Cat: A Collection of Short Stories

Level 2, $119.95.

Level 2 Teacher's Manual

Level 2 Student Packet

What Am I? A Collection of Short Stories, 3rd ed.

Queen Bee: A Collection of Short Stories, 3rd ed.

Level 3, $119.95.

Level 3 Teacher's Manual

Level 3 Student Packet

Chasing Henry: A Collection of Short Stories

Shipwreck! A Collection of Short Stories

Level 4, $119.95.

Level 4 Teacher's Manual

Level 4 Student Packet

Heirloom Antics: A Collection of Short Stories

The Voyage: A Collection of Short Stories

Readers

There are hundreds of good books and collections of poetry available to a child who is reading on a first- through fourth-grade level. The children's librarian at your local library or the children's books manager at a larger bookstore can direct you toward award-winning stories, novels, and poetry on your child's reading level. Also consider using the following resources:

Hirsch, E. D., Jr., and John Holdren. *Books to Build On: A Grade-by-Grade Resource Guide for Parents and Teachers.* New York: Delta, 1996.

Recommended titles divided by curricular areas: language arts, history, visual arts, music, science, math.

Lipson, Eden Ross. *The New York Times Parent's Guide to the Best Books for Children.* 3rd ed. New York: Three Rivers Press, 2000.

An annotated list of books in six age ranges, from "wordless books" for babies all the way up to young adults.

Wilson, Elizabeth L., and Susan Schaeffer Macaulay. *Books Children Love: A Guide to the Best Children's Literature.* Wheaton, IL: Crossway Books, 2002.

We have listed just a few of our favorite authors and beginning readers below. Also look for other titles by these authors and illustrators.

Cronin, Doreen. *Click, Clack, Moo: Cows That Type*. New York: Simon & Schuster, 2011.

Hoban, Russell. The Frances series. New York: Trophy Picture Books, 1960–1994.

Leaf, Munro. *The Story of Ferdinand*, illus. Robert Lawson. New York: Grosset & Dunlap, 2000.

McCloskey, Robert. *Make Way for Ducklings* and *Blueberries for Sal*. New York: Puffin, 1976 and 1991.

Meddaugh, Susan. The Martha series. Boston: Houghton Mifflin, 1992–2004.

Munsch, Robert. *The Paper Bag Princess*. Toronto: Annick Press, 1980.

Rey, Margret, and H.A. The Curious George series. Boston: Houghton Mifflin, 1958–1989.

Scieszka, John. *The True Story of the Three Little Pigs*, illus. Lane Smith. New York: Puffin, 1996.

Steig, William. *Sylvester and the Magic Pebble* and *The Amazing Bone*. New York: Simon & Schuster, 1969 and 1977.

Trivizas, Eugene. *The Three Little Wolves and the Big Bad Pig*, illus. Helen Oxenbury. New York: Margaret K. McElderry, 1997.

Van Leeuwen, Jean. The Amanda Pig series, illus. Ann Schweninger. New York: Penguin Young Readers, 1982–2008.

Viorst, Judith. *Alexander and the Terrible, Horrible, No Good, Very Bad Day*, reprint ed. New York: Atheneum, 1987.

Waber, Bernard. The Lyle the Crocodile series. Boston: Houghton Mifflin, 1965–1998.

Zion, Gene. The Harry series, illus. Margaret Bloy Graham. New York: HarperCollins, 1956–1966.

Reading: Literature

These titles are listed in order of use. Remember, you don't have to read all of these. But you can choose reading assignments from among the following names. Note that this list—especially the early-modern and modern sections—is merely a starting place. There are many other authors and books worth reading, and you'll discover them as you explore your library. Rather than organizing these books and authors alphabetically, we have listed them in chronological order, and we suggest that you read them in this order. In most cases, you can use any version of these stories. We have suggested a few specific editions that we particularly like.

Useful for All Four Years

Russell, William F. *Classics to Read Aloud to Your Children: Selections from Shakespeare, Twain, Dickens, O. Henry, London, Longfellow, Irving, Aesop, Homer, Cervantes, Hawthorne, and More.* New York: Crown Publishers, 1992.

Excerpts from classics appropriate for first grade ("The Ugly Duckling" and "How Arthur Was Crowned King", etc.) through fourth grade (*The Red Badge of Courage*, "The Highwayman," *The Call of the Wild*, etc.). A handy resource for all four years, covering ancients through the twentieth century; all excerpts are a good length for a single-session read-aloud, and pronunciation guides are included.

Ancients, 5000 B.C.–A.D. 400 (First Grade)

Work through these books and authors in the following order. Many other literature selections that correspond to history are provided in the activity guide to *The Story of the World*, one of our recommended history resources. (See Chapter 7.)

Stories and poems by, about, or from . . .

The Bible

Homer

Little, Emily. *The Trojan Horse: How the Greeks Won the War.* New York: Random House, 1988.

Part of the "Step into Reading" series, this second-grade-level text can also be read independently by strong first-grade readers.

McCaughrean, Geraldine. *The Odyssey*, illus. Victor G. Ambrus. New York: Puffin, 1997.

At most public libraries; worth asking for on interlibrary loan. Too difficult for first graders, but a wonderful read-to over several weeks (one chapter per session). Geraldine McCaughrean manages to keep the poetic flow of the original.

Sutcliff, Rosemary. *Black Ships Before Troy: The Story of the Iliad*, illus. Alan Lee. New York: Bantam, 2005.

Find at any bookstore or library. Another read-aloud with beautiful illustrations.

Greek and Roman Myths

Aliki. *The Gods and Goddesses of Olympus*. New York: HarperCollins, 1997.

An age-appropriate set of tales.

D'Aulaire, Ingri, and Edgar Parin D'Aulaire. *D'Aulaires' Book of Greek Myths*. New York: Delacorte Books for Young Readers, 1992.

Demi. *King Midas: The Golden Touch*. New York: Margaret K. McElderry, 2002.

Spectacular illustrations in this picture-book retelling.

Kimmel, Eric A. *The McElderry Book of Greek Myths*, illus. Pep Montserrat. New York: Margaret K. McElderry, 2008.

The stories of Prometheus, Pandora, Arachne, Theseus, and more, with art inspired by ancient friezes.

Lock, Deborah. *Greek Myths (DK Readers, Level 3)*. New York: DK Children, 2008.

A beginning book accessible to strong first-grade and most second-grade readers.

Mayer, Marianna. *Pegasus*, illus. Kinuko Y. Craft. New York: HarperCollins, 1998.

Russell, William F. *Classic Myths to Read Aloud: The Great Stories of Greek and Roman Mythology*. New York: Broadway Books, 1992.

Short and lively versions for students aged 5–12, complete with background for the parent and a pronunciation guide (very useful).

Osborne, Mary Pope. *Favorite Greek Myths*. New York: Scholastic, 1989.
A read-aloud collection that retells stories from Ovid in an age-appropriate manner.

Aesop's fables

Plato

Aristotle

Egyptian myths
Barker, Henry. *Egyptian Gods and Goddesses*, illus. Jeff Crosby. New York: Penguin, 1999.
From the All Aboard Reading series; some young students will be able to read this independently.

Indian folktales
Williams, Marcia. *The Elephant's Friend and Other Tales from Ancient India*. New York: Candlewick, 2014.
This colorful and entertaining text combines comic-book-style layout with clear, beginner-friendly text.

African folktales
Arkhurst, Joyce Cooper. *The Adventures of Spider: West African Folktales*, illus. Jerry Pinkney. New York: Little, Brown & Co., 1992.

Confucius

Chinese and Japanese folktales
Bishop, Claire. *The Five Chinese Brothers*. New York Puffin, 1996.
Try your local library. This favorite folktale is available in several different versions.

Ancient Chinese and Japanese poetry

Virgil
Emily Frenkel. *Aeneas: Virgil's Epic Retold for Younger Readers*. London: Bristol Classical Press, 1991.
An independent read for middle-school students, but perfectly accessible as a read-aloud to younger learners. Clear and accessible, with a pronunciation guide.

English, Irish, and Welsh fairy tales

Smith, Philip, ed. *Irish Fairy Tales (Dover Children's Thrift Classics)*. New York: Dover, 1993.

Well-told read-aloud tales with black-and-white illustrations.

Medieval/Early Renaissance, 400–1600 (Second Grade)

Work through these books and authors in the following order.

Stories and poems by, about, or from . . .

Saint Augustine

Beowulf

Green, John. *Beowulf (Dover Coloring Book)*. New York: Dover, 2007.

Brief clear text and thirty scenes to color; a fun way for elementary students to encounter the tale for the first time.

Sir Gawain and the Green Knight

Stories of Robin Hood

San Souci, Robert D. *Robin Hood and the Golden Arrow*, illus. Earl B. Lewis. New York: Orchard Books, 2010.

A beautifully illustrated version for students reading a little below grade level.

Pyle, Howard, John Burrows, and Lucy Corvino. *The Adventures of Robin Hood (Classic Starts)*. New York: Sterling, 2005.

An illustrated retelling accessible to third- and fourth-grade readers.

Geoffrey Chaucer, *Canterbury Tales*

McCaughrean, Geraldine. *The Canterbury Tales*, illus. Victor G. Ambrus. New York: Puffin, 1997.

The Junior Bookshelf calls this "one of the very finest interpretations of Chaucer for the young." A read-to for most second graders. Well worth the effort of ordering on interlibrary loan.

Edmund Spenser, *The Faerie Queene*

Hodges, Margaret. *Saint George and the Dragon*, illus. Trina Schart Hyman. New York: Little, Brown, 1990.

A Caldecott Medal winner; retells the story of Saint George from Edmund Spenser's *Faerie Queene*. Beautiful illustrations, and Hodges retains some of Spenser's original poetry. At most libraries.

William Shakespeare, all the plays

A Shakespeare Coloring Book. Santa Barbara, CA: Bellerophon, 1985.

Historical illustrations of famous scenes from Shakespeare's plays.

Burdett, Lois. The Shakespeare Can Be Fun series.

Designed for ages 6–8, these books retell the plays in rhyming couplets, illustrated by children's drawings.

Hamlet for Kids. Toronto: Firefly Books, 2000.

Macbeth for Kids. Buffalo, NY: Firefly Books, 1996.

Much Ado About Nothing for Kids. Toronto: Firefly Books, 2002.

Romeo and Juliet for Kids. Toronto: Firefly Books, 1998.

Twelfth Night for Kids. Buffalo, NY: Firefly Books, 1994.

Coville, Bruce. *William Shakespeare's A Midsummer Night's Dream,* illus. Dennis Nolan. New York: Puffin, 2003.

A beautiful picture-book version. Out of print but worth tracking down secondhand or at your local library. Coville has also done beautiful (out of print) versions of *The Tempest, The Winter's Tale, Macbeth, Romeo and Juliet,* and *Hamlet.*

Garfield, Leon. *Leon Garfield's Shakespeare Stories,* illus. Michael Foreman. New York: NYR Children's Collection, 2015.

Retellings of twenty-one plays, retaining much of the original language; a twentieth-century classic recently republished.

Lamb, Charles, and Mary Lamb. *Tales from Shakespeare.* New York: Puffin Classics, 2010.

These classic retellings of Shakespeare's stories use the original words wherever possible. Sixth-grade reading level; a read-to for grammar-stage students.

Nesbit, E. *Shakespeare's Stories for Young Readers.* New York: Dover, 2006.

Nesbit's retellings are read-aloud for younger students, independent reads for middle graders. Briefer and more lyrical than the classic Lamb retellings.

Dante, *The Inferno*

Thomas Malory, *Morte d'Arthur*

Translated, this means the "death of Arthur." Look for retellings of the Arthur legend, most of which are based on Malory.

Gross, Gwen. *Knights of the Round Table.* Stepping Stone series, illus. Norman Green. New York: Random House, 1985.

The Stepping Stone series adapts classic stories to a second- to third-grade level.

Hodges, Margaret. *The Kitchen Knight: A Tale of King Arthur,* illus. Trina Schart-Hyman. New York: Holiday House, 1993.

Erasmus
Martin Luther
John Calvin

Sir Thomas Wyatt

Wyatt, a poet in his own right, sometimes shows up as a secondary character in stories about Henry VIII and Anne Boleyn.

John Knox
René Descartes

Late Renaissance/Early Modern, 1600–1850 (Third Grade)

Work through these books and authors in the following order.

Stories and poems by, about, or from . . .

John Milton

French fairy tales

Many were collected by Charles Perrault, 1628–1703.

Daniel Defoe, *Robinson Crusoe*

Defoe, Daniel, Deanna McFadden, and Jamel Akib. *Robinson Crusoe (Classic Starts).* New York: Sterling, 2006.

An illustrated retelling accessible to third- and fourth-grade readers.

Jonathan Swift, *Gulliver's Travels*

Swift, Jonathan, and Martin Woodside. *Gulliver's Travels (Classic Starts).* New York: Sterling, 2006.

An illustrated retelling accessible to third- and fourth-grade readers.

Findlay, Lisa. *Gulliver in Lilliput,* illus. Antonio Caparo. New York: Random House, 2010.

For students who are still reading a little below grade level.

John Bunyan, *Pilgrim's Progress*

Victor Hugo

    Hugo, Victor, Deanna McFadden, and Lucy Corvino. *The Hunchback of Notre-Dame (Classic Starts)*. New York: Sterling, 2008.

        An illustrated retelling accessible to third- and fourth-grade readers.

    Hugo, Victor, and Monica Kulling. *Les Miserables*. Stepping Stone series. New York: Random House, 1995.

        Adapted to a second- to third-grade reading level.

Alexandre Dumas

    Dumas, Alexandre, and Deborah G. Felder. *The Three Musketeers*. Stepping Stone series. New York: Random House, 1994.

        Adapted to a second- to third-grade reading level.

    Dumas, Alexandre, Oliver Ho, and Jamel Akib. *The Three Musketeers (Classic Starts)*. New York: Sterling, 2007.

        An illustrated retelling accessible to third- and fourth-grade readers.

William Blake, *Songs of Innocence*
William Wordsworth, collected poems
Jane Austen
Alfred, Lord Tennyson
Robert Browning, *The Pied Piper of Hamelin*
Elizabeth Barrett Browning
Jacob and Wilhelm Grimm, *Grimms' Fairy Tales*

Charles Dickens

    Dickens, Charles, Deanna McFadden, Eric Freeberg. *Great Expectations (Classic Starts)*. New York: Sterling, 2010.

        An illustrated retelling accessible to third- and fourth-grade readers.

    Dickens, Charles, and Monica Kulling. *Great Expectations*. Stepping Stone series. New York: Random House, 1996.

        Adapted to a second- to third-grade reading level.

    Dickens, Charles, Kathleen Olmstead, and Dan Andreasen. *Oliver Twist (Classic Starts)*. New York: Sterling, 2006.

        An illustrated retelling accessible to third- and fourth-grade readers.

Dickens, Charles, Les Martin, and Jean Zallinger. *Oliver Twist*. Stepping Stone series. New York: Random House, 1990.

    Adapted to a second- to third-grade reading level.

Edward Lear, the nonsense poems

Christina Rossetti, children's poems

Lewis Carroll, *Alice in Wonderland* and *Through the Looking-Glass*

Mark Twain, all the stories

    Twain, Mark, and Deidre S. Laikin. *The Adventures of Tom Sawyer: Great Illustrated Classics*. New York: Baronet Books, 2008.

    Adapted to a third- to fourth-grade reading level.

James Fenimore Cooper, all the novels

Jules Verne, all the novels

    Verne, Jules, and Judith Conaway. *20,000 Leagues Under the Sea*, illus. Gino D'Achille. Stepping Stone series. New York: Random House, 1983.

    Verne, Jules, Deanna McFadden, Jamel Akib. *Around the World in 80 Days (Classic Starts)*. New York: Sterling, 2007.

    An illustrated retelling accessible to third- and fourth-grade readers.

    Verne, Jules, Kathleen Olmstead, and Eric Freeberg. *Journey to the Center of the Earth (Classic Starts)*. New York: Sterling, 2011.

    An illustrated retelling accessible to third- and fourth-grade readers.

Norwegian folktales

    Asbjronsen, Peter, and Jorgen Moe. *Norwegian Folk Tales*. New York: Pantheon, 1982.

    This book is an affordable version of the original 1849 collection.

Herman Melville, *Moby-Dick*

    Melville, Herman, Kathleen Olmstead, and Eric Freeberg. *Moby-Dick (Classic Starts)*. New York: Sterling, 2010.

    An illustrated retelling accessible to third- and fourth-grade readers.

Modern, 1850–Present (Fourth Grade)

Tell the children's librarian at your local library that you're looking for classic literature from 1850 to the present, on your child's reading level, and follow up on his or her suggestions. (Librarians may differ in their ideas about what's suitable for fourth graders, so glance through all the recommendations.) We also suggest the following (work through these books and authors in the following order).

Stories and poems by, about, or from . . .

Robert Louis Stevenson

Stevenson, Robert Louis. *A Child's Garden of Verses*, illus. Tasha Tudor. Rev. ed. New York: Simon & Schuster, 1999.

Stevenson, Robert Louis. *Kidnapped*. Narrated by John Sessions. Franklin, TN: Naxos Audiobooks, 2000.

Although this is an abridged audiobook, *Kidnapped* can be difficult to follow, and this version is worth checking out; it makes the storyline clear, and Sessions is a wonderful narrator.

Stevenson, Robert Louis, Chris Tait, and Lucy Corvino. *Treasure Island (Classic Starts)*. New York: Sterling, 2005.

An illustrated retelling accessible to third- and fourth-grade readers.

Arthur Conan Doyle

Johanna Spyri, *Heidi*

Carlo Collodi, *Pinocchio*

Collodi, Carlo. *The Adventures of Pinocchio: Story of a Puppet*, illus. Robert Ingpen. New York: Sterling, 2014.

Avoid the Disney version, which changes both the plot and the original moral message of the story.

H. G. Wells

Wells, H. G., Chris Sasaki, and Troy Howell. *The Time Machine (Classic Starts)*. New York: Sterling, 2008.

An illustrated retelling accessible to third- and fourth-grade readers.

Wells, H. G., and Malvina G. Vogel. *War of the Worlds: Great Illustrated Classics*. Edina, MN: Abdo Publishing Company, 2005.

Adapted to a third- to fourth-grade reading level.

Louisa May Alcott

Andrew Lang, collected tales

Lang, Andrew. *The Blue Fairy Book*. New York: Dover, 1965.

———. *The Orange Fairy Book.* New York: Dover, 1968.

———. *The Lilac Fairy Book.* New York: Dover, 1968.

Frances Hodgson Burnett, all the novels

Kenneth Grahame, *The Wind in the Willows*
Grahame, Kenneth. *The Wind in the Willows.* New York: Signet Classics, 2006.

James Barrie, *Peter Pan* and all the plays

Rudyard Kipling, *Just So Stories* and *The Jungle Book*s
Kipling, Rudyard. *The Elephant's Child,* illus. Tim Raglin. New York: Rabbit Ears Entertainment, 2013.

Kipling's original text along with young-reader-friendly illustrations.

———. *How the Camel Got His Hump,* illus. Tim Raglin. New York: Rabbit Ears Entertainment, 2012.

———. *How the Leopard Got His Spots,* illus. Tim Raglin. New York: Rabbit Ears Entertainment, 2012.

———. *How the Rhino Got His Skin,* illus. Tim Raglin. New York: Rabbit Ears Entertainment, 2012.

———. *The Jungle Book,* illus. Robert Ingpen. New York: Sterling, 2012.

Beatrix Potter, all the stories
Laura Ingalls Wilder, all the novels
Walter de la Mare, collected poems
Carl Sandburg, collected poems

John Ciardi, collected poems
Ciardi, John. *You Read to Me, I'll Read to You,* illus. Edward Gorey. New York: HarperCollins, 1987.

An award-winning book of poetry designed for parents and children to read to each other.

T. S. Eliot, *Old Possum's Book of Practical Cats*

Recordings to Supplement Literature

Storyteller Jim Weiss retells classic stories for children, including versions of some of the titles listed above. These MP3s and compact discs are wonderful listening; they won't replace reading, but they will serve as a valuable supplement. The list below is only partial; visit Well-Trained Mind Press at www.welltrainedmind.com for a full list. Very highly recommended for building knowledge of the classics and improving general literacy. Read-along print versions are also available for some titles. Titles include:

Ancient Times
Egyptian Treasures: Mummies and Myths
Greek Myths
Julius Caesar and the Story of Rome
She and He: Adventures in Mythology
Heroes in Mythology: Theseus, Prometheus, and Odin

Middle Ages/Early Renaissance
Arabian Nights
Celtic Treasures
King Arthur and His Knights
Romeo and Juliet
Shakespeare for Children
Three Musketeers/Robin Hood

Late Renaissance/Early Modern
The Prince and the Pauper: The Mark Twain Classic
Rip Van Winkle/Gulliver's Travels
A Christmas Carol and Other Favorites
A Tale of Two Cities
American Tall Tales
The Adventures of Tom Sawyer

Modern
The Jungle Book
Sherlock Holmes for Children
Treasure Island
Mystery! Mystery! Sherlock Holmes, Father Brown, Auguste Dupin
Spooky Classics for Children
Twenty Thousand Leagues under the Sea

Poetry Memorization Resources

Ferris, Helen, ed. *Favorite Poems Old and New,* illus. Leonard Weisgard. New York: Doubleday, 1957.

Hall, Donald, ed. *The Oxford Illustrated Book of American Children's Poems.* New York: Oxford University Press, 2001.

Kennedy, Caroline, ed. *Poems to Learn by Heart,* illus. Jon J. Muth. New York: Disney/Hyperion Books, 2013.

Prelutsky, Jack, ed. *The Random House Book of Poetry for Children: A Treasury of 572 Poems for Today's Child,* illus. Arnold Lobel. New York: Random House, 1983.

Spelling

There are dozens of spelling curricula and resources out there. We've listed three resources with very different approaches here; we selected these for ease of use, affordability, and their track record of effectiveness across a wide range of home-schooling families.

Modern Curriculum Press Spelling Workout series, rev. ed. Parsippany, NJ: Modern Curriculum Press (Pearson Learning Group), 2002.

> $12.97 for each student edition, $13.47 for each *Teacher's Edition* (you probably won't need these until you're into the fourth or fifth book at the earliest). Order from Pearson Learning. We've listed the entire series for your reference, but most children won't get past *E* or *F* by fourth grade. The grade levels are approximate, but will give you a guide as to where to begin with an older student.
>
> Spelling Workout is the most straightforward of the programs listed here: students progress through a series of workbook exercises that teach the rules of spelling ("The sound /oi/ can be spelled *oy* or *oi,* as in *toy* and *oil*"), the proper names for letter combinations ("A *consonant digraph* is two consonants that come together to make just one sound"), and the phonetic symbols used in dictionaries ("/ar/ makes the sound in *farm*"). The Spelling Workout series even teaches basic proofreading marks.
>
> Begin first grade with the first workbook, *Spelling Workout A.* This

workbook is the most basic one: it reviews the letters of the alphabet, asks children to connect pictures of objects that begin or end with the same letter, and then has the children write three-letter words. These exercises teach beginning spellers to hear the individual sounds in words and translate those sounds into written symbols. Most first-grade students who are reading well will find this book easy. Don't skip anything, though; the books build valuable skills and confidence through repetition. And don't try to match books to grade level; move on to *Spelling Workout B* whenever *A* is finished, and so on.

Spelling Workout works best for students who learn to read without much difficulty and who don't struggle with spelling; it will reinforce their intuitive knowledge of language, teach rules explicitly, and drill them in proofreading.

Caveats: Don't do the associated writing exercises, which are badly organized (as many writing assignments in spelling and grammar programs tend to be). Ignore anything which seems unnecessarily "school-ish" to you, such as the Pearson "Guide for Parents," which earnestly explains how important it is to have a detailed lesson plan for your spelling program that includes "potential field trip ideas" and "key concepts." (Guys: It's just spelling. *Spelling Workout*'s strength is its organization—you don't have to prepare, just open and go.) And if your student doesn't like puzzles, don't do the crosswords.

Otherwise, this is a clear, minimal-preparation-required, simple spelling program.

Spelling Workout A (first-grade level)
  Teacher's Edition A
Spelling Workout B (second-grade level)
  Teacher's Edition B
Spelling Workout C (third-grade level)
  Teacher's Edition C
Spelling Workout D (fourth-grade level)
  Teacher's Edition D
Spelling Workout E (fifth-grade level)
  Teacher's Edition E
Spelling Workout F (sixth-grade level)
  Teacher's Edition F
Spelling Workout G (seventh-grade level)

Teacher's Edition G

Spelling Workout H (eighth-grade level)

Teacher's Edition H

All About Spelling. Eagle River, WI: All About Learning Press, 2006–2014. Developed by dyslexia researcher Marie Rippel, *All About Spelling* is based on the Orton-Gillingham system. This seven-level workbook series is ideal for students who need more direct instruction than *Spelling Workout* provides. Students who struggled with the primer approach to reading outlined in Chapter 4 should go directly to *All About Spelling* (don't even try *Spelling Workout*). Each Teacher's Manual is "lightly scripted" (you, the parent, are told what to explain, how to explain it, and what visual aids and manipulatives to use). The accompanying Student Packets contain all cards, charts, and worksheets required. In keeping with our approach, *All About Spelling* allows spelling to be studied at its own pace, rather than connecting it to other language arts areas, and does not require significant handwriting in the early years. Directions are clear, there is little busywork, and teacher preparation is minimal. Samples are available at the publisher's website.

We have listed the entire series for your convenience, but most children will not progress past level 4 or 5 during the elementary years. When beginning the program, you'll need to purchase one Spelling Interactive Kit (containing letter tiles, magnets, cards, and app), which will serve you for the rest of the levels.

Samples may be viewed on the publisher's website, which also provides scope and sequence documents, video clips, apps, and more.

Level 1 (Teacher's Manual and Student Packet), $29.95.

Level 2 (Teacher's Manual and Student Packet), $39.95.

Level 3 (Teacher's Manual and Student Packet), $39.95.

Level 4 (Teacher's Manual and Student Packet), $39.95.

Level 5 (Teacher's Manual and Student Packet), $39.95.

Level 6 (Teacher's Manual and Student Packet), $39.95.

Level 7 (Teacher's Manual and Student Packet), $39.95.

Spelling Interactive Kit, $22.85.

Sequential Spelling. Clio, MI: AVKO Educational Research Foundation, various dates.

This seven-level series was developed by longtime teacher Don McCabe, himself a dyslexic reader. *Sequential Spelling* takes an entirely different approach: rather than teaching the rules that govern English spelling, the books teach words in "word families" that all have the same pattern. For example, one early lesson builds on the vowel-consonant combination *in* to teach the spelling of *bin, inn, spin, inner,* and *chin*; a much later lesson teaches the letter combination *ange,* and builds on that combination to form the words *range, ranges, arranges,* and *arrangement.*

Sequential Spelling requires more teacher preparation time than either *Spelling Workout* or *All About Spelling,* since you must understand and directly teach each lesson; there is no scripting and you will need to take some time to grasp the method and the aimed-for results. However, the program is often very effective for students who struggle with rule-based spelling. In addition, the publisher offers DVD lessons that teach the student directly, so that the parent needs only to supervise and check (a particularly good option for larger families).

Sequential Spelling does not teach rules at all ("Most people never need to be taught spelling rules in order to learn English"), instead focusing entirely on patterns. However, supplemental materials teaching spelling rules explicitly can be downloaded from the publisher's website; we suggest that you make as much use of these as possible.

The publisher recommends beginning in second grade; Level 1 is too intensive for first grade. The levels are not by grade, but rather by word family; always begin with Level 1.

Each level costs $15 for the Teacher Manual, $10 for the Student Response Book, and $30 for the DVD (ebook versions are also available for a lower cost, as are "bundles" of all required materials). Buy from the publisher, www.avko.org. Extensive samples of all materials are available at the publisher's website.

Sequential Spelling 1
Sequential Spelling 2
Sequential Spelling 3
Sequential Spelling 4
Sequential Spelling 5
Sequential Spelling 6
Sequential Spelling 7

Grammar

Wise, Jessie. *First Language Lessons for the Well-Trained Mind*. Charles City, VA: Well-Trained Mind Press.

First Language Lessons covers parts of speech, punctuation, types of sentences, and word use. Levels 1 and 2 are entirely oral (optional enrichment exercises involve small amounts of writing). Levels 3 and 4 introduce handwritten workbook assignments, using a separate student workbook for each level. The program is scripted for the parent's use, so that parents who are unfamiliar with grammar can use it with confidence. Review of all concepts and memory work is built into the lessons. Second and third graders just entering the program can begin at grade level; it is recommended that fourth graders begin with *First Language Lessons 3*. Purchase from the publisher's website or from any bookstore.

First Language Lessons for the Well-Trained Mind, Level 1, 2nd ed. (2010), $14.95

First Language Lessons for the Well-Trained Mind, Level 2, 2nd ed. (2010), $14.95

First Language Lessons for the Well-Trained Mind, Level 3 (2007). $29.95.

First Language Lessons, Level 3 Student Workbook. $18.95.

First Language Lessons for the Well-Trained Mind, Level 4 (2008). $29.95.

First Language Lessons, Level 4 Student Workbook. $19.95.

English for the Thoughtful Child. Lebanon, TN.: Greenleaf Press.

This revision of classic nineteenth-century grammar books updates and simplifies the original texts. Use as an oral language text for first and second grade; unless your child is an unusually willing and comfortable writer, skip the writing assignments. *English for the Thoughtful Child* does not have a great deal of teacher direction in it, and some users complain that it still feels dated, but it covers basic grammar skills with less repetition than the FLL series.

Incidentally, if you are relatively comfortable with English grammar, you can download and use the original texts for free (both are available at books.google.com and elsewhere, as well as at many libraries). Volume 1 is based on *Practical Lessons in the Use of English, Book I: For Primary and Intermediate Grades*, by Mary F. Hyde (Boston: D. C. Heath & Co., 1894). Volume 2 is based on *Lessons in English: Book One*, by Fred Newton Scott and Gordon A. Southworth (New York: B. H. Sanborn & Co., 1906, revised in 1912, 1916, and 1921). With some adjustments (such as leaving out the copperplate copywork, doing written exercises orally, and skipping the assigned compositions), you can easily adapt the texts for first- and second-grade use.

Whichever version you use, plan to move on to one of the other resources listed for third- and fourth-grade grammar.

English for the Thoughtful Child, Vol. 1, by Mary F. Hyde and Cynthia A. Shearer (1990).

English for the Thoughtful Child, Vol. 2, by Fred Newton Scott, Gordon A. Southworth, and Cynthia A. Shearer (2003). Revised for print-on-demand 2013.

Rod & Staff Grammar and Composition series

Parents who have finished *English for the Thoughtful Child* or do not wish to continue with the scripted style of *First Language Lessons* can instead use the textbook series published by Rod & Staff. The third-grade book is called *Beginning Wisely: English 3*, the fourth- grade book is called *Building with Diligence: English 4*, and the series is unabashedly Christian (Rod & Staff is a Mennonite publisher). (First- and second-grade grammar is integrated into their entire "language arts" curriculum, which we do not recommend.)

These texts provide an excellent, rigorous, thorough grounding in grammar. Remember, though, that this program was originally designed for a classroom, and there's enough repetition in the exercises to keep a roomful of students busy. Don't feel that you need to complete every exercise if the child understands the concept. The books are nonconsumable and the student is expected to copy out each exercise; be very careful how much physical writing you require of a third- or fourth-grade student, and feel free to do as many exercises orally as you think appropriate. Skip the writing assignments. We have provided information about the tests and extra practice worksheets, but most students will not need them.

Rod & Staff has no website and limited distribution; order from Milestone Books or Exodus Books.

Beginning Wisely: English 3. Crockett, KY: Rod & Staff, 1991.

Pupil Textbook. $14.25.

Worksheets (additional practice). $3.60.

Teacher's Manual. $17.55.

Test Booklet. $2.50.

Building with Diligence: English 4. Crockett, KY: Rod & Staff, 1992.

Pupil Textbook. $17.55.

Worksheets (additional practice). $3.60.

Teacher's Manual. $23.05.

Test Booklet. $2.50.

Hake Grammar & Writing series. Boston: Houghton Mifflin Harcourt, 2014. Previously known as Saxon Grammar, Hake Grammar & Writing offers a thorough and nonsectarian approach to grammar. The exercises are comprehensive and provide an excellent transition from oral language lessons into written grammar.

There is no third-grade book; the series begins with Book 4, but you can choose to extend *First Language Lessons* or *English for the Thoughtful Child* over three years and begin Hake in fourth grade, or begin Hake in third grade and take two years to complete the book.

You will need the Student Textbook and Teacher Edition; these contain all of the grammar instruction and exercises. We do *not* recommend the Student Workbook, which contains the writing component of the program. Hake introduces expository essays, personal narratives, descriptive essays, and even research papers in fourth grade, which is completely developmentally inappropriate. These are logic-stage skills. Buy the Student Textbook and Teacher Edition separately rather than buying the Homeschool Kit, which contains the Student Workbook as well.

Order from Houghton Mifflin Harcourt's home education site or from a home-school supplier such as Rainbow Resource. *Note:* HMH's main site sells the hardcover school version of the program, which is different only in format and cannot be purchased by individual users. Samples can be viewed on the publisher's website. ISBNs are provided because the site is very difficult to navigate.

Grammar and Writing 4 Student Textbook (ISBN 9780544044203). $43.25.

Grammar and Writing 4 Teacher Guide (ISBN 9780544044227). $29.75.

Voyages in English series. Chicago: Loyola Press, 2011.

Voyages in English is a series originally designed by Loyola Press for

Catholic schools and reissued in a nonsectarian version. The rules are clearly stated and the exercises are adequate; the program is not quite as rigorous or complete as the Rod & Staff program, and the writing exercises should be skipped (see the Writing section in this chapter). Most students will not need the additional practice books. Samples can be viewed on the publisher's website.

Order from Loyola Press or from Rainbow Resource Center.

Voyages in English, Grade 3, Student Edition. $52.95.

Voyages in English, Grade 3, Practice Workbook. $11.95.

Voyages in English, Grade 3, Teacher Guide. $81.95.

Voyages in English, Grade 4, Student Edition. $52.95.

Voyages in English, Grade 4, Practice Workbook. $11.95.

Voyages in English, Grade 4, Teacher Guide. $81.95.

Penmanship

Olsen, Jan Z. Handwriting Without Tears program, rev. ed. Cabin John, MD: Handwriting Without Tears.

Order from Handwriting Without Tears. The books below are listed in progressive order.

My Printing Book (first grade). $9.50.

1st Grade Printing Teacher's Guide. $10.50.

Printing Power (second grade). $9.50.

2nd Grade Printing Teacher's Guide. $10.50.

Cursive Handwriting (third grade). $9.50.

3rd Grade Cursive Teacher's Guide. $10.50.

Cursive Success (fourth grade). $9.50.

4th Grade Cursive Teacher's Guide. $10.50.

Double Lined Notebook Paper. Designed specifically to go along with the skills taught in this program.

Regular (grades 2–3). 100 sheets. $3.75.

Regular (grades 2–3). 500 sheets. $11.75.

Narrow (grades 4+). 100 sheets. $3.75.

Narrow (grades 4+). 500 sheets. $11.75.

Zaner-Bloser Handwriting series. Columbus, OH: Zaner-Bloser, 2008.

$11.49 each. Order from Zaner-Bloser. This is the Zaner-Bloser continuous-stroke alphabet method. See Chapter 4, Resources, for the first two books in the series (Grades K–1).

Handwriting: Grade 2C Student Book.

This book provides the transition into cursive writing. Use for second or third grade.

Handwriting: Grade 3 Student Book.

More practice in cursive writing.

Handwriting: Grade 4 Student Book.

Handwriting: Grade 5 Student Book.

Handwriting: Grade 6 Student Book.

Zaner-Bloser Handwriting Paper.

$10.99 each. Order these packs of writing paper for extra handwriting practice from Zaner-Bloser. A typical student uses one ream of writing paper per year. The ruled lines on these sheets narrow as the grades go on. See Chapter 4, Resources, for K–1 paper.

Grade 2 paper (½" wide).

Grade 3 paper (⅜" wide).

Grades 4–6 paper (⅜" wide with no center guide line).

Writing

The First Steps: Copywork, Dictation, Narration

While a writing curriculum is not necessarily required for parents who feel comfortable following the principles in this chapter, many families find a more structured program helpful.

Bauer, Susan Wise. *The Complete Writer: Writing With Ease.* Charles City, VA: Well-Trained Mind Press.

Susan has laid out a complete elementary program in her series *The Complete Writer: Writing with Ease.* The core text, *Strong Fundamentals*, gives a detailed overview of the skills that should be developed during the elementary-, middle-, and high-school years; outlines a complete four-year progression of copywork, dictation, and narration for elementary students, complete with weekly lesson plans; and provides troubleshooting for common writing problems. The core text allows the parent to plan out the four years of elementary writing and to choose the majority of the copywork, dictation, and narration exercises independently. *Strong Fundamentals* allows writing to be integrated across the curriculum, with narration and writing exercises chosen in literature, history, and science.

Parents who would prefer to have each day's lesson spelled out can use the accompanying workbooks. *The Complete Writer: Level 1 Workbook* lays out an entire year's worth of copywork and narration exercises, all based on classic literature, and provides a script for the instructor to follow. The *Level 2* and *Level 3* workbooks each cover one year of elementary writing, progressing from copywork into dictation and more complex narration exercises. After Level 3, elementary students may progress to one of the elementary writing courses listed below; the *Level 4* workbook is optional, for students who need additional practice before going into a composition course. The workbooks are open-and-go; no preparation time is required and all parent guidance is scripted. However, in exchange for ease of use and instructor support, you lose some of the integration across the curriculum.

Samples of all books are available at the publisher's website.

Choose which approach suits you best; all of them will teach the child to write.

Writing with Ease, Strong Fundamentals: A Guide to Designing Your Own Elementary Writing Curriculum, rev. ed. 2015. $29.95.

    Level 1 Workbook for Writing with Ease. 2008. $34.95.

    Level 2 Workbook for Writing with Ease. 2008. $34.95.

    Level 3 Workbook for Writing with Ease. 2009. $36.95.

    (Optional) *Level 4 Workbook for Writing with Ease.* 2010. $36.95.

Introduction to Composition. Louisville, KY: Memoria Press.

    This one-year course uses three classic children's novels (*Charlotte's Web, Farmer Boy,* and *The Moffats*) as the basis for exercises in narration, dictation, and beginning outlining. Best for fourth grade or advanced third graders, this can be used as a fourth year after *Writing With Ease* or as an independent one-year practice course.

    Introduction to Composition: Student Guide, 2nd ed. 2014. $10.

    Introduction to Composition: Teacher Key, 2nd ed. 2014. $10.

The Next Step

Most students need to continue with dictation and narration exercises through third grade, and many should continue to work on these skills through fourth grade. However, students who write with ease may wish to move on to a new challenge. They should continue to write narrations in history, science, and literature, but you may choose to add one of the following curricula.

Killgallon, Don and Jenny. *Sentence Composing for Elementary School: A Worktext to Build Better Sentences.* Portsmouth, NH: Heinemann, 2000. $27.50.

Developed by college writing teacher Don Killgallon and secondary writing teacher Jenny Killgallon, this one-year, one-volume course focuses on analyzing and imitating good sentences from accomplished writers. Excellent preparation for the middle-grade years and in line with classical principles of modeling work before asking students to complete it. The course does assume that students have had a basic grammar course. Suitable for fourth-grade writers. Answer key is in the back of the worktext. Samples can be viewed at the publisher's website.

Writing & Rhetoric: A Creative Approach to the Classical Progymnasmata. Camp Hill, PA: Classical Academic Press.

CAP's Writing & Rhetoric series brings the classical *progymnasmata* (a set of exercises assigned by ancient and medieval teachers of rhetoric in order to develop their students' persuasive skills) down to the elementary level. As we explain in greater detail in Chapter 25 (pages 574–576), we find the *progymnasmata* to be best suited to the high-school years. However, the first volume in the series spends an entire year on the first of the *progymnasmata* exercises: retelling a fable. This retelling builds on and improves skills in narration; students not only summarize, but begin to work on the skills of rewriting, using dialogue, changing points of view, and so on. A good challenge for young writers who don't struggle with the mechanics of getting words down on paper.

Suitable for a fourth-grade writer. Samples can be viewed on the publisher's website.

Kortepeter, Paul. *Writing & Rhetoric, Book 1: Fable.* 2013. $19.95.

———. *Writing & Rhetoric, Book 1: Fable, Teacher's Edition.* 2013. $19.95.

Writing Strands: Challenging Writing Programs for Homeschoolers series. Niles, MI: National Writing Institute, rev. ed.

This seven-book series begins with simple descriptions and progresses through paragraph construction, tense use, narrative voice, dialogue, reports, interviews, and short stories. Two additional books cover exposition and fiction on the high-school level. Since Writing Strands contains creative writing exercises as well, it should not be used with young students who find imaginative writing or journaling difficult.

Writing Strands is best suited to students who don't have trouble getting words down on paper, but who need the writing process broken down into small steps; students who are naturally creative, but resist expository writing; and students who prefer to work independently. Samples can be viewed at the publisher's website.

The first Writing Strands book is a prewriting book that can be skipped. Begin with *Writing Strands 2* and allow the student to progress at his own rate. (This is not exactly in line with the publisher's recommendations, but will suit most students.) One caution: The Writing Strands books declare that no one ever learned to write by studying grammar. While this is true, there's a strong flavor of "Therefore, nobody needs to study grammar" throughout the books. *Grammar is necessary.* So is writing. Contractors should be able to draw up plans *and* hammer nails; young writers should know their grammar rules and be able to put them to use in compositions.

Books 2–4 are elementary level; Book 5 begins dealing with the logical development of arguments (see Chapter 13).

The Writing Strands program can be purchased directly from the National Writing Institute or, at a small discount, from Rainbow Resource Center. The books aren't consumable; you do all the assignments on notebook paper, so you can reuse these books for another child.

Writing Strands 2. $20.

Writing Strands 3. $20.

Writing Strands 4. $20.

6

THE JOY OF NUMBERS:

MATH

Let no one ignorant of mathematics enter here.
—Plato (inscription written over the entrance to the Academy)

SUBJECT: Elementary mathematics
TIME REQUIRED: 30–60 minutes per day

The four years of elementary math—first through fourth grade—lay the foundation for the high-level abstract thinking required by algebra, trigonometry, and calculus later on. And foundation laying is what the grammar stage is all about.

The job of laying a mathematical foundation should be taken seriously. Basic mathematics—the skills of addition and subtraction, multiplication and division, the knowledge of basic geometrical shapes and patterns, the ability to think through word problems, a firm grasp of the relationships between numbers—is as vital to high-level mathematical achievement as an understanding of punctuation and sentence structure is to high-level language use. (The buzzword for this is *numeracy*: not just a grasp of basic arithmetic, but also an understanding of *how numbers work,* a "number sense.")

In fact, mathematics *is* a language because it uses symbols and phrases to represent abstract realities. And for many children, it's a foreign language because they don't grow up hearing it all around them.

The classical educator can change this by developing mathematical literacy: helping young students to master basic math operations, memorize math facts, and also *understand* the concepts behind both the operations and the facts.

This seems intimidating to many parents who don't consider themselves math-savvy. Don't worry; you can learn along with your student. Start by reading carefully through the following sections, which will acquaint you with some of the most important aspects of teaching elementary mathematics.

PROCEDURAL MATH AND CONCEPTUAL MATH

As soon as you start reviewing math curricula, you'll run across the phrase "conceptual math." What is conceptual math (and why should you care)?

"Conceptual math" is shorthand for mathematics instruction that clearly explains the reasons *why* operations work as they do. It is often contrasted with "procedural math," which teaches students to solve problems by giving them a series of steps to do. Procedural math approaches an elementary problem such as two-digit subtraction:

$$72$$
$$- 69$$

by teaching students to "borrow": since you can't subtract 9 from 2, strike through the 7 next to the 2, turn it into a 6, and "lend" the 1 that you've borrowed to the 2. That turns 2 into 12, and $12 - 9$ is 3, while $6 - 6$ is 0.

$$_6\cancel{7}{}^1 2$$
$$- 69$$
$$(0)3$$

This series of steps is known as an *algorithm:* a set process that you follow to find the answer to a problem.

Conceptual math explains *why* the algorithm works. First of all, these numbers are just shorthand ways to write

70 + 2 and 60 + 9

Rather than being taught to "borrow" a 1 from the 7 to make 12, the student instead might learn that 70 is made up of ones that are "bound up," or "composed," into seven sets of 10.

10 + 10 + 10 + 10 + 10 + 10 + 10 + 2

and that one of those sets will need to be "decomposed" back into ones and combined with the 2 ones in order to form a 12. So the subtraction problem can actually be written:

$$
\begin{array}{r}
60 + 12 \\
-60 + 9 \\
\hline
(0) 3
\end{array}
$$

This is the sort of problem that should be demonstrated using manipulatives such as toothpicks or pencils tied up in groups of tens that can be broken apart; see "The Way Children Think," below. (The language of "composed" and "decomposed" is suggested by Liping Ma in her classic work on conceptual math, *Knowing and Teaching Elementary Mathematics;* see the Resources at the end of this chapter.)

At the most elementary level, this might not seem like such a big difference in method. But the understanding that a larger number is "composed" of smaller groups bound up into larger sets will be crucial to a proper understanding of more complicated operations—such as long division. Students who only learn procedure will find themselves, at the upper levels, carrying out algorithms without understanding *why* the steps work. (In the words of one manual for math teachers, "Many students in the United States have given up on ever knowing *why* things work in mathematics. When they get an answer correct by simply following a procedure, regardless of conceptual understanding, they are satisfied.")[1]

---

[1] Margaret M. Pearse and Kate Walton, *Teaching Numeracy: 9 Critical Habits to Ignite Mathematical Thinking* (Thousand Oaks, CA: Corwin, 2011), pg. 4.

Procedural math is important; young students *should* learn the algo-rithms. But mathematical literacy involves learning both the procedures and the reasons why they work.

SPIRAL APPROACH AND MASTERY APPROACH

Math programs tend to take one of two approaches: spiral or mastery.

The spiral approach assumes that students learn best when they prac-tice a skill at a basic level, move away to other skills, and then return to the first skill and practice it at a slightly deeper level. Multiple skills are taught each year, and then revisited each following year; the student isn't expected to entirely master concepts and operations until they've been "spiraled" back to again and again.

The mastery approach teaches fewer topics per year but focuses in on each longer. Mastery programs also cover concepts at greater depth, expecting the student to develop a deeper understanding before moving on to the next concept; that knowledge then serves as a foundation for the next concept, but won't be explicitly revisited for a much longer period of time.

THE WAY CHILDREN THINK

No matter what program or approach you end up using (see below), the use of manipulatives to illustrate concepts is vital.

When you taught your student to write, the first step was to put a con-crete model—a written word or sentence—in front of the child so that she could copy it. Only when she mastered copying did you take away the concrete model and ask her to write from dictation. Only after copying from a written model was she able to form a mental picture of the spoken sentence.

This first step is necessary because young children tend to think in concrete terms. They don't do mathematical operations in their heads; if you ask a first grader to add 3 and 2, she'll look around for spoons, fingers, apples, or pennies to count so that she can find the answer. Just as you asked the beginning writer to copy a visible model, you'll ask the beginning mathematician to do arithmetic using "manipulatives"—objects that she can see, touch, and move around.

Math companies sell boxed manipulatives (see Resources at the end of this chapter), but you can also use beans, pennies, blocks, or chocolate chips. Toothpicks work well when you get to place value—you can move a bundle of 10 toothpicks from the 1s column to the 10s column to illustrate adding two-digit numbers, or you can break the bundles open to illustrate "borrowing." Every time you teach a new math skill, have the child work the problems out with real objects until the concept makes sense to her.

YOU: Put these three beans in one pile. Put these two beans in another pile. Now push them together. That's addition. How many do you have?
CHILD: *(Carefully counts the beans.)* Five.

Or . . .

YOU: Let's add thirty-six and twenty-seven. For thirty-six, we have three bundles of ten toothpicks—that's thirty—plus six extra toothpicks: the ones. For twenty-seven we have two bundles of ten, plus seven extra ones. How many bundles of toothpicks do we have?
CHILD: *(Counts the bundles.)* Five.
YOU: How many toothpicks are in those five bundles all together?
CHILD: Fifty.
YOU: How many ones—single toothpicks—do we have?
CHILD: *(Groups the six toothpicks with the seven.)* Thirteen.
YOU: Can we write thirteen in the ones column? No, because it won't fit. Where can we put the extra toothpicks?

(The child sees that she can bundle together ten of the thirteen and put them with the five bundles she already has. Now she has six groups of ten and three left over—sixty-three in all. She's just learned how to carry.)

Even older children can benefit from using manipulatives when learning a new skill; fractions, for example, may require division of an apple pie before they make sense.

When the concept is mastered on this concrete level, it is time to move on to mental arithmetic, where the child can picture the items in her mind instead of having actual apples, pennies, beans, or toothpicks in front of her.[2] Mental arithmetic requires abstract thinking because numerals now stand for concrete objects: 3 and 2 represent 3 beans and 2 beans; the number 27 represents 2 bundles of ten plus 7 single toothpicks. But don't push the child to dispense with her manipulatives until she's ready. Children's minds mature at different rates; if you require a child to do addition with numerals alone (no objects) before she's ready, the result will be math frustration.

Children aged 5 through 7 usually need concrete objects; children aged 8 through 10 begin to shift into "mental image" mode (but will still need manipulatives when new concepts are introduced). Ask a five-year-old how many people are in her family, and she'll turn around and count everyone present. Ask an eight-year-old the same question, and you'll see her summon a mental image of each person to mind and count the images: "Me, Mom, Dad, Jeremy. That's four."

True abstract thinking—the ability to use the symbols 5 + 7 or 27 × 2 without using or picturing concrete objects—is the third stage of mental development. Abstract thinking begins around age nine or ten, which coincides with the beginning of the logic stage. And the logic stage is the time to teach "higher-order critical thinking skills."

The goal of early elementary mathematics is to move the child from manipulating real objects to picturing those objects mentally. You achieve this through lots of practice with real objects. In later elementary mathematics (third or fourth grade), you'll begin to nudge the child, through much repetition, toward early symbolic thinking so that she can use written numbers and understand what those numbers represent.

You can't force a child to develop abstract thinking. Instead, lay the foundation for it with practice. You've got four years to get there. Take your time, and the child will have a strong foundation on which to build those higher-order skills.[3]

---

[2] Educators refer to this as moving from the *manipulative* or *preoperational* stage to the *mental image* or *concrete operational* stage.

[3] The concept of "higher-order skills" may seem to imply that "lower-order skills" (such as the knowledge of addition or division facts) are somehow inferior, less important, or unnecessary. But "higher" simply means "coming after." The tenth story of a building is "higher" than the foundation, but no one would argue that the foundation is less important simply because it is "lower."

MATH TABLES: A DEFENSE

We think that the memorization of mathematical facts—addition and subtraction facts, the multiplication and division tables—is essential in building a strong foundation. We feel that much of the protest over learning the math tables by rote arose because children were being taught to skip that important mental-image step of thinking. If a child goes straight from manipulative mode to symbolic mode, the symbols 2 + 4 = 6 don't mean anything to her. She's never practiced them with beans. If she's forced to memorize a whole sheet of these meaningless symbols (2 + 1 = 3, 2 + 2 = 4, 2 + 3 = 5), she's memorizing gobbledygook. That's rote learning at its worst, and, of course, it isn't productive.

But after you've practiced addition with manipulatives (2 beans and 1 bean equal 3 beans, 2 beans and 2 beans equal 4 beans, 2 beans and 3 beans equal 5 beans) and then practiced these same sums with imaginary beans, the child understands the concept of addition. At this point, the memorization of the math tables reinforces and strengthens the concept that the child comprehends.

The memory work also moves the child's mind toward abstract, symbolic thinking. Thorough knowledge of math facts leads to an instinctive understanding of math relationships. Consider, for example, the 9 times table:

$9 \times 2 = 18$
$9 \times 3 = 27$
$9 \times 4 = 36$
$9 \times 5 = 45$
$9 \times 6 = 54$

When you multiply a one-digit number by 9, the first digit of the resulting number is always one less than the number you began with:

$9 \times 2 = 1\_\_$
$9 \times 3 = 2\_\_$
$9 \times 4 = 3\_\_$

$9 \times 5 = 4\_\_$
$9 \times 6 = 5\_\_$

And the second digit of the resulting number, when added to the first digit, always adds up to 9.

$9 \times 2 = 18 \ (1 + 8 = 9)$
$9 \times 3 = 27 \ (2 + 7 = 9)$
$9 \times 4 = 36 \ (3 + 6 = 9)$
$9 \times 5 = 45 \ (4 + 5 = 9)$
$9 \times 6 = 54 \ (5 + 4 = 9)$

This little mental trick for remembering the 9 times table also reveals an important mathematical relationship: because 9 is 1 less than 10, multiplying a one-digit number (like 6) by 9 will never produce a number that has that same one-digit number in the 10s column. 6×9 *has* to be less than 60, because 9 groups of 6 must be less than 10 groups of 6.

$$
\begin{array}{cc}
6 & 6 \\
\underline{\times 9} & \underline{\times 10} \\
54 & 60
\end{array}
$$

Mastering basic facts now lays the foundation for true understanding later on. One of Jessie's eighth-grade relatives attended a well-regarded private school nearby. Instead of being required to memorize his math facts, he was allowed to use a calculator for math since a very early grade. When he reached algebra, he could work rote problems—problems that exactly followed the pattern in the textbook—but he lacked a true understanding of basic mathematical relationships. When more difficult or innovative problems appeared, he was helpless. The machine had done his computation for too many years.

This leads us to a firm principle of elementary mathematics: *no calculators*. No child who has not already memorized her mathematical facts should be allowed to use a calculator. We recommend the use of calculators beginning in seventh grade and not before.

KEEPING MATH IN VIEW

In Chapter 4, we recommended a number of math storybooks and manipulatives to use with your preschooler. When you begin an actual math curriculum, it's easy to let other math activities slide. But don't forget that mathematics isn't merely a school subject; it's a way of understanding the world.

In the first chapter of his book *How Not to Be Wrong: The Power of Mathematical Thinking*, mathematician Jordan Ellenberg points out that treating math simply as another part of the curriculum encourages students to think of it as irrelevant and pointless, particularly once they get into the higher levels. ("The number of adults who will ever make use of . . . synthetic division of polynomials," he remarks, "can be counted on a few thousand hands.") Rather, Ellenberg encourages readers to think of mathematical knowledge as "a pair of X-ray specs that reveal hidden structures underneath the messy and chaotic surface of the world. Math is a science of not being wrong about things, its techniques and habits hammered out by centuries of hard work and argument. With the tools of mathematics in hand, you can understand the world in a deeper, sounder, more meaningful way."[4]

So as you work through your math program, make an effort to check out math books and to practice everyday math. We've suggested resources for both in the lists at the end of this chapter. If integrating mathematics into your regular routine doesn't feel natural (probably because you never had it done for you during your school years), set a goal: read one math storybook and do one "real-life" math project every week.

And take this last section seriously.

EDUCATE YOURSELF

To teach your child mathematics, you have to develop your own understanding.

Don't worry: when your young student hits the higher levels, you can definitely choose to use a tutor, online class, or other outside instruction. You don't necessarily have to master the intricacies of algebra or pre-calculus in order to home-educate.

---

[4] Jordan Ellenberg, *How Not to Be Wrong: The Power of Mathematical Thinking* (New York: Penguin Books, 2015), pp. 2–3.

But you *do* need to understand the basics of mathematical thinking. If your first grader has to master place value (*really* master it, not just learn to perform steps), you can master it too. She's only six. You're a grown-up.

And you have a responsibility to help her learn. A 2015 study published by the Association for Psychological Science suggests that when parents who are anxious about math help first and second graders with homework, their assistance actually *decreases* their children's math performance. So if *your* "numeracy" is low, resolve to read at least one popular math book per year. Don't get hung up on trying to master every single equation or problem that these books present; instead, try to understand the type of *thinking* that mathematics requires. We've provided a list in the Resources section that follows.

HOW TO CHOOSE A PROGRAM

Picking the right math program for your child is always going to involve a compromise. Most curricula lean a little too far in one direction or the other. Conceptual math programs tend to score low on the "usability" front for parents who are not themselves mathematically inclined, low on the "affordability" scale, or both; they also generally give mastery of math facts short shrift. ("Write the numbers that add up to 6. Memorize these!" says Math Mammoth, but provides no memorization strategies or practice drills.) Curricula that lean toward the procedural are strong in practice and in drill, but often fall short on explaining the concepts clearly.

In addition, students learn differently. Very concrete thinkers may be frustrated by highly conceptual programs; some children need to learn the procedure and follow this up with more instruction in concepts. Others need to grasp the concept first and need little in the way of procedural teaching. Spiral learning suits some students and frustrates others. Mastery teaching sparks interest in some children, but feels like overkill for others.

We've indicated the approach of each curriculum that follows and have added a list of additional resources for teaching concepts and procedures. If you choose a conceptual program, supplement with additional math drills; if you choose a more procedural program, be sure to add some extra instruction in concepts.

Until you start math instruction, you may not know whether a spiral or mastery approach suits your child best. We highly recommend downloading the sample lessons from each publisher's website and doing a dry run before purchasing. But it might take six months or more of instruction to identify your student's preferred learning style. Don't worry: first- and second-grade math ought to be a time when you can experiment and switch programs as necessary without being concerned about "getting behind." Finding the right approach for your child should be a top priority.

Once you find a workable program, try to stick with it. All math programs build on what's been taught the year before. The more often you change systems, the more chances to confuse the student.

Many parents agonize over choosing the correct math program. But each of the math programs we list here is a good choice. Choosing a math program shouldn't cause you to stay awake at night.

If your child cries when you bring out the math book, switch programs, no matter how good everyone else tells you the program is. If your child is flourishing, stick with the program, even if everyone else in your home-school support group switches to something else.

If you want to check that your child *understands* what she's learning (rather than simply doing it by formula, with no comprehension of the principles involved), simply take a lesson or two from another math program or supplement and ask her to complete it. Make sure you pick lessons that involve material the child has covered several months before, since it takes time for math concepts to "sink in." If the child can do lessons from another program, she's understanding her work; she is able to take concepts from one program and transfer them to another. If she seems lost, she may be learning by formula—figuring out how to "plug in" answers that a particular math program requires, without really knowing why. If this happens, try another program.

SUGGESTED SCHEDULES

Math is best done daily, especially in the early grades. (And most home schoolers schedule math first thing in the morning, when children are the most alert and ready to tackle a challenge.) A typical school year is 36 weeks, or 180 days, although you can arrange your school year to fit your family situation (see Chapter 40 for more details). Count the lessons in whichever curriculum you've chosen. Then decide if you want to do your math lessons five days a week or four days a week (saving one day for field trips, library visits, math reading, or hands-on projects).

The Saxon first-grade home-study kit, for example, has 130 lessons, which means that you can do four lessons per week and save a day for something else, or four lessons per week with the option of doing a lesson or two over two days (some of the lessons are longer than others), or five lessons per week and take a week off from the curriculum now and then. When Susan's oldest was in first grade, he loved the playing-store lessons, so we would stretch those over a couple of days. We also took a week off from all of our curricula now and then to focus on some special history or science project: building a model of the Great Wall of China; assembling a nature notebook; planting a flower garden; going to the science museum.

Remember, in first and second grades especially, you won't want to take more than a week off at a time from math lessons. Unfamiliar math concepts are easily forgotten.

Sample Schedules
(only two of many possible schedules)

First Grade

30–40 minutes per day	Mon.	Math lesson
	Tues.	Math lesson, read math storybook
	Wed.	Math lesson
	Thurs.	Math lesson, do real-life math project
	Fri.	Project/library day

Second, Third, and Fourth Grade

40–60 minutes per day	Mon.	Math lesson
	Tues.	Math lesson, read math storybook

	Wed.	Math lesson
	Thurs.	Math lesson, do real-life math project
	Fri.	Project/library day

OR

First Grade

30–40 minutes per day	Mon./Wed./Fri.	Math lesson
	Tues.	Math lesson, read math storybook
	Thurs.	Math lesson, do real-life math project

Second, Third, and Fourth Grade

40–60 minutes per day	Mon./Wed./Fri.	Math lesson
	Tues.	Math lesson, read math storybook
	Thurs.	Math lesson, do real-life math project

RESOURCES

Most books can be obtained from any bookseller or library; most curricula can be bought directly from the publisher or from a major home-school supplier such as Rainbow Resource Center. Contact information for publishers and suppliers can be found at www.welltrainedmind.com. If availability is limited, we have noted it. Where indicated, resources are listed in chronological order (the order you'll want to use them in). Books in series are listed together. Remember that additional curricula choices and more can be found at www.welltrainedmind.com. Prices change constantly, but we have included 2016 pricing to give an idea of affordability.

Educating Yourself

Start with:

Ma, Liping. *Knowing and Teaching Elementary Mathematics: Teachers' Understanding of Fundamental Mathematics in China and the United States,* anniversary ed. New York: Routledge, 2010.

Ma's study of the differences between American and Chinese elementary math teachers is a wonderful introduction to mathematical thinking; it also provides plenty of insight into teaching concepts to younger students.

Then try tackling a few of these (as you read, you'll discover more titles):

Benjamin, Arthur. *The Magic of Math: Solving for x and Figuring Out Why*. New York: Basic Books, 2015.

Eastaway, Rob, and Jeremy Wyndham. *Why Do Buses Come in Threes? The Hidden Mathematics of Everyday Life*. New York: John Wiley & Sons, 2000.

Ellenberg, Jordan. *How Not to Be Wrong: The Power of Mathematical Thinking*. New York: Penguin Books, 2015.

Fernandez, Oscar E. *Everyday Calculus: Discovering the Hidden Math All Around Us*. Princeton, NJ: Princeton University Press, 2014.

Mlodinow, Leonard. *The Drunkard's Walk: How Randomness Rules Our Lives*. New York: Vintage, 2009.

Oakley, Barbara. *A Mind for Numbers: How to Excel at Math and Science (Even If You Flunked Algebra)*. New York: Tarcher, 2014.

Strogatz, Steven. *The Joy of x: A Guided Tour of Math, from One to Infinity*. New York: Mariner Books, 2013.

Math Curricula
(listed alphabetically)

Math Mammoth

Math Mammoth is a relatively new but highly regarded elementary program that is strongly mastery oriented and conceptual in approach—in fact, probably the most conceptual of the programs listed here. Presentation is simple (there's just one book for each level, containing both the explanations and all of the problems to be worked), concepts are explained clearly and in small steps, there are plenty of illustrations (although no manipulatives included), and you can download each level for an extremely affordable price.

The program is very strong on concepts, mental math, and problem solving. It is much weaker in practicing procedures, and very light on drill. (Occasionally the text notes, "Memorize these facts!" but you don't get a lot of help.)

In addition, there is practically no teacher guidance. The program is advertised as "self-teaching," which it is absolutely *not*. There's nothing wrong with the explanations in the text, but if your child doesn't understand on the first read-through, you'll have to figure out how to re-present the material on your own. Math Mammoth is definitely best for math-oriented parents (and I'd strongly suggest that you read Liping Ma's book before starting to teach it).

You'll want to add several elements to the program: math fact drills as needed, more frequent review of concepts that have been covered in the past, and manipulatives. Most elementary students will need to do some hands-on work with the concepts rather than just looking at the illustrations. The program's author recommends an abacus, but you'll also want to add some of the manipulatives listed in our resources section below.

Sample lessons and many additional resources are available at the publisher's website. The curriculum is available both as a download and on a CD. Each level contains two books: A for the first semester and B for the second. When you purchase the "Full Set" you also get answer keys, additional review, and an Internet-linked worksheet generator.

The download for each set is $37.50; the CDs are priced at $42.50.

Math Mammoth Light Blue Series

Grade 1 full set.

Grade 2 full set.

Grade 3 full set.

Grade 4 full set.

Grade 5 full set.

Math-U-See

The Math-U-See program is based on a series of teaching videos in which concepts are demonstrated using manipulatives; the student also works with these manipulatives when completing workbook exercises. It is suited to parents who are intimidated by the idea of teaching math and to children who are very hands-on or visual in their learning styles. The multisensory approach is particularly good for students who have some level of dyslexia.

The program is conceptual in approach; be sure to purchase additional MUS practice sheets or supplement with the resources suggested below, so that students will have plenty of opportunity to solidify their knowledge of the math facts.

Math-U-See is primarily a mastery program. Frequent reviews are provided. Rather than providing grade-by-grade texts, the Math-U-See Elementary Curriculum is divided into levels. The *Primer* level, for preschool and kindergarten, can probably be skipped by most students unless you feel a gentle introduction to formal math is necessary. Otherwise, progress through the six books of the Elementary Curriculum in order: *Alpha* (single-digit addition and subtraction), *Beta* (multiple-digit addition and subtraction), *Gamma* (multiplication), *Delta* (division), *Epsilon* (fractions), and *Zeta* (decimals and percentages). This progression will take you through fifth or sixth grade. (This description reflects the 2004 revision of the Math-U-See program; if you buy secondhand materials published in 2003 or before, you'll find the curriculum divided into *Foundations of Mathematics,* which covers first-, second-, and third-grade material, and *Intermediate Mathematics,* which covers fourth, fifth, and sixth grades.)

Each level includes a Student Pack (workbook and test booklet) and an Instruction Pack (Instruction Manual and DVD).

Visit the publisher's website for placement tests, a demonstration video, and other resources.

Manipulative Blocks. $38. These are necessary for all levels. The publisher recommends that you buy two sets.

Primer (preschool and kindergarten).

　Instruction Pack. $31.

　Student Pack. $22.

Alpha (single-digit addition and subtraction).

　Instruction Pack. $43.

　Student Pack. $30.

Beta (multiple-digit addition and subtraction).

　Instruction Pack. $43.

　Student Pack. $30.

Gamma (multiplication).
  Instruction Pack. $44.
  Student Pack. $30.
Delta (division).
  Instruction Pack. $44.
  Student Pack. $30.
Epsilon (fractions).
  Instruction Pack. $45.
  Student Pack. $30.
  Fraction Overlays. $40.
Zeta (decimals and percentages).
  Instruction Pack. $45.
  Student Pack. $30.
  Algebra/Decimal Inserts. $20.

Right Start Mathematics

Right Start Math is a hands-on program based on Montessori principles. The program, which makes heavy use of an abacus and manipulatives and de-emphasizes worksheets, is well designed for students who struggle with fine motor skills; learning is not tied to the student's ability to write.

Right Start Math is conceptual in orientation but also provides quite a bit of procedural teaching. While it is probably the most comprehensive program on our list, it is also by far the most expensive. Although the publisher claims that the program is both spiral *and* mastery in approach, it leans much more heavily towards the spiral.

The elementary program is divided into levels, not grades; Level A is preliminary, kindergarten-type preparation, and most first-grade students can progress directly into Level B. The Right Start website provides a placement test. Completion of Levels B through E should bring the student to the end of fourth grade; see Chapter 15, page 309, for thoughts about the transition out of Right Start into another math program.

As of 2015, the program was under revision; the second edition was partially complete, with the remaining levels due out by 2017.

Samples can be viewed at the publisher's website.

RS2 Math Set (all manipulatives for all levels). $280.
  Level A Book Bundle (2nd ed.) (optional). $85.
  Level B Book Bundle (2nd ed.). $85.

Level C Book Bundle (2nd ed.). $85.
Level D Book Bundle (2nd ed.). $85.
Level E Starter Kit. $215.

Saxon Math

Saxon Math is the most procedural of the programs we list. Some students will find it dry and uninspiring, while others need the careful step-by-step instruction, the concrete examples, and the repetition in order to find their way in mathematics. Saxon's *Home Study Kits* contain student workbooks and a teacher's manual that explains the concepts to the parent and tells her or him how best to teach them. Grades 1–3 also include a *Daily Meeting Book*, which takes the parent through practical skills like measuring, telling time, reading charts, and so on. Saxon Math has plenty of activities as well: playing story, measuring rooms, graphing the ages of everyone the child knows, and so on.

The manuals recommend that the young child study math for short periods twice per day: for the first session, explain the concept using manipulatives, and complete one side of a worksheet; later in the day, have the child review the material by completing the other side of the sheet. Most home schoolers (Susan included) find one session per day (and one side of the worksheet) to be plenty, and it isn't necessary to do the Daily Meeting unless you enjoy it. Be sure to use the manipulatives recommended.

Saxon is heavily spiral in approach.

Saxon Math is graded K, 1, 2, and 3 for kindergarten through third-grade students. After third grade, the textbooks switch to "skill level" rather than "grade level." Thus, Math 3 is followed by Math 5/4, which is for fourth graders who have finished the Math 3 book or for fifth graders who took two years to get through the Math 3 book. Math 5/4 is followed by 6/5, 7/6, 8/7 (general math for those who need extra practice), and then Algebra 1/2 (see Chapter 5). Ideally, you go from Math 7/6 straight to Algebra 1/2.

We strongly suggest that you combine Saxon with one of the conceptual supplements listed below. Also, timed fact drills are not appropriate for elementary students, who often panic when a clock begins to tick; do the drills, just don't time them.

Saxon Homeschool Mathematics. Boston: Houghton Mifflin Harcourt.

Saxon Math 1 Homeschool Complete Kit (1st ed.). $117.55.
Saxon Math 2 Homeschool Complete Kit (1st ed.). $117.55.

Saxon Math 3 Homeschool Complete Kit (1st ed.). $121.20.

Saxon Math 5/4 Homeschool Complete Kit (3rd ed.). $96.85.

For fourth-grade students.

Saxon Homeschool Manipulative Kit (1st ed.). $94.40.

Contains all manipulatives required for grades 1–3.

Singapore Primary Math

Singapore Math is the program used in Singapore's schools; it has become popular in the United States in large part because of the high scores earned by Singapore's children on international math tests. Singapore Math is highly conceptual; its focus is on teaching mathematical thinking from the very beginning and "mental math" exercises are assigned as soon as children learn to count. Because the goal of the Singapore program is to produce an understanding of the way mathematical processes work, skills are introduced differently than in American programs. Multiplication and division are begun very early (right at the beginning of second grade), so that the student is aware of the relationship between multiplication/addition and subtraction/division.

Each semester of the Singapore Primary Math program (for grades 1–6) consists of one textbook, one workbook, and a parent guide. The textbooks are colorful, with cartoon-like illustrations and pictures showing each new concept worked out with actual objects (very important for grammar-stage students). The accompanying workbooks are consumable.

Singapore is not as fact-oriented as Saxon or Math-U-See, and it lacks the procedural instruction found in Right Start. Many children flourish with it, but others simply need a less abstract approach in the early years. The Singapore method leads children into "logic-stage" thinking much earlier than other programs. If you try Singapore and your child is frustrated, this may signal a maturity gap; stick with another program for a couple of additional years. The Home Instructor's Guides (which are indispensable) provide lists of recommended manipulatives, but they are not included. The Singapore approach follows the *concrete > pictorial > abstract* method: you teach the concepts first with concrete objects, then with pictures, and finally with symbols, so it's essential to have the manipulatives on hand. Also, remember that this program produces high marks in Singapore because it is part of a math-oriented culture that provides plenty of additional reinforcement. The coursebooks and workbooks alone do not provide enough practice; invest in the additional resources the program offers, such as the *Extra Practice* and *Challenging Word Problems* books.

Singapore Math, U.S. edition. $12.50 for each textbook and workbook, $17.50 for each Home Instructor Guide. The program can be ordered from Singapore Math, Inc. (the U.S. distributor, not the program publisher), or from a home-school supplier. The U.S. edition uses American weights and money.

Primary Math US 1A Textbook.
Primary Math US 1A Workbook.
Primary Math US 1A Home Instructor's Guide.
Primary Math US 1B Textbook.
Primary Math US 1B Workbook.
Primary Math US 1B Home Instructor's Guide.
Primary Math US 2A Textbook.
Primary Math US 2A Workbook.
Primary Math US 2A Home Instructor's Guide.
Primary Math US 2B Textbook.
Primary Math US 2B Workbook.
Primary Math US 2B Home Instructor's Guide.
Primary Math US 3A Textbook.
Primary Math US 3A Workbook.
Primary Math US 3A Home Instructor's Guide.
Primary Math US 3B Textbook.
Primary Math US 3B Workbook.
Primary Math US 3B Home Instructor's Guide.
Primary Math US 4A Textbook.
Primary Math US 4A Workbook.
Primary Math US 4A Home Instructor's Guide.
Primary Math US 4B Textbook.
Primary Math US 4B Workbook.
Primary Math US 4B Home Instructor's Guide.

Extra Practice for Primary Math US Edition 1. $11.20.
Extra Practice for Primary Math US Edition 2. $11.20.
Extra Practice for Primary Math US Edition 3. $11.20.
Extra Practice for Primary Math US Edition 4. $11.50.

Extra Practice for Primary Math US Edition 5. $11.50.

Challenging Word Problems for Primary Mathematics Common Core Edition 1. $12.80.

Challenging Word Problems for Primary Mathematics Common Core Edition 2. $12.80.

Challenging Word Problems for Primary Mathematics Common Core Edition 3. $12.80.

Challenging Word Problems for Primary Mathematics Common Core Edition 4. $12.80.

Challenging Word Problems for Primary Mathematics Common Core Edition 5. $12.80.

Manipulatives

Abacus.

Wooden Abacus. $14.99. Self-standing frame, one hundred colored beads strung in 10 × 10 rows. Order from Rainbow Resource Center.

Cuisenaire Rods.

Cuisenaire Rods come in lengths from 1 cm to 10 cm, each color-coded. Use along with one of the listed books for visual and hands-on representations of place value and mathematical operations. All may be ordered from Hand2Mind.

Rods:

Cuisenaire Rods Introductory Set, Plastic, Set of 74. $9.25.

Books:

Bradford, John. *Everything's Coming Up Fractions with Cuisenaire Rods.* New Rochelle, NY: Cuisenaire Company of America, 1981.

Davidson, Patricia. *Addition and Subtractions with Cuisenaire Rods.* New Rochelle, NY: Cuisenaire Company of America, 1989.

Davidson, Patricia, and Robert E. Willcott. *From Here to There with Cuisenaire Rods: Area, Perimeter & Volume.* New Rochelle, NY: Cuisenaire Company of America, 1981.

Marolda, Maria R. *Cuisenaire Rods Alphabet Book: Problem Solving A to Z.* Vernon Hills, IL: Learning Resources, Inc., 2002.

Fraction Stax.

$22.99. Order from Carson-Dellosa Publishing Group. 51 stacking pieces allow the student to form halves, thirds, fourths, fifths, sixths, eighths, tenths, and twelfths.

Geared Clock.
Student Geared Clock. $3.99. Order from Rainbow Resource Center.

Number Line.
Student Number Lines with Wipeoff Crayon or Marker. $2.50. Order from Rainbow Resource Center.

Pattern Blocks.
Wood, plastic, or foam (larger for small hands). Consider ordering one of the listed guides as well. Order from Didax.
Blocks:
Plastic Pattern Blocks. 250 pieces, six shapes and colors, .5 cm thick. $17.95.
Pattern Blocks, Foam. 1,250 pieces, 1 cm thick. $47.
Wooden Pattern Blocks. 250 pieces, six shapes and colors. $22.95.
Guides:
Swan, Paul, and Geoff White. *Developing Mathematics with Pattern Blocks.* Greenwood, WA: RIC Publications, 2006.

Unifix Cubes.
Snap-together cubes allow you to teach patterning, counting, addition, subtraction, multiplication, and division, all with one set. Consider ordering the listed guide as well. Order all from Didax.
Cubes:
100 Unifix Cubes. $13.95.
300 Unifix Cubes. $37.95.
Guide:
Swan, Paul, and Geoff White. *Developing Mathematics with Unifix, Grades K–3.* Greenwood, WA: RIC Publications, 2006.

Conceptual Math Supplements

Khan Academy.
Founded by Salman Khan as a nonprofit educational organization, Khan Academy offers "microlectures" in all elementary mathematical concepts, along with online exercises and practice problems. Use to learn

or review specific topics, or design a personalized instructional plan. Highly recommended as a supplement to any math program. www .khanacademy.org.

Mathematics Enhancement Program.

A British version of a mathematics program developed in Hungary, MEP offers free online practice sheets, answers, and some teacher helps, along with number lines and number and shape cards. When followed sequentially, the lessons are spiral in approach. Download at the Centre for Innovation in Mathematics Teaching. www.cimt.plymouth.ac.uk

Miquon Math.

Miquon Math is a "discovery math" program that uses workbooks ("lab sheets") and Cuisenaire Rods to encourage students to find out mathematical principles through a combination of hands-on activities, critical thinking, and deduction. Particularly good as a supplement to Singapore Math, since it provides the hands-on illustration to round out Singapore's more abstract approach.

The program requires a fair amount of parent preparation. Some children will find Miquon's approach exciting; others will be frustrated due to a need to have the concepts laid out clearly for them from the beginning. However, using Miquon once the concept has been introduced and thoroughly explained elsewhere can add an additional level of understanding.

Samples and a scope and sequence are available at the publisher's website. Each book is $8.95.

Orange Book (Level 1)
Red Book (Level 2)
Blue Book (Level 3)
Green Book (Level 4)
Yellow Book (Level 5)
Purple Book (Level 6)
Cuisenaire Rods, introductory set. $9.95.

Procedural Math Supplements (Including Facts Drills)

Audio Memory Songs. Newport Beach, CA: Audio Memory.

$9.95 for each CD, $12.95 for each CD/workbook set. Order from

AudioMemory. These CDs contain the addition, subtraction, multiplication, and division facts, put to music. Play them in the car, and learn all your math facts.

Addition Songs.

Subtraction Songs.

Multiplication Songs.

Division Songs.

Developmental Mathematics: A Self-Teaching Program. Halesite, NY: Mathematics Programs Associates.

Each level offers a workbook ($10), teacher's guide ($4), and solution manual ($15). A full description of the twenty levels available and a placement test is available on the publisher's website. Lots of extra practice problems for elementary math operations; useful to review past concepts while using a mastery program, or to develop more mastery while using a spiral program. Best ordered from Rainbow Resource Center.

Level 1. Ones: Concepts and Symbols.

Level 2. Ones: Addition Concepts and Basic Facts.

Level 3. Ones: Subtraction Concepts and Basic Facts.

Level 4. Tens: Concepts, Addition and Subtraction of Tens.

Level 5. Two-Digit Numbers: Addition and Subtraction without Regrouping.

Level 6. Tens & Ones: Adding and Grouping.

Level 7. Tens & Ones: Subtracting with Exchange.

Level 8. Multiplication: Concepts and Facts.

Learning Wrap-Ups.

$8.99 each. Order from Learning Wrap-Ups. As you go through the facts printed on the front of each card, wrap the attached string through the notches of the correct answers to form a pattern.

Addition.

Division.

Fractions.

Multiplication.

Subtraction.

Montessori Flash Cards.

These flash cards provide not just numbers (3 + 4 =) but unit dots printed next to each number to provide a visual reminder. The reverse

side shows the answer in the same way. A good "first flash cards" drill
option. Order from Shiller Math or Rainbow Resource Center. $9.95 each.

Montessori Flash Cards: Addition
Montessori Flash Cards: Subtraction
Montessori Flash Cards: Multiplication
Montessori Flash Cards: Division

Snow, Kate. *Addition Facts That Stick: Mastering the Addition Tables in Six
Weeks.* Charles City, VA: Well-Trained Mind Press, 2016.

———. *Subtraction Facts That Stick: Mastering the Subtraction Tables in Six
Weeks.* Charles City, VA: Well-Trained Mind Press, 2016.

$14.95 each. Order from the publisher. Each book contains a simple,
effective six-week program of games and activities that not only explain
but cement the addition and subtraction facts. Appropriate for grades
1–4 (and above).

Timed Math Flash Cards.
Traditional flash cards with the math facts on them; don't time them, just
use the cards for drill. $11.99 each. Order from Rainbow Resource Center.

Timed Math Flash Cards: Addition
Timed Math Flash Cards: Subtraction
Timed Math Flash Cards: Multiplication
Timed Math Flash Cards: Division

Times Tales.
$19.95. Order from Times Tales. A nontraditional memory system for
the multiplication tables, based on pictures and a simple narrative.

Times Tales Print Edition. $26.95.
Times Tales DVD. $26.95.
Math Bundle Deluxe. $69.80.

Math Reading

This is only a beginning list; you will find more titles as you explore.

Adler, David A. *Perimeter, Area, and Volume: A Monster Book of Dimensions.*
New York: Holiday House, 2012.

————. *Shape Up! Fun With Triangles and Other Polygons.* New York: Holiday House, 1998.

Calvert, Pam. *Multiplying Menace: The Revenge of Rumpelstiltskin,* illus. Wayne Geehan. Watertown, MA: Charlesbridge, 2006.

————. *The Multiplying Menace Divides.* Watertown, MA: Charlesbridge, 2011.

Clements, Andrew. *A Million Dots.* New York: Simon & Schuster, 2006.

Dodds, Dayle Ann. *Full House: An Invitation to Fractions,* illus. Abby Carter. Cambridge, MA: Candlewick, 2009.

————. *The Great Divide: A Mathematical Marathon,* illus. Tracy Mitchell. Cambridge, MA: Candlewick, 1999.

————. *Minnie's Diner: A Multiplying Menu,* illus. John Manders. Cambridge, MA: Candlewick, 2004.

Ellis, Julie. *What's Your Angle, Pythagoras? A Math Adventure.* Watertown, MA: Charlesbridge, 2004.

Gifford, Scott. *Piece = Part = Portion,* illus. Shmuel Thaler. Berkeley, CA: Tricycle Press, 2008.

Giganti, Paul. *Each Orange Had 8 Slices: A Counting Book.* New York: Greenwillow Books, 1992.

Hulme, Joy N. *Wild Fibonacci: Nature's Secret Code Revealed.* Berkeley, CA: Tricycle Press, 2005.

Jenkins, Steve. *Actual Size.* Boston: Houghton Mifflin, 2004.

Juster, Norton. *The Dot and the Line: A Romance in Lower Mathematics.* San Francisco, CA: Chronicle Books, 2012.

Lasky, Kathryn. *The Librarian Who Measured the Earth.* Boston: Joy Street Books, 1994.

Neuschwander, Cindy. *Mummy Math: An Adventure in Geometry.* New York: Henry Holt, 2005.

————. *Patterns in Peru: An Adventure in Patterning.* New York: Henry Holt, 2007.

Pallotta, Jerry. *Apple Fractions,* illus. Rob Bolster. New York: Scholastic, 2002.

Pappas, Theoni. *The Adventures of Penrose the Mathematical Cat.* San Carlos, CA: Tetra, 1997.

————. *Fractals, Googols, and Other Mathematical Tales.* San Carlos, CA: Tetra, 1993.

Pinczes, Elinor J. *A Remainder of One.* Boston: Houghton Mifflin, 1995.

Reimer, Luetta. *Mathematicians Are People Too: Stories from the Lives of Great Mathematicians.* Palo Alto, CA: Dale Seymour Publications, 1995.

Schwartz, David M. *On Beyond a Million: An Amazing Math Journey,* illus. Mike Reed. New York: Simon & Schuster, 2006.

Silveria, Gordon. *The Greedy Triangle.* New York: Scholastic, 1994.

Tang, Greg. *Math Fables: Lessons That Count.* New York: Scholastic, 2004.

————. *Math Potatoes: Mind-Stretching Brain Food.* New York: Scholastic, 2005.

7

SEVENTY CENTURIES
IN FOUR YEARS:
HISTORY AND GEOGRAPHY

The history of the world is but the biography of great men.

—Thomas Carlyle

SUBJECT: History and geography

TIME REQUIRED: An average of 3 hours per week, about 60 minutes per day, three days per week or 1½ hours per day, two days per week

Documentary filmmaker Ken Burns appeared at the National Press Club in early 1997 to plug his latest project (the life of Thomas Jefferson). Afterward, he took questions. One questioner pointed out that an astronomical percentage of high-school graduates saw no purpose in studying history and asked for a response.

Ken Burns answered: History is the study of everything that has happened until now. Unless you plan to live entirely in the present moment, the study of history is inevitable.

History, in other words, is not *a* subject. History is *the* subject. It is the record of human experience, both personal and communal. It is the story of the unfolding of human achievement in every area—science, literature, art, music, and politics. A grasp of historical facts is essential to the rest of the classical curriculum.

When you first introduce the elementary student to history, you must keep one central fact in mind: *history is a story.*

The logical way to tell a story is to begin (as the King said to Alice) at the beginning and go on till you come to the end. Any story makes less sense when learned in bits and pieces. If you were to tell your five-year-old the story of Hansel and Gretel, beginning with the house made of candy and cookies (because that's likely to be the most interesting part of the story to the child), then backing up and telling about the woodchopper's unfortunate second marriage, then skipping to the witch's demise, and then scooting backward again and relating the story of Hansel and Gretel's walk in the woods, the story isn't going to form a coherent whole in the child's mind. Even if he listens to the end, you may have lost him long before that.

History is no different. Yet it's too often taught unsystematically—as a series of unrelated bits and pieces: American history this year, ancient history the next, eighteenth-century France the year after that. Think back. By the time you graduated high school or college, you'd studied King Tut and the Trojan War and the Bronze Age; you probably learned about the end of the Athenian monarchy and the rise of the city-state; you may have been taught about the Exodus or the Magna Carta or the early history of Ethiopia. Chances are you studied these subjects in different years, in different units, out of different textbooks. You probably have difficulty fitting them together chronologically.

Furthermore, if you grew up in the United States you probably started with American history (which is pretty near the end of the story as we know it) and then spent at least twice as much time studying American history as you did studying the rest of the world. Yes, American history is important for Americans, but this myopic division of the curriculum does the Founding Fathers a disservice. Children who plunge into the study of the American Revolution with no knowledge of the classical models used by Jefferson, Washington, and their colleagues can achieve only a partial understanding of American government and ideals. And American history ought to be kept in perspective: the history curriculum covers seventy centuries; America occupies only five of them.

A common assumption found in history curricula seems to be that children can't comprehend (or be interested in) people and events distant from their own experience. So the first-grade history class is renamed Social Studies and begins with what the child knows: first, himself and his family, followed by his community, his state, his country, and only then the rest of the world.

This intensely self-focused pattern of study encourages the student of history to relate everything he studies to himself, to measure the cultures and customs of other peoples against his own experience. And that's exactly what the classical education fights *against*—a self-absorbed, self-referential approach to knowledge. History learned this way makes *our* needs and wants the center of the human endeavor. This attitude is destructive at any time, but it is especially destructive in the current global civilization.

The goal of the classical curriculum is multicultural in the true sense of the word: the student learns the proper place of his community, his state, and his country by seeing the broad sweep of history from its beginning and then fitting his own time and place into that great landscape. The systematic study of history in the first four years lays the foundation for the logic stage, when the student will begin to understand the relationships between historical events—between Egypt and Greece, Greece and Rome, Rome and England, England and America.

From a practical point of view, starting the curriculum with ancient history makes sense. First graders are fascinated by ancient times—the mummies of Egypt, the myths of Greece, the great wars of Rome, the armies of China. The average first grader would much rather read about the embalming process than go on a field trip to his local center of government.

SEVENTY CENTURIES IN FOUR YEARS

Where's the text that supplies this comprehensive survey of history from its beginnings?

Well, there isn't one. The trivium in general steers away from "texts"—

predigested historical facts, analyzed and reduced by someone else—and requires the student to tackle original sources. In the years to come, your history student will read Herodotus, not a textbook version of his histories; *The Federalist Papers*, not a simplified explanation of the relationship between the states and the federal government.

Of course, students aren't reading at this level in first through fourth grades. But instead of limiting your elementary student to a text, you'll use a basic history survey (several different resources and approaches are listed at the end of this chapter) to anchor your study. Armed with a library card, you'll study history using the fascinating, inventive, colorful history books published for young children.

Over the four years of the grammar stage, you'll progress from 5000 B.C. to the present, accumulating facts the whole way. These four years will be an exploration of the *stories* of history: tales of great men and women of all kinds, battles and wars, important inventions, the world religions, details of daily life and culture, the creation of great books.

As you do this, it's important to remember that history isn't a skill or a "mastery" subject. You will never cover all of history (or even most of its more famous events), and your elementary student is not going to retain everything (or even most) that she learns. History is an exploration, a chance for even the youngest students to begin developing the skills she'll need for later humanities research, a place where your child can practice reading and writing with fascinating content as the subject matter. Elementary history study has three major goals: to give students an overall sense of the progression of historical events from ancient times to the present; to develop skills in reading and writing; and to teach geographic awareness.

And in the elementary grades, history should be *enjoyable*.

In the Resources at the end of this chapter, we suggest several different "spines," chronological world histories that can serve as your organizing outline and jumping-off point for the study of history. We suggest that, using one of these, you divide history into four segments, one segment per year of study. In first through fourth grades, the child will study history from 5000 B.C. through the present day. In fifth through eighth grades (the logic stage), he'll study it again, concentrating on cause-and-effect and chronological relationships. In grades 9 through 12, he'll repeat it yet again, this time studying original sources and writing thoughtful essays about them.˙

The classical method leans heavily on original sources. Because these increase as time goes on, the centuries aren't divided evenly among the four years of study (see the table). This breakdown, however, does allow for a fairly even division of labor from year to year. It takes notice of the fact that an immense amount of great literature was produced between the years 1600 and 1850 and that scientific discovery and technological changes accelerated at a tremendous rate between 1850 and the present day.

The Study of History

Period	Years	Studied during grades . . .
Ancients	5000 B.C.–A.D. 400 (5,400 years)	1, 5, 9
Medieval–early Renaissance	400–1600 (1,200 years)	2, 6, 10
Late Renaissance–early modern	1600–1850 (250 years)	3, 7, 11
Modern	1850–present (150 years)	4, 8, 12

This progression is not, of course, set in stone. You might choose to condense the four-year sequence into three years, and then spend a year doing national and state history. You might decide to wait on history studies until second grade (a good choice if your first grader is already spending hours per day on reading, writing, and math), and then condense the sequence into three years, or stretch it out so that it runs into the logic stage (see Chapter 17 for more about this). Just try to hold on to two principles: progressing chronologically from your chosen starting point gives students an organized and orderly way to think about history; and the majority of your history study should be done with a worldwide focus, not country by country.

WHAT IF YOU'RE STARTING IN THE MIDDLE?

If you're beginning to home-school a second or third grader, remember that history is a story and that you should usually start at the beginning. Most of the resources we recommend can be used and enjoyed by students between grades 1 and 6. No matter what grade you begin in, progress to the moderns; when the student reaches fifth grade (the "logic stage"), supplement his study with the *Kingfisher History Encyclopedia,* a time line, and the teaching techniques suggested in Chapter 17 (see "Starting in the Middle" for more details).

If you're teaching more than one child, you can certainly adjust your history lessons so that both students are covering the same period. Grammar skills, spelling, writing, and math should be taught individually, but both a first and third grader could study ancient history. Expect more writing, more discussion, and more outside reading from the third grader. When your third-grade student reaches fifth grade, incorporate the suggestions found in Chapter 17 into his study of history, no matter what *period* of history he is studying at that point.

HOW TO DO IT

To study history and geography, you'll need a 3-inch three-ring notebook with lots of paper, a three-hole punch, art supplies, your chosen history "spine," geography resources (a globe, a wall map of the world, and maps to color—see Resources for ordering information), and a library card.

The history notebook will contain your child's pictures, compositions, and narrations about history, and will organize the child's history study for grades 1 through 4.

Make four dividers:

Ancients, 5000 B.C.–A.D. 400
Medieval/Early Renaissance, 400–1600
Late Renaissance/Early Modern, 1600–1850
Modern, 1850–Present Day

In Chapter 5, we introduced you to narration: reading to the child (or giving the child a reading assignment), and then asking her to tell you what she's just read. You'll be using this technique extensively in the study of history. (Don't forget that narrations done for history, and copywork/dictation chosen from your child's history books, can be used to meet the writing goals in Chapter 5.)

You'll need to decide how many pages or chapters of your history spine to cover per week (see the notes in the Resource section for some guidance on this). If you're doing history twice a week, cover half of the material in each lesson; if three times a week, one-third. No matter how many pages or chapters you're studying, follow the same basic pattern:

1. Read the material to your child as she follows along. Once she's beginning to read independently, alternate reading paragraphs or sections out loud to each other. By third or fourth grade, some students are ready to read alone (although most will still get more out of the material if they read out loud to you; it's easy for young minds to wander when reading nonfiction).

2. Make a narration page. After your first or second grader tells you about what you've just read, write her version down on notebook or drawing paper for her. (By third grade, children should be starting to write down their own narrations; see page 78).

3. Ask the child to illustrate what she's just read (and help her make a caption), or let her color a picture related to the story.

4. Find the geographical area under discussion on a globe and on a wall map, and color the appropriate black-line map.

5. Go to the library to find out more about the subject.

You do not need to perform all five steps for every reading. If students are interested, stop and spend more time on a topic; if not, read, ask the student to narrate back to you orally, and then move on without worrying about making a page or doing additional work (although you should always locate the areas you've just read about on a map).

All of the child's narration pages and pictures should be placed in the history notebook. Once a month or so, read back through the notebook together; this will help the student remember what's been studied.

First Grade: Ancients (5000 B.C.–A.D. 400)

During first grade, aim to spend at least three hours per week on history.

Use common sense. History is important, but the first grader is learning all sorts of foundational skills from scratch: reading, writing, putting sentences together, keeping track of the dates, telling time, adding, subtracting, and so forth. If the child misses some ancient history in first grade, he'll pick it up in fifth grade, or in ninth grade, or in independent reading. If he doesn't learn to read, write, and understand basic mathematical operations, he'll be hampered for years. So in the early grades, give priority to reading, grammar, spelling, writing, and math. History and science follow on these basic abilities.

Ideally, you'll do history three days per week for an hour each day, or two days for a slightly longer period; or you'll do math, grammar, writing, and reading four days a week and devote the fifth to history and science. (See the Epilogue, "The Grammar Stage at a Glance," pages 253–258, for several sample schedules.)

Sit down on the sofa with your first grader and read a section of your chosen history spine aloud to him. Let him ask questions. When you've finished the section, move to a writing surface (a desk or the kitchen table). Get out a sheet of notebook paper, and give it the same title as the section you've just read ("The First Writing," for example, or "Making Mummies"). Then ask the child to tell back to you the most important or most interesting thing that you just read. Prompt him with questions, if necessary.[1] Write his narration down in your neatest printing—you want him to be able to read it. When this page is finished, ask the child to read it back to you. Then put it into the child's history notebook.

Now ask the child to complete a coloring page related to the history lesson (see the Resources at the end of this chapter), or to draw a picture of something from the lesson that strikes his fancy. Although the child should have fun, don't let him do unnecessarily sloppy work; encourage him to draw or color carefully (this will help to improve fine motor skills).

---

[1] See Chapter 5, pages 74–75, for a discussion of the narration method. You'll progress from writing what the child dictates to you, to writing his words out and asking him to copy part of the narration out in his own writing, to helping the child write his own original sentences without a written model in front of him.

When the coloring page or illustration is finished, write a caption for the page. By the end of first grade, you should write out the caption on another sheet of paper, and ask the child to copy it onto the drawing; by the end of second grade, he should be writing his own captions. Then put this drawing in the notebook as well. Keep these pages in chronological order. By the end of the year, this notebook will contain the child's own story of ancient history. (*Note:* Work done for the notebook should be carefully done; handwriting, cut edges, labels, and coloring should all be the child's best effort.)

Once the child has finished the narration and coloring page, look together at the map at the beginning of the chapter. Find the location of the map on your globe. Most children enjoy putting their finger on their own location and then traveling to the ancient country under discussion. Then go to the wall map, which is larger and more detailed than the globe, and find the location there. Finally, ask the child to color a black-line map of the area, either from the accompanying activity book or from one of the resources listed at the end of this chapter. Punch holes in the black-line map and put it into the notebook as well.

You may wish to finish all of this work in one long session; you may want to stretch it out over two. (Alternately, you can read an entire chapter or section in your first session, and then use your second session to do one narration, coloring page, and map exercise on the whole selection.) Once you've completed the process of read/narrate/color/map, it's time to go to the library. Find books in the children's section about anything in the lesson that interests the child. Your children's librarian can help you; most libraries have reference works that will help the librarian find, for example, picture books set in ancient Egypt. We have included a few recommended titles at the end of this chapter (you can use this either as a library list or as a shopping list if you decide to buy the books instead). Check these books out, and read them at home.

Then, move on to the next topic in the history book.

As you continue, you'll find that some topics provide very little opportunity for extra reading (so far as we know, there's no first-grade guide to Ur on your library shelves), while others will lead you to scads of wonderful books (ancient Egypt probably occupies an entire library shelf of its own). Use your common sense. You don't have to make a library visit for every chapter, or labor to find books on obscure topics; just do a narration, a coloring page, and move on. If, on the other hand, the child's interest is sparked by the invention of writing, mummification, or the Hanging Gardens of Babylon, take as much time as you please to investigate it thoroughly. History should be a delight-centered activity for the grammar-stage child. Allow him to explore, do activities and projects, and have fun; you can always hurry over (or skip) later chapters without injury.

Keep the following tips in mind as you study history:

Don't limit yourself to books the child can read on his own. Most children's history books are written on a third- to seventh-grade reading level. Check them out, and read them to your young student. Soon he'll be reading them on his own.

You'll never read every good book in the library, so don't even try. At the beginning, you may find it easier to go to the library on your own and bring books home. By second grade, however, you'll want to take your child with you at least part of the time so that he can learn to find books in the catalog and then locate them on the shelf. (A children's librarian will be glad to show him—and you—how the catalog works.)

Don't forget to check the audiobook section of the library; look for unabridged audio versions of children's history titles.

Use hands-on projects as well as books. We've recommended several resources for history projects: treasure chests with Egyptian beads inside, ancient Chinese games, books that tell you how to make Greek clothing or Roman food. You'll want the child to make notebook pages about some of the library books he reads and projects he does. Use your judgment. As with reading, don't make him do a page for every book, or the fun of discovery will quickly become drudgery.

A tip for recording history projects: Veteran home schoolers continually wonder what to do with all the maps, projects, crafts, and activities their children produce. We suggest that when you finish a project, you take a picture of it, tape the picture to a notebook page, and record the date. The project has thus been immortalized. Eventually, you can disassemble it or throw it away.

Pay special attention to biographies. Try to make a page for all the great men and women you encounter (Sargon, Moses, Hammurabi, Hatshepsut, Tutankhamen, Alexander the Great, Julius Caesar . . . the list goes on). These biographies can be wonderful "pegs" on which to hang the progression of history. You may not remember much about ancient history, but you probably remember that Alexander cried when he found no more worlds to conquer. We've supplied a list of great men and women at the end of this chapter, for your reference.

Again, don't feel that you have to read a biography of every historical figure. The elementary years are not the time to develop comprehensive knowledge, but to see how history progresses. First graders are not only learning how to record information, but the information itself, so you'll move slowly at first. If you spend a lot of time on the first Olympic games and end up skipping the Scythians, nothing dreadful will happen. Your child will come across this period again in fifth grade, when he's reading and writing well.

Remember, file all these pages in the history notebook chronologically. By the end of fourth grade, the history notebook will be crammed with fascinating information; the student's first trip through the entire expanse of world history, organized and recorded in his own hand (and yours).

What about testing?

Formal testing is unnecessary at this level. If the child can tell you what you've read to him, he's been listening. If he reads several books on the same subject, the information will be fixed in his mind. Once a month, sit down with the child and read through the pages he's already done so that he can review the history he's covered.

Memorization

The history notebook should be accompanied by a certain amount of memorization. Dates, personalities, and wars serve as pegs on which to hang incoming information. (Alexander Graham Bell invented the telephone in 1876. Quick: Was this before or after the Civil War?)

You can pick your own "pegs." Almost any series of major events or personalities will do, but these "mental pegs" will be most useful if they correspond to the child's interests. In first grade, people and events will probably be more meaningful than dates. A first grader could memorize the pharaohs of Egypt and the first twenty emperors of Rome. (Any six-year-old who can say *tyrannosaurus* can learn to say *Amenhotep* or *Pertinax*.) We've suggested some additional memorization resources at the end of this chapter.

For first graders, aim to memorize one list of twenty facts or so (rulers, major wars, birth dates of great inventors, etc.) or two different lists of nine to ten facts each over the course of the year. You can add more if your student finds memorization fun.

Second Grade: Medieval–Early Renaissance (400–1600)

Using narration, coloring pages, map work, and library trips, the second grader (or the student in the second year of history) will study history from about 400 to 1600. You'll follow the same basic procedure, but you'll find many more on-topic library books for this historical period.

At the beginning of second grade, write half of the child's narration, and ask her to copy from your model the other half. Aim to have her copying her own narrations by the end of the year. Again, don't do these narrations for all the books she reads; this would tie her reading skills to her writing skills, which are typically slower to develop. If she writes one narration for history, she can then dictate other narrations to you (or draw pictures).

Don't forget to review once a month, and look back at those first-grade pages several times during the year.

Memorization

A second grader could memorize the rulers of England from Egbert through Elizabeth I, along with each ruler's family allegiance (Saxon, Dane, Norman, Plantagenet, Lancaster, York, Tudor). Other options, depending on the child's interests and background, are the rulers of Scotland from Malcolm II through James VI, the later Holy Roman Emperors, or the rulers of other medieval countries—France, Spain, Japan, Russia. Second graders could also memorize the major wars and major discoveries. Aim for two lists of fifteen to twenty facts each over the course of the year: the rulers of England, perhaps, plus one other set of rulers, wars, or discoveries.

Second graders can also memorize a Shakespeare sonnet (Sonnet 18, "Shall I compare thee to a summer's day?" is probably the most familiar; see Shakespeare-online.com for all of the sonnets) and one Shakespearean soliloquy (along the lines of Macbeth's "Tomorrow, and tomorrow, and tomorrow" speech from act 5, scene 5; see Resources for more suggestions). It isn't necessary for young children to understand every word in a poem or speech in order to memorize and speak it; the process of memorizing and speaking will itself begin to accustom them to more complex language patterns and more difficult vocabulary.

Third Grade: Late Renaissance–Early Modern (1600–1850)

Third graders (or students in the third year of history study) will cover the years from 1600 to 1850. Continue on with narration (these narrations should now contain more detail and should begin to resemble one- to two-paragraph compositions; see Chapter 5 for more details), coloring pages, map work, library readings, and projects. By third grade, some children are ready to begin to make several written pages per week for the history notebook; aim for this if writing has become easier for the student.

Memorization

During the third-grade year, American students should memorize at least the beginning of the Declaration of Independence (most children can master the entire document, given enough time and repetition). The third grader should also memorize the first twelve presidents of the United States and the major wars for the period 1600 to 1850. (Parents in other countries should adjust this memorization goal to their own national histories.)

You can assign other lists—rulers of other countries, important discoveries and explorations—at your own discretion. Aim for at least three different lists of twelve to eighteen items each over the course of the year.

Fourth Grade: Modern (1850–Present)

The fourth grader will study the years 1850 to the present. Follow the same pattern: narration (now short compositions of about two paragraphs), illustrations or coloring pages, maps, and library visits. Even more library resources will be available for the student on contemporary topics, so don't feel obliged to read even a fraction of the supplemental books available; let the child pick the subjects that interest him for further reading.

American fourth graders should use additional map resources to learn the fifty states of the United States of America. Use one of the coloring or geography resources listed in Resources under "Modern, 1850–Present (Fourth Grade)" at the end of this chapter. By the end of the year, the fourth grader should be able to locate each state on a map of the United States. (Parents in other countries should choose comparable, but suitable, geographic goals.)

Also plan to spend several weeks (three to six, depending on the emphasis your state places on state history) studying the history of your own state, province, or region. In the United States, most public libraries carry several series of books about the states (see the Resources section). Use the same basic procedure to study these books: read, have the child complete a narration, and then look for additional library resources on subjects that interest your student.

Memorization

American fourth graders should know the Preamble to the Constitution, the Gettysburg Address, and the purpose (if not the exact words) of the amendments to the Constitution. Also, plan to finish memorizing the list of presidents from 1850 to the present, the dates of the major wars since 1850, and the capitals of the fifty states. At the end of this chapter, we've suggested songs, games, flash cards, and coloring books to help with this memory work.

As above, if you live in another country adjust this assignment to suit your own situation.

SUGGESTED SCHEDULES

You can study history either Monday/Wednesday/Friday, or Tuesday/Thursday for a longer time.

A good Monday/Wednesday/Friday schedule might look like this:

Monday   Read selected pages from your selected history spine.
             Look up locations on a globe and map. Ask the student
             questions about the reading; help him to answer in com-
             plete sentences.
Wednesday   Help the student to make a narration page about the mate-
             rial covered in the spine (first and second graders narrate
             to you, third and fourth graders can begin to write their

own narrations). Younger students may also choose to draw a picture and then narrate a sentence to you about the picture.

Friday   Read additional chapters or library books about the subject, or do a history project/activity. Go over memory work.

A Tuesday/Thursday schedule might look like this:

Tuesday   Read selected pages from your selected history spine. Look up locations on a globe and map. Ask the student questions about the reading; help her to answer in complete sentences. Read one additional chapter or library book.

Thursday   Read at least one more chapter or library book. Ask the student to make another narration page covering one of the additional resources. Or do a history activity or project. Go over memory work.

You could also choose to alternate weeks:

Week One   Read from your history spine MWF or T/Th; make at least one narration page about a topic covered.

Week Two   Read additional library books, or do history projects/activities based on at least one of the topics covered in Week 1. Do at least one narration page.

Whatever pattern you choose, plan to spend a *minimum* of 1½ hours per week doing history in first grade; a minimum of 2 hours in second grade; and at least 3 hours per week in third and fourth grade.

RESOURCES

Most books can be obtained from any bookseller or library; most curricula can be bought directly from the publisher or from a major home-school supplier such as Rainbow Resource Center. Contact information for publishers and suppliers can be found at www.welltrainedmind.com. If availability is limited, we have noted it. Where indicated, resources are listed in chronological order (the order you'll want to use them in). Books in series are listed together. Remember that additional curricula choices and more can be found at www.welltrainedmind.com. Prices change constantly, but we have included 2016 pricing to give an idea of affordability.

The titles we list are only a few of the many available. Plan on exploring library and bookstore shelves for yourself.

During first and second grades, you should plan on reading many of these biographies and histories aloud. We have suggested a few simple books that young children can read alone.

Basic texts for the four-year grammar stage are listed first. A supplementary list is provided for each year of study. The first section for each year lists books that provide general information about the historical period, including coloring books and other project resources. The second section lists some of the most useful biographies alphabetically by subject.

Because biographies are often the most useful supplemental reading for young children, we have supplied chronological lists of famous people to help you in your search for library titles. For third and fourth grade, when children are better able to understand historical "topics," we have also supplied a list of major historical events that the student can explore.

Basic Texts ("Spines")

Narrative Spines

These are told in story format, engaging the student's imagination and making retention simpler. They have few visuals, and only The Story of the World *has accompanying curriculum guides. Students who need pictures may benefit from one of the encyclopedias that follow. Narrative and encyclopedic spines can be used individually or together.*

Bauer, Susan Wise. *The Story of the World: History for the Classical Child* series. Charles City, VA: Well-Trained Mind Press.

This four-volume series provides an engaging narrative, connecting events around the world in a way grammar-stage children can easily grasp. Each volume covers one year of history study. Volumes 1 and 2 (*Ancient Times* and *The Middle Ages*) can be read aloud; Volumes 3 and 4 (*Early Modern Times* and *The Modern Age*) can be read independently. Each volume is written at a slightly higher reading level.

You can assemble your own maps, illustrations, and reading lists, using the suggestions we provide here; alternatively, each volume of *The Story of the World* can be ordered with an accompanying activity book which contains comprehension questions and answers, sample narrations for each section (to give you some idea of the appropriate level of detail you hope to hear from the child), both nonfiction and fiction library lists for additional reading, black-line maps and exercises for each chapter, coloring pages, and project instructions (for hands-on learning).

Each volume is available in paperback ($16.95) and hardback ($21.95), as well as in a PDF download.

Unabridged audiobook versions have been recorded by Jim Weiss and are available in CD and as an MP3 download.

Test booklets are also available. We don't think testing is necessary during the grammar stage, but the tests also make excellent review worksheets.

The Story of the World is not a heavily illustrated series; children who need visuals will appreciate using one of the encyclopedias below as a supplement.

Extensive samples can be viewed at the publisher's website.

Volume I: Ancient Times: From the Earliest Nomads to the Last Roman Emperor, rev. ed. (2006).
Covers world history 5000 B.C.–400 A.D.
Activity Book I: Ancient Times, 3rd ed. (2006). $34.95.
Volume 1 Audiobook, rev. ed. (2006). $39.95, MP3 download $25.
Rountree, Elizabeth. *Volume 1, Ancient Times: Tests and Answer Key* (2007). $12.95.

Volume II: The Middle Ages: From the Fall of Rome to the Rise of the Renaissance, rev. ed. (2007).
Covers world history 400–1600.
Activity Book II: The Middle Ages, rev. ed. (2008). $36.95.
Volume II Audiobook, rev. ed. (2008). $44.95, MP3 download $29.
Rountree, Elizabeth. *Volume 2, The Middle Ages: Tests and Answer Key* (2007). $13.95.

Volume III: Early Modern Times: From Elizabeth the First to the Forty-Niners (2004).
Covers world history 1600–1850.

Activity Book III: Early Modern Times (2004). $36.95.

Volume III Audiobook (2007). $49.95, MP3 download $32.

Rountree, Elizabeth. *Volume 3, Early Modern Times: Tests and Answer Key* (2007). $13.95.

Volume IV, The Modern Age (2004).
Covers world history 1850–present.

Activity Book IV: The Modern Age: From Victoria's Empire to the End of the USSR. (2004). $36.95.

Volume IV Audiobook (2006). $54.95, MP3 download $35.

Rountree, Elizabeth. *Volume 4, The Modern Age: Tests and Answer Key* (2007). $14.95.

Gombrich, E. H. *A Little History of the World.* New Haven, CT: Yale University Press, 2008.

$15 paperback; an illustrated paperback edition (2013) is available for $22. This one-volume world history takes young readers from the Stone Age through the mid-twentieth century in forty chapters. Ernst Gombrich, trained as an art historian, wrote the *Little History* in German in 1935, and at the end of his life revised it for English-speaking readers. It is a readable and entertaining history that covers world events in much less detail than *The Story of the World;* you will need to use at least one of the encyclopedias below to flesh out the details. Asian history gets very little space, and you may wish to consider using the fourth volume of *The Story of the World* as a supplement, since post–World War I history is covered in a very sparse fashion. However, this is a good option for parents who prefer to pull together more outside resources; also a good choice for older students who wish to do a one- or two-year survey of world history before entering the logic stage.

Sample chapters can be previewed at the publisher's website.

Encyclopedic Spines

These chronological encyclopedias offer brief, easily grasped chunks of text along with plenty of charts, graphs, and illustrations. The information is more fragmented than in the narrative spines, but some students may prefer the more visual approach; others will find it busy and distracting.

Unfortunately, all three publishers (DK, Kingfisher, and Usborne) are terribly unreliable, and these encyclopedias constantly go out of print and are replaced by new versions—sometimes for the same age group and sometimes considerably more advanced. Used versions of the resources can usually be located online.

The encyclopedias can also be used as handy supplements to the narratives listed above.

Bingham, Jane, Fiona Chandler, and Sam Taplin. *The Usborne Internet-Linked Encyclopedia of World History.* Tulsa, OK: E.D.C. Publishing, 2003.

This is the hardback; the paperback is currently dated 2010. Definitely the most age-appropriate encyclopedia for the grammar stage, but (annoyingly) out of print. Check online for used versions.

History Year by Year: The History of the World, From the Stone Age to the Digital Age, 1st American ed. New York: DK Publishing, 2013.

$24.99. More accessible than the Kingfisher encyclopedia for young students, but with more fragmented text (many one- to two- sentence "sound bites") than the Usborne encyclopedia. Visually appealing and very well organized, but plan to supplement with a narrative spine or plenty of storybook-type resources so that students become familiar with sustained historical writing. Samples can be viewed on the publisher's website.

The Kingfisher History Encyclopedia, 3rd ed. New York: Kingfisher, 2012.

$32.99. Really more appropriate for fifth grade and up (see Chapter 17), but can be adapted for use with younger children (with some parental effort), and more widely available than the Usborne encyclopedia. Expect to read aloud in grades 1–3. The "Ready Reference" section in the back provides useful memorization lists: dynasties, emperors, kings, prime ministers, presidents, and major wars.

Geography Resources

Up-to-date globes and wall maps can be found at the National Geographic online map store (maps.nationalgeographic.com).

Arnold, Caroline. *The Geography Book: Activities for Exploring, Mapping, and Enjoying Your World.* New York: Jossey-Bass, 2001/Wiley, 2002.

$15.95. For third grade and older. An excellent introduction to physical geography: the points of the compass, time zones, different types of maps, physical formations (continents, mountains, valleys, oceans, seas, etc.), and weather. Activities and projects throughout. Good for focused geography study.

Geography. Louisville, KY: Memoria Press.

For third grade and older. An organized, sequential course in political geography; exercises teach the current borders and features of each country, with a brief historical survey of the country's development and a "fast facts" chart that gives major cities, population, and other important figures. Use in the order listed below. Samples may be viewed at the publisher's website.

> *States & Capitals.*
>> *Student Guide.* $12.95.
>> *Teacher Manual.* $12.95.

> *Geography I: The Middle East, North Africa, & Europe.*
>> Memoria Press is a Christian publisher, and the sections on Middle Eastern history make use of the Old and New Testament accounts.
>> *Student Text.* $14.95.
>> *Workbook.* $12.95.
>> *Teacher Guide.* $14.95.

> *Geography II: Sub-Saharan Africa, Asia, Oceania, & the Americas.*
>> *Student Text.* $14.95.
>> *Workbook.* $12.95.
>> *Teacher Guide.* $14.95.

> *Geography III,* 2nd ed.
>> A more detailed review of world geography (definitely involving logic-stage skills).
>> *Student Text.* $16.95.
>> *Workbook.* $17.95.
>> *Teacher Guide.* $17.95.

Geography Songs Kit. Newport Beach, CA: AudioMemory, 1999.

$22.95 for CD. Thirty-three songs cover continents, oceans, planets, and 225 countries; includes 23 maps to label.

Johnson, Terri. *Blackline Maps of World History.* Boring, OR: Knowledge Quest Maps.

"Historical" geography; focus is on the changes in countries, empires, and kingdoms over time; useful as a supplement for all grades. Black-line maps to label and color; full-color teacher's maps plus blank student maps. Extensive samples and lesson plans also available at the publisher's website. All downloads are from the publisher's website.

Map Trek, V1: Ancient World. $14.95 for download.

Map Trek, V2: Medieval World. $14.95 for download.

Map Trek, V3: New World. $14.95 for download.

Map Trek, V4: Modern World. $14.95 for download.

Map Trek, US Edition. Historical and contemporary maps of the U.S. states. $19.95 for download.

Map Trek: The Complete Collection. $55 for hardcover book plus CD-ROM, $47 for download.

VanCleave, Janice. *Janice VanCleave's Geography for Every Kid.* New York: Wiley, 1993.

$16. For third grade and older. A combination of historical and physical geography; plenty of activities (making your own Mercator projection, drawing maps for others to follow) with some connection to historical events (such as the first trip around the African continent). Good for a one-year focused geography course.

Ancients, 5000 B.C.–A.D. 400 (First Grade)

List of Great Men and Women to Cover

Cheops, pharaoh of Egypt (2700–2675 B.C.)

Abraham (c. 2100 B.C.)

Hammurabi (c. 1750 B.C.)

Queen Hatshepsut of Egypt (c. 1480 B.C.)

Moses (c. 1450 B.C.)

Tutankhamen (c. 1355 B.C.)

Nebuchadnezzar (1146–1123 B.C.)

King David (c. 1000 B.C.)

Homer (c. 800 B.C.)

Romulus (753–716 B.C.)

Sennacherib (705–681 B.C.)

Lao-tse (b. 604 B.C.)

Pythagoras (581–497 B.C.)

Confucius (K'ung Fu-tsu) (551–479 B.C.)

Buddha (Siddhartha Gautama) (550–480 B.C.)

Socrates (470–399 B.C.)

Plato (427–347 B.C.)

Aristotle (384–322 B.C.)

Alexander the Great (356–323 B.C.)

Hannibal (fought with Rome c. 218–207 B.C.)

Cicero (106–43 B.C.)

Julius Caesar (100–44 B.C.)

Virgil (70–19 B.C.)

Caesar Augustus (c. 45 B.C.–A.D. 14)

Jesus Christ (c. 4 B.C.–A.D. 33)

Saint Paul (c. A.D. 45)

Nero (died A.D. 68)

Constantine the Great (ruled A.D. 306–337)

General Information

Ali, Daud. *Ancient India: Discover the Rich Heritage of the Indus Valley and the Mughal Empire.* Wigston, Leicester: Armadillo, 2014.

$12.99. Fifteen first-grade-friendly projects and over three hundred illustrations illuminate ancient Indian customs and history.

Broida, Marian. *Ancient Egyptians and Their Neighbors: An Activity Guide.* Chicago: Chicago Review Press, 1999.

$16.95. Includes information and activities about Mesopotamians, Nubians, and Hittites, as well as the more popular Egyptians.

Carlson, Laurie. *Classical Kids: An Activity Guide to Life in Ancient Greece and Rome.* Chicago: Chicago Review Press, 1998.

$16.95. Information and hands-on activities about these two ancient cultures.

A Coloring Book of Ancient Egypt. Santa Barbara, CA: Bellerophon Books, 1985.

$4.95. Museum-shop-quality coloring book with designs and images from Egyptian tombs and monuments.

A Coloring Book of Ancient India. Santa Barbara, CA: Bellerophon Books, 1989.

$4.95. Scenes drawn from ancient Indian paintings and carvings show everyday life as well as pictures from myth and legend.

A Coloring Book of Ancient Rome. Santa Barbara, CA: Bellerophon Books, 1988.

$4.95. Museum-shop-quality coloring book with Roman art depicting Caesars, senators, chariot races, and other scenes from Roman life.

Ford, Michael. *You Wouldn't Want to Be a Greek Athlete!* New York: Franklin Watts, 2014.

$9.95. The everyday life of an athlete, plus a glossary of terms.

Green, John. *Life in Ancient Egypt.* New York: Dover, 1989.

$3.99. Coloring book; an artist's detailed drawings of Egyptian life.

————. *Life in Ancient Greece.* New York: Dover, 1993.

$3.99. Coloring book; an artist's detailed drawings of Greek life.

————. *Life in Ancient Rome.* New York: Dover, 1997.

$4.99. Coloring book; an artist's detailed drawings of Roman life.

————. *Life in Old Japan.* New York: Dover, 1994.

$4.99. Coloring book; an artist's detailed drawings of ancient Japanese life.

Guerber, H. A. *The Story of the Greeks,* 3rd ed. Fort Collins, CO: Nothing New Press, 2003.

$26.95. An engaging narrative history, broken into small, readable sections, first published in the late nineteenth century; a great reference book to have on hand for extra reading through the year.

————. *The Story of the Romans,* 3rd ed. Fort Collins, CO: Nothing New Press, 2002.

$24.95. An engaging narrative history, broken into small, readable sections, first published in the late nineteenth century; a great reference book to have on hand for extra reading through the year.

Krebs, Laurie. *We're Sailing Down the Nile: A Journey Through Egypt,* illus. Anne Wilson. Cambridge, MA: Barefoot Books, 2007.

$7.99. A rhyming read-it-yourself book for the youngest students, with additional information about ancient Egypt for the parent/teacher.

Malam, John. *You Wouldn't Want to Be a Roman Gladiator! Gory Things You'd Rather Not Know.* New York: Franklin Watts, 2012.

$9.95. All about gladiators and the ancient Roman culture that surrounded them.

Mann, Elizabeth. *The Great Pyramid.* New York: Mikaya Press, 2006.

$9.95. A lavishly illustrated guide to the construction of this wonder of the ancient world, with fold-out sections.

———. *The Great Wall.* New York: Mikaya Press, 2006.

$12.95. Another beautiful book, covering the history and extent of the Great Wall of China, with a fold-out scene of an attack on the wall's center.

Morley, Jacqueline. *You Wouldn't Want to Be a Pyramid Builder! A Hazardous Job You'd Rather Not Have.* New York: Franklin Watts, 2013.

$9.95. An engaging look at life on the bottom of Egyptian society.

———. *You Wouldn't Want to Be a Sumerian Slave! A Life of Hard Labor You'd Rather Avoid.* New York: Franklin Watts, 2007.

$9.95. A rare (and funny) look at Sumerian customs.

———. *You Wouldn't Want to Be in Alexander the Great's Army! Miles You'd Rather Not March.* New York: Franklin Watts, 2005.

$9.95. Covers a number of the areas that Alexander conquered. (Some death and dismemberment, although it's cartoonish in nature.)

———. *You Wouldn't Want to Work on the Great Wall of China! Defenses You'd Rather Not Build.* New York: Franklin Watts, 2006.

$9.95. An entertaining examination of the Great Wall through the eyes of its builders.

Oakes, Lorna. *Mesopotamia: All About Ancient Assyria and Babylonia.* Wigston, Leicester: Armadillo, 2012.

$12.99. Fifteen first-grade-friendly projects and over three hundred illustrations illuminate ancient Mesopotamian customs and history.

O'Connor, Jane. *Hidden Army: Clay Soldiers of Ancient China (All-Aboard Reading).* New York: Grosset & Dunlap, 2011.

$3.99. A paperback beginning-reader guide to the terra-cotta soldiers of ancient China.

Payne, Elizabeth. *The Pharaohs of Ancient Egypt*. New York: Random House, 1981.

$5.99. Each chapter tells about one pharaoh. Fourth- to fifth-grade reading level but easily read aloud. Covers Egypt's history from the beginning to its conquest by Greece and Rome.

Queen Nefertiti Coloring Book. Santa Barbara, CA: Bellerophon Books, 1992.

$3.50. Museum-shop-quality coloring book with reproductions of actual images from tombs and monuments in Egypt.

Sanders, Nancy I. *Old Testament Days: An Activity Guide*. Chicago: Chicago Review Press, 1999.

$18.95. Activities and information about Near Eastern lands during ancient times.

Steele, Philip. *Ancient China: Step Into the Time of the Chinese Empire*. Wigston, Leicester: Armadillo, 2012.

$12.99. Fifteen first-grade-friendly projects and over three hundred illustrations illuminate ancient Chinese customs and history.

Tames, Richard. *Ancient Greece: Step Into the World of the Classical Greeks*. Wigston, Leicester: Armadillo, 2012.

$12.99. Fifteen first-grade-friendly projects and over three hundred illustrations illuminate ancient Greek customs and history.

Biographies

Alexander the Great

Demi. *Alexander the Great*. New York: Marshall Cavendish, 2010.

$19.99; less for the ebook version. A kid-friendly picture-book survey of Alexander's life, with beautiful illustrations.

Cleopatra

Stanley, Diane, and Peter Vennema. *Cleopatra*. New York: HarperCollins, 1997.

$7.99. The picture-book format makes this biography attractive to young readers, but you'll need to read the text aloud.

Eratosthenes

Lasky, Kathryn. *The Librarian Who Measured the Earth*, illus. Kevin Hawkes. New York: Little, Brown & Co., 1994.

$18.99. Unfortunately available only in an expensive library binding; check your library. This picture book tells the story of the ancient Greek librarian who managed to measure the earth's circumference, using the shadows cast by the sun.

Julius Caesar

Medina, Nico. *Who Was Julius Caesar?* illus. Tim Foley. New York: Grosset & Dunlap, 2014.

$5.99. An accessible read-aloud biography with short chapters.

Romulus and Remus

Rockwell, Anne. *Romulus and Remus (A Ready-to-Read Book).* New York: Simon Spotlight, 1997.

$3.99. The Ready-to-Read series is accessible to beginning readers.

Tutankhamen

Sabuda, Robert. *Tutankhamen's Gift.* New York: Aladdin, 1997.

$7.99. This picture-book biography tells about Tutankhamen's life, not just his tomb.

Medieval/Early Renaissance, 400–1600 (Second Grade)

List of Great Men and Women to Cover

Saint Augustine (writing c. 411)

Attila the Hun (c. 433–453)

King Arthur (probably killed in 537 at the Battle of Camlann)

Muhammad (570–632)

Charlemagne (ruled 768–814)

Alfred the Great (849–899)

Leif Eriksson (discovered North America c. 1000)

Edward the Confessor (1042–1066)

Genghis Khan (b. 1155)

Dante Alighieri (1265–1321)

Geoffrey Chaucer (c. 1340–1400)

Jan van Eyck (c. 1390–1441)

Johannes Gutenberg (c. 1396–1468)

Christopher Columbus (1451–1506)

Leonardo da Vinci (1452–1519)

Amerigo Vespucci (1454–1512)

Nicolaus Copernicus (1473–1543)

Michelangelo (1475–1564)

Ferdinand Magellan (1480–1521)

Martin Luther (1483–1546)

Raphael (1483–1520)

Nostradamus (1503–1566)

John Calvin (1509–1564)

Hernando Cortés (entered Mexican capital, 1519)

Tycho Brahe (1546–1601)

Walter Raleigh (1554–1618)

William Shakespeare (1564–1616)

Galileo Galilei (1564–1642)

General Information

Aliki. *A Medieval Feast*. New York: HarperTrophy, 1986.

$6.99. A colorful account of the journey of a medieval king and the preparations made for his arrival.

Apte, Sunita. *The Aztec Empire: A True Book*. New York: Scholastic, 2010.

$6.95. The origin of the Aztecs, the building of Tenochtitlan, daily life, the extent of the empire, and the conquest by Spain.

Carlson, Laurie. *Days of Knights and Damsels: An Activity Guide*. Chicago: Chicago Review Press, 1998.

$15.95. Activities and information about the Middle Ages, designed for elementary students.

A Coloring Book of the Middle Ages. Santa Barbara, CA: Bellerophon Books, 1985.

$4.95. Pictures from actual medieval drawings and paintings, showing daily life, worship, knights, kings, monks, and warfare.

Copeland, Peter F. *Exploration of North America*. New York: Dover, 1992.

$3.90. Informative coloring book.

———. *Indian Tribes of North America*. New York: Dover, 1990.

$3.99. Informative coloring book.

Green, John. *Life in a Medieval Castle and Village Coloring Book*. New York: Dover, 1990.

$4.99.

MacDonald, Fiona. *You Wouldn't Want to Be a Crusader! A War You'd Rather Not Fight*. New York: Children's Press, 2005.

$9.95. Centered around the earlier crusades.

————. *You Wouldn't Want to Be a Medieval Knight!*, rev. ed. New York: Franklin Watts, 2013.

$9.95. An entertaining walk through a knight's training, life, and duties.

————. *You Wouldn't Want to Work on a Medieval Cathedral! A Difficult Job That Never Ends*. New York: Franklin Watts, 2010.

$9.95. Kid-friendly look at the gargantuan task of cathedral-building.

Maloy, Jackie. *The Ancient Maya: A True Book*. New York: Scholastic, 2010.

$9.95. The development of the Mayan culture: daily life, achievements, beliefs, and decline.

Manning, Mick, and Brita Granstrom. *Viking Longship: See History as It Happened*. London: Frances Lincoln Children's Books, 2015.

$9.99. An interactive and entertaining guide to Viking life, from the well-done Fly on the Wall series.

Miller, Christine, H. A. Guerber, and Charlotte M. Yonge. *The Story of the Middle Ages*, 3rd ed. Fort Collins, CO: Nothing New Press, 2002.

$30.95. An engaging narrative history, broken into small, readable sections, that reworks two nineteenth-century texts into a chronicle of events and colorful personalities.

Mooney, Carla. *Explorers of the New World: Discover the Golden Age of Exploration*. White River Junction, VT: Nomad Press, 2011.

$15.95. Readable guide to the explorers of the fifteenth and sixteenth centuries, with twenty-two hands-on projects (using a compass, tying knots, etc.).

Newman, Sandra. *The Inca Empire: A True Book*. New York: Scholastic, 2010.

$6.95. The location, customs, rise, and fall of the Incas.

Olmon, Kyle, and Tracy Sabin. *Castle: Medieval Days and Knights*. London: Orchard Books, 2006.

> $19.99. Designed by paper engineers Robert Sabuda and Matthew Reinhart, this pop-up book lets you into a wonderfully detailed castle complete with prisoners, jousting, and a drawbridge. Out of print but worth searching for, particular for engineering-minded students.

Paper Soldiers of the Middle Ages: 100 Years' War. Santa Barbara, CA: Bellerophon, 1992.

> $3.95.

Paper Soldiers of the Middle Ages: The Crusades. Santa Barbara, CA: Bellerophon, 1992.

> $4.95.

Polin, C. J. *The Story of Chocolate*. New York: Dorling Kindersley, 2005.

> $3.99. A DK Reader designed for second and third graders, this history of chocolate gives details about its use in the Aztec world and in medieval times—a fun way to connect ancient America to the present day.

Queen Elizabeth I: Paper Dolls to Color. Santa Barbara, CA: Bellerophon, 1985.

> $4.95. Paper dolls of Elizabeth I, Sir Walter Raleigh, the earl of Essex, and others, with outfits, as well as some text written by Queen Elizabeth herself.

Renaissance. Santa Barbara, CA: Bellerophon, 1983.

> $4.95. Coloring book with images from Renaissance paintings, engravings, and frescoes.

Senior, Kathryn. *You Wouldn't Want to be Sick in the 16th Century! Diseases You'd Rather Not Catch*, rev. ed. New York: Children's Press, 2014.

> $9.95. A slightly tongue-in-cheek introduction to medieval medicine: humors, epidemics, battlefield wounds, and the slow progress of medicine in Padua.

Shakespeare Fandex Family Field Guide. New York: Workman Publishing, 2003.

> $9.95. Fifty cards, held together in an easy-reference fan shape, with plenty of color illustrations and fascinating facts about Shakespeare, his plays, and his times.

Smith, A. G. *Castles of the World Coloring Book*. New York: Dover, 1986. $4.99. Medieval castles not only from England and France, but from Spain, Portugal, Japan, and other countries.

———. *Knights and Armor Coloring Book*. New York: Dover, 1985. $3.99. Drawings of knights and armor at different periods in history.

———. *Life in Celtic Times Coloring Book*. New York: Dover, 1997. $4.99.

———. *Story of the Vikings Coloring Book*. New York: Dover, 1988. $4.99. Tells the story of the Viking presence in Europe as well as in Russia and other countries.

Vikings. Mahopac, NY: Z-Man Games. $59.99. A family game for up to four players; lead a Viking band, discover islands, build settlements, and conquer your neighbors.

Biographies

Christopher Columbus

DeKay, James T. *Meet Christopher Columbus*. New York: Random House, 2001.
$4.99. A Landmark Biography on a second- to fourth-grade reading level.

Foster, Genevieve. *The World of Columbus and Sons*. Sandwich, MA: Beautiful Feet Books, 1998.
$21.95. A read-aloud biography of Columbus and his sons, interwoven with other biographies: Erasmus, Copernicus, Richard III, and others.

Wade, Mary Dodson. *Christopher Columbus (Rookie Biographies)*. New York: Children's Press, 2014.
$5.95. One of the books in the wonderful Rookie Biography series for first- to third-grade readers.

Elizabeth I

Stanley, Diane. *Good Queen Bess*. New York: HarperCollins, 2001.
$17.99.

Galileo

Sis, Peter. *Starry Messenger*. New York: Square Fish, 2000.

$7.99. Tells the story of Galileo's discoveries, with illustrations based on Galileo's own journals and records.

Genghis Khan

Demi. *Genghis Khan*. Tarrytown, NY: Marshall Cavendish, 2009.

$19.99; ebook also available for much less. A lovely picture book biography for young students, with brief text and many illustrations.

Joan of Arc

Stanley, Diane. *Joan of Arc*. New York: HarperCollins, 2002. $8.99.

Leif Eriksson

d'Aulaire, Ingri, and Edgar Parin. *Leif the Lucky*. Minneapolis: University of Minnesota Press, 2014.

$16.95.

Marco Polo

Herbert, Janis. *Marco Polo for Kids*. Chicago: Chicago Review Press, 2001.

$16.95. A biography of Marco Polo that includes activities and projects.

Muhammad

Demi. *Muhammad*. New York: Margaret K. McElderry Books, 2003.

$19.95. Check your library; many used copies also available. An easy-to-read picture book with illustrations modeled on Persian miniatures and Muhammad depicted as a golden silhouette.

Who in the World Biography Series. Charles City, VA: Well-Trained Mind Press.

$9.50 each. Order from any bookstore or from Well-Trained Mind Press. This series, designed especially for second- to fourth-grade readers, meshes with Volume II of *The Story of the World*. Accompanying audiobooks, read by Jim Weiss, are also available on CD for $12.95.

Beckham, Robert. *Who in the World Was the Secretive Printer? The Story of Johannes Gutenberg*. 2005.

Clark, Connie. *Who in the World Was the Unready King? The Story of Ethelred*. 2005.

Lambert, Lorene, *Who in the World Was the Forgotten Explorer? The Story of Amerigo Vespucci*. 2005.

Phillips, Robin. *Who in the World Was the Acrobatic Empress? The Story of Theodora*. 2006.

Late Renaissance/Early Modern, 1600–1850 (Third Grade)

List of Historical Topics to Cover

Your children's librarian can point you to third-grade-level books exploring these major events (listed chronologically):

the *Mayflower*
early American settlements
Russia under Peter the Great and his successors
Prussia in the eighteenth century
the Enlightenment
the agricultural revolution
Native American cultures
the British in India
the French Revolution
British-French conflict in Canada
the American Revolution
the Napoleonic Wars
the industrial revolution
Simón Bolívar's fight for independence in South America
the siege of the Alamo
the California gold rush
Australia's beginnings as a penal colony.

List of Great Men and Women to Cover

Mary Stuart (Mary Queen of Scots) (1542–1587)
Tokugawa Ieyasu (1543–1616)
James I of England (1566–1652)
Queen Nzinga of Angola (1582–1644)
Shah Jahan (1592–1666)
Oliver Cromwell (1599–1658)
Charles I (1600–1649)
Rembrandt (1606–1669)
John Milton (1608–1674)
Robert Boyle (1627–1691)
Louis XIV of France (1638–1715)
Isaac Newton (1642–1727)
William Penn (1644–1718)

Peter I (Peter the Great) (1672–1725)

Yoshimune (1684–1751)

Johann Sebastian Bach (1685–1750)

Frederick William I (Frederick the Great) (1688–1740)

Benjamin Franklin (1706–1790)

Qianlong (1711–1795)

Maria Theresa (1717–1780)

Catherine the Great (1729–1796)

George Washington (1732–1799)

Franz Joseph Haydn (1732–1809)

Thomas Jefferson (1743–1826)

Betsy Ross (1752–1836)

Phyllis Wheatley (1753–1784)

Louis XVI (1754–1793)

Marie Antoinette (1755–1793)

Wolfgang Amadeus Mozart (1756–1791)

George III of England (1760–1820)

Eli Whitney (1765–1825)

Captain James Cook (1768–1771)

Tecumseh (1768–1813)

Napoleon (1769–1821)

Ludwig van Beethoven (1770–1827)

Meriwether Lewis (1774–1809) and William Clark (1770–1838)

Simón Bolívar (1783–1830)

Shaka Zulu (1787–1828)

Sacagawea (c. 1788–1812)

Nat Turner (1800–1831)

General Information

Aliki. *The King's Day: Louis XIV of France*. New York: Crowell, 1989.

   Out of print, but worth checking your library for; a day in the life of
   Louis XIV, with illustrations and descriptions of his lavish lifestyle.

Benchley, Nathaniel. *George the Drummer Boy*, illus. Don Bolognese. New
York: HarperCollins, 1987.

   $3.99. Historical fiction on a second- to fourth-grade reading level about
   the battles at Lexington and Concord.

————. *Sam the Minuteman*, illus. Arnold Lobel. New York: HarperCollins, 1987.

$3.99. Historical fiction on a second- to fourth-grade reading level about a Revolutionary War soldier.

Bliven, Bruce. *The American Revolution*. New York: Random House, 1981.
$5.99. Part of the excellent Landmark series.

Brill, Ethel. *Madeleine Takes Command*, illus. Bruce Adams. South Bathgate, ND: Bethlehem Books, 1996.

$13.95. A read-aloud that corrects the U.S.-centered focus of many books written about this time period by telling the story of a French Canadian heroine.

Copeland, Peter F. *Early American Trades Coloring Book*. New York: Dover, 1980.

$4.99. Drawings of the different occupations in Colonial America.

————. *Life in Colonial America Coloring Book*. New York: Dover, 2002.
$4.99.

————. *The Story of the American Revolution Coloring Book*. New York: Dover, 1988.
$4.99.

Daugherty, James. *The Landing of the Pilgrims*. New York: Random House, 1981.
$5.99. A classic account.

Dennis, Yvonne Wakim, and Arlene Hirschfelder. *A Kid's Guide to Native American History*. Chicago: Chicago Review Press, 2009.

$16.95. Projects, games, and crafts covering nine major geographical areas in North America, along with suggestions for additional reading and a time line.

Guerber, H. A. *The Story of the Great Republic*. Ed. Christine Miller. Fort Collins, CO: Nothing New Press, 2006.

$26.95. An engaging narrative history, broken into small, readable sections, first published in the late nineteenth century. The first half of the book deals with America before the Civil War.

———. *The Story of the Thirteen Colonies.* Fort Collins, CO: Nothing New Press, 2002.

$26.95. An engaging narrative history, broken into small, readable sections, first published in the late nineteenth century; a great reference book to have on hand for extra reading through the year.

Harness, Cheryl. *They're Off! The Story of the Pony Express.* New York: Simon & Schuster, 2002.

$7.99. The story of communications between the east and west coasts in the mid-1800s, written on a third- to fourth-grade reading level.

King, David C., and Bobbie Moore. *Colonial Days: Discover the Past with Fun Projects, Games, Activities, and Recipes.* New York: Jossey-Bass, 1997.

$14.95.

———. *Pioneer Days: Discover the Past with Fun Projects, Games, Activities, and Recipes.* New York: Jossey-Bass, 1997.

$12.95.

Maestro, Betsy. *A More Perfect Union: The Story of Our Constitution,* illus. Giulio Maestro. New York: HarperCollins, 2008.

$7.99. The simplest and clearest introduction to the Constitution and its history, written for grades 2–4.

———. *Struggle for a Continent: The French and Indian Wars: 1689–1763,* illus. Giulio Maestro. New York: HarperCollins, 2000.

$18.99. A nicely illustrated and clear guide to the wars on the North American continent.

Moore, Kay. *If You Lived at the Time of the American Revolution.* New York: Scholastic, 1998.

$6.99. Part of the Scholastic series written for young children; covers both daily life and history in an entertaining way.

Morley, Jacqueline. *You Wouldn't Want to Be an American Colonist.* New York: Children's Press, 2013.

$9.95. Leads young students step-by-step through the perils of life in the early American colonies.

Mullenbach, Cheryl. *The Industrial Revolution for Kids: The People and Technology That Changed the World.* Chicago: Chicago Review Press, 2014.

$16.95. A hands-on introduction to the worldwide changes that industrialism made; photographs, explanations, and twenty-one activities and projects.

San Souci, Robert, and N. C. Wyeth. *N. C. Wyeth's Pilgrims*. San Francisco, CA: Chronicle Books, 1996.

$6.95. Simple text accompanies N. C. Wyeth's wonderful full-color paintings of pilgrims. Generally informative, but ignore the page that explains how the first settlers threw a Thanksgiving feast to thank the *Indians* (!). Out of print, but worth tracking down secondhand.

Schwartz, Heather. *The French Revolution: Terror and Triumph*. Huntington Beach, CA: Teacher Created Materials, 2013.

$8.99. Part of the Primary Source Readers series, this illustrated paperback discusses the major players of the French Revolution (the royal family, Robespierre, and more) and covers the events leading up to the Declaration of the Rights of Man.

Tierney, Tom. *American Family of the Colonial Era: Paper Dolls in Full Color*. New York: Dover, 1987.

$6.95. Large, historically accurate paper dolls.

———. *Marie Antoinette Paper Doll*. New York: Dover, 2001.

$6.95. Paper dolls of the queen and her dressmaker, along with fifteen costumes (and wigs).

Biographies

Adams, Abigail

Wagoner, Jean Brown. *Abigail Adams: Girl of Colonial Days*. New York: Aladdin, 1992.

$6.99. Written on a third- to fifth-grade level, these imaginative biographies in the Childhood of Famous Americans series focus on the childhood of each subject. Highly recommended.

Adams, John

Benge, Janet. *John Adams: Independence Forever*. Lynnwood, WA: Emerald Books, 2002.

$8.99. One of the Heroes of History series, written on an entertaining fourth- to fifth-grade level.

Hopkinson, Deborah. *John Adams Speaks for Freedom*, illus. Craig Orback. New York: Simon Spotlight, 2005.

$3.99. One of the Ready-to-Read series, this is ideal for students reading on a second- to third-grade level (much simpler than the Heroes of History biography above).

Antoinette, Marie

Hockinson, Liz. *Marie Antoinette: "Madame Deficit" (The Thinking Girl's Treasury of Dastardly Dames)*. Foster City, CA: Goosebottom Books, 2011.

$18.95. Available as an ebook for less. A nicely illustrated, well-written biography of Marie Antoinette that covers her times as well; written on a third- to fourth-grade level with some advanced vocabulary.

Attucks, Crispus

Millender, Dharathula H. *Crispus Attucks: Black Leader of Colonial Patriots*. New York: Aladdin, 1986.

$6.99. A Childhood of Famous Americans biography.

Bach, Johann Sebastian.

Venezia, Mike. *Johann Sebastian Bach (Getting to Know the World's Greatest Composers)*. New York: Children's Press, 1998.

$6.95. Simple illustrated biography of Bach along with information about his greatest hits; a good independent read for most third graders.

Beethoven, Ludwig van

Venezia, Mike. *Ludwig Van Beethoven (Getting to Know the World's Greatest Composers)*. New York: Children's Press, 1996.

$6.95. Simple illustrated biography of Beethoven along with information about his greatest hits; a good independent read for most third graders.

Boone, Daniel

Stevenson, Augusta. *Daniel Boone: Young Hunter and Tracker*. New York: Aladdin, 1986.

$6.99. A Childhood of Famous Americans biography.

Buffalo Bill

Stevenson, Augusta. *Buffalo Bill: Frontier Daredevil*. New York: Aladdin, 1991.

$6.99. A Childhood of Famous Americans biography.

Crockett, Davy

Parks, Eileen Wells. *Davy Crockett: Young Rifleman*. New York: Aladdin, 1986.

$6.99. A Childhood of Famous Americans biography.

Franklin, Benjamin

Cousins, Margaret. *Ben Franklin in Old Philadelphia*. New York: Random House, 2004.

$5.99. One of the Landmark Biography series.

Giblin, James Cross. *The Amazing Life of Benjamin Franklin*, illus. Michael Dooling. New York: Scholastic, 2006.

$7.99. A well-written picture-book biography with plenty of additional information about Franklin's times.

Harness, Cheryl. *The Remarkable Benjamin Franklin*. Washington, DC: National Geographic Children's Books, 2008.

$7.95. Another fine, highly illustrated biography suitable for readers in grades 3–5.

Handel, George Frideric

Venezia, Mike. *George Handel*. Chicago: Children's Press, 1995.

$6.95. Part of the readable junior series Getting to Know the World's Greatest Composers.

Henry, Patrick

Adler, David A. *A Picture Book of Patrick Henry*. New York: Holiday House, 2001.

$7.99. A simple and interesting guide to Patrick Henry's life. From the Picture Book Biographies series.

Fritz, Jean. *Where Was Patrick Henry on the 29th of May?*, illus. Margot Tomes. New York: Puffin, 1997.

$6.99. A classic children's book, covering the history of the early Revolution as it tells the story of Patrick Henry.

Jackson, Andrew

Venezia, Mike. *Andrew Jackson: Seventh President, 1829–1837*. Chicago: Children's Press, 2005.

$7.95. A simpler read than the Jackson biography listed below, this is part of the Getting to Know the U.S. Presidents series.

Stanley, George Edward. *Andrew Jackson: Young Patriot*. New York: Aladdin, 2003.

$6.99. One of the Childhood of Famous Americans series.

Jefferson, Thomas

Barrett, Marvin. *Meet Thomas Jefferson*. New York: Random House, 2001.

$4.99. A Landmark Biography.

Giblin, James Cross. *Thomas Jefferson: A Picture Book Biography*. New York: Holiday House, 1991.

$7.99. A simple biography with attractive color illustrations; part of the Picture Book Biographies series.

Lafayette, Marquis de

Fritz, Jean. *Why Not Lafayette?*, illus. Ronald Himler. New York: Putnam, 2001.

$5.99. A fourth- to fifth-grade level biography of the Marquis; this would also make an entertaining read-aloud for younger students.

Monroe, James

Venezia, Mike. *James Monroe: Fifth President, 1817–1825*. Chicago: Children's Press, 2005.

$7.95. Part of the Getting to Know the U.S. Presidents series.

Mozart, Wolfgang Amadeus

Venezia, Mike. *Wolfgang Amadeus Mozart (Getting to Know the World's Greatest Composers)*. New York: Children's Press, 1995.

$6.95. Simple illustrated biography of Mozart along with information about his greatest hits; a good independent read for most third graders.

Nur Jahan

Bridges, Shirin Yim. *Nur Jahan of India (The Thinking Girl's Treasury of Real Princesses)*. Foster City, CA: Goosebottom Books, 2010.

$18.95. Available as an ebook for less. A nicely illustrated, well-written biography of Nur Jahan that also discusses Shah Jahan and the Mughal empire; written on a third- to fourth-grade level with some advanced vocabulary.

Nzinga

Havemeyer, Janie. *Njinga: "The Warrior Queen" (The Thinking Girl's Treasury of Dastardly Dames)*. Foster City, CA: Goosebottom Books, 2011.

$18.95. Available as an ebook for less. A nicely illustrated, well-written biography of Queen Nzinga; written on a third- to fourth-grade level with some advanced vocabulary.

Pitcher, Molly

Stevenson, Augusta. *Molly Pitcher: Young Patriot*. New York: Aladdin, 1986.

$8.99. One of the Childhood of Famous Americans series.

Pocahontas

Penner, Lucille Rech. *The True Story of Pocahontas*. New York: Random House, 1994.

$3.99. A Step Into Reading biography, written on a second-grade level.

Revere, Paul

Stevenson, Augusta. *Paul Revere: Boston Patriot*. New York: Aladdin, 1986.

$6.99. One of the Childhood of Famous Americans series.

Ross, Betsy

Greene, Stephanie. *Betsy Ross and the Silver Thimble*, illus. Diana Magnuson. New York: Simon Spotlight, 2002.

$3.99. A Step Into Reading easy reader for beginners.

Sacagawea

Seymour, Flora Warren. *Sacagawea: American Pathfinder*. New York: Aladdin, 1991.

$6.99. One of the Childhood of Famous Americans series.

Sitting Bull

Stevenson, Augusta. *Sitting Bull: Dakota Boy*. New York: Aladdin, 1996.

$6.99. One of the Childhood of Famous Americans series.

Squanto

Bulla, Clyde Robert. *Squanto, Friend of the Pilgrims*. New York: Scholastic, 1990.

$5.99.

Tecumseh
  Mayer, Cassie. *Tecumseh*. Portsmouth, NH: Heinemann, 2007.
    $5.99. A First Biography, written on a very simple reading level.

Washington, George
  Adler, David A. *A Picture Book of George Washington*. New York: Holiday
  House, 1990.
    $7.99. A simple biography with colorful illustrations; part of the Picture Book Biographies series.

Harness, Cheryl. *George Washington*. Washington, DC: National Geographic
Children's Books, 2006.
    $8.99. Large illustrations, straightforward text on a third- to fifth-grade level.

Heilbroner, Joan. *Meet George Washington*. New York: Random House, 2001.
    $4.99. A Step-Up Biography.

Washington, Martha
  Wagoner, Jean Brown. *Martha Washington: America's First First Lady*. New
  York: Aladdin, 1986.
    $6.99. One of the Childhood of Famous Americans series.

Wheatley, Phillis
  Weidt, Maryann. *Revolutionary Poet: A Story about Phillis Wheatley*, illus.
  Mary O'Keefe Young. Minneapolis, MN: Carolrhoda Books, 1997.
    $6.95.

Modern, 1850–Present (Fourth Grade)

List of Historical Topics to Cover

Your children's librarian can point you to fourth-grade level books exploring these major events (listed chronologically). For U.S. state history, you can also write to your state's Chamber of Commerce and request materials to study your state's history, geography, and commerce.
  Africa under European control
  the Indian mutinies
  the Crimean War
  the Victorian era
  suffrage movement and the Seneca Falls declaration

the War between the States (Civil War)
exploration of the American West
Euro-American conflict with the Native American tribes
the Boxer Rebellion
World War I
the Russian Revolution
the Soviet Union
the Great Depression
the New Deal
civil war in Spain
the Axis and the Allies
World War II
Nazi Germany/Hitler
the Holocaust
Zionism/the Jews' return to Palestine
apartheid/South African segregation
China under Mao
the Korean War
the American civil rights movement
the Vietnam War
space race and landing on the moon

List of Notable Men and Women to Cover

Andrew Jackson (1767–1845)
Louis Joseph Papineau (1786–1871)
Samuel Morse (1791–1872)
Commodore Matthew Perry (1794–1858)
Santa Anna (1794–1876)
Robert E. Lee (1807–1870)
Abraham Lincoln (1809–1865)
David Livingstone (1813–1873)
Otto von Bismarck (1815–1898)
Elizabeth Cady Stanton (1815–1902)
Karl Marx (1818–1883)
Queen Victoria (1819–1901)
Victor Emmanuel II (1820–1878)
Susan B. Anthony (1820–1906)

Florence Nightingale (1820–1910)

Harriet Tubman (1820–1913)

Ulysses S. Grant (1822–1885)

Catewayo of the Zulus (1826–1884)

Sitting Bull (1831–1890)

Empress Dowager Cixi (1835–1908)

Samuel Clemens (Mark Twain) (1835–1910)

George Custer (1839–1876)

Claude Monet (1840–1926)

Alexander Graham Bell (1847–1922)

Thomas Edison (1847–1931)

Mutsuhito (emperor of Japan) (1852–1912)

Theodore Roosevelt (1858–1919)

Henry Ford (1863–1947)

Wilbur Wright (1867–1912) and Orville Wright (1871–1948)

Mahatma Gandhi (1869–1948)

Vladimir Lenin (1870–1924)

Winston Churchill (1874–1965)

Josef Stalin (1879–1953)

Franklin D. Roosevelt (1882–1945)

Benito Mussolini (1883–1945)

Adolf Hitler (1889–1945)

Dwight D. Eisenhower (1890–1969)

Charles de Gaulle (1890–1970)

Francisco Franco (1892–1975)

Mao Zedong (1893–1976)

Czar Nicholas II (1895–1917)

Amelia Earhart (1897–1932)

Albert Einstein (1879–1955)

Charles Lindbergh (1902–1974)

John F. Kennedy (1917–1963)

Nelson Mandela (1918–2013)

Margaret Thatcher (1925–2013)

Martin Luther King, Jr. (1929–1968)

Neil Armstrong (1930–2012)

Saddam Hussein (1937–2006)

Bill Gates (1955–)

General Resources

If you are a U.S. home-schooling family, your district may ask you to spend fourth grade studying American history; we suggest that you continue with the study of world history, but focus your additional and supplemental readings on the American history resources listed below.

The books listed below are only a few of the many available.

Archambault, Alan. *Black Soldiers in the Civil War Coloring Book*. Santa Barbara, CA: Bellerophon, 1995.

$3.95. A museum-shop-quality coloring book of Civil War–era images.

———. *Civil War Heroes: A Coloring Book*. Santa Barbara, CA: Bellerophon, 1988.

$4.95. A museum-shop-quality coloring book of contemporary Civil War portraits.

Bernhard, Annika. *State Birds and Flowers Coloring Book*. New York: Dover, 1990.

$3.99.

Bunting, Eve. *The Wall*. Boston: Houghton Mifflin, 1992.

$6.99. A little boy is taken to find his grandfather's name on the Vietnam Veterans Memorial.

Carey, Charles W. *The Emancipation Proclamation*. Chanhassen, MN: Child's World, 2014.

$20.95. Part of the Journey to Freedom series, this informative book for young students is available as an ebook only.

A Coloring Book of Our Presidents, Washington through Clinton. Santa Barbara, CA: Bellerophon, 1999.

$4.95. Contemporary portraits of each president.

Conklin, Wendy. *The Cold War*. Huntington Beach, CA: Teacher Created Materials, 2013.

$8.99. Heavily illustrated introduction to communism, the arms race and the space race, the Berlin Wall, the Korean War, the Cuban crisis, and the Vietnam conflict, all readable on a fourth-grade level.

Copeland, Peter F. *Famous Women of the Civil War Coloring Book*. New York: Dover, 1999.

$3.99.

————. *Story of the Civil War Coloring Book*. New York: Dover, 1991.
$3.99.

Demuth, Patricia Brennan. *What Was D-Day?*, illus. David Grayson. New York: Grosset & Dunlap, 2015.
$5.99. Interesting and age-appropriate coverage of the events leading up to D-Day as well as the invasion itself.

————. *What Was Pearl Harbor?* illus. John Mantha. New York: Grosset & Dunlap, 2013.
$5.99. The events of December 7, 1941, and what came after.

Dubois, Muriel L. *The U.S. House of Representatives*. Mankato, MN: Capstone Press, 2003.
$7.29. Simple and heavily illustrated guide.

————. *The U.S. Presidency*. Mankato, MN: Capstone Press, 2003.
$7.29. Simple and heavily illustrated guide to one of the three branches of government.

————. *The U.S. Supreme Court*. Mankato, MN: Capstone Press, 2003.
$7.29. Simple and heavily illustrated guide.

Foster, Genevieve. *Abraham Lincoln's World*. Sandwich, MA: Beautiful Feet Books, 2003.
$21.95. Tells the story not only of Lincoln, but also of other men and women whose lives intersected his.

Fradin, Dennis Brindell. From Sea to Shining Sea series. Danbury, CT: Children's Book Press.
This series includes one title for each state and is written on a simple second- to fourth-grade reading level.

Graham, Ian. *You Wouldn't Want to Be a World War II Pilot! Air Battles You Might Not Survive*. New York: Franklin Watts, 2009.
$9.95. Engaging cartoon-illustrated guide to World War II combat flying.

Holling, Holling C. *Minn of the Mississippi*. Boston: Houghton Mifflin, 1978.
$11.95. The history of the Mississippi told through the adventures of a snapping turtle.

————. *Paddle-to-the-Sea*. Boston: Houghton Mifflin, 1980.

$11.95. A Caldecott-winning story about an Indian boy's toy canoe and its journey from the Great Lakes to the Atlantic.

————. *Tree in the Trail.* Boston: Houghton Mifflin, 1990.
$11.95. The history of the Great Plains and Santa Fe Trail, centered on a cottonwood tree.

King, David C. *Civil War Days: Discover the Past with Exciting Projects, Games, Activities, and Recipes.* New York: Jossey-Bass, 1999.
$16.95. Follows the lives of two families, one white and one black, through daily activities; plenty of suggestions for hands-on learning.

————. *World War II Days: Discover the Past with Exciting Projects, Games, Activities, and Recipes.* New York: Wiley, 2000.
$12.95. Explore the culture of America in the 1930s and '40s.

Levine, Ellen. *If You Lived at the Time of Martin Luther King.* New York: Scholastic, 1994.
$6.99. Simple reading about the civil rights movement.

Lincoln, Abraham. *The Gettysburg Address,* illus. Michael McCurdy. New York: Houghton Mifflin, 1998.
$7.99. Each sentence of the Gettysburg Address stands in large type above a woodcut illustration; this book will bring the famous speech to life.

Malam, John. *You Wouldn't Want to Be a Secret Agent During World War II! A Perilous Mission Behind Enemy Lines.* New York: Franklin Watts, 2010.
$9.95. Follow along as a spy goes behind enemy lines in France under German occupation.

Matthews, Rupert. *You Wouldn't Want to Be a Chicago Gangster! Some Dangerous Characters You'd Better Avoid.* New York: Franklin Watts, 2010.
$9.95. The Roaring Twenties in Chicago.

Meyer, Carolyn. *Anastasia: The Last Grand Duchess, Russia, 1914.* New York: Scholastic, 2013.
$6.99. Part of the "Royal Diaries" series, this story of the Russian Revolution is told in the form of brief diary entries kept by Anastasia, the youngest daughter of Tsar Nicholas II and Tsarina Alexandra. Historical notes flesh out the picture of early twentieth-century Russian society and its conflicts.

Moore, Kay. *If You Lived at the Time of the Civil War.* New York: Scholastic, 1994.

$6.99. Simple reading level.

Murphy, Jim. *The Boys' War.* Boston: Houghton Mifflin, 1993.

$8.95. Boys as young as eleven and twelve fought in the Civil War; this book tells their stories in their own words.

Pascal, Janet. *What Was the Great Depression?*, illus. Dede Putra. New York: Grosset & Dunlap, 2015.

$5.99. Eighty illustrations and kid-friendly text.

Presidents of the United States Pocket Flash Cards.

$2.99. All the U. S. presidents on cards: portraits, signatures, brief biographies, and trivia.

The Presidents Song. Animaniacs, 1995.

The catchiest memory aid around; Wakko and friends sing the first forty-three presidents. The song can be purchased as part of the *Animaniacs* series, Season 3, Episode 75; first aired on November 11, 1995. You can also find it on YouTube.com.

Rasmussen, R. Kent. *World War I for Kids: A History with 21 Activities.* Chicago: Chicago Review Press, 2014.

$17.95. Clear text about the conflict, good illustrations, and plenty of activities explaining how trench warfare worked.

Rickman, David. *Cowboys of the Old West Coloring Book.* New York: Dover, 1985.

$4.99.

Smith, A. G. *Easy-to-Make Plains Indians Teepee Village.* New York: Dover, 1990.

$6.99. A modeling project that needs no scissors!

———. *Union Army Paper Soldiers.* New York: Dover, 1995.

$6.95. Twenty-four large soldiers.

States and Capitals Songs. Newport Beach, CA: AudioMemory, 1998.

$12.95 for CD and kit. The kit includes the CD with states and capitals songs, plus a map to color.

Wyk, Chris van, ed. *Nelson Mandela: Long Walk to Freedom,* illus. Paddy Bouma. New York: Flash Point, 2009.

$18.99. This adaptation of Mandela's autobiography, aimed at readers in grades 3–5, is a good way to learn more about apartheid and its breakdown.

Biographies

Alcott, Louisa May

Meigs, Cornelia. *Invincible Louisa: The Story of the Author of Little Women.* Boston: Little, Brown, 1995.

$9. A 1937 Newbery winner.

Anthony, Susan B.

Monsell, Helen Albee. *Susan B. Anthony: Champion of Women's Rights.* New York: Aladdin, 1986.

$6.99. One of the Childhood of Famous Americans series, imaginative biographies written on a third- to fifth-grade level that focus on the childhood of each subject. Highly recommended.

Barton, Clara.

Stevenson, Augusta. *Clara Barton: Founder of the American Red Cross.* New York: Aladdin, 1986.

$6.99. One of the Childhood of Famous Americans series.

Bethune, Mary McLeod

Greenfield, Eloise. *Mary McLeod Bethune,* illus. Jerry Pinkney. New York: HarperCollins, 1994.

$6.99. A simple biography of the famous educator born the fifteenth child of former slaves.

Blackwell, Elizabeth

Henry, Joanne Landers. *Elizabeth Blackwell: Girl Doctor.* New York: Aladdin, 1996.

$6.99. One of the Childhood of Famous Americans series.

Carver, George Washington

Moore, Eva. *The Story of George Washington Carver,* illus. Alexander Anderson. New York: Scholastic, 1990.

$5.99. This Scholastic Biography is written for good third- to fifth-grade readers.

Chavez, Cesar
Krull, Kathleen. *Harvesting Hope: The Story of Cesar Chavez*, illus. Yuji Morales. New York: Harcourt, 2003.
$17.95. A fascinating picture-book account of Cesar Chavez's childhood and his rise to activism.

Churchill, Winston
Labracque, Ellen. *Who Was Winston Churchill?*, illus. Jerry Hoare. New York: Grosset & Dunlap, 2015.
$5.99. Engaging illustrated biography written on a fourth- to fifth-grade reading level.

Cixi
Yim, Natasha. *Cixi: "The Dragon Empress" (The Thinking Girl's Treasury of Dastardly Dames)*. Foster City, CA: Goosebottom Books, 2011.
$18.95. Available as an ebook for less. A nicely illustrated, well-written biography of the last Qing ruler; written on a third- to fourth-grade level with some advanced vocabulary.

Darwin, Charles
Hopkinson, Deborah. *Who Was Charles Darwin?*, illus. Nancy Harrison. New York: Grosset & Dunlap, 2005.
$5.99. A simple but thorough biography, written on about a fourth-grade level.

Douglass, Frederick
Adler, David A. *A Picture Book of Frederick Douglass*. New York: Holiday House, 1995.
$7.99. Order from any bookstore. A simple illustrated guide to Douglass's life.

Earhart, Amelia
Henderson, Meryl. *Amelia Earhart: Young Aviator*. New York: Aladdin, 2000.
$6.99. One of the Childhood of Famous Americans series.

Edison, Thomas
  Guthridge, Sue. *Thomas Edison: Young Inventor*. New York: Aladdin, 1986.
  $6.99. One of the Childhood of Famous Americans series.

Edmonds, Emma
  Reit, Seymour. *Behind Rebel Lines*. New York: HMH Books, 2001.
  $6.95. The true story of a Civil War–era girl who posed as a boy,
  became a soldier, and then became a spy.

Einstein, Albert
  Hammontree, Marie. *Albert Einstein: Young Thinker*. New York: Aladdin,
  1986.
  $6.99. One of the Childhood of Famous Americans series.

Ford, Henry
  Aird, Hazel B. *Henry Ford: Young Man with Ideas*. New York: Aladdin, 1986.
  $6.99. One of the Childhood of Famous Americans series.

Gandhi, Mohandas
  Demi. *Gandhi*. New York: Margaret K. McElderry, 2001.
  $21.99. A biography that most elementary students can read inde-
  pendently.

Keller, Helen
  Davidson, Margaret. *Helen Keller*, illus. Wendy Watson. New York: Scholastic, 1989.
  $5.99. This Scholastic Biography is written for good third- to fifth-
  grade readers.

Kennedy, John F.
  Frisbee, Lucy Post. *John F. Kennedy: America's Youngest President*. New
  York: Aladdin, 1986.
  $6.99. One of the Childhood of Famous Americans series.

King, Martin Luther, Jr.
  Millender, Dharathula H. *Martin Luther King, Jr.* New York: Aladdin, 1986.
  $6.99. One of the Childhood of Famous Americans series.

Lincoln, Abraham
  Freedman, Russell. *Lincoln: A Photobiography*. Boston: Houghton Mifflin,
  1989.

$9.95. This Newbery Medal winner shows the changes in Lincoln over time.

Harness, Cheryl. *Abe Lincoln Goes to Washington, 1837–1865.* Washington, DC: National Geographic Children's Books, 2008.

$7.95. Simple and well-illustrated biography covering the most important years in Lincoln's life.

Marshall, Thurgood

Adler, David A. *A Picture Book of Thurgood Marshall.* New York: Holiday House, 1999.

$7.99. A simple illustrated guide to Marshall's accomplishments.

Parks, Rosa

Mara, Will. *Rosa Parks.* Chicago: Children's Press, 2007.

$5.95. A very simple Rookie Biography.

Pasteur, Louis

Alphin, Elaine Marie. *Germ Hunter: A Story About Louis Pasteur,* illus. Elaine Verstrate. New York: Carolrhoda Books, 2003.

$8.95. Part of the Creative Minds Biography series, this book is written with an almost novelistic tone—enjoyable reading for grades 3–5.

Roosevelt, Eleanor

Weil, Ann. *Eleanor Roosevelt: Fighter for Social Justice.* New York: Aladdin, 1989.

$6.99. One of the Childhood of Famous Americans series.

Roosevelt, Franklin D.

Mara, Will. *Franklin D. Roosevelt.* Chicago: Children's Press, 2004.

$4.95. A very simple Rookie Biography.

Roosevelt, Theodore

Mara, Will. *Theodore Roosevelt.* Chicago: Children's Press, 2007.

$4.95. A very simple Rookie Biography.

Stanton, Elizabeth Cady

Fritz, Jean. *You Want Women to Vote, Lizzie Stanton?* New York: Puffin, 1999.

$6.99. An entertaining account of Stanton's life.

Tubman, Harriet

McDonough, Yona. *Who Was Harriet Tubman?*, illus. Nancy Harrison. New York: Grosset & Dunlap, 2002.

$4.99. A thorough but simple biography, written on about a fourth-grade level.

Twain, Mark

Mason, Miriam E. *Mark Twain: Young Writer*. New York: Aladdin, 1991.

$6.99. One of the Childhood of Famous Americans series.

Queen Victoria

Gigliotti, Jim. *Who Was Queen Victoria?*, illus. Jerry Hoare. New York: Grosset & Dunlap, 2014.

$5.99. Engaging illustrated biography written on a fourth- to fifth-grade reading level.

Wright, Wilbur and Orville

Schulz, Walter A. *Will and Orv*. New York: Carolrhoda Books, 2003.

$6.99. An easy-reader account of the day when the airplane first flew.

Stevenson, Augusta. *Wilbur and Orville Wright: Young Fliers*. New York: Aladdin, 1986.

$5.99. One of the Childhood of Famous Americans series.

8

INVESTIGATING THE WORLD: SCIENCE

All the world is a laboratory to the enquiring mind.
—Martin H. Fischer

SUBJECT: **Beginning science**
TIME REQUIRED: **An average of 2 to 3 hours per week, 60–90 minutes twice per week**

For the next four years, the beginning science student gets to explore the physical world: animals and people (biology), the earth and the sky (earth science and astronomy), the way the elements work together (chemistry), and the laws that govern the universe (physics).

GOALS FOR THE GRAMMAR STAGE

As in other areas of the curriculum, the grammar-stage student should be gathering basic information. For science, this means exploring the world around us: learning about animal anatomy and behavior, the functions of the human body, the movements of the planets and the position of the stars, the ways in which atoms interact.

Grammar-stage study has a larger goal, though. While grammar-stage students are gathering all of this information, you (the parent-teacher) should be cultivating two important attitudes: a sense of amazement and a commitment to *look hard* at the world around us.

The overall purpose of grammar-stage science study is not just to accumulate information, but to begin to develop a scientific viewpoint. The scientist doesn't take natural operations for granted. She asks: *Why* do objects fall to the earth? The sun *looks* as though it moves from one horizon to the other, but what is it *really* doing?

One of the very first scientists, Aristotle, began his study of nature by asking: Why do things grow? Why does a seed turn into a tree? Why does a kitten grow into a cat? These questions became the catalyst for the first Western scientific writing—Aristotle's *History of Animals*, a study that gave birth to the field of biology. Aristotle's countrymen had also seen kittens grow into cats and seeds into trees, but they took this change for granted; it didn't strike them as *amazing*, so they didn't look hard at it. Aristotle was thinking like a scientist. He was amazed, and so he tried to find an explanation.

That's the way young students should learn to think in the grammar stage. Clouds are *amazing*. Flowers and dolphins and chemical reactions and things that fall are *amazing*. Why do they behave the way they do?

So as you study, you'll keep these purposes in mind. You're not trying to teach your second grader everything that's important about the earth and sky (that would be overwhelming). You're learning basic information about our planet and about the universe, and then you're using that information as a springboard to ask: Why? Look *hard* at the information. Question it. (And be amazed.)

WHICH SUBJECTS TO STUDY, AND WHEN

Think of science as divided into five major fields of study: biology/ natural science (the study of animals, plants, and people), astronomy, earth science, chemistry, and physics. You could choose to add a sixth area of investigation, which we could call *technology*—how and why machines, electronics, robots, digital players, and Lego creations work the way they do.[1]

In earlier editions of this book, we suggested dividing the four years of science study into subjects that roughly correspond to the history periods. First graders, who are studying the Ancients, learn about those things that the ancients could see—animal life, the human body, and plants. They make collections, take nature walks, and sprout beans in jars. Second graders study the earth and sky while also studying the Middle Ages and early Renaissance, a time when astronomy was the queen of the sciences. Third graders work on basic chemistry—atoms and molecules, what elements are and how they interact—while they're also reading history from the period spanning 1600 to 1850 (the years when Robert Boyle, Georg Ernst Stahl, Antoine Lavoisier, and John Dalton lived). Fourth graders, studying modern times, learn basic physics and are introduced to modern technology.

These divisions—the study of life, the study of earth and sky, the study of chemistry, the study of physics—also correspond to the child's growing ability to think abstractly. A six-year-old can collect and examine plants and animals; a seven-year-old, who is a little more mature, can understand something about the vastness of space; an eight-year-old can comprehend atoms, even though she can't see them; and a nine-year-old can begin to understand what light and sound are made of.

This is one useful way to organize your science studies—but only one. Parents who are themselves scientists have told us that they prefer to teach the sciences as connected to each other rather than related to history. Other parents have found that their students are more engaged and have better retention if they cycle through all of the sciences in a single year, at six- or eight-week intervals, rather than covering one field over an entire year of study.

When and how you teach each field of science is much less important than keeping the primary goals (collecting basic information and facts,

---

[1] It is common to see the curriculum divided into two major fields: the humanities (language arts and social sciences) and what is often referred to as STEM areas (science, technology, engineering, and mathematics). Technically, "engineering" involves design and "technology" encompasses bringing those designs to life, but for the grammar stage both aspects can be combined.

learning to look hard and ask questions, and staying amazed) in mind. Any of the following schemes—or another scheme that you develop yourself—can work for elementary science study. (For more explanation of the methods used, see the "How to" sections below.)

First grade	Biology	Animal kingdom (18 weeks)
		Human body (10 weeks)
		Plant kingdom (8 weeks)
Second grade	Earth and sky science	Earth science (18 weeks)
		Astronomy (18 weeks)
Third grade	Chemistry	Basic chemistry (36 weeks)
Fourth grade	Physics & technology	Basic physics (18 weeks)
		Technology & engineering (18 weeks)

OR

First grade	The basic sciences of nature	Earth science (8 weeks)
		Astronomy (8 weeks)
		Animal kingdom (8 weeks)
		Human body (8 weeks)
		Plant kingdom (4 weeks)
Second grade	Looking below the surfaces	Basic chemistry (12 weeks)
		Basic physics (12 weeks)
		Technology & engineering (12 weeks)
Third grade	Repeat first grade topics: review and go deeper	
Fourth grade:	Review second grade topics: review and go deeper	

OR

First grade	All sciences	Earth science (5 weeks)
		Astronomy (5 weeks)
		Animal kingdom (6 weeks)
		Human body (5 weeks)

Plant kingdom (5 weeks)

Chemical reactions (5 weeks)

Physics (5 weeks)

Second grade	Same topics with more depth
Third grade	Same topics with more depth
Fourth grade	Same topics with more depth

As you plan, remember that the elementary years are the time when vital basic skills (reading, writing, and arithmetic) are a priority. A second grader who doesn't finish learning about the constellations won't be hampered later on. But a second grader who doesn't grasp the concept of writing complete sentences instead of fragments, or the basics of addition, will be hobbled. So be sure to devote enough time to skill development, even if it means spending less time in the content areas of history, science, art, etc.

Some classical academies even go so far as to leave science out of the poll-parrot stage altogether, which we think is a poor idea. Grades 1 through 4 are a time of discovery—why leave science out of the equation? But it's true that the elementary student—especially a first or second grader—will spend a large percentage of her time and energy on basic skills. Because of this, you may want to schedule science study only one or two days per week for younger students, and you may choose to introduce science study for the first time several weeks or months into the first-grade year, after the six-year-old has settled into her reading, writing, and math routines.

HOW TO TEACH SCIENCE: GENERAL METHODS

The only books more boring than basic history textbooks are standard science textbooks. They tend to lack good organization, decent writing, clear layout, and/or any sense of overall purpose. (One textbook we reviewed moved from rain forests to diet and nutrition to sound waves within a twelve-week period. Why?) So instead of using a single text, then, we suggest that you use encyclopedia-type works as a "spine," and supplement this with living books, kits, and projects—just as you do for history.

(We've listed a number of our favorites at the end of this chapter, but you will find many more as you investigate.)

You may also wish to use an actual science *curriculum,* particularly if you feel you need more structure. We've listed a few options for those as well.

As you pursue the study of science, we recommend that you make use of three general methods.

Read, Narrate, Investigate Further

The process is simple: Read aloud to the child from the science encyclopedia or "spine." Ask her to narrate—to tell back to you in her own words two or three important facts that she's learned (see Chapter 5 for a description of the narration process). Write this narration down (or ask the child to write it, if her skills permit). If the child shows interest, go find additional library books on the topic. Read the books together. And if not, move on to the next topic.

Don't forget that you can stop at any time and dig deeper into a subject. Your goal is *not* to complete some sort of predetermined survey of the entire scientific field. If the child develops a sudden devouring interest in guinea pigs or volcanoes or how fire works, that's fine. Spend some time checking books out of the library, reading, doing more narrations, and allowing the student to draw pictures and illustrate her narration pages. We suggest that you keep all of the science narrations and pictures in a science notebook for easy reference.

This is an excellent first-exposure method: it introduces students to a whole range of topics, facts, and ideas that they might otherwise not know, allows them to practice putting the new knowledge into words, and gives them the chance to dig deeper as interest dictates. (However, as we explain in the sections that follow, you'll probably want to skip this step when doing chemistry and physics, since hands-on learning suits these areas better.)

Do Projects, Talk About Them

In the grammar stage, students do not do "experiments" (in the strict sense of the word). An experiment requires you to have a hypothesis—

some theory of what the outcome might be—and grammar-stage students don't have enough background information to hypothesize. Rather, you should aim to give them projects: hands-on explorations of the world.

A project is something you *do,* rather than something you simply read about.

A project can be looking at something (*really* looking at it, not just seeing what you already know is there) and describing it: a mosquito under a microscope, a cloud formation, a moving gear.

A project can be watching a science documentary together and then listing three things you learned that you didn't already know.

A project can be building a simple machine from blocks or Legos and explaining how it works.

A project can be collecting pine cones and pulling them apart to see what's inside.

A project can be watching the mother bird in the backyard and recording how often she leaves her nest, how long she's gone, and when she returns.

Measuring and recording rainfall over the period of a week is a project. So is setting out bread and recording how long it takes to grow mold, watching a meteor shower and making note of the seconds between each meteor sighting, making homemade slime and figuring out which ingredients make it slimy, creating a salt map of a tectonic plate.

Projects make science concrete, in the same way that manipulatives make math concrete. We've listed a number of project resources at the end of this chapter; pick and choose or devise your own. There's only one requirement: make some record of your project. For first and second graders, have the student tell you in two or three sentences what she learned, or what questions she still has. Write down her answer and have her read it back to you. Put the sentences in the science notebook.

For third and fourth grade, have the student complete a Project Page with brief answers to the following questions:

What Did We Use?
What Did We Do?
What Happened?
What Did We Learn?

(If the student is still struggling with the writing process, give all necessary help.)

These Project Pages will prepare the student for the writing of lab reports in the years to come, and will also serve as a record of projects completed.

(For chemistry and physics, you'll probably want to combine this method with the method that follows; see our more detailed explanations below.)

Ask Why, How, or What: Find the Answer

Ask a question that you don't know the answer to.

Why does a kite fly?
Why does a plane fly?
What falls faster, light objects or heavy objects?
Why does bread get moldy?
What is the most common tree in my neighborhood?
What's in that blue water we pour on flowers that helps them grow?
How do we know what's at the core of the earth?
What do the chambers of the heart really look like?
How does a microwave oven work?

Go check out books and do projects to help find the answer. Take as long as you need. When you've found an answer, record it using the following form:

Initial Question.
Resources We Consulted.
Projects We Did.
Our Answer.

Place the record in the science notebook.

When you're working with a grammar-stage student, it's important to ask a question that can be answered in terms of their very basic and concrete knowledge. So, ask "Does a large stone fall faster than a small stone?" (something that can be easily researched and then tested), not

"Why do large and small stones fall at the same rate?" (a question which requires you to tackle the principles of gravitational pull—which a few, but by no means all, elementary students will be ready for).

Get into the habit of asking *why, how,* and *what* as often as possible. Every time the student does a project or reads a book, think to yourself: Is there a question we can ask about this? A project involving the use of two different fertilizers on two plants to see which one works better leads to the question: What chemicals in the fertilizer are affecting the plants, and why? A book about dolphin behavior might lead to the question: How does dolphin hearing work?

Developing this habit is vital to thinking scientifically—which means not taking anything for granted. Like Aristotle, question the obvious. And at the point when you suddenly realize that *answering* the question is going to involve high-school level mathematics or an advanced grasp of physics, don't be afraid to discard the question, back up, and ask a more appropriate one. Trial and error is also part of science.

Note: Suggestions for how to balance all three methods can be found under "Sample Weekly Schedules," pages 207–208.

HOW TO DO LIFE SCIENCE: ANIMALS, HUMAN BEINGS, AND PLANTS

During the grammar-stage study of living things, you'll examine, describe, and explore animals, human beings, and plants.

For a basic text, choose one of the colorful, large-print guides to the natural world listed in the Resources, and use this as a jumping-off point for further readings, projects, and investigations. If you're spending the whole year on life science, divide your thirty-six-week school year into approximately twenty weeks on the animal kingdom, ten weeks on the human body, and the last six weeks (or so) on the plant kingdom. Keep those same proportions if you decide to cover life science in less time.

How to Read, Narrate, Investigate Further

Begin by reading the encyclopedia entry (usually one page) to the child, and then ask her to narrate the information back to you while you write.

Note: The best way to prompt a science narration at this level is to say, "Can you tell me two things that you learned about this animal?" or "What was the most interesting thing we read about this plant?"

Then, go to the library and browse through the juvenile science books. You'll find plenty of titles with colorful pictures and clear, simple text. Read a few of these titles together. You don't have to make a narration page for every book, but try to make a narration page from one out of three (or so) outside sources. The child can illustrate the narration pages with pictures she's drawn, photocopied, or cut out of magazines.

Place these pages in your science notebook.

How to Do Projects and Talk About Them

We've listed a number of different project resources in the Resources at the end of this chapter; remember to have first and second graders tell you two or three sentences about what they've done, and ask third and fourth graders to complete a Project Page.

But for life science, *outside observation* can also serve as a "project" for the study of animals and plants. For animals, go outside and hunt for worms, butterflies, or spiders. Put the specimens in a jar or bug-house. Ask the child to draw a picture of the specimen. Then, write down the answers to three or more of the following questions:

> *Does it have a backbone?*
> *Does it have fur?*
> *Does it have wings?*
> *What does its skin feel like?*
> *How many feet does it have? What do its feet look like?*
> *How many legs does it have? What do the legs look like?*
> *What does its body look like?*
> *What does it eat? Where does it live? How big is it?*
> *What do its babies look like?*
> *Is it domesticated (tamed by man) or wild?*
> *Is it endangered?*

For a worm observation, the questions and answers might look like this:

Does it have a backbone? The worm has no backbone.

Does it have fur? The worm has no fur.

Does it have wings? The worm has no wings.

What does its skin feel like? The skin feels soft and slimy.

How many feet does it have? What do its feet look like? The worm has no
feet.

How many legs does it have? What do the legs look like? The worm has no
legs.

What does its body look like? The body is round and soft, with segments.

What does it eat? The worm eats soil.

Where does it live? It lives in dirt all over the world.

How big is it? [Measure the worm.]

What do its babies look like? We don't know. [Where can we find out?]

Is it domesticated (tamed by man) or wild? [Have you ever seen a tame
worm?]

Is it endangered? [Ask the child how many earthworms she's seen. Are
they in any danger of disappearing from the earth?]

This process builds the habit of looking closely—the child is *observing*
the animal in an attempt to answer certain questions about it and is beginning to learn how to deduce from what she sees.

For plants, you can pursue the same basic procedure, with a heavy
emphasis on identifying trees from their leaves and bark and wildflowers
from their blooms. Don't feel that it's necessary to teach actual *classification*
unless the student shows an interest (the difference between monocoty-
ledons and dicotyledons is pretty abstract for most elementary students).
Concentrate on close observation of what can be seen.

A number of human body project resources are suggested at the end
of this chapter. You can also keep records of the student's (and family's)
heartbeat and respiration rates after different activities, make fingerprints
and examine them, record all food eaten over a certain period and compare
intake of protein/carbohydrate/fats/vegetables, chart physical activity,
watch documentaries about the body's function—or simply do an online
search for *human body study for kids* and use any of the myriad of activities
that pop up.

How to Ask Why, How, or What and Find the Answer

Now that you've observed, begin to ask questions about the structures of living things and how they work. What do worms do for the earth? How do they do it? How does a plant work? What is the function of roots and leaves, how do plants manufacture chlorophyll, what nutrients do they need to survive, how do trees help the earth? Now that you know where the heart is and what its structure is, ask: Why does it *beat*? How does the circulation of blood help the body? What is blood made of?

For the study of animals, concentrate on how animal anatomy affects behavior and survival. For plants, look at the structure of the plant, how it functions, and what it does for the surrounding area. And for the human body, ask: How does the body react to different situations? Why are organs located in certain parts of the body and not in others? And what is the *function* of those organs?

The project resources at the end of this chapter contain plenty of why, how, and what projects; use them to help discover and answer questions.

Once you find an answer, help the student to write down both the question and the answer.

A Word About Classification

The animal encyclopedias listed at the end of this chapter are organized alphabetically, not by classification. We think this is appropriate for the youngest students, who (in most cases) aren't yet ready to sort and classify the world; classification is more likely to benefit the middle-grade student who is moving into the logic stage of study. However, if you would prefer to group animals together by phylum, use this simple chart and study animals in the same phylum and class at the same time:

The Animal Kingdom

Phylum	Class	Animals
Mollusca		Octopus, squid, slug, snail
Annelida		Earthworm
Echinodermata		Starfish, ray
Cnidaria		Jellyfish

Chordates

	Amphibia	Frog and toad, newt, amphibian
	Reptilia	Lizard, all snakes, turtle and tortoise, alligator and crocodile, chameleon, komodo dragon and iguana
	Chondroichthyes	Shark
	Osteichthyes	Eel, salmon and trout, fish, goldfish, seahorse, swordfish
	Aves	All birds, chicken and turkey, duck and goose
	Mammalia	Aardvark, anteater, antelope, armadillo, baboon, badger, bat, bear, beaver, bison and musk ox, buffalo, camel, cat, chimpanzee, cow and bull, deer, dog, dolphin, donkey, elephant, elk, fox, giraffe, goat, gorilla, guinea pig, hedge-hog, hippopotamus, horse, hyena, kangaroo and wallaby, killer whale, koala, wombat and opossum, lemur, leopard, lion, llama, meerkat, mole, monkey, mouse, orangutan, otter, panda, pig, polar bear, porcupine, puma, rabbit and hare, raccoon, rat, reindeer, rhinoceros, sea cow, seal and sea lion, sheep, skunk, sloth, squirrel, tiger, walrus, weasel, whale, wolf, yak, zebra

Arthropoda

	Chilopoda	Centipede
	Arachnida	Spider, scorpion
	Insecta	Ant and termite, bee and wasp, beetle, butterfly and moth, cricket and grass-hopper, dragonfly and damselfly, fly

Crustacea
(subphylum of
arthropoda)

	Malacostraca	Crab, lobster and crayfish, shrimp and prawn

If you decide to introduce classification to the young student, you should begin by explaining what classification is. *Classification is organizing things into groups.* For an example, use types of stores: grocery stores, hardware stores, toy stores, and clothes stores all sell different kinds of things. Help the child think through the differences between groceries, hardware, toys, and clothes. Then explain that the *kingdoms* (animal and plant) are like stores for organizing different types of living things—animals and plants.

You can play this game with your house as well. Why do you keep certain things in the bedroom, certain things in the kitchen, and certain things in the living room? Each room can represent a kingdom, where different types of household items are kept.

Go on to explain that within each kingdom, things are divided into smaller groups. The grocery store is the food kingdom. But the grocery store doesn't just put all the food into one big heap—meat is in one place, cereal in another, fresh vegetables in another. Use your next grocery trip as a classification exercise, and see if the two of you can figure out why food is classified as it is: Why do eggs, milk, and cheese all belong together?

Once the child understands this concept, you can explain the different *groups* (phyla) within the animal kingdom. When you read the section on worms, explain that earthworms are in the annelid group because they have bodies divided into segments, but that flatworms belong to another group because they have no segments. Explain that insects have bodies divided into three parts (head, thorax, and abdomen), six legs, and wings; spiders, therefore, aren't insects because they have only two body parts (head and abdomen), eight legs, and no wings. (Don't worry—all this information is clearly laid out in the books we recommend.) As you make your narrative pages, try to note the group (phylum) to which each animal belongs. You'll probably want to begin each grouping by reading the topic page ("Mammal," "Insect," "Amphibian") that describes the phylum or class under study.

HOW TO DO EARTH SCIENCE
AND ASTRONOMY

Now that your child has studied life on earth, she's ready to move on to the study of the planet itself.

As with life science, we suggest that you use one of the encyclopedia resources listed at the end of this chapter as a "spine." Begin with earth science, and then move on to astronomy.

How to Read, Narrate, Investigate Further

Read a page of your "spine" text aloud to the student. Encourage him to begin to read portions of the text aloud to you, if he's able. After reading, ask him to narrate back to you what he's just heard; use the prompting questions "Can you tell me two or three things that you learned?" and "What was the most interesting thing we just read?" to encourage him. This narration should be written down and put in the science notebook. By second grade, some children may be ready to write down at least the first sentence of their own narrations.

Then do additional reading. Again, use library visits; we've recommended a few excellent earth and space titles in our Resources list, and a search of the library catalog will provide others. Aim to make a narration page for at least one additional source.

Remember: don't try to cover every detail on every page! Pick out the topics that excite your child. If he gets excited about volcanoes or the sun, let him spend weeks in the library, discovering everything he can. Don't hurry him along! *You are not giving the child an exhaustive course in earth science and astronomy.* The goal of classical education is to teach the student to *enjoy* investigation and learning. If you can successfully introduce him to astronomy, you'll find him checking out books about the planets and stars—and reading them on his own time.

How to Do Projects and Talk About Them

Activity and project resources are listed at the end of this chapter; more ideas can be found by searching online for earth science for kids and astronomy for kids. Earth science activities might involve digging in the dirt to examine its layers, investigating weather, collecting rocks, watching documentaries about volcanoes and earthquakes, and charting tides; astronomy projects might include charting the phases of the moon, making a sundial, building a model of the solar system, and (above all) stargazing.

Stargazing can be difficult in urban areas; if you're surrounded by light pollution, plan a nighttime trip out of the city and away from city lights. Most major cities have astronomy clubs that sponsor star parties, with telescopes set up and resident experts on hand. Watch for these in your local newspaper, or call your local museum and ask for information.

If the student shows interest, you can spend several weeks on the constellations and do notebook pages on the legends behind favorite constellations.

Continue to ask younger students to describe the finished project in two or three sentences; ask third and fourth graders to complete a Project Page.

How to Ask Why, How, or What and Find the Answer

Why do certain types of clouds form? What sort of weather do they produce? How does the moon affect the tides? Why does the sun appear to move in the sky? Once the student has *observed* (above), look a little deeper into each phenomenon. Remember to ask questions with *concrete* answers; it's easy, particularly in astronomy, to suddenly find yourself in very advanced territory. "How long does it take the light from Sirius to reach the earth?" is a question that can be answered with a little bit of basic research. "How do we measure electromagnetic radiation from the stars?" is better saved for later years of study.

Help the student write down the question and the answer.

HOW TO DO CHEMISTRY

Many elementary science texts ignore chemistry altogether, and although there are a number of good "chemistry for kids" books available, they are written at the logic-stage level and above. So instead of trying to follow the three-step investigation described above (read and narrate, do projects and talk about them, then ask why) we suggest that you go straight to doing projects *and* asking why. Essentially, beginning chemistry combines the methods of doing projects and talking about them, and asking why/how/what, into a single activity-focused study.

We also suggest that you save chemistry for third or fourth grade, so that students can record each activity on a Project Page. The questions on the Project Page:

What Did We Use?
What Did We Do?
What Happened?
What Did We Learn?

are particularly useful for chemistry.

In the elementary grades, chemistry "experiments" are simply activities that teach the principles of chemistry in a hands-on way. (We have recommended several good resources at the end of this chapter.) Choose an experiment, carry it out together, and have the student complete the Project Page. This serves as the first part of the chemistry lesson.

Then, have the student look up each chemical term encountered during the experiment in a science encyclopedia. She should then make a Definition Page that contains the term (or terms), its definition, and a drawing or diagram that makes the term clear.

For example, the child might investigate molecular movement by using food coloring and a glass of water. He'll observe colored molecules spreading through the clear molecules of water, and then complete a Project Page, which will look something like this:

Project Page:
Do Molecules Move?

What Did We Use? We used food coloring and a glass of water.

What Did We Do? We dropped one drop of food coloring into the water and did not move the glass.

What Happened? The color spread out through the water even though the glass was still.

What Did We Learn? This showed us that the molecules in the water were moving.

The student has now learned from experimentation a basic principle of chemistry: molecules are in constant motion. He should then look up the definition of *molecule* in one of the recommended science encyclopedias, and make a Definition Page with a brief definition of a molecule and one or two simple drawings of different molecules.

Some experiments will contain multiple terms that need defining. An experiment with yeast that explores whether molecules can be broken into smaller molecules might include the terms *enzymes, yeast,* and *fermentation.* After doing the experiment, the child writes *enzyme* on a blank notebook page, along with the definition in the book: "Enzymes are complex molecules made by living organisms." When he looks up *enzymes* in the appropriate *Science Encyclopedia,* he will find a fuller explanation plus diagrams and pictures. With your help, he uses this information to make his notebook page and then places it in Definitions. He should do the same with the next two terms. Stretch the assignment out over as many days as necessary if the child is a slow writer.

Put the Project Page and the Definition Page into the student's science notebook.

On the one hand, we wish all this information had been published neatly in one book; on the other, the child is practicing how to look up and record information—a very scientific endeavor. Even if you're science-challenged, don't worry—all the recommended texts are written in plain, easy-to-understand language with lots of pictures.

HOW TO DO PHYSICS

Chemistry is the study of the way molecules react to each other to form different substances. Physics is the study of how those substances act in the universe.

Physics is simply the study of the physical world and how it works. The way sound travels, magnetism, the laws of electricity, energy, and motion—these are the concepts of physics.

Like basic chemistry, elementary physics should be activity focused. (See the Resources list at the end of this chapter.) After doing an "experiment" (for example, investigating friction by rubbing two blocks of wood against each other and then repeating the action after covering the blocks with soap or Vaseline), the student should fill out a Project Page:

Project Page:

Friction

What Did We Use? We used two blocks of wood and a bar of soap.

What Did We Do? We rubbed the blocks together. Then we coated the blocks with soap and rubbed them together again.

What Happened? The blocks were much easier to move when they were coated with soap.

What Did We Learn? The soap covered the surface of the wood so that the blocks didn't actually touch each other. This reduced the friction between them.

Then, she should complete the lesson by making a Definition Page: looking up *friction* in one of the recommended science encyclopedias and writing a brief (two- to three-sentence) explanation.

As with chemistry, we suggest saving physics for third grade or above.

HOW TO DO TECHNOLOGY

If you'd like to add technology to these basic fields of science, use one of the resources listed at the end of this chapter and follow the same basic procedure described for physics.

SUGGESTED SCHEDULES

Sample Yearly Schedules

Consider using one of the schedules suggested below:

Grade	Topic(s)
First grade	Animal kingdom (20 weeks)
2 times per week	Human body (10 weeks)
	Plant kingdom (6 weeks)
Second grade	Astronomy (18 weeks)
2 times per week	Earth science (18 weeks)

Third grade 3 times per week	Chemistry OR Physics (18 weeks) Technology (18 weeks)
Fourth grade 3 times per week	Chemistry OR Physics (18 weeks) Technology (18 weeks)

Grade	Topic(s)
First grade 2 times per week	Animal kingdom (12 weeks) Human body (6 weeks) Plant kingdom (4 weeks) Earth science (14 weeks
Second grade 2 times per week	Astronomy (10 weeks) Chemistry (10 weeks) Physics (10 weeks) Technology (6 weeks)
Third grade 3 times per week	Animal kingdom (12 weeks) Human body (6 weeks) Plant kingdom (4 weeks) Earth science (14 weeks
Fourth grade 3 times per week	Astronomy (10 weeks) Chemistry (10 weeks) Physics (10 weeks) Technology (6 weeks)

Grade	Topic(s)
First grade 2 times per week	Earth science (5 weeks) Astronomy (5 weeks) Animal kingdom (6 weeks) Human body (5 weeks) Plant kingdom (5 weeks) Chemical reactions (5 weeks) Physics (5 weeks)
Second grade 2 times per week	Same topics at greater depth

Third and fourth grades   Same topics at greater depth
3 times per week

Sample Weekly Schedules

You can arrange your weekly schedule in many different ways. Pick one of these methods as a base:

Alternating Weeks
    Week One: Read, narrate, investigate further.
    Week Two: Do a project and talk about it.
    Week Three: Ask a question about the reading and projects; answer it
        together.
    Repeat three-week sequence

Alternating Days
First and second grades:
    Week One
        Day One: Read and narrate.
            Make a narration page.
        Day Two: Do a project, talk about it.
            Make a project page.
    Week Two
        Day One: Read additional books.
            Make one more narration page.
        Day Two: Ask a question; answer it together.
            Record the question and the answer.
Third and fourth grades:
    Week One
        Day One: Read and narrate.
            Make a narration page.
        Day Two: Investigate additional books.
            Make one more narration page.
        Day Three: Begin a project.
    Week Two
        Day One: Finish the project.
            Make a project page.

Day Two: Ask a question and begin to answer it.
Day Three: Finish answering the question.
　　Record the question and the answer.

When doing chemistry and physics, alternate doing experiments and project pages, and looking up definitions and making definition pages.

Be guided by the student's interest; allow reading, projects, and asking/answering questions to flow into additional days as needed. Some topics will lend themselves to additional reading; others to more involved projects that take multiple days to complete. Some questions can be answered with a single day's work; others may take two or three days or even more.

Remember: The goal is to practice *doing science* and to *cultivate enthusiasm, not* to cover a certain amount of material each year!

RESOURCES

Most books can be obtained from any bookseller or library; most curricula can be bought directly from the publisher or from a major home-school supplier such as Rainbow Resource Center. Contact information for publishers and suppliers can be found at www.welltrainedmind.com. If availability is limited, we have noted it. Where indicated, resources are listed in chronological order (the order you'll want to use them in). Books in series are listed together. Remember that additional curricula choices and more can be found at www.welltrainedmind. com. Prices change constantly, but we have included 2016 pricing to give an idea of affordability.

Basic Texts ("Spines")

Any of these resources can help organize your study and serve as a jumping-off point for further investigation.

For project, activity, and experiment resources, see the supplemental lists that follow.

Life Science
Carlson, Laurie. *Green Thumbs: A Kid's Activity Guide to Indoor and Outdoor Gardening*. Chicago: Chicago Review Press, 1995.

$14.95. Although not an exhaustive guide to the plant kingdom, this project book explains the basic facts about seeds, plants, and trees, and offers both inside and outside gardening projects. Combine with supplementary readings and activities for an engaging introduction to botany.

DK First Animal Encyclopedia, reissue ed. New York: DK Children, 2015.
$16.99. Excellent for first- and second-grade study. Don't try to cover the whole book; choose from the available topics. Plan on covering one topic (one page) per week, along with additional reading (and if the child develops a passion for armadillos or rattlesnakes, don't hold yourself to this schedule). You might want to read through the table of contents with your student and allow her to pick the animals that she wants to study.

DK First Human Body Encyclopedia. New York: DK Children, 2005.
$16.99. Ideal for first and second graders. Don't try to cover the whole book; pick your favorite topics.

Human Body: A Visual Encyclopedia. New York: DK Publishing, 2012.
$24.99. Well suited to third grade and above, this beautifully illustrated encyclopedia covers the body systems in more detail than the *First Human Body* book.

Spelman, Lucy. *National Geographic Animal Encyclopedia.* Washington, DC: National Geographic Children's Books, 2012.
$24.95. Excellent for third grade and above: 2,500 animals with amazing photographs, clear text, and maps.

Earth Science

First Earth Encyclopedia. New York: DK Children, 2010.
$16.99. A good introduction to the study of the earth. Simple reading level for grades 1–3.

Woodward, John. *Geography: A Visual Encyclopedia.* New York: DK Publishing, 2013.
$19.99. Developed in cooperation with the Smithsonian Institute, this heavily illustrated reference work covers the major topics in earth science (the planet's structure, rocks and minerals, oceans, weather, etc.) as well as topics in geography and culture. Best for grades 3 and up.

Astronomy

Dickinson, Terence. *Exploring the Night Sky: The Equinox Astronomy Guide for Beginners.* Camden East, ON: Camden House, 1987.

$9.95. An illustrated paperback guide to the stars that begins in our solar system and travels out into the universe. Good for grades 3-4, although you will want to simplify some of the text.

Hughes, Catherine D. *National Geographic Kids First Big Book of Space.* Washington, DC: National Geographic Children's Books, 2012.

$14.95. For first- and second-grade students, a colorful and well-organized guide to the solar system, our galaxy, and the universe beyond.

Thompson, C. E. *Glow-in-the-Dark Constellations: A Field Guide for Young Stargazers,* illus. Randy Chewning. New York: Grosset & Dunlap, 1999.

$8.99. Brief retellings of the legends behind the constellations, descriptions and diagrams of each constellation, and, across from each diagram, a glow-in-the-dark picture of the sky so that you can practice finding a constellation in the dark before you go outside.

Chemistry

Heinecke, Liz Lee. *Kitchen Science Lab for Kids: 52 Family Friendly Experiments from Around the House.* Beverly, MA: Quarry Books, 2014.

$24.99. Basic chemical reactions, crystals, polymers, colloids, acids, bases, and more, all with common ingredients.

VanCleave, Janice. *Janice VanCleave's Chemistry For Every Kid: 101 Easy Experiments That Really Work.* New York: John Wiley & Sons, 1989.

$14.95. Simple and fun experiments illuminating the nature of matter, forces, gases, changes, solutions, acids and bases.

Physics

Hodge, Deborah. *Starting with Science: Simple Machines.* Tonawanda, NY: Kids Can Press, 1998.

$7.95. Thirteen experiments with levers, wheels and axles, pulleys, inclined planes, wedges and screws; combine with another resource to create a physics spine.

Mandell, Muriel. *Physics Experiments for Children.* New York: Dover, 1968.

$6.95. One hundred and thirteen experiments divided into seven chapters: Matter: Air; Matter: Water; Mechanical Energy and Machines; Heat; Sound; Light; and Magnetism and Electricity. There's a fair amount of overlap between the experiments, so you can eliminate those that call for materials not found around your house, since one or two of the experiments use items more common in the 1950s than today (a medicine bottle sealed with a cork?).

Osborne, Louise. *Starting With Science: Solids, Liquids, and Gases.* Tonawanda, NY: Kids Can Press, 1995.

$7.95. Thirteen experiments with matter in all three states; combine with another resource to create a physics spine.

VanCleave, Janice. *Janice VanCleave's Physics For Every Kid: 101 Easy Experiments in Motion, Heat, Light, Machines, and Sound.* New York: John Wiley & Sons, 2009.

$14.95. Simple and fun experiments with electricity, magnets, buoyancy, gravity, balance, simple machines, inertia, motion, light, heat, and sound.

Technology

Macaulay, David, and Neil Ardley. *The New Way Things Work,* rev. ed. Boston: HMH, 1998.

$35. A massive and fascinating book that will provide the curious with months of additional exploration, this book groups machines together by the principles that make them run. Gears, sound, magnetism, computer technology, and much, much more.

General Reference Encyclopedias

Use for definitions while studying chemistry and physics, and for general reference for all fields of science

DK First Science Encyclopedia. New York: DK Children, 2008.

$16.99. Written for grades 1–3, this contains simply written entries on major topics in life science, physical science, elementary chemistry, and earth and space science.

The Kingfisher Science Encyclopedia, 3rd ed. New York: Kingfisher, 2011.

$34.99. The most detailed and useful of the encyclopedias, written for fourth grade and above (too difficult for first- and second-grade students).

The New Children's Encyclopedia. New York: DK Children, 2013.
$19.99. For grades 3–6; more detail, slightly more difficult reading level than the First Science encyclopedia. Covers life science, basic chemistry, and physical forces as well as topics in history.

Formal Curricula

Some parents may prefer to use a developed curriculum rather than following the exploratory methods described in this chapter. The following programs are compatible with our approach, but consider supplementing with additional books, projects, and narration assignments.

Elemental Science. Wytheville, VA: Elemental Science, 2014.
Developed by a science-oriented home-schooling parent, the Elemental Science series loosely follows our recommendations for hands-on experimentation, supplemental outside reading, and narration pages. Lesson plans and plenty of teacher support. View samples at the publisher's website. Each set is one full year of study.

Biology for the Grammar Stage.
Teacher Guide. $21.99.
Student Workbook. $19.49.
Coloring Pages. $6.50.
Experiment Kit. $45.99.

Earth Science & Astronomy for the Grammar Stage.
Teacher Guide. $21.99.
Student Workbook. $19.49.
Coloring Pages. $5.
Experiment Kit. $45.99.

Chemistry for the Grammar Stage.
(Requires purchase or library use of additional books; see the publisher's website for details.)
Teacher's Guide & Student Workbook Combo. $28.99.
Experiment Kit. $60.99.

Physics for the Grammar Stage.
> (Requires purchase or library use of additional books; see the publisher's website for details.)
> Teacher's Guide & Student Workbook Combo. $28.99.
> Experiment Kit. $55.99.

Great Science Adventures, by Dinah Zike and Susan Simpson. Melrose, FL: Common Sense Press.
> As students progress through the lessons, they cut, fold, draw, and glue paper handouts into mini-books and construct paper models. The program is designed for teaching students of different ages together; each lesson provides three different projects on three different levels of difficulty. Most elementary students would do only the first and easiest project; some may be ready to progress to the second. The program is well organized and interesting, but it may frustrate students (and parents) who don't like to cut and paste. Order from Common Sense Press. Each book is $24, provides twenty-four lessons, and should take eight to twelve weeks to complete. Supplement with experiments and outside reading. Samples can be viewed at the publisher's website.
>> *Discovering the Human Body and Senses* (life science)
>> *The World of Insects and Arachnids* (life science)
>> *The World of Vertebrates* (life science)
>> *The World of Plants* (life science)
>> *Discovering Earth's Landforms and Surface Features* (earth science)
>> *Discovering the Ocean* (earth science)
>> *The World of Space* (astronomy)
>> *Discovering Atoms, Molecules, and Matter* (chemistry)
>> *The World of Light and Sound* (physics)
>> *The World of Tools and Technology* (technology)

R.E.A.L. Science Odyssey. Mount Dora, FL: Pandia Press.
> Developed for use by home-schooling parents and small classrooms, R.E.A.L. Science emphasizes hands-on learning. The elementary levels begin with a read-aloud lesson, followed by "lab" activities that are intended to teach the basics of the scientific method along with developing skills in close observation and recording findings. Each level is one full year of science. Student and instructor pages are bound together

into the books; additional supplies are necessary. Samples and supply lists can be viewed at the publisher's website. Cheaper ebook versions are also available.

Life, Level One. $68.

Earth & Space, Level One. $68.

Chemistry, Level One. $68.

Supplementary Resources

Life Science

Animals

Audubon, J. J., and Paul E. Kennedy. *Audubon Birds of America Coloring Book.* New York: Dover, 1974.

$3.99. Includes instructive captions and color pictures on the inside covers.

Bernath, Stefen. *Tropical Fish Coloring Book.* New York: Dover, 1978.

$3.99. Includes instructive captions and color pictures on the inside covers.

Green, John. *Birds of Prey Coloring Book.* New York: Dover, 1989.

$3.99. Includes instructive captions and color pictures on the inside covers.

——. *Horses of the World Coloring Book.* New York: Dover, 1985.

$3.95. Includes instructive captions and color pictures on the inside covers.

——. *Wild Animals Coloring Book.* New York: Dover, 1987.

$3.95. Includes instructive captions and color pictures on the inside covers.

Grow-A-Frog Kit.

$24.95. Order from Young Explorers. Raise a live hybrid frog with transparent skin (so that you can see its internal organs)!

National Audubon Society Pocket Guides. New York: Knopf.

If you're able to go out and search for wildlife while making your life-science notebook, consider the National Audubon Society Pocket Guides.

These are full of beautiful, clear color photographs with full descriptions; too difficult for six-year-olds, but a wonderful parent resource. Most libraries carry the field guides, or you can buy them through any bookstore.

> *Familiar Birds of North America: Eastern Region.* 1987. $11.95.
> *Familiar Birds of North America: Western Region.* 1987. $10.95
> *Familiar Insects and Spiders of North America.* 1988. $10.95.
> *Familiar Reptiles and Amphibians of North America.* 1988. $10.95

Quirk, Thomas C., Jr. *Reptiles and Amphibians Coloring Book.* New York: Dover, 1981.

> $4.99. Includes instructive captions and color pictures on the inside covers.

Rookie Read-About Science Series. San Francisco, CA: Children's Book Press.

> $4.95–$5.95 each. This beginning-reader series is heavily illustrated and has very brief, large-print text on each page. Excellent for encouraging young readers!
>
> Fowler, Allan. *The Chicken or the Egg?* 1993.
> ———. *Life in a Tide Pool.* 1997.
> ———. *These Birds Can't Fly.* 1999.
> Herrington, Lisa M. *Frogs and Toads.* 2015.
> ———. *It's a Good Thing There Are Spiders.* 2014.
> Mattern, Joanne. *It's a Good Thing There Are Ladybugs.* 2014.

Sovak, Jan. *Butterflies Coloring Book.* New York: Dover, 1992.

> $4.99. Includes instructive captions and color pictures on the inside covers.

———. *Insects Coloring Book.* New York: Dover, 1994.

> $4.99. Includes instructive captions and color pictures on the inside covers.

———. *Snakes of the World Coloring Book.* New York: Dover, 1995.

> $4.99. Order from Rainbow Resource Center. Includes instructive captions and color pictures on the inside covers.

TOPS Learning Systems Activities (Life). Watsonville, CA: TOPS Learning Systems.

> Developed by a science educator, TOPS lessons use simple materials and

emphasize inquiry, discovery, and experimentation. Extensive samples can be viewed at the publisher's website. For grades 3 and above.

 Animal Survival. Twenty activities centered around animal adaptability and survival. $18.

Human Beings

My First Skeleton (Tiny Tim). Baltimore, MD: Anatomical Chart Company (Lippincott, Williams & Wilkins).

 $24.96. A fully assembled 16½-inch plastic human skeleton on a stand with a moveable jaw and detachable limbs.

Cole, Joanna. *The Magic School Bus: Inside the Human Body.* New York: Scholastic, 1990.

 $6.99. A trip through all the major parts of the body!

Colombo, Luann. *Uncover the Human Body.* San Diego, CA: Silver Dolphin Books, 2003.

 $18.95. The thick pages allow you to construct and deconstruct a human body, one system at a time.

Hands On Lab. Torrance, CA: Artec-Educational.

 Order from the publisher. Fun hands-on project resources with study guides. For all elementary students.

 Build Your Own Internal Organs. $9.99.

 Cells of Life. $12.99. Build models of animal and plant cells.

 Model Eye with Liquid Lens. $14.99. Reproduces the inside of the eye; change lens from concave to convex and see the difference.

Human Anatomy Floor Puzzle. Wilton, CT: Melissa & Doug.

 $13. This 4-foot-tall two-sided floor puzzle has the skeletal system on the front and other body systems on the reverse.

Rookie Read-About Science Series. San Francisco, CA: Children's Press.

 $4.95–5.95 each. This beginning-reader series is heavily illustrated and has very brief, large-print text on each page. Excellent for encouraging young readers!

 Curry, Don L. *How Do Your Lungs Work?* 2004.

 ———. *How Does Your Brain Work?* 2004.

Fowler, Allan. *Arms and Legs and Other Limbs.* 1999.

———. *Knowing About Noses.* 1999.

———. *A Look at Teeth.* 2000.

Somebody: Five Human Anatomy Games. Plainwell, MI: Talicor-Aristoplay.
$30. Play five different games of increasing complexity with this body-parts game—wonderful for teaching anatomy as well as organ function.

Plants

Arbel, Ilil. *Favorite Wildflowers Coloring Book.* New York: Dover, 1991.
$4.99. Includes instructive captions and color pictures on the inside covers.

Bernath, Stefen. *Garden Flowers Coloring Book.* New York: Dover, 1975.
$4.99. Includes instructive captions and color pictures on the inside covers.

Hands On Lab. Torrance, CA: Artec-Educational.
Order from the publisher. Fun hands-on project resources with study guides. For all elementary students. $9.99 each.

Anatomy of a Plant. Ten different experiments illuminating plant structure.

Photosynthesis in a Tube. Watch the process happening.

Roots & Shoots. Clear tank allows students to observe root growth.

Sprout Garden. See how different conditions (air quality, sunlight, gravity, etc.) affect plant growth.

National Audubon Society Pocket Guides. New York: Knopf.
If you're able to go out and search for plants while making your life-science notebook, consider the National Audubon Society Pocket Guides. These are full of beautiful, clear color photographs with full descriptions; too difficult for six-year-olds, but a wonderful parent resource. Most libraries carry the Pocket Guides, or you can buy them through any bookstore.

Familiar Flowers of North America. 1987. $10.95.

Familiar Mushrooms. 1990. $11.95.

Familiar Trees of North America: East. 1987. $10.95.

Familiar Trees of North America: West. 1987. $10.95.

Rookie Read-About Science Series. San Francisco, CA.: Children's Press.
$4.95 each. Order from any bookstore or check your library; many can also be ordered from Rainbow Resource Center. This beginning-reader series is heavily illustrated and has very brief, large-print text on each page. Excellent for encouraging young readers!

Fowler, Allan. *Cactuses.* 2002.

———. *It's a Fruit, It's a Vegetable, It's a Pumpkin.* 1996.

———. *Pine Trees.* 2002.

———. *Plants That Eat Animals.* 2001.

Herrington, Lisa M. *Seed to Plant.* 2014.

Robinson, Fay. *Vegetables, Vegetables!* 1995.

Soffer, Ruth. *Coral Reef Coloring Book.* New York: Dover, 1995.
$4.99. Includes instructive captions and color pictures on the inside covers.

TOPS Learning Systems Activities (Life). Watsonville, CA: TOPS Learning Systems.
Developed by a science educator, TOPS lessons use simple materials and emphasize inquiry, discovery, and experimentation. Extensive samples can be viewed at the publisher's website. For grades 3 and above.

Green Thumbs: Radishes. Twenty activities all using easy-to-grow radish sprouts: understanding plant structure, experimenting with light and soil, the effects of gravity, and much more. $18.

Earth Science and Astronomy
Earth Science

Burns, T. D. *Rocks and Minerals.* New York: Dover, 1995.
$4.99. This is a high-quality coloring book with instructive captions and color illustrations on the inside covers.

Cole, Joanna. *The Magic School Bus Inside the Earth,* illus. Bruce Degen. New York: Scholastic, 1989.
$6.99.

Hands On Lab. Torrance, CA: Artec-Educational.
Order from the publisher. Fun hands-on project resources with study guides. For all elementary students.

Home Volcano. $12.99. Measure ash distribution, watch a magma chamber erupt, and more.

Planet Anatomy. $9.99. Make a model of the earth and its layers.

Shiny Earth Balls. $12.99. Investigate soil, rocks, and minerals.

Weather Watcher. $12.99. Basic projects in meteorology.

Rocks and Minerals of the U.S. Collection.

Order from Rainbow Resource Center. These are the most economical rock collections around and include study guides.

$31.50. Basic Collection, 35 pieces.

$22.80. Reference Collection, 24 pieces.

Rookie Read-About Science series. San Francisco, CA: Children's Press.

$4.95 each. Order from any bookstore or check your library. This beginning-reader series is heavily illustrated and has very brief, large-print text on each page. Excellent for encouraging young readers!

Fowler, Allan. *All the Colors of the Rainbow.* 1999.

———. *Icebergs, Ice Caps, and Glaciers.* 1998.

———. *The Top and Bottom of the World.* 1997.

———. *What's the Weather Today?* 1992.

Mara, Wil. *The Four Oceans.* 2005.

Robinson, Fay. *Where Do Puddles Go?* 1995.

Science in a Nutshell series. Nashua, NH: Delta Education.

$45. Order from Delta Education. These kits provide a complete science experiment and activity center, designed for grades 2–6. Consider sharing the cost with a neighbor, since the kits provide materials for two or three students.

Fossil Formations. The kit includes six actual fossil samples, sand, plaster of Paris, modeling clay, an activity guide, and a journal.

Rock Origins. Investigate the origins of twenty-two rock and mineral samples; includes actual samples.

Simon, Seymour.

$6.99. Simon's elementary science books, available through libraries and bookstores, have spectacular photographs and easy-to-follow text, written on a third- to fourth-grade reading level.

Earthquakes. New York: HarperCollins, 2006.

Hurricanes. New York: HarperCollins, 2007.

Icebergs and Glaciers. New York: HarperCollins, 1999.

Lightning. New York: HarperCollins, 2006.

Mountains. New York: HarperCollins, 1997.

Oceans. New York: HarperCollins, 2006.

Storms. New York: HarperCollins, 1992.

Tornadoes. New York: HarperCollins, 2001.

Volcanoes. New York: HarperCollins, 2006.

Weather. New York: HarperCollins, 2006.

Astronomy

Cole, Joanna. *The Magic School Bus: Lost in the Solar System*. New York: Scholastic, 1992.
  $6.99.

Hands On Lab. Torrance, CA: Artec-Educational.
  Order from the publisher. Fun hands-on project resources with study guides. For all elementary students.
    Planet Engineer. $9.99. Construct a planet in our solar system—or invent your own.
    World Time Sundial. $9.99. Build a sundial that can tell the time in any country.

Ghez, Andrea Mia, and Judith Love Cohen. *You Can Be a Woman Astronomer*, illus. David Katz. New York: Cascade Press, 1995.
  $6. Dr. Ghez has extensive experience in astronomy, ranging from a stint at a Chilean observatory to work on the Hubble Space Telescope. This title is one of a series depicting real women in science and math careers.

Lafontaine, Bruce. *Constellations in the Night Sky*. New York: Dover, 2003.
  $4.99. A coloring book of the constellations.

Rey, H. A. *The Stars: A New Way to See Them*, 2nd ed. New York: HMH, 2008.
  $11.99. The author of *Curious George* provides a way to picture the constellations that is much simpler than the classic drawings of Greek myths. Text is written for the middle grades and up, but the drawings are worth looking at with younger students.

Rookie Read-About Science series. San Francisco, CA: Children's Press.
$4.95 each. Order from any bookstore or check your library. This begin-

ning-reader series is heavily illustrated and has very brief, large-print text on each page. Excellent for encouraging young readers!

Bullock, Linda. *Looking Through a Telescope*. 2004.

Fowler, Allan. *Energy from the Sun*. 1998.

———. *So That's How the Moon Changes Shape!* 1992.

———. *The Sun's Family of Planets*. 2002.

———. *When You Look Up at the Moon*. 1994.

Simon, Seymour.
$7.99 each. Simon's elementary science books, available through libraries and bookstores, have spectacular photographs and easy-to-follow text, written on a first- to third-grade reading level. Some are available as ebooks.

Comets, Meteors, and Asteroids. HarperCollins, 1998.

Destination: Jupiter. New York: HarperCollins, 2000.

Destination: Mars. New York: HarperCollins, 2004.

Destination: Space. HarperCollins, 2006.

Galaxies. New York: HarperCollins, 1991.

Saturn. New York: HarperCollins, 1988.

Stars. New York: HarperCollins, 2006.

The Sun. New York: HarperCollins, 1989.

The Universe. New York: HarperCollins, 2006.

Uranus. New York: HarperCollins, 1990.

Venus. New York: HarperCollins, 1998.

Solar System Floor Puzzle. Wilton, CT: Melissa & Doug.
$13. Order from Fat Brain Toys. A 2×3-foot floor puzzle of the solar system and asteroid belt.

Solar System: Glow in the Dark. San Francisco, CA: Great Explorations.
$24. Order from Fat Brain Toys. Nine glow-in-the-dark planets, 200 glow-in-the-dark stars, and supplies to turn them into a mobile.

Star Theater Home Planetarium. Agoura Hills, CA: Uncle Milton Toys.
$30.95. Order from Home Science Tools. Project constellations onto the walls and ceiling of a dark room; learn the position of the major stars and constellations throughout the year.

Chemistry

Atom Chartlet.

$2.49. Order from Rainbow Resource Center. A 17 × 22-inch chart showing the parts of an atom.

Fizzy Foamy Science. Seattle, WA: Scientific Explorer.

$19.95. Safe kit of acids and bases and a set of experiments that foam and bubble.

Hands On Lab. Torrance, CA: Artec-Educational.

Order from the publisher. Fun hands-on project resources with study guides. For all elementary students.

Fun With Polymers. $12.99. Investigate the properties of polymers.

Marvelous Molecules. $12.99. Build models of atoms and a variety of molecules.

Unmixables: Water and Oil. $12.99. Experiment with the properties of both.

The Magic School Bus Slime, Gel & Goop Science Kit.

$19.95. Order from Home Science Tools. Transform liquids into solids, experiment with polymers, grow gel crystals.

My First Chemistry Kit. Seattle, WA: Scientific Explorer.

$21. Order from Fat Brain Toys. A chemistry set and microscope designed especially for elementary students.

Rock Candy Crystal Growing Experiment Kit.

$16.95. Order from Home Science Tools. Grow large crystals within a week; all ingredients included.

Rookie Read-About Science series. San Francisco, CA: Children's Press.

$4.95 each. Order from any bookstore or check your library. This beginning-reader series is heavily illustrated and has very brief, large-print text on each page. Excellent for encouraging young readers!

Garrett, Ginger. *Solids, Liquids, and Gases.* 2005.

Trumbauer, Lisa. *What Are Atoms?* 2005.

Science Wiz Chemistry Kit.

$21.99. Order from Home Science Tools. Thirty activities; some items (wax, test tubes, sand, etc.) provided, others make use of common household items.

Physics

Hands On Lab. Torrance, CA: Artec-Educational.

Order from the publisher. Fun hands-on project resources with study guides. For all elementary students.

Light Rays: Reflection and Refraction. $12.99.

Moving Heat. $14.99. Multiple experiments exploring the properties of heat.

Pendulums and Collisions. $12.99. Build Newton's Cradle and more.

Pulley Systems. $12.99. Moving pulleys, compound pulleys, and systems.

Sound Waves: Frequency and Pitch. $9.99.

Waves in Motion. $14.99. View waves with LED lights and more.

Our Amazing Bridges Architecture Kit. Plymouth, MI: Poof-Slinky, Inc.

$20. Order from Fat Brain Toys. Slightly more difficult than the other kits listed, but appropriate for fourth graders interested in the physics of bridges; build three different model bridges.

Science in a Nutshell series. Nashua, NH: Delta Education.

$45. Order from Delta Education. These kits provide a complete science experiment and activity center, designed for grades 2–6. Consider sharing the cost with a neighbor, since the kits provide materials for two or three students.

Bubble Science.

Variables affecting the size, shape, color, and durability of bubbles.

Charge It! Static Electricity.

Positive and negative charges, static electricity.

Electrical Connections.

Simple and complex circuits, current, batteries.

Energy and Motion.

Stored energy, motion; weights, marbles, and ramps.

Gears at Work.

Gear systems and interaction.

Magnet Magic.

Magnetic materials, polar strength.

Sound Vibrations.

Sound waves and their interaction with various materials.

Work: Plane and Simple.

Inclined planes; force and friction.

Rookie Read-About Science series. San Francisco, CA: Children's Press. $4.95 each. Order from any bookstore or check your library. This beginning-reader series is heavily illustrated and has very brief, large-print text on each page. Excellent for encouraging young readers!

Barkan, Joanne. *What Is Density?* 2006.

———. *What Is Velocity?* 2005.

Bullock, Linda. *You Can Use a Balance.* 2004.

Curry, Don L. *What Is Mass?* 2005.

———. *What is Matter?* 2005.

Fowler, Allan. *Simple Machines.* 2001.

———. *What Magnets Can Do.* 1995.

Murphy, Patricia J. *Push and Pull.* 2002.

Stewart, Melissa. *Energy in Motion.* 2006.

Trumbauer, Lisa. *All About Light.* 2004.

———. *All About Sound.* 2004.

———. *What Is Electricity?* 2004.

———. *What Is Friction?* 2004.

———. *What Is Gravity?* 2004.

———. *What Is Volume?* 2006.

Young, June. *Energy Is Everywhere.* 2006.

TOPS Learning Systems Activities (Physics I). Watsonville, CA: TOPS Learning Systems.

Developed by a science educator, TOPS lessons use simple materials and emphasize inquiry, discovery, and experimentation. Extensive samples can be viewed at the publisher's website. For grades 3 and above.

Diving Into Pressure and Buoyancy. Fourteen activities involving displacement, volume, Archimedes' principles, etc. Downloadable PDF from publisher's website. $7.50.

Electricity. Twenty activities based on building elementary circuits. $18.

Magnetism. Twenty activities using mapping and graphing of fields and construction of basic machines. $18.

Perfect Balance. Twenty activities exploring mass and weight. $18.

9

DEAD LANGUAGES FOR LIVE KIDS: LATIN (AND OTHER LANGUAGES STILL LIVING)

Docendo discitur.[1]
—Seneca

SUBJECT: **Latin and other foreign languages**
TIME REQUIRED: **2 ½–4 hours per week, beginning in third or fourth grade.**

As you've no doubt noticed, we don't consider Latin to be the defining element of a classical education. Classical education has to do with setting up solid foundations, with learning how to learn, with mental discipline and intellectual curiosity and a willingness to grapple with the lessons of the past. All of this is much more important than a single foreign-language course.

But you should still study Latin.

[1] "One learns by teaching" (something you'll have the opportunity to do as you go through Latin with your third grader).

Elementary students are perfectly capable of beginning Latin. In third and fourth grade, the students do basic memory work (vocabulary and parts of speech), work on English derivations from Latin words, and study elementary Latin grammar.

At the end of this chapter, we'll recommend systematic, easy-to-follow Latin courses that you can teach to your third- or fourth-grade child. And you'll have the opportunity to learn along with him.

WHY LATIN?

Why bother with Latin? It is, after all, a dead language (a pejorative phrase)—no literature is being produced in it, no one's speaking it or doing business in it.

We bother with it for a number of reasons.

Latin trains the mind to think in an orderly fashion. Latin (being dead) is the most systematic language around. The discipline of assembling endings and arranging syntax (grammar patterns) according to sets of rules is the mental equivalent of a daily two-mile jog. And because Latin demands precision, the Latin-trained mind becomes accustomed to paying attention to detail, a habit that will pay off—especially when studying math and science.

Latin improves English skills. The grammatical structure of English is based on Latin, as is about 50 percent of English vocabulary. The student who understands how Latin works is rarely tripped up by complicated English syntax or obscure English words. And for decades, critical studies have confirmed that children who are taught Latin consistently score higher than their peers in reading comprehension, vocabulary, and even critical thinking and problem solving.[2]

---

[2] See, for example, Nancy A. Mavrogenes, "The Effect of Elementary Latin Instruction on Language Arts Performance," in *The Elementary School Journal* 77, 4 (March 1977), pp. 268–73; Richard L. Sparks et al., "An Exploratory Study on the Effects of Latin on the Native Language Skills and Foreign Language Aptitude of Students With and Without Learning Disabilities," in *The Classical Journal* 91, 2 (January 1996), pp. 165–84; Timothy V. Rasinski et al., "The Latin-Greek Connection: Building Vocabulary Through Morphological Study," in *The Reading Teacher* 65, 2 (October 2011), pp. 133–41; and many, many more.

Latin prepares the child for the study of other foreign languages: French, Spanish, and Italian are all related to Latin. Even non-Latinate languages can be more easily learned if Latin has already been studied. The child who has been drilled in Latin syntax understands the concepts of agreement, inflected nouns, conjugated verbs, and grammatical gender, no matter what language these concepts appear in.

Latin guards against arrogance. The study of the language shows the young child that his world, his language, his vocabulary, and his way of expression are only one way of living and thinking in a big, tumultuous, complicated world. Latin forces the student to look at words and concepts anew:

> *What did this Latin word really mean?*
> *Is this English word a good translation for it?*
> *Doesn't the Latin word express something that English has no equivalent word for?*
> *Does this reveal a gap in my own thinking?*

A foreign language, as Neil Postman writes in *The End of Education*, "provides one with entry into a worldview different from one's own. . . . If it is important that our young value diversity of point of view, there is no better way to achieve it than to have them learn a foreign language."[3]

HOW DOES LATIN WORK?

You can learn Latin along with your child, but it will help if you have some basic understanding of how the language works. Latin is an *inflected language*, which means that *word endings are more important than word order.*

If I want to say that my husband just planted his shoe in the dog's ribs, I say:

Peter kicked the dog.

---

[3] Neil Postman, *The End of Education: Redefining the Value of Schools* (New York: Knopf, 1995), p. 147.

(although he would never do such a thing). How do you know that the dog was the receiver of the kick and that Peter was the giver of the kick? Because Peter comes before the verb, and the dog comes after. This tells English speakers that the dog is the *object* (receiver) of the kick and that Peter is the *subject* (the doer) of the kick.

But Latin works slightly differently. A set of endings called *inflections* tell the reader whether a noun is the subject or the object. It's as though, in English, every noun acting as a subject had an *s* on the end and every noun acting as an object had an *o* on the end:

Peter-s kicked the dog-o.

If English worked this way, we could reverse the sentence:

The dog-o kicked Peter-s.

and the reader would still realize that Peter had done the kicking and that the dog had received it—because of the ending.

That's how Latin works. Case endings take the place of word order. Case endings tell you whether a word is being used as a subject, object, possessive, and so on.

You also need to know that Latin uses these word endings on verbs to take the place of pronouns. If I say:

I kicked the dog

you know who did the action, because "I" comes before "kicked." But instead of using pronouns *before* verbs, Latin *conjugates* verbs by tacking the pronouns onto the ends of the verbs:

Kicked-I the dog.

Now I could say "The dog kicked-I" and mean the same thing.

There's more to Latin than this, of course, but the above explanations will get you started.

There are several different ways to pronounce Latin: the so-called classical pronunciation (in which, for example, *v* is pronounced as *u* or *w*) and the "Christian" or "ecclesiastical" pronunciation, used by choirs, are the two most common. We prefer not to worry overmuch about pronunciation. Even in ancient times, Latin pronunciation varied widely by region and by century. The ecclesiastical pronunciation will be useful if the child ever gets to sing in Latin; otherwise, don't get too sidetracked trying to master pronunciation.

HOW TO DO IT

If you decide to begin Latin in third or fourth grade (see Chapter 19 for other options), you'll take advantage of the child's most natural "window" for language learning. The resources that we suggest at the end of this chapter are suitable for elementary students, and do not require that you have previous knowledge of the language.

The curricula we suggest are "parts to whole" (conjugations and declensions are taught all at once rather than incidentally), rather than "whole to parts."[4] Here's what we mean: In Latin, every verb (such as *amo*, "I love") has a *root*, which carries the verb's basic meaning (*am-*, "love"), and *endings*, which serve as pronouns: *-o* means "I," *-as* means "you" singular, and so on. These pronoun endings are the same for every verb the child encounters in the first two years of study. So once the student learns the list of endings for *I, you* (singular), *he/she/it, we, you* (plural), *they* (the endings are *-o, -as, -at, -amus, -atis, -ant*), he can put them on any verb he wants:

amo	I love	*voco*	I call
amas	You love	*vocas*	You call
amat	He/she/it loves	*vocat*	He/she/it calls
amamus	We love	*vocamus*	We call
amatis	You love	*vocatis*	You call
amant	They love	*vocant*	They call

This is parts-to-whole instruction: first the student learns the parts, *then* he learns how to put them together to form a whole.

---

[4] See pages 271–275 for a further explanation of "whole to parts" versus "parts to whole" instruction.

Whole-to-parts Latin primers, on the other hand, tell the child that the word *amamus* means "we love," never explaining that the word has both a root and a personal ending. Later, the child will meet *vocamus* in a sentence and discover that this word means "we call"—again with no explanation. Sooner or later, he'll figure out that *-amus* means "we." Or he may get frustrated with this apparently patternless language and quit. Either way, he'll have wasted a great deal of time and energy trying to understand how Latin works. But if he is simply given the list of personal endings to memorize, he will have the power to form any Latin verb he likes as well as the knowledge to decode the Latin words he encounters in his reading. Whole-to-parts Latin instruction is frustrating and counterproductive, and breaks down the very skill that systematic Latin lessons develop—the habit of systematic thinking.

WHAT ABOUT OTHER LANGUAGES?

Why do we recommend beginning Latin when everyone knows that starting a modern foreign language at a young age is the best way to achieve fluency?

Well, we agree. The elementary grades *are* the best time to learn a modern foreign language, and we think every American child should learn to speak Spanish (at the very least). At the end of this chapter we've recommended a couple of modern language programs suitable for home use. However, in our experience, *none* of these programs will get you speaking a foreign language. This only happens if you're able to *speak* the language (with a live person) at least twice a week. Conversation, which requires you to think in the language you're learning, is the only path to fluency.

If you speak a foreign language fluently and would like to teach it to your student, go ahead and do this during the third- and fourth-grade years, and save Latin until later. Or if you can arrange for a tutor (preferably a native speaker) to come in and converse with your child at least twice a week, go ahead and study a modern language now and wait on Latin until sixth or seventh grade. Many parents have also told us that attendance at Saturday language school was the only way their children attained even basic fluency in another language.

But if you can't arrange for modern-language conversation, make Latin central to your foreign-language learning for right now. The study of Latin syntax and vocabulary will provide many of the same benefits as modern-language study, as well as improving the child's general language skills. The student who has completed a Latin course will have much less difficulty when she encounters a modern foreign language later on. And since Latin isn't a spoken language, you won't need to worry about the conversational component.

As you study Latin, you may want to use one of the modern language programs listed below as an additional resource, perhaps adding it to your schedule once or twice a week. This will give the student exposure to a modern language and prepare her for later learning.

SUGGESTED SCHEDULES

Plan on spending between 2 ½ and 4 hours per week on Latin, depending on maturity and interest. It's more productive to spend thirty minutes every day than to do one long session or even two shorter ones per week. Three days per week is an absolute minimum; four is better.

RESOURCES

Most books can be obtained from any bookseller or library; most curricula can be bought directly from the publisher or from a major home-school supplier such as Rainbow Resource Center. Contact information for publishers and suppliers can be found at www.welltrainedmind.com. If availability is limited, we have noted it. Where indicated, resources are listed in chronological order (the order you'll want to use them in). Books in series are listed together. Remember that additional curricula choices and more can be found at www.welltrainedmind.com. Prices change constantly, but we have included 2016 pricing to give an idea of affordability.

Online language instruction and practice designed for elementary students can be found for many, many more languages. Visit www.welltrainedmind.com for links and descriptions!

Basic Texts

Latin

Lowe, Leigh. *Prima Latina: An Introduction to Christian Latin*, 2nd ed. Louisville, KY: Memoria Press, 2003.

Prima Latina consists of a student book, teacher manual, and pronunciation CD; you can also buy an instructional DVD and premade flash cards. The program is called "Christian Latin" because it teaches ecclesiastical pronunciation (although the publisher's website gives tips on using other pronunciation styles) and also uses early Christian hymns and prayers in some of the lessons. The teacher's manual has a summary of Latin grammar in the front. Read it over, but don't let it confuse you. In the twenty-five lessons provided, you can learn the basic grammar needed along with your child.

You can begin *Prima Latina* in either third or fourth grade; the program will take a year or less to complete. When you complete this introduction to Latin, you can continue on to *Latina Christiana I*, which is put out by the same press and is designed to follow *Prima Latina*. Both of these programs are written for parents who do not know Latin and feature very clear instruction. The optional DVDs provide instruction from one of the program's authors, Leigh Lowe.

Order from Memoria Press. Samples available on the publisher's website.

Prima Latina Text Set (student book, teacher manual, pronunciation CD). $34.95.

Prima Latina Complete Set (Text Set plus instructional DVDs and flash cards). $90.90.

Lowe, Cheryl. *Latina Christiana: An Introduction to Christian Latin*. Louisville, KY: Memoria Press, 2001.

Follows *Prima Latina* and introduces more complex Latin grammar; in most cases students will need to be working on at least a fourth-grade level in English grammar to begin the series.

Latina Christiana I Set (student book, teacher manual, pronunciation CD). $41.95.

Latina Christiana I Complete Set (also includes instructional DVDs and flash cards). $98.90.

Latina Christiana II Set (student book, teacher manual, pronunciation CD). $41.95.

Latina Christiana II Complete Set (also includes instructional DVDs and flash cards). $98.90.

Song School Latin. Camp Hill, PA: Classical Academic Press.

Song School Latin is a first Latin course with a very different approach than *Prima Latina*. Instruction is far more aural (songs, chants, conversation) and teaches Latin phrases and vocabularies much more in the style of a modern foreign language. Either pronunciation can be used. The course is both more elaborate (more activities, games, and worksheets) and more time-consuming than *Prima Latina*. Good for multisensory teaching and for parents who want to make Latin a higher priority. Note that although the first book is marketed for grades 1–3, we do not suggest beginning this program before third grade; there is too much pencil work.

Order from Classical Academic Press. Samples are available at the publisher's website.

Song School Latin Book 1 Program. Includes student book, teacher's manual, DVD teaching set, and a flash card game. $82.95.

Song School Latin Book 2 Program. Includes student book, teacher's manual, DVD teaching set, and another flash card game. $82.95.

Latin for Children. Camp Hill, PA: Classical Academic Press.

Designed to follow *Song School Latin 2*, this primer begins on a fourth- to fifth-grade level. An online supplement provides additional games and opportunities for reinforcement. Order from Classical Academic Press. Samples are available at the publisher's website.

Latin for Children Primer A Program. Includes student workbook, answer key, DVD and CD set, activity book, and a simple reader. $99.95.

Drown, Catherine. *The Big Book of Lively Latin.* San Marcos, CA: Lively Latin, 2008.

Good for those beginning with an advanced third-grade or fourth-grade student. Written by Latin teacher and home-schooling parent Catherine Drown, the *Big Book* provides good basics in grammar and vocabulary as well as supplementary material (historical background, activities and games, studies in mythology and Roman society). *The Big Book* is self-explanatory, intended for parents and students to work through together. After completing the second *Big Book*, students can continue on to one of the programs suggested in Chapter 19.

Samples can be seen at the publisher's website.

Big Book 1. $55 for the online PDF version, $79 for the PDF on a 2-CD set, $125 for the print version plus CD.

Big Book 2. $70 for the online PDF version, $89 for the PDF on a 2-CD set, $140 for the print version plus CD.

Modern Languages

Song School Spanish. Camp Hill, PA: Classical Academic Press.

A fun first introduction to Spanish vocabulary and grammar; begin anytime from third grade on (second grade if children are comfortable with handwriting). Plenty of songs and basic conversation; games, puzzles, and additional online supplementary activities. Order from Classical Academic Press. Samples available at publisher's website.

Song School Spanish Program. Student book, teacher's edition, flash card game, and online access; note that there is no instructional DVD or CD. $66.95.

Kraut, Julia, et al. *Spanish for Children.* Camp Hill, PA: Classical Academic Press, 2008.

Designed to follow *Song School Spanish*, but you can begin it in fourth grade or later even if you haven't used the Song School materials. Order from Classical Academic Press. Samples can be viewed on the publisher's website.

Spanish for Children Primer A Program. Includes student book, answer key, DVD and CD set, reader, and online access to games and drills. $94.95.

La Clase Divertida. Holly Hills, FL: La Clase Divertida.

Order from La Clase Divertida. This Spanish program, developed by a home-school father with twenty years of Spanish teaching experience, is designed as a family learning project. The Rosetta Stone courses listed below are focused primarily on language learning; this program provides games, stories, cooking and project activities, and other resources along with video and audio cassette instruction, turning Spanish into something closer to a mini-unit study. Good for family fun. Each kit provides enough material (workbooks and craft supplies) for two students.

Level 1 Kit. $120.

Additional Student Packet. $15.

Level II Kit. $130.

Additional Student Packet. $25.

Linney, William E., and Antonio L. Orta. *Getting Started with Spanish: Beginning Spanish for Homeschoolers and Self-Taught Students of Any Age.* Burke, VA: Armfield Academic Press, 2009.

$20.95. Systematic clear grammar designed for home use, along with MP3 files for pronunciation help. Parents can learn alongside children.

Schultz, Danielle. *First Start French.* Louisville, KY: Memoria Press, 2008.

Order from Memoria Press. This beginning French program takes the same approach as *Prima Latina.* The pronunciation CD features a native speaker. Each book offers one year of study. Samples can be viewed on the Memoria Press website.

First Start French I Set. Student book, teacher manual, and pronunciation CD. $43.95.

First Start French II Set. Student book, teacher manual, and pronunciation CD. $43.95.

10

ELECTRONIC TEACHERS:
USING COMPUTERS
AND OTHER SCREENS

New York Times reporter Nick Bilton: So, your kids must love the iPad?

Steve Jobs, CEO of Apple Inc. and Pixar Animation: They haven't used it.
We limit how much technology our kids use at home.

You'll notice that, so far, we haven't recommended online instruction,
or very much in the way of computer-based learning, in our Resources
lists.

Yes, we know they exist (and we'll suggest various ways to use technology with your middle- and upper-grade students in the sections to come).
We just don't think this should be your preferred method of teaching
grammar-stage students.

Reading is mentally active and forces the student to use a brand-new and
difficult set of skills. Watching a presentation online is mentally passive.

Writing is labor intensive. Clicking icons is effortless.

Print that stays still and doesn't wiggle, talk, or change colors makes
the brain work hard at interpretation. Print that jumps up, changes colors, and sings a song interprets itself for you and doesn't make the brain
work at all.

All children prefer ease to effort. It seems reasonable to us to limit their exposure to the easier way until the harder way has been mastered.

There's a growing body of scientific evidence to back us up on this. The brain activity created by reading and writing is significantly different from the brain activity created by image-based technologies. Jane Healy, PhD in education psychology and the author of *Endangered Minds,* points out that while reading and writing depend on left-hemisphere brain development, children's television programming depends almost entirely on right-hemisphere stimuli—quickly changing visual images instead of stability; noises (booms, crashes, single-word exclamations) rather than complex sentences; bright colors, rapid movement, and immediate resolutions rather than logical sequencing of actions.[1]

In the early grades, the brain develops more quickly than at any other time. Connections are made. Neural pathways are established. The grammar stage is a particularly crucial time for verbal development: the brain is mapping out the roads it will use for the rest of the child's life. (This is why foreign languages acquired during early childhood are almost always completely fluent, while languages learned later are never as natural.) It is vital that the child become fluent in reading and writing during the elementary years—and the brain development required for this fluency is markedly different from that used for comprehending visual images. And online learning for the youngest students tends to be image-centered, not word-centered. "In print culture," Neil Postman writes in *The End of Education,* "we are apt to say of people who are not intelligent that we must 'draw them pictures' so that they may understand. Intelligence implies that one can dwell comfortably without pictures, in a field of concepts and generalizations."[2] Indeed, the higher stages of classical education require the child to think without pictures—to be so comfortable with nonvisual concepts such as responsibility, morality, and liberty that she can ponder their meanings in widely different circumstances. Word-centered education requires the student to interact with the material—to comprehend

[1] See Jane Healy, *Endangered Minds: Why Our Children Don't Think and What We Can Do about It* (New York: Touchstone, 1990), ch. 10, "TV, Video Games, and the Growing Brain," esp. p. 211.

[2] Neil Postman, *The End of Education: Redefining the Value of School* (New York: Knopf, 1995), p. 25.

it, interpret it, and talk about it. A student must be *actively* involved in the learning process in order to benefit; this is why we lay such stress on reading history and science and then writing about the knowledge gained.

Watched too often and too early, screens can begin to replace the child's own imagination. Susan once checked out a movie version of the children's classic *The Lion, the Witch, and the Wardrobe* for her six-year-old son, Christopher. They'd read the book aloud together, and although he enjoyed the video, he heaved a big sigh when it was over.

"What's wrong?" Susan asked.

"Mommy," he said, "I had another picture of Lucy in my head, and that girl didn't look *anything* like her."

"Well, you can still think of her in your head however you want."

"No," he said. "Now that picture's in my head and I can't get it out."

And there can be developmental implications when software takes priority over traditional reading and writing. In 2013, the American Academy of Pediatrics recommended that toddlers avoid all screen time and that young children be limited in their use of computers, iPads, and other devices; when swiping and tapping take precedence over drawing, writing, and moving around, fine motor skills remain underdeveloped and muscle strength is affected.

What about online learning? We're fans of using online classes and tutorials, as long as the online component is a delivery method that helps more students and parents work with great teachers on fascinating content. But grammar-stage students are still learning the basics of human communication. They need to interact with real people in real time; this is how they learn to interpret expressions, tones of voice, body movements. Face-to-face learning is a vital stage in their maturing process.

We're not saying that you should make *no* use of online resources. We've just recommended a few for language learning, after all. But formal online classes should wait until the middle grades.

And we're not saying that you should ban screens. Limit their use, particularly in education. Supervise content. As much as possible, steer away from highly visual, quickly changing programs with a constant barrage of sound effects. Don't enroll your grammar-stage child in online classes; teach her yourself.

When you have the flu, or when you're trying to teach fractions to your third grader while your four-year-old sprints around and around the kitchen, or when company's coming and the bathroom hasn't been cleaned, put on a movie. But, every once in a while, ask yourself: What am I giving up? If I didn't put this on, would the kids go play basketball out back, or drag out Chutes and Ladders out of sheer boredom? Would they read a book? Would I be forced to give the four-year-old a math lesson to keep him happy, too? If my twelve-year-old doesn't watch this movie, will he go build a model? If my ten-year-old is told she can't play this computer game, will she wander off and read fairy tales?

Educational videos can be useful in science. We've enjoyed the spectacular photography of the *Eyewitness* science videos, and we watch National Geographic specials with rapt attention (lava flowing down a mountain has to be seen to be believed). But we watch screens in the evening— curled up with a bowl of popcorn—not during schooltime. During schooltime, we read books, do experiments, and write about what we're learning. It's hard work, but the more the student reads and writes, the more natural reading and writing become.

Unfortunately, the same is true of watching, and using, screens. The brain becomes expert at whatever it does the most of during the formative years. So do your best to limit the young child's lessons with the "electronic teacher."

We guarantee you that she won't have any trouble catching up later on.

11

꒰꒱

MATTERS OF FAITH:
RELIGION

Man is by his constitution a religious animal.
—Edmund Burke, *Reflections on the Revolution in France*

The old classicists called theology the "queen of sciences" because
it ruled over all other fields of study. Theology still does, either in
its presence or its absence. The presence or absence of the divine has
immense implications for every area of the curriculum: Are we animals or
something slightly different? Do math rules work because of the coincidental shape of space and time or because God is an orderly being, whose
universe reflects his character? Is a man who dies for his faith a hero or
a fool?

Public schools, which have the impossible task of teaching children of
many different faiths, must proclaim neutrality. *We don't deal in matters of
faith,* the teachers explain. *We're neutral.*

Think about this for a minute. Arguing for the presence of God is generally considered "biased." Assuming his absence is usually called "neutral."
Yet both are statements of faith; both color the teacher's approach to any

subject; both make a fundamental assumption about the nature of men and women.

To call this neutrality is intellectually dishonest.

Education cannot be neutral when it comes to faith: it is either supportive or destructive. The topic of education is humanity, its accomplishments, its discoveries, its savage treatment of its own kind, its willingness to endure self-sacrifice. And you cannot learn—or teach—about humanity without considering God.

Let's take biology as an example. Mammals are characterized by, among other things, their tendency to care for and protect their young. Do mothers love their babies because of sheer biological imperative? If so, why do we come down so hard on fathers who neglect their children? It's a rare male mammal that pays much attention to its young. Do fathers love their babies because of the urge to see their own genetic material preserved or because fathers reflect the character of the father God? How should a father treat a disabled child? Why?

We don't blame the public schools for sidestepping these sorts of questions. In most cases, it's the only strategy they can adopt.

Yet this separation of religious faith from education yields an incomplete education. We're not arguing that religion should be "put back" into public schools. We'd just like some honesty: an education that takes no notice of faith is, at the very least, incomplete.

Since you're teaching your child yourself, you can rectify this situation. Don't ignore instruction in (at the bare minimum) the facts of the world's major religions. Do try to relate the child's studies to your own faith, to your own religious heritage.

Your child will probably start asking the tough questions in the logic stage (something to look forward to): Why did the Crusades take place? Isn't it wrong to try to change people's religion by forcible means? Well, how about peaceful means? Was the pope wrong to put all of England under an interdict? Why would a medieval scholar risk excommunication? Why did Newton believe in God? And what about that father and his disabled child?

The elementary-level student won't be thinking on this level, so you can relax for a few years. But now is the time to understand the basics of the faiths that have shaped both history and science. Explain Islam and Buddhism and Hinduism and ancestor worship. Discuss the elements of Christianity and Judaism. Teach the Exodus and the Conquest and the Exile and the birth of Christ right along with ancient history. Show how these world religions have collided—why, for example, the English ruling India were so appalled over suttee (widow burning) while the Indians considered it an honorable act. Don't be afraid of America's Puritan and Dissenter past. And don't fall into the "Thanksgiving trap."[1]

If you don't do this now, your child will reach the logic stage badly equipped—unable to understand fully the events of history and why they have unfolded in their present pattern. Religion plays a major role in the formation of any culture. For this reason, it is imperative that the continuing education of the child include how religion has influenced art, music, literature, science, and history itself.

We believe that religion's role in both past and present cultures is best taught by the parents from the strength of their own faith. I (Susan) don't want my six-year-old taught religion in school. That's my job. It is my responsibility to teach my children what I believe, why I believe it, and why it makes a difference.

RESOURCES

For the teaching of religion, use family resources or check with your own religious community for suggestions.

---

[1] Many elementary-school history texts, unwilling to run the risk of lawsuits, tell third graders that the Pilgrims gave thanks at Thanksgiving but never mention God. One particularly bad text informs children that the Pilgrims gave thanks to the Indians.

12

FINER THINGS:
ART AND MUSIC

Oh, the world is so full of a number of things.
—Robert Louis Stevenson

SUBJECT: Art and music
TIME REQUIRED: 1–4 hours per week

One of the distinctive traits of classical education is the attention it pays to basics. Classical education takes great care in laying the proper foundations for reading, writing, math, history, and science.

Laying foundations is time-consuming. If you learn these subjects thoroughly and well, you may find that you don't have a great deal of time for other areas of study at this level.

In the science chapter (Chapter 8), we told you not to try to cover all of the animal kingdom or all of astronomy. The purpose of the elementary years is to accumulate knowledge, yes, but the focus of your teaching should not be sheer amount of material covered. Rather, your child ought to be learning how to *find* information, how to *fit* information together, and how to *absorb* information through narration, notebook pages, and memorization.

What is true for science holds true for the entire elementary curriculum. You will never be able to cover every subject taught in elementary schools. Resist the temptation to spread your instruction too thin. Give the academic basics your best time and teaching energy during these early years.

Having said that, we now go on to say that art and music have great value for elementary students. Instruction in drawing and art appreciation improves muscle coordination and perception skills. Recent studies have shown that piano lessons improve the reasoning skills of preschool children. We suggest that you try to schedule at least one block of time (an hour or two) per week for art and music appreciation. If you can manage two blocks of time during the week, do art appreciation one day and music appreciation another. If you can only cope with one more teaching period per week, alternate—art appreciation one week, music the next.

ART

Art for elementary students should involve basic training in two areas: learning about art techniques and elements (drawing, color, and so forth), and learning about great artists.

You can alternate actual art projects and reading books about great artists. For art projects, we've recommended several drawing resources at the end of this chapter. You can also make use of picture study, the method used by Charlotte Mason, the educator who originated narration as a teaching tool. Like narration, picture study requires the student to take in information and then repeat it back to the teacher.

Using the children's art books we've recommended in the Resources, ask the child to look intently at a painting for a while—two or three minutes for younger children, up to ten for fourth graders. Then take the picture away, and ask the student to tell you about it.

At first, you may have to ask leading questions. "What color is _____ ?" "What is the man at the side doing?" With practice, though, the student will start to notice more and more details and retain them longer and longer.

Whenever you read an artist's biography, be sure to use at least one of her or his paintings for picture study.

MUSIC

As with other subjects, music in grades 1 through 4 is a matter of accumulation—getting familiar with what's out there. You can require the child, twice a week, to spend half an hour or so listening to classical music. Most public libraries have a fairly extensive classical music selection available for checkout. Start with music designed for children, such as *Peter and the Wolf*, and then explore together. You'll find additional suggestions in the Resources section.

The first time the child listens to a piece of music, have her listen to it two or three times in a row. Then make sure she plays it again at the beginning of her next listening period. Familiarity breeds enjoyment. She can do handwork such as Play-Doh or coloring books about the composer she is listening to (see Resources at the end of this chapter) but nothing that involves words; her attention should be focused on what she hears, not on what she reads.

There's no easy way to "narrate" symphonies. Asking the child how the music made her feel is of dubious value; asking her to hum the melody only works if she can hum and the melody is uncomplicated. We suggest that you simply make sure she listens to the piece at least twice. (Dancing along is always a good idea.)

Just as math and reading are easier for children who've heard sums and stories all their lives, so music appreciation comes more naturally to children whose parents play music in the house. The best way to follow up on the child's music-appreciation lesson is to play the piece yourself a couple of weeks later and listen to it as a family. Playing lively classical music while doing housework and playing quiet classical music during meals are two ways to have your family become familiar with classical music.

If you can afford them, piano lessons are good. I (Jessie) feel that every child should take two years of piano (all of mine did). My experience has been that if they showed no interest in it after two years of study, keeping them at it was a waste of time and energy, counterproductive to their love and appreciation of music.

If they show any interest in an instrument, do your best to provide lessons. If possible, as with piano, require two years of lessons before allowing the student to drop; two years is the minimum time that it takes to begin to *enjoy* an instrument, rather than simply struggling with it.

SUGGESTED SCHEDULES

First and second grade

Week One	1 art lesson, 60–90 minutes
Week Two	Read an artist biography, do picture study, 60–90 minutes
Week Three	Listen to classical music for 2 hours at some point during the week
Week Four	Read a composer's biography

Repeat sequence

Third and fourth grade

Week One	Day 1: Art lesson, 60 minutes
	Day 2: Read an artist biography
	Day 3: Do picture study, 15–20 minutes
Week Two	Day 1: Listen to classical music for 1 hour
	Day 2: Listen to classical music for 1 hour
	Day 3: Read a composer's biography

Repeat sequence

Note: You could also choose to focus in on music during the first semester and art during the second semester, or vice versa.

RESOURCES

Pick and choose from among these books and tapes in order to familiarize children with a wide range of art and music skills and styles. Most of these titles (and some of the CDs) will be at your local library or bookstore.

Art Appreciation

Dover Art Postcards. New York: Dover.

Order from Rainbow Resource Center. These sets of art postcards (24 each) provide a simple way to do picture study. $5.95–$6.95 per set.

Berthe Morisot

Dalí

Degas Ballet Dancers (small format postcard book for $1.99)

Leonardo da Vinci

Manet Paintings

Masterpieces of Flower Painting

Monet

Picasso

Pre-Raphaelite Paintings

Renoir

Van Gogh

Vermeer

Winslow Homer

Martin, Mary, and Steven Zorn. *Start Exploring Masterpieces: A Fact-Filled Coloring Book.* Philadelphia: Running Press, 2011.

$11.95. Sixty famous paintings to color, along with the stories behind them.

Venezia, Mike. *Getting to Know the World's Greatest Artists.* Chicago: Children's Press.

$6.95 each. Order from Rainbow Resource Center or check your library. These short, 32-page children's books provide an entertaining introduction to some of the most important artists of the Renaissance and later, along with very nice reproductions of paintings. The text is written on a third- to fourth-grade level.

Botticelli. 1994.

Bruegel. 1994.

Mary Cassatt. 1994.

Paul Cézanne. 1998.

Dalí. 1994.

Da Vinci. 1994.

Gauguin. 1994.

Francisco Goya. 1994.

Edward Hopper. 1994.

Paul Klee. 1994.

Henri Matisse. 1997.

Michelangelo. 1991.

Monet. 1994.

O'Keeffe. 1994.

Picasso. 1994.

Pollock. 1994.

Rembrandt. 1988.

Renoir. 1996.

Diego Rivera. 1995.

Toulouse-Lautrec. 1995.

Van Gogh. 1989.

Grant Wood. 1996.

Wolf, Aline D. *How to Use Child-size Masterpieces for Art Appreciation.* Hollidaysburg, PA: Parent Child Press, 1996.

$12. Order from Parent Child Press or from Rainbow Resource Center. This Montessori-method art appreciation course for ages three through nine begins with simple matching and progresses through more complicated exercises. This instruction manual tells the parent how to use the postcard-sized art reproductions listed below; children are encouraged to match, pair, and group paintings, to learn the names of artists and their works, to learn about schools of art, and finally to place paintings on a time line.

Child-size Masterpieces. $16 each. Each book below has postcard-sized reproductions of paintings for you to remove and use in picture study, as described in the handbook above. Use these three books to match and group paintings and artists:

Child-size Masterpieces: Level 1—Easy Level.

Child-size Masterpieces: Level 2—Intermediate Level.

Child-size Masterpieces: Level 3—Advanced Level.

Use the next three books to learn names of paintings and artists:

Child-size Masterpieces: Step 4—Learning the Names of the Artists.

Child-size Masterpieces: Step 5—Learning About Famous Paintings.

Child-size Masterpieces: Steps 6 & 7—Modern Schools of Art.

Art Skills

Artistic Pursuits, *The Curriculum for Creativity*, rev. ed. Arvada, CO: Artistic Pursuits, 2008.

> Order from Artistic Pursuits. The books are $47.95 each.
>
> > *Grades K–3 Book One: An Introduction to the Visual Arts.*
> > *Grades K–3 Book Two: Stories of Artists and Their Art Grades.*
> > *Grades K–3 Book Three: Modern Painting and Sculpture.*
> > *Elementary 4–5 Book One: The Elements of Art and Composition.*
> >
> > Art supplies can be purchased from one of several art supply companies (links and lists for each book are provided on the Artistic Pursuits website) or in a preassembled kit.
> >
> > > *Supply Kit Grades K–3 Kit 1. $76.*
> > > *Supply Kit Grades K–3 Kit 2. $92.*
> > > *Supply Kit Grades K–3 Kit 3. $81.*
> > > *Supply Kit Grades 4–5 Kit 1. $45.*

Press, Judy, and Loretta Trezzo Braren. *The Little Hands Art Book: Exploring Arts and Crafts with 2- to 6-Year-Olds.* Charlotte, VT: Williamson Publishing, 2008.

> $12.99. For younger children, art (glue, paint, paper, crayons, markers) and crafts (clothespins, popsicles, paper bags, etc.) projects that are simple to do (and use common household items).

Usworth, Jean. *Drawing Is Basic.* Parsippany, NJ: Dale Seymour Publications, 2000.

> $21.47 each. Order from Rainbow Resource Center. For the busy parent who wants to do art but can't find the time, these books offer fifteen-minute "drawing breaks" for you to guide the student in; these breaks teach beginning skills and grow a little more demanding with each year.
>
> > *Drawing Is Basic: Grade 1.*
> > *Drawing Is Basic: Grade 2.*
> > *Drawing Is Basic: Grade 3.*
> > *Drawing Is Basic: Grade 4.*

Music Appreciation

Beethoven's Wig. Cambridge, MA: Rounder Records.

$11.99 at iTunes. A favorite at the Bauer household, this puts (silly) words to great music, builds familiarity, and reveals the underlying structure of symphonies and other music forms.

Sing-Along Symphonies. 2002.

Vol. 2: More Sing-Along Symphonies. 2004.

Vol. 3: Many More Sing-Along Symphonies. 2006.

Vol. 4: Dance-Along Symphonies. 2008 ($14.98).

Brownell, David. *A Coloring Book of Great Composers: Bach to Berlioz.* Santa Barbara, CA: Bellerophon.

$4.95. Order from Bellerophon. Portraits to color along with biographical sketches for fifteen composers each.

Vol. One: Bach to Berlioz.

Vol. Two: Chopin to Tchaikovsky.

Vol. Three: Mahler to Stravinsky.

American Composers.

Classical Composers Collections: 50 Best of series. Chicago: GIA Publications, Inc.

Another set of "greatest hits" and excerpts, this one encompassing more recent classical masters. Prices range from $7.99–$10.99 on iTunes; an average of four to five hours of music on each album.

50 Best of Bach.

50 Best of Brahms.

50 Best of Grieg and Dvorak.

50 Best of Haydn.

50 Best of Liszt, Strauss, and Mendelssohn.

50 Best of Prokofiev.

50 Best of Rachmaninov.

50 Best of Ravel and Schubert.

50 Best of Rimsky-Korsakov, Borodin, Mussorgsky.

50 Best of Smetana, Bizet, Orff.

50 Best of Vivaldi.

Hammond, Susan, producer. Classical Kids series. Toronto: Children's Group.

$16.98. Order from any music store, from Rainbow Resource Center, or check your library. These CDs combine music with history and dramatic storytelling to familiarize children with great composers and their works. Very highly recommended.

Beethoven Lives Upstairs. 2000.

A young boy learns about Beethoven's life through letters to his uncle.

Hallelujah Handel. 2000.

The composer gets involved in a fictional plan to help an orphan boy who sings but won't speak.

Mozart's Magic Fantasy: A Journey Through "The Magic Flute." 2000.

A young girl is magically transported into the middle of *The Magic Flute.*

Mr. Bach Comes to Call. 1999.

An eight-year-old practicing the Minuet in G is startled when Bach shows up in her living room. Includes over twenty excerpts from Bach's works.

Tchaikovsky Discovers America. 1998.

The composer arrives in New York in 1891 for the opening of Carnegie Hall.

Vivaldi's Ring of Mystery. 1998.

An orphaned violinist tries to find out more about her family in Vivaldi's Venice. Over twenty-four Vivaldi works are included.

Rise of the Masters: 100 Supreme Classical Masterpieces series. Stockholm, Sweden: X5 Music Group.

Ranging from $4.99 to $7.99 on iTunes, each of these collections from the digital-only music publisher X5 Music Group contains one hundred pieces or excerpts (as much as twelve hours of music) from each composer. Excerpts are a good way to get young children "hooked" on classical music; they're usually the most tuneful and attractive parts of longer, more complicated works.

Beethoven

Chopin

Debussy

Grieg

Handel

Mozart

Schubert

Schumann

Tchaikovsky

Tomb, Eric. *Early Composers Coloring Book*, illus. Nancy Conkle. Santa Barbara, CA: Bellerophon, 1988.

$3.95. From Palestrina through Corelli, with a biographical note and a portrait (to color) of each.

Music Skills

John Thompson's Modern Course for the Piano.

Although you will want to find an experienced music teacher before long, you can use the John Thompson piano course for an early introduction to piano; the books begin by assuming no piano knowledge at all. Order from J. W. Pepper or through a local music store.

Teaching Little Fingers to Play: A Book for the Earliest Beginner/CD. $9.99.

First Grade: Book/CD. $10.99.

Popular Piano Solos, First Grade: Book/CD. $10.99.

The Violin Book Series. Clearwater, FL: Ebaru Publishing.

Order from Ebaru Publishing. Eden Vaning, a concert violinist and violin teacher, developed this series of self-teaching books for parents and students. Like the Thompson course above, it provides an affordable introduction to instrument skills. In our opinion, you'll want to find a teacher by the second year, but the Ebaru series builds good basics. Susan (who knew nothing about violin) began one of her sons on this series; when he began formal lessons the following year, his teacher praised the fundamentals that the Ebaru books had built. (He went on to four years of high-school youth orchestra and became a music major in college.) Learn more (and order both books and reasonably priced student violins) at Vaning's website, www.theviolinbook.com. Beginning levels are listed below.

The Violin Book

Book 0: Let's Get Ready for Violin/Practice and Performance CD. $43.96.

Book 1: Beginning Basics/Practice and Performance CD. $43.96.

Book 2: The Left Hand//Practice and Performance CD. $51.96.

Student violins (see website).

PART I

EPILOGUE: CHARTS, SCHEDULES, WORKSHEETS, ETC.

The Grammar Stage at a Glance

Guidelines to how much time you should spend on each subject are general; parents should feel free to adjust schedules according to child's maturity and ability.

Kindergarten (Ages Four and Five)

Reading	Spend time every day reading out loud, as much time as you can afford. Learn basic phonics for fluent reading. Begin with 10 minutes, gradually working up to 30 minutes. Practice reading easy books.
Writing	Practice printing. Work up to 10 minutes per day. Copy short sentences from a model.
Mathematics	Learn to count from 1 to 100. Use actual objects to understand what numbers mean, 1 to 100. Be able to write the numbers from 1 to 100. Practice skip-counting by 2s, 5s, and 10s. Teach about math as you go about life. If you use a kindergarten math program, plan on no more than 30 minutes a day.

General Learning	Do fine motor work (coloring, cutting and pasting, stickers, etc.) for 10–15 minutes every day. Schedule active play daily.

First Grade

Reading	15 to 20 minutes per day of phonics work. 30 minutes of reading (skill building), 3 times per week; one instructional, one at-level, one below-level.
Literature	20 to 30 minutes, 3 days per week, focusing on ancient myths and legends; make notebook pages (narrations) once or twice per week; memorize a poem every 3 to 6 weeks.
Spelling	10 to 15 minutes per day, 3 to 4 days per week.
Grammar	10 to 15 minutes per day, 3 to 4 days per week.
Writing	Penmanship, 5 to 10 minutes per day. Copy short sentences 2 or 3 days per week (may be completed as a history or science assignment). Do a total of three narrations per week (may be completed as a literature, history, or science assignment).
Mathematics	30 to 40 minutes per day (math lesson and storybook reading); try to do one real-life math project per week.
History	Study ancient times (5000 B.C.–A.D. 400). Read biographies and easy history books to the child; ask the child to tell you what you've just read; make one narration page each week for the history notebook. Do this for at least 1½ hours per week, divided into two or three sessions.
Science	Spend at least 2 hours per week, either 1 or 2 days per week, reading science books, doing science activities and projects, or asking and answering scientific questions. Write out at least one of the following as the child dictates: a narration page about the science book, a brief description of the project or activity, or a question and its answer.
Religion	Learn about world religions through the study of

	history; learn the basics of the family's faith for 10 to 15 minutes per day as part of "family time."
Art & Music	OPTIONAL: Spend 1 to 2 hours per week on art projects, reading biographies of composers and artists, or listening to music.

Second Grade

Reading	20 to 25 minutes per day of phonics work until program is finished. 30 minutes of reading (skill building), 3 times per week; one instructional, one at-level, one below-level.
Literature	30 minutes, 3 days per week, focusing on stories of the Middle Ages; make notebook pages (narrations) 1 or 2 times per week; memorize a poem every 3 to 6 weeks.
Spelling	20 minutes per day, 3 to 4 days per week.
Grammar	20 minutes per day, 3 to 4 days per week.
Writing	Penmanship, 10 minutes per day, introducing cursive script halfway through the year. Short dictation exercises 2 or 3 days per week (may be completed as a history or science assignment). Do a total of three narrations per week (may be completed as a literature, history, or science assignment).
Mathematics	40 to 60 minutes per day (math lesson and story-book reading); try to do one real-life math project per week.
History	Study medieval–early Renaissance times (400–1600). Read biographies and easy history books to the child; ask the child to tell you what you've just read; make at least one narration page per week for the history notebook. Do this for a minimum of 2 hours per week, divided into 2 or 3 sessions.
Science	Spend at least 2 hours per week, either 1 or 2 days per week, reading science books, doing science activities and projects, or asking and answering

scientific questions. Write out at least one of the following as the child dictates: a narration page about the science book, a brief description of the project or activity, or a question and its answer.

Religion   Learn about world religions through the study of history; learn the basics of the family's faith for 10 to 15 minutes per day as part of "family time."

Art & Music   OPTIONAL: Spend 1 to 2 hours per week on art projects, reading biographies of composers and artists, or listening to music. Begin instrumental instruction if desired.

Third Grade

Reading   20 to 25 minutes per day of phonics work until program is finished. 30 minutes of reading (skill building), 3 times per week; one instructional, one at-level, one below-level.

Literature   30 to 45 minutes, 3 days per week, focusing on literature of the late Renaissance and early modern eras; make notebook pages (narrations) once or twice per week; memorize a poem every 3 to 6 weeks.

Spelling   20 minutes per day, 3 to 4 days per week.

Grammar   20 to 30 minutes per day, 3 to 4 days per week.

Writing   Penmanship, 10 to 15 minutes per day. Dictation exercises 3 days per week (may be completed as a history or science assignment). Do a total of three narrations per week (may be completed as a literature, history, or science assignment).

Mathematics   40 to 60 minutes per day (math lesson and storybook reading); try to do one real-life math project per week.

History   Study late Renaissance–early modern times (1600–1850). Read history books to the child; assign easy biographies and histories for the child to read; ask the child to tell you what you've just read; make at least one narration page for the history notebook. The child should be writing at least part of his own narrations now. Do this for 3 hours per week, divided into 2 or 3 sessions.

Science Spend at least 3 hours per week, either 2 or 3 days per week, reading science books, doing science activities and projects, or asking and answering scientific questions. Help the child write out at least one of the following: a narration page about the science book, a brief description of the project or activity, or a question and its answer.

Latin/Foreign Language OPTIONAL: Spend 30 minutes per day on basic vocabulary and grammar.

Religion Learn about world religions through the study of history; learn the basics of the family's faith for 10 to 15 minutes per day as part of "family time."

Art & Music OPTIONAL: Spend 2 to 3 hours per week on art projects, reading biographies of composers and artists, or listening to music. Begin or continue instrumental instruction if desired.

Fourth Grade

Reading 30 minutes of reading (skill building), 3 times per week; one instructional, one at-level, one below-level.

Literature 30 to 45 minutes, 3 days per week, focusing on literature of the modern era; make notebook pages (narrations) 1 or 2 times per week; memorize a poem every 3 to 6 weeks.

Spelling 20 minutes per day, 3 to 4 days per week.

Grammar 30 minutes per day, 3 to 4 days per week.

Writing Penmanship, 15 minutes per day. Student should write her own narrations 3 times per week (may be completed as literature, history, or science assignments). Optional: add practice in sentence and paragraph construction if student is writing easily.

Mathematics	40 to 60 minutes per day (math lesson and story-book reading); try to do one real-life math project per week.
History	Study modern times (1850–present). Read history books to the child; assign easy biographies and histories for the child to read; ask the child to tell you what you've just read; make at least one narration page per week for the history notebook. The child should be doing most of her own writing. Do this for at least 3 hours per week, divided into 2 or 3 sessions.
Science	Spend at least 3 hours per week, either 2 or 3 days per week, reading science books, doing science activities and projects, or asking and answering scientific questions. Ask the child to write out at least one of the following: a narration page about the science book, a brief description of the project or activity, or a question and its answer.
Latin/Foreign Language	OPTIONAL: Spend at least 30 minutes per day on basic vocabulary and grammar.
Religion	Learn about world religions through the study of history; learn the basics of the family's faith for 10 to 15 minutes per day as part of "family time."
Art & Music	OPTIONAL: Spend 2 to 3 hours per week on art projects, reading biographies of composers and artists, or listening to music. Begin or continue instrumental instruction if desired.

Notebook Summary, Grades 1 through 4

Literature. Use the same notebook for grades 1–4 or begin a new binder each year. This notebook contains two sections:

1. *My Books.* Use for summaries or illustrations of books from the literature lists in Chapter 5.
2. *Memory Work.* All pieces learned by heart and recited in front of family or friends.

Writing. All copywork, dictation, and narration exercises not filed under Literature, History, or Science.
Optional: stories done by students who enjoy creative writing.

History. If possible, use the same notebook for grades 1–4.
This notebook contains four divisions; each has pictures, compositions, historical narrations, and photographs of projects, arranged in chronological order. Also place copies of memorized lists, speeches, etc., in the notebook for periodic review.

1. Ancients
2. Medieval–Early Renaissance

3. Late Renaissance–Early Modern
4. Modern

Science (use a new notebook each year)
Notebooks used for life science, astronomy, and earth science should have three divisions.

1. *Narrations.* For narrations of science books.
2. *Project Pages.* Two- to three-sentence descriptions for first and second graders, answers to all four Project Page questions for third and fourth graders.
3. *Answers to Questions.* Use the form on page 194.

For chemistry and physics, add an additional section:

4. *Definitions.* All terms, briefly defined and illustrated if appropriate.

Sample Weekly Checklists

Note: These are intended only as illustrations of how your weeks might be organized. Adjust and change or make your own checklists. If particular curricula areas are a challenge and take additional time, eliminate optional studies until the core skills are mastered. Be alert for exhaustion and give plenty of breaks!

First Grade (average of 2 ½ to 3 ½ hours on task per day)
Note: Writing assignments are completed as part of history, science, and literature. They can also be scheduled as a separate course (see Second Grade).

Monday
Phonics (20 minutes) _____
At-level reading (30 minutes) _____
Grammar (10 minutes) _____
History (40–45 minutes) _____
   (Includes copying 1 sentence)

Literature (20 minutes) _____
Penmanship (5 minutes) _____
Math (30–40 minutes) _____

Tuesday
Phonics (20 minutes) _____
Spelling (15 minutes) _____

Listen to music and color
   (30 minutes) _____

Grammar (10 minutes) _____

Math (30–40 minutes) _____

Penmanship (5 minutes) _____

Science (1 hour) _____
   (Includes 1 narration)

Wednesday

Phonics (15 minutes) _____

Instructional-level reading
   (30 minutes) _____

Math (30–40 minutes) _____

Art project/drawing
   (30–40 minutes) _____

Literature (25 minutes) _____
   (Includes copying 1 sentence)

History (40–45 minutes) _____
   (Includes 1 narration)

Thursday

Phonics (20 minutes) _____

Spelling (15 minutes) _____

Grammar (10 minutes) _____

Penmanship (10 minutes) _____

Math (30–40 minutes) _____

Science (1 hour) _____
   (Includes copying 1 sentence)

Friday

Phonics (20 minutes) _____

Below-level reading
   (30 minutes) _____

Spelling (15 minutes) _____

Grammar (10 minutes) _____

Literature (25 minutes) _____
   (Includes 1 narration)

Math (30–40 minutes) _____

Penmanship (5 minutes) _____

Second Grade (average of 3 ½ to 4 hours on task per day; adjust for maturity level!)

Note: Writing assignments are done as a separate course, so slightly less time has been allowed for history, science, and literature. They could also be completed as part of longer history, science, and literature lessons (see First Grade).

Monday

Phonics (25 minutes) _____

At-level reading (30 minutes) _____

Grammar (20 minutes) _____

Literature (25 minutes) _____

Penmanship (10 minutes) _____

Math (45 minutes) _____

History (40 minutes) _____

Writing (dictation,
   15 minutes) _____

Tuesday

Phonics (25 minutes) _____

Spelling (20 minutes) _____

Writing (narration,
   25 minutes) _____

Science (1 hour) _____

Listen to music and color
   (30 minutes) _____

Penmanship (10 minutes) _____

Math (45 minutes) _____

Grammar (20 minutes) _____

Wednesday

Phonics (20 minutes) _____

Instructional-level reading
   (30 minutes) _____

Writing (dictation,
   15 minutes) _____

Math (45 minutes) _____

Literature (25 minutes) _____

History (40 minutes) _____

Art project/drawing
   (45 minutes) _____

Thursday

Phonics (25 minutes) _____

Spelling (20 minutes) _____

Grammar (20 minutes) _____

Writing (narration,
   25 minutes) _____

Penmanship (10 minutes) _____

Math (45 minutes) _____

Science (1 hour) _____

Latin (30 minutes) _____

Friday

Phonics (25 minutes) _____

Below-level reading
   (30 minutes) _____

Spelling (25 minutes) _____

Grammar (10 minutes) _____

Penmanship (10 minutes) _____

Literature (25 minutes) _____

Latin (30 minutes) _____

Math (45 minutes) _____

Writing (dictation,
   15 minutes) _____

Writing (narration,
   25 minutes) _____

Third Grade (average of 3 ½ to 4 ½ hours on task per day; adjust for maturity level!)

Note: Writing assignments are completed as part of history, science, and literature. They can also be scheduled as a separate course (see Second Grade).

Monday

Phonics (20 minutes) _____

At-level reading (30 minutes) _____

Math (45 minutes) _____

History (60 minutes) _____
    (Includes narration exercise)

Literature (30 minutes) _____
    (Dictation exercise as part of
    literature)

Penmanship (15 minutes) _____

Latin (30 minutes) _____

Tuesday

Phonics (20 minutes) _____

Spelling (20 minutes) _____

Grammar (10 minutes) _____

Listen to music and color
    (30 minutes) _____

Penmanship (15 minutes) _____

Math (45 minutes) _____

Science (90 minutes) _____
    (Includes 1 narration)

Latin (30 minutes) _____

Wednesday

Grammar (30 minutes) _____

Instructional-level reading
    (30 minutes) _____

Math (45 minutes) _____

Art project/drawing
    (30–40 minutes) _____

Literature (30 minutes) _____
    (Narration exercise as part
    of literature)

History (60 minutes) _____
    (Includes dictation exercise)

Latin (30 minutes) _____

Thursday

Phonics (20 minutes) _____

Spelling (20 minutes) _____

Grammar (10 minutes) _____

Latin (30 minutes) _____

Penmanship (15 minutes) _____

Math (45 minutes) _____

Science (90 minutes) _____

Friday

Below-level reading
    (30 minutes) _____

Spelling (20 minutes) _____

Grammar (30 minutes) _____

Penmanship (15 minutes) _____

Literature (40 minutes) _____

Math (45 minutes) _____

History (60 minutes) _____
    (Includes dictation exercise)

Latin (30 minutes) _____

Fourth Grade (average of 3½ to 4½ hours on task per day; adjust for maturity level!)

Note: This student has begun a sentence/paragraph writing course. Others might still be doing narration and dictation (see Second or Third Grade).

Monday

Literature (45 minutes) _____

At-level reading (30 minutes) _____

Math (45 minutes) _____

History (60 minutes) _____

  (Includes brief written summary)

Penmanship (15 minutes) _____

Latin (30 minutes) _____

Tuesday

Penmanship (15 minutes) _____

Spelling (20 minutes) _____

Grammar (10 minutes) _____

Listen to music and color

  (30 minutes) _____

Writing course

  (25 minutes) _____

Math (45 minutes) _____

Science (90 minutes) _____

Latin (30 minutes) _____

Wednesday

Grammar (30 minutes) _____

Instructional-level reading

  (30 minutes) _____

History (60 minutes) _____

Art project/drawing _____

  (30–40 minutes)

Literature (30 minutes) _____

  (Includes brief written summary)

Math (45 minutes) _____

Latin (30 minutes) _____

Thursday

Writing course

  (25 minutes) _____

Spelling (20 minutes) _____

Grammar (30 minutes) _____

Latin (30 minutes) _____

Penmanship (15 minutes) _____

Math (45 minutes)

Science (90 minutes) _____

Friday

Below-level reading

  (30 minutes) _____

Spelling (20 minutes) _____

Grammar (30 minutes) _____

Latin (30 minutes) _____

Literature (45 minutes) _____

Math (45 minutes) _____

History (60 minutes) _____

  (Includes brief written summary)

Curriculum Planning Worksheet

Use this worksheet to start planning out each year of study. *Download a PDF version of this worksheet at welltrainedmind.com.*

READING SKILLS

Primer Approach

     Ordinary Parents' Guide _____ *Phonics Pathways* _____ *Other* _____

O-G Approach

     All About Reading _____ *Other* _____

Possible readers to have on hand as the year begins: _____

_____

_____

_____

_____

Poems to memorize this year: _____

_____

_____

_____

_____

SPELLING

Spelling Workout _____   *All About Spelling* _____
Sequential Spelling _____   *Other* _____

GRAMMAR

First Language Lessons _____
English for the Thoughtful Child (Grades 1 & 2 only) _____
Rod & Staff (Grades 3 & 4 only) _____
Hake Grammar (Grades 4 or 3–4 only) _____
Voyages in English (Grades 3 & 4 only) _____   *Other* _____

PENMANSHIP

Handwriting Without Tears _____   *Zaner-Bloser* _____   *Other* _____

WRITING

Writing with Ease _____
Copywork, dictation, and narration across curriculum _____
Introduction to Composition (Grades 4 or advanced 3–4 only) _____
Sentence Composing (Grade 4 only) _____
Writing & Rhetoric 1: Fable (Grade 4 only) _____
Writing Strands _____   *Other* _____

MATH

Conceptual Approach
    Math Mammoth _____   *Math-U-See* _____   *Right Start* _____
    Singapore _____   *Other* _____
Procedural Approach
    Right Start _____   *Saxon* _____   *Other* _____
Conceptual Supplements (for Procedural Courses)
    Khan Academy _____   *MEP* _____   *Miquon* _____   *Other* _____
Procedural Supplements (for Conceptual Courses)
    Audio Memory _____   *Developmental Mathematics* _____
    Montessori Flash Cards _____   *Timed Math Flash Cards* _____
    Times Tales _____   *Learning Wrap-Ups* _____   *Other* _____

Possible math readers to have on hand as the year begins: _____

_____
_____
_____
_____

HISTORY

Narrative Spine Approach

 Story of the World _____ *Little History* _____ *Other* _____

Encyclopedic Spine Approach

 Usborne I-L Encyclopedia _____ *History Year by Year* _____

 Kingfisher History Encyclopedia _____ *Other* _____

Tentative Chapters/Pages to Cover Per Semester: _____

Tentative Chapters/Pages to Cover Per Week: _____

Additional readers to have on hand as the year begins: _____

_____
_____
_____

GEOGRAPHY

Geography Songs Kit _____ *Black-line Maps* _____

The Geography Book (Grades 3 & 4 only) _____

MP Geography (Grades 3 & 4 only) _____

Janice VanCleave's Geography (Grades 3 & 4 only) _____ *Other* _____

LITERATURE

Possible titles to have on hand as the year begins: _____

_____
_____
_____

SCIENCE

Fields(s) to cover this year and how many weeks to take to study them

Animal kingdom _____ / _____ Plant kingdom _____ / _____

Human body _____ / _____

Earth science _____ / _____ Astronomy _____ / _____

Chemistry _____ / _____ Physics _____ / _____
Technology _____ / _____

Life Science Spines/Curricula
DK First Animal Encyclopedia _____
National Geographic Animal Encyclopedia _____ *Green Thumbs* _____
DK First Human Body Encyclopedia _____ *Human Body: Visual Encyclopedia* _____
Elemental Biology _____ *Great Science Adventures* _____
R.E.A.L. Science, Life _____
Other(s) _____

Earth Science and Astronomy Spines/Curricula
First Earth Encyclopedia _____ *Geography: A Visual Encyclopedia* _____
Exploring the Night Sky _____ *National Geographic Kids. . . . Space* _____
Glow-in-the-Dark Constellations _____
Elemental Earth Science & Astronomy _____
Great Science Adventures _____ *R.E.A.L Science, Earth & Space* _____
Other(s) _____

Chemistry Spines/Curricula
Kitchen Science Lab _____ *Janice VanCleave's Chemistry* _____
Elemental Chemistry _____ *Great Science Adventures* _____
R.E.A.L. Science, Chemistry _____ *Other* _____

Physics Spines/Curricula
Starting with Science: Simple Machines _____
Starting with Science: Solids, Etc. _____
Physics Experiments for Children _____ *Janice VanCleave's Physics* _____
Elemental Physics _____ *Great Science Adventures* _____
Other _____

Technology Spines/Curricula
The New Way Things Work _____ *Great Science Adventures* _____

Encyclopedia
DK First Science _____ *Kingfisher Science* _____ *New Children's* _____
Other _____

FOREIGN LANGUAGES (Grades 3 & 4 only)

Prima Latina _____ *Latina Christiana* _____
Song School Latin _____ *Latin for Children* _____
Big Book of Lively Latin 1 _____ *Big Book of Lively Latin 2* _____
Song School Spanish _____ *Spanish for Children* _____
La Clase Divertida _____ *Getting Started with Spanish* _____
Getting Started with French _____
First Start French _____ *Other* _____

ART & MUSIC (optional)

Art Appreciation
Dover Art Postcards _____ *Start Exploring Masterpieces* _____
Child-Size Masterpieces _____
Getting to Know the World's Greatest Artists _____ *Other* _____

Art Skills
Artistic Pursuits _____ *Little Hands Art Book* _____
Drawing is Basic _____ *Other* _____

Music Appreciation
Beethoven's Wig _____ *Coloring Book of Great Composers* _____
Classical Composers Collections _____ *Classical Kids* _____
Rise of the Masters _____ *Early Composers Coloring Book* _____
Other _____

Music Skills
John Thompson _____ *Violin Book* _____ *Lessons* _____
Other _____

Whole Language and Phonics:
Whole to Parts versus Parts to Whole Teaching
(A Brief Explanation)

Using phonics—the method of teaching children the sounds of letters and combinations of letters—is the best way to teach reading. "Whole language" instruction, popular in many classrooms, is based on an innovation of the 1930s—the so-called "look-say" method.

The inventors of look-say reading thought that teaching children the sounds of letter combinations (phonics) required lots of drill and memorization, resulting in tedium. Couldn't this unnecessary step be eliminated? After all, good readers don't sound a word out from beginning to end; good readers glance at a word and take it all in in one gulp. Children ought to learn this from the start. So a new method of reading took over: "whole word" or "look-say." Instead of learning letter combinations and sounding words out, children were taught each word separately and in isolation.

Whole-word teaching, meant to preserve children from the drudgery of drill, actually increased the amount of drill needed. It also prevented children from reading anything that contained words they hadn't yet learned, which is why it took Theodore Geisel (Dr. Seuss) almost a year to write *The Cat in the Hat*. "That damned *Cat in the Hat* took nine months until I was satisfied," Geisel later wrote. "I did it for a textbook house and they sent me . . . two hundred and twenty-three words to use in this book. I read the list three times and I almost went out of my head." Children taught that same list could read *The Cat in the Hat* and practically nothing else.

And parents weren't able to teach whole-word reading.[1] Look-say required expert teachers. You couldn't just start teaching a child words; you had to teach the words in a particular order so that the child could read his lessons. And you had to reinforce this memory work with a complex system of drills and word games.

Look-say is generally acknowledged to have been a disaster. It's true that some children—those whose subconsciouses were very well stocked with words and sounds because they came from homes where print was important—were able to figure the process out. But many more simply gave up. Whole-word reading might have died a quick and ignoble death but for the phonics teachers, who had been laboring to turn phonics into a science. Instead of learning how to pronounce the alphabet, six-year-olds in phonics classrooms were taught phonetic notation and drilled on individual sounds for months before they were allowed to read actual sentences. Eventually, both "scientific phonics" and look-say reading gave way to the "whole language" classroom, where students—rather than being taught to sound out words—are "immersed" in language. Teachers read stories, point to words, talk to the children, and generally surround them with words, as we suggest you do during the preschool years.

Unfortunately, illiteracy is still soaring in states where whole-language classrooms dominate. There are several reasons for this. First, many whole-language teachers, while insisting that their methods differ from look-say, are still using look-say drills. They read texts over and over again, pointing to each word and encouraging the children to join in. Children eventually learn to recognize many of the words through sheer repetition. This, of course, does nothing to teach them how to read real literature, which might contain words they haven't seen in the classroom.

---

[1] This antiparent mood still has a voice in many "whole language" classrooms, expressed in such phrases (encountered by us in our research) as "No parent should tutor a child without the teacher's knowledge," "Maybe the parent shouldn't be tutoring the child," and "Reading instructional material is not designed for parents." If a teacher has ever told you not to tutor your child in phonics, you've experienced this legacy.

Second, most whole-language teachers will insist that they don't rely on look-say alone; they also teach something called "incidental phonics." If, for example, the child has seen the words *smile, smoke, small, smog,* and *smith* over and over again, the teacher will finally point out that *sm* makes the same sound *every time.* Incidental phonics teaches the connections between words and sounds *only* as the child runs across them in texts. Which means that a child who doesn't encounter many words ending in *-ough* could get to sixth grade or so before finding out that *-ough* can make an *f* sound.

This guessing game is labeled "developing phonemic awareness." It's also called "whole-to-parts phonics instruction" because the student is given the "whole" (the entire word) and only later is told about the "parts" (the letter sounds) that make it up. Granted, it's an improvement on pure look-say, which never lets on that there's any connection between words and the letters that make them up. But whole-language teaching still encourages children to guess. They see a familiar combination of letters, but they haven't learned the letters that come after. They see a word that starts with *in-,* but then they have to use *context* to figure out whether the word is *incidental, incident, inside, incite,* and so forth. And unless a teacher is standing over them to help, they have no tools to read the rest of the word.[2]

But why force the children to guess? Why not simply put them in a systematic phonics program and give them the rules?

A good systematic phonics program does just that—it tells children the rules up front. This is called "parts-to-whole" instruction because the student is taught the parts of words and then shown how they fit together. A good phonics program has the children reading books as soon as possible. Most phonics-taught children can read picture books with easy text after a few weeks. Many move on to chapter books after only a few months of instruction.[3]

---

[2] The whole-language method is infamous for suggesting that it doesn't really matter whether the child reads *incite* or *incident* as long as the sentence makes sense to the child.

[3] And, yes, English *is* a phonetic language. Rudolph Flesch writes, "About 13 per cent of all English words are partly irregular in their spelling. The other 87 per cent follow fixed rules. Even the 13 per cent are not 'unphonetic,' as Dr. Witty calls it, but

Whole-language teachers want to saturate children with language; the classical education requires it. Yet whole-language philosophy collides with the philosophy of classical education. Whole-language teachers put the highest priority on the child's mental process, not on the information that is on the page. If the child is constructing *a* meaning while reading, that's good enough. It doesn't matter if the meaning may not correspond to what's in front of them. Guessing (whole-language teachers prefer to call this "predicting by context") is perfectly all right. Ken Goodman, professor of education at the University of Arizona and a whole-language proponent, says that "accuracy is not an essential goal of reading."[4]

This attitude is one of the most troubling aspects of whole-language reading. A classical education tries to equip a child to join the Great Conversation, to understand and analyze and argue with the ideas of the past. Those *ideas* are important. Those *words* are important. Aristotle chose his terms with care; the reader must struggle to understand why, not substitute another phrase to simplify matters.

Furthermore, whole-language rejects all drill and repetitive memory work. Granted, drill can be overdone (and has been in many phonics-based classrooms). But the goal of classical education is to show a child how subjects—reading, writing, science, history—are assembled, from the most basic elements to the finished structure. And drill is important because it equips a child's mind with the most basic tools needed for understanding language.

Teaching reading by a pure whole-language approach is like trying to train a house builder by showing him a manor house, explaining to him how to construct those parts that catch his interest—a chimney here, a porch front there—and then leaving him to figure out the rest on his own. A classical approach first explains the properties of brick, wood, concrete, plaster, and steel; then teaches the prospective builder to read a plan; and only then sets him on the task of house building. A builder who knows his

---

usually contain just one irregularly spelled vowel: *done* is pronounced 'dun,' *one* is pronounced 'wun,' *are* is pronounced 'ar,' and so on" (Rudolph Flesch, *Why Johnny Can't Read and What You Can Do about It* [New York: Harper & Row, 1985], p. 13).

[4] Art Levine, "Education: The Great Debate Revisited," *Atlantic Monthly*, December 1994, p. 41.

work from the bottom up can fix a leak or a sagging floor, instead of staring helplessly at the problem and wondering what went wrong.

In the early grades, teaching should be parts to whole, rather than whole to parts. Parts-to-whole teaching gives the student all the facts—the building blocks—and then lets him assemble them into a meaningful structure. Whole-to-parts instruction presents the child with the entire structure and then pulls bits and pieces out and explains them, one at a time, as the child encounters them.

Parts-to-whole teaching tells the young historian about the gods and goddesses of ancient Rome and explains how the Romans used omens and auguries to tell the future. Whole-to-parts teaching gives the child stories about Roman religious customs and asks, "What gods did the Romans worship? Why? How is this like modern religion in America? How is this like your own experience with religion?"

Parts-to-whole science informs the budding entomologist that insects have five different types of leg and foot (swimming leg, digging leg, jumping leg, pollen-carrying leg, and food-tasting brush foot), and then asks the student to place the insects he finds into these categories. Whole-to-parts science lays out a tray full of insects and asks, "What differences do you see between these legs and those legs?"

What's the matter with whole-to-parts instruction? Nothing, except that it can be immensely frustrating for children who are at the poll-parrot stage. Whole-to-parts instruction requires analytical thought, an ability that is developed later (in our experience, around fourth or fifth grade). And whole-to-parts teaching assumes a certain knowledge base that untaught children don't yet have. Examine the instances above. The history example requires the immature mind to reflect on religious practices about which it knows very little. And the whole-to-parts science assignment can't be done unless the student knows that different insects do different things with their legs.

Learning through deduction and analysis is a valuable method—but primarily *in the second stage of the trivium*, the logic years, when the student has the accumulated knowledge of the poll-parrot years to build on. Trying to instruct children by deduction and analysis without first laying the foundation of good, solid, systematic knowledge is like building a house from the top down. Many popular school texts are whole to parts in the elementary grades; when you recognize whole-to-parts instruction, avoid it.

PART II

THE
LOGIC
STAGE

Fifth Grade through Eighth Grade

13

THE ARGUMENTATIVE CHILD

The Pert age . . . is characterized by contradicting, answering back, liking to "catch people out" (especially one's elders); and by the propounding of conundrums. Its nuisance-value is extremely high.

—Dorothy Sayers, "The Lost Tools of Learning"

Somewhere around fourth grade, the growing mind begins to switch gears. The child who enjoyed rattling off her memorized spelling rules now starts noticing all the awkward exceptions. The young historian says, "But *why* did Alexander the Great want to conquer the whole world?" The young scientist asks, "What keeps the earth in orbit around the sun?" The mind begins to generalize, to question, to analyze—to develop the capacity for abstract thought.

In the second stage of the trivium, the student begins to connect all the facts she has learned and to discover the relationships among them. The first grader has learned that Rome fell to the barbarians; the fifth grader asks why and discovers that high taxes, corruption, and an army made up entirely of mercenaries weakened the empire. The second grader has learned that a noun names a person, place, thing, or idea; the sixth grader discovers that gerunds, infinitives, and noun clauses can also act as nouns.

The third grader has learned how to multiply two two-digit numbers to produce an answer; the seventh grader asks, "What if I have only one two-digit number and an answer? Can I discover the missing number if I call it x?"

Now it's time for critical thinking.

"Critical thinking skills" has become the slogan of educators from kindergarten through high school. Critical-thinking books, software, and curricula abound. Catastrophe is predicted for children who miss out on this vital training. "Are you going to wait until schools teach thinking directly?" asks the back cover of one critical-thinking tome. "That may be too late for your children."

But what are these "critical thinking skills," and how are they to be taught?

A quick look through education materials reveals certain phrases popping up again and again: "higher-order thinking," "problem solving," "metacognitive strategies." All these boil down to one simple concept: critical thinking means that the student stops absorbing facts uncritically and starts to ask "Why?": "Why did the U.S. wait so long to enter World War I?" "Why do scientists believe that nothing can go faster than the speed of light?" "Why do words that begin with pre- all have to do with something that comes 'before'?" "How do we know that water boils at 212 degrees Fahrenheit?"

The student who has mastered "higher-order thinking" and "problem-solving techniques" doesn't simply memorize a formula. ("To find the area of a square, multiply the length of a side by itself.") Instead, she memorizes the formula and then figures out why it works. ("Hmmm . . . the sides of a square are the same, so the area inside the square is always going to measure the same horizontally and vertically. That's why I multiply the side by itself.") Once she knows why the formula works, she can extrapolate from it to cover other situations. ("How would I find the area of a triangle? Well, this triangle is like half a square . . . so if I multiply this side by itself, I'll get the area of a square . . . and then if I take half of that, I'll know how much area the triangle covers. The area of a triangle is this side, times itself, times one-half.")

Some critical-thinking advocates suggest that "thinking skills" can somehow replace the acquisition of specific knowledge. "Traditional teaching" is often referred to, with scorn, as "mere fact assimilation" or "rote memorization," an outdated mode of learning that should be replaced with classes in "learning to think." The popular teacher's journal *Education Week* defines critical thinking as "the mental process of acquiring information, then evaluating it to reach a logical conclusion or answer," and adds, "Increasingly, educators believe that schools should focus more on *critical thinking* than on memorization of facts."[1]

But you shouldn't consider critical thinking and fact gathering to be mutually exclusive activities. Critical thinking can't be taught in isolation (or "directly," as the critical-thinking manual quoted above suggests). You can't teach a child to follow a recipe without actually providing butter, sugar, flour, and salt; piano skills can't be taught without a keyboard. And focusing on the whys and wherefores doesn't mean that your child will no longer learn facts. A fifth grader can't analyze the fall of Rome until she knows the facts about Rome's decay. A seventh grader can't track dominant and recessive traits unless he knows what an allele is.

So we won't be simply recommending workbooks that claim to develop isolated "critical-thinking skills." Instead, as we cover each of the subjects—math, language, science, history, art, music—we'll offer specific instructions on how to teach your middle schooler to evaluate, to trace connections, to fit facts into a logical framework, and to analyze the arguments of others. The middle-grade student still absorbs information. But instead of passively accepting this information, she'll be interacting with it—deciding on its value, its purpose, and its place in the scheme of knowledge.

BUILDING ON THE FOUNDATION

The poll-parrot stage has prepared the middle-grade student for the logic stage in two important ways.

First, the middle-grade student should no longer be struggling with the basic skills of reading, writing, and arithmetic. A child must read fluently and well before entering the logic stage; the student who still battles his way through a sentence cannot concentrate on what that sentence means. The logic-stage student will write extensively as he evaluates, analyzes,

---

[1] "Critical Thinking," *Education Week on the Web,* www.edweek.org.

and draws conclusions; the study of grammar and punctuation will continue through high school, but the basic mechanics of spelling, comma placement, capitalization, and sentence construction should no longer act as barriers to expression. The middle-grade child will begin to move toward increasingly abstract mathematics; he can't do this unless the basic facts and concepts of arithmetic are rock solid in his mind.

Second, the student has already been exposed to the basics of history, science, art, music, and other subjects. Now he has a framework of knowledge that will allow him to think critically.

On pages 271–275, we discussed the differences between parts-to-whole and whole-to-parts instruction. When you taught bugs in first grade, you used parts-to-whole instruction. You got out all the pictures of bugs (or used actual bugs) and described the five different types of legs and feet. Then you asked the child to tell you what he just heard, to point out the different types of legs, to write a sentence or draw a picture. In other words, you taught the bits of information—the parts—to the child and then helped him assemble them into a whole.

The middle grader has already learned something about bugs, though. And his mind has matured and developed beyond the need for spoon-feeding. In the middle grades, you'll move toward a whole-to-parts method of teaching—presenting the student with a piece of information or a phenomenon and asking him to analyze it. When you study biology with a fifth grader, you can lay out a tray full of insects and ask: "What differences do you see between these legs and those?" "How would you describe each leg?" "What function does each have?" He now has enough basic knowledge about insects to apply categories to the raw information in front of him.

In the following chapters, we'll guide you through this type of teaching in the middle-grade curriculum.

LOGIC AND THE TRIVIUM

A classical education isn't a matter of tacking logic and Latin onto a standard fifth-grade curriculum. Rather, logic trains the mind to approach every subject in a particular way—to look for patterns and sets of relationships in each subject area.

But *formal logic* is an important part of this process. The systematic study of logic provides the beginning thinker with a set of rules that will help her to decide whether or not she can trust the information she's receiving. This logic will help her ask appropriate questions: "Does that conclusion follow the facts as I know them?" "What does this word really mean? Am I using it accurately?" "Is this speaker sticking to the point, or is he trying to distract me with irrelevant remarks?" "Why is this person trying to convince me of this fact?" "Why don't I believe this argument—what do *I* have at stake?" "What other points of view on this subject exist?"

These are questions that very young minds cannot easily grapple with. A seven-year-old has difficulty in understanding that (for example) a public figure might twist the facts to suit himself or that a particular text might not be trustworthy because of the writer's bias or that newspaper reports might not be accurate. But in the expanding universe of the middle-grade child, these questions have begun to make sense.

You may find yourself indebted to formal logic as well. Any parent of a fifth grader should be able to point out such logical fallacies as the *argumentum ad nauseam* (the belief that an assertion is likely to be accepted as true if it is repeated over and over again) and the *argumentum ad populum* (if everyone's doing it, it must be okay).

LOGIC IN THE CURRICULUM

In language, the logic-stage student will begin to study syntax—the logical relationships among the parts of a sentence. He'll learn the art of diagramming (drawing pictures of those relationships). The grammar-stage student wrote compositions that summarized information—how the Egyptians wrote, the important battles of the Civil War, the life of George Washington. Now, compositions will begin to focus on *structure:* how to assemble facts and ideas into central and supporting points, how to develop an argument in a way that makes sense, how to present information in an orderly, clear manner. Logic-stage students will also begin to read literature more critically, looking for character and plot development.

Properly speaking, grammar-stage math is concerned with *arithmetic*—adding, subtracting, multiplying, and dividing actual numbers. Arithmetic isn't theoretical. Arithmetic problems can be worked out in apples and oranges and pieces of bread. But in the second stage of the trivium, the student begins mathematics proper—the study of the many different relationships between numbers both known (10^{13}) and unknown ($2y \div 6x$). In other words, arithmetic is the foundation for mathematics proper.

In science, students will learn scientific *concepts*, how they relate to each other, and how they work themselves out in the physical world. They will use experiments and demonstrations to make those concepts clear and will practice recording those experiments and demonstrations properly.

History in the logic stage will take on a new character. The student will still be responsible for dates and places, but you'll encourage him to dig deeper into the motivations of leaders, into the relationships between different cultures that existed at the same time, into forms of government and causes of war. Morality should become a matter of discussion as well. Was this action (this war, this threat) justified? Why, or why not?

The study of art and music at this point will become synchronized with the study of history. The student will learn about broad developments in society and culture and will try to understand how these are reflected in the creative works of the times.

HOW TO TEACH THE LOGIC STAGE

For you, the teacher, the teaching process will change slightly. In first through fourth grades, your focus was on memorization—on the learning of rules, dates, stories, and scientific facts. You *told* the student what she needed to learn, either by reading to her or by giving her a little lecture, and you expected her to be able to repeat that information back to you. You used narration and notebook pages to bring this about.

Now, you won't be feeding the child with a spoon. You'll be asking her to dig a little deeper, to do more discovering on her own. Instead of lecturing, you'll concentrate on carrying on a dialogue with your child, a conversation in which you guide her toward the correct conclusions, while permitting her to find her own way. You'll allow the child to disagree with your conclusions, if she can support her points with the facts. And you'll expect her not simply to repeat what she's read, but to rework the material to reflect her own thoughts. Once she's done this, she'll have learned the material once and for all.

Here, one-to-one tutoring has an obvious advantage over the large public-school classroom. Classrooms encourage children to answer questions set to them; one-on-one instruction encourages children to formulate their own questions and then pursue the answers. Even the most dedicated teacher can't allow a class of thirty to dialogue their way to comprehension—the noise would be overwhelming.

As the logic stage progresses, you'll be using more and more original sources, steering away from "textbooks" in the content areas. Many textbooks are boring. And most present information in a way that's actively incompatible with the intent of the logic stage. History, for example, is often given as a series of incontrovertible facts. As Neil Postman observes, there is usually "no clue given as to who claimed these are the facts of the case . . . no sense of the frailty or ambiguity of human judgment, no hint of the possibilities of error."[2] A textbook leaves nothing for the child to investigate or question; it leaves no connections for the student to discover.

How do you guide this journey toward discovery?

Start with logic. In the next chapter, we'll introduce you to the formal study of logic. In the chapters that follow, we'll guide you in applying the categories and structures of logic to the various subjects.

We cover logic itself first; then, science and mathematics; then since the middle-grade humanities curriculum is structured around the logic of history, we present history before continuing on to reading, writing, grammar, foreign languages, art, and music.

PRIORITIES

The logic-stage student is doing much more independent work than the grammar-stage student and is requiring much less one-on-one attention from you. Home-educated students typically spend an hour in self-directed work for every ten minutes of parental tutoring.

[2] Neil Postman, *The End of Education: Redefining the Value of Schools* (New York: Knopf, 1995), p. 115.

Because of this new time economy, and because the student has now mastered the most basic elements of reading, writing, and math, you'll find that you're able to cover more material. Language, mathematics, logic, history, and science are staples of the logic stage; art and music should be pursued, if possible.

While you won't need to do as much one-on-one teaching with the student, maintain close supervision. Every home-schooling parent has made the mistake of relying a little too much on the self-reports of a seemingly mature seventh grader, only to find at Thanksgiving that most of the work has been left undone. Check assignments on a weekly basis.

Because home education is flexible, you can structure your academic day to allow a child to follow an interest. If, for example, your seventh grader acquires a passion for King Arthur, let her follow the knights of the Round Table throughout literature and history for several months; don't insist that she move to the Reformation right on schedule. If she wants to immerse herself in a complex crystal-growing project that accounts for a whole range of variables (temperature, outside impurities, different concentrations of chemicals, different mixing techniques), don't insist that she bring the experiment to an end so that you can move on to the next science topic; let her work.

During the middle grades, many students begin to develop a clear preference for either the humanities or the STEM subjects (science, technology, engineering, mathematics). This may require you to do some tricky balancing. On the one hand, it's good teaching to encourage students to explore more deeply in areas where they're talented. On the other hand, middle-grade students aren't yet ready to choose a specialty; that's something that happens closer to the high-school years (see Chapter 34). A fifth-grade student who prefers history to math may be a born humanities scholar—or she may still be struggling with foundational math concepts and feel lost in the face of increasingly difficult assignments. A sixth grader who hates literature and would rather work on technological projects may be a budding engineer—or he may be an immature reader who will hit his stride once his reading ability catches up to his technological knowledge.

So insist that your young students keep up in each core subject area, while you allow them to follow their interests in the less essential fields of study. Your STEM-inclined student should still be doing a full complement of grammar, writing, spelling, literature, and history assignments, but you might want to give art and music short shrift so that she can spend more time with her science projects. Your young novelist should still be encouraged to pursue rigorous mathematics and science, but don't insist on science fair projects if she'd rather be creating character sketches.

14

SNOW WHITE WAS IRRATIONAL: LOGIC FOR THE INTUITIVE

Captain, that is an illogical conclusion.
—Mr. Spock

SUBJECT: **Formal logic and puzzle solving, grades 5–8**
TIME REQUIRED: **3 hours per week**

How do you teach logic when you've never studied it?

If you can read, you can understand the logic texts we recommend at the end of this chapter. None of them require any previous knowledge of logic. The most important background knowledge for the study of logic is (you might be surprised to discover) *grammatical*: you have to be able to distinguish between a statement and a question, between a linking verb and an action verb, between a subject and an object.

If you can do that, you can understand logic.

AN INTRODUCTION TO LOGIC

What is logic, anyway?

Logic is simply the study of rules of reasoning. Think of logic as a roadmap that keeps you driving in the correct direction. The roadmap has no control over where you start, just as the rules of logic won't automatically guarantee that an argument begins with the correct assumptions. If you begin an argument about affirmative action, for example, by stating that one race is naturally inferior to another, logic won't prevent you from arriving at a bigoted conclusion. But if you have your facts straight, the rules of logic will guide you to the correct destination.

Logic has a three-part structure, which is used to help you examine an argument:

1. the *premise*, the facts you start with—statements
2. the *argument*, the deductions you make from these facts
3. the *conclusion*, your final deduction—another statement

A *fallacy* is a flaw in the process: a lousy premise, an incorrect argument, or an irrelevant statement in the middle.

Let's demystify this with the help of Snow White and the Seven Dwarfs (the Brothers Grimm version). At the beginning of the story, a queen is sitting at her ebony window, looking out at the falling snow. She pricks her finger, and blood falls on the snow. "Ah," she sighs, "I wish I had a child as white as snow, as red as blood, and as black as ebony." Some (unspecified) time later, this does indeed happen. The queen names the baby Snow White and dies immediately after her birth.

Already we've got material to work with here. The story contains a number of *statements*, sentences that tell us something that can be true or false. The first lesson of logic is that statements (which are the foundation of logical arguments) must be distinguished from other types of sentences.

Was the queen happy with her baby?

This isn't a statement. It doesn't give us information, and it can't be classified as true or false, so it can't be used as part of an argument. Neither can a command, such as

Finish reading the story.

Only sentences that give information can be used in a logical argument.

> The queen pricked her finger.
> The queen wished for a white, red, and black baby.
> Snow White was born after the queen's wish.
> The queen died after Snow White's birth.

All of these sentences give information, so they pass the test: they're statements (as opposed, say, to questions or commands). Now we have to decide on their *truth value*.

> The queen pricked her finger.

is true.

> The queen didn't want a baby.

is false.

A valid argument is made up of two types of statements: true statements called *premises*, and a statement of *conclusion*.

> *Premise A:* The queen wished for a white, red, and black baby.
> *Premise B:* Afterward, the queen had a white, red, and black baby.
> *Conclusion:* Therefore, the queen got her wish.

This is a valid argument. The premises are true, and the conclusion comes directly from information contained in the premises.

But it's unexpectedly easy to trip up. Consider this:

> *Premise A:* The queen wished for a white, red, and black baby.
> *Premise B:* Afterward, the queen had a white, red, and black baby.
> *Conclusion:* Therefore, the queen's wish was granted.

What's the problem? Well, the premises don't say anything about the wish being *granted*. Just because one event follows another event in time (the baby came after the wish), we can't assume that the first event *caused* the second. This fallacy has a nice Latin tag—*post hoc, ergo propter hoc*—and shows up all the time in politics.

Premise A: I was elected in 2008.
Premise B: The economy began to improve in 2009.
Conclusion: My policies caused economic improvement.

Notice that both the premises are true, but the conclusion isn't valid because it doesn't come directly from the premises.

This kind of fallacy is called an *inductive fallacy*—the conclusion might be true, but you just don't have enough information in the premises to be sure. Inductive fallacies show up when you make a conclusion (an "induction") on insufficient evidence.

Another type of inductive fallacy is the *hasty generalization:*

Premise A: Snow White's stepmother was wicked.
Premise B: Cinderella's stepmother was wicked.
Premise C: Hansel and Gretel's stepmother was wicked.
Conclusion: All fairy-tale stepmothers are wicked.

This could well be true (I can't think of any exceptions offhand), but unless you do an exhaustive survey of fairy-tale stepmothers, you can't be sure.

To continue. Snow White's father, misguided man, marries a witch who can't bear any rival to her beauty. Every morning she asks her magic mirror, "Mirror, mirror on the wall, who is the fairest of them all?" And the mirror, which never lies, replies, "You are the fairest of them all." But one day, Snow White surpasses the witch in beauty, and the mirror informs the witch, "You, my queen, have beauty rare, but Snow White is beyond compare." The queen, unable to live with this competition, tells her chief huntsman to take Snow White into the forest, kill her, and bring back her lungs and liver.

The huntsman agrees but has an attack of conscience in the forest and lets Snow White go. He brings back the lungs and liver of a boar as proof that Snow White is dead. According to the Brothers Grimm, the wicked queen then eats the organs for dinner (with salt).

Notice the queen's logic here:

Premise A: Snow White is more beautiful than I am.
Premise B: I believe that I cannot live if anyone is more beautiful than I am.
Conclusion: I cannot let Snow White live.

Is this a valid argument?

Well, let's start with the premises. After all, one of the first rules of logic is: Be sure of your premises because false premises will always yield a false conclusion.

Premise A: The earth is a flat surface.
Premise B: It is possible to fall off the edge of a flat surface.
Conclusion: It is possible to fall off the edge of the earth.

That's an impeccably valid argument in form, but since the first premise is wrong, the conclusion is useless.

How does the queen's argument look? Premise B is fine; it's called a *self- supporting statement*—a statement that has to be accepted as true. There are three types of self-supporting statements: those that have to be true because they cover all the possibilities ("Snow White is either alive or dead"), those that have to be true because they contain their own definitions ("The mirror reflects"), and those that have to do with personal belief (called "self-reports"). To say "I believe that the sun is blue" has to be accepted as logically valid, even by those who don't agree. I can prove to you that the sun is yellow, but I have to accept as fact that you *believe* it's blue. Premise B is a self-report—it has to do with the queen's feelings. Logically, it's valid.

But notice. We've already encountered one limit of logic. Is it morally acceptable to believe that you have to be the most beautiful person on earth? No, of course not. But logic is concerned with the form of the argument, not its content. You can always discount a valid conclusion if you disagree with one of its premises.

Let's apply this to history for a moment. A typical sixth-grade history-book account of the American Civil War might proceed in this way:

Premise A: Lincoln believed that it was necessary for the federal government to stop slavery.
Premise B: Only a civil war could stop slavery.
Conclusion: It was necessary for the federal government to fight a civil war.

Case closed? Not for the classically trained student, who has learned in his formal-logic class to be wary of self-reports when they show up as premises of arguments. Recast this argument without a self-report as premise A, and the argument appears quite different:

Premise A: It was necessary for the federal government to stop slavery.
Premise B: Only a civil war could stop slavery.
Conclusion: It was necessary for the federal government to fight a civil war.

This is still a valid conclusion, but now that premise A is no longer a self-report, the student cannot automatically accept it as valid. Was it truly necessary for the federal government to stop slavery? This statement has now ceased to be self-supporting and is now a *supported statement:* outside evidence has to be brought in to support it. Premise B is a supported statement as well. Before the sixth grader can accept this argument, he has to investigate other remedies for slavery and conclude that they were inadequate. And once he's done that, he'll understand the Civil War in a new and vivid way.

Now back to Snow White and the egomaniacal stepmother.

If we allow the wicked queen her self-report in premise B, we still have to deal with premise A: "Snow White is more beautiful than I am." This isn't a self-supporting statement: it doesn't cover all the possibilities ("Snow White is either beautiful or not beautiful") or contain its own definition ("Snow White is snow white"), and it doesn't have to do with personal belief. So this statement is a supported statement. There's a hidden argument in this premise:

Premise A: The mirror always tells the truth.
Premise B: The mirror says Snow White is more beautiful than I am.
Conclusion: Snow White is more beautiful than I am.

Because the mirror is magical, premise A is true and the conclusion is valid.

Snow White flees through the forest until she finds the house of the seven dwarfs, where she dines on leftovers and falls asleep in one of the dwarfs' beds. The dwarfs come home, discover their things in disarray, and exclaim, "Who's been eating our food? Who's been sitting in our chairs?" in an echo of the three bears. When they find Snow White, they decide she can stay as long as she cooks and cleans for them.

Meanwhile, the wicked queen discovers (with the help of her magical mirror) that Snow White is still alive. She disguises herself as an old peasant woman and arrives at the dwarfs' cottage with a poisoned apple—half red, half white, and magically constructed so that all the poison is in the red half. The dwarfs have warned Snow White not to let anyone in while they're at the mines, but Snow White really wants that apple.

"Look here," says the disguised queen. "I'll cut it in half and eat half myself." She eats the white half. And when Snow White sees that the apple seems harmless, she lets the woman in, takes a bite from the red half, and falls down dead. Eventually, a prince comes along and carries her body away, which jolts her so that the poisoned apple falls from her throat, and she wakes up, marries him, and lives happily ever after.

Now, there are any number of logical fallacies—statements that sound like valid arguments but aren't—implied in this story:

- *anecdotal evidence fallacy*—using a personal experience to prove a point. "I've met peasant women before, and none of them ever poisoned me."
- *argumentum ad hominem*—an attack on the speaker rather than on the argument itself. "Did the dwarfs tell you not to let anyone in? They just want you to keep on cooking their meals and scrubbing their floors."
- *argumentum ad misericordiam*—appeal to pity. "I'm just a poor peasant woman trying to earn a penny for my sick children, so you have to let me in."
- *argumentum ad verecundiam*—appeal to authority; it uses the name of a famous person in support of an assertion. "I just sold an apple to the king, and he said it was the best apple he ever ate!" (Unless the king is a noted apple connoisseur, this is irrelevant.)

- *argumentum ad lazarum*—the assumption that a poor person is automatically more virtuous than a rich person. "I'm just a simple beggar
  woman, so I'd never hurt you."

Once you've studied these and a host of other logical fallacies, you'll find
them everywhere: policy speeches, ad campaigns, election slogans, newspaper editorials, and junior-high history textbooks.

As logic continues, the student will begin to learn that all statements
can be placed into one of four categories—the *universal affirmative* ("All
stepmothers are witches"), the *universal negative* ("No princes are villains"),
the *particular affirmative* ("Some dwarfs are miners"), and the *particular negative* ("Some fairy-tale heroines are not intelligent"). These are known as
categorical statements.

The *syllogism* is a type of logical argument used for evaluating categorical statements. Snow White's syllogism probably went something like this:

My stepmother is a witch.
This peasant woman is not a witch.
Therefore, this peasant woman is not my stepmother.

Syllogisms have particular rules. For one thing, the first statement in
the syllogism

My stepmother is a witch.

ought to describe the last phrase of the conclusion, the so-called *major
term*—in this case, "my stepmother."

Also, the second statement in the syllogism

This peasant woman is not a witch.

ought to describe the first phrase of the conclusion, the *minor term*—"this
peasant woman."

Furthermore, the syllogism has to have a *middle*—a term that appears
in both of the premises, but not in the conclusion. The *middle* in Snow
White's syllogism is "witch." So far, so good.

But Snow White's middle has problems. In a syllogism, the middle has to refer to *every member of its class* in at least one of the premises (this is called a *distributed middle*). Snow White never makes a sweeping statement (a *universal* categorical statement) about witches. She has committed the fallacy of the *undistributed middle,* which always yields a false conclusion.

If she had constructed this syllogism properly, it would have looked like this:

> My stepmother is a witch.
> No peasant woman is a witch.
> Therefore, this peasant woman is not my stepmother.

In this syllogism, the statement "No peasant woman is a witch" has a *distributed middle* because it says something about *all* witches (none of them is a peasant woman). But if Snow White had made this argument—which is logically valid—she might have hesitated over that middle premise. How does she *know* that no peasant women are witches? Has she met them all?

Snow White pays for her muddled thought: she chokes to death on the apple. Fortunately, she lives in an enchanted forest and so revives and lives happily ever after—something that violates *all* known laws of logic.

HOW TO TEACH LOGIC

Logic is only one kind of critical thinking; studying the art of argumentation will not, in itself, turn your young student into an analytical thinker. But logic is a useful tool. It teaches students to pay attention to the exact words used in arguments—a skill vital to critical thinking in all areas of the curriculum. Logic trains the mind to follow certain patterns and gives students a new way to think about the categories *true* and *false*.

There are three basic sorts of logic: informal, formal, and symbolic. Informal logic pays close attention to arguments made in words, with a particular focus on finding fallacies. Formal logic takes this one step further, distilling verbal arguments into formulas (such as the major premise, minor premise, and conclusion) and paying much more attention to form and syntax than meaning. And symbolic logic reduces the patterns of argumentation even further, into symbolic expressions. (Propositional logic is the major subset of symbolic logic and is the type of symbolic logic you will most often encounter in advanced logic texts.)

Symbolic logic is a senior high-school/college-level subject, and not all students need to advance forward into propositional logic; it's most useful for philosophy and advanced mathematics. In the middle grades, you'll begin with the study of informal logic. Once the student is comfortable with informal logic, aim to advance forward into at least one year of formal logic.

Be sensitive to the student's level of understanding. Not all fifth graders are ready for informal logic. A student who is still struggling with grammar should wait at least a year to begin the study of informal logic and may not be ready for formal logic until ninth grade. You cannot force mental maturity; be willing to be flexible.

We suggest that you begin with a year of what we call "casual" informal logic: a year of exploring terms and methods of informal logic through storybooks, puzzles, and other fun activities. This will serve as a warm-up for a more organized study of informal logic. Plan on spending two more years working through an informal logic course, and then wrap up with at least one year of formal logic. Progressing on to the second year of formal logic is optional, and the progression may well run over into the high-school years.

Sample progressions might look like this:

For the student comfortable with both grammar and mathematics:

GRADE	TIME PER WEEK	SUBJECT
Fifth	2 hours	"Casual" informal logic
Sixth	3 hours	Informal logic I
Seventh	3 hours	Informal logic II
Eighth	4 hours	Formal logic I

Optional progression forward, for students inclined toward mathematics and philosophy:

| Ninth | 4–5 hours | Formal logic II |
| Tenth | 5–6 hours | Symbolic/propositional logic, introduction |

Slower progression:

GRADE	TIME PER WEEK	SUBJECT
Fifth	———	———
Sixth	2 hours	"Casual" informal logic
Seventh	3 hours	Informal logic I
Eighth	3 hours	Informal logic II
Ninth	4 hours	Formal logic I

Optional:

Tenth	4 hours	Formal logic II

RESOURCES

Most books can be obtained from any bookseller or library; most curricula can be bought directly from the publisher or from a major home-school supplier such as Rainbow Resource Center. Contact information for publishers and suppliers can be found at www.welltrainedmind.com. If availability is limited, we have noted it. Where indicated, resources are listed in chronological order (the order you'll want to use them in). Books in series are listed together. Remember that additional curricula choices and more can be found at www.welltrainedmind .com. Prices change constantly, but we have included 2016 pricing to give an idea of affordability.

"Casual" Informal Logic

(Pick from among the following. They are listed in order of difficulty.)

Langman, Kris. *Adventures in Reason* series. Boston: Post Hoc Publishing.
   Logic to the Rescue: Adventures in Reason. 2008.
   The Prince of Physics: Adventures in Reason. 2014.
      Entertaining ebook series about a heroine who enters a magical land filled with knights, talking scarecrows, castles, wishing wells, and logical fallacies. A fun introduction written on a fifth-grade level, excellent for students who enjoy reading.

Risby, Bonnie. *Blast Off With Logic* series. Austin, TX: Prufrock Press, 2005.
   Logic Countdown (Grades 3–4).

Logic Blastoff (Grades 4–6).

Orbiting with Logic (Grades 5–7).

> A very different approach, this workbook series focuses in on teaching deductive thinking: using grids, diagrams, charts, sequence completion, analogies, and other tools to sharpen the student's thinking skills. The first book will be simple for most fifth graders, but is worth completing as preparation for the more advanced material in the second and third books. Good for students who are more comfortable with mathematical notation than with written explanations.

Baker, Michael. *The Basics of Critical Thinking*. North Bend, OR: Critical Thinking Company, 2015.

> Combines the workbook approach of the *Blast Off* series with some attention to logical fallacies; a one-year course that begins on a low fifth-grade level but then grows more complex. Sample pages can be viewed at the publisher's website.

Almossawi, Ali. *An Illustrated Book of Bad Arguments*, 2nd ed. New York: The Experiment Publishing, 2013.

> Engaging cartoons illustrating logical fallacies, each one followed by a brief explanation of the fallacy itself. Well suited to fifth grade and above.

Givler, Ray. *Don't Get Fooled! How to Analyze Claims for Fallacies, Biases, and Other Deceptions*. Ray Givler, 2013.

> This self-published book (available through Amazon.com as an ebook and print-on-demand paperback) offers clear explanations of logical fallacies and how they look in real life. Fifth- to sixth-grade reading level; you'll probably want to spend a little extra time finding additional examples of the fallacies (in real life, news reports, Facebook debates, etc.).

Informal Logic

Classical Academic Press informal logic sequence. Camp Hill, PA: Classical Academic Press.

> Larsen, Aaron, and Joelle Hodge. *The Art of Argument: An Introduction to the Informal Fallacies*.

Student Text. $22.95.

Teacher's Edition. $24.95.

DVD Set. $54.95.

Johnson, Shelly. *The Argument Builder: Constructing an Argument Piece by Piece.*

Student Text. $22.95.

Teacher's Edition. $24.95.

> Together, these two sets provide a two-year course in informal logic (fallacies, an introduction to Aristotle's "common topics" and sub-topics, and the development of valid arguments). Begin with *The Art of Argument* (which includes an optional teaching DVD) and continue with the *Argument Builder.* Samples are available at the publisher's website. Although the publisher lists this as seventh grade and above, the books are easily accessible to younger students who are good readers and have completed a year of casual study as described above.

Critical Thinking series. North Bend, OR: Critical Thinking Company.

Harnadek, Anita. *Critical Thinking Book One: Problem Solving, Reasoning, Logic, and Arguments.* 1998.

Student Text. $24.99.

Instruction/Answer Guide: $10.99

———. *Critical Thinking Book Two: Problem Solving, Reasoning, Logic, and Arguments.* 2014.

Student Text. $26.99.

Instruction/Answer Guide. $10.99

O'Meara, William, and Daniel Flage. *James Madison Critical Thinking Course.* 2011.

Student Text. $39.99.

Answer Guide. $10.99.

> The workbook format of this logic course is well suited to students who find complex text difficult or who do not learn primarily through reading. Books One and Two cover informal logic, including deduction, inference, and logical fallacies, and also provide a brief introduction to some formal logic terms and categories. The *James Madison Critical Thinking Course* provides problem-solving in the context of mystery stories and goes more deeply into beginning

formal logic. Complete all three books over two years; complete one book per year and begin formal logic one year later; or skip the *James Madison* course and go directly into formal logic after *Critical Thinking Book 2.*

Formal Logic

Cothran, Martin. *Traditional Logic.* Louisville, KY: Memoria Press, 2000.
  Traditional Logic I: An Introduction to Formal Logic.
    Basic Set (student book, teacher key, quizzes). $38.
    Complete Set (student book, teacher key, quizzes, instructional DVDs). $75.
  Traditional Logic II: Advanced Formal Logic.
    Basic Set (student book, teacher key, quizzes). $38.
    Complete Set (student book, teacher key, quizzes, instructional DVDs). $75.

A straightforward course in basic formal logic. The student and teacher books are concise; the instructional DVDs are highly recommended. Good for mathematical/philosophical/scientific thinkers who intend to do a full two years of formal logic. The publisher also offers an online version of the course. Memoria Press is a Christian publisher and a significant number of the examples are drawn from biblical writers and the Church fathers. Not all students will need to complete Book II. Samples can be viewed at the publisher's website.

Hodge, Joelle, Aaron Larsen, and Shelly Johnson. *The Discovery of Deduction: An Introduction to Formal Logic.* Camp Hill, PA: Classical Academic Press, 2009.
  Student Text. $26.95.
  Teacher's Edition. $29.95.

A one-year introduction to formal logic, well suited to students who do not intend to go on to the second year of study. Instead of the combination of brief text and DVD teaching found in the Memoria Press course, this is a more developed text at a slightly more complex reading level. Most examples are drawn from the classics rather than from Christian writers. Samples can be viewed at the publisher's website.

15

THE LANGUAGE OF REASON:
MATH

Mathematics is the extension of common sense by other means.
—Jordan Ellenberg, *How Not to Be Wrong*

SUBJECT: **Mathematics and algebra, grades 5–8**
TIME REQUIRED: **45 to 60 minutes per day**

During the logic stage, the study of math begins to move away from the elementary-level focus on *arithmetic* (understanding and carrying out mathematical operations such as adding, subtracting, dividing, multiplying, and so on) to a wider understanding of *mathematics* (how numbers and quantities and shapes relate to one another and explain the world). Arithmetic uses numbers; mathematics also makes use of symbols and signs and proofs. Algebra, trigonometry, and calculus are all branches of mathematics; they depend, and build, on a strong understanding of arithmetic.

The broader focus on mathematics becomes possible because the child's mind is making the transition from the *mental image* mode (picturing objects to go along with numerical symbols) to the *symbolic* mode (using numerals alone). Until this transition is complete, the abstract operations demanded by pre-algebra and algebra are impossible. A problem such as 9×2 simply requires you to picture two sets of nine objects. But a problem such as $-5x = -15$ requires you to deal with symbols that have no easily pictured reality behind them. If I don't know what x is, how can I picture it? And what mental image can I make of a negative number?

This transition to the symbolic mode happens for most students some-time between grades five and eight—but it's impossible to lay down a strict rule for exactly when. The move from concrete to abstract thinking depends on mental maturity, which can't be rushed. However, the better the student's grasp of arithmetical concepts and operations, the simpler the transition will be.

HOW TO PLAN MIDDLE-GRADE MATH

Everything we said about math approaches in Chapter 6 also applies to logic-stage curricula, so we won't repeat it all here. But if you haven't read Chapter 6, go back now and review the distinction between procedural and conceptual math. Like grammar-stage programs, logic-stage programs lean toward one approach or the other, and you'll need to continue to make sure that the student has the opportunity to both practice operations *and* understand concepts.

Likewise, review the explanation of the spiral versus the mastery approach to mathematics instruction; this continues to apply to middle-grade programs.

And although you may choose to make use of tutorials, online classes, or other helps as your student nears algebra, our Chapter 6 exhortation to improve your own mathematical understanding still holds true. You don't have to master quadratic equations along with your student, but you should at least be able to grasp what a quadratic equation is. One or two of the self-education resources listed at the end of Chapter 6 should still be on your bedside table.

At the beginning of the logic stage, you should concentrate on solidify-ing the student's understanding of, and skill in, arithmetical operations. You'll begin to introduce more abstract concepts: negative numbers, percentages, probabilities, and decimals. Increase the time spent doing word problems and move toward more complex problems that require both logic and abstract mathematical reasoning. Your curriculum should involve plenty of practice—and *no* use of calculators. Until the transition to the symbolic mode of thought is complete, students must continue to carry out their own math operations.

We suggest that you also do some practical, hands-on math work during these years. The middle-grade student grows easily impatient with material that doesn't seem to have any logical connection to real life, which is why the National Council of Teachers of Mathematics suggests that middle-grade math curricula place "math in the context of students' everyday lives . . . giving students hands-on activities"[1] and real-life problems to solve.

Most math curricula can be finished in a year if you do four lessons per week and set aside one extra day to do testing, consumer math, a real-life math problem, or math games. We've suggested a few consumer math and math game books at the end of this chapter. Real-life problems might include

- figuring out the family's grocery budget for a week (or a month), or finding the best buys at the grocery store
- figuring out expenses and profits for a kid-run home business—grass cutting, pet tending, baby-sitting, baking
- balancing a checkbook (better now than in college)
- figuring out the monthly and yearly interest on a credit-card debt (ditto)
- calculating the area of a room, a wall, or the entire house for wallpapering, carpeting, or another home project
- figuring out the cost of driving the car to and from a special event
- figuring out how much a restaurant meal would cost if it were cooked at home
- calculating the cost in work hours of movie tickets, concert passes, or other types of entertainment

[1] Debra Viadero, "Math Texts Are Multiplying," *Education Week on the Web*, May 8, 1996, www.edweek.org.

- altering a recipe so that it serves a different number of people—for example, reducing a six-person dish so that it will now serve two or (more complicated) rewriting a four-person recipe so that it will now serve nine or eleven
- working out the itinerary for a family trip, complete with routes, time-tables, and scheduled stops

Your own family life will yield plenty of additional problems. Try to stay alert for those times you use numbers, measurements, or calculations, and then ask yourself whether this problem is within the reach of your young math student.

In most math programs, the reorientation toward symbolic mathematics begins in earnest with pre-algebra. It's normal for a student to be ready for pre-algebra any time between sixth and ninth grade. As you look forward to the high-school years, remember that students need three years of high-school math—algebra I, algebra II, and geometry—in order to graduate from high school, so ninth grade is the absolute latest that any student should take pre-algebra. (Even if pre-algebra is taken in ninth grade, you can't award a high-school credit for it, since it is considered a middle-grade course.) Many colleges prefer to see four years of mathematics, so beginning pre-algebra no later than eighth grade keeps one year of high school open for pre-calculus or trigonometry. STEM-oriented students (those focusing in on science, technology, engineering, and mathematics) should take pre-algebra no later than seventh grade so that the twelfth-grade year is open for an advanced math elective.

Mastery of algebra has implications that go far beyond successful college admissions. Algebra, even at its most basic level, requires the student to work with unknowns, which means that she cannot memorize set answers and fill them in mechanically. Instead, she must analyze each problem, discover its central point, and then apply the knowledge she has already acquired to its solution. Algebra, like logic, teaches the mind to think straight. It demands not only the memorization of information, but also the ability to apply that information in a number of different situations. *That* is higher-order thinking.

We can't emphasize enough that higher-order thinking requires mastery of the lower-order skills. Calculators are only acceptable once the student is completely fluent in arithmetic. Again, we depart from the opinion of the National Council of Teachers of Mathematics, which recommends the use of calculators beginning in fourth grade—a standard that inevitably produces seventh graders with little intuitive understanding of mathematics.

The resources listed at the end of this chapter are divided into "Before Algebra" (curricula that firm up arithmetical understanding, typically used for fifth and sixth grade) and "Algebra" (including pre-algebra, which introduces algebraic concepts). Use the "Before Algebra" resources until your student is confident and working problems with ease; then, introduce pre-algebra. If after a good two-month trial, the student is frustrated, try switching programs; if there's no improvement in six weeks or so, go back to the "Before Algebra" programs and give the student another six months or so to mature. It's not always easy to tell when a student is ready to step forward into algebraic thinking, and you should be willing to experiment without panicking that your child isn't progressing "fast enough."

SUGGESTED SCHEDULES

45–60 minutes per day	M, T, W, Th	Math lesson
60 minutes or more	F	Real-life math project or activity

RESOURCES

Most books can be obtained from any bookseller or library; most curricula can be bought directly from the publisher or from a major home-school supplier such as Rainbow Resource Center. Contact information for publishers and suppliers can be found at www.welltrainedmind.com. If availability is limited, we have noted it. Where indicated, resources are listed in chronological order (the order you'll want to use them in). Books in series are listed together. Remember that additional curricula choices and more can be found at www.welltrainedmind.com. Prices change constantly, but we have included 2016 pricing to give an idea of affordability.

Before Algebra

Curricula listed alphabetically.

Note: If you've been using an elementary program with success, stick with it until at least the end of the fifth-grade year; notes about the transition to pre-algebra are found below. If you're just beginning to home school now, see the descriptions below for guidance about where to start.

Math Mammoth

Math Mammoth is strongly mastery oriented, and highly conceptual in approach. Presentation is simple (one book for each level, containing both the explanations and all of the problems to be worked); concepts are explained clearly and in small steps; there are plenty of illustrations (although no manipulatives included); and you can download each level for an extremely affordable price.

The program is very strong on concepts, mental math, and problem solving. It is much weaker in practicing procedures, and very light on drill. In addition, there is practically no teacher guidance. The program is advertised as "self-teaching," which it is absolutely *not*. There's nothing wrong with the explanations in the text, but if your child doesn't understand on the first read-through, you'll have to figure out how to re-present the material on your own.

Continue to add math-fact drills as needed along with more frequent review of concepts that have been covered in the past. Sample lessons and many additional resources are available at the publisher's website. The curriculum is available both as a download and on a CD. Each level contains two books: A for the first semester and B for the second. When you purchase the "Full Set" you also get answer keys, additional review, and an Internet-linked worksheet generator.

The download for each set is $37.50; the CDs are priced at $42.50.

Students who are new to the program should take the placement test at the publisher's website. Students who have been using Math Mammoth with success can simply continue at their own pace until the Grade 7 book is complete. Grade 7 covers pre-algebra; most students should be able to transition into another Algebra I program without difficulty. However, since most algebra options offer a systematic four-year program (pre-algebra, algebra I, geometry, and algebra II), you may also choose to stop the program after Grade 6 and begin the algebra sequence with the pre-algebra book related to that series.

Math Mammoth Light Blue Series

Grade 5 full set. Arithmetical operations, place value, decimals, simple equations, graphing, fractions, basic geometry.

Grade 6 full set. Arithmetical operations; decimal review; fraction review; statistics; ratios and percentages; prime factorization; first introduction to pre-algebraic topics.

Grade 7 full set. Introduction to algebra: basic concepts, one-step equations, negative numbers, linear equations, ratios and proportions, geometry, probability, statistics.

Math-U-See

Math-U-See is a conceptual program, mastery in approach, based on a series of teaching videos in which concepts are demonstrated using manipulatives. It is suited to parents who are intimidated by the idea of teaching math, and to children who are very hands-on or visual in their learning styles. The multisensory approach is particularly good for students who have some level of dyslexia. Supplement the program with additional drill as necessary (see the "Procedural" supplements listed below).

Students who are already using Math-U-See should continue on through the remaining books of the Elementary Curriculum (they are, in order, *Alpha* (single-digit addition and subtraction), *Beta* (multiple-digit addition and subtraction), *Gamma* (multiplication), *Delta* (division), *Epsilon* (fractions), and *Zeta* (decimals and percentages). Students new to the program should take the placement test provided on the publisher's website.

The Elementary Curriculum is followed by Math-U-See's algebra sequence. Students who finish Zeta and are not ready for pre-algebra should consider moving sideways into one of the other "Before Algebra" programs listed.

Each level includes a Student Pack (workbook and test booklet) and an Instruction Pack (Instruction Manual and DVD).

Gamma (multiplication).

Instruction Pack. $44.

Student Pack. $30.

Delta (division).
  Instruction Pack. $44.
  Student Pack. $30.
Epsilon (fractions).
  Instruction Pack. $45.
  Student Pack. $30.
  Fraction Overlays. $40.
Zeta (decimals and percentages).
  Instruction Pack. $45.
  Student Pack. $30.
Algebra/Decimal Inserts. $20.

Right Start Mathematics

Right Start Math, a hands-on program based on Montessori principles, is primarily conceptual but also provides extensive procedural practice. It leans toward the spiral approach and is well designed for students who struggle with fine motor skills.

Students new to the program should take the placement test on the publisher's website. First-time users should purchase the "starter kit," which includes manipulatives; students who have been using the program in earlier grades simply need the individual manuals and worksheets. All students should have the Level G Starter Kit, which contains tools not previously used.

The elementary program is divided into levels, not grades. Currently, the program goes directly from Level E (which can be finished in fifth grade or even as early as fourth grade) to Level G, a quite advanced geometry/pre-algebra course that is equivalent to the seventh-grade level offered by other programs. Except for mathematically precocious students, we would recommend moving sideways from Level E into one of the other Before Algebra programs recommended.

The publisher is currently planning a Level F to serve as a bridge between Levels E and G, but as of this writing Level F is not available. Check the publisher's website for updates and sample lessons.

  Level E Starter Kit. $215.
  Or *Level E Lessons* ($70) and *Level E Worksheets* ($20).
  Level G Starter Kit. $150.

Saxon Math

Saxon Math is a procedural and heavily spiral program. Some students will find it dry and uninspiring, while others need the careful step-by-step instruction, the concrete examples, and the repetition. The *Home Study Kits* contain student workbooks and a teacher's manual. Saxon contains more drill than many students need, so you should feel free to assign every other problem or tailor the program to your child's needs in some other way.

After third grade, Saxon is organized by "skill level" rather than "grade level." The first middle-grade level, Math 5/4, can be taken in either the fourth- or fifth-grade year and is followed by 6/5, 7/6, 8/7 (an optional year), and then Algebra 1/2 (pre-algebra), which can be started right after 7/6 unless students need additional work and practice.

Placement tests are available at the publisher's website, under the "Resources" link for Saxon Math Homeschool.

We strongly suggest supplementing Saxon with Khan Academy or another of the conceptual resources listed below.

Saxon Homeschool Mathematics. Boston: Houghton Mifflin Harcourt.

Saxon Math 5/4 Homeschool Complete Kit, 3rd ed. $96.85.

Saxon Math 6/5 Homeschool Complete Kit, 3rd ed. $96.85.

Saxon Math 7/6 Homeschool Complete Kit, 4th ed. $107.75.

Saxon Math 8/7 Homeschool Complete Kit, 3rd ed. $107.75.

> This is the transitional book for students who aren't ready to begin pre-algebra. If your student goes through *Math 7/6* without unusual difficulty, skip *Math 8/7* and go straight into *Algebra* 1/2 or another algebra sequence

Singapore Primary Math

Singapore Math is highly conceptual; its focus is on teaching mathematical thinking from the very beginning and "mental math" puzzles are assigned as soon as children learn to count. Each Primary Math semester for grades K–6 consists of one course book and one workbook. Singapore is not as fact-oriented as Saxon or Math-U-See, and it lacks the procedural instruction found in Right Start; the coursebooks and workbooks alone do not provide enough practice, so invest in the additional resources the program offers, such as the *Extra Practice* books. Be sure to add the *Challenging Word Problems* into your fifth- and sixth-grade years.

Students who complete Level 6 should be prepared for pre-algebra, but if an extra year of maturity is needed, consider going sideways into one of the other recommended programs.

Singapore Math, U.S. edition.
$12.50 for each textbook, $11.20 for each workbook, $17.50 for each Home Instructor Guide. The program can be ordered from Singapore Math, Inc. (the U.S. distributor, not the program publisher) or from a home-school supplier. The U.S. edition uses American weights and money.

Primary Math US 5A Textbook.
Primary Math US 5A Workbook.
Primary Math US 5A Home Instructor's Guide.
Primary Math US 5B Textbook.
Primary Math US 5B Workbook.
Primary Math US 5B Home Instructor's Guide.
Primary Math US 6A Textbook.
Primary Math US 6A Workbook.
Primary Math US 6A Home Instructor's Guide.
Primary Math US 6B Textbook.
Primary Math US 6B Workbook.
Primary Math US 6B Home Instructor's Guide.
Extra Practice for Primary Math US Edition 5. $11.50.
Extra Practice for Primary Math US Edition 6. $11.50.
Challenging Word Problems for Primary Mathematics Common Core Edition 5. $12.80.
Challenging Word Problems for Primary Mathematics Common Core Edition 6. $12.80.

Algebra

Curricula listed alphabetically.
Note: There are many programs available to home educators; explore more algebra options and read user reviews at www.welltrainedmind.com.

Art of Problem Solving

The Art of Problem Solving math program is a highly conceptual, discovery-oriented program. Designed (in the publisher's words) for "outstanding math students," it is probably best suited to students who

312   THE LOGIC STAGE

flourished with the approach taken by Singapore and Math Mammoth. Rather than learning concepts and then practicing skills to reinforce them, students are challenged to solve problems in order to find their way to mastery; puzzlement is an important part of the program. Students work their way through sets of problems that slowly increase in difficulty in order to uncover a concept, and are then given an explanation of the concept itself *afterward*.

This will suit students who enjoy a challenge and who prefer to find their way independently, but frustrate those who need a little more specific guidance and leading from a teacher. For those whose learning style suits the program, AOPS can lead to high achievement.

Diagnostic tests and samples are available at the publisher's website; online classes using the books, and online versions of the texts, are also offered.

For additional advanced texts, see Chapter 28.

Art of Problem Solving mathematics curriculum. Alpine, CA: AOPS Press.

> *Prealgebra.* Richard Rusczyk, David Patrick, and Ravi Boppana. Text and solutions, $54.
>
> *Introduction to Algebra.* Richard Rusczyk. Text and solutions, $59.
>
> A complete Algebra I course with some Algebra II material included.
>
> *Introduction to Geometry.* Richard Ruscyzk. Text and solutions, $57.

Math-U-See

In the upper levels, Math-U-See continues on with the workbook/video/manipulative combination previously used (see above). The algebra sequence follows the standard progression of pre-algebra, first-year algebra, geometry, second-year algebra, and trigonometry.

Each Universal Set includes all manipulatives as well as instructional DVD, solution manual, student workbook, and tests. Students who have used previous levels of Math-U-See may already have the manipulatives and can simply order the Base Set for pre-algebra and algebra I for $90.

Placement tests, online samples, and more ordering options can be found at the publisher's website.

Math-U-See. Lancaster, PA: Math-U-See, Inc.

> *Pre-Algebra Universal Set* ($169) or *Base Set* ($90).
>
> *Algebra I Universal Set* ($169) or *Base Set* ($90).
>
> *Geometry Universal Set* ($92).

Saxon

The upper levels of Saxon continue with the same careful procedural approach as the elementary and middle grades (see above). Placement tests can be downloaded from the publisher's website. Supplement with conceptual resources as necessary.

Previous editions of Saxon math had "integrated geometry"; rather than being divided into the traditional American sequence of algebra I, geometry, and algebra II, the three books (Algebra I, Algebra II, and Advanced Mathematics) spread algebraic and geometric topics out over three years. The current edition follows the standard American pattern instead. If you are using an older version, be aware that all geometry topics will not be covered until the end of the third year, which may affect testing results (since most American standardized tests assume all geometry has been covered in the second year).

Saxon Homeschool Mathematics. Boston: Houghton Mifflin Harcourt.

Saxon Algebra 1/2 Kit with Solutions Manual, 3rd ed. $120.60.
   Pre-algebra.

Saxon Algebra I Homeschool Kit with Solutions Manual, 3rd ed. $129.20.
Saxon Homeschool Geometry Kit with Solutions Manual, 1st ed. $135.80.

VideoText

Developed by mathematics teacher Tom Clark, VideoText takes a different approach to algebra. The first course, *Algebra: A Complete Course*, covers pre-algebra, algebra I, and algebra II in a single course that stretches over 176 lessons (and can take up to three years to complete), while *Geometry: A Complete Course* is 176 lessons covering geometry, trigonometry, and pre-calculus. Since the geometry course follows the algebra course, students will not complete geometry topics normally taught after algebra I until later years of study; this is a perfectly reasonable strategy, but may affect test results (particularly SAT scores) for students who begin the sequence late.

VideoText, recommended by the developer of RightStart as a good follow-up to the RightStart elementary course, is mastery-oriented (not spiral) and nicely blends conceptual teaching with procedural practice. Students watch a DVD lesson, pausing when instructed to answer questions or complete assignments, and then work through practice problems.

The program is particularly well suited to students who are ready to begin pre-algebra relatively early, giving them a good chance to get through both courses before SAT testing begins. Students who do not wish to go on to trigonometry may want to substitute a separate geometry course.

Scope and sequence and further explanations of the method are available at the publisher's website. Instructional materials include DVDs, workbook, print version of DVD instruction, solutions manual, progress tests, and instructor's guides; the publisher also offers an online version of the program with varied pricing depending on the number of students taking part.

Algebra: A Complete Course.
Algebra Modules A-B-C. $279.
Algebra Modules D-E-F. $279.
Geometry: A Complete Course with Trigonometry. $529.

Online Math Options

Pre-algebra is often the point at which parents decide to outsource math instruction. There are a number of good, live, interactive algebra classes offered online. Web addresses, teachers, and materials often change; for a continuously updated list of recommended classes, visit www.welltrained mind.com.

Real-Life Math

Checkbook Math: Detailed Exercises for Learning to Manage a Checkbook. Scottsdale, AZ: Remedia Publications, 2010.
$7.99. Order from Remedia Publications. Students learn to write checks, keep a register, and balance a checkbook.

Math on the Menu. Berkeley, CA: GEMS, 1999.
$20. Order from the Lawrence Hall of Science Museum Store. Developed by teachers Jaine Kopp and Denise Davila, this 144-page math unit will lead you through a real-life math scenario: the Rosada family is opening and then expanding their Mexican restaurant, and they need help pricing the menu, combining ingredients, analyzing costs, opening a second location, and more.

Menu Math: Market Math and Extra Price Lists. Scottsdale, AZ: Remedia Publications, 2009.
$17.99. Order from Remedia Publications. A colorful grocery price list

and real-life math problems for students to solve: comparing prices and quantities, using coupons, and more.

Moneywise Kids. Ann Arbor, MI: Aristoplay, 1994.
$12. Order from Talicor. Two games that require kids seven and up to budget and dispose of a hypothetical paycheck.

Stanmark, Jean, et al. *Family Math.* Berkeley, CA: Equals, 1996.
$19.95. Order from a bookstore, Rainbow Resource Center, or the Lawrence Hall of Science Museum Store. Published by the Family Math program at the Lawrence Hall of Science, this series is designed for use by the entire family (K–6 especially). It contains hands-on math activities, games, and reference charts. A good guide to real-life math problems.

Thompson, Virginia, et al. *Family Math: The Middle School Years, Algebraic Reasoning and Number Sense.* Berkeley, CA: Equals, 1998.
$20.95. Order from a bookstore or from the Lawrence Hall of Science Museum Store. The sequel to *Family Math*, this book provides more family-oriented math activities, including some that reinforce algebra skills.

Conceptual Math Supplements

Arbor Algebra series.
An engaging narrative approach to algebraic skills, with plenty of examples and accompanying workbooks. Order from Arbor Algebra.
Samples are available on the publisher's website. Additional titles dealing with more advanced topics are listed in Chapter 28.
Rollman, Linus. *Jousting Armadillos & Other Equations: An Introduction to Algebra.*
Student text and workbook. $25.
Answer book and tests. $35.

Gardner, Martin.
Martin Gardner, mathematician and magician, created science and math puzzles for *Scientific American,* the *New York Times,* and *NPR.* Although much of Gardner's work is better used with high-school students, a selection of his puzzles has been reprinted by Dover Press for younger thinkers; an entertaining way to encourage logic-stage students to exercise those "higher-level" thinking skills.

Classic Brainteasers (1995).

Entertaining Mathematical Puzzles (1986).

My Best Mathematical and Logic Puzzles (2013).

Perplexing Puzzles and Tantalizing Teasers (1988).

Hands-On Equations. Allentown, PA: Borenson and Associates.

Hands-On Equations is a supplemental problem-solving method, excellent for introducing younger students to algebraic thinking. Manipulatives and activities make abstract math concepts clear for visual and kinesthetic learners, who are taught to make models of how equations work. An app version is also available (see welltrainedmind.com).

Additional buying options are available at the publisher's website.

Hands-On Equations Deluxe Home Set. $69.95.

Instructor's manual, verbal problems workbook, manipulatives, worksheets, and DVD. Can be purchased separately as well.

Khan Academy.

Founded by Salman Khan as a nonprofit educational organization, Khan Academy offers "microlectures" in all elementary mathematical concepts, along with online exercises and practice problems. Use to learn or review specific topics, or design a personalized instructional plan. Highly recommended as a supplement to any math program.

www.khanacademy.org.

Mathematics Enhancement Program.

A British version of a mathematics program developed in Hungary, MEP offers free online practice sheets, answers, and some teacher helps, along with number lines and number and shape cards. When followed sequentially, the lessons are spiral in approach. Download at the Centre for Innovation in Mathematics Teaching.

www.cimt.plymouth.ac.uk.

Procedural Math Supplements

Developmental Math: A Self-Teaching Program. Halesite, NY: Mathematics Programs Associates.

Each level offers a workbook ($10), teacher's guide ($4), and solution manual ($15). A full description of the twenty levels in the program and a placement test is available on the publisher's website. Lots of extra practice problems for elementary math operations; useful to review past concepts while using a mastery program, or to develop more mastery while using a spiral program. Best ordered from Rainbow Resource Center.

Level 9. Division: Concepts and Facts.

Level 10. Hundreds and Three-Unit Numbers.

Level 11. Three-Unit Numbers: Multiplication and Division Skills.

Level 12. Thousands and Large Numbers: Concepts and Skills.

Level 13. Decimals, Fractions, and the Metric System: Concepts and Basic Skills.

Level 14. Fractions: Concepts and Skills.

Level 15. Fractions: Advanced Skills.

Level 16. Special Topics: Ratio, Percent, Graphs and More.

Level 17. Algebra 1: Signed Numbers.

Level 18. Algebra 2: Equations.

Level 19. Geometry 1: Foundations of Geometry.

Level 20. Geometry 2: Two-Dimensional Figures.

16

RECOGNIZING THE PATTERNS:
SCIENCE

Science is organized knowledge.
—Herbert Spencer

SUBJECT: Science: biology, astronomy and earth science, chemistry, physics

TIME REQUIRED: 3 hours per week—90 minutes per day, two days per week—plus additional time working on independent experimentation

In logic-stage science, the student begins to make connections.

Grammar-stage science was a time of discovery. The youngest students explored the world around them, dipping into life science and astronomy, physics and chemistry, and collecting interesting bits of information. During the logic stage, the budding scientist digs deeper and finds out how those bits of information are connected.

The first grader learned about animals; the fifth grader will learn about the cells that make up the animal's body, how they function, how they keep the animal alive. The second grader memorized the constellations; the sixth grader will learn how and why stars are born and die. The third grader experimented with food coloring and water; the seventh grader will study the atoms and molecules that make up water itself, their construction, and the rules that govern their movement. The fourth grader did experiments with weights and planes; the eighth grader will learn about the laws of motion and the principles of gravity.

Elementary students discovered facts; middle-grade students will begin to grasp the scientific concepts that link those facts together. They'll start to see *patterns*. "To do science," ecologist Robert MacArthur once observed, "is to search for repeated patterns, not simply to accumulate facts." During the logic stage, your child will actually begin to *do* science.

YOUR GOALS

Your focus in grades 5–8 should be on scientific concepts: not just *how* but *why* the world works as it does. And whenever possible, the logic-stage student should not just learn *about* concepts, but reinforce that knowledge with hands-on work: experiments, demonstrations, and projects.

Think of the concepts that you'll teach in the middle grades as falling into three categories.

The first category: *scientific principles*. Scientific principles are statements (the student's logic study should help him recognize these) about how the world works. Scientific principles hold true when they are demonstrated in the real world or tested through experimentation. Principles can simply express how something works: "Living organisms grow and reproduce through cell division." (The student can watch cells dividing on YouTube: that's a demonstration.) Or principles may be stated as laws: Newton's Third Law of Motion, "For every action there is an equal and opposite reaction," is a scientific law. (The middle-grade student can test this out by standing up in roller skates and throwing a ball—the action of throwing produces the reaction of rolling backward.)

The second category: *scientific descriptions*. When you describe a chemical reaction from beginning to end, outline the life cycle of a salmon, investigate the steps of a volcanic eruption, or read about the birth, life, and death of a star, you are making use of scientific description: a chronological narrative laying out a series of orderly steps that occur again, and again, and again. When you describe the rings of Saturn, the parts of a tuber plant, or the features of the Marianas Trench, you are also making use of scientific description.

The third category: *scientific classifications*. The periodic table, the taxonomic categories, the grouping of planets into types (metallic, rocky, gaseous, fluid), the categorization of stars as red giants, blue giants, red dwarfs, yellow dwarfs, brown dwarfs, binary stars—all of these are examples of scientific classification.

Paying attention to these three categories will help you give your logic-stage student a thorough grounding in the concepts of science and the patterns that bring order to our knowledge of the world.

WHICH SUBJECTS TO STUDY, AND WHEN

As in the grammar stage, you'll want to cover the five major scientific fields—biology/natural science, astronomy, earth science, chemistry, and physics—possibly adding technology as a sixth field. And, as in the grammar stage, you can divide your studies by year:

Fifth grade	Biology	Animal kingdom (18 weeks)
		Human body (10 weeks)
		Plant kingdom (8 weeks)
Sixth grade	Earth science and astronomy	Earth science (18 weeks)
		Astronomy (18 weeks)
Seventh grade	Chemistry	Concepts in chemistry (36 weeks)
Eighth grade	Physics	Concepts in physics (36 weeks)
	OR	
	Physics and technology	Concepts in physics (18 weeks)
		Technology and engineering (18 weeks)

This scheme has two advantages: first, the concepts in biology and earth science tend to be a little simpler for younger students to grasp than those in astronomy, chemistry, and physics, so the more abstract principles are encountered when the student is more mature; second, the student who is simultaneously studying history in the order we recommend in Chapter 17 will encounter many of the innovators in each field in history as well as science.

However, you can also choose one of the following patterns of study:

Fifth grade	The basic sciences of nature	Earth science (8 weeks) Astronomy (8 weeks) Animal kingdom (8 weeks) Human body (8 weeks) Plant kingdom (4 weeks)
Sixth grade	Looking below the surfaces	Basic chemistry (12 weeks) Basic physics (12 weeks) Technology and engineering (12 weeks)
Seventh grade	Repeat fifth grade topics: review and go deeper	
Eighth grade	Repeat sixth grade topics: review and go deeper	

OR

Fifth grade	All sciences	Earth science (5 weeks) Astronomy (5 weeks) Animal kingdom (6 weeks) Human body (5 weeks) Plant kingdom (5 weeks) Chemical reactions (5 weeks) Physics (5 weeks)
Sixth grade	Same topics with more depth	
Seventh grade	Same topics with more depth	
Eighth grade	Same topics with more depth	

(See the "How to Teach Scientific Concepts" section, below, for suggestions on how to advance in depth and difficulty each year.)

We warned you in the grammar stage against attempting a "comprehensive" study of any field of science. This wouldn't be possible even in high school (or college, for that matter); scientific discovery hurtles forward while students pick their way carefully through new material. So we'll repeat the warning: Middle-grade students have more maturity and better reading and writing skills than elementary students, but they still can't be stuffed with an exhaustive knowledge of science. Your goal is not to cover *all* of the important concepts in science, but to begin to train the student to *do science*.

HOW TO TEACH SCIENTIFIC CONCEPTS: GENERAL METHODS

As in the grammar stage, you'll want to use a science "spine" of some kind to organize your work. In the Resources at the end of this chapter, we've suggested some possible spines that can serve as your basic science text(s), as well as some fully developed curricula for parents who prefer not to plan their own science study.

In order to plan out your year, decide how many weeks you'll devote to each field of science and how many pages of your science spine you'll cover during those weeks. Then, we suggest that you once again use the notebook method to organize your study. Make four divisions in the notebook:

Definitions
Scientific Principles
Scientific Classifications
Scientific Descriptions

Using the science notebook, no matter what texts or curricula you choose, has three benefits. First: the student is practicing beginning note-taking, learning how to distill information down into shorter forms and write it down for reference. (See Chapter 18 for an explanation of how this sort of writing fits into the overall logic-stage writing program.) Second: the student is learning to keep neat and careful records, an important skill for any developing scientist. And third: the notebook will become a reference guide for him as he moves into more complex science.

Definitions

Use the first section of the notebook to collect the basic facts that the student should be able to remember—the facts that he's probably already met in the grammar stage, but now needs to be able to keep in mind. Whenever the student runs into a term and an explanation of that term, he should write it down in the Definitions section of the notebook.

This helps the student create a reference list of important information, but also forces him to winnow out the most important information rather than simply writing everything down (a vital logic-stage skill). A definition generally takes the form noun, linking verb, descriptive phrase. For example, if the student reads the following text:

> **Around the sun.** The sun's gravity holds in thrall a diverse assortment of celestial objects, as well as the eight planets, with their own families of rings and moons. The solar system comprises billions of pieces of rocky and icy debris.
>
> The planets all orbit the Sun in the same direction, and in almost the same flat plane. Closest to the Sun's heat are four small, rocky worlds: Mercury, Venus, Earth, and Mars. In the chilly farther reaches of the solar system lie the giant planets: Jupiter, Saturn, Uranus, and Neptune. They are composed mostly of substances more volatile than rock, such as hydrogen, helium, methane, and water.
>
> The asteroids, most of which reside between Mars and Jupiter, are lumps of rocky debris left over from the birth of the planets. The edge of the planetary system is marked by icy chunks—comets and the Kuiper belt objects—that have survived from the earliest days of the solar system.[1]

[1] Heather Couper et al., *The Planets: The Definitive Visual Guide to Our Solar System* (New York: DK/Smithsonian, 2014), p. 12.

he should write down in the Definitions section

asteroids: lumps of rocky debris left over from the birth of the planets

The other information in the passage is interesting, but this is the only *definition*.

Scientific Principles

Every time the student encounters a scientific principle in his encyclopedia, book, or curriculum, he should write it down and place it in the Scientific Principles section of the notebook.

A principle explains *how the world works*. A principle may be a simple statement, a rule, or a law. In biology, principles would include Mendel's rules of inheritance and (for middle-grade students) the principle that DNA transfers information from generation to generation. (A more precise understanding of what DNA does will come later.). In earth science, "the continents drift" can be considered a principle; in astronomy, Kepler's laws of planetary motion; in chemistry, "atoms form molecules by sharing their electrons"; in physics, the First Law of Thermodynamics. In the sections that follow, we've provided a few more examples from each field of science.

(Keep in mind that technology is a slightly different kind of study: technology is the application of scientific principles to real-world situations, so it doesn't produce *new* principles. If you choose to spend some time studying technology, the student will be reviewing principles from other fields of science.)

Then, ask the student to take part in some kind of experiment, demonstration, or active illustration of the principle.

Technically, an "experiment" happens when you come up with a question ("How does temperature affect the growth of crystals?"), do some research to get a hint of what the answer might be, come up with a possible answer ("Crystals grow faster in colder temperatures"), and test the answer through experimentation (growing crystals in solutions at three different temperatures, with all other variables accounted for). The results of the experiment can confirm or deny the hypothesis—or they can be inconclusive, which means you have to redo the experiment (possibly in a different way).

Some principles are within reach of actual experimentation for middle-grade students: "Photosynthesis converts the sun's energy to food and energy for plants" can be the basis of an experiment where some radish sprouts are placed in sunlight, others in the dark, and their vigor is then measured. But experimentation is only one way to do science. Many principles—particularly the foundational laws in physics and chemistry—are way out of the reach of even advanced students. (Your seventh grader is not going to be able to measure the bend of starlight as it passes the sun; it took Einstein's colleagues over a decade to observe this after he proposed it.) Instead, students can draw diagrams, build models, or watch video demonstrations (both live and animated). Your goal is simply to get the principle off the page and into the real world.

In the Resources at the end of this chapter, we've listed a number of hands-on kits, experiment books, and projects to help. But you can also find numerous simple demonstrations and experiments online, simply by searching. For example, if you search for "Newton" + "second law of motion" + "demonstration," you'll find several YouTube demonstrations, an illustration of Newton's Cradle, and a number of activities (one with a yo-yo, several making use of marbles and ball bearings, and one with a dart gun).

Once the student has done the experiment, watched the demonstration, or carried out the project, he should write a brief summary of the activity and put it in the notebook with the statement of the principle itself. He's been prepared for this by the grammar-stage science assignment of keeping "project pages" and the grammar-stage writing assignment of composing summaries. Fifth-grade students should write three or four sentences; sixth grade students, two paragraphs; seventh- and eighth-grade students, half a page or more.

If the activity is an actual experiment, this written summary should resemble a lab report. Real lab reports are a high-school level assignment, but logic-stage students need training in careful and orderly record keeping. In the Resources section, we've suggested a few basic guides to experimentation and lab reports; use them for reference as needed. Generally, the middle-school lab report should be a neatly written page with the following:

1. *What question am I trying to answer?* (state the question)
2. *What could the answer be?* (form a hypothesis)
3. *How will I test this answer?*
   a. *Materials used*
   b. *Steps of the experiment*
4. *What results did I get?*
5. *Does this agree with the answer I thought I would get? If not, what answer should I give instead?*

Scientific Description

As the student works through his science spine, he'll encounter *descriptions*: physical descriptions of objects in nature (the parts of a cell, the layers of the earth, the structure of an atom) and narrative descriptions of natural processes (the fission of an atom, the journey of a tree from seed to sapling, the orbit of a planet). Whenever he encounters one of these descriptions, he should summarize it briefly in his own words, write it down, and place it in the Scientific Description section of his notebook.

For example, a student doing life science might come across this description of an invertebrate family:

The word *cephalopod* means "head-feet" in Greek, which reflects their anatomy. Their size is recorded by the length of their body cavity, called a mantle, which sits behind the head. Their large brains and advanced senses make them sociable creatures able to communicate with one another—they sometimes even shoal with fish for company.

Cephalopods can change the colour and pattern of their bodies to camouflage themselves or ward off predators. They have sucker-like tentacles, and move by taking in water and shooting it out to move forward by jet propulsion. Cephalopods produce ink and, when threatened, they release an inky cloud to confuse predators. Some can produce a ghost-like cloud a similar size, shape and colour to their own body, which acts as a decoy and gives the cephalopod a chance to escape.[2]

[2] Jenny Broom, *Animalium*, illus. Katie Scott (Somerville, MA: Big Picture Press, 2014), pp. 12–13.

He would then write a summary, resembling this one:

> Cephalopods have a body cavity, the mantle, that sits behind the head.
> They have large brains and tentacles with suckers. They can change their
> color and pattern for camouflage. They move by jet propulsion, and they
> can release ink and clouds to protect themselves from predators.

This is a physical description of an object in nature.

While doing earth science, he might come across this description of a
natural process:

> In 1960, Hess proposed a radical idea. He suggested that the ocean floors
> move like conveyor belts, carrying the continents along with them. This
> movement begins at the mid-ocean ridge. The mid-ocean ridge forms
> along a crack in the oceanic crust. At the mid-ocean ridge, molten mate-
> rial rises from the mantle and erupts. The molten material then spreads
> out, pushing older rock to both sides of the ridge. As the molten material
> cools, it forms a strip of solid rock in the center of the ridge. Then more
> molten material flows into the crack. This material splits apart the strip
> of solid rock that formed before, pushing it aside.
>
> Hess called the process that continually adds new material to the
> ocean floor sea-floor spreading. He realized that the sea floor spreads
> apart along both sides of the mid-ocean ridge as new crust is added.[3]

He could summarize this in two or three sentences:

> Sea-floor spreading happens when molten material rises up out of the
> mantle through the ocean floor, spreads out, cools, and forms a strip of
> solid rock. Then more molten material rises out, splits that strip, and
> cools. This adds new crust to the ocean floor.

The student can always add sketches to the descriptions to make them
clearer (colored pencils are fun!).

---

[3] Michael J. Padilla et al., *Prentice-Hall Science Explorer Inside Earth* (Needham, MA:
Pearson Prentice-Hall, 2005), p. 35.

Scientific Classification

Finally, whenever the student encounters an explanation of a scientific classification, he should note it down and place it in the Scientific Classification section of his notebook.

Classification happens whenever natural processes or objects are placed into categories. For example, while doing chemistry, the student might come across this paragraph:

> The world of chemicals can be divided broadly into organic and inorganic compounds. The name *organic compound* intuitively feels soft, like something you might find growing in the garden. Indeed, many organic compounds are closely associated with life. On the other hand *inorganic compound* sounds gritty, like a rock, and in fact rocks generally are inorganic. But this hard-versus-soft definition doesn't really work out—there are just too many exceptions.
>
> So how, exactly, is the division between organic and inorganic defined?[4]

It isn't necessary for the student to write down every detail of the discussion that follows; he just needs to note:

Chemicals

Organic   Inorganic

and place this in the notebook. As he comes across additional categories and divisions, he can add this to his chart, or redraw it to show the new groups.

Note: It's important not to get bogged down in trying to write down *every* definition, principle, description, and classification. You are *not* attempting to give the student a thorough grounding in each scientific field; high-school study will be much more technical, systematic, and advanced. Instead, you are training the student to keep good records; the student is

---

[4] Theodore Gray, *Molecules: The Elements and the Architecture of Everything*, illus. Nick Mann (New York: Black Dog & Leventhal, 2014), p. 47.

practicing his note-taking and writing skill; and he is beginning to grasp the larger patterns of science. Logic-stage science should be more challenging, and more *organized,* than grammar-stage science, but it should still be enjoyable—not tedious.

Use these basic rules of thumb:

Fifth-grade students should make at least two to three entries in the science notebook each week.

Sixth-grade students should make three to four entries per week.

Seventh- and eighth-grade students should make five to seven entries per week.

HOW TO DO LIFE SCIENCE: ANIMALS, HUMAN BEINGS, AND PLANTS

Use a selection of the recommended spines in the Resources at the end of this chapter and supplement with the experiment and project kits and books listed, or search online for activities and demonstrations.

Look out for these scientific principles:

Mendel's rules of inheritance (dominant and recessive characteristics)

DNA's transfer of information from generation to generation

Natural selection

The food chain

Try to include these descriptions over the course of your study:

Parts and structure of a cell

Parts of a flower (receptacle, petals, sepals, nectaries, stamens, pistil)

Major human body systems (could include skin, skeletal system, muscular system, digestive system, respiratory system, circulatory system, urinary system, reproductive system, endocrine system, and nervous system)

Major bones (cranium, mandible, clavicle, scapula, rib cage, ulna,
    radius, pelvis, carpus, femur, patella, fibula, tibia)
Components of blood and what each does (red blood cells carry oxy-
    gen, white blood cells fight disease, platelets stop bleeding)
Basic structure and function of genes

Important categories of classification:

Animal kingdom: phylum and class (see Chapter 8, pages 00)
Plant kingdom: phylum and class
Types of compound leaves (palmate, trifoliate, ternate, pinnate,
    bipinnate)
Types of roots (taproot, fibrous root, adventitious root, aerial root,
    prop root)

HOW TO DO EARTH SCIENCE
AND ASTRONOMY

Use a selection of the recommended spines in the Resources at the end
of this chapter and supplement with the experiment and project kits and
books listed, or search online for activities and demonstrations.

Look out for these scientific principles:

Heliocentric theory (Copernicus)
Kepler's laws of planetary motion
Continental drift
Expansion of the universe
The speed of light

Try to include these descriptions over the course of your study:

Solar system (planets, in the proper order)
Parts and layers of the earth, from core to crust
Plates of the earth (North American, Cocos, Caribbean, South
    American, Nazca, African, Eurasian, Indo-Australian, Pacific)

Layers of the earth's atmosphere
Major constellations
Birth, life, and death of a star
Phases of the moon
Tides
The "Big Bang"

Important categories of classification:

Types of clouds
Types of rocks/minerals
Types of stars and their characteristics (red giants, white dwarfs,
    variable stars, supernovas, pulsars, binary stars, black holes,
    neutron stars, etc.)
Classification of galaxies
Classes of planets

HOW TO DO CHEMISTRY

Use a selection of the recommended spines in the Resources at the end
of this chapter and supplement with the experiment and project kits and
books listed, or search online for activities and demonstrations.

Look out for these scientific principles:

Formation of molecules from atoms (how they share/exchange
    electrons)
Boyle's law

Try to include these descriptions over the course of your study:

Parts and structure of an atom: electron, proton, neutron, nucleus
Structure of major molecules
Fission of an atom

Important categories of classification:

Periodic table of elements
Organic/inorganic
Three states of matter

HOW TO DO PHYSICS

Use a selection of the recommended spines in the Resources at the end of this chapter and supplement with the experiment and project kits and books listed, or search online for activities and demonstrations.

Look out for these scientific principles:

Archimedes' principle
Newton's three laws of motion
Newton's law of gravitation
Laws of thermodynamics
Law of conservation of energy

Try to include these descriptions over the course of your study:

Colors of the spectrum of light
Direct current and alternating current
Mass, force, and weight
Sound waves

Important categories of classification:

Types of energy
Types of heat flow (conduction, convection, radiation)

HOW TO DO TECHNOLOGY

Use a selection of the recommended spines in the Resources at the end of this chapter and supplement with the experiment and project kits and books listed, or search online for activities and demonstrations.

Since technology is the application of scientific principles to real-world problems, pursue it in a slightly different manner than the other scientific fields. If you decide to spend some time on technology, create a separate division in the notebook labeled "Technology." For each technological project, answer the following two questions, writing three or four sentences for each:

What problem or need does this invention/project/machine solve or address?
What scientific principles am I putting to use?

Place the written answers in the notebook. You may also add a sketch or photo of the finished project.

SUGGESTED SCHEDULES

Sample Yearly Schedules

Consider using one of the schedules suggested below:

Grade	Topic(s)	Notebook Entries
Fifth grade 3 times per week	Animal kingdom (20 weeks) Human body (10 weeks) Plant kingdom (6 weeks)	2–3 entries per week; distribute among definitions, principles, descriptions, and notes on classification
Sixth grade 3 times per week	Astronomy (18 weeks) Earth science (18 weeks)	3–4 entries per week; distribute as above
Seventh grade 3 times per week	Chemistry OR Physics (18 weeks) Technology (18 weeks)	For chemistry or physics, 5–7 entries, distribute as above. For technology, try to complete at least 7 projects, with a page for each

Eighth grade	Chemistry OR Physics (18	For chemistry or
3 times per week	weeks) Technology (18	physics, 5–7 entries
	weeks)	per week; distribute as above. For
		technology, try to
		complete at least
		7 projects, with a
		page for each

Grade	Topic(s)	Notebook Entries
Fifth grade	Animal kingdom (12	2–3 entries per
3 times per week	weeks)	week; distribute
	Human body (6 weeks)	among definitions,
	Plant kingdom (4 weeks)	principles, descrip-
	Earth science (14 weeks)	tions, and notes on
		classification
Sixth grade	Astronomy (10 weeks)	3–4 entries per
3 times per week	Chemistry (10 weeks)	week; distribute as
	Physics (10 weeks)	above. For technol-
	Technology (6 weeks)	ogy, try to complete
		2–3 projects, with a
		page for each
Seventh grade	Animal kingdom (12	5–7 entries per
3 times per week	weeks)	week; distribute as
	Human body (6 weeks)	above
	Plant kingdom (4 weeks)	
	Earth science (14 weeks)	
Eighth grade	Astronomy (10 weeks)	5–7 entries per
3 times per week	Chemistry (10 weeks)	week; distribute as
	Physics (10 weeks)	above. For technol-
	Technology (6 weeks)	ogy, try to complete
		3–4 projects, with a
		page for each

Grade	Topic(s)	
Fifth grade	Earth science (5 weeks)	2–3 entries per
3 times per week	Astronomy (5 weeks)	week; distribute
	Animal kingdom (6 weeks)	among definitions,

	Human body (5 weeks)	principles, descriptions, and notes on classification
	Plant kingdom (5 weeks)	
	Chemical reactions (5 weeks)	
	Physics (5 weeks)	
Sixth grade 3 times per week	Same topics at greater depth	3–4 entries per week; distribute as above
Seventh and eighth grades 3 times per week	Same topics at greater depth	5–7 entries per week; distribute as above

About Weekly Scheduling

In the middle grades, allow your science spine to dictate your work each day. Read; as definitions, principles, descriptions, and classification are addressed, make notebook entries; stop after each principle to reinforce with an experiment or demonstration; do experiments and projects in the text according to the student's interest.

Be guided by the student's interest; allow reading, projects, and asking/answering questions to flow into additional days as needed. Some topics will lend themselves to additional reading, experimentation, and activities; others, to more involved projects that take multiple days to complete. Some topics can be covered in a single day's work; others may extend over a week or more.

Remember: As in the grammar stage, the goal is to practice *doing science* and to *cultivate enthusiasm,* not to cover a certain amount of material each year!

RESOURCES

Most books can be obtained from any bookseller or library; most curricula can be bought directly from the publisher or from a major home-school supplier such as Rainbow Resource Center. Contact information for publishers and suppliers can be found at www.welltrainedmind.com. If availability is limited, we have noted it. Where indicated, resources are listed in chronological order (the order you'll want to use them in). Books in series are listed together. Remember that additional curricula choices and more can be found at www.welltrainedmind.com. Prices change constantly, but we have included 2016 pricing to give an idea of affordability.

Reference materials for all four logic-stage years are listed first. For each field of science, options for central "spines" are listed first, followed by supplemental resources for experiments and demonstrations, and then options for full curricula.

Reference Materials for All Four Years

Blister Microscope. Minneapolis, MN: General Science Service Co.

$65. Order from Blister Microscope. This affordable microscope can be used with regular slides or with the custom-fitted Blister Slides, which have a small depression for the easy viewing of insects and small organisms in liquid. One hundred slides come with the microscope ($57.50 without slides included).

Brock Magiscope. Maitland, FL: Brock Optical, Inc.

$179 and up. Order from Brock. If you want better optics than those provided by the $65 microscope above, use a Brock Magiscope—tough, reliable, easy to use, good magnification.

Dinwiddie, Robert, et al. *Science: The Definitive Visual Guide.* New York: DK Children, 2011.

$24.99. An illustrated encyclopedia written on a sixth- to eighth-grade level.

Kramer, Stephen P. *How to Think Like a Scientist: Answering Questions by the Scientific Method,* illus. Felicia Bond. New York: HarperCollins, 1987.

$16.89. A readable story-based introduction to the scientific method; aimed at grades 5 and 6.

Lemke, Donald B. *Investigating the Scientific Method with Max Axiom, Super Scientist,* illus. Tod G. Smith. North Mankato, MN: Capstone Press, 2008.

$8.10. Part of the Graphic Science series, this is designed for middle-school/junior-high students. The graphic novel format is excellent for slow or reluctant readers.

Taylor, Charles. *The Kingfisher Science Encyclopedia,* 3rd ed. New York: Kingfisher, 2011.

$34.99. Written on a fifth- to seventh-grade level.

Woodford, Chris, and Steve Parker. *Science: A Visual Encyclopedia.* New York: DK Children/Smithsonian, 2014.

$29.99. Nicely illustrated, written on a fourth- to sixth-grade level.

Yomtov, Nel. *How to Write a Lab Report*. Ann Arbor, MI: Cherry Lake Publishing, 2014.
$12.79. A late elementary-/early middle-school guide to producing good lab reports; highly recommended as a clear and simple manual even for slightly older students (who may need to ignore the cartoon mice).

Life Science: Animals, Human Beings, and Plants

Basic Texts ("Spines")

Choose from among the following.

Alderton, David. *The Encyclopedia of Animals*. New York: Chartwell Books, 2013.
$19.99. Gorgeous photographs and detailed text.

Broom, Jenny. *Animalium*, illus. Katie Scott. Somerville, MA: Big Picture Press, 2014.
$35. Part of the Welcome to the Museum series, this guide to the animal kingdom has clear text and gorgeous pen-and-ink illustrations. Engaging, excellent for fifth- and sixth-grade study. Supplement with plant kingdom and human body spines.

CPO Life Science. Nashua, NH: CPO Science, 2007.
This one-year life science course is a nicely produced, well-written text designed for schools; it is more expensive than the other options (as classroom materials tend to be) but includes animal and plant kingdoms as well as the human body. Purchase from the publisher or from School Specialty.
CPO Science Middle School Life Science Student Book Set (includes Student Text and Investigations Manual with lab activities). $72.95.
CPO Science Middle School Life Science Teacher's Guide. Lesson plans, review questions, and teaching suggestions; helpful but not necessary. $129.95.

Macaulay, David. *The Way We Work: Getting to Know the Amazing Human Body*. Boston: HMH Books for Young Readers, 2008.
$35. This carefully illustrated book in David Macaulay's distinctive style

is thorough, readable, and fascinating. From the cell level up through the body's major systems.

McHenry, Ellen Johnston. *Botany in 8 Lessons.* Ellen McHenry's Basement Workshop, 2013.
$32.95. A full (and interesting) botany curriculum, plus activities, in one book. Student and teacher pages both included.

Prentice Hall Science Explorer: Life Science. Needham, MA: Prentice Hall School Division.
The basics of cells and heredity, as well as a survey of living things from bacteria all the way up to human beings. A full one-year life science text, developed for classrooms but useful for home educators. Good illustrations, clear text. The two most recent editions are 2005 and 2009; both are useful, but if you buy the accompanying workbook, make sure it is from the same year as the text. Order from Amazon, textbook.com, or another textbook supplier. The new copies are priced like textbooks (which means: ridiculously expensive), but you can find lightly used and even new copies from online booksellers for less than a third of the cover price.
Student edition, $95.51 cover price but available for $29 and up online.
Guided Reading and Study Workbook, $10 cover price. Useful review and study worksheets but not essential.

Rothman, Julia, and John Niekrasz. *Nature Anatomy: The Curious Parts and Pieces of the Natural World.* North Adams, MA: Storey Publishing, 2015.
$16.95. A fun visual guide to the plant kingdom with some attention to the animal kingdom as well. Good for a fifth- to sixth-grade tour of plants; you'll want to supplement for the animal kingdom and human body.

Spilsbury, Louise, and Richard Spilsbury. *The Life of Plants* series, 2nd ed. New York: Heinemann, 2008.
This heavily illustrated series provides a simple and engaging introduction to the plant kingdom and the individual features of different plant families. Suggested activities included. $7.99 each.
Plant Classification.
Plant Parts.
Plant Growth.

Supplementary Resources: Life Sciences
Animal Kingdom

Arnold, Nick. The Horrible Science series. New York: Scholastic, 2014.
This fun, insightful, kid-friendly series combines tongue-in-cheek text and cartoon illustrations with clear explanations and doable experiments. Some paperbacks are out of print but all are available as ebooks (and secondhand).

  Nasty Nature.

  Ugly Bugs.

Basic Animal Dissection Kit. Burlington, NC: Carolina Biological Supply Company.
$22.95. Order from Carolina Biological Supply.

Burnie, David. *Eyewitness: Bird.* New York: Dorling Kindersley, 2008.
$16.99. A good resource to have on hand for the study of birds.

Carolina Bio Lab: Pig. Burlington, NC: Carolina Biological Supply Company.
$87.50. Purchase from Carolina Biological Supply. A "virtual dissection" software program that allows students to investigate anatomy, observe heart, muscle, and kidney function, and more. Actual fetal pigs and dissection manuals can also be found at the Carolina website.

Gilpin, Daniel. The Animal Kingdom Classification series. New York: Compass Point Books, 2006.
These lavishly illustrated books cover the physical characteristics, habitats, and habits of different animal families. The focus on classification is ideal for logic-stage science, and the series covers unusual animals often ignored in other guides. $29.99 each but should be at your local library.

  Lobsters, Crabs, and Other Crustaceans.

  Nematodes, Leeches, and Other Worms.

  Snails, Shellfish, and Other Mollusks.

  Sponges, Jellyfish, and Other Simple Animals.

  Starfish, Urchins, and Other Echinoderms.

Graphic Science series. New York: Capstone Press.
$8.10 each. Engaging and intelligent graphic novels, ideal for slow or reluctant readers.

Biskup, Agnieszka. *Decoding Genes with Max Axiom, Super Scientist.* 2010.

———. *A Journey into Adaptation with Max Axiom, Super Scientist.* 2007.

———. *The Surprising World of Bacteria with Max Axiom, Super Scientist.* 2010.

———. *Understanding Viruses with Max Axiom, Super Scientist.* 2010.

Keyser, Amber J. *The Basics of Cell Life with Max Axiom, Super Scientist.* 2009.

O'Donnell, Liam. *Understanding Photosynthesis with Max Axiom, Super Scientist.* 2007.

———. *The World of Photosynthesis with Max Axiom, Super Scientist.* 2007.

Kneidel, Sally Stenhouse. *Creepy Crawlies and the Scientific Method: Over One Hundred Hands-On Science Experiments for Children,* 2nd ed. Golden, CO: Fulcrum Publications, 2015.

$24.95. Shows parents how to teach the five steps of the scientific method: question, hypothesis, methods, result, and conclusion.

Owl Pellet Dissection Kit.

$4.99. Order from Discover This.

Parker, Steve, and Dave King. *Eyewitness: Mammal.* New York: Dorling Kindersley, 2004.

$16.99. Another good reference book to have on hand for the study of mammals.

———. *Eyewitness: Seashore.* New York: Dorling Kindersley, 2004.

$16.99. A good reference book to have on hand for the study of saltwater fish and amphibians.

Parker, Steve, and Philip Dowell. *Eyewitness: Pond and River.* New York: Dorling Kindersley, 2011.

$16.99. A good reference book to have on hand for the study of fish, amphibians, and reptiles.

Peterson, Roger Tory, et al. *Birds (Peterson Field Guide Color-In Books).* Boston: Houghton Mifflin Harcourt, 2013.

$8.95. This coloring book, based on the Peterson's Field Guide series, contains detailed drawings with information about each specimen.

————. *Butterflies (Peterson Field Guide Color-In Books)*. Boston: Houghton Mifflin Harcourt, 2013.

$8.95. This coloring book, based on the Peterson's Field Guide series, contains detailed drawings with information about each specimen.

————. *Reptiles and Amphibians (Peterson Field Guide Color-In Books)*. Boston: Houghton Mifflin Harcourt, 2011.

$8.95. This coloring book, based on the Peterson's Field Guide series, contains detailed drawings with information about each specimen.

VanCleave, Janice. *A+ Projects in Biology: Winning Experiments for Science Fairs and Extra Credit*. New York: Jossey-Bass, 2003.

$14.95. Includes experiments in both animal and plant science.

————. *Biology for Every Kid*. New York: Wiley, 1990.

$16.

Human Beings

Arnold, Nick. The Horrible Science series. New York: Scholastic, 2014.

This fun, insightful, kid-friendly series combines tongue-in-cheek text and cartoon illustrations with clear explanations and doable experiments. Some paperbacks are out of print but all are available as ebooks (and secondhand).

Blood, Bones, and Body Bits.
Body Owner's Handbook.
Bulging Brains.
Deadly Diseases.
Disgusting Digestion.
Microscopic Monsters.

Cumbaa, Stephen. *The Bones Book and Skeleton*, illus. Kim La Fave. New York: Workman Publishing, 2006.

$19.95. Assemble a twelve-inch, twenty-five-piece plastic skeleton with moving joints.

Fingerprint Kit. Plymouth, MI: Slinky Science.

$9.88. Order from Are You Game.

Genetics & DNA. Portsmouth, RI: Thames & Kosmos.

$36.95. Order from Thames & Kosmos. Experiment kit with manual;

isolate plant DNA, build a model of the double-stranded helix, chart inherited characteristics, and more.

Matt, Margaret, et al. *Human Anatomy Coloring Book*. New York: Dover, 1982.

$4.99. Detailed, scientifically accurate drawings of body organs and systems, with charts listing names of body parts.

Optical Science Experiment Kit. Portsmouth, RI: Thames & Kosmos.

$34.95. Order from Thames & Kosmos. Experiment with light, lenses, optical illusions, and other phenomena related to sight.

Science in a Nutshell series. Nashua, NH: Delta Education.

$45 each. Order from Delta Education. These kits provide a complete science experiment and activity center; consider going in with a friend, since the kits provide material for two or three students.

Body Basics.

Kit includes materials for an overview of the human body, along with an activity guide and student journal.

The Human Machine.

Kit includes materials for the study of bones, muscles, and joints, along with an activity guide and student journal.

A Peek Inside You.

Respiration, digestion, and circulation.

Smell, Taste, and Touch.

The senses.

Vision and Hearing.

Experiments based on illusions in sight and sound.

Stark, Fred. *Gray's Anatomy: A Fact-Filled Coloring Book*. Philadelphia: Running Press, 2011.

$12.95. This simplified black-line version of *Gray's Anatomy* is more difficult and more interesting than the Dover coloring book listed above.

The Visual Dictionary of the Human Body. New York: Dorling Kindersley, 1991.

$18.99. Big clear drawings, exploded views, cutaways and sections, all labeled with proper Latin names. A beautiful book.

Plant Kingdom

Arbel, Ilil. *Medicinal Plants Coloring Book*. New York: Dover, 1993.
$4.99.

Bernath, Stefen. *Herbs Coloring Book*. New York: Dover, 1977.
$3.99.

Botanical Discoveries: Science Fair Kit. Chagrin Falls, OH: DuneCraft.
$24.99. Order from Discover This or Home Science Tools. Grow unusual
and odd plants.

Burnie, David. *Eyewitness: Plant*. New York: Dorling Kindersley, 2011.
$16.99. A good resource to keep on hand during the study of the plant
kingdom.

Carnivorous Creations Terrarium Kit. Chagrin Falls, OH: DuneCraft.
$24.99. Order from Discover This or Home Science Tools.

Graphic Science series. New York: Capstone Press.
$8.10 each. Engaging and intelligent graphic novels, ideal for slow or
reluctant readers.
  O'Donnell, Liam. *Understanding Photosynthesis with Max Axiom, Super
  Scientist*. 2007.

Peterson, Roger Tory, et al. *Wildflowers (Peterson Field Guide Color-In Books)*.
Boston: Houghton Mifflin Harcourt, 2013.
$8.95. Order from Rainbow Resource Center. This coloring book, based
on the Peterson's Field Guide series, contains detailed drawings with
information about each specimen.

Formal Curricula

Some parents may prefer to use a developed curriculum rather than following the exploratory methods described in this chapter. The following
programs are compatible with our approach, but consider supplementing
with the science notebook suggestions in this chapter.

Elemental Science. Wytheville, VA: Elemental Science, 2014.
Developed by a science-oriented home-schooling parent, the Elemental
Science series loosely follows our recommendations for hands-on exper-
imentation and supplemental outside reading. Lesson plans and plenty

of teacher support. View samples at the publisher's website. Each set is one full year of study.

> *Biology for the Logic Stage.*
> Printed Combo (Teacher's Guide and Student Guide). $40.99.
> Experiment Kit. $65.99.

Great Science Adventures, by Dinah Zike and Susan Simpson. Melrose, FL: Common Sense Press.

As students progress through the lessons, they cut, fold, draw, and glue paper handouts into mini-books and construct paper models. The program is designed for teaching students of different ages together; each lesson provides three different projects on three different levels of difficulty. Logic-stage students should aspire to do the second and third projects in each level. The program is well organized and interesting, but it may frustrate students (and parents) who don't like to cut and paste. Order from Common Sense Press. Each book is $24, provides twenty-four lessons, and should take eight to twelve weeks to complete. Supplement with experiments and outside reading. Samples can be viewed at the publisher's website.

> *Discovering the Human Body and Senses* (life science).
> *The World of Insects and Arachnids* (life science).
> *The World of Vertebrates* (life science).
> *The World of Plants* (life science).

R.E.A.L. Science Odyssey. Mount Dora, FL: Pandia Press.

Developed for use by home-schooling parents and small classrooms, R.E.A.L. Science emphasizes hands-on learning. Each written lesson is followed by labs, activities, and research assignments. The writing of lab reports is emphasized. Each level is one full year of science. Student and instructor pages are bound together into the books; additional supplies are necessary. Samples and supply lists can be viewed at the publisher's website. Cheaper ebook versions are also available.

> *Biology, Level Two.*
> *Biology 2* (student book). $132.
> *Biology 2 Teacher Guide.* $42.

Earth Science and Astronomy
Basic Texts ("Spines")

Choose from among the following.

Allaby, Michael. *National Geographic Visual Encyclopedia of Earth*. Washington, DC: National Geographic Children's Books, 2008.
  $24.95. Illustrated guide to earth science for grades 5 and 6.

CPO Earth Science. Nashua, NH: CPO Science, 2007.
  This one-year earth science course is a nicely produced, well-written text designed for schools; it is more expensive than the other options (as classroom materials tend to be) but can be bought more cheaply from online textbook stores. Purchase from the publisher or from School Specialty.
  CPO Science Middle School Earth Science Student Text Book. $54.95.
  CPO Science Middle School Earth Science Investigation Manual. Useful review questions and activity suggestions. $18.95.

Dinwiddie, Robert, et al. *Universe: The Definitive Visual Guide*, rev. and updated ed. New York: DK Publishing, 2012.
  $50. A detailed and beautiful guide to the cosmos, including a star atlas with all known constellations, a planetary chart, and hundreds of photographs. Developed in cooperation with the Smithsonian Institute. Seventh grade and up.

————. *Earth: The Definitive Visual Guide*, rev. and updated ed. New York: DK Publishing, 2013.
  $50. A detailed and beautiful guide to our planet, including 3-D cutaway illustrations of many of the earth's features. Developed in cooperation with the Smithsonian Institute. Seventh grade and up.

Space: A Visual Encyclopedia. New York: DK Children, 2010.
  $24.99. A guide to all space topics, from our solar system to the farther reaches of the universe. Text on a fifth- to sixth-grade level and spectacular NASA photographs.

Space: The Universe as You've Never Seen It Before. New York: DK Publishing, 2015.

$24.99. Developed in association with the Smithsonian Institute, this is a good text for fifth and sixth graders. Plenty of photographs and a good survey of astronomy topics.

Supplementary Resources: Earth Science

Crystal PRO Crystal Growing & Crystallography Kit.
$29.95. Order from Discover This.

Graphic Science series. New York: Capstone Press.
$8.10 each. Engaging and intelligent graphic novels, ideal for slow or reluctant readers.

Krohn, Katherine. *The Earth-Shaking Facts about Earthquakes with Max Axiom, Super Scientist.* 2008.

——. *The Whirlwind World of Hurricanes with Max Axiom, Super Scientist.* 2010.

Harbo, Christopher L. *The Explosive World of Volcanoes with Max Axiom, Super Scientist.* 2008.

Introductory Earth Science Collection.
$79. Order from Rainbow Resource Center. Seventy-five rock samples, along with a study guide and equipment for testing properties.

National Geographic Earthquakes & Volcanoes Experiment Kit.
$36.95. Order from Thames & Kosmos.

Science in a Nutshell series. Nashua, NH: Delta Education.
$45 each. Order from Delta Education. These kits provide a complete science experiment and activity center; consider going in with a friend, since the kits provide material for two or three students.

Fossil Formations.
Six fossil samples, sand, plaster of Paris, and modeling clay, along with an activity guide and student journal.

Rock Origins.
Twenty-two rock and mineral samples and materials for investigating their properties.

TOPS Learning System Activities (Earth & Space). Watsonville, CA: TOPS Learning Systems.
Developed by a science educator, TOPS lessons use simple materials and

emphasize inquiry, discovery, and experimentation. Extensive samples can be viewed at the publisher's website.

The Earth, Moon and Sun. $18. Observation-based activities and demonstrations.

Rocks and Minerals. $18. Test and classify the rocks in your own backyard.

VanCleave, Janice. *Earth Science for Every Kid.* New York: John Wiley, 1991. $14.95. One hundred and one experiments.

———. Spectacular Science: Mind-Boggling Experiments You Can Turn into Science Fair Projects series. New York: John Wiley.
These experiments are more complex (and interesting) than those in the Every Kid series. Suitable for exhibition.

Rocks and Minerals. 1996. $12.95.

Volcanoes. 1994. $16.

Weather. 1995. $16.

Van Rose, Susanna. *Eyewitness: Earth.* New York: Dorling Kindersley, 2013. $16.99. A good reference work for report writing.

Wind Power 2.0: Renewable Energy Science Kits. Portsmouth, RI: Thames & Kosmos.
$49.95. Order from Thames & Kosmos.

Supplementary Resources: Astronomy

Arnold, Nick. The Horrible Science series. New York: Scholastic, 2014.
This fun, insightful, kid-friendly series combines tongue-in-cheek text and cartoon illustrations with clear explanations and doable experiments. Some paperbacks are out of print but all are available as ebooks (and secondhand).

Space, Stars and Slimy Aliens.

Lafontaine, Bruce. *Exploring the Solar System Coloring Book.* New York: Dover, 1998.
$4.99. Order from Rainbow Resource Center.

Lippincott, Kirsten. *Eyewitness: Astronomy.* New York: Dorling Kindersley, 2013.
$16.99. Wonderful pictures.

Mars 2020. Dexter, MI: Aristoplay.

$30. In this family board game, a race to Mars teaches about space and space exploration.

The Planets: The Definitive Visual Guide to Our Solar System. New York: DK Publishing, 2014.

$30. For good readers, a detailed, heavily illustrated study of the solar system. 3-D models of the structure of each planet and excellent texts.

Primer for the Beginning Astronomer/Astromax Introductory Astronomy Binocular Kit.

$5 for the five-lesson primer, $99 for the high-powered binocular/star chart kit. Order from Astromax.

Staal, Julius D. *The New Patterns in the Sky: Myths and Legends of the Stars.* Granville, OH: McDonald & Woodward, 1988.

$27.95. For good readers, a complete guide to the myths behind the constellations from a number of different countries.

Styrofoam Solar System Kit

$23.99. Order from Rainbow Resource Center. Paint and construct a styrofoam ball model of the solar system.

TOPS Learning System Activities (Earth & Space). Watsonville, CA: TOPS Learning Systems.

Developed by a science educator, TOPS lessons use simple materials and emphasize inquiry, discovery, and experimentation. Extensive samples can be viewed at the publisher's website.

Pi in the Sky. $18. Developed in cooperation with NASA; use pi to measure heavenly objects; investigate radian angles, visual acuity, and parallax.

The Planets and Stars. $18. Constellations, measuring space, and more.

Scale the Universe. $18. Distance and time over forty- plus orders of magnitude.

VanCleave, Janice. *Astronomy for Every Kid.* New York: Jossey-Bass, 1991.

$16.

———. *Constellations for Every Kid.* New York: Wiley, 1997.

$16. Straightforward astronomy experiments.

Formal Curricula

Some parents may prefer to use a developed curriculum rather than following the exploratory methods described in this chapter. The following programs are compatible with our approach, but consider supplementing with the science notebook suggestions in this chapter.

Elemental Science. Wytheville, VA: Elemental Science, 2014.

> Developed by a science-oriented home-schooling parent, the Elemental Science series loosely follows our recommendations for hands-on experimentation and supplemental outside reading. Lesson plans and plenty of teacher support. View samples at the publisher's website. Each set is one full year of study.
>
> *Earth Science & Astronomy for the Logic Stage.*
> Printed Combo (Teacher's Guide and Student Guide). $40.99.
> Experiment Kit. $60.99.

Great Science Adventures, by Dinah Zike and Susan Simpson. Melrose, FL: Common Sense Press.

> As students progress through the lessons, they cut, fold, draw, and glue paper handouts into mini-books and construct paper models. The program is designed for teaching students of different ages together; each lesson provides three different projects on three different levels of difficulty. Logic-stage students should aspire to do the second and third projects in each level. The program is well organized and interesting, but it may frustrate students (and parents) who don't like to cut and paste. Order from Common Sense Press. Each book is $24, provides twenty-four lessons, and should take eight to twelve weeks to complete. Supplement with experiments and outside reading. Samples can be viewed at the publisher's website.
>
> *Discovering Earth's Landforms and Surface Features* (earth science)
> *Discovering the Ocean* (earth science)
> *The World of Space* (astronomy)

Chemistry

Basic Texts ("Spines")/Formal Curricula

Although there are many different chemistry books and kits aimed at younger students, they tend to be scattershot in approach: experiment-centered workbooks often don't explain the concepts, and beautifully presented concept books usually don't include experiments. Because of this, we suggest that you use one of the following chemistry curricula as your "spine." Continue to make use of the notebook system that we recommend, asking the student to write about definitions, principles, descriptions (there will be only a few of these), and classification. Supplement with the concept and experiment books listed in the next section.

CPO Physical Science. Nashua, NH: CPO Science, 2007.

The entire first half of this one-year course covers basic chemistry. A nicely produced, well-written text designed for schools; more expensive than the other options (as classroom materials tend to be) but can be bought more cheaply from online textbook stores. You can also purchase from the publisher or from School Specialty. An excellent choice if you don't intend to spend the entire year on chemistry; in the second half of the year, you could also use the TOPS or McHenry resources listed.

CPO Science Middle School Physical Science Student Book Set. $72.95. Student text plus investigation manual with useful review questions and activity suggestions.

CPO Science Middle School Physical Science Teacher's Guide. $129.95. Answers, teaching suggestions, review, and other supporting material; helpful but not at all essential.

Elemental Science. Wytheville, VA: Elemental Science, 2014.

Developed by a science-oriented home-schooling parent, the Elemental Science series loosely follows our recommendations for hands-on experimentation and supplemental outside reading. Lesson plans and plenty of teacher support. View samples at the publisher's website. Each set is one full year of study. Appropriate any time between grades 5 and 8.

Chemistry for the Logic Stage.

Printed Combo (Teacher's Guide and Student Guide). $40.99.

Experiment Kit. $65.99.

Keller, Rebecca W. *Focus on Middle School Chemistry.* Albuquerque, NM: Gravitas Publications, 2013.

$67 for the Middle School Chemistry Book Bundle, which includes the student text, teacher's manual, a lab workbook, and a downloadable lesson plan. Order from the publisher; samples are available at the publisher's website. A one-year course; good coverage of essential chemistry concepts with ten experiments (you'll want to supplement).

McHenry, Ellen Johnston. Basement Workshop chemistry series. Ellen McHenry's Basement Workshop, 2013.

You will want to supplement this course with additional experiments from the supplemental resources listed in the next section. Order from the author's website or from a home-school supply company.

The Elements: Ingredients of the Universe. $24.95 for book and accompanying CD. This is an excellent introduction to chemistry that covers difficult topics in a clear and entertaining way with plenty of activities built in. Teacher and student pages are both included. A sample can be read at the author's website. Highly recommended as a first foray into chemistry; ten weeks of study.

Carbon Chemistry: An Introduction to Organic Chemistry and Biochemistry for Ages 9–14. $24.95 for book and accompanying CD. Designed to follow *The Elements,* this twelve- to sixteen-week course covers a range of topics in organic chemistry, including polymers and the structure of DNA.

Prentice Hall Science Explorer: Physical Science. Needham, MA: Prentice Hall School Division.

The first eight chapters of this twenty-two-chapter middle-school text deal with the basics of chemistry. Well-presented and clear, but only about twelve weeks of study; good for students who are studying chemistry for a shorter period. Could be the basis for a full year of study if combined with the Ellen McHenry or selected TOPS materials. Order from Amazon, textbook.com, or another textbook supplier. The new copies are priced like textbooks (which means: ridiculously expensive), but you can find lightly used and even new copies from online booksellers for less than a third of the cover price.

Student edition, $89.40 cover price but available for $29 and up online.

Guided Reading and Study Workbook, $14.14 cover price. Useful review and study worksheets but not essential.

TOPS Learning System Activities (Chemistry). Watsonville, CA: TOPS Learning Systems.

Developed by a science educator, TOPS lessons use simple materials and emphasize inquiry, discovery, and experimentation. Extensive samples can be viewed at the publisher's website. Do all five of the following in order; best for seventh and eighth grades; you will want to supplement this course with additional experiments from the supplemental resources listed in the next section. Order from the publisher; ebook versions available for less.

Analysis. Forty-eight-page introduction to chemistry with sixteen activities.

Analysis Starter Kit. $25.50. All of the supplies and chemicals needed to complete the experiments in *Analysis*.

Cohesion/Adhesion. $14. Twenty-four projects demonstrating cohesion, adhesion, surface tension, and capillary action. Uses common household objects.

Oxidation. $12. Sixteen activities dealing with the reactions caused by oxygen. Common household objects.

Oxidation Starter Kit. $30.50. Nothing unusual here (D batteries, steel wool, garden lime, ceramic magnet, etc.) but convenient to have it all in one place.

Solutions. $16. Twenty-eight experiments demonstrating suspensions, solutions, coagulation, chlorination, crystallization, concentration, saturation, and solubility.

Solutions Supplies. $18.50. Seven not-so-common chemicals to round out the common ingredients used in the experiments.

Kinetic Model. $14. Solids, liquids, gases, and how they behave.

Kinetic Model Starter Kit. $54. Common items assembled for you, along with graduated cylinders, test tubes, syringe, pipettes, and tubing.

Supplementary Resources

Arnold, Nick. The Horrible Science series. New York: Scholastic, 2014.
This fun, insightful, kid-friendly series combines tongue-in-cheek text and cartoon illustrations with clear explanations and doable experiments. Some paperbacks are out of print but all are available as ebooks (and secondhand).
Chemical Chaos.

CHEM C2000 Chemistry Kit, version 2. Portsmouth, RI: Thames & Kosmos.
$149.95. Order from Thames & Kosmos.

ElementO.

$34.95. Order from Rainbow Resource Center. In this Monopoly-type game, players collect elements and pay each other with proton and neutron certificates. Keep track with the Periodic Table of Elements in the middle of the board. A great way to memorize the basic properties of chemistry.

Elements series. Danbury, CT: Grolier.

Check your library; most will carry a few of these titles. The books contain clear and detailed explanations of the elements, so consider reading through at least a couple of them. They are listed here in the order they appear on the periodic table.

Hydrogen and the Noble Gases.

Sodium and Potassium.

Calcium and Magnesium.

Iron, Chromium, and Manganese.

Copper, Silver, and Gold.

Zinc, Cadmium, and Mercury.

Aluminum.

Carbon.

Silicon.

Lead and Tin.

Nitrogen and Phosphorus.

Oxygen.

Sulfur.

Chlorine, Fluorine, Bromine, and Iodine.

Uranium and Other Radioactive Elements.

Graphic Science series. New York: Capstone Press.

$8.10 each. Engaging and intelligent graphic novels, ideal for slow or reluctant readers.

Biskup, Agnieszka. *The Dynamic World of Chemical Reactions with Max Axiom.* 2010.

———. *Super Cool Chemical Reactions with Max Axiom.* 2015.

Gray, Theodore. *Elements: A Visual Exploration of Every Known Atom in the Universe.* New York: Black Dog & Leventhal, 2012.

$19.95. Double-page spreads on the first one hundred elements in the periodic table, with color photographs of the element accompanied by images and explanations of the ways in which each element is used. Highly recommended.

————. *Molecules: The Elements and the Architecture of Everything*. New York: Black Dog & Leventhal, 2014.
$29.95. The follow-up volume to *Elements: A Visual Exploration*; how elements make up materials all over the world.

Newmark, Ann. *Eyewitness: Chemistry*. New York: Dorling Kindersley, 2005.
$16.99. A good guide to the history of chemistry.

Periodic Table of Elements Chartlet.
$2.49. Order from Rainbow Resource Center. A 17 × 22-inch reference chart of the table of elements.

Trombley, Linda, and Thomas G. Cohn. *Mastering the Periodic Table: Exercises on the Elements*. Portland, ME: J. Weston Walch, 2000.
$24. Order from J. Weston Walch or from Rainbow Resource Center.

VanCleave, Janice. *Janice VanCleave's Chemistry for Every Kid: 101 Easy Experiments That Really Work*. Boston: Jossey-Bass, 1989.
$14.95.

————. *Janice VanCleave's A+ Projects in Chemistry: Winning Experiments for Science Fairs and Extra Credit*. New York: John Wiley, 1993.
$14.95. These experiments, slightly more complex than those in the Every Kid series, are suitable for exhibition.

————. *Molecules: Mind-Boggling Experiments You Can Turn Into Science Fair Projects*. New York: John Wiley, 1995.
$15.

Physics

Basic Texts ("Spines")

Choose from among the following.

Prentice Hall Science Explorer: Physical Science. Needham, MA: Prentice Hall School Division.
The final fourteen chapters of this twenty-two-chapter middle-school text deal with the basics of physics. Well-presented and clear, but not

quite a full year of study unless supplemented with other units (such as the TOPS units listed below.) Order from Amazon, textbook.com, or another textbook supplier. The new copies are priced like textbooks (which means: ridiculously expensive), but you can find lightly used and even new copies from online booksellers for less than a third of the cover price.

You will need a number of supplies. Online versions of some of the tools are available at Explore Learning; see our link at www.well trainedmind.com.

Student edition, $89.40 cover price but available for $29 and up online. *Guided Reading and Study Workbook*, $14.14 cover price. Useful review and study worksheets but not essential.

Reynolds, Helen. *Complete Physics for Cambridge Secondary 1*. Oxford: Oxford University Press, 2014.

This U.K. course is ideal for advanced seventh- or eighth-grade students; a good and systematic grounding in physics concepts. Usually available in the U.S. from online booksellers, but if it appears out of stock it can be ordered from amazon.co.uk for U.S. delivery. The teacher pack is recommended but not absolutely essential. View samples online at the publisher's website.

Student Book: For Cambridge Checkpoint and Beyond. $31. (£19.50)
Teacher Pack. $113. (£63.25)

TOPS Learning System Activities (Physics I and Physics II). Watsonville, CA: TOPS Learning Systems.

Developed by a science educator, TOPS lessons use simple materials and emphasize inquiry, discovery, and experimentation. Extensive samples can be viewed at the publisher's website. The list below progresses from simple to more difficult; we suggest doing them in order and progressing at the student's natural pace through as many as will fit into the year. Each softback book contains multiple activities, but you don't need to do them all; once the student has grasped the concepts you can move to the next book. A good hands-on grounding that prepares students for high-school physics; easily adaptable to study ranging from six weeks to a full year.

Order from the publisher; ebook versions are available for less. The starter kits contain the supplies required; many are common household items, but you may find it more convenient to have them all in one place; contents listed at publisher's website.

Individual titles may also be used to supplement the other resources listed in this section.

Perfect Balance. $18. Cut and fold paper balance beams as an introduction to mass and weight.

Diving Into Pressure and Buoyancy. $7.50 for PDF download.

Electricity. $18. Introduction to circuits.

Electricity Starter Kit. $29.50.

Magnetism. $18. Using magnets to build compasses, motors, and other inventions.

Magnetism Starter Kit. $20.75.

Pendulums (I). $18. Cycles, measurement, graphing data, ratios, all using pendulums.

Focus Pocus. $18. Use lenses to explore refraction.

Weighing. $13. Building a gram balance to explore mass vs. weight, restoring forces, and more.

Balancing. $13. Exploring the mathematics of balance with mobiles and cantilevers.

Light. $18. Use lenses to examine the particle and wave nature of light.

Light Starter Kit. $31.50.

Floating and Sinking. $14. Displacing volumes, densities, weight, and buoyancy.

Pressure. $17. Build systems that are airtight and watertight to explore pressure.

Sound. $13. Amplitude, wavelength, pitch, frequency.

Motion. $18. Mass, inertia, balanced and unbalanced forces, acceleration, action and reaction.

Machines. $13. Building simple machines to calculate efficiency and effort.

Pendulums (II). $13. Focus on length and amplitude. Requires algebraic skills.

Heat. $14. Heat in solids, in fluids, and in space.

Electricity (II). $18. Like and unlike charges, current flow, parallel and series circuits, and much more.

Electricity Supplies. $12.50. The five most hard-to-locate items required; highly recommended.

Magnetism (II). $116. Twenty-eight activities exploring the nature of magnetism.

Supplementary Resources

Arnold, Nick. The Horrible Science series. New York: Scholastic, 2014.
This fun, insightful, kid-friendly series combines tongue-in-cheek text and cartoon illustrations with clear explanations and doable experiments. Some paperbacks are out of print but all are available as ebooks (and secondhand).

Fatal Forces.

Frightful Flight.

Killer Energy.

Shocking Electricity.

Terrible Time.

Eyewitness Science series. New York: Dorling Kindersley.
$16.99 each. Check your library for these titles.

Burnie, David. *Light.* 2001.

Challoner, Jack. *Energy.* 2012.

Gribbon, Mary, and John R. Gribbon. *Time and Space.* 2000.

Lafferty, Peter. *Force and Motion.* 1999.

Parker, Steve. *Electricity.* 2013.

Graphic Science series. New York: Capstone Press.
$8.10 each. Engaging and intelligent graphic novels, ideal for slow or reluctant readers.

Biskup, Agnieszka. *The Powerful World of Energy with Max Axiom, Super Scientist.* 2009.

———. *The Solid Truth About States of Matter with Max Axiom, Super Scientist.* 2009.

Gianopoulos, Andrea. *The Attractive Story of Magnetism with Max Axiom, Super Scientist.* 2008.

O'Donnell, Liam. *The Shocking World of Electricity with Max Axiom, Super Scientist.* 2007.

Sohn, Emily. *Adventures in Sound with Max Axiom, Super Scientist.* 2007.

———. *A Crash Course in Forces and Motion with Max Axiom, Super Scientist.* 2007.

————. *The Illuminating World of Light with Max Axiom, Super Scientist.* 2008.

Great Science Adventures, by Dinah Zike and Susan Simpson. Melrose, FL: Common Sense Press.

As students progress through the lessons, they cut, fold, draw, and glue paper handouts into mini-books and construct paper models. The program is designed for teaching students of different ages together; each lesson provides three different projects on three different levels of difficulty. Logic-stage students should aspire to do the second and third projects in each level. The program is well organized and interesting, but it may frustrate students (and parents) who don't like to cut and paste. Order from Common Sense Press. Each book is $24, provides twenty-four lessons, and should take eight to twelve weeks to complete. Samples can be viewed at the publisher's website.

Discovering Atoms, Molecules, and Matter.

The World of Light and Sound.

Gurstelle, William. *Backyard Ballistics: Build Potato Cannons, Paper Match Rockets, Cincinnati Fire Kites, Tennis Ball Mortars, and More Dynamite Devices,* 2nd ed. Chicago: Chicago Review Press, 2012.

$16.95.

Horemis, Spyros. *Visual Illusions.* New York: Dover, 1973.

$3.95. Order from Rainbow Resource Center. You won't know whether the lines are straight or curved until you color them. Finished, the designs are spectacular.

Mercer, Bobby. *Junk Drawer Physics: 50 Awesome Experiments That Don't Cost a Thing.* Chicago: Chicago Review Press, 2014.

$14.95. A great supplement to any physics program; fifty unique experiments that don't require specialized equipment. Covers force, energy, momentum, light, magnetism, and pressure.

Physics Discovery. Portsmouth, RI: Thames & Kosmos.

$31.95. Order from Thames & Kosmos. Build twelve different models to explore force and simple machines.

Physics Pro. Portsmouth, RI: Thames & Kosmos.

$99.95. Order from Thames & Kosmos. Hands-on exploration of more advanced topics in physics: fluid dynamics, energy, oscillation, hydraulics, pneumatics.

Physics Solar Workshop. Portsmouth, RI: Thames & Kosmos.
$69.95. Order from Thames & Kosmos. Thirty experiments and twelve model-building projects using solar cells and transforming this power into energy.

Physics Workshop. Portsmouth, RI: Thames & Kosmos.
$54.95. Order from Thames & Kosmos. Build thirty-six models and conduct experiments with them to explore mechanical physics: basic forces, centripetal force, and more.

Sato, Koichi. *Optical Illusions Coloring Book*. New York: Dover, 1994.
$3.99. Order from Rainbow Resource Center. Mind-bending pictures to color. Eighth-grade level.

Science in a Nutshell series. Nashua, NH: Delta Education.
$45 each. Order from Delta Education. These kits provide a complete science experiment and activity center, designed for grades 2 to 6. Consider sharing the cost with a neighbor, since the kits provide materials for two or three students.
  Bubble Science.
    Variables affecting the size, shape, color, and durability of bubbles.
  Charge It! Static Electricity.
    Positive and negative charges, static electricity.
  Clever Levers.
    Build a wheelbarrow, balance a scale, lift weights, and more.
  Electrical Connections.
    Simple and complex circuits, current, batteries.
  Energy and Motion.
    Stored energy, motion; weights, marbles, and ramps.
  Flight! Gliders to Jets.
    Build designs for parachutes, gliders, propeller and jet craft; teaches principles of air pressure and Newton's third law of motion.
  Gears at Work.
    Gear systems and interaction.

Magnetic Magic.

Magnetic materials, polar strength.

Pulley Power.

Using fixed and movable pulleys to reduce the force needed to lift objects.

Sound Vibrations.

Sound waves and their interaction with various materials.

Work: Plane and Simple.

Inclined planes; force and friction.

VanCleave, Janice. *Magnets: Mindboggling Experiments You Can Turn into Science Fair Projects.* New York: John Wiley, 1993.

$16.

———. *Physics for Every Kid.* New York: John Wiley, 1991.

$14.95. Simpler experiments than the Spectacular Science series. Deals with motion, heat, light, machines, and sound.

Formal Curricula

Some parents may prefer to use a developed curriculum rather than following the exploratory methods described in this chapter. The following programs are compatible with our approach, but consider supplementing with the science notebook suggestions in this chapter.

Elemental Science. Wytheville, VA: Elemental Science, 2014.

Developed by a science-oriented home-schooling parent, the Elemental Science series loosely follows our recommendations for hands-on experimentation and supplemental outside reading. Lesson plans and plenty of teacher support. View samples at the publisher's website. Each set is one full year of study.

Physics for the Logic Stage.

Printed Combo (Teacher's Guide and Student Guide). $40.99

Keller, Rebecca W. *Focus on Middle School Physics.* Albuquerque, NM: Gravitas Publications, 2013.

$67 for the Focus On Middle School Physics Book Bundle, which includes the student text, teacher's manual, a lab workbook, and a downloadable lesson plan. Order from the publisher; samples are available at the publisher's website. A one-year course; good coverage of essential chemistry concepts with ten experiments (you'll want to supplement).

Technology

If you decide to devote some focused time to technology, you can use the resources from the elementary science lists in Chapter 5 (particularly *The New Way Things Work*) as well as any of the suggestions listed below. See www.welltrainedmind.com for computer programming resources.

Arnold, Nick. The Horrible Science series. New York: Scholastic, 2014.
This fun, insightful, kid-friendly series combines tongue-in-cheek text and cartoon illustrations with clear explanations and doable experiments. Some paperbacks are out of print but all are available as ebooks (and secondhand).
Evil Inventions.
Really Rotten Experiments.

Brain, Marshall. *How Stuff Works.* New York: Chartwell Books, 2010.
$14.99. An illustrated encyclopedic guide to the technology of everyday objects.

———. *More How Stuff Works.* New York: John Wiley, 2002.
$14.99. Available secondhand or as an ebook.

Fuel Cell 10 Experiment Kit. Portsmouth, RI: Thames & Kosmos, 2009.
Build a model car that runs on water.

Great Science Adventures, by Dinah Zike and Susan Simpson. Melrose, FL: Common Sense Press.
As students progress through the lessons, they cut, fold, draw, and glue paper handouts into mini-books and construct paper models. The program is designed for teaching students of different ages together; each lesson provides three different projects on three different levels of difficulty. Logic-stage students should aspire to do the second and third projects in each level. The program is well organized and interesting, but it may frustrate students (and parents) who don't like to cut and paste. Order from Common Sense Press. Each book is $24, provides

twenty-four lessons, and should take eight to twelve weeks to complete. Samples can be viewed at the publisher's website.

The World of Tools and Technology.

LEGO Mindstorms. Billund, Denmark: The LEGO Group.
Build and program robots with touch, color, and infrared sensors. Visit the LEGO website for many more options.

LEGO Mindstorms EV3. $349.99. 601-piece kit to build five different robots.

Mercer, Bobby. *The Robot Book: Build and Control 20 Electric Gizmos, Moving Machines, and Hacked Toys.* Chicago: Chicago Review Press, 2014.
$14.95. Simple designs using household tools and items, along with a few specialty supplies (LED lights, etc.) that should be easily located at a hardware store.

Nanotechnology: Experiment Kit. Portsmouth, RI: Thames & Kosmos, 2015.
For STEM-inclined students, a kit-based series of experiments aimed at understanding and even using nanoparticles.

Platt, Charles. *Make: Electronics. A Hands-On Primer for the New Electronics Enthusiast.* Sebastopol, CA: Maker Media, Inc., 2009.
$34.99. A thorough, discovery-based exploration of electronics, including clear explanations, shopping lists, and project directions.

Salvadori, Mario. *The Art of Construction: Projects and Principles for Beginning Engineers & Architects,* 3rd ed., illus. Saralinda Hooker. Chicago: Chicago Review Press, 2001.
$16.95. Learn the principles behind bridges, skyscrapers, and more; all projects done with household items.

Snap Circuits. Wheeling, IL: Elenco Electronics, Inc.
These easy-to-assemble circuits come in kits of varying complexity, along with detailed manuals. Excellent for all sorts of electronics projects, from AM radios to digital voice recorders. We've listed just a few of the available options; view the whole range of products at the Snap Circuits website.

Snap Circuits Basic Electricity Mini-Kit. $19.95.

Snap Circuits Beginner. $24.95.

Snap Circuits Electromagnetism Mini-Kit. $16.50.

Snap Circuits Jr. Educational 100 Experiments. $54.95.

Snap Circuits Motion Detector Mini-Kit. $26.95.

Snap Circuits Pro 500 Experiments. $99.95.

Snap Circuits 300 Experiments. $66.95.

VanCleave, Janice. *Janice VanCleave's Engineering for Every Kid.* New York: John Wiley, 2007.
$14.95. 25 projects (structural, solar, electrical, and chemical) applying scientific problems to real-life situations.

17

WHY 1492?

HISTORY AND GEOGRAPHY

All things from eternity are of like forms and come round in a circle.
—Marcus Aurelius, *Meditations* II.14

SUBJECT: History and geography, grades 5–8

TIME REQUIRED: 3 hours of intensive study, 90 minutes per day, two days per week, or 60 minutes per day, three days per week, plus as much additional time as possible to be spent in free reading and investigation.

During the logic stage, the student learns how to find connections. In formal logic, he discovers connections between a set of propositions and a conclusion. In math, he's taught the connections between the parts of an equation. In science, he begins to recognize the patterns that play out in the natural world.

In history, he'll concentrate on finding connections between world events. Instead of simply reading the story of Rome's fall, the fifth grader will look at what happened before that fall—the events that led to the empire's destruction. Instead of studying the Revolutionary War as a single event, the seventh grader will read about the early days of the colonies and ask: What happened to make Americans discontent? What happened after the war that allowed America to stay independent as a nation? In the logic stage, history changes from a set of stories into one long, sequential story filled with cause and effect.

Beginning in the logic stage, the study of history becomes the backbone of classical humanities study. Literature, art, and music are organized around the outline provided by history. History is the training ground where the student learns how to organize and evaluate information. And that's the goal of the classical education—to produce an adult who can take in new knowledge, evaluate its worth, and then discard it or put it to good use.

In Part I, we referred to the mind of an elementary student as a storeroom that must be stocked with all sorts of images and words. Imagine what would happen to that storeroom if you kept cramming in more and more stuff without ever stopping to organize it. Greek history, Chinese fairy tales, biological classifications, the life of Bach, the concentration camps of the Third Reich—all lie stacked together. The student who can't get beyond this point will never realize that the laws of Hammurabi, the Magna Carta, and the Bill of Rights are linked. The information will remain jumbled together and ultimately unusable. And unless the student is given the mental skills to sort through and classify all this knowledge, he'll become an adult with (in the words of classical schoolmaster David Hicks) a "cluttered, disorderly mind—helpless to make the fundamental connections between basic ideas, or to . . . participate intelligently in the public debate over the great issues confronting his nation and his times."[1]

As in the grammar stage, students will not use a predigested interpretation of world history. Rather, they should make use of a core text that lays out the events in world history and allows them to investigate further. See the Resources at the end of this chapter for options.

---

[1] David Hicks, *Norms and Nobility: A Treatise on Education* (New York: Praeger, 1981), p. 132.

KEEPING IT ORGANIZED

How does the student sort through and classify all this material?

He'll still make up history notebooks as he did in the elementary grades. But the study of history will now incorporate four elements:

1. creating a time line
2. outlining
3. using and evaluating primary sources
4. organizing this information using the history notebook

Each of these activities has a separate role in the mind's development. Creating a time line teaches the student to trace chronological connections; outlining trains the student to look past rhetorical smoke and mirrors in order to find the "bare bones" argument of a speech or essay; the use of primary sources teaches the student to interpret material himself instead of relying on "experts"; organizing information into the divisions of the history notebook helps the student to classify similar events and historical trends together.

The Time Line

The time line is simply a piece of paper long enough to stretch along one (or more) walls of the student's room. (Hallways are also good places for time lines.) You can tape sheets of oversized construction paper together or use a commercial time line; see the Resources section for ordering information.

Time lines help the student make visual connections between events. A young historian could study the conquests of Genghis Khan, Francis of Assisi's founding of the Franciscan order, and the death of Richard the Lionhearted without realizing that these events all occurred within the same decade[2]—until she saw them marked on a time line.

---

[2] Richard the Lionhearted was killed in France in 1199. He was succeeded by King John. Genghis Khan defeated his greatest rival in 1203 and was crowned chief prince of the Mongols in 1206. John himself was excommunicated in 1209, the same year that the Franciscan order was founded.

The time line should begin with a reasonable date in ancient history. We suggest 5000 B.C.,[3] when farming begins in earnest in China, Mesopotamia, and the Nile River valley. Make the time line as long as you can, measure it, and divide it by the number of centuries you'll be studying that year. You'll be repeating the divisions you used during the grammar stage:

Ancients	5000 B.C.–A.D. 400
Medieval–early Renaissance	400–1600
Late Renaissance–early modern	1600–1850
Modern	1850–present

During the first year of logic-stage history, since you'll be covering fifty-four centuries, you'll want to divide the time line into fifty-four equal parts and label each one. Don't forget that years B.C. run backward, while A.D. years run forward:

200 B.C.	100 B.C.	1	A.D. 100	A.D. 200

(A peculiarity of chronology: there's no year 0. Dating goes from 1 B.C. to A.D. 1 without a break.)

Try to make the century divisions as long as possible. There's not much going on between 5000 and 3000 B.C., but resist the temptation to make the early centuries short just to save space—*the time line must be kept in proportion.* Each year's time line should have centuries of equal length. The 3500–3400 B.C. space may remain bare, compared with the crowded space between 300 and 200 B.C. But part of the time line's purpose is to give some sense of the quickening pace of recorded history.

The time line can be simple (birth and death dates recorded in red pencil, political events in green, scientific discoveries in purple, and so forth).

---

[3] Western civilization has traditionally divided time into the centuries before Christ's birth (B.C.) and the centuries after Christ's birth (A.D., or *anno domini*—the "year of our Lord"). Some people prefer to use the abbreviations C.E. ("Christian Era" or "Common Era") and B.C.E. ("before the Christian Era" or "before the Common Era"). As Westerners, we're accustomed to B.C. and A.D.

Or it can be as complicated as the student likes (adorned with drawings and cutout pictures: notebook-paper-sized inserts hung above or below a particular date to allow for expansion—for example, a month-by-month account of the Civil War or a year-by-year description of the Arab conquests of the seventh century). You can purchase published time lines, but avoid those with dates and events already printed on them. Writing up the dates is part of the learning process.

We suggest that you leave two spaces at the beginning of the ancients time line, one marked "before 9000 B.C." and the other marked "9000–5000 B.C." You can put in these two spaces the small amount of information provided about very early civilizations and ages.

| Before | 9000 B.C. | 5000 B.C. | 4900 B.C. | 4800 B.C. |
| 9000 B.C. | | | | |

The time line will not only be an at-a-glance reference tool, but it will also act as a synthesizer of areas of knowledge. Birth and death dates of great writers, scientific advances made in biology and chemistry, dates of symphonies, paintings, and cathedrals—all will be recorded on the time line. Astronomers, poets, kings, wars, discoveries, and publication dates will appear, breaking down the walls between science, history, and literature. Since the stories of the Old Testament have influenced so much of Western thought, you may want to integrate them with recorded secular history.

Outlining

You'll use outlining as an exercise at least once a week. In the elementary grades, the student created narrations—at first telling you what he'd just read while you wrote it down, and then writing the narration down himself. This process developed the student's comprehension skills and taught him how to tell the difference between irrelevant details and important elements of plots or argument.

But as texts grow more complex, the simple narration process will no longer be adequate. Instead of doing narrations, the student will begin to outline what he's read. Eventually, he'll be able to pick out the central idea from a chapter in any book and distinguish it from supporting ideas. This is an invaluable skill for note-taking during college lectures; it also prepares the student to do advanced research. Once he can write a good, succinct précis of a scholarly work, he'll be ready to tackle the research paper without thrashing around in masses of unnecessary information.

Outlining involves finding the main ideas of a work and listing the supporting ideas beneath it. In fifth grade, the student will begin to develop this skill by simply summarizing each paragraph he reads. By eighth grade, he'll be able to condense a book chapter into Roman-numeral outline form. He'll also learn to use these outlines as the basis for short original compositions.

This outlining does not have to be done from the main text (some of the more encyclopedic suggestions do not lend themselves to outlining). Instead, the student can choose to outline several paragraphs or pages from a supplementary resource. We lay out the how-tos of outlining for each grade in the sections that follow.

(Outlining helps the student remember and understand his history lessons, but it also serves as a vital composition exercise; see Chapter 18, pages 450–453 for a fuller explanation.)

Primary Sources

In the logic stage, the child will still use paraphrases of difficult works such as the *Aeneid*, the *Odyssey*, and *The Canterbury Tales*. But he'll also begin to explore *primary source material*—original letters, reports, engravings, journals, and essays. Use of primary sources is vital to logic-stage history; the student can't evaluate historical events unless she has firsthand knowledge of them.

In the Resources at the end of this chapter, we've listed ways to find primary sources for each historical period. A primary source is anything that has its origins in the actual time under study. The *Epic of Gilgamesh*, for example, is a primary source if you read it in a good translation (a retelling in picture-book form wouldn't be a primary source because the story has been substantially changed and simplified). The Magna Carta, the poetry of Henry VIII, Martin Luther's journals, the Declaration of Independence, and the letters of Civil War soldiers are all primary sources. (A book about the Magna Carta, a biography of Henry VIII or Martin Luther, or the story of the creation of the Declaration would be a secondary source.)

Whenever the student encounters a primary source, she needs to evaluate it. As she studies history, she will develop her own ways of evaluating primary sources. To start, we suggest that the student go through the following checklist whenever she finishes reading a primary source:

> *What does this source say?* (Content)
> *Who is the author?* (Social position, profession, political affiliations, age, any other relevant personal detail)
> *What is the writer's purpose?*
> *What does he/she have to lose or gain by convincing others of his/her position?*
> *What events led to this piece of writing?*
> *What happened as a result of this writing?*

For each primary source, have the student head a sheet of notebook paper with the name of the source ("The First Amendment to the Constitution") and answer the above questions. In this way, she will learn how to ask critical questions of historical documents. File these sheets of paper in the history notebook.

The Notebook

Logic-stage history involves both *synthesis* (fitting information into one overall framework) and *analysis* (understanding individual events). The time line will be the student's tool for synthesis. To help in analysis, he'll be creating another history notebook—a fat three-ring binder full of notebook paper. Label this notebook with the period under study (for example, "Ancients: 5000 B.C. to A.D. 400"), and divide it into nine sections:

1. Facts
2. Great Men and Women
3. Wars, Conflicts, and Political Events
4. Inventions, Science, and Discoveries
5. Daily Life, Beliefs, and Customs
6. Literature and the Arts
7. Cities and Settlements

8. Primary Sources
9. Outlines

Basic resources for the logic stage of history are the core text you've chosen, a wall map, a globe, and an atlas. Consider having two atlases on hand: a contemporary atlas, showing current political boundaries and locations, and a "historical" atlas that illustrates changes in countries over time. (See our Resources for suggestions.) History and geography fall naturally together; every time you study an event or person, you'll want to look up the location on the globe, on the wall map, and in the atlas (which will give you not only political borders, but also a brief history of the region).

Note: Don't neglect the use of a globe—all wall maps and atlases distort land masses by laying them out flat.

Now the student is ready to begin. For the next four years, he'll follow the same basic pattern. He will

1. read a section from the core text and list important facts.
2. mark all dates on the time line.
3. find the region under study on the globe, on the wall map, and in the atlas.
4. do additional reading from the library or from the Resources list.
5. prepare summaries of information on one or more of the above topics and file them in the history notebook.
6. practice outlining one to four pages of text, once per week.

Once a month or so, he should look back through the history notebook, review his lists of facts and outlines, and glance back through his summaries. This will help him remember what's been studied.

Additional Help for Parents

The student who does history using the methods described below will learn by using three basic study skills: reading, outlining, and summarizing. She'll then follow her interests to learn more with additional history books, hands-on projects, models, detailed coloring books, and more resources (listed at the end of this chapter).

The student who reads well and who has been following a good standard grammar and composition course in the grammar stage of education shouldn't have too much trouble with the methods we're about to suggest. However, some students need additional practice—either to build confidence or to reinforce basic skills.

In the Resources section, we've listed a few resources to help with nonfiction reading, note-taking, and outlining. If necessary, use them to sharpen the student's ability to handle the history assignments.

STARTING IN THE MIDDLE
(OR WITH MORE THAN ONE)

We describe a pattern of study that takes the student through four years of history chronologically, once in the grammar stage (grades 1–4) and again in the logic stage (grades 5–8). However, you can certainly adapt this progression for a student who doesn't begin the history cycle neatly in first or fifth (or ninth) grade. Pick one of the strategies below.

1. Start with the ancients and progress more quickly so that the student finishes the modern age by the end of eighth grade and begins the high-school progression with the ancients in ninth grade. Hit the "high points" of history rather than attempting to cover it all (which you'll never manage to do in any case); do less outside reading.
2. Start with the period of history your student would fall into if you'd begun the progression in fifth grade: Medieval/early Renaissance for sixth grade, late Renaissance/early modern for seventh, modern for eighth. Go forward from that point. After all, the student is going to start over again with the ancients when you reach high school.
3. Start in whatever period of history you please, progress at a normal rate, and transition into the Great Books study recommended for high school when the student reaches ninth grade—no matter what *period* the student has reached. For example, a student who begins chronological history study in seventh grade might follow this pattern:

Seventh grade   Ancients. Keep a time line, do outlining,
                           and use the resources recommended for

	fifth grade (most of the books listed in the Resources section at the end of this chapter are appropriate for use anytime between grades 5 and 8).
Eighth grade	Medieval/early Renaissance. Keep a time line, do outlining, and use the resources recommended for sixth grade.
Ninth grade	Begin Great Books study with the late Renaissance/early modern period.
Tenth grade	Modern Great Books.
Eleventh grade	Ancient Great Books.
Twelfth grade	Medieval/early Renaissance Great Books.

The chronological progression forward provides the student with coherence, even if you choose a later starting point. (As a matter of fact, there can be a useful trade-off in doing the Great Books in this way: The ancient and medieval lists are technically very challenging, and the student will meet them with more mature reading skills. However, the subject matter of the modern list can be disturbing, although the work itself is technically easier; it is usually best to encounter these books at tenth grade or later.)

If you're doing history with several children, follow the same basic principle: do the same year of history with all of them, so that you're not trying to keep up with two or three historical periods simultaneously—a sure path to burnout. When each student reaches fifth grade, begin the logic-stage process of outlining and keeping a time line, no matter what period of history you're in; whenever the student reaches modern times, he can then go back to the ancients and start filling in the beginning of the time line. When each student reaches ninth grade, begin the transition into Great Books study (see Chapter 27 for more detail).

If you are educating younger and older students at the same time, you can use the elementary core text to keep all of your students on the same basic topic. First, read the pages or chapter from the grammar-stage text together. Then, ask the older students to (1) read the pages from the more difficult core text that corresponds to the topic, and (2) complete the other work described below.

A WORD ABOUT
AMERICAN HISTORY

Many U.S. states ask that middle-school students do at least one full year of American history. In most cases, home educators are not obliged to follow this standard. And the program that we outline does cover American history; it just spreads it out over seventh and eighth grade in order to put the history of the United States into global perspective.

However, if you would prefer to do a one-year American history course, consider scheduling it for seventh grade, and then cover world history (without a focus on the United States) from 1600 to the present day in the following year. Eighth graders have more capacity to move quickly and still remember what they've studied the previous month.

A number of American history resources are recommended in the supplements for seventh and eighth grade. A suggested core text is also included in the list of basic texts at the end of this chapter.

HOW TO DO IT

Fifth Grade: Ancients
(5000 B.C.–A.D. 400)

Let's assume that your fifth grader has just opened his chosen history spine to a section about the Phoenicians. What does his study look like?

(1) As described on page 371, he begins his assignment by reading the section and making a list of six to eight important facts about the Phoenicians. This list does not need to include every fact on the page (the student can choose the facts that he finds most interesting) and should be in the form of complete sentences.

So, if the text in the section reads:

Traders from Phoenicia. The Phoenicians were descended from the Canaanites, who lived at the eastern end of the Mediterranean Sea. From around 1200 B.C., they became the most successful traders in the ancient world.

Cities by the sea. The main Phoenician trading ports were the cities of

Tyre, Sidon and Byblos. The cities were protected by strong walls and each one had its own king, who lived in a luxurious palace.

Ships and sailing. The Phoenicians were expert sailors. Their sturdy trading ships sailed all over the Mediterranean and beyond, probably even reaching the British Isles. One expedition sailed all the way around Africa.

Crafts. Skilled craftworkers made objects for traders to sell abroad. The Phoenicians were known for their fine ivory carvings and their beautiful glass bottles and beads.

Purple people. The Phoenicians used a shellfish, called a murex, to make an expensive purple dye. The name "Phoenicians" comes from a Greek word meaning "purple men."

The city of Carthage. Merchants set up trading posts and colonies around the Mediterranean. The most famous one was Carthage on the north coast of Africa. It was set up by a Phoenician princess called Dido, who tricked the local African ruler into giving her enough land to build a city.

Writing. The Phoenicians invented a simple alphabet with just 22 letters. It gradually developed into the alphabet we use today.

The end of the Phoenicians. Although the Phoenicians became part of the mighty empires of Assyria, Babylon, and Persia, their way of life survived until they were conquered by Alexander the Great in 332 B.C. The city of Carthage remained powerful for another 200 years, but was totally destroyed by the Romans in 146 B.C.[4]

then the student's list of facts might look like this:

1. The ancestors of the Phoenicians came from Canaan.
2. The cities of Tyre, Sidon, and Byblos were the main trading posts.
3. The Phoenicians sailed around Africa.
4. They made purple dye from shellfish.

---

[4] This particular text is taken from Jane Bingham et al., *The Usborne Internet-Linked Encyclopedia of World History* (London: Usborne, 2003), pp. 144–45. It is now out of print, although used copies can be located very easily. The example is merely intended to show an appropriate level of detail for a fifth-grade student; the same procedure should be followed no matter what spine the student has chosen to use.

5. They invented an alphabet with 22 letters.
6. They were conquered by Alexander the Great.
7. Carthage was destroyed by the Romans.

Remember that the list of facts is not intended to be exhaustive; it should be a record of the information the student finds most interesting. (Also, in illustrated encyclopedia-type texts, some important facts may be found in the captions of pictures; those can be included.) Place the list of facts in the history notebook under Facts (the first section), which will serve as a running summary of information learned.

(2) Now it's time to mark dates on the time line. This passage has three important dates:

c. 1200–1000 B.C.	The Phoenicians became successful traders
332 B.C.	Phoenicia is conquered by Alexander the Great
146 B.C.	Carthage is destroyed by the Romans

Each of these dates should go on the time line, along with the accompanying information about what happened. (If there are other important dates elsewhere on the page, in call-out boxes or as part of picture captions, these should also be entered on the time line.)

(3) Once the dates have been placed on the time line, the student should find the Mediterranean Sea on his globe, wall map, and atlas. He should also make use of historical maps, either in his core text or in another historical map resource (several are listed at the end of this chapter), to find the most important countries and cities mentioned in the passage: Phoenicia, Babylon, and Persia, and Tyre, Sidon, Byblos, and Carthage.

(4) and (5) Now the student is ready to do extra reading. He could pursue any of the following topics:

The port cities of Tyre, Sidon, and Byblos
Phoenician expeditions to the British Isles and Africa
Ivory carvings
Glass bottles and beads
Purple dye
Phoenician trading posts and colonies
Carthage

The Phoenician princess Dido
The Phoenician alphabet
Conquest by Assyria, Babylon, and Persia
Conquest by Alexander the Great
Destruction of Carthage by the Romans

At first, you may need to read through the section and help the student pick out these topics, but fifth graders will soon be able to do this independently.

Any one of these topics could serve as the subject for additional reading—from the library, from another history encyclopedia or history book on hand, or from a trustworthy online source. (See "Using the Internet for Research and Reading" at the end of this chapter.) If, for example, he's interested in Phoenician crafts, he can look for books or search online for information on ancient dyes and glasswork. And he can also investigate the library's catalog—the children's librarian will be glad to help.[5]

After the student has done additional reading, ask him to write several sentences (a minimum of three; five to six is better as students grow more practiced) about how the Phoenicians built warships or first began to blow glass.[6] If he has trouble extracting the relevant facts, glance through his book with him and ask questions: Where did the murex come from? How did the Phoenicians get the dye out? What did it smell like? Was the process difficult to do? Remember, in the logic stage, conversation becomes your primary teaching tool. *Talk* to the student about what he's reading; encourage him to talk to you in complete sentences.

Pay special attention to biographies. Try to make a page for many of the great men and women you encounter (personalities act as memorable "pegs" on which to hang the progression of history). Actual names will be in short supply at first. But by the time you get to 3000 B.C., you'll be finding many great individuals (mostly men). For the centuries between 3000 and 2500, for example, you'll have the pharaohs Zoser, Cheops (Khufu),

---

[5] The classically educated student learns library skills as he researches—hands-on training in research is one of the benefits of the classical method.

[6] The writing programs recommended in Chapters 5 and 18 will help prepare the student to do this sort of short composition.

and Khafre (the sphinx was built to guard Khafre's pyramid) as well as Gilgamesh, who reigned in Sumer around 2700 B.C.

As in the early grades, some topics (Egyptian pharaohs and life in ancient Rome) will turn up dozens of useful library books, while others will produce nothing. Don't waste time digging for obscure details. If our resource list is silent and the library catalog yields no useful titles, move on.

For primary source work, see the Resources list at the end of this chapter. Online archives and anthologies provide plenty of accessible primary resources for middle-grade students. Aim to consult at least two primary sources per semester in fifth grade—four over the course of the year. Study each primary source, answer the questions suggested above in writing (and in complete sentences), and file the written responses in the Primary Sources section of the notebook.

The student will use the Arts and Great Books section of the notebook to file pages created during literature and art study (see Chapters 18 and 21). Whenever you run across a writer, musician, or artist—Homer, Virgil, Cicero, Praxiteles—make a biographical page listing his or her works and details about his or her life. Although these pages will be filed under Great Men and Women, those notebook pages covering the books, paintings, and compositions themselves will be created outside of the history lesson and filed in the history notebook.

By the end of fifth grade, the student will have created two historical resources: a time line that synthesizes all of his knowledge about historical events, personalities, and achievements; and a notebook that shows him at a glance the development of specific areas of human endeavor. He can flip through the Wars, Conflicts, and Political Events section of his notebook and see the progression of conflict from the war uniting Upper and Lower Egypt, through the Greek siege of Troy, all the way to the wars of Alexander the Great and the Punic Wars. Or she can trace the development of science in the ancient world, or review the establishment of great cities from Jericho to Mohenjo-daro to Alexandria.

(6) Ask the student to choose one page of text (approximately 250 to 300 words, or five to six paragraphs) from the most interesting history resource he's read during the week. He should outline this page of text on his own notebook paper.

This outlining practice will begin to prepare the student for more advanced composition. (See Chapter 18 for a fuller explanation of the middle-grade writing process.) As he moves into high school, he'll need to know how to write his own history essays from an outline. Before he can do this, however, he needs to study the outlines of *other* writers. The best and simplest way to do this is to create an outline from a finished piece of writing. The fifth grader needs to master the most basic element of the outline: the main point. Ask him to boil down each paragraph into one sentence by asking, "What is the most important statement in this paragraph?" This statement should be put into his own words, and each statement should be given a Roman numeral:

I. Main point of first paragraph
II. Main point of second paragraph
III. Main point of third paragraph

and so on. See "How to Outline" on pages 391–396 for more detailed directions.

This outline should be placed in the Outlines section of the history notebook. (The student can do this outlining practice either before or after completing the summary; choose whichever sequence seems more natural.)

Suggested Schedule

Once you've selected your core text, calculate how many pages or chapters you'll need to complete each week in order to cover the years until 400 A.D. This will serve as your basic weekly assignment.

But remember that your goal is to teach the student *how* to study history, not to do an exhaustive survey of all possible history topics! If you get behind or the student simply needs to move more slowly, skip sections. (Nothing terrible will happen if the student doesn't study the Hittites.) Or take a week now and then to spend history time doing nothing but reading through the text (no compositions, outlines, or outside reading) in order to catch up.

If you're studying history Mondays, Wednesdays, and Fridays:

Monday   Complete the week's reading from the core history
                resource. Make a list of facts and place in the history
                notebook. Mark all dates on the time line; find locations
                on the globe, the wall map, and in the atlas.

Wednesday   Do additional reading on one or two chosen topics, using library books or books recommended in the Resources list. Pick one resource and outline one page (five to six paragraphs). Place the outline in the history notebook.

Friday   Prepare a written summary of the information on the chosen topic and file it in the appropriate section of the history notebook.

If you're studying history on Tuesdays and Thursdays:

Tuesday   Complete the week's reading from the core history resource. Make a list of facts and place it in the history notebook. Mark all dates on the time line; find locations on the globe, the wall map, and in the atlas. Begin additional reading on one or two chosen topics, using library books or books recommended in the Resources list.

Thursday   Finish additional reading. Pick one resource and outline one page (five to six paragraphs). Place the outline in the history notebook. Prepare a written summary of the information on the chosen topic and file it in the appropriate section of the history notebook.

Twice during each semester, spend your history time during the week reading, evaluating, and completing a notebook page on your chosen primary source instead.

A note to busy parent-teachers: Logic-stage history involves a great deal of reading and writing. The classical curriculum is centered around reading and writing as the primary means of gaining knowledge. If you're wondering how time-consuming all this is, note that you'll be spending several hours per week helping the child find topics and locating library books, in addition to providing assistance in composition and checking over the finished work. But home schoolers inevitably find that the time parents need to spend in one-on-one instruction decreases dramatically in the middle grades. Your fifth grader may spend an hour reading history on Wednesdays, but that's not time-intensive on your part; you'll spend ten minutes at the beginning of the period giving directions and guidance, and ten minutes at the end talking to him about what he's read so that he can put the facts down in a composition.

Sixth Grade:
Medieval–Early Renaissance (400–1600)

For the years 400 to 1600, you'll be following the same basic pattern as you did in the fifth grade (see pages 374–379).

The List of Facts

The sixth grader will read her history pages and make her list of six to eight important facts to place in the history notebook.

Remind her to choose the most *important* facts rather than just listing the first few she encounters. For example, if one section of the student's text reads:

In 1240 Sundiata Keita, the ruler of the small Malinke kingdom in West Africa, brought about the collapse of the nation of Ghana, and established a new nation called Mali. He set up a well-organized state that possessed fertile farmlands beside the Niger River. Under Sundiata's rule, Mali controlled the gold trade and became rich and powerful. Many of the camel caravan routes across the Sahara Desert led to Mali's fine cities, such as Koumbi Saleh, Djenne, and Timbuktu.

Mali's trading cities exported ivory, gold, and slaves to the Muslim world, and to Venice and Genoa in Europe. In exchange, they imported salt, cloth, ceramics, glass, horses, and luxuries. Timbuktu and Djenne became centers of learning, where Muslims mingled with Africans. Timbuktu had a university and 100 schools. Mali reached the height of its power, and also became Muslim, under Sundiata's grandson Mansa Musa (1307–37). He made a pilgrimage to Mecca in 1324, taking 500 slaves and 90 camels loaded with gold. In 1325, Mali overpowered Songhay, lower down the Niger River, but in 1464 Songhay's ruler declared independence. Mali's decline had begun in 1350, and by 1500, it had been conquered by Songhay.[7]

---

[7] *The Kingfisher History Encyclopedia* (New York: Kingfisher, 2004), p. 164.

then the student's list of facts might look like this:

1. Sundiata Keita established Mali in 1240.
2. Mali controlled the gold trade.
3. Mali became Muslim under Mansa Musa (1307–1334).
4. Mansa Musa made a pilgrimage to Mecca in 1324.
5. Mali was conquered by Songhay in 1500.

The Time Line

The student should enter the dates found in the text on her time line. Begin the school year by creating a time line that covers the medieval–early Renaissance period—twelve centuries, or twelve equal divisions. You'll have much more space for each century, which is good—the centuries are crowded.

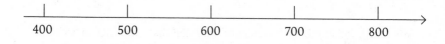

| | | | | |
| 400 | 500 | 600 | 700 | 800 |

The Outline

The student should still choose pages from her additional reading to outline. But now, instead of simply condensing the reading into one sentence per paragraph, she'll identify one main point and two to four subpoints for each paragraph. These will be written out in proper outline form, using Roman numerals and uppercase letters. Even though she's already learned this in fifth-grade grammar (see Chapter 17), it bears repeating:

   I. First main point
     A. First supporting point
     B. Second supporting point
  II. Second main point
     A. First supporting point
     B. Second supporting point
     C. Third supporting point

and so on. In this type of outlining, two short paragraphs covering the same subject can be combined together; a long paragraph can be broken in half, if it begins a new thought halfway through. The goal: to create an outline that lays out the logical development of the text. In a good outline, each supporting point is related to the main point. See "How to Outline" on pages 391–396 for more detailed direction; note that, as the student grows more practiced, she should aim to outline up to two pages from her chosen resource.

In the passage above, the life of Mansa Musa could be researched to create a notebook page for the Great Men and Women section; the export of ivory, gold, and slaves and the importation of salt, cloth, ceramics, glass, horses, and luxuries could provide material for a page to be filed in Daily Life, Beliefs, and Customs; the city of Timbuktu could be covered for a page in Cities and Settlements. These short compositions will follow the rules for composition taught in the student's language arts study (see Chapter 18). Aim for one-half to one full page for each composition (that is, 200–400 words). (See the summary at the end of this section for the total amount of writing the student should be doing during the logic stage.)

Primary Sources

The student will continue to use primary sources, evaluating them by asking herself the same questions she did in fifth grade (see page 370). Aim to cover four to six primary sources over the course of the year (two to three per semester). Try to include the Magna Carta, which is a foundational document in Western culture. You will find a longer list of available materials in the Resources at the end of this chapter; substitute other topics if you wish.

The Notebook

Label a new three-ring binder "Medieval-Early Renaissance: 400–1600," and divide it into the same nine sections as in fifth grade (see pages 370–371).[8] The student will complete the same five steps: reading and outlining, marking dates, finding locations, doing extra reading, and filing summaries in the history notebook.

Once again: be sure to remember that you're not trying to cover every

---

[8] Some parents choose to keep the same notebook for all four years, filing pages chronologically within each section, so that (for example) the "Famous Men and Women" sections would begin with an ancient hero and end with a modern person of note.

detail of the years 400–1600. And the student will find many possible topics for additional research. You should feel free to skip some topics, or spend additional time on others; the text is a springboard, not a prison.[9]

On the other hand, if you've only progressed a hundred years from September to Christmas, you may need to reevaluate. Is the student dawdling? Does she need remedial writing or reading work? Do you need to drop back to the simpler history text for a while? Or are you letting other things— phone calls, jobs, visits from friends, housework—crowd out school? If so, you may need to adjust the child's daily schedule.

Suggested Schedule

If you're studying history Mondays, Wednesdays, and Fridays:

Monday	Complete the week's reading from the core history resource. Make a list of facts and place in the history notebook. Mark all dates on the time line; find locations on the globe, the wall map, and in the atlas.
Wednesday	Do additional reading on one or two chosen topics, using library books or books recommended in the Resources list. Pick one resource and outline one or two pages (five to ten paragraphs). Place the outline in the history notebook.
Friday	Prepare a written summary of the information on the chosen topic and file it in the appropriate section of the history notebook.

If you're studying history on Tuesdays and Thursdays:

Tuesday	Complete the week's reading from the core history resource. Make a list of facts and place it in the history notebook. Mark all dates on the time line; find locations

---

[9] This is one of the keys to successful home tutoring: You're the boss. You set the schedules. *Use common sense.* If the child spends three hours outlining her history lesson, you're doing too much. Start skipping sections. Or don't finish the book. How many textbooks did your teacher actually finish in high school or college?

	on the globe, the wall map, and in the atlas. Begin additional reading on one or two chosen topics, using library books or books recommended in the Resources list.
Thursday	Finish additional reading. Pick one resource and outline one or two pages (five to ten paragraphs). Place the outline in the history notebook. Prepare a written summary of the information on the chosen topic and file it in the appropriate section of the history notebook.

Two or three times per semester, spend your history time during the week reading, evaluating, and completing a notebook page on your chosen primary source instead.

Seventh Grade:
Late Renaissance–Early Modern (1600–1850)

The List of Facts

As in the previous years, the seventh grader will read his history pages and make his list of six to eight important facts to place in the history notebook.

Although you can continue on with the same history core text used in sixth grade, very strong readers may wish to move on to one of the more difficult narrative-style texts recommended in the Resources. This will require more careful distillation of the important facts. For example, if the student's text reads

India splintered into many states in the 1700s as the Moguls who ruled the subcontinent began to lose power. While a dwindling Mogul Empire endured near Delhi, old provinces became independent kingdoms, a Hindu hill people called the Marathas spread out from central India, and Sikhs assumed control of the Punjab in the northwest. Meanwhile European trade with India flourished, with the British becoming the principal traders. To protect their economic interests, the British established armies composed mostly of local troops called sepoys. Armed and equipped like the British Army, the sepoys were the most efficient fighters on the subcontinent.

As businessmen, British traders wanted to acquire wealth, not territory. But over time, one aim led to the other. Calcutta, in the rich province of Bengal, was a prime center of British commerce. On June 20, 1756, the Indian ruler of Bengal seized Calcutta's British garrison for violations of local trading laws. As part of the takeover, scores of British prisoners were held overnight in a hot, poorly ventilated cell, later called the Black Hole of Calcutta. By morning, most had died. The incident— often retold with the numbers exaggerated—became a symbol to the British of Indian brutality. In January 1757 Col. Robert Clive retook Calcutta, then went on to seize all of Bengal.[10]

then the student's list of facts might look like this:

1. In the 1700s, the Moguls lost power and India divided into many states.
2. The Marathas and the Sikhs began to gain power.
3. Calcutta became the center of British trade.
4. The British kept local soldiers called sepoys.
5. In 1756, the Indian ruler of Bengal took the British in Calcutta prisoner.
6. The Black Hole of Calcutta was the cell where the prisoners were kept (most of them died).
7. The British recaptured Calcutta and then took the rest of the province of Bengal.

The Time Line

For the years 1600 to 1850, you should create a new time line. Divide this one into ten twenty-five-year segments:

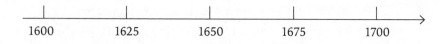

| 1600 | 1625 | 1650 | 1675 | 1700 |

---

[10] Patricia S. Daniels and Stephen G. Hyslop, *National Geographic Almanac of World History*, 2nd ed. (Washington, DC: National Geographic, 2011), pp. 219–20.

The Outline

The seventh grader should continue the sixth-grade method of outlining until he is comfortable with it. He can try to introduce more supporting points than before:

I. First main point
   A. First supporting point
      1. First subpoint
      2. Second subpoint
   B. Second supporting point
      1. First subpoint
      2. Second subpoint
II. Second main point
   A. First supporting point
   B. Second supporting point
   C. Third supporting point

The seventh grader should only begin to do this when the sixth-grade method has become easy. This point may be reached at any time during the seventh-grade year or at the beginning of the eighth-grade year.

Each subpoint must relate to the supporting point it follows. See "How to Outline" on pages 391–396 for more detailed direction; note that, as the student grows more practiced, he should aim to outline two to three pages from his chosen resource.

Primary Sources

Primary sources for this period include the founding documents of America (from the Pilgrims through the Revolution) as well as many other topics; choose from the list provided in the Resources section of this chapter.

Primary resource evaluation, when done, can replace library reading and notebook-page creation. The student should continue to make evaluation pages for these primary sources (see page 370) and file them in the Primary Sources section of the history notebook. Aim to cover three to four primary sources each semester, six to eight over the course of the year.

The Notebook

Label a new three-ring binder "Late Renaissance–Early Modern: 1600–1850," and divide it into the same nine sections as in fifth and sixth grades (see pages 370–371).

This period is heavy on wars—the Glorious Revolution, the annexation of Ireland, the Great Northern War, the Seven Years' War, the American Revolution, the French Revolution, the Napoleonic Wars, the War of 1812, and more. You will find a great deal of material in the library on these topics, as well as on the creation of the Declaration of Independence and on the persons who defined early American political life. The Industrial Revolution also takes place during this period.

Memorization

American seventh graders should take time out during the year to memorize the opening sections of the Declaration of Independence and the Preamble to the Constitution.

Suggested Schedule

For Monday-Wednesday-Friday and Tuesday-Thursday schedules, see the sixth-grade year (pages 386–387).

Eighth Grade: Modern (1850–Present)

Again, the student will read a section from the core text, prepare a list of facts, mark all dates on the time line, find locations on the globe/wall map/atlas, do additional reading, outline selected pages from one of the additional resources (eighth graders should aim to outline three or four pages), and prepare notebook pages.

The List of Facts

If the student has not already transitioned into a more difficult core text, eighth grade is a good time to do so. If you are already using a more complex history core text, continue on as you have before.

Create a new time line. Divide this one into fifteen ten-year segments since you'll be recording a number of events that occur close together. In the case of World War II, for example, you may need to mark a series of events taking place over a matter of months. The time line should look like this:

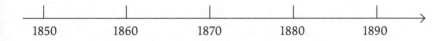

1850   1860   1870   1880   1890

The Outline

The student should make three-level outlines of selected pages from his additional resources. See "How to Outline" on pages 391–396 for more detailed guidance; note that, as the student grows more practiced, he should aim to outline three to four pages from his chosen resource.

Primary Sources

Military documents and letters from the American Civil War are simple to find; since the Civil War was one of the earliest wars photographed, look in the adult nonfiction section of the library for books of Civil War photos. They bring the conflict to life as nothing else can. (And remember, a photograph is a type of primary source.)

Other primary sources for the modern period are not difficult to locate. Letters and speeches of world leaders—Queen Victoria, Abraham Lincoln, Winston Churchill, Benito Mussolini, Adolf Hitler, just to name a few—abound. Check the library for juvenile and young adult nonfiction on the great men and women of the modern age; many of these books will contain primary information. (We've listed a few suggestions in our Resources.) When the student encounters a primary document such as the Gettysburg Address or Edward VIII's abdication speech, he should fill out the primary-source evaluation and file it in Primary Sources. Aim to cover at least three to four primary sources each semester, six to eight over the course of the year.

As you move into the twentieth century, you should be making use of another type of primary source—oral history. Whenever the student encounters a major event in the twentieth century, make an effort to bring him into contact with someone who lived during that time. If you're fortunate enough to have grandparents (or great-grandparents) and great-uncles or great-aunts nearby, send the child over to interview them. What was rationing like during World War II? Did you have to look out for airplanes? Did you get to eat chocolate? What were cars like in 1950? How much did you pay for rent in 1952? What music did you listen to? As you come closer to modern times, these recollections will become easier to find: friends may be willing to tell about tours of duty in Vietnam; older relatives and neighbors might recall the days of segregation; and most people born in the fifties will remember the first moon landing and where they were when they heard of Kennedy's assassination.

These oral histories should be written down and filed in Primary Sources (see "The Notebook," pages 370–371). If you can't find friends and relatives to fill in these accounts, you might consider a trip to a retirement community or nursing home; the staff should be able to direct you toward residents who can tell stories about the early twentieth century. Once you reach the 1930s and 1940s, try to conduct an oral-history interview at least twice per month, even if you have to sacrifice some library time to do so.

The oral-history project has two purposes. It develops the student's ability to "do" history by recording events and stories firsthand instead of relying on the written work of others. And it brings recent history to life— the student is able to connect the stories in books to real people's lives for the first time. Reading about the Holocaust is powerful; discovering that a nursing-home resident has a tattoo on her forearm is explosive.

We've supplied a list of questions at the end of this book (see the Appendix, Taking an Oral History, pages 785–787). Although the student can use these questions to give oral-history interviews direction, he shouldn't feel tied to them.

As in fourth grade, American students should plan to take one to two weeks at the end of the year to read through the history of their home state (see Resources, page 426).

The Notebook

Label a new three-ring binder "Modern Times: 1850–Present," and divide it into the same nine sections as in fifth through seventh grades (see pages 370–371). Add one additional section: Eyewitness Accounts.

Memorization

American eighth graders should take time during the year to memorize the Gettysburg Address. Optional memory work might be done on the

Emancipation Proclamation, the amendments to the Constitution, the wartime speeches of Winston Churchill, the speeches of Martin Luther King, Jr., or anything else the student finds and likes.

Suggested Schedule
For Monday-Wednesday-Friday and Tuesday-Thursday schedules, see the sixth-grade year (pages 384–385). As an alternative, you might take one week to do reading, outlining, and map work and then devote a full week to reading, research, and oral-history taking.

HOW TO OUTLINE

The student should begin to develop her outlining skills by finding the main idea in each paragraph and assigning it a Roman numeral. Remember that the goal is not to write a single sentence that incorporates *all* (or even most) of the information in the paragraph. Instead, the student should try to find a *topic sentence* in the paragraph—the one that summarizes the paragraph's central theme. Topic sentences can often be found at the beginning or end of a paragraph (remind the student to put the information into her own words), but many paragraphs have no single topic sentence and the student will need to write her own.

It can be useful to ask the student two questions for each paragraph:

1. What is the main thing or person that the paragraph is about?
2. Why is that thing or person important?

For purposes of illustration, consider the following paragraph from *The Story of Canada*, by Janet Lunn and Christopher Moore.

Five hundred years ago, 60 million bison—or buffalo, as they are more often called—roamed the grasslands of North America. They meant life itself to plains nations like the Blackfoot of what is now southern Alberta. The Blackfoot moved slowly across the land, following the herds and carrying with them everything they had. They hunted deer and antelope, they grew tobacco, and they gathered wild turnips and onion. But for centuries it was the buffalo that provided for the Blackfoot people. Buffalo hides made their tipis and their clothing. Buffalo sinews were their thread. Buffalo bones made clubs and spoons and needles. They even used dried buffalo dung as fuel for their campfires. To the Blackfoot, buffalo meat was "real" meat and nothing else tasted so good. They trusted the buffalo to keep them strong.

What is the main thing that the paragraph is about? Buffalo. Why is the buffalo important? Because the Blackfoot people used it for food, clothing, and other purposes. If the student combines these answers into one sentence, she will have her topic sentence:

I. The Blackfoot people used buffalo for food, clothing, and many other purposes.

The next paragraph in *The Story of Canada* reads:

The Blackfoot had always gone on foot, using dogs to help carry their goods, for there were no horses in North America until Spanish colonists brought them in the 1500s. Soon after that, plains people captured animals that had gone wild, or stole them in raids. They traded the horses northward and early in the 1700s, horses came to the northern plains. Suddenly the Blackfoot were a nation on horseback. How exciting it was, learning to ride a half-wild mustang and galloping off to the horizon!

Ask the question: What is the main thing that the paragraph is about? Horses. Why are horses important? The Blackfoot tribe learned how to ride them in the 1700s.

II. The Blackfoot tribe learned to use horses in the 1700s.

You will have to remind the student continually that she is not trying to summarize the entire paragraph; she is finding the central idea in it. Leaving facts out is a difficult skill, and also involves a judgment call on the part of the student. As long as she can answer the two questions above with information that makes sense, don't agonize over whether she's chosen the "right" sentence for her outline.

Once the student is comfortable finding the main idea in each paragraph (something that can take the entire fifth-grade year), ask her to move on to a two-level outline. In this level of outlining, the main Roman-numeral point still provides the central idea of the paragraph, while each capital-letter subpoint should provide a specific piece of information that relates *directly* to the main idea.

After writing the main Roman-numeral point, the student should ask herself: What additional information does the paragraph give me about each of the people, things, or ideas in the main point? For the first paragraph above, the student would ask: What other important thing does the paragraph tell me about buffalo? There were 60 million buffalo in North America. What other important thing does the paragraph tell me about the Blackfoot's use of the buffalo? They relied on the buffalo to keep them strong.

The two-level outline of the paragraph would read:

I. The Blackfoot people used buffalo for food, clothing, and other purposes.
   A. There were 60 million buffalo in North America.
   B. The Blackfoot relied on the buffalo to keep them strong.

It is tempting for the sixth-grade student to use the capital letter subpoints to give specific details about the paragraph:

I. The Blackfoot people used buffalo for food, clothing, and other purposes.
   A. They hunted deer and antelope too.
   B. They made clothing from buffalo.
   C. They ate buffalo meat.
   D. They made clubs and spoons and needles from buffalo bones.

These are actually details about the extent to which the Blackfoot relied on the buffalo, so they would only appear in a three-level outline:

I. The Blackfoot people used buffalo for food, clothing, and other purposes.
   A. There were 60 million buffalo in North America.

B. The Blackfoot relied on the buffalo to keep them strong.
  1. They made clothing from buffalo.
  2. They ate buffalo meat.
  3. They made clubs and spoons and needles from buffalo bones.

(Note that the detail about deer and antelope is a random statement that doesn't fit into the outline at all.)

Before the student can do three-level outlines (which she'll begin in seventh grade), she needs to master the basic two-level outline; each capital-letter subpoint should make an independent statement relating directly to something in the main Roman-numeral point. This means that the student will need to work on the skill of eliminating unnecessary detail, picking out only the central statements in each paragraph. A two-level outline of the second paragraph would answer the questions: What is the most important additional information that this paragraph gives me about the Blackfoot? What is the most important additional information that it gives me about the horses? An acceptable outline might look like this:

II. The Blackfoot tribe learned to use horses in the 1700s.
  A. They had always gone on foot before.
  B. The horses were brought to North America by Spanish colonists.

As the student grows more comfortable with two-level outlining, encourage her to outline up to two pages rather than merely outlining one.

Around seventh grade, the student can begin to construct three-level outlines. The third level of the outline uses Arabic numerals:

I. Main point.
  A. Additional information about the main point.
    1. Detail about that additional information.

Third-level details are relatively simple to find; the student merely needs to ask, "What else is important to know in this paragraph?" A full three-level outline of the two paragraphs above might look like this:

I. The Blackfoot people used buffalo for food, clothing, and other purposes.

   A. There were 60 million buffalo in North America.
      1. The buffalo are also called bison.
      2. They roamed North America 500 years ago.
   B. The Blackfoot relied on the buffalo to keep them strong.
      1. They made clothing from buffalo.
      2. They ate buffalo meat.
      3. They made clubs and spoons and needles from buffalo bones.
      4. They used buffalo dung for fuel.
II. The Blackfoot tribe learned to use horses in the 1700s.
   A. They had always gone on foot before.
      1. There were no horses in North America.
      2. They used dogs to carry their goods.
   B. The horses were brought to North America by Spanish colonists.
      1. The horses first came in the 1500s.
      2. Some of the horses escaped or were stolen.
      3. The horses came to the northern plains in the 1700s.

Once the student is reasonably comfortable with the three-level outline, encourage her to expand the number of pages that she outlines: up to three pages for seventh graders, three to four pages for eighth graders.

Developing outlining takes practice—and don't forget that this history outlining should be paired with a grammar program that teaches the basics of outlining skills. However, remember three things.

First, many guides to outlining will tell you that you should never have an A unless you have a B, and that you should never use 1 unless you use 2. While this might be a useful guide when you're constructing your own outlines to write from, it's not workable when you're outlining someone else's material; the writer might not have provided two subpoints per main point, and it's pointless to make one up to preserve some sort of ideal outline form.

Second, there may be several different ways to outline any given paragraph. If the student can give good reasons why she's chosen her main points and subpoints, don't worry about whether she's constructed the best possible outline.

Third, if the student struggles with outlining a particular resource, it is possible that the book itself is either badly written or written in "encyclopedic" form (many main points packed into single paragraphs of text). Put it away and try outlining from a different book.

SUMMARY OF LOGIC-STAGE HISTORY WORK

Fifth grade
: 60 minutes, three days per week, or 1½ hours, twice per week: study ancient times (5000 B.C.–A.D. 400), using selected history resources, including primary sources (four over the course of the year); do at least one outline (one sentence per paragraph) of five to six paragraphs; prepare at least one written summary; mark dates on the time line; do map work.

Sixth grade
: 60 minutes, three days per week, or 1½ hours, twice per week: study medieval–early Renaissance times (400–1600), using selected history resources, including primary sources (four to six over the course of the year); do at least one two-level outline of a five- to ten-paragraph selection; prepare at least one written summary; mark dates on the time line; do map work.

Seventh grade
: 60 minutes, three days per week, or 1½ hours, twice per week: study late Renaissance–early-modern times (1600–1850), using selected history resources, including primary sources (six to eight over the course of the year); do at least one two-level or three-level outline of a two- to three-page selection; prepare at least one written summary; mark dates on the time line; do map work.

Eighth grade
: 60 minutes, three days per week, or 1½ hours, twice per week: study modern times (1850–present), using selected history resources, including primary sources (six to eight over the course of the year); do at least one oral history project; do at least one three-level outline of a three- to four-page selection; prepare at least one written summary; mark dates on the time line; do map work.

RESOURCES

Most books can be obtained from any bookseller or library; most curricula can be bought directly from the publisher or from a major home-school supplier such as Rainbow Resource Center. Contact information for publishers and suppliers can be found at www.welltrainedmind.com. If availability is limited, we have noted it. Where indicated, resources are listed in chronological order (the order you'll want to use them in). Books in series are listed together. Remember that additional curricula choices and more can be found at www.welltrainedmind.com. Prices change constantly, but we have included 2016 pricing to give an idea of affordability.

The titles we list are only a few of the many available. Plan on exploring library and bookstore shelves for yourself. Basic texts for the four-year logic stage are listed first, followed by basic geography resources. A three-part supplementary list is provided for each year of study. The first section for each year lists, in chronological order, great men and women (for grades 5 and 6) or major events (for grades 7 and 8) that you might want to cover during the year—this is simply a checklist to help you organize your history study. The second section lists primary sources—books and texts written during the period under study. The third section lists books that provide general information about the historical period, including coloring books and other project resources.

Many of the resources recommended in Chapter 7, such as the detailed Bellerophon coloring books, are still suitable for middle-grade students. Older students may also enjoy reading elementary-level biographies as a refresher. Check the Resources section at the end of Chapter 7 for details.

Basic Texts

Texts are listed in order of difficulty, from simplest to most complex. All of these options are colorful and beautifully illustrated and presented. Samples of all can be viewed online.

History Year by Year. New York: DK Children, 2013.
$24.99. The simplest text, written on an upper fourth-grade/fifth-grade level. Produced in cooperation with the Smithsonian Institute. Double-page spreads on most topics, with plenty of captions. Good for slower readers or students who have difficulty absorbing large amounts of written information.

Kingfisher History Encyclopedia, 3rd ed. New York: Kingfisher, 2012.
> $32.99. Fifth- to lower seventh-grade reading level; the third edition of a long-standing, highly regarded reference work.

National Geographic Visual History of the World. Washington, DC: National Geographic, 2005.
> $35. Moves away from brief encyclopedic entries toward narrative text, with one-page summaries on most topics. Grades 6 and 7.

Daniels, Patricia, and Stephen G. Hyslop. *National Geographic Almanac of World History,* 3rd ed. Washington, DC: National Geographic, 2014.
> $40. Narrative style text; two- to three-page summary essays. Best for grades 7 and up.

American History Basic Texts

Use alongside core texts above or as the basis for a one-year study.

Children's Encyclopedia of American History. New York: Dorling Kindersley, 2014.
> $29.99. Produced in cooperation with the Smithsonian, this encyclopedia has short entries with plenty of illustrations, photographs, and maps; less narrative and more visual than the Davidson text below.

Davidson, James West. *A Little History of the United States.* New Haven, CT: Yale University Press, 2015.
> $25. A brisk, readable narrative history of the U.S., ideal for sixth grade and above. Excellent writing but few visual aids (the occasional black-and-white illustration or map).

Basic Geography Resources

Up-to-date globes and wall maps can be found at the National Geographic online map store (www.shopnationalgeographic.org) and at www.maps .com. See Chapter 7 for the Knowledge Quest black-line maps, which are also useful for logic-stage history study.

National Geographic Family Reference Atlas, 4th ed. Washington, DC: National Geographic Society, 2015.

$70 list price, but you can often find it discounted at the National Geographic online store or from other booksellers. Before buying, though, visit the National Geographic store for the most recent edition. Contemporary national boundaries and geographical features.

National Geographic Kids World Atlas. Washington, DC: National Geographic Society, 2013.
$14.99. Visit the National Geographic store for the most recent edition. Simplified atlas with contemporary political boundaries and geographical features.

New Historical Atlas of the World. Skokie, IL: Rand McNally, 2015.
$12. One hundred maps showing changes in political borders from ancient times to the present. Simpler than the O'Brien atlas listed below.

O'Brien, Patrick, ed. *Atlas of World History*, 2nd ed. Oxford: Oxford University Press, 2010.
$49.95. Four hundred and fifty historical maps; a much more complete collection of maps showing changes in empires and kingdoms from ancient times to the present. An excellent resource to keep on hand for all four years.

Penguin Atlas of . . . series. New York: Penguin.
Accessible, colorful softcover books showing political changes every thirty to forty years throughout history. Listed in chronological order.
Kinder, Hermann, and Werner Hilgemann. *The Penguin Atlas of World History, Vol. 1: From Prehistory to the French Revolution*, 2004. $15.
McEvedy, Colin. *The New Penguin Atlas of Ancient History*, rev. ed. 2003. $17.
McEvedy, Colin. *The New Penguin Atlas of Medieval History*, rev. ed. 1992. $16.
McEvedy, Colin. *The Penguin Atlas of Modern History: To 1815*. 1986. $16.
Kinder, Hermann, and Werner Hilgemann. *The Penguin Atlas of World History, Vol. 1: From the French Revolution to the Present*. 2004. $16.
McEvedy, Colin. *The New Penguin Atlas of Recent History: Europe Since 1815*, rev. ed. 1992. $16.

Historical Atlases of South Asia, Central Asia, and the Middle East series. New York: Rosen Publishing Group, 2003–2004.
$32.95 each (library binding only), but check your library or buy used

for a fraction of the price. Excellent, colorful maps showing changes over time in some of the world's most troubled areas; perfect for families who want to focus in more deeply on a country with a complex history.

Draper, Allison Stark. *A Historical Atlas of Egypt.*

———. *A Historical Atlas of Syria.*

Greenberger, Robert. *A Historical Atlas of Pakistan.*

Isaac, Michael. *A Historical Atlas of Oman.*

Khan, Aisha. *A Historical Atlas of Kyrgyzstan.*

———. *A Historical Atlas of Uzbekistan.*

Liberman, Sherri. *A Historical Atlas of Azerbaijan.*

Phillips, Larissa. *A Historical Atlas of Iraq.*

Ray, Kurt. *A Historical Atlas of Kuwait.*

Romano, Amy. *A Historical Atlas of Afghanistan.*

———. *A Historical Atlas of Israel.*

———. *A Historical Atlas of the United Arab Emirates.*

———. *A Historical Atlas of Yemen.*

Time-Line Resources

Blank Timeline Templates.

$4.50 for 10. Order from Rainbow Resource Center. These 22-inch time-line segments are each divided into twenty sections, which can be divided in numerous ways. Designate each section as one, five, ten, twenty, or more years; tape them together to form a custom time line; bind them into a booklet.

Add-A-Century Timeline. Sauk Rapids, MN: Add-A-Century.

For those who want a slightly more elaborate time-line system, Add-A-Century offers coated card stock panels that can be connected together or bound into a book, along with category labels (Art & Music, Government & Politics, Science & Technology, etc.), stickers, and supplies to make "flip-up" panels where the time line gets crowded. Makes it simple to insert additional panels into the middle of an already constructed time line. More details on the publisher's website.

Starter Pack. $49.50. panels, connectors, category labels, stickers, flip-ups, and accessories.

Starter Pack/Binder Set. $63. Includes an oversize binder to make a time-line book.

Resources for Teaching Skills

Boynton, Alice, and Wiley Blevins. *Teaching Students to Read Nonfiction.* Scholastic Teaching Strategies, Grades 4 and Up. New York: Scholastic, 2003.

$23.99. Order from any bookstore or from Social Studies School Service. Designed for grades 4 to 7, this book guides students through the basics of reading nonfiction, with an emphasis on history. A good way to build skills and confidence. Strategies for comprehension, tips on how to study maps, time lines, and other elements of history texts, and plenty of practice. You could work your way through the fifteen lessons in this book before beginning history study, if necessary—or return to it if the student begins to have difficulty.

Broadwater, Deborah White. *Note Taking: Lessons to Improve Research Skills and Test Scores.* Greensboro, NC: Mark Twain Media/Carson Dellosa Publishing, Inc., 2003.

$8.99, print and ebook. Buy directly from Carson Dellosa. For grades 4 to 8. Direct instruction and practice in finding the most important facts in a reading selection; good practice for students who have difficulty condensing and summarizing. View samples at Carson Dellosa's website.

Mueller, Mary. *Study Skills Strategies: Outlining.* Portland, ME: Walch Education, 2003.

$26. Order through any bookstore or from Walch Education. High-school skills.

Pearce, Q. L. *Note Taking and Outlining.* Greensboro, NC: Frank Schaffer Publications/Carson Dellosa Publishing, Inc., 2003.

$6.99. Available as an ebook directly from Carson Dellosa. Designed for grades 3 to 5, this is an excellent resource for students who are struggling with basic outlining skills. View samples at Carson Dellosa's website.

Ancients, 5000 B.C.–A.D. 400 (Fifth Grade)

List of Great Men and Women

Cheops, pharaoh of Egypt (2700–2675 B.C.)

Abraham (c. 2100 B.C.)

Hammurabi (c. 1750 B.C.)

Queen Hatshepsut of Egypt (c. 1480 B.C.)

Moses (c. 1450 B.C.)

Tutankhamen (c. 1355 B.C.)

Nebuchadnezzar (1146–1123 B.C.)

King David (c. 1000 B.C.)

Homer (c. 800 B.C.)

Romulus (753–716 B.C.)

Sennacherib (705–681 B.C.)

Lao-tse (b. 604 B.C.)

Pythagoras (581–497 B.C.)

Confucius (K'ung Fu-tsu) (551–479 B.C.)

Buddha (Siddhartha Gautama) (550–480 B.C.)

Darius I of Persia (522–485 B.C.)

Socrates (470–399 B.C.)

Hippocrates (b. 460 B.C.)

Plato (427–347 B.C.)

Aristotle (384–322 B.C.)

Alexander the Great (356–323 B.C.)

Shi Huangdi (first emperor of unified China, 221–207 B.C.)

Hannibal (fought with Rome c. 218–207 B.C.)

Judas Maccabaeus (c. 168 B.C.)

Cicero (106–43 B.C.)

Julius Caesar (100–44 B.C.)

Virgil (70–19 B.C.)

Caesar Augustus (c. 45 B.C.–A.D. 14)

Jesus Christ (c. 4 B.C.–A.D. 33)

Caligula (died A.D. 42)

Saint Paul (c. A.D. 45)

Nero (died A.D. 68)

Marcus Aurelius (ruled A.D. 161–180)

Constantine the Great (ruled A.D. 306–337)

Primary Sources: Suggested Topics

You will discover many more options, but the following are particularly accessible to middle-grade students.

The Palette of Narmer (c. 3200 B.C.)

Excerpts from the Pyramid Texts (c. 2425–2300 B.C.)

Birth legend of Sargon (c. 2240 B.C.)

Code of Hammurabi (c. 1780 B.C.)

The Twelve Tables of Roman law (c. 450 B.C.)

Thucydides, "The Plague of Athens" (c. 430 B.C.)

Julius Caesar, "The Germans" from Book VI of *The Gallic Wars* (c. 51 B.C.)

Augustus Caesar, "Acts of the Divine Augustus (A.D. 14)

Josephus, "Siege and Fall of Jerusalem" and "Masada" from *The Wars of the Jews* (c. A.D. 70)

Procopius of Caesarea, "Alaric's Sack of Rome" from *History of the Wars* (c. A.D. 410)

Codex Theodosianus (A.D. 438)

Primary Sources: Resources

The Internet Ancient History Sourcebook. legacy.fordham.edu/halsall/ancient/asbook.asp

> Hosted by Fordham University, this invaluable website is an easy-to-navigate online archive of primary sources (translated into English) ranging from Sumer (artwork, Akkadian prayers, multiple translations of *Gilgamesh*, Sumerian king lists, and much more) to the third-century church (Pliny's letters, excerpts from the Church Fathers, official edicts, and more). Highly useful for the curious student.

Mellor, Ronald, and Amanda H. Podany. *The World in Ancient Times: Primary Sources & Reference Volume.* Oxford: Oxford University Press, 2005.

> $36.95. Excerpts from seventy-six ancient documents (letters, historical records, inscriptions, epics, and more), spanning the world from Mesopotamia to Asia and the Americas. Well-presented, usable, and clear. Highly recommended.

Plato. *The Last Days of Socrates.* Trans. Hugh Tredennick. New York: Penguin, 2003.

> $12. For good readers, this primary source contains dialogues that you and your middle-grade student could read together; the dialogue is often funny, and ideas are thought-provoking. (Remember, this is a first introduction to ancient thought; the student doesn't need to understand every word!)

General Information

Aldred, Cyril. *A Coloring Book of Tutankhamun*. Santa Barbara, CA: Bellerophon, 1978.

> $3.50. Order from Bellerophon. Uses actual images from the ancient world to tell the story of Tutankhamen's reign and burial. Detailed and challenging.

Anderson, John. *Alexander the Great Coloring Book*. Santa Barbara, CA: Bellerophon, 1981.

> $4.95. Order from Bellerophon. These illustrations of Alexander the Great are taken from Persian and Indian drawings as well as from the art of ancient Greece and medieval Europe. Includes biographical material.

Art, Suzanne Strauss. Ancient Times and Early Times series.

> $22.95 each. Art, an ancient history teacher, wrote these series because she couldn't find history texts for fifth graders that covered the ancient world in a systematic way, while still providing plenty of interesting detail. These books are well worth having on hand for additional reading; they cover civilizations and stories neglected in other texts, and include projects, maps, writing assignments, personality profiles, and suggested additional readings. Order from the publisher or from Amazon.com or another bookstore.

> *Ancient Times: The Story of the First Americans*. Freeport, ME: Wayside Publishing, 1999.
> *Early Times: The Story of Ancient Egypt*, 4th ed. Freeport, ME: Wayside Publishing, 2013.
> *Early Times: The Story of Ancient Greece*, 4th ed. Freeport, ME: Wayside Publishing, 1994.
> *Early Times: The Story of Ancient Rome*, 2nd ed. Freeport, ME: Wayside Publishing, 2012.
> *The Story of Ancient China*, 3rd ed. Freeport, ME: Wayside Press, 2012.
> > From Neolithic times to the Tang dynasty; includes explanations of Taoism, Confucianism, and Buddhism.
> *West Meets East: The Travels of Alexander*. Concord, MA: Wayside Publishing, 1996.

Calliope. Peterborough, NH: Cobblestone Publishing.

$43.95 for one year's subscription, a combination of print and web issues. Order from Cobblestone Publishing. A world history magazine for readers aged nine to twelve; each 52-page issue has a theme ("The City-States of Sumer," "Tang Dynasty") and includes articles, maps, art, and a question-and-answer feature about world history.

Conkle, Nancy. *A Coloring Book of the Trojan War: The Iliad, Vol. 1.* Santa Barbara, CA: Bellerophon, 1995. (Also Knill, Harry. *A Coloring Book of the Trojan War: The Iliad, Vol. 2.* Santa Barbara, CA: Bellerophon, 1994.)
   $4.95 each. Order from Bellerophon. Detailed drawings, taken from Greek sculpture and architecture, can be turned into works of art with careful coloring.

Diez-Luckie, Cathy. *Famous Figures of Ancient Times: Movable Paper Figures to Cut, Color, and Assemble.* Oakland, CA: Figures In Motion, 2009.
   $19.95. Order from the publisher or from Well-Trained Mind Press. Great for kids who like crafts: detailed, colored figures from history, from Narmer to Augustine, to cut out and assemble. The figures are on cardstock with movable joints. Good for decorating time lines (or just for fun).

Eyewitness Books series. New York: Dorling Kindersley.
   $16.99 hardcover, $9.99 paperback for each. Available in libraries and bookstores; the pictures, designs, and layout will provide more information than you need. Consider keeping these on hand so that you can refer back to them as you progress through the time line.
   Ayo, Yvonne, et al. *Africa.* 2000.
   Farndon, John. *Mesopotamia.* 2007.
   Hart, George, et al. *Ancient Egypt.* 2014.
   James, Simon, et al. *Ancient Rome.* 2008.
   Pearson, Anne, et al. *Ancient Greece.* 2014.
   Putnam, James, et al. *Pyramid.* 2011.

Green, John. *Egyptian Stained Glass Coloring Book.* New York: Dover, 1994.
   $6.99. Order from Rainbow Resource Center. Color on translucent paper with crayons or colored pencils and end up with a stained-glass effect. (You can also order the *Little Coloring Book* for $1.50 for little brother or sister.)

Langley, Andrew, et al. *The Roman News*. New York: Candlewick Press, 2009.

$7.99. Headline stories from ancient history, along with facts, quotes, news flashes, and even want ads. Entertaining and informative; written for fifth graders.

Macaulay, David. *City: A Story of Roman Planning and Construction*. Boston: Houghton Mifflin Harcourt, 1983.

$10.99. All the stages of construction in a Roman city. Fascinating for the mechanically minded. Incorporates history and culture into descriptions of the building process.

————. *David Macaulay's World of Ancient Engineering*. Alexandria, VA: PBS, 2006.

$24.99 each. Order from PBS (or try your local library). These splendid DVDs use both live action and animation to explore the engineering marvels of the ancient world.

Pyramid.

Roman City.

————. *Pyramid*. Boston: Houghton Mifflin Harcourt, 1982.

$9.95. The book on which the video above was based, this offers incredibly detailed drawings and explanations of pyramid construction.

Mills, Dorothy. The Book of the Ancient . . . series, ed. by Memoria Press. Louisville, KY: Memoria Press.

Dorothy Mills wrote popular middle-grade history texts in the early twentieth century. Slightly outdated, these are nevertheless readable, entertaining, and packed with information. If you're using an encyclopedic resource, these provide invaluable practice in reading narrative text and can also serve as a basis for outlining exercises. Memoria Press, which has edited and reissued the texts, has also published Teacher Guides (written by Matthew Anderson) for each with comprehension questions, short answer exercises, and other supplements.

The Book of the Ancient Greeks. 2012. $16.95.

The Book of the Ancient Greeks Teacher Guide. 2012. $17.95.

The Book of the Ancient Romans. 2012. $16.95.

The Book of the Ancient Romans Teacher Guide. 2012. $17.95.

The Book of the Ancient World. 2013. $16.95. Egypt and ancient Near Eastern civilizations.

The Book of the Ancient World Teacher Guide. 2010. $17.95.

Payne, Elizabeth. *The Pharaohs of Ancient Egypt.* New York: Random House, 1981.

$5.99. Covers Egypt's history from the beginning until its conquest by Greece and Rome. Each chapter tells about one pharaoh; on a fifth-grade reading level.

Perspective: The Timeline Game.

$29.95. Order from Rainbow Resource Center. Each player challenges others to put cards bearing historical events into the proper order on a time line.

Powell, Anton, and Philip Steele. *The Greek News.* New York: Candlewick Press, 2009.

$7.99. Headline stories from ancient history, along with facts, quotes, news flashes, and even want ads. Entertaining and informative; written for fifth graders.

Queen Nefertiti. Santa Barbara, CA: Bellerophon, 1992.

$3.50. Order from Bellerophon. The story of one of the great women of the ancient world, told through a coloring book that uses complex images from Egyptian art itself.

Roehrig, Catharine. *Fun with Hieroglyphs.* New York: Simon & Schuster, 2008.

$24.99. Designed by the New York Metropolitan Museum of Art, this set includes rubber stamps, an ink pad, and a key.

Roman Arch Set. Hamburg, Germany: HABA Toys.

$48. Order from Fat Brain Toys. Wooden blocks make it possible to construct (and understand the dynamics of) a Roman arch.

Steedman, Scott, ed. *The Egyptian News.* New York: Candlewick Press, 2009.

$7.99. Headline stories from ancient history, along with facts, quotes, news flashes, and even want ads. Entertaining and informative; written for fifth graders.

Walton, John. *Chronological and Background Charts of the Old Testament*. Grand Rapids, MI: Zondervan, 1994.

$19.99. A highly valuable resource that gives dates for Old Testament events, helping you to fit them into secular history; where there is controversy over a date, a brief note is provided.

Wiese, Jim. *Ancient Science: 40 Time-Traveling, World-Exploring, History-Making Activities for Kids*, illus. Ed Shems. San Francisco, CA: John Wiley, 2003.

$16. Hands-on experience with inventions across the ancient world, from ancient candy and kites to counting systems and compasses.

Winters, Kay. *Voices of Ancient Egypt*. Washington, DC: National Geographic Children's Books, 2009.

$6.95. The daily occupations of Old Kingdom Egypt told in the poetic voices of the Egyptians themselves; illustrated and engaging.

The World in Ancient Times series. Oxford: Oxford University Press, 2005.

$36.95 each in hardcover, but check your local library. A collaboration between historians and YA novelists, this series has short engaging chapters, each based on a primary source selection.

Cline, Eric H., and Jill Rubalcaba. *The Ancient Egyptian World*.

Fash, William, and Mary E. Lyons. *The Ancient American World*.

Kenoyer, Jonathan Mark, and Kimberley Heuston. *The Ancient South Asian World*.

Kleeman, Terry, and Tracy Barrett. *The Ancient Chinese World*.

Mellor, Ronald, and Marni McGee. *The Ancient Roman World*.

Podany, Amanda H., and Marni McGee. *The Ancient Near Eastern World*.

Roberts, Jennifer T., and Tracy Barrett. *The Ancient Greek World*.

Robertshaw, Peter, and Jill Rubalcaba. *The Early Human World*.

You Wouldn't Want To . . . series. New York: Franklin Watts.

$9.95. Entertaining history series at a fourth- to fifth-grade reading level, reviewing the lifestyles of unfortunate people from ancient times with plenty of historical detail.

Ford, Michael. *You Wouldn't Want to Be a Greek Athlete!* 2014.

Malam, John. *You Wouldn't Want to Be a Roman Gladiator!* 2001.

———. *You Wouldn't Want to Live in Pompeii!* 2008.

Morley, Jacqueline. *You Wouldn't Want to Be a Pyramid Builder!* 2013.

———. *You Wouldn't Want to Be a Sumerian Slave!* (2007.

———. *You Wouldn't Want to Be in Alexander the Great's Army!* 2005.

———. *You Wouldn't Want to Work on the Great Wall of China!* 2006.

Pipe, Jim. *You Wouldn't Want to Be Cleopatra!* 2007.

Stewart, David. *You Wouldn't Want to Be an Egyptian Mummy!* 2012.

Medieval/Early Renaissance, 400–1600 (Sixth Grade)

List of Great Men and Women

This list includes a few early rulers of major countries up until about 1050. After Edward the Confessor, any ruler of England, Holy Roman Emperor, ruler of France, emperor of Japan, or emperor of China is worth making a notebook page on; we don't list them here (there are simply too many). Check the encyclopedia for complete listings.

Saint Augustine (writing c. 411)

Attila the Hun (c. 433–453)

King Arthur (probably killed in 537 at the Battle of Camlann)

Theodora (500–548)

Gregory of Tours (540–594)

Muhammad (570–632)

The Venerable Bede (672–735)

Charles Martel (688–741)

Charlemagne (ruled 768–814)

Alfred the Great (849–899)

Leif Eriksson (discovered North America c. 1000)

Omar Khayyam (1027–1123)

Edward the Confessor (1042–1066)

Anna Comnena (1083–1153)

Hildegard of Bingen (1098–1179)

Empress Matilda (1102–1167)

Eleanor of Aquitaine (1122–1204)

Chrétien de Troyes (1144–1190)

Genghis Khan (b. 1155)

Thomas Aquinas (1225–1274)

Dante Alighieri (1265–1321)

Geoffrey Chaucer (c. 1340–1400)

Thomas à Kempis (1380–1471)

Jan van Eyck (c. 1390–1441)

Johannes Gutenberg (c. 1396–1468)

Catherine of Valois (1401–1437)

Joan of Arc (1412–1431)

Sandro Botticelli (1444–1510)

Christopher Columbus (1451–1506)

Leonardo da Vinci (1452–1519)

Amerigo Vespucci (1454–1512)

Erasmus (1465–1536)

Nicolaus Copernicus (1473–1543)

Michelangelo (1475–1564)

Titian (1477–1576)

Thomas More (1478–1535)

Ferdinand Magellan (1480–1521)

Martin Luther (1483–1546)

Raphael (1483–1520)

Ignatius Loyola (1491–1556)

Correggio (1494–1534)

Giovanni Angelo de' Medici (1499–1565)

Thomas Wyatt (1503–1542)

Nostradamus (1503–1566)

John Knox (1505–1572)

John Calvin (1509–1564)

Hernando Cortés (entered Mexican capital, 1519)

Pieter Brueghel (1520–1569)

Giovanni Pierluigi da Palestrina (1525–1594)

Tycho Brahe (1546–1601)

Philip Sidney (1551–1586)

Walter Raleigh (1554–1618)

William Shakespeare (1564–1616)

Galileo Galilei (1564–1642)

Jan Brueghel (1568–1625)

John Donne (1572–1631)

Inigo Jones (1573–1652)

René Descartes (1596–1650)

Primary Sources: Suggested Topics

You will discover many more options, but the following are particularly accessible to middle-grade students.

Procopius, "On Justinian" from *The Secret History* (c. 540)

Muhammad, "Last Sermon" (630)

Bede, "The Conversion of England" from *The Ecclesiastical History* (c. 700)

William of Malmesbury, "The Battle of Hastings" (1066)

Urban II's Speech at Clermont (1095)

The Magna Carta (1215)

"Peasant Uprising of 1381," from *Anonimalle Chronicle* (1381)

"The Discovery of North America by Leif Ericsson" from *The Saga of Eric the Red* (1387)

Joan of Arc, "Letter to the King of France" (1429)

Christopher Columbus, "Selections from Journal" (1492)

Vasco da Gama, "Round Africa to India" (1498)

Martin Luther, "95 Theses" (1517)

Thomas Cranmer, "Letter on Henry VIII's Divorce" (1533)

Primary Sources: Resources

The Internet Medieval Sourcebook. legacy.fordham.edu/halsall/sbook .asp. Hosted by Fordham University, this invaluable website is an easy-to-navigate online archive of primary sources (translated into English) ranging from decrees of Justinian to the Ballad of Bosworth Field. Highly useful for the curious student.

Kelley, Donald R., and Bonnie G. Smith. *The Medieval and Early Modern World: Primary Sources & Reference Volume.* Oxford: Oxford University Press, 2005.

$32.95. From A.D. 400 to 1800, excerpts from letters, historical records, inscriptions, epics, and more, from Europe to Asia. Well-presented, usable, and clear. Highly recommended.

Stanley, George Edward. *The European Settlement of North America, 1492–1763: A Primary Source History of the United States.* World Almanac Library, 2005.

$14.05. The history of colonization told in well-chosen primary sources with interpretative essays.

General Resources

Art, Suzanne Strauss. *China's Later Dynasties*. Lincoln, MA: Pemblewick Press, 2002.

$12.49. Tells about China during the time of the Song, Yuan, Ming, and Qing dynasties.

———. *The Story of the Renaissance*. Freeport, ME: Wayside Publishing, 1997.

$14.95. A readable guide to major developments in the West during the fourteenth to sixteenth centuries; a good reference work to have on hand for additional reading.

Calliope. Peterborough, NH: Cobblestone Publishing.

$43.95 for one year's subscription, combination of print and web-based issues. Order from Cobblestone Publishing. A world history magazine for readers aged nine to twelve; each 52-page issue has a theme ("The Qu'ran," "Mary Queen of Scots") and includes articles, maps, art, and a question-and-answer feature about world history.

Cathedral: The Game of the Medieval City. Pukekohe, New Zealand: Brightway Products, 1997.

$40. Order from Rainbow Resource Center. In this high-quality wooden game, players place their pieces ("buildings") inside a walled city, trying to claim enough space to rule the city and become its lord. *Cathedral* has become a classic strategy game, winning a *Games* magazine award twice.

Chorzempa, Rosemary A. *Design Your Own Coat of Arms: An Introduction to Heraldry*. New York: Dover, 1987.

$4.99. Explains the symbolism and history of coats of arms so that you can design your own.

Davis, Courtney. *Celtic Stained Glass*. New York: Dover, 1993.

$6.99. The Dover stained-glass coloring books reproduce medieval windows on translucent paper. Color them and put them against a window for a beautiful effect.

Deary, Terry. *Horrible Histories*, illus. Martin Brown. London: Scholastic.

$7.99. Order from horriblebooks.com, used from Amazon.com, or (if you can stomach the exchange rate) from Amazon.com.uk where you can also find a DVD version. This British series highlights the more disgusting aspects of medieval life and does a good bit of history along the way; a sure middle-grade hit.

The Angry Aztecs. 2008.

The Cut-throat Celts. 2008.

Dark Knights and Dingy Castles. 2011.

The Incredible Incas. 2008.

Knights. 2006.

The Measly Middle Ages. 2007.

The Smashing Saxons. 2007.

The Stormin' Normans. 2007.

The Terrible Tudors. 2007.

The Vicious Vikings. 2007.

Eyewitness Books. New York: Dorling Kindersley.

$16.99. These books are available in libraries and bookstores. The pictures and designs are beautiful, and the books will give you more information than you'll ever need. Consider keeping these on hand for several months, referring back to them as you progress through the time line.

Baquedano, Elizabeth, et al. *Aztec, Inca, and Maya.* 2011.

Byam, Michelle, et al. *Arms and Armor.* 2011.

Cole, Alison, et al. *Renaissance.* 2000.

Gravett, Christopher, et al. *Castle.* 2008.

———. *Knight.* 2007.

Langley, Andrew, et al. *Medieval Life.* 2004.

Margeson, Susan M., et al. *Viking.* 2009.

Green, John. *Cathedrals of the World Coloring Book.* New York: Dover, 1995.

$3.95. Over forty great cathedrals; floor plans, overhead, interior, and exterior views.

Macaulay, David. *Castle.* Boston: Houghton Mifflin Harcourt, 1982.

$9.95. Macaulay's books are engrossing, with detailed drawings and explanations of how things work; particularly good for the mechanically minded. This book traces the social, cultural, and political role of a castle through its construction.

———. *Cathedral,* full-color ed. Boston: Houghton Mifflin Harcourt, 2013.

$19.99. Order from any bookstore. The story of a cathedral's construction, beginning in a French town in 1252.

————. *David Macaulay's World of Ancient Engineering.* Alexandria, VA: PBS. $24.99 each. Order from PBS (or try your local library). These splendid DVDs use both live action and animation to explore the engineering marvels of the medieval world.

> *Castle*
>
> *Cathedral*

A Medieval Alphabet to Illuminate. New York: Bellerophon, 1983. $4.95. Order from Bellerophon. Ornate capital letters from medieval alphabets. Each is a full-page drawing, ready to be colored.

The Medieval and Early Modern World series. Oxford: Oxford University Press, 2005. $32.95 each in hardcover, but check your local library or shop used. Excellent overview of medieval and early modern topics, organized thematically and written for sixth- and seventh grade and above. Each volume also has a $9.95 Student Study Guide with activities, review worksheets, short answer and writing assignments, and note-taking helps. Highly recommended.

> Bingham, Marjorie Wall. *An Age of Empires, 1200–1750.*
>
> Des Forges, Roger V. *The Asian World, 600–1500.*
>
> Hanawalt, Barbara A. *The European World, 400–1450.*
>
> Pouwels, Randall L. *The African and Middle Eastern World, 600–1500.*
>
> Wiesner-Hanks, Merry E. *An Age of Voyages, 1350–1600.*

Medieval Siege Engines. Victoria, BC: Pathfinders Design and Technology. Order from Amazon.com. These historically accurate model kits can be put together with glue; the wooden pieces are pre-cut. Sturdy and fun.

> Catapult. $24.99.
>
> Siege Tower. $39.99.
>
> Trebuchet (shoots over twenty feet!). $36.99.

Medieval World series. New York: Crabtree Publishing. $8.95 each. Readable 32-page guides to different aspects of life in the Middle Ages. Much simpler than the Oxford University Press series listed above.

> Cels, Marc. *Life on a Medieval Manor.* 2004.
>
> Eastwood, Kay. *The Life of a Knight.* 2003.

———. *Places of Worship in the Middle Ages.* 2003.

———. *Women and Girls in the Middle Ages.* 2003.

Elliot, Lynne. *Children and Games in the Middle Ages.* 2004.

———. *Clothing in the Middle Ages.* 2004.

———. *Food and Feasts in the Middle Ages.* 2004.

———. *Medieval Medicine and the Plague.* 2005.

———. *Medieval Towns, Trade, and Travel.* 2004.

Findon, Joanne. *Science and Technology in the Middle Ages.* 2004.

Groves, Marsha. *Manners and Customs in the Middle Ages.* 2005.

———. *Medieval Projects You Can Do!* 2005.

Mills, Dorothy. *The Book of the Middle Ages,* ed. by Memoria Press. Louisville, KY: Memoria Press, 2012.

Dorothy Mills wrote popular middle-grade history texts in the early twentieth century. Slightly outdated, these are nevertheless readable, entertaining, and packed with information. If you're using an encyclopedic resource, these provide invaluable practice in reading narrative text and can also serve as a basis for outlining exercises. Memoria Press, which has edited and reissued the texts, has also published Teacher Guides (written by Matthew Anderson) for each with comprehension questions, short answer exercises, and other supplements.

The Book of the Middle Ages. $16.95.

The Book of the Middle Ages Teacher Guide. $17.95.

Nicole, David. *Paper Soldiers of the Middle Ages.* Santa Barbara, CA: Bellerophon, 1992.

Vol. 1: The Crusades.

$4.95. Order from Bellerophon. Approximately sixty detailed, two-sided figures to be colored; includes Byzantine, Mongol, and Iranian cavalry, Muslim soldiers, crusader knights, and even Richard the Lionhearted.

Vol. 2: The Hundred Years' War.

$3.95. Order from Bellerophon. Approximately sixty detailed, two-sided figures to be colored; includes knights, archers, kings, queens, and peasants.

Platt, Richard. *Castle Diary.* Cambridge, MA: Candlewick Press, 2003.

$6.99. This fictionalized diary of a thirteenth-century page, filled with detailed illustrations, describes the daily routine of medieval life: hunts, tournaments, Latin lessons, doctor visits, feasts, and more.

Queen Elizabeth I. New York: Bellerophon, 1985.
$4.95. Order from Bellerophon. Paper dolls to color include Sir Walter Raleigh, the earl of Essex, and Mary, Queen of Scots.

Sansevere-Dreher, Diane. *Explorers Who Got Lost.* New York: Starscape, 2016.
$12.99. Order from Rainbow Resource Center. A good survey of the achievements (often unintentional) of a whole range of medieval and Renaissance explorers, from da Gama to Henry Hudson.

Smith, A. G. *Cut and Assemble a Medieval Castle.* New York: Dover, 1984.
$12.95. Order from Dover Publications. A full-color model of Caernarfon Castle, built by Edward I in 1283.

Late Renaissance/Early Modern, 1600–1850 (Seventh Grade)

List of Topics to Explore

the *Mayflower*
early American settlements
Russia under Peter the Great and his successors
Prussia in the eighteenth century
the Enlightenment
the agricultural revolution
Native American cultures
the British in India
the French Revolution
British-French conflict in Canada
the American Revolution
the Napoleonic Wars
the industrial revolution
Simón Bolívar's fight for independence in South America
the siege of the Alamo
the California gold rush
the Lewis and Clark expedition

the U.S. acquisition of North American territories

Australia's beginnings as a penal colony

Primary Sources: Suggested Topics

You will discover many more options, but the following are particularly accessible to middle-grade students.

Samuel de Champlain, "The Foundation of Quebec" (1608)

The Mayflower Compact (1620)

Patrick Henry, "Give Me Liberty or Give Me Death" (1775)

The Declaration of Independence (1776)

United States Constitution (1787)

Bill of Rights (U.S.) (1789)

The Tennis Court Oath (1789)

Declaration of the Rights of Man (1789)

Olympe de Gouges, "Declaration of the Rights of Women" (1791)

Seneca Falls Declaration (1848)

Primary Sources: Resources

The Internet Modern History Sourcebook. legacy.fordham.edu/Halsall/mod/modsbook.asp

Hosted by Fordham University, this invaluable website is an easy-to-navigate online archive of primary sources (translated into English). Highly useful for the curious student.

Kelley, Donald R., and Bonnie G. Smith. *The Medieval and Early Modern World: Primary Sources & Reference Volume.* Oxford: Oxford University Press, 2005.

$32.95. From A.D. 400 to 1800, excerpts from letters, historical records, inscriptions, epics, and more, from Europe to Asia. Well-presented, usable, and clear. Highly recommended.

Lepore, Jill. *Encounters in the New World: A History in Documents.* Oxford: Oxford University Press, 2002.

$33.95. A collection of first-person accounts, written between the fifteenth and eighteenth centuries, by Europeans and Africans arriving in the New World.

Stanley, George Edward. *The European Settlement of North America, 1492–*

1763: A Primary Source History of the United States. Milwaukee, WI: World Almanac Library, 2005.

$14.05. The history of colonization told in well-chosen primary sources with interpretative essays.

General Resources

Anderson, J. K. *Castles to Cut Out and Put Together.* Santa Barbara, CA: Bellerophon, 1985.

$4.95. Order from Bellerophon. These are models of the Tower of London and Chateau Gaillard, with all the turrets, towers, and walls. They need to be colored before assembly.

Anderson, J. K., and Nick Taylor. *Castles of Scotland to Cut Out and Put Together.* Santa Barbara, CA: Bellerophon, 1985.

$5.95. Order from Bellerophon. Doune Castle and Caerlaverock Castle. To be colored and assembled.

Bliven, Bruce. *The American Revolution.* New York: Random House, 1981.

$5.99. This history for young people was first published in 1958. It gives a very detailed account of the struggle for independence and of George III's misdeeds.

Blos, Joan W. *A Gathering of Days: A New England Girl's Journal 1830–32.* New York: Atheneum Books, 1990.

$5.99. This is a Newbery Medal-winning novel. Not "history" as such, but provides a well-researched look into everyday life in nineteenth-century America. The story is told through the journal of a teenage girl in colonial New Hampshire.

Brownell, David, ed. *A Coloring Book of Kings and Queens of England.* Santa Barbara, CA: Bellerophon, 1985.

$4.95. Order from Bellerophon. Portraits in royal dress, with quotes from Shakespeare as a bonus.

Cobblestone. Peterborough, NH: Cobblestone Publishing.

$43.95 for one year's subscription, a combination of print and web-based issues. Order from Cobblestone Publishing. An American history magazine for readers aged nine to twelve; each 52-page issue has a theme

("Medicine," "The Constitution," "The Circus") and includes articles, maps, art, and a question-and-answer feature about history.

Copeland, Peter F. *Early American Crafts and Occupations Coloring Book*. New York: Dover, 1994.

$4.99. Order from Dover. Historically accurate, detailed drawings with interesting text.

———. *Everyday Dress of the American Colonial Period*. New York: Dover, 1975.

$4.99. Order from Dover.

———. *Indian Tribes of North America Coloring Book*. New York: Dover, 1990.

$3.99. Order from Dover.

———. *Lewis and Clark Expedition Coloring Book*. New York: Dover, 1984.

$4.99. Order from Dover.

———. *Western Pioneers Coloring Book*. New York: Dover, 1997.

$4.99. Order from Dover.

Daugherty, James. *The Landing of the Pilgrims*. New York: Random House, 1981.

$5.99. First published in the 1950s, this Landmark Book is a classic young-adult text on the Pilgrims and their settlements.

Eyewitness Books. New York: Dorling Kindersley.

$16.99 each. Available in libraries and online bookstores. The pictures and designs are beautiful, and the books will give you more information than you'll ever need. Consider keeping these on hand for several months, referring back to them as you progress through the time line.

Cole, Alison, et al. *Renaissance*. 2000.

Holmes, Richard, et al. *Battle*. 2009.

Matthews, Rupert O., et al. *Explorer*. 2012.

Murdoch, David, et al. *North American Indian*. 2005.

Murray, Stuart, et al. *American Revolution*. 2005.

Platt, Richard, et al. *Pirate*. 2007.

Freedman, Russell. *Children of the Wild West*. Boston: Houghton Mifflin Harcourt, 1990.

$9.95. With well-written text and plenty of photographs, Freedman explores the lives of children traveling west in the 1840s.

Fritz, Jean. *Why Not Lafayette?*, illus. Ronald Himler. New York: Puffin Books, 2001.
$6.99. A readable biography of the French hero of the American Revolution that also brings the French Revolution into view.

History Songs Kit. Newport Beach, CA: AudioMemory, 1998.
$15.95 for book and CD. Order from AudioMemory. Eleven songs teach major events and dates in American history from 1492 to 1991. A painless way to review!

Johnston, Robert D. *The Making of America: The History of the United States from 1492 to the Present,* rev. ed. Washington, DC: National Geographic, 2010.
$29.95. This one-volume history of the United States is brief but thorough, readable (on about a sixth- to seventh-grade reading level), and well-illustrated.

Knill, Harry, and Nancy Conkle. *A Coloring Book of the American Revolution.* Santa Barbara, CA: Bellerophon, 1987.
$4.95. Order from Bellerophon. Based on a set of eighteenth-century caricatures.

Macaulay, David. *Mill Times.* Alexandria, VA: PBS, 2001.
$24.99. Order from PBS. This splendid DVD, which covers the construction and use of a nineteenth-century New England mill, uses both live action and animation.

————. *Mill.* Boston: Houghton Mifflin Harcourt, 1989.
$9.95. The *Mill Times DVD* is based on this book. Macaulay tells the story of a nineteenth-century New England mill, tracing its social, political, and cultural roles with detailed, fascinating drawings and eloquent text.

Made for Trade. Plainwell, MI: Talicor Aristoplay.
$25. Order from Fat Brain Toys. Players "shop" and barter in a colonial American town in this game for two to four players.

The Medieval and Early Modern World series. Oxford: Oxford University Press, 2005.

$32.95 each in hardcover, but check your local library or shop used. Excellent overview of medieval and early modern topics, organized thematically and written for sixth to seventh grade and above. Each volume also has a $9.95 Student Study Guide with activities, review worksheets, short answer and writing assignments, and note-taking helps. Highly recommended.

Bingham, Marjorie Wall. *An Age of Empires, 1200–1750.*

Huff, Toby E. *An Age of Science & Revolutions, 1600–1800.*

O'Reilly, Kevin. Critical Thinking in United States History series. Pacific Grove, CA: Critical Thinking Press, 1995.

$24.99 for each ebook package of student book plus teacher's guide. Download from the publisher's website. Each book begins with a "Guide to Critical Thinking," which reviews the basics of logic: fallacies, proper use of sources, generalizations, and so on. The table of contents clearly identifies the historical event on which each lesson is based ("Was the Stamp Act Justified?" "Foreign Views of the Constitution"). Have the student complete these lessons when he reaches the corresponding historical event in the core history text.

Book One: Colonies to Constitution.

Book Two: New Republic to Civil War.

Petrillo, Valerie. *Sailors, Whalers, Fantastic Sea Voyages.* Chicago: Chicago Review Press, 2003.

$14.95. A hands-on, activity-centered guide to sea life, from China in the 1700s to the rise of the New England whaling trade. Cook ship's food, paint china, make a lighthouse, and more.

Spier, Peter. *The Star-Spangled Banner.* New York: Dragonfly Books, 1992.

$10.99. Order from Rainbow Resource Center. An illustrated national anthem, with historical notes and maps describing the War of 1812, as well as a history of the anthem's composition.

Stanley, George Edward. *A Primary Source History of the United States* series. Milwaukee, WI: World Almanac Library, 2005.

$14.05 each. Well-chosen primary sources with interpretive essays.

The New Republic: 1763–1815.

The Crisis of the Union: 1815–1865.

Waldman, Carl. *Encyclopedia of Native American Tribes,* rev. ed., illus. Molly
Braun. New York: Checkmark Books, 2006.
$26.95. The history and customs of over 150 North American Indian
nations, readable and illustrated.

Waters, Kate. The Day series, illus. Russ Kendall. New York: Scholastic.
The Kate Waters series on early American life uses reenactors and inter-
preters for photographic illustration. Excellent information.
Samuel Eaton's Day. 1996.
$6.99. A typical day for a young boy at Plymouth.
Sarah Morton's Day. 2008.
$6.99. The daily life of a young girl in Plymouth colony.
Tapenum's Day. 1996.
$18.95 (hardback only). The daily life of a Native American boy liv-
ing near Plymouth.

Wicked History series. New York: Franklin Watts.
$5.95 for paperbacks. Wonderful historical series for grades 7 and up
with a biographical focus.
Brooks, Philip. *King George III: America's Enemy.* 2009.
DiConsiglio, John. *Robespierre: Master of the Guillotine.* 2008.
Nick, Charles. *Sir Frances Drake: Slave Trader and Pirate.* 2009.
Heuston, Kimberly Burton. *Napoleon: Emperor and Conqueror.* 2010.
Vincent, Zu. *Catherine the Great: Empress of Russia.* 2009.

Modern, 1850–Present (Eighth Grade)

List of Topics to Explore

Africa under European control
the Indian mutinies
the Crimean War
the Victorian era
the American Civil War
exploration in the American West
Euro-American conflict with the Native American tribes
the Boxer Rebellion
World War I
the Russian Revolution

the Soviet Union
the Great Depression
the New Deal
civil war in Spain
the Axis and the Allies
World War II
Nazi Germany/Hitler
the Holocaust
Zionism/the Jews' return to Palestine
apartheid/South African segregation
China under Mao
the Korean War
the civil-rights movement
the Vietnam War
landing on the moon
Chernobyl nuclear disaster
fall of the Berlin Wall
9/11

Primary Sources: Suggested Topics

You will discover many more options, but the following are particularly accessible to middle-grade students.

Sojourner Truth, "Ain't I a Woman" (1851)

Abraham Lincoln, "Gettysburg Address" (1863)

Susan B. Anthony, "On Women's Right to Vote" (1873)

Florence Nightingale, "Rural Hygiene" (1894)

Mohandas K. Gandhi, "Indian Home Rule" (1909)

Proclamation of the Abdication of the Manchus (February 24, 1912)

Private Donald Fraser, "War Diary, September 1915" (1915)

John McCrae, "In Flanders Fields" (1915)

Proclamation of the Irish Republic (Easter 1916)

Tsar Nicholas II, "Abdication" (March 15, 1917)

Franklin D. Roosevelt, "First Inaugural" (March 4, 1933)

Neville Chamberlain, "Peace in Our Time" (1938)

Winston S. Churchill, "We Shall Fight on the Beaches" (June 4, 1940)

Franklin D. Roosevelt, "A Date Which Will Live in Infamy" (December 8, 1941)

U.S. Declaration of War on Germany (December 11, 1941)

Bishop Desmond Tutu, "The Question of South Africa" (1984)

George W. Bush, "Post 9/11 Speech" (2001)

Primary Sources: Resources

Aten, Jerry. *Our Living Constitution, Then and Now,* 2nd ed. Carthage, IL: Good Apple Press, 2002.

$16.99. The original text of the Constitution in one column, interpretation in another column; also includes games and writing activities.

Blaisdell, Bob, ed. *Great Speeches of the 20th Century.* New York: Dover, 2011.

$4.50. A handy and cheap way to hear the voices of twentieth-century leaders.

Frank, Anne. *Anne Frank: The Diary of a Young Girl.* Trans. B. M. Mooyaart. New York: Bantam, 1993.

$5.99. This classic journal is a good place to begin discussions of the Holocaust.

The Internet Modern History Sourcebook. legacy.fordham.edu/Halsall/mod/modsbook.asp

Hosted by Fordham University, this invaluable website is an easy-to-navigate online archive of primary sources (translated into English) ranging from an eyewitness account of the lives of plantation slaves in the American South to a report on the pope's visit to Cuba in 1998. Highly useful for the curious student.

Murphy, Jim. *The Boys' War: Confederate and Union Soldiers Talk about the Civil War.* Boston: Houghton Mifflin Harcourt, 1993.

$8.95. Journal entries and letters from boys sixteen and under who fought in the Civil War. Sepia photographs.

General Information

Allen, Thomas B. *Remember Pearl Harbor: American and Japanese Survivors Tell Their Stories.* Washington, DC: National Geographic Society, 2015.

$7.99. An illustrated account of the attack that brings the Japanese perspective into view.

Archambault, Alan. *Black Soldiers in the Civil War Coloring Book*. Santa Barbara, CA: Bellerophon, 1995.
$3.95. Order from Bellerophon.

Archambault, Alan, and Jill Caron. *Civil War Heroes: A Coloring Book*. Santa Barbara, CA: Bellerophon, 1988. Also *Civil War Heroines*, 1989.
$4.95 each. Important personalities from both sides, each with a full-page drawing and a one-page biography.

Bachrach, Susan D. *Tell Them We Remember: The Story of the Holocaust*. Boston: Little, Brown, & Co., 1994.
$18. This oversized softcover book, produced by the United States Holocaust Memorial Museum, is a good middle-grade introduction. The black-and-white photographs are disturbing but not horrifying, and include many portraits of children and families who perished (rather than focusing on graphic descriptions of the camps themselves).

Blumenthal, Karen. *Six Days in October: The Stock Market Crash of 1929*. New York: Atheneum Books, 2002.
$21.99. A lucid and readable account of the stock market crash; this valuable book will also give students (and parents) a good basic grasp of how the stock market works. Highly recommended.

Cobblestone. Peterborough, NH: Cobblestone Publishing.
$43.95 for one year's subscription, mixed print and web-based issues. Order from Cobblestone Publishing. An American history magazine for readers aged nine to twelve; each 52-page issue has a theme ("Whaling," "The Great Depression," "The Korean War") and includes articles, maps, art, and a question-and-answer feature about history.

Coloring Book of Our Presidents. Santa Barbara, CA: Bellerophon, 1999.
$4.95. Order from Bellerophon. From George Washington to Bill Clinton; full-page portraits, each from a historical source (paintings, campaign posters, and so forth). Great memory aid.

Freedman, Russell. *Lincoln: A Photobiography*. Boston: Houghton Mifflin Harcourt, 1989.
$11.99. The personal and public story of Abraham Lincoln, with a series

of profiles that shows him aging during his terms in office. A Newbery Medal winner.

————. *The Wright Brothers: How They Invented the Airplane.* New York: Holiday House, 1994.

$16.95. Uses the brothers' own photographs along with a readable account of their achievements. Lots of quotes from the Wrights' own writings.

Giblin, James Cross. *The Life and Death of Adolf Hitler.* Boston: Houghton Mifflin Harcourt, 2015.

$21. A very well-done biography, detailed and appropriate for eighth-grade reading.

Heinrichs, Ann. America the Beautiful series. San Francisco, CA: Children's Book Press.

This series includes one title for each state and will provide the eighth-grade student with a good basic review of state history (required by most state educational boards).

History Songs Kit. Newport Beach, CA: AudioMemory, 1998.

$15.95 for book and CD. Order from AudioMemory. Eleven songs teach major events and dates in American history from 1492 to 1991. A painless way to review!

Houston, Jeanne Wakatsuki, and James D. Houston. *Farewell to Manzanar: A True Story of Japanese American Experience During and After the World War II Internment.* New York: Ember, 2012.

$9.99. The true story of a Japanese family's experience in America during World War II; the author spent part of her childhood in a Japanese internment camp after the attack on Pearl Harbor.

Johnston, Robert D. *The Making of America: The History of the United States from 1492 to the Present,* rev. ed. Washington, DC: National Geographic, 2010.

$29.95. This one-volume history of the United States is brief but thorough, readable (on about a sixth- to seventh-grade reading level), and well-illustrated.

Krull, Kathleen. *A Kids' Guide to America's Bill of Rights: Curfews, Censorship, and the 100-Pound Giant.* New York: Festival, 1999.

$16.99. A simple and readable guide to the Bill of Rights, with plenty of real cases used as illustration; written on a sixth- to seventh-grade level.

McPherson, James M. *Fields of Fury: The American Civil War*. New York: Atheneum Books, 2002.
$24.95. This history of the Civil War, heavily illustrated and full of maps, charts, and contemporary photographs and posters, was written by a Pulitzer Prize–winning historian for middle-grade readers. Highly recommended.

O'Reilly, Kevin. Critical Thinking in United States History series. Pacific Grove, CA: Critical Thinking Press, 1995.
$24.99 for each ebook package of student book plus teacher's guide. Download from the publisher's website. Each book begins with a "Guide to Critical Thinking," which reviews the basics of logic: fallacies, proper use of sources, generalizations, and so on. The table of contents clearly identifies the historical event on which each lesson is based ("Was the Stamp Act Justified?" "Foreign Views of the Constitution"). Have the student complete these lessons when he reaches the corresponding historical event in the core history text.
Book Three: Reconstruction to Progressivism.
Book Four: Spanish-American War to Vietnam War.

Our America: Growing Up... series. Minneapolis, MN: Lerner Publications.
$26.60 for each hardback. These are expensive, but the contrasts between modern adolescence and the middle-school experience in previous decades makes them well worth finding. Try your local library.
Josephson, Judith Pinkerton. *Growing Up in a New Century, 1890 to 1914.* 2002.
————. *Growing Up in Pioneer America, 1800 to 1890.* 2003.
————. *Growing Up in World War II, 1942 to 1945.* 2003.
Ruth, Amy. *Growing Up in the Great Depression, 1929–1941.* 2003.

Presidents: Fandex Family Field Guide. New York: Workman Publishing, 1998.
$12.95. Order from any bookstore (the ISBN for the set is 0-7611-1203-0). This set of presidential fact cards, connected at the bottom so that you can fan them out, has portraits, dates, brief biographies, and interesting facts. Great for review and memorization.

Stanley, George Edward. A Primary Source History of the United States series. Milwaukee, WI: World Almanac Library, 2005.

$14.05 each. Well-chosen primary sources with interpretative essays.

The Era of Reconstruction and Expansion: 1865–1900.

An Emerging World Power: 1900–1929.

The Great Depression and World War II: 1929–1949.

America in Today's World: 1969–2004.

Taylor, Theodore. *Air Raid–Pearl Harbor! The Story of December 7, 1941.* Boston: Houghton Mifflin Harcourt, 2001.

$6.99. A vivid account of the attack, written for middle-grade readers.

Thimmesh, Catherine. *Girls Think of Everything: Stories of Ingenious Inventions by Women.* Boston: Houghton Mifflin Harcourt, 2002.

$7.99. A fun look at modern inventions, from Liquid Paper to spacecraft bumpers, invented by women; includes information for young women on how to get started inventing.

Uncovering the Past: Analyzing Primary Sources series. New York: Crabtree Publishing, 2015.

$10.95. Written on a fifth- to sixth-grade level, these are excellent for students who read slowly or have difficulty absorbing written information.

Flatt, Lizann. *Immigration.*

———. *The Underground Railroad.*

Hyde, Natalie. *Black Tuesday and the Great Depression.*

Peppas, Lynn. *The Holocaust.*

———. *Women's Suffrage.*

Staton, Hilarie. *Civil Rights.*

U.S. States and Capitals Flash Cards.

$7.49. Order from Rainbow Resource Center. Fifty-one flash cards (one extra for Washington, DC) with maps and capitals, along with fifty-seven fact cards covering not only capitals but also birds, flowers, trees, and other fun facts; these also cover U.S. territories. The cards can be used for games as well.

Wicked History series. New York: Franklin Watts.

$5.95 for paperbacks. Wonderful historical series for grades 7 and up with a biographical focus.

Dougherty, Steve. *Idi Amin*. 2010.

Goldberg, Enid A. *Grigory Rasputin: Holy Man or Mad Monk?* 2009.

Heuston, Kimberley Burton. *Otto Von Bismarck: Iron Chancellor of Germany*. 2010.

———. *Mao Zedong*. 2010.

McCollum, Sean. *Joseph Stalin*. 2010.

Olson, Tod. *Leopold II: Butcher of the Congo*. 2008.

Price, Sean. *Adolf Hitler*. 2010.

———. *Cixi: Evil Empress of China?* 2009.

The World in Conflict series. Minneapolis, MN: Lerner Publications.
Check your local library for titles in this series; your student may find them helpful in understanding some of the ongoing conflicts that continue to afflict the twenty-first century. Written on an eighth- to ninth-grade level.

Black, Eric. *Bosnia: Fractured Region*. 1998.

———. *Northern Ireland: Troubled Land*. 1998.

Bodnarchuk, Kari. *Kurdistan: Region Under Siege*. 2000.

———. *Rwanda: A Country Torn Apart*. 1999.

Kizilos, Peter. *Quebec: Province Divided*. 1999.

———. *South Africa: Nation in Transition*. 1998.

———. *Tibet: Disputed Land*. 2000.

McGuinn, Taro. *East Timor: Island in Turmoil*. 1998.

Streissguth, Thomas. *Cyprus: Divided Island*. 1998.

Turk, Mary C. *Haiti: Land of Inequality*. 1999.

Zwier, Lawrence J. *Sri Lanka: War-Torn Island*. 1998.

———. *Sudan: North Against South*. 1999.

18

⁂

THINKING STRAIGHT:
SPELLING, GRAMMAR,
READING, AND WRITING

Writing . . . isn't a special language that belongs to English teachers and a few other sensitive souls who have a "gift for words." Writing is thinking on paper. Anyone who thinks clearly should be able to write clearly.

—William Zinsser, *Writing to Learn*

SUBJECT: **Spelling, grammar, reading, and writing, grades 5–8**
TIME REQUIRED: **5 to 10 hours per week**

In the grammar years, your child learned to spell, to name the parts of speech and assemble them into properly punctuated sentences, to gather information through reading, and to write simple compositions—summaries, narratives, descriptions. She absorbed the basic rules and skills of language use.

Now, in grades 5 through 8, she will shift focus. Acquiring information is still important, but instead of simply absorbing facts about language use, the middle-grade student will learn to *analyze* language. Now that she knows the basic rules that govern language use, she'll dig deeper into *how* and *why* language works. She'll diagram the structure of English sentences, find out why they succeed (or fail), investigate the organization of written compositions to discover why they convey—or fail to convey—clear meaning. And when she's finished, she'll be prepared to use language with precision and eloquence. She'll be ready for rhetoric.

Grammar-stage language study was organized around four subjects: spelling, grammar, reading, and writing. In the logic stage, the student will make the transition from spelling (learning how words are put together) to word study (discovering why words are formed the way they are). She's already studied the names and qualities of parts of speech; now she'll concentrate on how those parts of speech are connected into sentences. She'll begin to look at her reading assignments with a more critical eye: Why did this character act the way he did? How did the writer construct this particular plot? Is the argument in this essay sound? And in writing, she'll begin to construct longer compositions—well-reasoned arguments, logical descriptions.

Like the elementary student, the middle-grade student will spend a good part of her study time working with the English language. Plan on a minimum of an hour per day, with extra time allotted for writing at least twice a week (often this writing will overlap with history or science work) and a separate time for imaginative reading.

As in the grammar stage, students may be at different levels in spelling and word study, grammar, reading, and writing. We'll discuss each language skill separately, providing a year-by-year schedule at the end of the chapter.

KEEPING IT ORGANIZED

As in the grammar stage, we suggest that you keep the student's work organized using three-ringed notebooks. For middle-grade students, label one notebook "Writing" and a second notebook "Literature." Divide the Writing notebook into four sections: Spelling, Word Study, Grammar, and Compositions. (The first three sections will act as reference tools, the last as a way to organize the student's writing.) Divide the Literature notebook into two sections: Reading and Memory Work.

You'll still need plenty of art supplies, but as the child grows older, you'll shift away from stickers and glitter and lean toward high-quality colored pencils, watercolors, and other "real art" materials.

SPELLING AND WORD STUDY

Generally, spelling remains part of the middle-school curriculum in fifth and sixth grades, but then begins to transition to word study in seventh and eighth grades.

The fifth grader should already be familiar with the basic rules of spelling and the common exceptions. In the logic stage, she'll begin to study more words that are unusual because they come from outside the English spelling system—they're derived from other languages. Spelling these words correctly requires an understanding of their meaning and origin.

If you're already making use of a spelling program and are satisfied with the student's progress, continue on until the program is complete. Most spelling programs listed in the Resources begin to transition into word study and vocabulary building in the upper levels (see the fuller descriptions at the end of this chapter for more).

If you are just now beginning spelling with a middle-grade student, you'll need to evaluate the student's comfort level with spelling. A fifth grader who reads willingly (even if slowly) and spells common four- to six-letter words without too much difficulty can be started in the simplest spelling curriculum we recommend, a program that teaches the rules of spelling and gives the student lists of words to practice; you can plan to spend fifteen to twenty minutes per day, three to four days per week, going through the spelling exercises.

A reluctant reader who misspells common words will benefit from a more complex approach. Middle-grade students who struggle with spelling usually have not grasped the basic principles of phonetic reading either. We suggest making use of the Orton-Gillingham method described in Chapter 5 (see pages 62–64), which uses a multisensory approach to teach seventy-two phonograms (letters and letter combinations that represent single sounds) and gives students plenty of hands-on practice (written, aural, and visual) in combining them into words. We've listed several O-G spelling programs in the Resources, along with suggestions for placing your middle-grade speller. These programs require more time and direct teaching, but the effort will pay off; you should see improvement in your student's reading skills, as well as in her spelling.

As you progress through your spelling curriculum, make use of the first two sections of the Writing notebook. In the Spelling section, begin to make a list of commonly misspelled words. Every young writer has certain troublesome words; keep a reference list of the proper spelling of these words to help her as she writes. Also have her copy any spelling rules that she has particular trouble remembering and applying (such as the infamous "i before e" rule) into this section of the notebook.

You'll begin to notice that the rules in upper-level spelling are increasingly concerned with *meaning*. For example, the fifth grader might run into this "spelling rule": *The prefixes* em- *and* en- *add the meaning* in, into, cause to be, *or* to make *to the word.* (A fifth grader who's studied Latin already knows this; she can also figure out that *embitter,* for example, means "to make bitter.")

So the student should also begin to keep lists of prefixes, suffixes, word roots, and their meanings in the Word Study section of the notebook. Entitle a notebook page "Prefixes and Suffixes," and structure your list like this:

Prefixes and Suffixes

Prefix	Suffix	Meaning/function	Language (if given)
contra-		opposite, against	Latin
	-able	makes an adjective out of a noun	
mal-		bad	Latin
pan-		all	Latin
myria-		countless	Greek

Create a similar page headed "Word Roots." Follow this pattern:

Word Roots

Root	Meaning	Language
functio	to perform	Latin
cedere	to go forward	Latin
polis	city	Greek
annu	year	Latin

You can keep the same Language Arts notebook for all four years or make a new one each year; but if you make a new notebook, transfer the lists of spelling rules, the "Prefixes and Suffixes" list, and the "Word Roots" list into the Word Study section of the new notebook. And continue to fill out these lists of prefixes and suffixes and word roots with their meaning and language of origin.

When the spelling curriculum is completed—usually, sometime around seventh grade—vocabulary study will replace spelling as a formal subject. And the best way to build a good vocabulary is by reading a large variety of things. But while your seventh grader is reading, she should also study word origins and meanings to reinforce and sharpen her word skills. We've suggested several possible programs at the end of this chapter.

This study doesn't need to take up huge amounts of time; aim for fifteen to twenty minutes, three or four times per week. Continue to list all new word roots provided on the Word Roots page in the Word Study section of the notebook. And keep on with that list of frequently misspelled words in the Spelling section of the notebook.

GRAMMAR

The logic-stage student must use a formal grammar program to build the language skills so necessary for good writing. The fifth grader knows what elements make up a sentence (nouns, pronouns, verbs, adverbs, adjectives) and how to string them together (proper punctuation, capitalization, word use). Now he's ready to study relationships between words—how they combine into clauses and how those clauses relate to form sentences.

These relationships are governed by rules. And as the student encounters these rules, he should memorize them. He should also learn to draw a picture of the rule—through diagramming.

We don't think diagramming sentences ought to be optional. Sentence diagrams reveal the logic of sentence structure, just as syllogisms reveal the logic of arguments. Diagramming is a hands-on grammar activity. Visual learners will benefit from "seeing a picture" of grammatical structure, and drawing the diagram will help kinesthetic learners to understand the abstractions of grammar. Most importantly, diagramming prevents the child from simply parroting back rules that he doesn't fully understand.

He may be able to quote the definition of a dependent clause, but if he can't properly diagram a sentence that contains dependent clauses, you'll know that he doesn't really comprehend how they work. And until he understands how dependent clauses work, he won't be able to use them as he writes and talks. The study of grammar has as its goal the creation of a clear, persuasive, forceful, fully equipped speaker and writer.

Learning how to diagram in the middle grades will also benefit the high-school student. When students begin to do more complex rhetoric-stage compositions, they often struggle with sentence structure; as they strive to express complex thoughts, they write convoluted and unclear sentences. If you read a sentence in your ninth grader's composition and think, "There's something wrong with that sentence," ask the young writer to diagram it. Usually, the sentence will break one of the rules of proper sentence construction. Diagramming it is a diagnostic tool that will highlight its problems; learning *how* to diagram in the middle grades will equip the student to use this tool with ease.

Don't be intimidated by diagramming. It starts simply—writing a subject and a verb on a horizontal line and drawing a vertical line between them. Each sentence part has its own place on the diagram. But both you and your fifth grader will get plenty of practice in identifying those parts before you start diagramming them. (And you'll have the teacher's book!)

In the middle grades, you should plan to spend forty to sixty minutes, four days per week, working through a grammar text and its accompanying exercises.

One caution about the Resources list at the end of this chapter: Many grammar texts include composition exercises. Almost without exception, these should be skipped. In our experience, texts either teach grammar well (systematically and clearly) and composition poorly, or vice versa. Use the grammar texts for grammar, and ignore the composition exercises in favor of the approach we describe in this chapter.

As you progress through your grammar program, have the student write down any grammar or punctuation rule that gives him particular trouble. (For example, "Periods and commas go inside the closing quotation marks.") Keep a list of these "Trouble Rules" in the Grammar section of the Writing notebook.

If you're just beginning grammar for the first time with a middle-grade student, you can begin on grade level with students who have already been working in a systematic grammar program. Students who have done little (or scattershot) grammar should generally begin with the fifth-grade level of any given program and work forward. Older students will probably progress more quickly, but most grammar programs are designed to be completed around tenth grade, so don't worry about being "behind"; the student will still be able to complete a full grammar sequence before the end of high school.

READING: LITERATURE

Follow this schedule:

Fifth grade	Ancients (5000 B.C.–A.D. 400)
Sixth grade	Medieval–early Renaissance (400–1600)
Seventh grade	Late Renaissance–early modern (1600–1850)
Eighth grade	Modern (1850–present)

During the logic stage, plan to spend forty-five to sixty minutes, three days per week, reading and creating narration pages.

As in the grammar stage, literature is keyed to the historical period being studied. The student should place narrations of historical novels and other imaginative literature in the Reading section of the notebook.

However, she can put narrations of any great books—original literature written *during* the historical period under study—in the Arts and Great Books section of the history notebook. If she reads a novel about the Borgia in seventh grade, she should put it in the Literature notebook under Reading. But if she reads *Gulliver's Travels*, she can put this in her History notebook. In a way, it's a primary source, written by an eyewitness to the history she's working on. These notebooks are tools; use them in whatever way makes the most sense.

You shouldn't feel that you have to confine the child to stories during her reading time. Although the fifth grader should be reading tales from ancient Egypt, if she shows interest in a biography of Tutankhamen, let her read that, too. She needs to read a version of the *Iliad* and *Odyssey*, but she can also read nonfiction books about Homer or Socrates or the wars of Alexander the Great. Reading and history will inevitably overlap. Just try to keep a balance: at least one work of imagination for every biography or book of history. Historical novels are fine, but make sure that the child also reads versions of the classics, if not the classics themselves.

During the grammar stage, the student's narration pages aimed to answer one question: What happened? But during the logic stage, you'll begin to encourage the student to think more critically about literature. After she reads, you'll *converse* with her about the book—carrying on a dialogue about what is or isn't important in plots, about whether characters are heroes or villains, about the effects that books have on readers.

Does this mean you have to read the book yourself?

Ideally, yes. We've done our best, in this book, to guide you toward books and work texts that don't demand unnecessary preparation. But if you're going to discuss books with your child, you should (at the very least) skim through the story yourself. You don't have to do this with every book the child reads, just those literature books that you plan to discuss with the student. During the logic stage, your conversations with the student will guide her as she begins, for the first time, to think critically about what she reads. (And think of all the great literature you'll catch up on.)

However, we do know that you live in the real world, which means that jobs, family responsibilities, and home-schooling other children might scuttle your plans to read along with your child. Remember that your goal, in talking to your young student about the literature she's just read, is to give her practice forming thoughts about the book into complete sentences and expressing them out loud. You don't necessarily have to read the whole book in order to carry on this sort of dialogue; if necessary, the jacket flap and back cover copy might do the trick.

What questions should you ask?

Use the following list to begin your dialogue. As you grow more comfortable with the process, you'll think of others.

For a novel or story:

Whom is this book about? (central character[s])
What do the central characters want?
What keeps them from getting it?
How do they get what they want?

Do they have an enemy or enemies? Is there a villain?
What does the villain want?
What do you think is the most important event in the story?
What leads up to this event?
How are the characters different after this event?
What is the most important event in each chapter?
How many different stories does the writer tell?

For a biography:

What kind of family did the subject come from?
What were his parents like?
Where did he go to school?
What did he want the most as a child? As a grown-up?
How did he go about getting it?
Name three or four important people in his life.
Did he get married? To whom? When?
Did they have children?
What was the most important event in his life?
Name three other important events in his life.
Did he get what he wanted in life? Why or why not?
Why do we still remember this person?

For evaluation:

What was the most exciting part of the book?
What was the most boring part of the book?
Did you like the character[s]? Why or why not?
Did you hope that she would get what she wanted?
Did any part of the book seem particularly real?
Did any part of the book seem unlikely to you?
Did you hope it would end in another way? How?
Would you read this book again?
Which one of your friends would enjoy this book?

During fifth grade, concentrate on helping the student answer these questions orally. If a young reader knows that she'll have to write down everything she says, she's likely to answer as concisely as possible—which defeats the purpose. And even coming up with answers to these questions is hard at first; you don't want to add a second difficult task to the process. Sixth graders can begin to write their answers down (see the progression outlined below).

Aim to spend at least three days per week, forty-five to sixty minutes per day, on reading—that is, reading the books, talking about them, and following the writing pattern we describe in the sections that follow. It is normal for a fifth-grade student to struggle with these questions at first. Putting thoughts into words and articulating them clearly to someone else is hard work. Be patient and take your time.

READING: FOR FUN
(CONTINUING SKILL DEVELOPMENT)

Throughout the logic stage, don't forget to provide a full hour (at least), four days per week or more, some other time during the day for free reading.

Children need to be encouraged to read for fun on a regular basis—and they should *not* have to summarize or discuss these books. Visit the library regularly (many home-schooling families make library visits a weekly school activity), and help your fifth grader choose good novels and nonfiction books on interesting subjects. Consider requiring your child to pick out two science books and two history books on each library trip. Don't scold the child for picking out easy books (those are important for continuing to develop speed and ease), but also challenge him to check out one or two more difficult books on each visit.

Realize that not all Caldecott or Newbery winners are suitable for all children. Skim through books you aren't familiar with; just because a book is recommended by a librarian doesn't mean that it will provide age-appropriate entertainment.

We've suggested a few resources for finding good books at the end of this chapter. Many libraries keep their own lists of recommended books for middle-grade readers; ask your librarian.

Fifth Grade: Ancients (5000 B.C.–A.D. 400)

The fifth grader returns to the ancients. In first grade, you read myths and fairy tales to your beginning reader. Now she can read them for herself. She'll begin the year with tales of ancient Egypt and end the year with the works of the Romans. Plan on spending forty-five to sixty minutes on reading. Since her history curriculum is also centered on the ancients, the history and reading curricula will reinforce and strengthen each other.

As in the grammar stage, avoid "reading textbooks." Go to the library, and check out the many middle-grade versions of classic literature—myths, legends, the works of Plato and Confucius, the tales of Homer and Virgil. At the end of this chapter, we've listed a number of adaptations suitable for fifth graders. We've also listed historical novels that can give the student an excellent picture of the ancient world.

Don't limit yourself to our suggestions, though. Go to the library catalog or children's librarian with the following chronological list, suitable for fifth to eighth graders (adaptations, biographies, and historical novels):

Confucius
Chinese folktales
Japanese folktales
ancient Chinese poetry
ancient Japanese poetry
myths of ancient Egypt
tales of the pharaohs
the Bible
Moses
Abraham
David
Solomon
Esther
Ruth
Homer
Buddha
Socrates
Plato
Aristotle

Alexander the Great

Roman emperors

the Iliad and the Odyssey

Greek and Roman myths

Aesop's fables

Indian folktales

African folktales

Cicero

Virgil

After each book is finished, spend some time talking to the student about the literature she's just read, using the questions above. At first, just ask two or three questions about each book, encouraging the student to answer in complete sentences. Slowly add additional questions as her comfort level increases. Be sensitive to frustration and boredom; you don't want to kill her interest in the book through over-discussion.

After you've talked about the book, ask the student to write a simple narrative summary—the sort of summaries she's been writing about books in fourth grade. This will allow her to continue to practice her narrative writing skills. These should be a half-page to one page long. As she moves on to longer and more complex books, she may take a week or so to read a single book and write a one-page summary. Try to enforce the one-page limit even though this is difficult for longer books (the child typically wants to include every detail in her summary). If she has difficulty condensing, talk to her about the book. Ask her to tell you the story (or relate the information, in the case of a nonfiction book). Help her to evaluate each detail by asking questions: "Is that important later on?" "Would the story still make sense if you left that part out?" "Does that character show up again at the end of the book?" "What does he do?" "If you leave him out of your report, will the story end the same way?" Talk about the book together until the child has pinpointed the most important events and is able to weave them into a narration.

At the end of the narration, ask the child to write a one- or two-sentence evaluation of the book that includes *specific* reasons why she did or didn't like the book. "I liked the *Odyssey* because Odysseus came back home to Penelope and she didn't have to marry someone she hated" is acceptable; "I liked the *Odyssey* because it was interesting" is not. Again, talk through this paragraph with your child. Ask: "What was your favorite part?" "Who was your favorite character?" "Why?" "Did you find this boring?" "How could it have been more interesting?" This will begin to give the student elementary practice in writing critically.

This process of selecting, evaluating, and criticizing will move the fifth grader from grammar-stage reading (where she simply repeats what she reads back to you) into logic-stage reading. During the logic stage, the student *thinks* about what she's read: "What makes it interesting?" "What parts of it are most important?" "Why do I react the way I do?"

Sixth Grade: Medieval–Early Renaissance (400–1600)

In sixth grade, the student will concentrate on literature from and about the Middle Ages and early Renaissance, a period that coincides with her study of history. If she's a good reader, she can tackle a few originals this year (many sixth graders are capable of reading some Malory, Chaucer, and *Beowulf* in modern English translation as well as scenes from Shakespeare). Sixth grade is the first year the student will actually complete a reading list. Aim to read parts of the following works, in the following chronological order:

> *Beowulf*
> *Sir Gawain and the Green Knight*
> *The Canterbury Tales*
> Dante Alighieri, *Inferno*
> Edmund Spenser, "Saint George and the Dragon" from *The Faerie Queene*
> Thomas Malory, a version of *Le Morte d'Arthur*
> One Shakespeare play: *Macbeth, Henry V,* or *A Midsummer Night's Dream*

Try to find the editions we've specified (nothing turns a reader from Shakespeare faster than a wrinkled, tiny-print edition with no explanatory footnotes). Our recommended editions should be readily available at libraries and bookstores.

For *Sir Gawain and the Green Knight,* the "Prologue" to *The Canterbury Tales,* and the introduction to the *Inferno,* we strongly recommend reading the texts aloud with your child (poems that seem obscure on the page come to life when read out loud). Also look for audiobook versions; the whole family might enjoy Derek Jacobi's reading of *Le Morte d'Arthur* on a long drive.

What about Shakespeare?

Sixth grade is the earliest that Shakespeare is taught. If you think your sixth grader is ready, try an original play. Otherwise, stick with the retellings and versions we list. Rely on your own judgment, and don't force an unready sixth grader to read Shakespeare. The goal of early Shakespeare studies is to create love, not loathing.

When you tackle Shakespeare for the first time, follow this three-step process:

1. Read a summary of the play's plot. The editions we suggest provide a synopsis, a summary of each act, and a character list.
2. Now that you know what's going on, go to or watch at least one staged production. Shakespeare was written to be watched. Borrow a DVD or watch online, and eat popcorn.
3. Now read the text.

Which play should you choose? *Romeo and Juliet* is the high-school standard, but the sexual elements make it unsuitable for many sixth graders, who will be either embarrassed or bored. We suggest you choose *Macbeth* (tragedy), *Henry V* (history), or *A Midsummer Night's Dream* (comedy). *A Midsummer Night's Dream* is the easiest of the comedies to follow, but the available staged versions are so-so. Good productions of *Macbeth* and *Henry V* are available, and the plays are about equal in terms of difficulty. Both require a fair amount of background historical knowledge (provided in the editions we suggest). Susan leans toward *Henry V* because the Kenneth Branagh movie is one of the best introductions to Shakespeare for any young student—it's got sword fighting, romance, comedy, and moral dilemmas.

Continue to discuss these books, using the discussion questions above. During sixth grade, encourage the student to begin to write answers to at least two of the discussion questions for each book; move toward answering three or four. Alternate writing answers to the discussion questions with writing brief summaries that end with a sentence or two of evaluation.

Because these books actually originated in the time period under study, you can file the summaries and written answers in the history notebook under The Arts and Great Books, or in the Literature notebook, whichever makes the most sense to you and the student.

Besides following the list above, you should explore the library. Consult the catalog or ask your librarian for sixth- to-eighth-grade books (adaptations, biographies, historical novels) by and about these writers and thinkers (listed chronologically):

St. Augustine
Geoffrey Chaucer
Erasmus
Edmund Spenser
Sir Thomas More
John Donne
William Shakespeare
Martin Luther
Sir Thomas Wyatt (try stories of Henry VIII and Anne Boleyn)
Dante Alighieri
Sir Thomas Malory
John Knox
John Calvin
René Descartes

Search for additional adaptations or versions of these specific works:

Beowulf
Sir Gawain and the Green Knight
The Canterbury Tales
The Faerie Queene (including "Saint George and the Dragon")
Inferno
Le Morte d'Arthur ("The Death of Arthur") or anything based on this work
the plays of Shakespeare

In sixth grade, try to spend at least three days per week, sixty minutes per day, on reading—reading the books, talking about them, writing about them.

Continue to provide free reading time.

Seventh Grade: Late Renaissance–Early Modern
(1600–1850)

The seventh grader will read literature from the late Renaissance through the early modern period.[1]

With an extra year under his belt, the seventh-grade student can read even more originals than he did in sixth grade, starting with the simpler novels of the writers he'll meet again in eleventh grade. Specific editions are important only where we've noted in the Resources at the end of this chapter; otherwise, an easily located edition such as a Penguin Classic or Dover Thrift will do. Try to complete the following reading list in order:

Miguel de Cervantes, *Don Quixote,* abridged and simplified only!

Charles Perrault, *Perrault's Complete Fairy Tales*

Jonathan Swift, "A Voyage to Lilliput" and "A Voyage to Brobdingnag," from *Gulliver's Travels*

John Bunyan, *The Pilgrim's Progress*

Daniel Defoe, *Robinson Crusoe*

William Wordsworth, "We Are Seven," "Lines Written in Early Spring," "Lines Composed a Few Miles above Tintern Abbey," "Lucy Gray," "Composed upon Westminster Bridge, September 3, 1802," and "I Wandered Lonely As a Cloud"

Samuel Taylor Coleridge, "The Rime of the Ancient Mariner"

Washington Irving, *The Legend of Sleepy Hollow* and *Rip Van Winkle*

Robert Browning, "The Pied Piper of Hamelin"

Jacob and Wilhelm Grimm, *Grimm's Fairy Tales*

Benjamin Franklin, "The Way to Wealth," in *Benjamin Franklin: The Autobiography and Other Writings*

Christina Rossetti, "Goblin Market," "A Birthday," "Sister Maude," "No, Thank You, John"

Lewis Carroll, *Alice's Adventures in Wonderland*

Jane Austen, *Pride and Prejudice*

Mark Twain, *The Adventures of Tom Sawyer*

Jules Verne, *20,000 Leagues under the Sea*

---

[1] Although some of the titles in this list were written after 1850, we've placed them in the early modern period if most of the author's life passed before mid-century.

Charles Dickens, *A Christmas Carol*

Alfred, Lord Tennyson, "The Lady of Shalott" and "The Charge of the Light Brigade"

Edgar Allan Poe, "The Raven"

Peter Christen Asbjornsen, *East o' the Sun and West o' the Moon: Fifty-nine Norwegian Folk Tales*

Frederick Douglass, *Narrative of the Life of Frederick Douglass, an American Slave, Written by Himself*

Most seventh graders will find that this list ranges from fairly simple to extremely challenging. As always, use your common sense. If you glance over a book and think it's too difficult or if the student begins it and struggles for more than a couple of chapters, skip it and move on. Good readers can certainly go on to explore the more difficult works of Dickens, Austen, Twain, and any of the writers listed below. Slower readers can simply skip some of these titles.

In seventh grade, the student can drop the writing of simple summaries (a skill which should be well established by this point) and move to answering four or more of the critical questions in writing, ending with one or two answers to evaluation questions. These written responses should be three-quarters of a page or more; these are basic critical essays on literature, excellent preparation for high-school writing. File them either in the Literature notebook, or in the History notebook under The Arts and Great Books.

Also explore the library for seventh- to ninth-grade-level books, adaptations, biographies, and historical novels by and about these writers and thinkers listed here in chronological order:

Daniel Defoe

Jonathan Swift

John Bunyan

Alexander Pope

John Milton

William Blake

Alfred, Lord Tennyson

William Wordsworth

Robert Browning

Elizabeth Barrett Browning
Charles Dickens
Jane Austen
Edward Lear
Percy Bysshe Shelley
Mary Shelley
Christina Rossetti
Lewis Carroll
Mark Twain
James Fenimore Cooper
Frederick Douglass
Jules Verne
Herman Melville

This is a bare outline—any literary figure encountered during the student's exploration of the years 1600 through 1850 is acceptable. Aim to spend at least three days per week, one hour per day, on reading the books, talking about them, writing about them.

Continue to require regular free reading.

Eighth Grade: Modern (1850–Present)

The eighth grader will read literature from the modern period. A complete reading list for this period would take a lifetime to work through, so consider the following a skeleton that you can clothe with any number of additional authors and books. The goal of the list is to introduce the student to a wide range of genres—adventure, poetry, mystery, science fiction, short stories—spanning a century and a half. Each list (fiction, poetry, and drama) is organized in chronological order. The more challenging works (and more difficult authors) of this period will be read in the senior year of high school, when the student encounters this period for the last time. We haven't suggested specific editions since these titles are so widely available.

Classical education demands a great deal of reading—ideally, the eighth grader will read every title on the list. But because the list is long, we've divided it into fiction, poetry, and drama. If you're unable to complete the entire list, make sure you select titles from each category.

Fiction
Robert Louis Stevenson, *Kidnapped* or *Treasure Island*
Edward E. Hale, "The Man without a Country"
Louisa May Alcott, *Little Women*
Arthur Conan Doyle, any of the Sherlock Holmes stories or *The Hound of the Baskervilles*
Rudyard Kipling, *The Jungle Book*
H. G. Wells, *The Time Machine* or *The War of the Worlds*
Jack London, *The Call of the Wild*
G. K. Chesterton, any of the Father Brown stories
Baroness Orczy, *The Scarlet Pimpernel*
O. Henry, any of the short stories
Lucy Maud Montgomery, *Anne of Green Gables*
Agatha Christie, *Murder on the Orient Express*
Dorothy Sayers, *Strong Poison*
Margaret Mitchell, *Gone With the Wind*
Marjorie Kinnan Rawlings, *The Yearling*

Poetry
Henry Wadsworth Longfellow, "The Song of Hiawatha"
Robert Frost, "The Road Not Taken" and other poems
E. E. Cummings, collected poems
Walter de la Mare, *Poems 1919–1934*, any selections
Langston Hughes, *The Dream Keeper and Other Poems* or *The Block: Poems*

Drama
Oscar Wilde, *The Importance of Being Earnest*
George Bernard Shaw, *Pygmalion*
Arthur Miller, *The Crucible*
Robert Bolt, *A Man for All Seasons*

Discuss these works with your student. After you've talked through them, ask her to write a basic critical essay, as she did in seventh grade.

Although this list ought to keep you busy all year, you can also look for biographies on and works by the following writers listed chronologically:

Beatrix Potter

Laura Ingalls Wilder

Frances Hodgson Burnett

K. D. Wyss

Gerard Manley Hopkins

Alexandre Dumas

Willa Cather

Wilfred Owen

Thomas Hardy

Carl Sandburg

A. A. Milne

W. Somerset Maugham

T. S. Eliot

Ezra Pound

F. Scott Fitzgerald

Sinclair Lewis

Amy Lowell

Ernest Hemingway

W. B. Yeats

Pearl S. Buck

Robert Lowell

Isaac Bashevis Singer

Toni Morrison

The eighth grader should plan on spending an hour per day, three or four days per week, reading, discussing, and writing about literature.

Free reading should continue. This is a good time for the student to go on with the novels of Agatha Christie, Thomas Hardy, Isaac Asimov, Terry Pratchett, or another newly discovered writer she enjoys.

MEMORY WORK

Each year, ask the student to select and memorize three to five favorite poems or passages from her reading. She should recite these for you before the end of the school year. Keep a page entitled "Memory Work" at the back of her notebook; write down the names of the pieces she has memorized and the dates she recited them for you. Fifth graders can choose English translations of classical poems or dramatic passages; sixth graders, passages from Chaucer or Dante; seventh graders have a wide range of choices, including poems of Wordsworth, Rossetti, and Poe, as well as Lewis Carroll's "Jabberwocky"; eighth graders have the entire range of modern poetry to choose from. Allow flexibility—the student ought to be able to memorize something that interests and attracts her.

WRITING

In the preceding chapters on science and history, and in the section above on literature, we've already covered much of what needs to be done in the middle-school writing curriculum: students need to continue to practice narrative summaries, learn how to write brief critical responses to literature, and—above all—learn to outline.

By now, the logic-stage student should be able to put ideas into words and get those words down on paper (the grammar-stage challenge). Once he can do this, the technical difficulties involved in the act of writing have been conquered. But until the student can begin to think about the *order* in which ideas should be set down, he'll continue to struggle with written composition. Thoughts will spin around in his head like a tangled ball of yarn; until he can reach into that ball and find the end (the starting place, the main idea that his paragraph, or page, will be organized around) he won't be able to get those thoughts down on paper. He needs an entrance point, an orderly plan that will tell him: First explain this idea; then explain how *this* and *this* relate to it; then move on to this observation. Without such a plan, he will either panic, or wildly set down ideas in random order (which describes much middle-grade writing).

So the focus of logic-stage writing should be *learning how to order ideas.* Making an outline is an exercise in ordering ideas: outlines require you to identify the organizing thought of a paragraph of composition (the topic sentence), figure out what pieces of information support it, and choose important details to flesh that information out.

In the classical tradition, students always have the chance to see skills demonstrated before trying to exercise them independently; they should always be able to observe a model, before being asked to carry out a task themselves. So rather than suddenly demanding that your middle-grade student construct an outline for his compositions (as many writing programs do), you'll encourage the student to examine how *other* writers organize their thoughts.

We've already touched on this skill in the last chapter, when we described how outlining slowly replaces simple narration in history study. As you plan out the middle-grade student's writing program, focus on assigning outlining all across the curriculum so that the student can see a number of different ways that writers develop their topics: narratives, descriptions, definitions, explanations, comparisons, and contrasts. Begin by asking the fifth-grade student to simply pick out the main point (the "topic sentence") in each paragraph of a nonfiction selection (perhaps one page of good writing). When the student is comfortable with this level of outlining, begin to require a two-level outline, and then a three-level outline (as described in "How to Outline" on pages 391–396).

While the student is learning to outline, continue to ask him to write narrative summaries, using this now-familiar form as a platform to practice sentence style and structure. But by sixth and seventh grade, the narrative summaries can give way to a more advanced form of writing: writing from an outline.

After making an outline of a passage, the student will put the original away and then rewrite the passage, using only the outline. Then he'll compare his assignment with the original. Again, this is preparation for mature high-school writing; before the student is given the task of coming up with an outline and writing from it, he needs to see how other writers flesh out the bones of an outline.

Up to this point, the student has not been required to do a great deal of original composition. But the student is nevertheless doing an enormous amount of writing practice: every day from first grade on, he's been either copying, taking dictation, writing down narrations, outlining, or writing from someone else's outline. All of this practice is necessary so that the student can come up to the high-school start line equipped and ready to go, prepared to launch into the full-fledged study of rhetoric.

In the classical tradition, early writing instruction focused on *imitation* rather than on originality. Young students need models, examples, and practice, practice, practice. Most writing programs—and almost all classroom writing instruction—require originality far too early, before students have had a chance to understand the writing process and practice writing based on models. And most classrooms assign too much advanced writing, too early. Your neighbor's seventh grader may be doing a big research paper, while your seventh grader is still outlining and rewriting. Don't fret. Those research papers have been thrown at that seventh grader without a great deal of preparation. He's probably struggling to figure out exactly what he's doing, making false start after false start, and ending up with a paper that is largely rehashed encyclopedia information. Susan has taught scores of college freshmen who went through classroom programs that had them doing book reports, research papers, and other long assignments as early as third grade. This doesn't improve writing skill; it just produces students who can churn out a certain number of pages when required. As someone who's had to read those pages, she can testify that this approach is not, across the board, working.

A decent research paper or essay requires skills in outlining and in persuasive writing that the majority of fifth, sixth, and seventh graders have not yet developed. Instead, in fifth through eighth grade, students should be writing constant short compositions, developing necessary skills before being required to carry those skills through into an extended piece of work. They will begin to learn the skills of researching, documentation, and argumentation, but the full exercise of these skills will not take place for several more years.

In summary: in the middle grades, students should learn to diagram, outline, and then write from an outline, following this pattern:

Grade	Weekly writing assignments
Fifth	1. Write at least two narrative summaries from history, literature, or science.
	2. Construct at least one outline of a nonfiction selection. Begin with a one-level outline of one or two selected pages. Work toward a two-level outline of three or more selected pages.

          3. Answer discussion questions orally about literature.

Sixth   1. Write at least two narrative summaries from history, literature, or science.

          2. Construct at least one outline of a nonfiction selection. Begin with a two-level outline of three or more selected pages. Work toward a three-level outline of three or more selected pages.

          3. Write one basic "literary essay" around one page in length (answering discussion questions about literature in writing).

Seventh   1. Write one narrative summary, drawn from history, literature, or science.

          2. Construct at least two three-level outlines of three or more selected nonfiction pages.

          3. Rewrite one selection, using the three-level outline, and compare it with the original.

          4. Write one basic "literary essay" around one page in length (answering discussion questions about literature in writing).

Eighth   1. Construct at least two three-level outlines of three or more selected nonfiction pages.

          2. Rewrite both selections, using the three-level outline, and compare them with the originals.

          3. Write one basic "literary essay" around one page in length (answering discussion questions about literature in writing).

A parent who is comfortable with writing can carry this program out without a formal writing curriculum, integrating the assignments into the student's history, literature, and science studies.

However, many parents don't have the confidence to teach writing in this way, so in the Resources section we've listed several different formal writing curricula that are compatible with the classical approach. If you use one of these programs, also try to incorporate at least one outlining exercise per week into history and science, following the pattern above; and do your best to follow the pattern described earlier in this chapter for the study and discussion of literature.

OVERVIEW OF LANGUAGE WORK

Fifth Grade

Spelling	15–20 minutes, 3–4 days per week	Begin or continue with formal spelling curriculum.
Grammar	40–60 minutes, 4 days per week	Formal grammar
Reading: Literature	45–60 minutes, 3 days per week	Read ancient myths and legends, versions of classics, and books about ancient writers. Write brief narrative summaries, ending with a short evaluation. Begin to discuss critical issues orally. Memorize and recite poems or passages, three to five for the year.
Reading: Skills	1 hour, 4 or more days per week	Free reading
Writing	Daily, time will vary	Two narrative summaries per week (overlaps with literature, history, and science assignments); at least one one-level outline per week of a nonfiction source; work toward two-level outlines

Sixth Grade

Spelling/ Word Study	15–20 minutes, 3–4 days per week	Continue with formal spelling curriculum.
Grammar	40–60 minutes, 4 days per week.	Formal grammar

Reading: Literature	45–60 minutes, 3 days per week	Read stories of the Middle Ages and Renaissance; begin to read some original writings; alternate writing brief narrative summaries with writing answers to two or more discussion questions; memorize and recite poems or passages, three to five for the year.
Reading: Skills	1 hour, 4 or more days per week	Free reading
Writing	Daily, time will vary	Two narrative summaries per week (overlaps with literature, history, and science assignments); at least one two-level outline per week of a nonfiction source (overlaps with history and science); work toward three-level outlines

Seventh Grade

Spelling/Word Study	15–20 minutes, 3–4 days per week	Continue or finish formal spelling curriculum; transition into word study.
Grammar	40–60 minutes, 4 days per week	Formal grammar
Reading: Literature	45–60 minutes, 3 days per week	Read late Renaissance through early modern literature; answer four or more critical questions about literature in writing; memorize and recite poems or passages, three to five for the year.
Reading: Skills	1 hour, 4 or more days per week	Free reading

| Writing | Daily, time will vary | One narrative summary per week (overlaps with literature, history, and science assignments); at least two three-level outlines per week of nonfiction sources (overlaps with history and science); rewrite one selection from an outline each week. |

Eighth Grade

Word Study	15–20 minutes, 3–4 days per week	Continue with word study.
Grammar	40–60 minutes, 4 days per week	Formal grammar
Reading: Literature	45–60 minutes, 3–4 days per week	Read modern literature; answer four or more critical questions about literature in writing; memorize and recite poems or passages, three to five for the year.
Reading: Skills	1 hour, 4 or more days per week	Free reading
Writing	Daily, time will vary	At least two three-level outlines per week of nonfiction sources (overlaps with history and science); rewrite both selections from the outlines each week.

RESOURCES

Most books can be obtained from any bookseller or library; most curricula can be bought directly from the publisher or from a major home-school supplier such as Rainbow Resource Center. Contact information for publishers and suppliers can be found at www.welltrainedmind.com. If availability is limited, we have noted it. Where indicated, resources are listed in chronological order (the order you'll want to use them in). Books in series are listed together. Remember that additional curricula choices and more can be found at www.welltrainedmind.com. Prices change constantly, but we have included 2016 pricing to give an idea of affordability.

Spelling

There are dozens of spelling curricula and resources out there. We've listed four resources with very different approaches here; we selected these for ease of use, affordability, and their track record of effectiveness across a wide range of home-schooling families.

All About Spelling. Eagle River, WI: All About Learning Press, 2006–14.
  Developed by dyslexia researcher Marie Rippel, *All About Spelling* is based on the Orton-Gillingham system. Each Teacher's Manual is "lightly scripted" (you, the parent, are told what to explain, how to explain it, and what visual aids and manipulatives to use). The accompanying Student Packets contain all cards, charts, and worksheets required. Samples are available at the publisher's website.

  We have listed the entire series for your convenience. The publisher's website suggests that students who are beginning the program for the first time start with Level 2 if they have some familiarity with phonograms, or Level 1 if they don't; older students will progress very quickly through the first levels. Additional placement advice is available at the publisher's website.

  When beginning the program, you'll need to purchase one Spelling Interactive Kit (containing letter tiles, magnets, cards, and app), which will serve you for the rest of the levels.
  Level 1 (Teacher's Manual and Student Packet), $29.95
  Level 2 (Teacher's Manual and Student Packet), $39.95
  Level 3 (Teacher's Manual and Student Packet), $39.95
  Level 4 (Teacher's Manual and Student Packet), $39.95
  Level 5 (Teacher's Manual and Student Packet), $39.95
  Level 6 (Teacher's Manual and Student Packet), $39.95
  Level 7 (Teacher's Manual and Student Packet), $39.95
  Spelling Interactive Kit, $22.85

Modern Curriculum Press Spelling Workout series, rev. ed. Parsippany, NJ: Modern Curriculum Press (Pearson Learning Group), 2002.
  $12.97 for each student edition, $13.47 for each Teacher's Edition. Order from Pearson Learning. The grade levels are approximate; students who are new to the series should begin with Level E. Most students will fin-

ish Level H, which introduces word study, in sixth or seventh grade and progress on to more advanced word study.

The program is a well-organized, low-preparation, open-and-go workbook series. Spelling Workout works best for students who read easily and don't struggle with spelling; it will reinforce their intuitive knowledge of language, teach rules explicitly, and drill them in proofreading.

Caveats: Don't do the associated writing exercises and ignore anything that seems unnecessarily "schoolish" to you.

Spelling Workout E (fifth-grade level)

Teacher's Edition E

Spelling Workout F (sixth-grade level)

Teacher's Edition F

Spelling Workout G (seventh-grade level)

Teacher's Edition G

Spelling Workout H (eighth-grade level)

Teacher's Edition H

Sequential Spelling. Clio, MI: AVKO Educational Research Foundation, various dates.

This seven-level series was developed by longtime teacher Don McCabe, himself a dyslexic reader. *Sequential Spelling* takes an entirely different approach: rather than teaching the rules that govern English spelling, the books teach words in "word families" that all have the same pattern. The program is often very effective for students who struggle with rule-based spelling. In addition, the publisher offers DVD lessons that teach the student directly, so that the parent needs only to supervise and check (a particularly good option for larger families).

Sequential Spelling does not teach rules at all ("Most people never need to be taught spelling rules in order to learn English"), instead focusing entirely on patterns. However, supplemental materials teaching spelling rules explicitly can be downloaded from the publisher's website; we suggest that you make as much use of these as possible.

The levels are not by grade, but rather by word family; always begin with Level 1 if you have not used the program before.

Each level costs $15 for the Teacher Manual, $10 for the Student Response Book, and $30 for the DVD (ebook versions are also available for a lower cost, as are "bundles" of all required materials). Buy from the publisher, www.avko.org. Extensive samples of all materials are available at the publisher's website.

Sequential Spelling 1
Sequential Spelling 2
Sequential Spelling 3
Sequential Spelling 4
Sequential Spelling 5
Sequential Spelling 6
Sequential Spelling 7

The Writing Road to Reading, 6th rev. ed. Phoenix, AZ: Spalding Education International.

The Writing Road to Reading, also known as the Spalding method, was developed in the 1950s by Romalda Spalding, an educator who studied with Samuel Orton (of the Orton-Gillingham method) and worked with severely dyslexic students. Much like the O-G approach, the Spalding method teaches seventy phonograms using multisensory methods, and combines a strong focus on spelling with instruction in phonics.

WRTR is much more complex and labor-intensive than the other O-G curricula we suggest, and its heavy emphasis on writing makes it a poor choice for younger students. However, middle-grade students who spell badly and read with reluctance can benefit from the approach. (They should also be evaluated for dyslexia, a condition that WRTR was designed to meet.)

Parents who want to use WRTR should strongly consider investing in the ten-hour online training session, "Spalding for Home Educators," offered through the Spalding Education International website. An online assessment is also available to help place your student in the correct level. Visit the web page for fuller explanations.

Home Educator's Kit. $206.60. Contains the core text, teacher's guide (select the correct grade level after completing the online assessment with your student), phonogram and word builder cards, supplemental testing and notebook materials, CD and DVD supplements, and accessories.

Word Study

Fifer, Norma, and Nancy Flowers. Vocabulary from Classical Roots series. Cambridge, MA: Educators Publishing Service.

Order from Educators Publishing Service. Core texts are $13.25, Teacher's Guide and Answer Key books (useful but not essential) are $22.90.

The books are part reference book and part workbook; they use classical quotes, definitions, and exercises to build vocabulary skills. The core books in the series are Books A through E, and each is sixteen lessons long. If you do one lesson per week, you can easily complete two books per year.

The *Vocabulary from Classical Roots* series provides exercises, but they aren't extensive. Instead of doing word study for fifteen minutes a day, as you did for spelling, we suggest that you follow this pattern:

Monday	30–45 minutes	Read through the word roots, definitions, and sample sentences; make 3 × 5-inch flash cards for each Latin root and unfamiliar English word.
Tuesday–Thursday	5–10 minutes	Drill with flash cards.
Friday	10 minutes	Review flash cards; complete exercises; check.

Aim to do one lesson per week. If you're able to begin *Vocabulary from Classical Roots* in seventh grade, you'll complete A and B in the seventh-grade year, and C and D in the eighth-grade year. If you don't finish the *Spelling Workout* texts until the middle of the seventh grade (or later), just stick to this same pattern—one lesson per week.

Vocabulary from Classical Roots A
Teacher's Guide and Answer Key A
Vocabulary from Classical Roots B
Teacher's Guide and Answer Key B
Vocabulary from Classical Roots C
Teacher's Guide and Answer Key C
Vocabulary from Classical Roots D
Teacher's Guide and Answer Key D

Vocabulary from Classical Roots E
Teacher's Guide and Answer Key E

Wordly Wise 3000, 3rd ed. Cambridge, MA: Educators Publishing Service.
This direct instructional vocabulary program focuses less on roots and
prefixes and more on word use. Particularly good for improving standardized testing, but also an excellent vocabulary builder. Lessons are
open-and-go. We suggest beginning with Book 7, but you can view word
lists and sample lessons from each book on the publisher's website and
choose the level that will challenge your student.

Student Book 7. $12.40.

Teacher's Resource Book 7. $49.55.

Student Book 8. $12.49.

Teacher's Resource Book 8. $49.55.

Student Book 9. $13.25.

Teacher's Resource Book 9. $49.55.

Student Book 10. $13.25.

Teacher's Resource Book 10. $49.55.

Grammar

Rod & Staff Grammar and Composition. Crockett, KY: Rod & Staff.
After reviewing a number of grammar texts, we still think that the Rod
& Staff grammar series, which now extends through tenth grade, is the
most thorough. Students new to the program can go directly into the
fifth-grade book, *Following the Plan,* which builds on the material taught
in the fourth-grade book we recommended in Chapter 5. The student can
continue on with *Progressing with Courage* (sixth grade), *Building Securely*
(seventh grade), and *Preparing for Usefulness* (eighth grade). Each nonconsumable text contains clear explanations of grammatical concepts
and plenty of exercises for practice. Don't feel that you have to complete
every grammar exercise; if your child understands the concepts and is
able to put them into practice, there's no need to be compulsive about
finishing the page.

Diagramming and outlining are included.

Rod & Staff is a Mennonite press, and the examples and exercises
sometimes refer to biblical passages and Christian theology.

Rod & Staff has no website and limited distribution; order from Milestone Books or Exodus Books.

Following the Plan: English 5. 1993.
  Pupil Textbook. $18.65.
  Worksheets (additional practice). $3.60.
  Teacher's Manual. $25.25.
  Test Booklet. $2.50.

Progressing with Courage: English 6. 1994.
  Pupil Textbook. $19.75.
  Worksheets (additional practice). $3.60.
  Teacher's Manual. $27.94.
  Test Booklet. $2.50.

Building Securely: English 7. 1996.
  Pupil Textbook. $19.75.
  Worksheets (additional practice). $3.60.
  Teacher's Manual. $27.45.
  Test Booklet. $2.50.

Preparing for Usefulness: English 8. 1997.
  Pupil Textbook. $19.75.
  Worksheets (additional practice). $3.60.
  Teacher's Manual. $27.45.
  Test Booklet. $2.50.

Hake Grammar & Writing, 2nd ed. Boston: Houghton Mifflin Harcourt, 2014.

Previously known as Saxon Grammar, Hake Grammar & Writing offers a thorough and nonsectarian approach to grammar, with outlining, diagramming, and plenty of review. You will need the Student Textbook, which contains all of the grammar instruction and exercises, and the Teacher Packet, which contains loose-leaf tests and answers to the exercises in the Student Textbook. We do *not* recommend the Student Workbook, which contains the writing component of the program; the Hake writing provides very little modeling and is not well organized. Buy the Student Textbook and Teacher Packet separately rather than buying the Homeschool Kit, which contains the Student Workbook as well.

Order from an online textbook supplier or from a home-school supplier such as Rainbow Resource. *Note:* HMH's main site sells the hardcover school version of the program, which is different only in format and cannot be purchased by individual users; HMH's home education site makes it very difficult to buy just the textbooks and teacher materials. ISBNs are included here to make ordering easier.

Samples can be viewed on the publisher's website.

Grammar and Writing 5 Student Textbook (ISBN 9780544044234). $43.25.

Grammar and Writing 5 Teacher Packet (ISBN 9780544044258). $29.75.

Grammar and Writing 6 Student Textbook (ISBN 9780544044265). $43.25.

Grammar and Writing 6 Teacher Packet (ISBN 9780544044289). $29.75.

Grammar and Writing 7 Student Textbook (ISBN 9780544044296). $43.25.

Grammar and Writing 7 Teacher Packet (ISBN 9780544044319). $29.75.

Grammar and Writing 8 Student Textbook (ISBN 9780544044326). $43.25.

Grammar and Writing 8 Teacher Packet (ISBN 9780544044340). $29.75.

Voyages in English. Chicago: Loyola Press, 2011. Order from Loyola Press. This series, originally designed by Loyola Press for Catholic schools, has been reissued in a nonsectarian version. The rules are clearly stated and the exercises are adequate; the program is not quite as rigorous or complete as the Rod & Staff program, and the writing exercises should be skipped (see the Writing section in this chapter). Voyages in English is a little more colorful and eye-appealing than Hake. Samples can be viewed on the publisher's website.

Voyages in English, Grade 5, Student Edition. $52.95.

Grade 5 Practice Book. $11.95.

Grade 5 Teacher Edition. $81.95.

Grade 5 Answer Key for Practice and Assessment Books. $15.95.

Voyages in English, Grade 6, Student Edition. $54.95.

Grade 6 Practice Book. $12.95.

Grade 6 Teacher Edition. $83.95.

Grade 6 Answer Key for Practice and Assessment Books. $18.95.

Voyages in English, Grade 7, Student Edition. $54.95.

Grade 7 Practice Book. $12.95.

Grade 7 Teacher Edition. $83.95.

Grade 7 Answer Key for Practice and Assessment Books. $18.95.

Voyages in English, Grade 8, Student Edition. $54.95.

Grade 8 Practice Book. $12.95.

Grade 8 Teacher Edition. $83.95.

Grade 8 Answer Key for Practice and Assessment Books. $18.95.

Supplementary Resources

Daly, Mary. *The First Whole Book of Diagrams*, rev. ed. Garretson, SD: Hedge School, 2010.

$26. Order from the Hedge School or from Emmanuel Books. A useful diagramming supplement.

Elementary Diagramming Worktext. $10.00 when ordered along with the text above. Provides students with plenty of practice.

Mueller, Mary. *Study Skills Strategies: Outlining.* Portland, ME: Walch Education, 2003.

$26.99. Order through any bookstore or from Walch Education (you can also read samples at www.walch.com). High-school level instruction in outlining skills.

Reading: Literature

These are listed in order of use. Remember, you don't have to read all of these. But you can choose reading assignments from among the following names. Note that this list—especially the early-modern and modern sections—is merely a starting place. There are many other authors and books worth reading, and you'll discover them as you explore your library. Rather than organizing these books and authors alphabetically, we have listed them in chronological order, and we suggest that you read them in this order; we have also included a few historical novels where appropriate. In most cases, you can find various versions of these stories. We have suggested a few specific editions that we particularly like.

For fifth grade, we have provided a number of different retellings of Greek myths and stories; pick one or several. From sixth grade on, the lists are divided into two parts. The first part, the formal reading list that we describe in detail in the chapter itself, is listed in chronological order. The supplementary list, containing books and novels that you can use to support the reading list, is listed alphabetically by author.

Ancients, 5000 B.C.–A.D. 400 (Fifth Grade)

Work through these books and authors in the following order.

Green, Roger Lancelyn. *Tales of Ancient Egypt*. New York: Puffin, 2001.
$4.99. A minor classic in its own right. Green's retelling is clear and vivid.

McGraw, Eloise Jarvis. *The Golden Goblet*. New York: Puffin, 1986.
$6.99. A young Egyptian boy solves the mystery of a goblet stolen from the City of the Dead.

————. *Mara, Daughter of the Nile*. New York: Puffin, 1985.
$6.99. An Egyptian slave girl gets involved with rivals who battle over the throne.

Fang, Linda. *The Ch'i-lin Purse: A Collection of Ancient Stories*, illus. Jeanne M. Lee. New York: Square Fish/FSG, 2012.
$8.99. Nine well-told stories from the Warring States period.

McAlpine, Helen, and William McAlpine. *Tales from Japan*. New York: Oxford University Press, 2002.
$12.95. Part of the Myths and Legends series. Engrossing and well-written stories.

Khan, Noor Inayat. *Twenty Jataka Tales*, illus. H. Willebeek Le Mair. Rochester, VT: Inner Traditions, 1985.
$14.95. Illustrated tales from ancient India.

Arnott, Kathleen. *Tales from Africa*. New York: Oxford University Press, 2000.
$12.95. Part of the Myths and Legends series. Engrossing and well-written stories.

Evslin, Bernard. *Heroes, Gods and Monsters of Greek Myths*, illus. William Hofmann. New York: Laurel Leaf, 1984.
$6.99. Vivid retellings of the "greatest hits" of Greek myth.

Coolidge, Olivia. *Greek Myths*. Boston: Houghton Mifflin Harcourt, 2001.
$6.99. A classic retelling.

Colum, Padraic. *The Golden Fleece and the Heroes Who Lived before Achilles*. New York: Aladdin, 2004.
$9.95. A classic retelling.

Green, Roger Lancelyn. *Tales of Greek Heroes*. New York: Puffin, 2009.
$4.99. A minor classic in its own right. Green's retelling is clear and vivid.

———. *The Tale of Troy*. New York: Puffin, 2012.
$4.99. A minor classic in its own right. Green's retelling is clear and vivid.

Morden, Daniel, and Hugh Lupton. The Greek Tales series, illus. Carole Henaff. Cambridge, MA: Barefoot Books.
$7.99. Accessible paperback chapter book retellings of Greek myths and epics.
  The Adventures of Achilles. 2012.
  The Adventures of Odysseus, illus. Christina Balit. 2006.
  Demeter and Persephone. 2013.
  Orpheus and Eurydice. 2013.
  Theseus and the Minotaur. 2013.

Coolidge, Olivia. *The Trojan War*. Boston: Houghton Mifflin Harcourt, 2001.
$6.95. A classic retelling.

Colum, Padraic. *The Children's Homer: The Adventures of Odysseus and the Tale of Troy*, illus. Willy Pogany. New York: Aladdin, 2004.
$9.99. A classic retelling.

Sutcliff, Rosemary. *Black Ships before Troy: The Story of the Iliad*, illus. Alan Lee. New York: Laurel Leaf, 2005.
$6.99. An excellent retelling with eerie, vivid illustrations.

Lively, Penelope. *In Search of a Homeland: The Story of the Aeneid*, illus. Ian Andrew. New York: Delacorte, 2001.
Out of print, but try your local library. This is one of the few retellings of the *Aeneid* available, and it's a good one, with excellent illustrations.

McGovern, Ann. *Aesop's Fables*. New York: Scholastic, 2013.
$4.99. A good retelling of sixty fables, illustrated.

Plato. *The Last Days of Socrates*. Trans. Hugh Tredennick. New York: Penguin, 2003.
$14. Contains the two dialogues "On Piety" and "The Death of Socrates." Most fifth graders can read this if you take one of the parts.

Coolidge, Olivia. *Caesar's Gallic Wars.* North Haven, CT: Linnet Books, 1998.

> Out of print, but worth hunting for. Based on Julius Caesar's Commentaries, the story of Caesar's wars in Gaul, 58–51 B.C. The only retelling of Caesar we've ever seen, difficult to find, but try your library or buy used.

Vennema, Peter. *Cleopatra,* illus. Diane Stanley. New York: HarperCollins, 1997.

> $7.99. Well-researched and beautifully illustrated life of the Egyptian queen.

Speare, Elizabeth George. *The Bronze Bow.* Boston: Houghton Mifflin Harcourt, 1997.

> $6.95. A Jewish rebel in first-century Galilee encounters the itinerant preacher Jesus. A Newbery Medal winner.

Sutcliff, Rosemary. *Outcast.* New York: Farrar, Straus and Giroux, 1995.

> $10.99. A Roman infant is rescued from a shipwreck and raised in a British village.

————. *The Eagle of the Ninth.* New York: Square Fish, 2011.

> $8.99. In A.D. 119, a Roman legion disappears in the wilds of Britain. Fifteen years later, the commander's son sets out to find the missing company.

————. *The Silver Branch.* New York: Square Fish, 2010.

> $9.99. In the sequel to *The Eagle of the Ninth,* Saxons raid Britain, and the Roman provinces fight for their land.

Medieval/Early Renaissance, 400–1600 (Sixth Grade)
Formal Reading List

Work through the list in this order. Titles can be ordered from any bookstore.

Nye, Robert. *Beowulf: A New Telling.* New York: Laurel Leaf, 1982.

> $5.99. A good (and very exciting) adaptation for sixth graders.

Tolkien, J. R. R. *Sir Gawain and the Green Knight.* New York: Del Rey, 1978.

> $6.99. Not a scholarly standard, but a wonderful verse translation of the

original. Fans of Tolkien will enjoy echoes of *The Hobbit* and *The Lord of the Rings*.

McCaughrean, Geraldine. *The Canterbury Tales.* New York: Puffin, 1997.
$3.99. An accessible prose retelling.

Chaucer, Geoffrey. "Prologue" to *The Canterbury Tales.* Trans. Nevill Coghill. New York: Penguin, 2003.
$11. This edition is in modern English.

Alighieri, Dante. *The Inferno of Dante: A New Verse Translation.* Trans. Robert Pinsky. New York: Farrar, Straus and Giroux, 1996.
$12. We like this free translation by the former poet laureate. Another standard is Allen Mandelbaum's translation (New York: Everyman's Library, 1995). Read Cantos I–V.

Hodges, Margaret. *Saint George and the Dragon.* New York: Little, Brown, 1990.
$8. From Spenser's *The Faerie Queene.* A better rendition is Geraldine McCaughrean's retelling (Doubleday, 1989), but it is out of print and sometimes difficult to find (check your library for it or buy used online).

Malory, Thomas. Versions of *Le Morte d'Arthur:*
Malory himself is pretty thick even for high-school students, but choose one (or more) of the following:

> *The Boy's King Arthur: Sir Thomas Malory's History of King Arthur and His Knights of the Round Table,* edited by Sidney Lanier, original illustrations by N. C. Wyeth (New York: Dover, 2006).
> > $14.95. Pardon the sexist title, but this is a classic adaptation of Malory, and the Wyeth illustrations are spectacular.
> Rosemary Sutcliff, *The Sword and the Circle: King Arthur and the Knights of the Round Table* (New York: Puffin, 1994).
> > $6.99. Paperback retelling of Malory.
> T. H. White, *The Sword in the Stone* (New York: Philomel, 1993).
> > This is the first in T. H. White's four-novel adaptation of Malory. All four are collected together into *The Once and Future King* (New York: Ace, 1987). A classic in its own right. An illustrated version is published by Philomel (1993).

Le Morte d'Arthur, abridged (Minneapolis, MN: Highbridge Audio, 2005).

$34.95. This audiobook version, read by Derek Jacobi, is an excellent introduction to Malory. Order directly from the publisher.

Shakespeare. Begin with one of the following retellings:

Garfield, Leon. *Leon Garfield's Shakespeare Stories.* New York: NYR Children's Collection, 2015.

$24.95. Twenty-one plays beautifully retold, with much of the original dialogue.

Nesbit, E. *Shakespeare's Stories for Young Readers.* New York: Dover, 2006.

$4.99. By the author of *The Railway Children,* clear and readable retellings of twelve plays with direct quotes.

Good readers can then move on to read a full play. Choose one of the following:

Shakespeare, William. Oxford School Shakespeare series. Ed. Roma Gill. New York: Oxford University Press.

$9.95 each.

A Midsummer Night's Dream. 2009.

Henry V. 2003.

Macbeth. 2002.

Supplementary Resources

The Chaucer Coloring Book. Santa Barbara, CA: Bellerophon Books, 1991.

$3.95. Order from Bellerophon Books. Contains the "Prologue" to *The Canterbury Tales* in the original Middle English, along with woodcuts from the earliest published editions. A nice introduction to Middle English.

Chute, Marchette Gaylord. *Stories from Shakespeare.* New York: Meridian Books, 1959.

$16. All thirty-six plays in story form; gives a straightforward plot summary along with famous lines from each play. Good for reading along with the plays themselves.

Colum, Padraic. *Nordic Gods and Heroes,* illus. Willy Pogany. New York: Dover, 1996.

$11.95. Myths rewritten in the style of the Eddas, for young readers; excellent.

Columbus, Christopher. *First Voyage to America: From the Log of the Santa Maria*. New York: Dover, 1991.

$9.95. The actual log, abridged for ages nine to twelve.

de Angeli, Marguerite. *The Door in the Wall*. New York: Laurel Leaf, 1998.

$5.99. A historical novel. The 1950 Newbery winner about a crippled boy who longs to be a knight.

de Trevino, Elizabeth Borton. *I, Juan de Pareja*. New York: Square Fish, 2008.

$7.99. A novel about the painter Velazquez and his African slave.

French, Allen. *The Story of Rolf and the Viking Bow*. Vancouver, WA: Bethlehem Books, 1995.

$15.95. A classic novel (first published around 1900 and still in print) about a young Viking boy's search for justice and his murdered father.

Gray, Elizabeth. *Adam of the Road*. New York: Puffin, 2006.

$6.99. In 1294, a young minstrel searches for his stolen dog—and his father. A Newbery Medal–winning novel.

Green, Robert Lancelyn. *The Adventures of Robin Hood*. New York: Puffin, 2010.

$4.99. Read this classic retelling when you study the Crusades in history.

Kelly, Eric P. *The Trumpeter of Krakow*. New York: Aladdin, 1992.

$6.99. A Newbery Medal winner about a young fifteenth-century Polish boy and a mysterious jewel.

Matthews, John. *Arthur of Albion*, illus. Pavel Tatarnikov. Cambridge, MA: Barefoot Books, 2008.

$12.99. A nice chapter book retelling of Arthurian legends with special attention to England during Arthur's day.

Pyle, Howard.

Howard Pyle wrote a series of modern classics—young adult novels of Arthurian and medieval times. They range from $7.99 to $11.99.

The Merry Adventures of Robin Hood. New York: Dover, 1968.

Otto of the Silver Hand. New York: Dover, 1976.

The Story of King Arthur and His Knights. New York: Sterling, 2005.

The Story of Sir Lancelot and His Companions. New York: Dover, 1991.

The Story of the Champions of the Round Table. New York: Dover, 1968.

The Story of the Grail and the Passing of Arthur. New York: Dover, 1992.

Shakespeare Coloring Book. Santa Barbara, CA: Bellerophon Books, 1985.
$4.95. Historical illustrations of famous scenes. A good memory aid.

Sperry, Armstrong. *Call It Courage*. New York: Simon Pulse, 2008.
$6.99. A novel about Mafatu, the son of a Polynesian chief, who must prove that he isn't a coward.

Sutcliff, Rosemary. *The Lantern Bearers*. New York: Square Fish, 2010.
$9.99. A historical novel. In 450, a Roman soldier in Britain fights against invading Angles and Saxons.

Tarnowska, Wafa'. *The Arabian Nights*, illus. Carole Henaff. Cambridge, MA: Barefoot Books, 2010.
$12.99. A nicely done chapter book retelling of stories from *A Thousand and One Nights*.

Willard, Barbara. *Augustine Came to Kent*. Warsaw, ND: Bethlehem Books, 1996.
$12.95. A historical novel. The story of a Saxon boy who accompanies Augustine on his mission to England.

Late Renaissance/Early Modern, 1600–1850 (Seventh Grade)
Formal Reading List

Work through this list in order. Unless otherwise noted, these are standard editions available at most bookstores or from Amazon.com. Many of the titles can be found in more than one edition. Prices will no longer be noted unless a book is unusually expensive or difficult to find.

We recommend against CreateSpace versions, since these are generally poorly done, badly edited, print-on-demand versions of public domain titles. Instead, look for quality paperback editions from Penguin, Oxford World's Classics, Wordsworth Editions, and other major presses. These have decent typesetting and readable layout.

Miguel de Cervantes, *Don Quixote*, abridged.

Dover Children's Thrift Classics: Adventures of Don Quixote, abridged. New York: Dover, 1999.

Perrault, Charles. *Perrault's Complete Fairy Tales.* Trans. Christopher Betts. Oxford: Oxford University Press, 2010.

Swift, Jonathan. "A Voyage to Lilliput" and "A Voyage to Brobdingnag." From *Gulliver's Travels.*
The Dover Thrift edition (New York: Dover, 1996) is cheapest, but any edition will do.

Bunyan, John. *The Pilgrim's Progress.*
Any edition is fine; Dover and Penguin both produce good paperbacks. You can also use *The Pilgrim's Progress: A Retelling* by Gary D. Schmidt (Grand Rapids, MI: Eerdmans, 1994) if the original seems too difficult.

Defoe, Daniel. *Robinson Crusoe.* New York: Penguin, 2003.
You can also order the hardback with N. C. Wyeth's illustrations (Atheneum, 2015) for $24.99.

Wordsworth, William. *Favorite Poems.*
Try the Dover Thrift edition (New York: Dover, 1992). Be sure to read "We Are Seven," "Lines Written in Early Spring," "Lines Composed a Few Miles above Tintern Abbey," "Lucy Gray," "Composed upon Westminster Bridge, September 3, 1802," and "I Wandered Lonely As a Cloud."

Coleridge, Samuel Taylor. "The Rime of the Ancient Mariner."
Found in most collections. You can buy the Dover Thrift edition of this poem and other works (New York: Dover, 1992).

Irving, Washington. *The Legend of Sleepy Hollow and Rip Van Winkle.* Dover Thrift edition. New York: Dover, 1995.

Browning, Robert. "The Pied Piper of Hamelin."
This is contained in the Dover Thrift edition of Browning, *My Last Duchess and Other Poems* (New York: Dover, 1993).

Grimm, Jacob, and Wilhelm Grimm. *Grimm's Fairy Tales.* New York: Puffin Classics, 2011.

Franklin, Benjamin. "The Way to Wealth." In *Benjamin Franklin: The Autobi-*

ography and Other Writings. New York: Penguin, 2003. The Oxford World's
Classics version (2009) is also a good one.

Rossetti, Christina. "Goblin Market," "A Birthday," Sister Maude," "No,
Thank You, John."
   All are contained in the Dover Thrift edition, *Goblin Market and Other
   Poems* (New York: Dover, 1994).

Carroll, Lewis. *Alice in Wonderland*.
   Any edition.

Austen, Jane. *Pride and Prejudice*.
   Any edition.

Twain, Mark. *The Adventures of Tom Sawyer*.
   Any edition.

Verne, Jules. *20,000 Leagues under the Sea*.
   Any edition.

Dickens, Charles. *A Christmas Carol*.
   Any edition. Make sure you don't get an abridged version by accident—
   this book is often abridged.

Tennyson, Alfred, Lord. "The Lady of Shalott" and "The Charge of the
Light Brigade."
   In any Tennyson collection.

Poe, Edgar Allan. "The Raven."
   In any collection or anthology.

Asbjornsen, Peter Christen. *East o' the Sun and West o' the Moon: Fifty-nine
Norwegian Folk Tales*. New York: Dover Children's Evergreen Classics, 2001.

Douglass, Frederick. *Narrative of the Life of Frederick Douglass, an American
Slave, Written by Himself*.
   Any edition.

Supplementary Resources

Brady, Esther Wood. *Toliver's Secret*. New York: Yearling, 1993.
   A teenaged girl disguises herself as a boy to carry a message from New
   York to the American rebels in New Jersey.

Brink, Carol Ryrie. *Caddie Woodlawn*. New York: Aladdin, 2006.
The novel of a pioneer girl and her family, who have to decide whether to stay in America or return to an inherited title in England.

Collier, James Lincoln. *My Brother Sam Is Dead*. New York: Scholastic, 2005.
The novel of a Connecticut family divided by the Revolutionary War.

Dalgliesh, Alice. *The Courage of Sarah Noble*. New York: Aladdin, 1991.
A Newbery Medal–winning novel about a young girl in the Connecticut wilderness, 1707.

Field, Rachel. *Hitty: Her First Hundred Years*. New York: Aladdin, 1998.
This Newbery winner tells the story of the first hundred years in a doll's life.

Forbes, Esther. *America's Paul Revere*. Boston: Houghton Mifflin Harcourt, 1990.
A novel of the life and adventures of Paul Revere by the Newbery Medal–winning author.

———. *Johnny Tremain*. Boston: Houghton Mifflin Harcourt, 2011.
The classic story of a silversmith's apprentice caught in the Revolutionary War.

Speare, Elizabeth George. *Calico Captive*. Boston: Houghton Mifflin Harcourt, 2001.
The story of a young girl, captured by Indians in 1754 and sold to the French. Based on an actual eighteenth-century diary.

———. *The Sign of the Beaver*. Boston: Houghton Mifflin Harcourt, 2011.
A novel about a boy who learns survival skills from Indians in eighteenth-century Maine.

———. *The Witch of Blackbird Pond*. Boston: Houghton Mifflin Harcourt, 2011.
A Puritan girl in Connecticut makes friends with a suspected witch.

Vernon, Louise. *The Beggar's Bible*. Grand Rapids, MI: Herald Press, 1971.
The biography of Bible translator John Wycliffe.

———. *The Man Who Laid the Egg*. Scottsdale, PA: Herald Press, 1977.

The story of Renaissance scholar Erasmus.

Yates, Elizabeth. *Amos Fortune, Free Man*. New York: Puffin, 1989.
The 1951 Newbery Medal–winning novel about an African prince brought to the United States as a slave.

Modern, 1850–Present (Eighth Grade)
Formal Reading List

These are available in standard editions at bookstores or from Amazon.com. Ebook versions are also available, some of them for free. Read each section in the order listed.

Fiction

Robert Louis Stevenson. *Kidnapped* or *Treasure Island*.
Edward E. Hale. "The Man Without a Country."
Louisa May Alcott. *Little Women*.
Arthur Conan Doyle. Any of the Sherlock Holmes short stories or *The Hound of the Baskervilles*.
Rudyard Kipling. *The Jungle Book*.
H. G. Wells. *The Time Machine* or *The War of the Worlds*.
Jack London. *The Call of the Wild*.
G. K. Chesterton. Any of the Father Brown stories.
Baronness Orczy. *The Scarlet Pimpernel*.
O. Henry. Any of the short stories.
Lucy Maud Montgomery. *Anne of Green Gables*.
Agatha Christie. *Murder on the Orient Express*.
Dorothy Sayers. *Strong Poison*.
Margaret Mitchell. *Gone With the Wind*.
Marjorie Kinnan Rawlings. *The Yearling*.

Poetry

Henry Wadsworth Longfellow. "The Song of Hiawatha."
Robert Frost. "The Road Not Taken."
E. E. Cummings. Collected poems.
Walter de la Mare. *Poems 1919–1934*. Any selections.
Langston Hughes. *The Dream Keeper and Other Poems*. New York: Knopf, 1996.

Drama

Oscar Wilde. *The Importance of Being Earnest.*

George Bernard Shaw. *Pygmalion.*

Arthur Miller. *The Crucible.*

Robert Bolt. *A Man for All Seasons.*

Supplementary Resources

Burnett, Frances Hodgson. *Little Lord Fauntleroy.* New York: Dover, 2002.
A children's classic; worth reading.

———. *A Little Princess.* New York: Puffin, 2014.
Another much-loved classic.

Gipson, Fred. *Old Yeller.* New York: HarperPerennial Modern Classics, 2009.
A fourteen-year-old tries to run the family farm in Texas after the Civil War. (Much better than the movie.)

Hunt, Irene. *Across Five Aprils.* New York: Berkley, 2002.
Jethro Creighton comes of age during the turbulent years of the Civil War.

Keith, Harold. *Rifles for Watie.* New York: HarperTeen, 1987.
A sixteen-year-old chooses sides in the Civil War.

Lowry, Lois. *Number the Stars.* Boston: Houghton Mifflin Harcourt, 2011.
A Newbery Medal winner. A Danish girl and her family work to save their Jewish friends and neighbors from the invading Nazis.

O'Dell, Scott. *Sing Down the Moon.* Boston: Houghton Mifflin Harcourt, 2010.
The story of a Navajo girl captured by Spanish soldiers in 1864.

Taylor, Mildred D. *Roll of Thunder, Hear My Cry.* New York: Puffin, 2004.
A sharecropper's family deals with prejudice and poverty in Depression-era Mississippi.

Ten Boom, Corrie. *The Hiding Place.* New York: Bantam, 1984.
Literary nonfiction; the ten Boom family was arrested for hiding Jews. This is Corrie's first-person account of the concentration camps. May be too intense for some eighth graders.

Wyss, J. D. *The Swiss Family Robinson.* New York: Bantam Classics, 1992.

Reading: Skills

Ask your local librarian for lists of recommended titles for young readers. A good annotated list of books for young readers is found in *Books Children Love* by Elizabeth L. Wilson (Wheaton, IL: Crossway Books, 2002), available at most bookstores.

Also look for these authors, who produced classic tales that have been loved by generations of young readers.

Aiken, Joan
Alexander, Lloyd
Brink, Carol Ryrie
Bulla, Clyde Robert
Burnett, Frances Hodgson
Carroll, Lewis
Cleary, Beverly
Cooper, Susan
de Angeli, Marguerite
Enright, Elizabeth
Estes, Eleanor
Fisher, Dorothy Canfield
George, Jean
Henry, Marguerite
Holling, Holling Clancy
Irving, Washington
Jacques, Brian
Juster, Norton
Kipling, Rudyard
Kjelgaard, Jim
Lawson, Robert
L'Engle, Madeleine
Lewis, C. S. (Narnia series)
Little, Jean
Norton, Mary
Nesbit, E.
O'Brian, Robert C.
O'Dell, Scott
Pratchett, Terry

Sewell, Anna

Sharp, Margery

Sobel, Donald J.

White, E. B.

Wiggin, Kate Douglas

Wilder, Laura Ingalls

Writing

Parents who are not confident with teaching writing may wish to make use of a developed writing curriculum. The programs listed below are compatible with the process we describe for middle-grade writing. They are listed alphabetically.

Bauer, Susan Wise, *Writing With Skill*. Charles City, VA: Well-Trained Mind Press, 2012–14.

> This three-level series was designed to provide a parent-friendly, easy-to-use, step-by-step guide to the writing process outlined in this chapter. Young writers begin by reviewing narration skills, and then progress through outlining (one-, two-, and three-level outlines) and analyzing a number of well-written nonfiction texts. They then model their own compositions (narratives, descriptions, definitions, explanations, and more) on the texts analyzed. Full instructor support in the teacher's guides, including rubrics for evaluation and sample compositions; all texts to be outlined and analyzed are included in the student workbooks. *Writing With Skill* makes it more difficult to integrate writing across the curriculum, but in exchange provides an open-and-go classical writing program.
>
> Young engineers will flourish with this program. Young creative writers will find it frustrating (try Killgallon or Writing & Rhetoric instead).
>
> The first level is best begun in sixth grade or later; for the fifth-grade year, consider one of the other resources listed here, or concentrate on one-level outlining and perfecting narrative summaries. The Killgallon series is a particularly good program to use between *Writing With Ease* and *Writing With Skill;* the initial levels of Writing & Rhetoric can also work well.
>
> After completing Level 3, the student should be prepared to go directly into the Basic Rhetoric recommendations in Chapter 25.

Samples, placement suggestions, and more available on the publisher's website (where you can download the first ten weeks of each year to try out). Online classes making use of this series are offered through the Well-Trained Mind Academy.

Writing With Skill, Level 1: Student Workbook. $28.95.

Writing With Skill, Level 1: Instructor Text. $32.95.

Writing With Skill, Level 2: Student Workbook. $30.95.

Writing With Skill, Level 2: Instructor Text. $34.95.

Writing With Skill, Level 3: Student Workbook. $30.95.

Writing With Skill, Level 3: Instructor Text. $34.95.

Institute for Excellence in Writing series. Atascadero, CA: Institute for Excellence in Writing.

The Institute for Excellence in Writing teaches *parents* how to guide children in writing across the curriculum. Models are used, and students are taught to use basic keyword outlines to write (although they do not outline other works of nonfiction). You progress through the nine-unit course each year, increasing the difficulty as the student matures. IEW can serve as a one-year or multiple-year program.

One caution: De-emphasize IEW's "dress-up" exercises, which teach a stilted and artificial method of varying sentences. The structural part of IEW is much sounder than the stylistic part.

After completing two to four years of work with IEW, the student will be prepared to go either into the Basic Rhetoric recommendations in Chapter 25, or into IEW's advanced program (see Chapter 25, pages 575–576).

Order from IEW. Visit the publishers website for additional options, samples, and placement help.

Teaching Writing: Structure and Style.

Video seminar instructs parents on how to teach writing and provides a syllabus. The package includes nine units, the syllabus, and a student workshop/demo class.

Complete Set (for those teaching grades 2–11). $189.

Killgallon, Don, and Jenny Killgallon. Sentence-Composing Approach series. Portsmouth, NH: Heinemann.

Developed by college writing teacher Don Killgallon and secondary writing teacher Jenny Killgallon, these programmed volumes focus on analyzing and imitating good sentences and good paragraphs from accomplished writers. In line with classical principles of modeling work before asking students to complete it. Answer key is in the back of the worktext. Samples can be viewed at the publisher's website.

Use *Sentence Composing* for the fall and *Paragraphs* for the spring to create an excellent one-year program that can give students enough maturity to move on to one of the other programs listed.

Sentence Composing for Middle School. 1997. $27.50.

Paragraphs for Middle School. 2013. $30.

Kortepeter, Paul. *Writing and Rhetoric: A Creative Approach to the Classical Progymnasmata*. Camp Hill, PA: Classical Academic Press, 2013–14.

$19.95 for each student book and each teacher's edition. CAP's Writing & Rhetoric series brings the classical *progymnasmata* (a set of exercises assigned by ancient and medieval teachers of rhetoric in order to develop their students' persuasive skills) down to the elementary and middle-grade level. We find the *progymnasmata* to be best suited to the high-school years; however, Writing & Rhetoric does teach writing based on models and encourages students to order compositions logically.

Books 1–4 are appropriate for upper elementary and middle-grade writers. Combine with outlining exercises, and note the caveats below. Samples can be viewed on the publisher's website.

Creative writers will enjoy this series; young engineers will find the lack of specific step-by-step guidance frustrating. There is a little too much focus on the structure of fiction, and not quite enough on expository writing, but the series will certainly develop skills in prose writing.

The series currently continues through Book 6. We have listed the entire series for your convenience. Students using this program should complete all available levels before beginning the Basic Rhetoric recommendations for high school; see Chapter 25. Expect to complete the series in ninth or tenth grade.

Writing & Rhetoric, Book 1: Fable.

Writing & Rhetoric, Book 1: Fable, Teacher's Edition.

Fourth grade and above. Analyzing and retelling fables (also recommended in Chapter 5); good for developing basic skills in narrative writing.

Writing & Rhetoric, Book 2: Narrative I .

Writing & Rhetoric, Book 2: Narrative I, Teacher's Edition.

Fifth grade and above. Despite the title, covers parables, dialogues, descriptions, and narrative structure. Plenty of analysis and practice.

Writing & Rhetoric, Book 3: Narrative II.

Writing & Rhetoric, Book 3: Narrative II, Teacher's Edition.

Follows Book 2. Yet more analysis and imitation of narrative structures. *Note:* Lesson 4 asks students to outline a fable. Outlining is *not* an appropriate tool to apply to fiction; stories work differently than expository writing. Skip the outlining exercise.

Writing & Rhetoric, Book 4: Chreia & Proverb.

Writing & Rhetoric, Book 4: Chreia & Proverb, Teacher's Edition.

Focus on proverbs and wise sayings.

Writing & Rhetoric, Book 5: Refutation & Confirmation.

Writing & Rhetoric, Book 5: Refutation & Confirmation, Teacher's Edition.

Confirming or disproving story elements; some outlining practice; comparison and contrast, introductions and conclusions.

Writing & Rhetoric, Book 6: Commonplace.

Writing & Rhetoric, Book 6: Commonplace, Teacher's Edition.

More focus on stating and developing a thesis.

Writing Strands. Challenging Writing Programs for Homeschoolers series. Niles, MI: National Writing Institute.

$20 for each book. The Writing Strands program can be purchased directly from the National Writing Institute or at a small discount from Rainbow Resource Center. The books aren't consumable; you do all the assignments on notebook paper, so you can reuse these books for another child.

Writing Strands is best suited to students who need the writing process broken down into small steps; students who are naturally creative, but resist expository writing; and students who prefer to work independently. Samples can be viewed at the publisher's website. You will want to add outlining practice to the program.

If you used this program in the grammar stage, simply continue on with it now. The entire series consists of seven books: Levels 2 through 7 and the final book, *Writing Exposition*, which contains thirteen lessons that prepare the student for college-writing assignments (story analysis, reaction papers, term papers, evaluations). *Writing Exposition* also reviews logic in writing (propaganda technique), library use, comparison and contrast, use of the first person in formal writing, and the SAT II writing test.

The Writing Strands levels don't necessarily correspond to grade levels; progress through them at a pace natural to the student. If you're just beginning with the program, try Level 4 or 5 for your fifth-grade writer.

The final level of the program, *Writing Exposition*, introduces techniques of rhetoric and will probably take students into the high-school years. After completing *Writing Exposition*, students should move into the Basic Rhetoric recommendations listed in Chapter 25.

Writing Strands 4.

Writing Strands 5.

Writing Strands 6.

Writing Strands 7.

Writing Exposition. Evaluating Writing.

This booklet for parents/teachers reviews common problems and how to fix them. A good parent resource.

19

LOOKING INTO OTHER WORLDS: LATIN AND LANGUAGES

Litterarum radices amarae, fructus dulces.[1]
—Anonymous

SUBJECT: Foreign languages (classical and modern)
TIME REQUIRED: 3 hours or more per week

The middle-grade student learns how her own language works. But that's not the end of her language study. She must also learn how other languages work.

For the middle-grade student, the study of a foreign language becomes an exercise in logic. Every culture puts words together to form thoughts in different ways. Language study is a way to explore these new ways of thinking. To master the syntax (the grammatical structure) of a foreign language is to discover a fresh way of looking at the world. It's become an educational cliché that most European students know several languages, but

---

[1] "The roots of language study are bitter, but the fruits are sweet."

American students generally learn only their own (if that). The classically educated student isn't limited by knowing only the thought patterns of her own language. She also studies the way other cultures express themselves.

Your goal in the middle grades is to expose the student to both ancient and modern languages. The study of Latin can continue, but the fifth- and sixth-grade years are also a fruitful time to introduce the child to a modern spoken language such as Spanish, French, or Japanese. The student is still young enough to develop fluency, but she's already been exposed to grammar and to beginning foreign-language work. (And if you didn't begin foreign language study in the grammar stage, now's the time to start.)

TEACHING OPTIONS

Unless you already know Latin, your fifth grader will rapidly move beyond your ability to teach her. And unless you're already fluent in a modern language, you won't be able to teach that either. You have four basic options for middle-grade language studies.

1. Use a tutor. If you live near a university, you can call the classics or foreign-language departments and ask the department secretaries to recommend a responsible student tutor.[2] Even if the school doesn't offer Latin classes, several foreign-language majors are bound to have had three or four years of high-school Latin. Or one of your local high schools may have a Latin teacher or responsible senior student who would enjoy tutoring. Using a tutor has drawbacks—cost, getting the student to her lesson—as well as advantages: you don't have to keep up with one more subject, and the student gets a break from your teaching style.

2. Use an online tutorial service. Several different reputable online academies offer foreign-language instruction for middle-grade students; we maintain an updated list at www.welltrainedmind.com. When middle-grade students take online courses, parents still need to provide plenty of supervision, support (i.e., helping them schedule

---

[2] See Chapter 45 for caveats about student tutors and advice on finding a reliable one.

and turn in their assignments on time), and instructor interaction. (See Chapter 22 for a few more thoughts on middle-grade students and online classes.)

3. Use a self-teaching course. This is probably your best at-home option for French, Spanish, German, or another modern language. The courses we recommend in the Resources are designed for self-teaching and include pronunciation tapes and conversational practice as well as grammatical instruction and reading drills.

   But don't fool yourself: no self-teaching course is going to develop fluency unless you combine it with Saturday language school (these schools are offered in many different languages by a number of different organizations across the country), daily or weekly conversational interaction, or some other regular practice and reinforcement. (This, incidentally, is why American students don't tend to speak foreign languages; unlike European students who are within a train ride of other countries, most of us don't have regular contact with speakers of other languages. But that doesn't excuse us from our shameful lack of knowledge of Spanish, which should be high on the list of any students who live south of the Mason-Dixon line and of most others who live north of it.)

4. Learn along with your child (perhaps using one of the courses with accompanying instructional DVDs that we recommend below). If your middle-school student can master this material, so can you. You might even consider Saturday school together.

WHICH LANGUAGES, AND WHEN?

We recommend continuing with Latin until the student has mastered a standard (high-school level) second-year Latin course; this can happen any time between sixth and twelfth grade. At that point, the student who's interested in Greek can switch; the student who's not interested at all can quit. Other students should continue on to the reading of actual Latin texts.

Around sixth grade, you can also add a modern foreign language to your studies (or add Latin, if you studied the modern language first).

Unless you have a personal reason for choosing another language, we suggest Spanish as the first modern language. A good first experience with modern-language learning is important. Since Spanish is full of Latinate vocabulary and structures, the student who has already studied Latin won't struggle. And Spanish is rapidly becoming the unofficial second language of the United States. The beginning Spanish student can easily find Spanish signs, directions, instruction manuals, children's books, TV shows, and more to exercise his growing skills. And he'll have more opportunity to converse in Spanish than in other languages.

Other Romance languages—French, Italian, Portuguese—are also Latin-influenced and easier for the Latin student to understand. But if you can arrange for your student to have regular conversational practice in Japanese, Chinese, Polish, Russian, or Vietnamese, add whatever language excites and interests your child.

A caveat: Not all students will have the inclination or time to study two foreign languages, particularly during middle school. At least *some* foreign-language learning is highly beneficial during the logic-stage years, but students who struggle with language arts, or who are heavily invested in STEM subjects and projects, will find the prospect of two languages overwhelming. Use your judgment. You may decide to simply continue on with your current language studies and wait for a second language until high school.

If the student has done *no* language learning up to this point, begin either a modern language (if you have good options for conversational practice) or Latin (if your opportunities for speaking are limited) now; we've recommended resources for both at the end of this chapter. Take the study at the student's natural pace. Two years of a high-school language are required by most university admissions offices, and in most cases admission counselors won't consider a language taken before ninth grade to be high-school level unless the achievement is confirmed through outside testing—national language proficiency exams, AP or SAT II tests. So your goal is to get to ninth grade with a student who is ready to pursue language studies at a high level—not to push students who are still mastering language skills to complete a particular curriculum.

WHEN DO I DO IT?

Ideally, you could study both Latin and a modern foreign language every year, each for three to four hours per week (option 1—see page 488).

We realize, though, that a six- to eight-hour commitment per week to foreign-language studies may not be possible.

Instead, you might want to study both languages—for example, Spanish and Latin—but progress more slowly through each (option 2—see page 488). Study Spanish on Mondays and Tuesdays, Latin on Wednesdays and Thursdays; take two years to go through each Latin book and four years to complete a two-year middle-grade modern language course. (If you're using a language tutor, explain that you only want to go at half speed.) You'll probably find that you don't need the full four years to finish the modern-language courses.

If the student finds two languages overwhelming, you can choose option 3: studying only one language each year, alternating your study (see page 488). To do this, begin your modern-language studies in fifth grade; continue with Latin in sixth grade; go back to your modern-language studies in seventh grade; then do Latin again in eighth grade. This works best if you're studying a Romance language (Spanish, French, or Italian) because the similarities between these languages and Latin will prevent the student from forgetting too much during the "year off." Whatever language you choose, be sure to schedule regular review sessions (every two weeks is good; once a month is minimum) for the student to read over the previous year's lessons. If you're studying Spanish in fifth grade, for example, stop every other Friday and review Latin vocabulary and grammar from the fourth-grade Latin book. If you're studying Latin in sixth grade, use every other Friday to listen to the Spanish tapes and/or read through Spanish lessons from the fifth-grade year. (See our caveat above as you plan, however.)

One caution: language skills tend to disappear if they're not constantly used. Don't simply stop Latin for grades 5 and 6 so that you can study a modern language and then try to pick up Latin again in grade 7. The effects of early exposure will fade almost completely.

SUGGESTED SCHEDULES

Plan on studying at least one foreign language for at least three hours per week. Five to seven hours per week is ideal; you may also choose to study more than one language, using one of the options below.

Option 1: Two Languages Quickly

Modern language	1 hour per day, 3–4 days per week
Latin	1 hour per day, 3–4 days per week

Option 2: Two Languages More Slowly

Modern language	1 hour per day, 2 days per week
Latin	1 hour per day, 2 days per week

Option 3: Two Languages, One at a Time

Fifth grade	Modern language	1 hour per day, 3–4 days per week
Sixth grade	Latin	1 hour per day, 4 days per week; use the fourth day to review modern language studied previous year
Seventh grade	Modern language	1 hour per day, 4 days per week; use the fourth day to review Latin or Greek studied previous year
Eighth grade	Latin	1 hour per day, 4 days per week; use the fourth day to review modern language studied previous year

RESOURCES

Most books can be obtained from any bookseller or library; most curricula can be bought directly from the publisher or from a major home-school supplier such as Rainbow Resource Center. Contact information for publishers and suppliers can be found at www.welltrainedmind.com. If availability is limited, we have noted it. Remember that additional curricula choices and more can be found at www.well trainedmind.com. Prices change constantly, but we have included 2016 pricing to give an idea of affordability.

Latin

Curricula

The following programs are listed in order, from the simplest to the most advanced.

The Latin program you choose for the logic-stage years will depend in part on what you decided to use in the grammar stage.

If you chose to work through *Prima Latina* or *The Big Book of Lively Latin*, progress on to *Latina Christiana I*. After completing *Latina I*, the student can continue on to *First Form Latin*; *First* through *Fourth Form Latin* are essentially a fleshed-out version of the first level of Henle's Latin, a classic high-school course. According to the publisher, *Latina Christiana II* and *First Form Latin* overlap so much that it isn't necessary to complete *II* before moving on. If you began with *Song School Latin* and progressed to *Latin for Children Primer A*, or simply began with *Latin for Children Primer A*, you can continue on with *Primer B* and *Primer C*. *Primer C* is then followed by *Latin Alive!*

If you begin Latin for the first time in fifth or sixth grade, you may start directly into *Latina Christiana I* and progress on to *First Form Latin*. Or you may begin with *Latin for Children Primer A* and progress through the next two levels, and from there into *Latin Alive!*

If you begin Latin in seventh grade or later, *Latina Christiana* and *Latin for Children* will seem too elementary. You may begin directly with *First Form Latin* or *Latin Alive!* An alternative is *The Latin Road to English Grammar*, a program designed for parents and students who know no Latin. This text makes no assumption about skills and also reviews English grammar. Start with *The Latin Road to English Grammar, Volume 1* in seventh grade and continue on with *Volume 2* in eighth grade.

Latin for Children. Camp Hill, PA: Classical Academic Press.
> This primer begins on a fourth- to fifth-grade level with *Primer A*, and continues on to *Primer B* and *Primer C* (designed to take you through grades 6 and 7). An online supplement provides additional games and opportunities for reinforcement. Order from Classical Academic Press. Samples are available at the publisher's website.
> > Follow with *Latin Alive!* Each program set includes a student workbook, answer key, DVD and CD set, activity book, and a simple reader.
> > *Latin for Children Primer A*. $99.95.
> > *Latin for Children Primer B*. $114.95.
> > *Latin for Children Primer C*. $114.95.

Lowe, Cheryl. *Latina Christiana: An Introduction to Christian Latin*. Louisville, KY: Memoria Press, 2001.
> Order from Memoria Press.
> > *Latina Christiana I*.
> > > *Basic Set*. $41.95.

Student book, teacher guide, pronunciation CD.

Complete Set. $98.90.

Student book, teacher guide, pronunciation CD, instructional DVDs, flash cards.

Latina Christiana II.

Basic Set. $41.95.

Student book, teacher guide, pronunciation CD.

Complete Set. $98.90.

Student book, teacher guide, pronunciation CD, instructional DVDs, flash cards.

Beers, Barbara. *The Latin Road to English Grammar, Volume I.* Redding, CA: Schola Publications.

The curriculum guide claims that you don't have to study English grammar while using the program. We think this is a mistake; the *Latin Road* is an excellent Latin program, but doesn't cover the grammar needed to develop excellent English writing skills.

Order from the publisher; combination packages are offered at a discount.

Volume I.

Teacher Curriculum Set. $199.

Complete Student Package. $63.95.

Teacher Training DVDs. $129.

Extra parent support for the truly intimidated.

Volume II.

Teacher Curriculum Set. $199.

Complete Student Package. $63.95.

Teacher Training DVDs. $129.

Form Latin series. Louisville, KY: Memoria Press.

This series, designed to follow *Latina Christiana I,* uses ecclesiastical pronunciation and has a heavy emphasis on traditional grammar instruction. Best for grades 7 and up unless used as a follow-up to *Latin Christiana.* Each basic set contains a student text and workbook, a teacher manual and key, quizzes and tests, and a pronunciation CD. The complete sets add instructional DVDs and flash card sets.

Most students will not reach the final level, *Fourth Form,* until high school.

First Form Latin Set. $65.

First Form Latin Complete Set. $125.

Second Form Latin Set. $65.

Second Form Latin Complete Set. $125.

Third Form Latin Set. $65.

Third Form Latin Complete Set. $125.

Fourth Form Latin Set. $65.

Fourth Form Latin Complete Set. $125.

Latin Alive! Camp Hill, PA: Classical Academic Press.

Designed to follow CAP's *Latin for Children, Latin Alive!* can be started as soon as *Latin for Children* is completed; students who have not done *Latin for Children* can begin the first *Latin Alive!* book in seventh grade. According to the publisher, completion of all four levels (not completed until high school) will prepare students for the National Latin Exam.

Order from the publisher. Each "program" level in Books 1–3 includes a student text with exercises, teacher's edition with answers and additional explanations, more than fifteen hours of DVD lessons, a pronunciation CD, and access to the program website, with quizzes, readings, games, and more.

Latin Alive! Book 1 Program. $139.95.

Latin Alive! Book 2 Program. $139.95.

Latin Alive! Book 3 Program. $139.95.

Latin Alive! Book 4 Program.

Reader. $29.95.

Teacher's Edition. $29.95.

Supplementary Resources

Lundquist, Joegil. *English from the Roots Up,* Vol. 1. Medina, WA: Literacy Unlimited, 1989.

———. *English from the Roots Up,* Vol. 2. Seattle, WA: Cune Press, 2003. $29.95 each. Vocabulary-building books built around Greek and Latin root words. Each page gives the original definition of the root along with related English words that incorporate the root word. Use this along with Latin to develop English vocabulary (and to teach your student why Latin is important).

Schlosser, Franz. *Latine Cantemus: Cantica Popularia Latine Reddita.* Wauconda, IL: Bolchazy-Carducci Publishers, 1996.

$10. Order from Bolchazy-Carducci. A songbook with nursery rhymes, familiar folk songs, and Christmas carols, all translated into Latin; a good way to begin to develop fluency.

Seuss, Dr., Jennifer Morrish Tunberg, and Terence O. Tunberg. *Cattus Petasatus: The Cat in the Hat in Latin.* Wauconda, IL: Bolchazy-Carducci Publishers, 2000.

$31. Order from Bolchazy-Carducci.

————. *Quomodo Invidiosulus Nomine Grinchus: How the Grinch Stole Christmas in Latin.* Wauconda, IL: Bolchazy-Carducci Publishers, 1998.

$25. Order from Bolchazy-Carducci.

————. *Virent Ova! Viret Perna! Green Eggs and Ham in Latin.* Wauconda, IL: Bolchazy-Carducci Publishers, 2003.

$26.75. Order from Bolchazy-Carducci.

Modern Languages

Most reasonably effective modern language programs are now web-based, giving students better access to conversational resources, drills, interactive exercises, etc. Visit welltrainedmind.com for links to the following programs and links to additional interactive live instruction options.

Duolingo. Pittsburgh, PA: Duolingo.

Thirteen different languages, including Esperanto and Irish, taught through interactive online modules. At the moment, a free program; most grammar and writing instruction is done through quick "tip sheets" that will be hard for middle-grade students to absorb, but the aural and oral instruction is very well done.

Visit the Duolingo website for online tutorials and language options.

Fluenz. Miami Beach, FL: Fluenz, Inc.

A full program that can be downloaded, with a substantial online component. Grammar, pronunciation, online taught sessions. Currently six languages available. Visit the website for pricing and options.

Rosetta Stone Homeschool. Harrisonburg, VA: Rosetta Stone.

An interactive computer-based language-learning program that uses photos, graphics, and interactive lessons to encourage students to think in a foreign language. The home-school editions include both student materials and parent resources, including lessons plans, multiple paths emphasizing different skills (grammar, speech, reading, etc.), tests, and the ability to generate reports. Visit the Rosetta Stone website for pricing options and the twenty-five available language programs. (Actually twenty-three for English speakers, since Rosetta Stone classifies American English and British English as two different languages.)

20

AWAY WITH ABUSIVE
FALLACIES!
RELIGION

Homo sine religione sic ut equus sine freno.[1]
—Medieval saying

In history, your middle-grade student will continually ask why. Why was that war fought? Why did this statesman make this decision? Why did the Crusades dominate the religious life of medieval Europe?

These questions cannot be answered unless you take the role of religion in public life seriously. People of faith have influenced history at every turn. Until the student is willing to examine honestly and soberly the claims of religion in the history of mankind, his study will be incomplete.

In the effort to offend no one, the public schools have managed to offend practically everyone—either by leaving religion and ethics out of curricula altogether or by teaching them in a way that satisfies neither believers nor skeptics. In sympathy, we'll say that the public schools are in an impossible situation. They are legally bound to avoid the appearance

[1] "Man without religion is like a horse without a bridle."

of promoting one religion over another. And in a mixed classroom, how can you take one religion seriously without antagonizing those who don't share it? The inevitable result is summed up by a character in P. D. James's mystery *Original Sin:*

> There were a dozen different religions among the children at Ancroft Comprehensive. We seemed always to be celebrating some kind of feast or ceremony. Usually it required making a noise and dressing up. The official line was that all religions were equally important. I must say that the result was to leave me with the conviction that they were equally unimportant.[2]

When you're instructing your own child, you have two tasks with regard to religion: to teach your own convictions with honesty and diligence, and to study the ways in which other faiths have changed the human landscape.

Only you and your religious community can do the first. As for the second, in high school the student will make a formal study of ethics. For middle school, we suggest you simply keep the following guidelines in mind as you do your history, science, and literature.

1. Include religious works in your study of primary sources. As you progress through history, stop and read the Old and New Testaments; they are foundational to Western thought and ought to be treated as serious philosophical documents.
2. Read about major faiths that have shaped our world: Judaism, Buddhism, Hinduism, Christianity, Islam. Compare them. Ask the most basic questions about them: What do these religions say about the nature of man? the nature of God? the purpose of living?
3. As you choose biographies for history reading, try to seek out works about those who have changed people's minds and ways of living— not only religious figures such as Confucius and Muhammad, but the theologians and prophets who followed them: among many, many others, Augustine, Anselm, Abraham ibn Ezra, Ibn Rushd (Averroes), Francis of Assisi, Julian of Norwich, Ignatius of Loyola, Martin Luther, the Dalai Lamas.

[2] P. D. James, *Original Sin* (New York: Warner, 1994), p. 303.

4. Watch out for logical fallacies. When writers start talking about religion—especially in books for young children—fallacies abound. Keep your eyes open for the three most common errors: chronological snobbery, which assumes that people long ago were more stupid than people today ("the Virgin Birth was accepted by theologians of the Middle Ages, but no modern scholar can seriously believe in it"); the black-and-white fallacy, which assumes that there can be no alternatives between extreme positions ("the Catholic Church tried Galileo for heresy because he said the earth wasn't at the center of the universe; therefore the churchmen involved were either blind to the truth, or else hypocritically protecting their own power");[3] and the poisoning-the-well fallacy, which discredits an argument by attacking its source rather than its content ("that legislator is a religious man, so his opinions are obviously biased by his religious beliefs").

5. Don't ignore the deep religious faith held by many of the West's greatest scientists. The theism of scientists and mathematicians, from Pascal to Einstein, deeply affected their professional and intellectual pursuits.

6. Finally, discuss the moral and ethical questions of history with your middle-grade student. Don't shy away from the errors made by religious men and women (adherents to every faith have mounted a version of Holy War at some point), but don't identify the mistakes of religious figures with the requirements of faith itself.

   You might start by reading together and discussing stories that bring the rewards and costs of ethical behavior to the forefront. We've suggested a few options at the end of this chapter; choose an evening once a week to read and talk—as a family—about ethical issues that come up. This will serve as great preparation for the formal study of ethics in high school.

We've also listed a couple of beginning introductions to world religions. As you work through history, pay attention to the development of religious

---

[3] The alternative is that the churchmen were honestly trying to work out a theological picture of the universe that made proper reference to scientific discovery—something they eventually did manage to do.

faiths and practices across the world. Without this, the study of the human experience is incomplete.

RESOURCES

These books are easily available through any bookstore or your local library.

Bowker, John. *World Religions: The Great Faiths Explored & Explained.* New York: Dorling Kindersley, 2006.

The Church History Time Line. Camino, CA: Brimwood Press.
$27. Order from Tools for Young Historians. Six-foot wall time line to accompany your regular history time line; shows the branching off of the Christian church into its multiple denominations as history progresses.

Greer, Colin, and Herbert Kohl, eds. *A Call to Character: A Family Treasury of Stories, Poems, Plays, Proverbs, and Fables to Guide the Development of Values for You and Your Children.* New York: Harper Perennial, 1997.

Guroian, Vigen. *Tending the Heart of Virtue: How Classic Stories Awaken a Child's Moral Imagination.* New York: Oxford University Press, 2002.

Kilpatrick, William. *Books That Build Character: A Guide to Teaching Your Child Moral Values through Stories.* New York: Touchstone, 1994.

Novak, Philip. *The World's Wisdom: Sacred Texts of the World's Religions.* San Francisco, CA: HarperOne, 1994.
A good and accessible way to look at primary sources for religious belief.

Stack, Peggy Fletcher, and Kathleen Peterson. *A World of Faith*, 2nd ed. Salt Lake City, UT: Signature Books, 2001.

21

THE HISTORY OF CREATIVITY:
ART AND MUSIC

Music creates order out of chaos; for rhythm imposes unanimity upon the divergent, melody imposes continuity upon the disjointed, and harmony imposes compatibility upon the incongruous.

—Yehudi Menuhin

SUBJECT: **Art and music**

TIME REQUIRED: **1 to 2 hours or more, once per week per subject**

The classical education is distinguished by its emphasis on fine arts—not necessarily performance (although classical education has traditionally included drawing as a foundational skill), but certainly appreciation and participation.

You started this process in the grammar stage. The young child studied art by looking at it and music by listening to it.

Now, as the student's mind matures, you'll tie this appreciation more closely to history. She'll study artists and musicians when she encounters them in her history readings; she'll enter birth and death dates and the dates of great artistic achievements on the time line.

As with other subjects, art and music will be subjected to analysis during the logic stage. Your middle-grade student will learn about the basic structure of musical pieces, the differences among the instruments of the orchestra, the way paints and other artistic media are used, and the different art movements and their practitioners.

Plan on keeping the same schedule you used during the elementary years. Reserve a one- to two-hour period once a week for music study; reserve the same amount of time on another day for art. In Chapter 12, we suggested the option of scheduling only one period per week and alternating the study of art and music. Now we strongly encourage you to make time for both subjects each week. Remember, much of this work can be done independently by the student. Your job is to supervise and provide resources.

The study of art and music is a good late-afternoon or early-evening project. You might schedule art appreciation for Mondays from 3:30 to 5:00 and music appreciation for Thursdays from 3:30 to 5:00. Or make it an after-dinner assignment, to be completed between 7:00 and 8:30 two evenings per week.

ART

The study of art is twofold: practicing the actual skills of art (drawing, painting, modeling), and learning to understand and appreciate the works of great artists.

You should alternate art skills and art appreciation. During the first week, spend one to one and a half hours on art projects; during the second week, use the time to study paintings and artists.

Art Skills

Art skills fall into three basic categories—drawing, painting, and modeling. During the logic stage, try to spend some time in each category. You can divide each year into three sections (if you're doing art lessons every other week, you'll have approximately eighteen lessons; you'll be able to divide the lessons into six drawing lessons, six painting lessons, and six modeling lessons). Or spend a year on each skill, allowing the child to return in the fourth year to her favorite one. Always begin with drawing, progress to painting, and finish up with modeling.

Your goal isn't to turn out a polished artist. You just want to introduce the child to the basic techniques and possibilities of art. With any luck, her interest will be sparked, and she'll continue working on her own time. But even if this doesn't happen, she'll have gained valuable and increasingly rare skills in a basic human activity.

In Resources, we have listed several basic texts suitable for middle-school instruction in drawing, painting, and modeling, along with additional ideas for drawing, painting, and modeling projects.

Art Appreciation

Let your study of history guide your study of art. Whenever the student comes across the name of a great artist during her history readings, she should jot it down. During art-appreciation sessions, she'll follow a four-step process. She will

1. read about the artists she's encountered in history during the previous two weeks,
2. enter the birth and death dates of each artist on the history time line,
3. prepare a brief biographical sketch for each artist and file it in the history notebook under Great Men and Women,
4. spend some time looking at, reading about, and coloring the work of the artists under study.

During this time, the student can use either art books that treat a single artist, or books that cover an entire school. There's no need for the student to write about what she's learning, but she should enter on her time line the dates of famous works of art (the completion of the Sistine Chapel ceiling or the year the *Mona Lisa* was finished). You can be flexible about art appreciation. If the student wants to spend some time learning more about a particular school of painting, don't insist that she read biographies instead.

At the end of this chapter, we've listed a number of art books for young people that include both interesting text and full-color reproductions of paintings. Use them alongside your other historical resources when you study history.

Because artists often go unmentioned in history texts, a reference list follows below. This isn't meant to be exhaustive, merely to provide you with a basic skeleton for your study of art history.

Giovanni Cimabue (1240–1301)
Giotto di Bondone (1266–1337)
Hieronymus Bosch (1450–1516)
Albrecht Dürer (1471–1528)
Michelangelo Buonarroti (1475–1564)
Titian (1477–1576)
Raphael (1483–1520)
Giorgio Vasari (1511–1574)
Tintoretto (1518–1594)
Peter Brueghel (1525–1569)
Peter Paul Rubens (1577–1640)
Rembrandt van Rijn (1606–1669)
Gerrit Dou (1613–1675)
Jan Vermeer (1632–1675)
Antoine Watteau (1684–1721)
William Hogarth (1697–1764)
Joshua Reynolds (1723–1792)
George Stubbs (1724–1806)
Jean Honoré Fragonard (1732–1806)
Benjamin West (1732–1820)
Jacques-Louis David (1748–1825)
Gilbert Stuart (1755–1828)
William Blake (1757–1827)
Joseph Mallord William Turner (1775–1851)
John Constable (1776–1837)
Jean-Auguste-Dominique Ingres (1780–1867)
John James Audubon (1785–1851)
Honoré Daumier (1808–1879)
Jean Francois Millet (1814–1874)
John Ruskin (1819–1900)
Carl Bloch (1834–1890)

Edgar Degas (1834–1917)

James Abbott McNeill Whistler (1834–1903)

Henri Fantin-Latour (1836–1904)

Winslow Homer (1836–1910)

Paul Cézanne (1839–1906)

Claude Monet (1840–1926)

Berthe Morisot (1841–1895)

Pierre Auguste Renoir (1841–1919)

Mary Cassatt (1844–1926)

Vincent Van Gogh (1853–1890)

John Singer Sargent (1856–1925)

Frederic Remington (1861–1909)

Edvard Munch (1863–1944)

Charles Marion Russell (1864–1926)

Emil Nolde (1867–1956)

Kathe Kollwitz (1867–1945)

Henri Matisse (1869–1954)

Georges Rouault (1871–1958)

Raoul Dufy (1877–1953)

André Derain (1880–1954)

Edward Hopper (1882–1967)

Georgia O'Keeffe (1887–1986)

Grant Wood (1892–1942)

Norman Rockwell (1894–1978)

Frida Kahlo (1907–1954)

MUSIC

Music Skills

If time and your budget make it possible—and if the child shows an interest—private music lessons are great. We think that every student should have two years of piano lessons early in his academic career. After two years, he can quit, switch to another instrument, or keep going. Consult friends and your local newspaper to find private music teachers; if you live near a university or community college, you can call the music department for recommendations.

Jessie adds—from years of experience with kids and music lessons—that forcing a reluctant child to keep taking lessons for more than two years is pointless. If interest hasn't developed after two years of study, let the student change instruments or turn his attention to other things.

Music Appreciation

Whether or not the student is taking music lessons, he should spend one and a half to two hours every week doing music appreciation. This time should involve the study of composers' lives, as well as an introduction to musical instruments and musical forms.

Reading about the lives of composers (and musicians) should be part of the study of history. Composers tend to get shorted in history texts, so we've supplied a reference list below. Make an effort to read biographies of these musical greats at the appropriate point in your chronological history study. (This is not intended to be an exhaustive list, merely a guide; nor do you have to read about everyone on it. Pick and choose.) Specific titles and series are suggested at the end of this chapter, but your library will yield others; look in the Junior Biography section, or ask your librarian for help. If you can't find a biography, at least look the musician up in an encyclopedia and make a brief time-line entry.

John Dunstable (1390–1453)
Guillaume Dufay (1400–1474)
Thomas Tallis (1505–1585)
Giovanni Pierluigi da Palestrina (1525–1594)
Michael Praetorius (1571–1621)
Henry Purcell (1659–1695)
Antonio Vivaldi (1678–1741)
Georg Philipp Telemann (1681–1767)
Johann Sebastian Bach (1685–1750)
Domenico Scarlatti (1685–1757)
George Frederic Handel (1685–1759)
Franz Joseph Haydn (1732–1809)
Wolfgang Amadeus Mozart (1756–1791)
Ludwig van Beethoven (1770–1827)
Niccolò Paganini (1782–1840)

Antonio Rossini (1792–1868)

Franz Schubert (1797–1828)

Hector Berlioz (1803–1869)

Felix Mendelssohn (1809–1847)

Frederic Chopin (1810–1849)

Robert Schumann (1810–1856)

Franz Liszt (1811–1886)

Richard Wagner (1813–1883)

Giuseppe Verdi (1813–1910)

Anton Bruckner (1824–1896)

Johannes Brahms (1833–1897)

George Bizet (1838–1875)

Piotr Ilyich Tchaikovsky (1840–1893)

Antonin Dvořák (1841–1904)

Arthur Sullivan (1842–1900)

Edvard Grieg (1843–1907)

Edward William Elgar (1857–1934)

Giacomo Puccini (1858–1924)

Gustav Mahler (1860–1911)

Claude Debussy (1862–1918)

Richard Strauss (1864–1949)

Jean Sibelius (1865–1957)

Ralph Vaughan Williams (1872–1958)

Sergei Vasilievich Rachmaninoff (1873–1943)

Gustav Holst (1874–1934)

Arnold Schoenberg (1874–1951)

Maurice Ravel (1875–1937)

Ottorino Respighi (1879–1936)

Igor Stravinsky (1882–1971)

Sergei Prokofiev (1891–1953)

Dimitri Shostakovich (1906–1975)

Samuel Barber (1910–1981)

Gian Carlo Menotti (1911–2007)

John Cage (1912–1992)

Benjamin Britten (1913–1976)

Leonard Bernstein (1918–1990)

Kenneth Leighton (1929–1988)

Because the study of composers' lives will take place mostly in the third and fourth years of history (from 1600 on, seventh and eighth grades), fifth and sixth grades are the perfect time to concentrate on appreciating musical forms, the instruments of the orchestra. We've suggested several guides at the end of this chapter.

The student should spend his time reading and listening. Writing about music is difficult, and there's no need for the beginning listener to write a summary unless he wants to. Put any dates mentioned in the resources on the history time line.

Beginning in sixth grade, the student can also begin to listen to music from the periods studied in history: medieval and early Renaissance music (sixth grade), music of the late Renaissance, Baroque, and classical periods (seventh grade), and music of the Romantic and modern periods (eighth grade). As in art appreciation, whenever the student encounters a great composer in his history reading, he should jot down the name. During music appreciation, he should record the birth and death dates on the time line, read a brief biography, and spend the rest of his music-appreciation period listening to the composer's works. (Again, plan on making use of your library's collection.)

Although you should generally try to keep music appreciation in step with history reading, don't worry if you get a little behind or ahead. When the student encounters a major musical figure—J. S. Bach, Handel, Mozart, Schubert—on the music time line, he can spend several weeks on each figure, even as he's going forward with his history reading.

SUGGESTED SCHEDULES
Sample Schedules

| Fifth grade | Mondays, 1–2 hours | Alternate art projects with studying ancient art. |
| | Thursdays, 1–2 hours | Study the orchestra and its instruments. |

Sixth grade	Mondays, 1–2 hours	Alternate art projects with making biographical pages and studying the works of medieval and early Renaissance artists; enter dates on time line.
	Thursdays, 1–2 hours	Listen to medieval and early Renaissance music; make biographical pages for musicians; enter dates on time line.
Seventh grade	Mondays, 1–2 hours	Alternate art projects with making biographical pages and studying the works of artists from the late Renaissance through the early modern periods; enter dates on time line.
	Thursdays, 1–2 hours	Listen to late Renaissance, Baroque, and classical music; make biographical pages for musicians; enter dates on time line.
Eighth grade	Mondays, 1–2 hours	Alternate art projects with making biographical pages and studying the works of modern artists; enter dates on time line.
	Thursdays, 1–2 hours	Listen to Romantic and modern music, including musical theater and light opera; make biographical pages for musicians; enter dates on time line.

RESOURCES

Most books can be obtained from any bookseller or library; most curricula can be bought directly from the publisher or from a major home-school supplier such as

Rainbow Resource Center. Contact information for publishers and suppliers can be found at www.welltrainedmind.com. Remember that additional curricula choices and more can be found at www.welltrainedmind.com. Prices change constantly, but we have included 2016 pricing to give an idea of affordability.

Art Skills

Basic Texts

Consider using one of the following as a basic spine for developing art skills.

Drawing

Artistic Pursuits: The Curriculum for Creativity, rev. ed. Arvada, CO: Artistic Pursuits, 2013.

A family-friendly art skills curriculum, with some art appreciation included. We recommended the earlier levels of this program for the elementary grades; continue on with it, or start with the Elementary series in grade 5 or the Middle School series in grade 6 or above. Order from Artistic Pursuits; extensive samples are available at the publisher's website. The books are $47.95 each.

Elementary 4–5 Book One: The Elements of Art and Composition.
Elementary 4–5 Book Two: Color and Composition.
Middle School 6–8 Book One: The Elements of Art and Composition.
Middle School 6–8 Book Two: Color and Composition.

Art supplies can be purchased from one of several art supply companies (links and lists for each book are provided on the Artistic Pursuits website) or in a preassembled kit.

Elementary 4–5 Pack One. $45.
Elementary 4–5 Pack Two. $66.
Middle School Pack One. $54.
Middle School Pack Two. $72.

Edwards, Betty. *Drawing on the Right Side of the Brain: The Definitive 4th Edition.* New York: Tarcher, 2012.

$19.95.

———. *New Drawing on the Right Side of the Brain Workbook: Guided Practice in the Five Basic Skills of Drawing.* New York: Tarcher, 2002.

$18.95. This classic book/workbook combo teaches logical drawing skills, perfect for the middle-grade student. Work progressively through the lessons in the time that you've scheduled. When you've finished, you can move on to any of the drawing projects (colored pencil, calligraphy, portrait drawing, and so forth) listed at the end of the chapter.

Painting

Start painting with watercolors, which are readily available and easy to clean up, and progress to acrylics if the student is interested. Beginning watercolor and acrylics books abound; you can also find instructional DVDs at your library and more instruction on YouTube. The books below are good starting places. Some painting instruction is also provided in the Artistic Pursuits curriculum listed above.

Powell, William F. *The Art of Watercolor.* Laguna Hills, CA: Walter Foster, 2004.
$19.95.

The Art of Acrylic Painting. Laguna Hills, CA: Walter Foster, 2005.
$19.95.

Modeling

Use one or more of the following, depending on the student's interest. They are listed in order of difficulty. Some projects may require simple modeling tools, easily located at Amazon or at a local craft store. Sculpey polymer clay also required.

Carlson, Maureen. *Clay Characters for Kids.* Cincinnati, OH: North Lights Books, 2003.
$12.99.

————. *How to Make Clay Characters.* Cincinnati, OH: North Light Books, 1997.
$22.99.

Dewey, Katherine. *Creating Life-Like Animals in Polymer Clay.* Cincinnati, OH: North Light Books, 2000.
$22.99.

————. *Creating Lifelike Figures in Polymer Clay: Tools and Techniques for Sculpting Realistic Figures.* New York: Watson-Guptill, 2008.
$21.99.

Sculpey, Elk Grove Village, IL: Polyform Products.
Order from Rainbow Resource Center or from Polyform Products.
Sculpey is an easy-to-work clay that fires in a regular oven in twenty minutes without shrinking. Many more colors and options available online.
1 lb. White Block. $8.24
8 lb. White Block. $54.22
Liquid Sculpey 2 oz. $8.60
Liquid Sculpey 8 oz. $13.68
Sculpey III Sampler. $28.18
Sculpey Bake & Bend. $18.26
Sculpey Glaze–Glossy 1 oz.: $3.88
Sculpey Glaze–Satin 1 oz.: $3.88

Supplementary Resources

Use these for additional project ideas.

Draw Today kits. Laguna Hills, CA: Walter Foster Publishing.
Order from Walter Foster directly. The kits offer step-by-step instruction in classical drawing technique. Each kit includes all supplies. Creator Walter Foster includes a toll-free 800 number to call if you have specific questions.

Blair, Preston. *Cartoon Animation.* 1994. $24.95.

Butkus, Michael, William F. Powell, and Mia Tavonatti. *Pencil Drawing Kit.* 2013. $19.99.

Newhall, Arthur, and Eugene Metcalf. *Calligraphy Kit.* 2014. $19.99.

Stoddard, Joseph. *Watercolor Painting Kit.* 2012. $19.99.

Cassidy, John, and Quentin Blake. *Drawing for the Artistically Undiscovered.* Palo Alto, CA: Klutz, 1999.
$19.95. A whole different approach to drawing, using Quentin Blake's scribble-style drawings.

Kistler, Mark. *Mark Kistler's Draw Squad.* New York: Touchstone, 1988.
$20. Thirty enjoyable lessons in drawing basics. Mark Kistler's "Draw Squad" is also a TV show; he has videos and many other resources available.

Schwake, Susan, and Rainer Schwake. *Art Lab for Kids: 52 Creative Adven-*

tures in Drawing, Painting, Printmaking, Paper, and Mixed Media for Budding Artists of All Ages. Beverly, MA: Quarry Books, 2012.

$22.99. A year's worth of well-designed projects that go beyond drawing and painting.

The Virtual Instructor.

Video lessons, live instruction, and full courses are available at The Virtual instructor's website. Visit welltrainedmind.com for live links.

Art Appreciation

Basic Texts

Hodge, Susie. *Ancient Art* series, 2nd ed. (Art in History). Chicago: Heinemann Library, 2006.

$7.99 each. This series offers a good introduction to the appreciation of ancient art.

Ancient Egyptian Art.

Ancient Greek Art.

Ancient Roman Art.

Prehistoric Art.

Art That Changed the World. New York: DK Publishing, 2013.

$40. Great works of art, entire artistic schools, and well-known artists, all put into historical context and placed on a time line. Lovely illustrations; ideal for logic-stage study.

Martin, Mary, and Steve Zorn. *Start Exploring Masterpieces: A Fact-Filled Coloring Book.* Philadelphia, PA: Running Press, 2011.

$11.95. Sixty famous paintings, done in detail for you to color. The book includes the story behind each painting. A great way to learn about particular works. The work is best done with good-quality colored pencils.

Wilkins, David G. *The Collins Big Book of Art: From Cave Art to Pop Art.* New York: HarperDesign, 2005.

$39.95. An excellent family reference book: a chronological survey of masterpieces from around the world, with explanations of major movements, styles, and themes. The text may be too difficult for some middle-grade students, but all can benefit from the photographs.

Supplementary Resources

Dillon, Patrick. *The Story of Buildings: From the Pyramids to the Sydney Opera House and Beyond*, illus. Stephen Biesty. Somerville, MA: Candlewick Press, 2014.

> $19.99. A fascinating introduction to architecture, with detailed, elaborate cross-section illustrations.

The Famous Artists series. New York: Barron's Educational Series, 1994.

> $8.99 for each. These provide a neat 32-page introduction to each artist, his life, and his major works. Color reproductions.
>
> Green, Jen, et al. *Michelangelo.*
>
> Hughes, Andrew S. *Van Gogh.*
>
> Mason, Antony. *Cézanne.*
>
> ———. *Leonardo da Vinci.*
>
> ———. *Matisse.*
>
> ———. *Monet.*

The Great Names biography series. Broomall, PA: Mason Crest Publishers.

> $19.95 each. Try your library for this series, which is written on a higher level than the Getting to Know series listed below.
>
> Bowen, Richard. *Van Gogh.* 2014.
>
> Cook, Diane. *Henri Toulouse-Lautrec.* 2003.
>
> ———. *Michelangelo: Renaissance Artist.* 2013.
>
> ———. *Paul Gauguin.* 2013.
>
> January, Brendan. *Da Vinci: Renaissance Painter.* 2014.

Krull, Kathleen. *Lives of the Artists: Masterpieces, Messes (and What the Neighbors Thought)*, illus. Kathryn Hewitt. New York: HMH, 2014.

> $8.99. A fun biography resource full of interesting (and obscure) snippets. (You may want to pre-read, since the lives of some of these artists were, to say the least, colorful.)

Strickland, Carol. *The Illustrated Timeline of Art History: A Crash Course in Words & Pictures.* New York: Sterling, 2006.

> $12.95. Beautifully illustrated time line of painting, sculpture, and architecture, from cave paintings all the way up to the present.

Taschen Basic Art series. Los Angeles: Taschen.

> $9.99 each. This series of 96-page books provides full-page annotated

illustrations, guiding readers into an understanding of specific artists and their styles. More difficult than the Getting to Know series listed below. Some are out of print, but worth checking your library for, or buying used.

Baur, Eva Gesine, and Ingo F. Walther. *Rococo.* 2007.

Becks-Malorny, Ulrike. *James Ensor, 1860–1949: Masks, Death, and the Sea.* 2001.

————. *Paul Cezanne, 1839–1906: Pioneer of Modernism.* 2001.

Emmerling, Leonhard. *Jackson Pollock, 1912–1956.* 2003.

Hendrickson, Janis. *Roy Lichtenstein, 1923–1997.* 2001.

Hess, Barbara. *Lucio Fontana, 1899–1968.* 2006.

Holzhey, Magdalena. *Giorgio de Chirico, 1888–1978: The Modern Myth.* 2005.

Kennedy, Ian G. *Titian, 1490–1576.*

Kettenmann, Andrea. *Diego Rivera, 1886–1957: A Revolutionary Spirit in Modern Art.* 2001.

Masanes, Fabrice. *Gustave Courbet, 1819–1877.* 2006.

Neret, Gilles. *Edouard Manet, 1832–1883: The First of the Moderns.* 2003.

————. *Henri Matisse.* 2006.

————. *Peter Paul Rubens, 1577–1640: The Homer of Painting.* 2004.

————. *Rubens.* 2004.

Neret, Gilles, and Gilles Lambert. *Caravaggio, 1571–1610.* 2000.

Scholz-Hansel, Michael. *El Greco, 1541–1614: Domenikos Theotokopoulos.* 2004.

Wolf, Norbert. *Albrecht Dürer.* 2006.

————. *Giotto Di Bondone, 1267–1337.* 2006.

————. *Hans Holbein the Younger, 1497/98–1543: The German Raphael.* 2004.

Venezia, Mike. Getting to Know the World's Greatest Artists series. Danbury, CT: Children's Press.
$7.95 each. Thirty-two-page biographies illustrated with masterpieces, on a simple reading level.

Andy Warhol. 1997.

Botticelli. 1991.

Da Vinci. 2015.

Diego Rivera. 2009.

Edgar Degas. 2001.

Frida Kahlo. 1999.

Georges Seurat. 2003.

Georgia O'Keeffe. 2015.

Giotto. 2000.

Henri Matisse. 1997.

Jackson Pollock. 1994.

Johannes Vermeer. 2002.

Marc Chagall. 2000.

Mary Cassatt. 1991.

Michelangelo. 2014.

Monet. 2014.

Paul Cezanne. 1998.

Paul Klee. 1991.

Picasso. 2014.

Pierre Auguste Renoir. 1996.

Raphael. 2001.

Rembrandt. 1988.

Rene Magritte. 2003.

Roy Lichtenstein. 2002.

Salvador Dali. 1993.

Van Gogh. 1989.

Music Appreciation

Basic Texts

Start with the following two texts. Move through both, and then progress on to the composer and music resources listed in the next section.

Helsby, Genevieve. *Those Amazing Musical Instruments! Your Guide to the Orchestra Through Sounds and Stories.* Naperville, IL: Sourcebooks Jabberwocky, 2007.
    $24.99. An introduction to the instruments of the orchestra, with an overview of each section, descriptions of instruments, and an interactive CD with examples of what each section/instrument does.

Levine, Robert. *The Story of the Orchestra: Listen While You Learn About the*

Instruments, the Music and the Composers Who Wrote the Music!, illus. Meredith Hamilton. New York: Black Dog & Leventhal, 2000.

> $19.95. Heavily illustrated, nicely written guide to the instruments of the orchestra, the most famous orchestral composers, and musical eras. Accompanying seventy-minute CD offers musical examples to illuminate the text. Highly recommended.

Supplementary Resources

The listening resources from Chapter 12 can (and should) be reused for the middle grades. Add some of the following:

Brownell, David, and Nancy Conkle. *Great Composers I: Bach to Berlioz Coloring Book*. Santa Barbara, CA: Bellerophon Books, 1985.

> $4.95. Order from Bellerophon. Portraits to color along with biographical sketches for fifteen composers, including Bach, Handel, Beethoven, and Mozart.

Brownell, David. *Great Composers II: Chopin to Tchaikovsky Coloring Book*. Santa Barbara, CA: Bellerophon Books, 1991.

> $4.95. Order from Bellerophon. Twenty-nine composers, including Schumann, Liszt, Wagner, Verdi, Brahms, and Grieg.

————. *Great Composers III: Mahler to Stravinsky Coloring Book*. Santa Barbara, CA: Bellerophon Books, 1993.

> $4.95. Order from Bellerophon. Twenty-seven composers.

Classical Composers Collections. Chicago, IL: GIA Publications, Inc.

> A collection of lesser-known, contemporary, and some off-the-beaten-path composers. Great for exploring new music! Prices range from $7.99 to $19.99 (for more recent composers) on iTunes; an average of two hours of music on each album.
>
> *Cindy McTee.*
> *Donald Grantham.*
> *Frank Ticheli.*
> *Gordon Jacob.*
> *Gustav Holst.*
> *Jack Stamp.*
> *Joseph Schwantner.*
> *Michael Colgrass.*

Paul Hindemith.

Percy Aldridge Grainger.

Ralph Vaughan Williams.

Vincent Persichetti.

The Great Names biography series. Broomall, PA: Mason Crest Publishers. $19.95 each. Try your library for this series, which is written on a higher level than the Getting to Know series listed below.

Carew-Miller, Anna. *Ludwig van Beethoven.* 2014.

Cook, Diane, and Victoria Fomina. *Mozart: World-Famous Composer.* 2013.

January, Brendan. *Louis Armstrong.* 2003.

Krull, Kathleen. *Lives of the Musicians: Good Times, Bad Times (and What the Neighbors Thought),* illus. Kathryn Hewitt. New York: HMH, 2013. $12. A fun biography resource full of interesting (and obscure) snippets.

The Music Masters series. $4.95 for each CD; MP3 downloads also available. Order from Amazon.com. Each contains a narration of the composer's life, with significant events illustrated by selections from the works composed at that time and eighteen to twenty minutes of unbroken music at the end. Good introduction to classical music.

The Stories of Foster and Sousa.

The Stories of Schumann and Grieg.

The Stories of Vivaldi and Corelli.

The Story of Bach.

The Story of Beethoven.

The Story of Berlioz.

The Story of Brahms.

The Story of Chopin.

The Story of Dvořák.

The Story of Handel.

The Story of Haydn.

The Story of Mendelssohn.

The Story of Mozart.

The Story of Schubert.

The Story of Strauss.

The Story of Tchaikovsky.
The Story of Verdi.
The Story of Wagner.

Tomb, Eric, and Nancy Conkle. *Early Composers Coloring Book.* Santa Barbara, CA: Bellerophon Books, 1988.

$3.95. Order from Bellerophon. The first in the Composers Coloring Books series. A detailed coloring book of composers' portraits from Palestrina through Corelli, with a biographical note for each. Also a good guide to early composers.

Venezia, Mike. Getting to Know the World's Greatest Composers series. Danbury, CT: Children's Press.

$6.95 each. Thirty-two-page biographies with historical images, on a simple reading level.

Aaron Copland. 1995.
The Beatles. 1997.
Duke Ellington. 1996.
Frederic Chopin. 2000.
George Gershwin. 1995.
George Handel. 1995.
Igor Stravinsky. 1997.
Johann Sebastian Bach. 1998.
Johannes Brahms. 1999.
John Philip Sousa. 1999.
Leonard Bernstein. 1998.
Ludwig van Beethoven. 1996.
Peter Tchaikovsky. 1995.
Wolfgang Amadeus Mozart. 1995.

22

∿

TEXTS AND TECHNOLOGY:
HOW TO USE SCREENS
IN THE LOGIC STAGE

Computers should work. People should think.
—IBM slogan

Since the first edition of this book came out in 1999, technology has (to put it mildly) changed.

Here's what we said then:

Software and videos are easier to use than books. They teach through images, not words; they encourage passive reception instead of active engagement. This is directly opposed to the goal of the logic stage. In grades 5 through 8, you're constantly teaching the student to analyze and make connections; software and (especially) videos tend to push the brain into a state of uncritical observation.

More than a decade and a half later, this has become a bit of an overstatement. The first generations of educational software *were* more flash than substance, relying on entertainment to keep students interested. But educational software, online learning programs and tutorials, and Internet research sources have improved beyond recognition.

We continue to believe that elementary students need to spend much more time with people than with screens, but beginning in the logic stage, you can make careful use of technology to deepen your student's education. Just remember that classical education is language-based, and that learning to deal with long chunks of uninterrupted *text* remains a primary goal of the logic stage. Use software, online learning, and other screen-based learning methods in service of this goal, not to replace it.

BASIC SKILLS IN TECHNOLOGY

Every middle-grade student should learn to keyboard (once known as typing) and to use a word-processing program. (We've recommended a few options at welltrainedmind.com.) Begin typing instruction any time from fifth grade on, and continue until students are completely at ease with the keyboard.

Our general recommendation is that students continue to prepare handwritten papers for the first year or two of the logic stage, since fine motor skills are often still developing into the middle-grade years. By seventh grade, students can move to word processing for most or all written work. But an important caveat: Students who struggle with handwriting to the point of tears should be allowed to type their papers as early as fourth grade. Continue on with regular penmanship practice, since the student clearly needs this muscle development; also consider having the child evaluated by a learning specialist who can recommend other types of therapy to help with the problem. But don't let handwriting become the equivalent of *writing* in the child's mind; pull the two subjects apart so that the student's physical difficulty doesn't stand in the way of his developing composition skills.

Students with a STEM orientation may also enjoy making a first run at educational programming (programming languages designed to teach students *how* to program, rather than to carry out real-life tasks). All students should have some exposure to programming skills, but the high-school years are a more appropriate time for many to begin this study.

However, if your logic-stage student has a bent toward technology, visit welltrainedmind.com for programming language recommendations.

EDUCATIONAL SOFTWARE

Our 1999 caution actually remains completely valid: When choosing software programs, beware of those that reduce complex subjects (science, history, literature, and history) to ten-second flashes of information narrated by constantly animated figures.

Instead, look for programs that replicate the role of an instructor, grader, or lab situation, or that allow the student to explore a physical reality that would otherwise be out of reach. Math drills, dynamic illustrations of math operations and problem-solving methods, virtual dissections, demonstrations of volcanic eruptions or atmospheric movements or planetary motion—educational software can put all of these within reach. Look for programs and apps that improve the *delivery methods* for good teaching (for example, the Khan Academy instructional videos, which essentially give you a way to access a good teacher lecturing in front of a blackboard), rather than those that promise to change the very experience of learning itself through tacking on multiple bells and whistles.

Educational software mutates so quickly that we've decided to keep our recommendations online, where they can be constantly updated; visit well trainedmind.com.

As you make use of these recommendations, remember to *keep a balance.* Books do not appear to be going away, as many futurists had gleefully predicted. And even if the delivery method for arguments shifts in a digital direction, the ability to develop and understand a complex and many-faceted argument is essential for every citizen in a democracy. Reading and writing *texts* builds this ability as nothing else can. So whatever educational software or online teaching tools you use, try to spend at least that amount of time reading and understanding books (ebooks or print books: both force you to interpret and grasp thoughts told in uninterrupted prose), and writing and polishing words on paper.

ONLINE LEARNING

Beginning in the logic stage, it may be appropriate for you to enroll your student in online courses. As we explained in Chapter 10, grammar-stage students are still learning how to respond to real human beings; it's best to keep their instruction face-to-face. But by fifth or sixth grade, many students are ready to try out an online class.

There are many live instructional options now available to home-educated students, making it possible for you to access expert teaching in math, science, writing, history, and any other area where you don't feel comfortable taking on all of the teaching. Visit welltrainedmind.com for a continually updated list of subjects and classes available online.

As you decide whether to make use of online teaching, keep four things in mind.

1. Logic-stage students are still children. They still need face-to-face teaching, lots of personal interaction, supervision, and guidance. Enroll your middle-grade student for one or two online courses; don't turn the entire logic-stage education over to someone who is physically very far away, even if that distant teacher uses the label "classical."

2. Just because you've enrolled the student in a course with deadlines, tests, and papers doesn't mean that the student is equipped to meet the deadlines, prepare for the tests, and finish the papers. (In fact, we can pretty much guarantee you that he won't do any of those things.) During most of middle school, you will need to be deeply and regularly involved in helping the student keep up with assignments. You'll need to prompt him to turn work in on time, teach him how to communicate with the teacher about difficulties, and help him work out a schedule of when to do his work. Middle-grade students don't naturally know how to do *any* of this. You can outsource actual academic instruction, but you'll still have to be the one who teaches your student *how* to learn. So don't sign your student up, take a deep breath, and move to the next thing. You've got to stay involved. (This tends to be true in any middle-school situation, but it is even *more* true in online learning, where the distance of the teacher

often means out of sight, out of mind; once the computer is switched off, your sixth-grade student will demonstrate an uncanny ability to forget that the online class exists—until the next sign-on time.)

3. Don't rely on your student for status updates. Middle-school students are, by definition, immature—which means "I'm doing fine" might well mean "I'm getting a D, but at least I'm not failing." Check grades yourself, and schedule regular update times where you communicate directly with the teacher or tutor.

4. Most middle-grade students need the structure and direction of a regular class. Don't assign a series of self-taught, self-administered online modules and expect quality learning to happen. Either teach the student yourself and carry out your own evaluations, or outsource this to an organized class situation that will accomplish the same goal.

INTERNET RESEARCH

There's plenty of information online, much of it highly useful. There's also much more that is either garbage or simply a waste of time.

Logic-stage students should begin to use the Internet for research purposes, but it's important that they (and you) know the difference between the two major types of information found online.

Once upon a time, it was relatively simple to distinguish between legitimate and sketchy online sources. Legitimate sources were those that had been published in book or newspaper form, while blogs, forums, and online compendiums such as Wikipedia were considered untrustworthy. But this is no longer the case. Anyone can use CreateSpace or some other self-publishing service to create a book that *looks* as though it comes from a major publisher, when in fact no one other than the author has any interest in (or stake in) the book's contents. And more and more carefully researched and fact-checked texts are available online—through books. google.com, JSTOR, Scholarpedia, and many other sites.

Instead, it's important that both you and your student distinguish between *mediated* and *unmediated* information, whether it's printed or online. "Mediated" information has been passed under the eyes of someone other than the author: a publisher who has a vested interest in selling the book, and so also cares whether or not the book is halfway decent; other experts in the field (this process is called "peer review"); an editorial board that is responsible for making sure that certain standards are upheld. Mediated information can be found in book form, in articles and newspapers, on web pages, and even in online compendiums.

"Unmediated" information has been put up without being fact-checked or peer reviewed. Unmediated information comes straight from the author to you. Blogs, personal web pages, self-published books, self-produced podcasts, personal YouTube channels—these are all sources of unmediated information.

Both mediated and unmediated information can be true or false—and the student's continuing studies in logic and critical thinking will help her begin to sort out the difference (a process that will go on through high school and college . . . and afterward). But for the purposes of researching and writing, logic-stage students need to understand that they should not cite unmediated information in a paper unless they can back it up from another source. They can cite a book from HarperCollins, but not one from Scribd; an article from the *L.A. Times*, but not one from the personal web page of a friend.

If this seems confusing, consider the difference between Wikipedia and Scholarpedia. Both are "wiki-based," meaning that they can be edited and changed by numerous online users. But Wikipedia is essentially unmediated. Anyone can change or add to a Wikipedia article at any time. There's some protection in this; if one user posts something blatantly untrue in a Wikipedia entry, someone else is bound to notice and change it before long. But if your fifth grader happens to visit that entry in the five minutes when the false information is still available, she'll write down the wrong information. Wikipedia can be useful—but its facts should always be verified elsewhere, and Wikipedia should *never* be cited in a footnote.

Scholarpedia entries, on the other hand, are written by experts who are selected by a committee and can be edited only by other members who have been approved for membership (also by a committee) based on their credentials. Those experts can be wrong, but they aren't likely to say something clearly and obviously stupid, because the other members would object. That's mediation.

So allow your logic-stage student to do (supervised) online research, but make sure that she always knows who has *mediated* the information (a publisher, an academic department, an organization) before she decides to use it.

MOVIES, ETC.

Rule one for the use of movies, YouTube videos, online series, and other dramatic presentations: *add* them to, don't substitute them for, bookwork.

Watch after preparation. Once you've already studied a subject, a program becomes a vehicle for building more connections, rather than one for passive absorption of ideas. After you've read about sea life, a National Geographic program can not only reinforce, but make vivid the concepts that the student has learned. If you've just studied volcanoes, watching the Mount St. Helens eruption can cement that information in the student's mind forever.

A YouTube documentary about Peru's "City of Ghosts" can bring history to life—once the student knows who the Nazca were, where they lived, what their cities were, and when their civilization flourished.

Movies made from classic novels can be great fun—*after* the student has read the book. Filmed versions of *Ivanhoe* or *Pride and Prejudice* can fill invaluable historical details of dress and daily life. But vast areas of plot and character development are, of necessity, eliminated.

The exception to this rule can be filmed versions of plays, which, after all, were written to be seen. The print versions of *Henry V* or *Murder in the Cathedral* will probably be more interesting and easier to understand *after* the student has seen a performance.

RESOURCES

See welltrainedmind.com for up-to-date recommendations.

23

MOVING TOWARD
INDEPENDENCE:
LOGIC FOR LIFE

What we have to learn to do, we learn by doing.

—Aristotle, *Nicomachean Ethics*

Your middle-grade student is busy learning about logic, cause and effect, valid and invalid arguments, clear thinking. All this knowledge isn't limited to academic work. Logic applies to daily life as well.

The logic stage is a time of growing independence, both mental and practical. As the student begins to form her own opinions, she also should begin to take responsibility for parts of her daily life.

Educationally, this new independence assumes the form of increased time spent in self-study. As you move through the middle-grade years, you—the parent—should start to step back from minute-to-minute supervision of the child's study. Begin in fifth grade by giving the child a single assignment. ("Read these two pages in your history book, and choose which topics you want to study further. Then see me.") If the child completes the assignment responsibly, she enjoys the rewards. ("Now you're done. Take some free time.") If she doesn't, she pays the price. ("It's time for swimming. But you've been lying on your bed reading a comic book instead of doing your history, so you'll need to stay in and finish it before going outside.")

This is the practical application of logic. Certain behaviors have certain consequences. And responsibility leads to freedom. If the child does her assignments regularly, you can begin to assign her a day's work at a time and check in with her at the end of the day to make sure she's finished. If she doesn't complete the work, supervise more closely.

During the logic stage, the home-educated student should begin to understand the logical relationships of daily living as well as the connection between responsibility and freedom—that is, between work and money, preparation and success. During the middle grades, students should begin to manage their own finances and keep their own daily schedules.

We suggest that seventh graders open a checking account at a local bank (many offer free checking without a minimum balance to students). Help the student draw up a budget so that she knows what portion of her money (earned or allowance) is available for spending, what part should be saved for a long-term goal (at least 20 percent), what part should be kept for family responsibilities (clothing, presents), and what part should be given away to charity or the religious community.

We also think that the logic stage is the perfect time for students to learn how to keep to a schedule independently. At the beginning of fifth grade, go together to an office supply store and buy a daily planning calendar and a large wall calendar with enough space to write on for each day of the month.

In the fall, sit down together and make preliminary plans for the entire year. On the large wall calendar, write down the weeks you plan to spend in school, the weeks you'll take off, family holidays, and other commitments. (Now is a good time to explain to the student that schedules are flexible.) At the beginning of each month, the two of you should make lists of goals. What do you want to accomplish in each subject? What days will the student "go to school"? What other appointments (library visits, music lessons, sports, doctors' visits, birthday parties, holidays, science fairs) need to be written on the calendar? Keep this calendar in a prominent place, and make it a cardinal rule that the student *must* write all new appointments (baby-sitting jobs, nights out, visits with friends) on both calendars as they come up. *A good rule:* If it isn't on the calendar, it doesn't happen. (If you're schooling two or more children, this rule is necessary for your sanity.)

In her daily calendar, the student should keep a basic daily schedule ("Mondays: up by 7, math 8–9, science 9:30–11 . . .") and refer to it. Each week, she should list her responsibilities. What should she complete in each subject? How much time can she spend watching TV, playing on the computer, talking on the phone? She should have her own alarm clock and watch so that she can begin to keep track of her own time.

This basic training in the logic of daily life yields three rewards. First, the student gains structure to her days. We understand that different personalities cope well with different degrees of structure, but we firmly believe that everyone needs a daily schedule of some kind in order to be productive.

Second, the student begins to understand that you, the parent, are not the sole motivating force in her life. She doesn't do her assignments because you're nagging her; she does them because the assignments have to be done by Friday so that she can move on to the next week's lessons because she wants to have enough time over the summer to do no school at all. She doesn't turn off the TV because you ordered her to; she turns off the TV because she's used up her TV quota for the day.

Third, she's getting ready for college and a career. Freshmen who fail classes or get fired from jobs often do so because they've never been responsible for their own schedules. They've always gotten up because Mom called them, changed classes because the bell rang, done homework because the teacher told them to. When they reach the relative freedom of college life, they often founder.

Your classically trained student won't founder if she has been well trained—not only for academics, but for the responsibilities of daily life.

RESOURCES

Bauer, Susan Wise. *Teaching Students to Work Independently.* Charles City, VA: Well-Trained Mind Press, 2009.

$3.99. A one-hour audio download lecture with accompanying PDF handout, detailing a step-by-step method of moving students toward greater self-responsibility and independent work during the middle grades. Order from Well-Trained Mind Press.

Dawson, Peg, and Richard Guare. *The Work-Smart Academic Planner: Write It Down, Get It Done*. New York: Guilford Press, 2015.

$16.50. More elaborate than the Student Planner listed below, this contains multiple planning forms plus helps for discovering organizational style, managing distractions, keeping track of materials, etc. Ignore the academic advice on writing five-paragraph essays and summaries and just use the scheduling tools.

Student Planner, Grades 4–8, 2nd ed. Columbus, OH: School Specialty Publishing (American Education Publishing), 2003.

$3.95. An easily customized, three-hole-punched calendar for recording daily assignments, activities, events, and more.

PART II

EPILOGUE:
CHARTS, SCHEDULES,
WORKSHEETS, ETC.

The Logic Stage at a Glance

Guidelines to how much time you should spend on each subject are general; parents should feel free to adjust schedules according to the child's maturity and ability.

Fifth Grade

Logic	2 hours per week of "casual" informal logic each week, or delay until next year.
Mathematics	45–60 minutes, 5 days per week: use one day for real-life math project or activity.
Science	60 minutes, 3 days per week; aim for two to three notebook entries per week; study life science, divide the year between life science and earth science, or do 5–6-week rotations through all major scientific topics.
History	60 minutes, 3 days per week, or 1½ hours, 2 times per week: study ancient times (5000 B.C.–A.D. 400), using selected history resources, including primary sources (four over the course

of the year); do at least one outline (one sentence per paragraph) of five to six paragraphs; prepare at least one written summary; mark dates on the time line; do map work.

Spelling/word study
15–20 minutes, 3–4 days per week; begin or continue formal spelling program.

Grammar
40–60 minutes, 4 days per week; formal grammar program.

Literature
45–60 minutes, 3 days per week; read ancient myths and legends, epics, versions of classics, books about ancient writers; write brief narrative summaries, ending with a short evaluation; begin to discuss critical issues orally; memorize and recite poems or passages, three to five for the year.

Reading
1 hour, at least 4 days per week; student's choice.

Writing
Daily, time will vary; two narrative summaries per week (overlaps with literature, history, and science assignments); at least one one-level outline per week of a nonfiction source (overlaps with history); work toward two-level outlines; adjust as necessary if also completing a formal writing program.

Latin/foreign language
3 or more hours per week, depending on pace: study Latin and/or begin a modern foreign language.

Religion
Varies per family; learn the basics of personal faith; learn about world religions through the study of history.

Art
1–2 hours, once per week: alternate art projects with studying ancient art.

Music
1–2 hours, once per week: study the instruments of the orchestra.

Sixth Grade

Logic	2 hours of "casual" informal logic or 3 hours of informal logic I each week.
Mathematics	45–60 minutes, 5 days per week: use one day for real-life math project or activity; aim to move toward pre-algebra if not already begun.
Science	60 minutes, 3 days per week; aim for three to four notebook entries per week; study life science, divide the year between life science and earth science, or do 5–6-week rotations through all major scientific topics.
History	60 minutes, 3 days per week, or 1½ hours, 2 times per week: study medieval–early Renaissance times (400–1600), using selected history resources, including primary sources (four to six over the course of the year); do at least one two-level outline of a five- to ten-paragraph selection; prepare at least one written summary; mark dates on the time line; do map work.
Spelling/word study	15–20 minutes, 3–4 days per week; continue formal spelling program.
Grammar	40–60 minutes, 4 days per week; formal gram-mar program.
Literature	45–60 minutes, 3 days per week; read stories of the Middle Ages and Renaissance; begin to read some original writings; alternate writing brief narrative summaries with writing answers to two or more discussion questions; memorize and recite poems or passages, three to five for the year.
Reading	1 hour, at least 4 days per week; student's choice.
Writing	Daily, time will vary; two narrative summaries per week (overlaps with literature, history, and science assignments); at least one two-level out-

line per week of a nonfiction source (overlaps with history and science); work toward three-level outlines; adjust as necessary if also completing a formal writing program.

Latin/foreign language 3 or more hours per week, depending on pace: study Latin and/or begin a modern foreign language.

Religion Varies per family; learn the basics of personal faith; learn about world religions through the study of history.

Art 1–2 hours, once per week: alternate art projects with making biographical pages about medieval and early Renaissance artists and studying medieval and early Renaissance art; enter dates on time line.

Music 1–2 hours, once per week: listen to medieval and early Renaissance music; read biographies of the composers; make biographical pages for musicians; enter dates on time line.

Seventh Grade

Logic 3 hours per week of informal logic II or informal logic I.

Mathematics 45–60 minutes, 5 days per week: use 1 day for real-life math project or activity. Aim for pre-algebra or algebra I.

Science 60 minutes, 3 days per week; aim for five to seven notebook entries per week; study life science, divide the year between life science and earth science, or do 5–6-week rotations through all major scientific topics.

History 60 minutes, 3 days per week, or 1½ hours, 2 times per week: study late Renaissance–early-modern times (1600–1850), using selected history resources, including primary sources (six to eight over the course of the year); do at least one two-level or three-level outline of a two- to three-page selection; prepare at least one written summary; mark dates on the time line; do map work.

Spelling/word study   15–20 minutes, 3–4 days per week; continue or finish formal spelling curriculum; transition into word study.

Grammar   40–60 minutes, 4 days per week; formal grammar program.

Literature   45–60 minutes, 3 days per week; read late Renaissance through early modern literature; answer four or more critical questions about literature in writing; memorize and recite poems or passages, three to five for the year.

Reading   1 hour, at least 4 days per week; student's choice.

Writing   Daily, time will vary; one narrative summary per week (overlaps with literature, history, and science assignments); at least two three-level outlines per week of nonfiction sources (overlaps with history and science); rewrite one selection from an outline each week; adjust as necessary if also completing a formal writing program.

Latin/foreign language   3 or more hours per week, depending on pace: study Latin and/or begin a modern foreign language.

Religion   Varies per family; learn the basics of personal faith; learn about world religions through the study of history.

Art   1–2 hours, once per week: alternate art projects with making biographical pages and studying the works of artists from the late Renaissance through the early modern periods; enter dates on time line.

Music	1–2 hours, once per week: listen to Renaissance, baroque, and classical music; read biographies of the composers; make biographical pages for musicians; enter dates on time line.

Eighth Grade

Logic	3 hours per week of formal logic I or informal logic II.
Mathematics	45–60 minutes, 5 days per week: use 1 day for real-life math project or activity. Aim for algebra I if not yet begun.
Science	60 minutes, 3 days per week; aim for five to seven notebook entries per week; study life science, divide the year between life science and earth science, or do 5–6-week rotations through all major scientific topics.
History	60 minutes, 3 days per week, or 1½ hours, 2 times per week: study modern times (1850–present), using selected history resources, including primary sources (six to eight over the course of the year); do at least one oral history project; do at least one three-level outline of a three- to four-page selection; prepare at least one written summary; mark dates on the time line; do map work.
Word study	15–20 minutes, 3–4 days per week; begin or continue with word study.
Grammar	40–60 minutes, 4 days per week; formal grammar program.
Literature	45–60 minutes, 3 days per week; read modern literature; answer four or more critical questions about literature in writing; memorize and recite poems or passages, three to five for the year.
Reading	1 hour, at least 4 days per week; student's choice.

Writing	Daily, time will vary; at least two three-level outlines per week of nonfiction sources (overlaps with history and science); rewrite both selections from the outlines each week; adjust as necessary if also completing a formal writing program.
Latin/foreign language	3 or more hours per week, depending on pace: study Latin and/or begin a modern foreign language.
Religion	Varies per family; learn the basics of personal faith; learn about world religions through the study of history.
Art	1–2 hours, once per week: alternate art projects with making biographical pages and studying the works of modern artists; enter dates on time line.
Music	1–2 hours, once per week: listen to Romantic and modern music, including musical theater and light opera; make biographical pages for musicians; enter dates on time line.

Notebook Summary, Grades 5 through 8

Since middle-grade students are doing significantly more writing than elementary students, you will probably need to use a new notebook each year for each subject.

Science. Make four divisions in the notebook.
1. Definitions
2. Scientific Principles
3. Scientific Classifications
4. Scientific Descriptions
(Optional: Add "Technology" as a separate division.)

History. The History notebook contains nine divisions.
1. Facts
2. Great Men and Women
3. Wars, Conflicts, and Political Events
4. Inventions, Science, and Discoveries
5. Daily Life, Beliefs, and Customs
6. Literature and the Arts
7. Cities and Settlements

8. Primary Sources
9. Outlines

Writing. Divide the Writing notebook into four sections.
1. Spelling
2. Word Study
3. Grammar
4. Compositions

Literature. The Literature notebook has two divisions.
1. Reading
2. Memory Work

Sample Weekly Checklists

Note: These are intended only as illustrations of how your weeks might be organized. Adjust and change, or make your own checklists. If particular curricula areas are a challenge and take additional time, eliminate optional studies until the core skills are mastered.

Fifth Grade (average of 5–6 hours on task per day, including free reading time)

Note: In this sample schedule, writing assignments are completed as part of history, science, and literature. This student is also doing "casual" informal logic rather than saving it until next year, and is doing only one foreign language.

Monday

Mathematics
(45–60 minutes) _____
Science (60 minutes) _____
Spelling (15–20 minutes) _____

Literature (40–60 minutes) _____
Latin (1 hour) _____
Music (2 hours) _____

Tuesday

Mathematics
   (45–60 minutes) _____

Logic (1 hour) _____

Spelling (15–20 minutes) _____

Reading (1 hour) _____

History (90 minutes) _____

Grammar (40–60 minutes) _____

Wednesday

Mathematics (45–60 minutes) _____

Science (60 minutes) _____

Spelling (15–20 minutes) _____

Grammar (40–60 minutes) _____

Literature (40–60 minutes) _____

Reading (1 hour) _____

Latin (1 hour) _____

Thursday

Mathematics (45–60 minutes) _____

Logic (1 hour) _____

History (90 minutes) _____

Grammar (40–60 minutes) _____

Literature (40–60 minutes) _____

Reading (1 hour) _____

Spelling (15–20 minutes) _____

Friday

Mathematics, project or activity
   (45–60 minutes) _____

Science (60 minutes) _____

Spelling (15–20 minutes) _____

Grammar (40–60 minutes) _____

Reading (1 hour) _____

Art (1 hour) _____

Latin (1 hour) _____

Sixth Grade (average of 5–6 hours on task per day, including free reading time)

Note: In this sample schedule, writing assignments are done as a separate course, so slightly less time has been allowed for history, science, and literature; grammar has also been reduced to 3 days per week to allow more space for the writing program. This student is doing two foreign languages so has decided not to do formal art and music study this year

Monday

Mathematics (45–60 minutes) _____

Science (50 minutes) _____

Spelling (15 minutes) _____

Writing (45 minutes) _____

Literature (40–60 minutes) _____

Latin (1 hour) _____

Logic (1 hour) _____

Tuesday

Mathematics (45–60 minutes) _____   Reading (1 hour) _____
Logic (1 hour) _____   History (45 minutes) _____
Spelling (15 minutes) _____   Grammar (40 minutes) _____
Spanish (1 hour) _____   Writing (45 minutes) _____

Wednesday

Mathematics (45–60 minutes) _____   Literature (40–60 minutes) _____
Science (50 minutes) _____   Reading (1 hour) _____
Spelling (15 minutes) _____   Latin (1 hour) _____
Grammar (40 minutes) _____   Writing (45 minutes) _____

Thursday

Mathematics   Literature (40–60 minutes) _____
   (45–60 minutes) _____   Reading (1 hour) _____
Logic (1 hour) _____   Spelling (15 minutes) _____
History (45 minutes) _____   Spanish (1 hour) _____
Grammar (40 minutes) _____

Friday

Mathematics, project or activity   Reading (1 hour) _____
   (45–60 minutes) _____   History (45 minutes) _____
Science (50 minutes) _____   Latin (1 hour) _____
Spelling (15 minutes) _____   Spanish (1 hour) _____
Grammar (40 minutes) _____

*The seventh- and eighth-grade years resemble the fifth- and sixth-grade years with
small adjustments in time. Older students may be able to spend a full 6 hours or more
on task, depending on interest, maturity, and extracurricular schedules.*

Curriculum Planning Worksheet

Use this worksheet to start planning out each year of study. Download a PDF version of this worksheet at welltrainedmind.com.

MATH

Before Algebra

Conceptual Approach

Math Mammoth _____

Math-U-See _____

Right Start _____

Singapore _____

Other _____

Procedural Approach

Saxon _____

Other _____

Pre-Algebra/Algebra

Conceptual Approach

AOPS _____

Math-U-See _____

VideoText _____

Other _____

Procedural Approach

Saxon _____

Other _____

Real-Life Math

Checkbook Math _____ Math on the Menu _____ Menu Math _____

Moneywise Kids _____ Family Math _____

Family Math: Middle School Years _____ Other _____

Conceptual Supplements (for Procedural Courses) _____
Khan Academy _____ *MEP* _____ *Arbor Algebra* _____
Gardner Puzzles _____ *Hands-On Equations* _____ *Other* _____

Procedural Supplements (for Conceptual Courses) _____
Developmental Mathematics _____ *Other* _____

SCIENCE
Fields(s) to cover this year/Weeks to study

Animal kingdom _____ / _____ Plant kingdom _____ / _____
Human body _____ / _____
Earth science _____ / _____ Astronomy _____ / _____
Chemistry _____ / _____ Physics _____ / _____
Technology _____ / _____

Reference Materials
Blister Microscope _____ *Brock Magiscope* _____ *Other* _____
Science: Definitive Visual Guide _____ *Kingfisher Science Encyclopedia* _____
How to Think Like a Scientist _____ *Investigating the Scientific Method* _____
How to Write a Lab Report _____

Life Science Spines/Curricula
The Encyclopedia of Animals _____ *Animalium* _____
CPO Life Science _____ *Prentice Hall Science Explorer* _____
Botany in 8 Lessons _____ *Nature Anatomy* _____ *The Life of Plants* _____
The Way We Work _____
Other(s) _____

Earth Science and Astronomy Spines/Curricula
National Geographic Visual Encyclopedia of Earth _____
CPO Earth Science _____
Universe: The Definitive Visual Guide _____
Space: A Visual Encyclopedia _____
Space: The Universe as You've Never. . . . _____
Elemental Science: Earth Science & Astronomy _____
Great Science Adventures _____
Other(s) _____

Chemistry Spines/Curricula

CPO Physical Science _____ *Elemental Science Chemistry* _____
Focus on Middle School Chemistry _____ *Basement Workshop* _____
Prentice Hall Science Explorer _____ *TOPS Learning System* _____
Other(s) _____

Physics Spines/Curricula

Prentice Hall Science Explorer _____
Complete Physics for Cambridge Secondary 1 _____
TOPS Learning System _____ *Other(s)* _____

Technology Spines/Curricula

The New Way Things Work _____ *Great Science Adventures* _____
Horrible Science _____ *How Stuff Works* _____ *Fuel Cell 10 Kit* _____
LEGO Mindstorms _____ *The Robot Book* _____ *Nanotechnology Kit* _____
Electronics: Hands-On Primer _____ *Art of Construction* _____
Snap Circuits _____
Janice VanCleave's Engineering _____ *Other(s)* _____

HISTORY

History Year by Year _____ *Kingfisher History Encyclopedia* _____
National Geographic Visual History _____
National Geographic Almanac _____
Children's Encyclopedia of American History _____
Little History of the U.S. _____
Other(s) _____
Tentative Chapters/Pages to Cover Per Semester _____
Tentative Chapters/Pages to Cover Per Week _____

Geography Resources

National Geographic Family _____ *National Geographic Kids* _____
New Historical Atlas of the World _____ *Atlas of World History* _____

Possible primary sources to cover: _____
_____
_____
_____

Additional resources to have on hand as year begins: _____

_____

_____

_____

SPELLING

Spelling Workout _____ *All About Spelling* _____
Sequential Spelling _____ *WRTR* _____ *Other* _____

WORD STUDY (only after spelling is completed)

Vocabulary from Classical Roots _____ *Wordly Wise* _____
Other _____

GRAMMAR

Rod & Staff _____ *Hake Grammar* _____ *Voyages in English* _____
Other _____

WRITING

Summarizing, outlining, and rewriting across curriculum _____
Writing With Skill _____ *IEW* _____ *Killgallon* _____
Writing & Rhetoric _____ *Writing Strands* _____ *Other* _____

LITERATURE

Possible titles to have on hand as year begins: _____

_____

_____

_____

FREE READING

Possible authors or titles to have on hand as year begins: _____

_____

_____

_____

FOREIGN LANGUAGES

Latin Sequence 1:

Prima Latina _____ OR *Big Book* _____

followed by

Latina Christiana I _____

First Form Latin _____

Second Form Latin _____

Third Form Latin _____

Latin Sequence 2:

Latin for Children Primer A _____

Latin for Children Primer B _____

Latin for Children Primer C _____

Latin Alive! _____

Latin, Beginning Later:

First Form Latin, 1–4 _____ *Latin Alive!* _____ *Latin Road* _____

Other _____

Modern Languages

Language of Choice _____

Duolingo _____ *Fluenz* _____ *Rosetta Stone* _____

Other _____

ART & MUSIC

Art Skills

Artistic Pursuits _____ *Drawing on the Right Side of the Brain* _____

Art of Watercolor _____ *Art of Acrylic Painting* _____

Clay Characters for Kids _____ *Creating Life-Like Animals* _____

How to Make Clay Characters _____

Creating Lifelike Figures _____ *Other(s)* _____

Art Appreciation

Ancient Art series _____ *Art that Changed the World* _____

Start Exploring Masterpieces _____ *Collins Big Book of Art* _____

Other(s) _____

Music Appreciation

Those Amazing Musical Instruments! _____

Story of the Orchestra _____

Composers and pieces to listen to this year: _____

_____

_____

_____

Music Skills

Plans for instruction: _____

_____

_____

_____

PART III

THE
RHETORIC
STAGE

Ninth Grade through Twelfth Grade

24

PREPARING FOR HIGH SCHOOL:
AN OVERVIEW

A goal without a plan is just a wish.
—Antoine de Saint-Exupéry

Many home-schooling parents view the beginning of ninth grade with something like terror. The details of the high-school curriculum (what is a credit? how many does my student need? in what?), the need for careful record keeping that looks official (transcripts and more), and the looming challenge of college applications make high-school home education seem like a gargantuan task. And often, as high school approaches, families start casting around for a more traditional school solution.

Moving into a classroom may be the right answer for some students, but don't make this decision out of fear. High school isn't nearly as complicated as it looks from the outside.

The chapters that follow outline a classical approach to the high-school subjects. They are very focused on *what* to teach, and how to teach it *well*: the intellectual and academic aspects of an excellent high-school education. (Part IV dedicates much more space to the pragmatic side of home education: issuing grades, keeping records, preparing high-school transcripts, doing college applications, and more.)

But you'll find it helpful to have an understanding of the technical side of the high-school curriculum in mind as you read through our description of rhetoric-stage academics. So bear with us while we go over some of the less inspiring aspects of teaching high-school students at home: state and college requirements, definitions of terms, and a few other important details.

(Most of what follows applies specifically to U.S. students; readers from other countries can skim, out of interest, or else skip to Chapter 25 now.)

HIGH-SCHOOL REQUIREMENTS

Each U.S. state has slightly different requirements for high-school graduation. (For example, as of this writing, Virginia requires three lab sciences, while New Mexico also requires three sciences but only two of them have to have a lab component.) In most states, home educators aren't required to demonstrate that they've met these exact standards. However, you should be familiar with your state high-school requirements; we've provided links to each state's website at welltrainedmind.com.

State graduation requirements are slightly less demanding than what colleges will be looking for on the high-school transcript. So for the sake of this chapter, we'll be assuming that your child plans to apply to college (see Chapters 39, 40, and 44 for more details), and we'll be describing a typical high-school curriculum for a university-bound student.

Definitions

First, let's define some terms.

Transcript. A transcript is simply a document that shows the subjects, credits, and grades taken by the student each year in grades 9–12. Home educators create their own transcripts. (In other words, there's no single magic form that you have to fill out—see Chapter 44 for examples and details.)

Credit. A full credit is one year of work in one subject. Generally speaking, 1 credit is equivalent to 160 45–50-minute class periods, or at least

120 full hours of study. Half credits may be awarded. (Driver's ed, for example, is usually a .5 credit in public high schools.)

Area. All high-school subjects are divided into seven "areas," or categories. They are:

Language Arts
Maths
Social Sciences
Natural Sciences
Foreign Languages
Physical Education
Electives

Requirements are often phrased in terms of these areas (i.e., "4 credits in Language Arts") rather than as individual subjects.

Subject. A subject is a specific class within each area. They are generally classified as follows:

Language Arts
    Reading
            Phonics
            Literature
    Writing
            Handwriting
            Composition
            Rhetoric
    Grammar
    Spelling
    Vocabulary
    Rhetoric

Maths
    Geometry
    Algebra
    Pre-calculus and Calculus
    Trigonometry

Social Sciences
    History

Government
Psychology
"Social Studies"

Natural Sciences
Biology
Chemistry
Physics
Geology
Environmental Science
Labs (hands-on)

Foreign Language
Study of any language other than English

Physical Education
Instruction in sports
General fitness

Electives
Fine Arts
  Music
  Art
Practical Arts
  Shop
  Driver's ed
Business
  Accounting
Other
  Computer programming
  Logic/thinking skills
  Health
  Test preparation

An elective can also be any subject taken in excess of the required number—so, if your student needs 3 lab sciences to fulfill the Natural Sciences requirement, but actually takes 4 classes, the fourth science is considered an "elective."

High-School Requirements for College Admissions

The requirements listed below are those that a college admissions officer would generally look for on a reasonably competitive high-school
transcript.

Subject	Required Credits	Area
Language Arts	4	Language Arts
Mathematics	3–4	Maths
Foreign Language	2–4	Foreign Languages
World History	1	Social Sciences
American History	1	Social Sciences
American Government	1	Social Sciences
Science	3–4, at least 2 of which include lab work	Natural Sciences
Physical Education	2	Physical Education
Electives	4–8	Any area

Remember, each one of these credits represents approximately 120 hours
of work on the part of the student.

At the end of each chapter in this section, we'll tell you how to represent the material on a transcript. Generally, keep the following in mind:

- Time spent reading, writing, and doing spelling and vocabulary can
  all count toward the Language Arts credit.
- Algebra I, Geometry, Algebra II, and upper-level mathematics can
  count toward the Mathematics credits. Pre-algebra cannot be counted
  for high school credit, even if taken in ninth grade.
- Foreign Language credits can be any modern or ancient language.
- World History can be Ancient, Medieval, Renaissance, or Modern.
- Science can be Biology, Chemistry, Physics, Astronomy, Meteorology,
  Geology, Ecology, or any topics that are subsets of those. Generally
  speaking, Earth Science is not considered high-school level, even
  when taken in ninth grade or later.
- Physical Education credits can be awarded for 120 hours of purpose-
  ful physical activity, as long as the student logs those hours in a journal or diary.

- Electives are made up of additional high-school credits beyond those listed in the core areas. For example, if a high-school student takes Expository Writing 3 and American Literature, she would earn two Language Arts credits on the high-school transcript. One credit would fulfill the Language Arts requirement for that year; the other would go toward the Elective credit.
- Colleges will expect to see the Electives filling out the areas in which the student is strongest; so, a prospective humanities major will probably graduate from high school with 3 credits in Maths and 3 in Natural Sciences, but with 6–8 credits in Language Arts and 4–5 in Social Sciences.

PLANNING AHEAD

As you read through the remaining chapters in this section, use the following worksheet to make preliminary plans to fulfill your student's high-school requirements. List the courses that will fulfill each required credit. Note that there's a great deal of flexibility in which subjects can round out those Electives. Be sure to pay special attention to Chapter 34, "The Specialist," as you plan out the elective courses.

A college admissions office will expect to see most of the electives drawn from the five core areas (language arts, mathematics, foreign language, social sciences, natural sciences), fewer from Fine Arts, and almost none from Physical Education or Practical Arts.

A PDF of this worksheet can be downloaded from welltrainedmind .com.

Subject/Area	Required Credits
Language Arts	1. _____
	2. _____
	3. _____
	4. _____
Mathematics	1. _____
	2. _____
	3. _____

Foreign Language   1. _____
                         2. _____

World History   1. _____

American History   1. _____

American Government   1. _____

Natural Sciences   1. _____ (with lab)
                        2. _____ (with lab)
                        3. _____

Physical Education   1. _____
                        2. _____

Electives   1. _____
                        2. _____
                        3. _____
                        4. _____
                        5. _____
                        6. _____
                        7. _____
                        8. _____

STAYING ORGANIZED

As you begin high school, I (Susan) strongly suggest that you set up the following system—developed through getting three boys into good colleges and, too often, finding out that I had to scramble to re-create or find information that I should have kept on hand all along.

In a special file cabinet drawer or dedicated file box, keep six file folders for each high-school student. Label them:

Course Descriptions
Books Read
Papers Written
Recommendations
Extracurricular Activities
Other

1. Course Descriptions

As soon as the student finishes each course, write a one- or two-sentence description of the course, list the major texts used, and note whether the course was completed with a tutor or service of any kind. Many colleges (and almost all smaller schools) will ask home educators to submit a list of course descriptions along with the transcript.

Here are a few sample descriptions that I used on the college application forms for my sons.

Course	Grades	Curriculum followed
Algebra 1 & 2/ Geometry	9, 11	Saxon Home School Study course along with *Geometry: An Integrated Course* (Larson, Boswell & Stiff), pursued with tutor.
American Literature	11–12	Reading and discussion of American literature classics including *The Scarlet Letter, Moby-Dick, Uncle Tom's Cabin, The Red Badge of Courage;* regular response and critical papers.
American History/ Gov't	11–12	In-depth study of *America: A Narrative History,* by George Brown Tindall (Norton) along with *A Guide to American Government* and outside resources; regular response papers, outlines, time lines.
Expository Writing	11	Study of forms (response paper, critical paper, research paper) under guidance of parent (professional writer).
Physical Education	10–11	Programmed course of cardiovascular & strength workouts.
Rhetoric & Communication	11	Study of rhetorical techniques using Thomas Kane, *New Oxford Guide to Writing,* and Edward Corbett, *Classical Rhetoric for the Modern Student.*
American History & Gov't	12	Based around the text *American Stories: A History of the United States,* 2nd ed. Pursued through the Well-Trained

		Mind Academy online; exploration of the competing cultural ideals, economic drives, political affiliations, and ethical dilemmas of American life; examination of the foundations and current form of the three branches of American government.
Anatomy & Physiology	11	Text: Elaine N. Marieb, *Essentials of Human Anatomy & Physiology*. Taken through Memoria Press Academy, a private online service, this course followed on general biology and focused in on structure and function of the human body.
Chemistry (Lab)	12	Text: *Conceptual Chemistry*, 4th ed. Comprehensive introduction to the structure, properties, and behaviors of atoms and molecules, chemical reactions, acid-base chemistry, and oxidation-reduction reactions. Weekly instructor-graded labs. Taken through the Well-Trained Mind Academy.
French I, II, III	10, 11, 12	Pursued with Rosetta Stone, *French for Reading*, and supplemental literature reading texts provided by private tutor.

Writing these descriptions as soon as you finish the course is much easier than reconstructing them later. Label each description with the year and grade, and drop it into the file folder.

2. Books Read

Every time the student finishes reading a book that's considered high-school level or above, whether it's read for school or independently, note the title, author, and date finished on a slip of paper or index card and drop it into this folder.

Many high-school students simply don't read—especially for fun. If you have the option to include a list of books read on the college application (see Chapter 44), do so. This folder will guarantee that you *remember* what those books were.

3. Papers Written
Whenever the student finishes a composition that strikes both of you as particularly good, put a copy in this folder. She'll need writing samples to send in with her applications.

4. Recommendations
Any time a student works with a tutor, teacher, or adult leader for at least a year and has a good experience, consider asking him or her for a written recommendation as soon as the course or activity is finished. You'll need these for applications, but coming back two years later and asking for a recommendation pretty much guarantees that you'll get something generic; memories, even of good students, fade.

5. Extracurricular Activities
Whenever the student takes part in a club, activity, team, individual pursuit, play, competition, etc., jot the details down on a piece of paper and drop it in this folder. You'd be amazed how hard it is to reconstruct these details later.

6. Other
Use this folder for any piece of information that might be helpful in documenting the student's high-school years, but that doesn't fit into the other categories.

ONE LAST NOTE

When you educate at home, you often don't have to show anyone your student's immunization records until it's time to register for freshman classes. All three of my boys ended up getting unnecessary shots because I relied on the doctor's office to keep a record of their shots—and the office merged with other practices and lost their records.

If they'd been in school, the school would have required me to give them a copy every year, and we'd have had proof. Instead, before they could register for classes during their freshman year of college, they had to get repeat MMR and tetanus shots.

So ask for a copy, signed by the physician, of every routine immunization and keep it yourself. Your child's arm will thank you.

25

꧁

SPEAKING YOUR MIND:

THE RHETORIC STAGE

It is absurd to hold that a man should be ashamed of an inability
to defend himself with his limbs, but not ashamed of an inability to
defend himself with speech and reason; for the use of rational speech
is more distinctive of a human being than the use of his limbs.

—Aristotle, *Rhetoric*

SUBJECT: Rhetoric (and optional debate)
TIME REQUIRED: 3 hours per week for two years (plus any time spent
in extracurricular debate activities), continuing on for two more
years if desired

Rhetoric is the art of expression. During the rhetoric stage—grades 9
through 12, the traditional high-school years—the student learns to
express herself with fluency, grace, elegance, and persuasiveness.

Since self-expression is one of the greatest desires of adolescence,
high-school students should have training in the skills of rhetoric so
that they can say, clearly and convincingly, what's on their minds. Without these skills, the desire for self-expression is frustrated. Expression
itself becomes inarticulate. External objects—clothes, jewelry, tattoos,

hairstyles—assume an exaggerated value as the clearest forms of self-expression possible.[1]

"To a certain extent," Aristotle writes in *Rhetoric*, the classic text on the subject, "all men attempt to discuss statements and to maintain them, to defend themselves and to attack others. Ordinary people do this either at random, or through practice and from acquired habit."[2] The study of rhetoric is designed to make success in speech a matter of skill and practice, not accident.

A GENERAL GUIDE TO THE RHETORIC STAGE

The rhetoric stage is dependent upon the first two stages of the trivium. The grammar stage laid a foundation of knowledge; without knowledge, the rhetorician has nothing of substance to say. The logic stage taught the student to think through the validity of arguments, to weigh the value of evidence. In the rhetoric stage, the student uses knowledge and the skill of logical argument to write and speak about all the subjects in the curriculum.

The last four years of classical education stress expression. The student expresses himself by continually writing and speaking about what he's learning. At first, rhetoric is a specific subject for study, just as logic was during the middle grades. But the skills acquired in the study of rhetoric are then exercised in history, science, literature, and mathematics. In the last two years of schooling, the student will undertake two major projects in an area of his own choice, which will show his mastery of rhetorical skills (see Chapter 34).

This emphasis on written and spoken expression is just one of the three distinctive aspects of the classical high-school curriculum. The second is an increasing *specialization* on the part of the student. Flexibility becomes paramount, particularly in the junior and senior years. When the high schooler decides on the fields she'll study in depth, other subjects in which

---

[1] Susan has a completely unscientific theory about this—she believes that students who are skilled in rhetoric will never feel the need for a tongue stud.

[2] Aristotle, *Rhetoric* I.i.

she has already received a good basic grounding can begin to take up less time and energy.

"Those who are likely never to have any great use or aptitude for mathematics," writes Dorothy Sayers in "The Lost Tools of Learning," "[should] be allowed to rest, more or less, upon their oars." The same can be said for every field of study.

In Chapter 13, we cautioned you against allowing logic-stage students to settle too quickly into a specialization, since basic skills are still being developed in grades 5 through 8. But in high school, most students will show a clear inclination toward either the humanities or the STEM subjects (science, technology, engineering, and mathematics). You should allow your rhetoric-stage student to spend more time in the subjects for which he shows a natural aptitude, while still fulfilling the suggested number of credits in other areas of study.

Use this basic principle as a way to adjust the recommendations in this section. In Chapter 27, for example, we describe a combined history and literature course with an intense focus on the Great Books. A humanities student will spend two hours or more per day on this pursuit and will write numerous papers. But a student with a strong STEM focus might need to cut that time back to 90 minutes, do less writing, and cover fewer books, in order to put additional time toward advanced mathematics and science. And a student who has already decided on a career in programming or molecular biology might decide to skip the great books approach to history altogether, and instead work through a standard history text and literature course in order to devote yet more thought and time to the sciences.

Young adults find their passions in widely differing time frames: some know their path very early, while others are still searching in the last years of college. This is normal. The more undecided your student is, the more you should work to keep him engaged in all of the areas across the curriculum; the more focused he is, the more you can allow him to specialize.

What if a student specializes in one field, and then changes his mind in the last year of high school?

This too is normal. Don't worry about it. As long as he completes the basic requirements we listed in the last chapter, he'll be fully equipped to enter into any college major offered by a liberal arts school. And the energy, skill, and discipline developed in the study of his specialty will serve him well in any other field he decides to pursue.

A third distinctive characteristic of the rhetoric stage is its focus on original works: great books in all areas of study. History and literature meld together as the student reads the works of great minds, from ancient Greece to the present day. The classic texts of science, from Aristotle to Darwin and beyond, lend depth and context to the study of scientific principles.

Great books are rhetoric in action; their persuasion has stood time's test. As the high schooler studies the rhetoric of these skilled authors, he analyzes the force of their arguments. Great books provide historical perspective on the accepted truths of our own age; they can prevent the student from swallowing the rhetoric of modern-day orators undigested.

THE STUDY OF RHETORIC

During the rhetoric stage, the student will study the principles of self-expression and exercise them in both writing and speech, using modern texts that build on the classical foundations.

The study of rhetoric involves developing skill in five areas, or "canons": *inventio, dispositio, elocutio, memoria,* and *pronuntiatio.* The first three of these apply to both written and spoken rhetoric, while *memoria* and *pronuntiatio* apply specifically to debate and speechmaking.

Inventio, "invention," is the process of formulating an argument and gathering all the supporting evidence. It requires both logic and knowledge. In every subject, *inventio* occurs when you select a thesis and research it, lining up all the proof needed to make your thesis convincing.

Dispositio, "disposition," or "arrangement," is the skill of putting all that information into persuasive order. The way you present an argument depends on a slew of factors—the makeup of the audience, the setting you'll be arguing in, the emotional effect various types of information might produce, and so on. *Dispositio* teaches you to arrange all your evidence in the most convincing way. (The question of whether this is also the best and truest way is a source of tension within the study of rhetoric, which continually brings ethical issues to the fore.)

Elocutio, "elocution," teaches you how to evaluate the words you use when you give your argument. Which words will most clearly reveal the truth? (Alternately, which words will produce the desired emotions in the listener?) Which types of metaphors, parallelisms, figures of speech should you use? How can you structure your sentences for maximum effect?

Students who choose to take part in speech and debate will also need skills in *memoria* (memorizing important points or entire speeches) and *pronuntiatio* (effective methods of delivering the speech).

Rhetoric, Aristotle tells us, leads to fair-mindedness. The student of rhetoric must be able to argue persuasively on both sides of an issue, not in order to convince her audience of that which is wrong, but "in order that we may see clearly what the facts are."[3] And this is true for every subject in which rhetoric is employed. Rhetoric, Aristotle concludes, is universal.[4]

HOW TO DO IT

During ninth and tenth grades, the student should study rhetoric during those hours previously devoted to logic. Plan on three hours per week, divided into two sessions of one and a half hours each or three sessions of one hour each.

As with other advanced subjects, you can use a tutor or online tutorial for the study of rhetoric (see options in the Resources at the end of this chapter). However, good readers should be able to pursue this study independently by following this pattern:

1. Read a section in the recommended text.
2. Outline the content of the text.
3. Provide two examples of the text's lesson, either from someone else's rhetoric or of your own creation, or else do any exercises provided.

For example, the student might encounter the following text:

(17) Personal attacks do not disqualify a source. Supposed authorities may be disqualified if they are *not* informed, impartial, or largely in

---

[3] Aristotle, *Rhetoric* I.1.
[4] Ibid., I.2.

agreement. *Other* sorts of attacks on authorities are not legitimate. Ludwig von Mises describes a series of illegitimate attacks on the economist Ricardo:

> In the eyes of the Marxians the Ricardian theory is spurious because Ricardo was a bourgeois. The German racists condemn the same theory because Ricardo was a Jew, and the German nationalists because he was an Englishman. . . . Some German professors advanced all three arguments together against the validity of Ricardo's teaching.[5]

This is the "ad hominem" fallacy: attacking the *person* of an authority rather than his or her qualifications. Ricardo's class, religion, and nationality are irrelevant to the possible truth of his theories. To disqualify him as an authority, those "German professors" have to show that his evidence was incomplete—that is, they have to show that his judgments were not fully *informed*—or that he was not impartial, or that other equally reputable economists disagree with his findings. Otherwise, personal attacks only disqualify the *attacker!*[6]

A good outline of this passage might look like this:

I. An authority can be attacked for three reasons.
   A. Not being informed.
   B. Not being impartial.
   C. Being out of agreement with most other authorities.
II. An authority cannot be attacked for his *person*.
   A. This is the "ad hominem" fallacy.
   B. Class, religion, nationality, or other personal attacks are irrelevant.
   C. Ad hominem attacks disqualify the attacker.

The student would follow this by finding two examples of ad hominem attacks in a political speech (a depressingly easy exercise, particularly

---

[5] L. von Mises, *Human Action* (New Haven: Yale University Press, 1963), p. 75.

[6] Anthony Weston, *A Rulebook for Arguments* (Indianapolis: Hackett, 1992), pp. 35–36.

during an election year) or by writing her own ad hominem refutation of something she's read. Either exercise will show that she understands the concept.

Here is another example, drawn from *The New Oxford Guide to Writing*. Each chapter deals with a particular rhetorical strategy and is divided into sections with bold-print headings; these sections are then divided further by subheadings in regular type. The student's first step should be to outline the chapter, using the bold headings as major outline points. Chapter 16, "Paragraph Development: Cause and Effect," is divided into the following headings and subheadings:

Cause
  Ordering Reasons within a Paragraph
Effects
  Multiple Effects
Cause and Effect

A good outline of this chapter might look like this:

  I. Cause.
   A. Explaining "why" is a major purpose of writing.
   B. The simplest strategy: ask "Why" and then give the answer.
   C. A writer may also choose to give cause and effect implicitly, without using the word "Why."
 II. How to write a paragraph containing reasons for a cause.
   A. Give a single reason and repeat it or expand it.
   B. Arrange several reasons in order.
    1. If each reason causes the next, this is "serial order."
    2. If the reasons are independent of each other, they are "parallel."
     a. Parallel reasons that have an order in time should be listed chronologically.
     b. Otherwise, they should be listed from least to most important.
III. How to write a paragraph containing the effects or consequences of a cause.
   A. The cause should be found in the topic sentence.

B. The effects should be found in the rest of the paragraph.
   1. There may be a single effect.
   2. There may be more than one effect.
      a. The effects may be independent of each other.
      b. Or each effect may actually be the cause of the next.

The text also gives clear examples of each kind of paragraph.

After outlining the chapter (an exercise that may take the whole week or perhaps longer, for more detailed chapters), the student would complete the practice exercises at each chapter's end. For example, Chapter 16 ends with several practice exercises, the first involving analysis ("Analyze the cause-effect relationship in the following paragraph") and the next two involving composition ("Compose a single paragraph developing three or four reasons to support one of the following topics: The enormous increase in the cost of housing, the contemporary mania for exercise, the expansion of professional sports in the last twenty-five years . . . ," etc.). The student could certainly substitute his own topics (perhaps drawn from his study of history, science, or another subject) for those suggested in the book.

Students should spend at least two years working on the techniques of rhetoric; this will provide a good grounding in the basics of written argumentation. Students who are putting a high level of effort into the study of upper-level mathematics or science may need to end their study of rhetoric here in order to have enough time to specialize. However, most students (and all those interested in the humanities) should go on to the upper-level text(s) recommended, spending at least one or two more years in rhetoric study.

To complete the above rhetoric study, students should be skilled at outlining. This skill is covered in the grammar programs we recommend in Chapters 18 and 26. If necessary, the rhetoric-stage student can return to these resources.

What about evaluation?

Remember that writing is a subjective activity and that even expert writing teachers can differ over whether a particular assignment is well-done or incompetent. Often, there is no "right" answer to a writing assignment. However, if you'd like some additional help in evaluating your high-school student's writing, consider one of the following options:

1. An assessment service; see the Resources for recommendations.
2. Call your local private or parochial school and ask whether the composition teacher would be willing to evaluate your student's work. Make sure that you take the rhetoric text with you, so that the teacher knows the principles the student is trying to put into place. Generally, offering an honorarium of forty to fifty dollars for an evaluation session is a nice gesture.
3. Call the secretary of the English department at your local university or community college and ask whether any of the writing teachers might be willing to evaluate your student's papers; the same honorarium is acceptable.

ALTERNATIVES

The process we've outlined above walks the student through foundational training in rhetoric; the texts we recommend at the end of this chapter are based on the model of the *progymnasmata*, the training exercises used in classical rhetoric, and the skills covered will equip the high-school student to write persuasive essays.

However, some parents may feel the need for a more structured curriculum—a "writing program"—particularly for students who continue to struggle with writing, or who have come out of a classroom situation and are not yet used to working independently. If you'd prefer to investigate a structured curriculum for rhetoric, we have suggested several options in the Resources section.

Important note: Students who are not yet writing on a high-school level should spend at least two years in one of the curricula recommended for logic-stage writing in Chapter 18 before moving on to our rhetoric-stage recommendations. If you feel that your student still needs more foundational writing instruction before trying the rhetoric study that we recommend, read through the next chapter, "Skill with Words," and adopt our suggestions there.

A WORD ABOUT STEM KIDS AND RHETORIC

Budding engineers, computer scientists, and electronics whizzes are often very terse writers. They can say what they mean perfectly well; they just don't see why they should say it at length.

Our advice: Don't fight it. Good writing is writing that uses as many words as necessary, no more, and no less. Terse writers should still study the techniques of persuasion; they too will need to convince others of an argument or a position. But there's nothing wrong with no-frills writing. Require good grammar, good mechanics, and clear thought. Don't torment your young scientist with mandatory word counts or particular stylistic demands. Accept clarity as beauty.

DEBATE

Involvement in a debate club or society provides invaluable, hands-on training in rhetoric. If possible, find a local debate society, and enroll your ninth grader in it. Try to pursue debate throughout ninth and tenth grades. If the eleventh grader no longer wants to take part, debate can then be dropped from the curriculum—it has served its purpose.

Your local university or college is a good starting place. Call the theater department, which is generally connected with the debate club because debate is a spoken performance. Ask who coaches the debate team. Once you've found the coach, explain what you're doing, list the rhetoric texts you're using, and ask how your ninth grader can practice debating skills. The coach may invite the student to sit in on the college sessions. At the very least, he should be able to direct you to an age-appropriate debate group nearby.

You can also call a parochial school, if you happen to have a good one nearby. Ask for the debate-team coach, and explain your situation. Some private schools welcome home schoolers to extracurricular clubs.

Finally, you can call your state home-education organization (see welltrainedmind.com for links) and ask about debate clubs for home schoolers.

More and more of these are popping up. The quality of the coaching tends to be mixed—you can end up with anyone from an overworked parent who's never studied rhetoric to a moonlighting university professor. Ask about the qualifications of the coach before you commit. But these groups are often very resourceful, mounting regular competitions and even state-wide championships for home schoolers.

SUGGESTED SCHEDULES

Ninth and tenth grade   3 hours per week   Work through
                                                 basic rhetoric texts

Eleventh and twelfth grade   3–5 hours per week   Work through
                                                 advanced rhetoric
                                                 texts

HOW TO PUT IT ON THE TRANSCRIPT

Course	Name of class on transcript	Area	Credit
Rhetoric	"Rhetoric I," "Rhetoric II," etc.	Language Arts	1 credit for 120 hours or more, .5 credit for 60–100 hours
Debate	Speech	Elective	1 credit for 120 hours or more, .5 credit for 60–100 hours

RESOURCES

Most books can be obtained from any bookseller or library; most curricula can be bought directly from the publisher or from a major home-school supplier such as Rainbow Resource Center. Contact information for publishers and suppliers can be found at www.welltrainedmind.com. If availability is limited, we have noted it. Remember that additional curricula choices and more can be found at www.well trainedmind.com. Prices change constantly, but we have included 2016 pricing to give an idea of affordability.

Rhetoric

For progressing out of a structured middle-grade curriculum into Rhetoric, see our specific recommendations in Chapter 18, pages 478–482.

Basic Texts

Work through in the following order.

Weston, Anthony. *A Rulebook for Arguments*, 4th ed. Indianapolis, IN: Hackett, 2008.

$11. This introduction to rhetoric provides a quick review of logic as applied to written essays; a straightforward transition from logic to rhetoric.

OR

Morrow, David R., and Anthony Weston. *A Workbook for Arguments: A Complete Course in Critical Thinking.* New York: Hackett, 2011.

$27. This workbook pairs the entire text of the Rulebook for Arguments with exercises, outlining practice, examples from books and the movies, and model answers. Highly recommended.

Kane, Thomas S. *The New Oxford Guide to Writing.* Oxford: Oxford University Press, 1994.

$19.95. A complete, accessible guide to colorful and persuasive writing, from the sentence level to essay organization and construction, with plenty of examples from great writers.

Supplementary Texts

Heinrichs, Jay. *Thank You for Arguing: What Aristotle, Lincoln, and Homer Simpson Can Teach Us About the Art of Persuasion*, rev. and updated ed. New York: Three Rivers Press, 2013.

$15. A very different approach, focused more on argumentation in real-life scenarios than on written rhetoric. However, used along with or just after the basic texts, this clever guide to argumentation can help bring rhetoric to life.

Advanced Texts

Work through in the following order.

Corbett, Edward P. J., and Robert J. Connors. *Classical Rhetoric for the Modern Student*, 4th ed. Oxford: Oxford University Press, 1999.
   $99.95 cover price. This is a complete and excellent text but is (obviously) priced for the college market. You can rent it online for much less, buy it used, or buy a previous edition; the fourth edition is not necessary.
   Corbett's six-chapter study of rhetoric uses models ranging from Socrates to Rachel Carson to teach students the art of persuasion. The student should begin by simply reading the first chapter, "Introduction," carefully. The second chapter, "Discovery of Arguments," deals with *inventio*, choosing a topic for writing (in Corbett's words, "how to 'discover' something to say on some given subject"). The chapter is quite long (over two hundred pages!) and should be outlined, section by section (the sections are set off by bold-print headings). After outlining, the student should either give a written example or (where provided) complete the "Practice" provided by Corbett. For example, after outlining "Formulating a Thesis," the student should choose a general topic, ask three questions about it (Corbett writes that you should define a topic for argument by asking whether you intend to prove that the topic is a fact, to define it, or to show what kind of thing it is—three classic strategies for narrowing the subject of an argument), and then state a thesis in a "single declarative sentence."
   Most students will need a month or more to work through this chapter. The following chapters are not quite as lengthy; the student should follow the same basic procedure in working through them. The fifth chapter, "The Progymnasmata," walks students through a set of writing exercises which have long been used in classical tutorials to develop writing skills; the student begins by retelling a folktale and then continues, writing a narrative, explaining an anecdote, arguing for or against

a proverb (a "maxim or adage"), and so on through the final step of the *progymnasmata*, the "legislation," in which the student argues "for or against the goodness of a law." These exercises will ask the student to put into practice all of the skills learned throughout the book, and will give her all the tools needed for the junior and senior projects (see Chapter 34).

The final chapter, "A Survey of Rhetoric," can be simply read for information or can be skipped.

Cothran, Martin. *Classical Rhetoric with Aristotle: Traditional Principles of Speaking and Writing.* Louisville, KY: Memoria Press, 2002.

Order from Memoria Press. Students who wish to continue the study of rhetoric as a specialization—and particularly those with an interest in political rhetoric—will benefit from this thirty-three-week rhetoric course, based on the reading and analysis of Aristotle's *Rhetoric*, a foundational ancient text on the subject. It also includes reading exercises from Mortimer Adler's classic *How to Read a Book* and exercises to reinforce Latin and logic skills (these are optional). The rhetoric course outlined in this chapter is focused more toward preparation for college writing; Cothran's course is a more traditional "ancient rhetoric" course, in that it gives equal preparation for speaking and writing and also focuses on the motivations of the men (and women) who seek to persuade.

Text and DVD Set. $95.95.

Includes student text, teacher key, DVD instruction, and *Aristotle's Rhetoric*.

Complete Set. $140.

Includes the above plus *Figures of Speech* and *How to Read a Book*.

Assessment Helps

Writing Assessment Services. Slippery Rock, PA.

Longtime writing instructor Cindy Rinaman Marsch offers individual writing assessment to home-educated students.

Structured Curricula

Note: The following recommendations assume that students are ready to write on a high-school level. Students who are struggling should make use of our remedial recommendations on pages 587–588.

Selby, James A. *Classical Composition.* Louisville, KY: Memoria Press.

This complete series takes the student through all nine levels of the *progymnasmata*: exercises used by classical rhetoric teachers to develop their pupils' skills in argumentation. It is the most user-friendly of the structured curricula listed here.

Although Memoria Press suggests beginning the course in fourth or fifth grade, we find it much more valuable for students to work on the outlining and organization skills we describe in the middle grades and turn to the *progymnasmata* in high school. Students who have made use of our earlier recommendations will be able to move quickly through the early books. We suggest the following plan:

Ninth grade	I: *Fable Stage*
	II: *Narrative Stage*
	III: *Chreia/Maxim Stage*
Tenth grade	IV: *Refutation/Confirmation Stage*
	V: *Common Topic Stage*
Eleventh grade	VI: *Encomium/Invective/Comparison Stage*
	VII: *Characterization Stage*
Twelfth grade	IX: *Thesis & Law*
	Kane, *New Oxford Guide*

$19.95 for each Student Book, $29.95 for each Teacher Guide (necessary). Order from the publisher. Online classes making use of this series are offered by the Memoria Press Online Academy.

I. *Fable Stage: Student Book.*

I. *Fable Stage: Teacher Guide.*

II: *Narrative Stage: Student Book.*

II: *Narrative Stage: Teacher Guide.*

III: *Chreia/Maxim Stage: Student Book.*

III: *Chreia/Maxim Stage: Teacher Guide.*

IV: *Refutation/Confirmation Stage: Student Book.*

IV: *Refutation/Confirmation Stage: Teacher Guide.*

V: Common Topic Stage: Student Book.

V: Common Topic Stage: Teacher Guide.

VI: Encomium/Invective/Comparison Stage: Student Book.

VI: Encomium/Invective/Comparison Stage: Teacher Guide.

VII: Characterization Stage: Student Book.

VII: Characterization Stage: Teacher Guide.

IX: Thesis & Law: Student Book.

IX: Thesis & Law: Teacher Guide.

Institute for Excellence in Writing series. Atascadero, CA: Institute for Excellence in Writing.The Institute for Excellence in Writing (see Chapter 18, page 479) offers an Advanced Communication Series DVD set, intended for high-school persuasive writing, and a one-year rhetoric course, *Classical Rhetoric through Structure and Style: Writing Lessons Based on the Progymnasmata.*

The courses assume previous experience with the IEW "Teaching Writing: Structure and Style" program. Students and parents who have already completed at least one year of the IEW course could progress in the following order:

1. The Advanced Communication Series set
2. The *Classical Rhetoric through Structure and Style* curriculum

    Depending on the student's ease with writing, this is a two- to three-year course. Afterward, the student should progress directly to the *New Oxford Guide to Writing*, as described above.

    Students and parents who have not used IEW before should complete one year of "Teaching Writing: Structure and Style" before beginning the Advanced Communication Series.

    Order from IEW.

    Teaching Writing: Structure and Style.

        $189. Prerequisite to the advanced levels; video seminar instructs parents on how to teach writing. The package includes ten DVDs and a workbook/syllabus. A streaming option is slightly cheaper.

    Advanced Communication Series.

        $69. Three-DVD seminar and student ebook (PDF download).

    Classical Rhetoric through Structure and Style: Writing Lessons Based on the Progymnasmata.

        $29. Student Text with Answer Key included. No DVD; assumes

that you (the parent/instructor) have completed the Teaching Writing: Structure & Style seminar, either live or on DVD.

The Lost Tools of Writing, 5th ed. Concord, NC: The Circe Institute, 2015. This two-level classical rhetoric curriculum makes use of the three elements of rhetoric: invention, arrangement, and elocution. Level One teaches the persuasive essay, the foundation of all rhetoric-stage writing; Level Two progresses on to additional essay forms.

The Lost Tools of Writing is the most rigorous of the structured programs we recommend, and offers a great deal of flexibility and integration, since students can exercise their skills on essays across the curriculum, choosing topics from their studies in history, literature, and science. However, in our opinion it scores low on the "user-friendly" scale. You will need to spend a fair amount of time acquainting yourself with how the program works before starting, and you should be prepared to put in significant preparation and teaching time on a weekly basis. You will want to make use of the Online Instructional Videos, which are included with the "Complete Set" purchase.

Recommended for parents who enjoy the writing process and are looking for a challenge.

We suggest beginning Level One in tenth grade or later. After completing Level Two, students can either do a quick pass through the *New Oxford Guide* or continue on to Corbett's more challenging text.

Order from the Circe Institute. Visit the publisher's website for scope and sequence, sample lessons, and introductory videos.

The Lost Tools of Writing Level One Complete Set. $147.
The Lost Tools of Writing Level Two Complete Set. $88.

Debate

The National Forensic League (www.nflonline.org) provides manuals, forums, support, and links for debaters and debate societies.

If you're inspired to start your own debate club, look for these useful titles through any bookstore:

Freeley, Austin J. *Argumentation and Debate,* 13th ed. Boston: Wadsworth Publishing, 2013.

The standard textbook on the subject. Comprehensive survey of argumentation and debate, with models, scenarios, and guides for real-life situations. A ridiculous cover price of $232.95, but you can rent, buy used, or buy an earlier edition for a fraction of the price.

Oberg, Brent C. *Forensics: The Winner's Guide to Speech Contests.* Colorado Springs, CO: Meriwether Publishing, 1995.

$19.95. A guide to debate, specifically geared toward competition skills.

Phillips, Leslie, William S. Hicks, and Douglas R. Springer. *Basic Debate,* 5th ed. New York: Glencoe/McGraw-Hill, 2005.

$64.24. A standard hardcover textbook on the subject.

26

SKILL WITH WORDS:
GRAMMAR AND WRITING

Reading maketh a full man, writing an exact man, and conference a
ready man.

—Francis Bacon

SUBJECT: **Grammar and writing skills**
TIME REQUIRED: **3 hours or more per week**

In many classical programs, English as a subject drops out of the schedule by high school. Reading and writing aren't separate "subjects," after
all, but skills that cut across the entire curriculum. Reading means coming in contact with the philosophical and creative minds of the past and
present, something that occurs in both history and science. Writing takes
place every day in every subject. So why do we need English as a subject
anymore?

Overall, we agree with this point of view. It does assume, though, that
the ninth grader has a complete grasp of grammar, syntax, and usage, and
is able to write effectively in all the subject areas. We haven't found this to
be generally true.

The middle-grade language topics—spelling and word study, grammar, reading, and writing—do change in high school. In the rhetoric stage, the student finally begins to put the knowledge and skills he's acquired during the first eight years of education to work. Once mastered, basic skills (such as spelling, constructing paragraphs and essays, and developing logical arguments) can be eliminated as specific subjects of study (unless they are not yet mastered—read on). The skills acquired during the logic stage don't disappear, but the student's focus is now on using those skills rather than acquiring them. A painter may take a special class in art school on mixing colors. He won't stay in this class for the rest of his painting career, but he will continually mix colors as he creates works of art.

HOW TO DO IT

During the rhetoric stage, we suggest that the student keep a single notebook, the language reference notebook. This notebook will serve not as an exercise book, but as a handbook of basic skills. One notebook should be used for the four years of high school.

Divide the language reference notebook into two sections: Words and Grammar.

Spelling and Word Study

Continue on with the word study program recommended for logic-stage students until finished. If you're just now entering the classical arena, go back to Chapter 18 and adopt one of our suggestions for word study.

Ninth graders who have followed the program outlined in Chapter 18 know how to spell. They've already studied the rules of spelling and the principles of word formation. Any new words they encounter can be spelled by comparing them to words they already know. Words that consistently trip them up (and we all have a few) should be kept on a list in the Words section of the language reference notebook. No other formal spelling work is necessary.

The reading and language study done during the middle grades should have developed the student's vocabulary skills so that he can tackle classic works without trouble. Even though his vocabulary will continue to grow for the rest of his life, during the rhetoric stage vocabulary acquisition will come "on the job"—from constant reading (exposure to new words in context) and writing (searching for just the right word to use).

Once you've finished this program no further formal vocabulary and spelling work is required. As the student encounters unfamiliar words in his reading, though, he should copy them into the Words section of the notebook, along with pronunciation, origin, definition, and the sentence in which they are used.

When reading *Jane Eyre*, for example, the eleventh-grade student will come across this paragraph:

> In her turn, Helen Burns asked me to explain; and I proceeded forthwith to pour out, in my own way, the tale of my sufferings and resentments. Bitter and truculent when excited, I spoke as I felt, without reserve or softening.

If he's not familiar with the word "truculent," he should look it up in the dictionary and make an entry in his language reference notebook:

> *Truculent.* 'trəkyələnt. From the Latin *truculentus,* wild or fierce. "Feeling or showing savage ferocity, harsh, aggressively self-assertive." *Jane Eyre:* "Bitter and truculent when excited, I spoke as I felt, without reserve or softening."

This word-study exercise will help build both Latin and English vocabulary skills.[1] The student will need some encouragement to stop and do this when he sees an unfamiliar word, rather than skimming over it and going on. As the rhetoric stage continues, though, he'll find himself stopping less often.

During the rhetoric stage, you *must* have two reference works on hand: a dictionary (unabridged, if you can afford it) and *Roget's Thesaurus.* Encourage the student to use the thesaurus continually while writing, choosing the exact word for every occasion.

---

[1] A side benefit: excellent performance on the verbal section of the SAT.

Grammar

Grammar study should be continued through at least tenth grade, and then grammar principles should be regularly reviewed in the junior and senior years of high school. Grammar, usage, and mechanics must become completely automatic for truly mature reading and writing to take place. And although the logic-stage student has been exposed to all the grammar skills she needs, the skills haven't yet had time to become part of her mental apparatus. To keep on reinforcing these skills, continue with the formal study of grammar.

Most grammar programs stop workbook exercises after tenth grade and offer an "English Handbook" with review worksheets for eleventh and twelfth grades. The student simply needs a grammar handbook and regular review of grammatical principles while writing.

So if you are just now beginning a formal grammar program, start with the seventh-grade book; this will allow you to work through the final four years of the program before your student graduates.

Plan on spending around thirty minutes per day, four days per week on grammar skills during ninth and tenth grade; you can reduce this time in eleventh and twelfth grades as long as the student has finished the tenth-grade-level text. Whichever program you select, the student should use the Grammar section of the language notebook to keep a running list of grammar rules and principles that consistently trip her up.

Reading

The rhetoric stage is centered around the study of great books of philosophy, politics, religion, poetry, fiction, biography. Rather than studying history and literature as two separate subjects, the classically educated student recognizes that these pursuits are essentially the same.

Because of this, "reading" as such is swallowed up by the Great Books study outlined in the next chapter.

Writing

Rhetoric-stage writing has two parts: essays written all year in each subject, across the curriculum; and the study of rhetorical techniques described in the previous chapter.

We also suggest that the student buy William Strunk and E. B. White's classic *The Elements of Style*. Keep it on hand as a reference work. Ideally, the student should reread it, taking notes as he reads, at the beginning of each year, and should refer to it constantly as he edits and revises his own writing.

However, rhetoric-level instruction assumes that students can write summaries fluently and with correct grammar and mechanics; are able to create a three-level outline of three or more pages of high-school level non-fiction; and know how to construct an effective paragraph. If your ninth-grader still struggles with the basics of writing, you'll need to go back and build basic writing skills before progressing on to rhetoric-level writing. See "Catching Up" in the Resources section at the end of this chapter for our suggestions.

SUGGESTED SCHEDULES

Adjust as suggested above for students who need to do catch-up work in grammar, vocabulary work, or writing.

Ninth grade	Finish word study program, 15–20 minutes per day, 4 days per week; work on formal grammar program, 30 minutes per day, 4 days per week; follow rhetoric recommendations from Chapter 25; read *Elements of Style*.
Tenth grade	Work on formal grammar program, 30 minutes per day, 4 days per week; follow rhetoric recommendations from Chapter 25; reread *Elements of Style*.
Eleventh grade	Use English handbook for reference; follow rhetoric recommendations from Chapter 25; reread *Elements of Style*.

Twelfth grade   Use English handbook for reference; follow rhet-
                       oric recommendations from Chapter 25; reread
                       Elements of Style.

HOW TO PUT IT ON THE TRANSCRIPT

Course	Name of class on transcript	Area	Credit
Grammar, word study and related exercises	Grammar & Composition	Language Arts	1*

*You may award one credit for Grammar & Composition *and* one credit for Rhetoric if the student spends at least 240 hours per year on grammar, word study, rhetoric, and related exercises.

If you award one credit for 120 hours of Rhetoric work (as suggested in the previous chapter) and the student spends at least 60 hours per year on grammar and word study, award .5 credit for Advanced Grammar rather than a full Grammar & Composition credit. (Students do not need the specific course "Grammar & Composition" on the high-school transcript as long as they have an appropriate total number of Language Arts credits. Rhetoric is recognized as an advanced composition course.)

If the student completes grammar and word study along with one of the "catch-up" sequences below rather than progressing directly into Rhetoric, award 1 credit for Grammar & Composition and no credit for Rhetoric.

RESOURCES

Most books can be obtained from any bookseller or library; most curricula can be bought directly from the publisher or from a major home-school supplier such as Rainbow Resource Center. Contact information for publishers and suppliers can be found at www.welltrainedmind.com. Remember that additional curricula choices and more can be found at www.welltrainedmind.com. Prices change constantly, but we have included 2016 pricing to give an idea of affordability.

Word Study

Kipfer, Barbara Ann, ed. *Roget's International Thesaurus.* 7th ed. New York: HarperCollins, 2010.

$26.99. Much better than an online thesaurus.

Fifer, Norma, and Nancy Flowers. Vocabulary from Classical Roots series. Cambridge, MA: Educators Publishing Service, 1994.

Order from Educators Publishing Service. For the entire series, see Chapter 18.

Vocabulary from Classical Roots C. $13.25.

Teacher's Guide and Answer Key C. $22.90.

Vocabulary from Classical Roots D. $14.20.

Teacher's Guide and Answer Key D. $22.90.

Vocabulary from Classical Roots E. $14.20.

Teacher's Guide and Answer Key E. $22.90.

Wordly Wise 3000, 3rd ed. Cambridge, MA: Educators Publishing Service.

Order from the publisher. For the entire series, see Chapter 18. Lessons are open-and-go. View word lists and sample lessons from each book on the publisher's website and choose the level that will challenge your student. $13.25 for each student book, $49.55 for each Teacher's Resource Book.

Student Book 9.

Teacher's Resource Book 9.

Student Book 10.

Teacher Resource Book 10.

Student Book 11.

Teacher's Resource Book 11.

Student Book 12.

Teacher's Resource Book 12.

Grammar

Continue with your logic-stage program through completion, or choose one of the following.

Finlay, R. Robin. *Analytical Grammar: A Systematic Approach to Language Mastery.* Cary, NC: Analytical Grammar, 1996.

This program, good for grades 9 and 10, reviews and reinforces all grammatical concepts learned in earlier grades and introduces a few more advanced concepts; it provides exercises and also guides the student in making a grammar notebook that will serve as a handbook. *Analytical Grammar* consists of a student workbook, a teacher book, and an additional set of "Review and Reinforcement" worksheets. Divide this course in two and complete half in grade 9 and half in grade 10.

If you choose this program, we suggest that you follow up in grades 11 and 12 with the Stewart English Program (below), published by Educators Publishing Service.

$94.95. Includes student workbook and teacher book. Order from Analytical Grammar.

Review and Reinforcement Worksheets and Answer Keys. $19.95. Order from Analytical Grammar.

Rod & Staff Grammar and Composition. Crockett, KY: Rod & Staff.
See full program description in Chapter 18. Do not do the composition exercises. If just starting this program, begin with English 7 and complete 7, 8, 9 and 10 in grades 9, 10, 11 and 12; this is the equivalent of completing the full program. Order from Milestone Books or Exodus Books.

Building Securely: English 7. 1996.
Pupil Textbook. $19.75.
Worksheets (additional practice). $3.60.
Teacher's Manual. $27.45.
Test Booklet. $2.50.
Preparing for Usefulness: English 8. 1997.
Pupil Textbook. $19.75.
Worksheets (additional practice). $3.60.
Teacher's Manual. $27.45.
Test Booklet. $2.50.
Communicating Effectively, Book One: English 9. 2003.
Pupil Textbook. $17.55.
Teacher's Manual. $21.95.
Tests and Editing Sheets. $3.20.
Communicating Effectively, Book Two: English 10. 2001.
Pupil Textbook. $17.55.

Teacher's Manual. $21.95.

Tests and Editing Sheets. $3.20.

English Handbook. $17.35.

Stewart, Donald S. The Stewart English Program. Cambridge, MA: Educators Publishing Service, 1998.

Order from Educators Publishing Service. An excellent follow-up to *Analytical Grammar* (above), or good as a standalone refresher for tenth grade and above. The three books should take three or four semesters to finish.

Book 1, Principles Plus . . . $11.45.

Teacher's Guide, Book 1. $7.55.

Book 2, Grammar Plus . . . $13.20.

Teacher's Guide, Book 2. $9.90.

Book 3, Writing Plus . . . $11.15.

Teacher's Guide, Book 3. $9.90.

Holt Traditions: Warriner's Handbook. Boston: Houghton Mifflin Harcourt.

Order from the publisher's website. Based on John Warriner's classic English grammar handbook, this is a complete grammar course for grades 7 through 12. Students who have had little or no formal grammar should begin with the First Course (approximately grade 7) and go forward; others can begin with the Grade 9 (Third Course) book. Softcover prices are $22.50 for each Student Edition and $9.60 for each Chapter Tests with Answer Key book. Teacher Editions are hardcover, $106.65. Most can be found online secondhand for much less.

HMH has the most dreadful website of any major publisher. Search by ISBN (provided below) or you won't be able to find anything.

7th grade

Student Edition First Course. ISBN 9780030990007 (available in hardcover only, $39.80)

Teacher's Edition First Course Grade 7. ISBN 9780030990366

Chapter Tests With Answer Key, First Course Grade 7. ISBN 9780030998447

8th grade

Student Edition Second Course. ISBN 9780030993343

Teacher's Edition Second Course Grade 8. ISBN 9780030990373

Chapter Tests With Answer Key, Second Course Grade 8. ISBN 9780030998454

9th grade

Student Edition Third Course. ISBN 9780030993398

Teacher's Edition Third Course Grade 9. ISBN 9780030990380

Chapter Tests With Answer Key, Third Course Grade 9. ISBN 9780030998461

10th grade

Student Edition Fourth Course. ISBN 9780030993367

Teacher's Edition Fourth Course Grade 10. ISBN 9780030990427

Chapter Tests With Answer Key, Fourth Course Grade 10. ISBN 9780030998478

11th grade

Student Edition Fifth Course. ISBN 9780030993404

Teacher's Edition Fifth Course Grade 11. ISBN 9780030990397

Chapter Tests With Answer Key, Fifth Course Grade 11. ISBN 9780030998485

12th grade

Student Edition Sixth Course. ISBN 9780030993381

Teacher's Edition Sixth Course Grade 12. ISBN 9780030990403

Chapter Tests With Answer Key, Sixth Course Grade 12. ISBN 9780030998492

Writing

Strunk, William, and E. B. White. *The Elements of Style*, 4th ed. New York: Longman, 1999.

$9.95. Buy at any bookstore.

Catching Up

Ninth-grade students who struggle with writing should adopt one of the following strategies. Visit welltrainedmind.com for more helps and suggested catch-up programs.

Begin with *Classical Composition, Book 1* and progress through as many levels as possible. This is a very low starting level for a high school student; ninth graders who are truly writing-phobic will find this approach helpful, but will have to put in significant extra time getting caught up. Writing assignments in the following chapters will have to be simplified until at least eleventh grade.

A full description of this program can be found on pages 574–575.

OR

Begin with *Writing with Skill, Level 1* in ninth grade and progress through the next two levels; follow up with the Weston/Morrow workbook and Kane's *New Oxford Guide* in twelfth grade. This will bring the student up to the writing level expected for freshman composition in college. This is best for students who are comfortable writing sentences and simple paragraphs but have difficulty organizing more complex compositions.

A full description of *Writing with Skill* can be found on pages 478–479.

27

✹

GREAT BOOKS:
HISTORY AND READING

Reading is to the mind what exercise is to the body.
—Richard Steele, *The Tatler*

SUBJECT: **History and reading**
TIME REQUIRED: **10 hours per week**

If grammar-stage learning is fact-centered and logic-stage learning is skill-centered, then rhetoric-stage learning is idea-centered. During the rhetoric stage, the student actively engages with the ideas of the past and present—not just reading about them, but evaluating them, tracing their development, and comparing them to other philosophies and opinions. This sounds abstract, but fortunately there's a very practical way to engage in this conversation of ideas: read, talk about, and write about the great books of the world.

To some extent, the division between history and literature has always been artificial; we know about history from archaeology and anthropology, but our primary source of historical knowledge is the testimony of those who lived in the past. Without the books written by Aristotle, Homer, Plato, Virgil, and Julius Caesar, we would know very little about the politics, religion, culture, and ideals of Greece and Rome.

By ninth grade, the student has already traveled twice through the story of mankind; she's already been exposed to the major writers and thinkers of each historical period. Although the student will record dates and read summaries of historical events, the focus of rhetoric-stage history is on ideas rather than on facts. The study of great books allows the past to speak for itself, combining history, creative writing, philosophy, politics, and ethics into a seamless whole.

The goal of the rhetoric stage is a greater understanding of our own civilization, country, and place in time, stemming from an understanding of what has come before us. "The old books," writes classical schoolmaster David Hicks, "lay a foundation for all later learning and life."[1] The student who has read Aristotle and Plato on human freedom, Thomas Jefferson on liberty, Frederick Douglass on slavery, and Martin Luther King, Jr., on civil rights will read Toni Morrison's *Beloved* with an understanding denied to the student who comes to the book without any knowledge of its roots.

Remember, again, that the goal of classical education is not an exhaustive exploration of great literature. The student with a well-trained mind continues to read, think, and analyze long after classes have ended.

We have supplied lists of great books for each year of study, the ninth-grade list being the shortest, the twelfth-grade list the longest and most complex.

A few words about list making:

1. The lists are flexible. Depending on speed of reading and comprehension, the student might read eight books or fifteen or twenty. No one will read all the books listed. Also, if the student finds a work impossible to understand after she's had a good try at it, let her move on.
2. The lists are made up of books that are from the historical period being studied; the date of composition or publication of each entry

---

[1] David Hicks, *Norms and Nobility: A Treatise on Education* (New York: Praeger, 1981), p. 138.

follows in parentheses. Read the titles in chronological order—as they appear on the lists.

List making is dangerous. We have, of necessity, left some important books off this list.

We've put titles on it that you may find trivial. You will encounter many lists of important books as you home-school, created by people of different ideologies; those lists inevitably reflect those ideologies. You can always add or drop titles from our list.

HOW TO DO IT

Once again, you'll be dividing your study into four years: ancients (5000 B.C.–A.D. 400) in ninth grade; medieval–early Renaissance (400–1600) in tenth grade; late Renaissance–early modern (1600–1850) in eleventh grade; modern (1850–present) in twelfth grade.

For each year of study, the student should keep a large three-ringed binder, labeled "History and the Great Books." Each binder should be divided into four sections: The History Foundation, Book Contexts, Book Notes, and Compositions.

Half of each week's study time will be devoted to laying a foundation of historical knowledge; the second half, to the study of the Great Books.

The History Foundation

The student will begin by once again progressing through the story of history, as he did in the grammar and logic stages of learning. In this third journey through time, his reading will set the stage for his encounter with the Great Books.

In the Resources at the end of this chapter, we have suggested a number of readable narrative history texts that can serve as your student's "spine" for this third progression through history. The student's task, over the course of each year, is simply to read through these books in chronological order.

Your lesson planning is straightforward: count the total number of chapters assigned for the year and divide by the number of weeks you intend to do school—thirty-six weeks is a useful benchmark. Fast readers should have no difficulty completing the work. For slower readers, you may choose to eliminate some of the chapters. As with previous years of study, the student's task isn't to grasp all of history (an impossible task at any age!); it is to develop a sense of the historical context of great works, a familiarity with cultures of the past, and a working knowledge of major events, eras, and historical characters.

At the end of each chapter, the student should stop and record the following on a sheet of notebook paper:

1. A list of the most important dates in the chapter, and why they stand out.
2. The names of the two or three most important individuals in the chapter.
3. Three or four events that stand out in the chapter.
4. Two events, people, or ideas he'd like to investigate further.

Study of the Great Books

The second half of each week's study will be devoted to reading, thinking about, and writing about the Great Books.

Try to make a realistic assessment of how many books the student will be able to cover in the course of a year. Eight books is a minimum; twelve is better; eighteen is stellar. Choose eight (or twelve, or eighteen) titles from the lists that follow, and read them in chronological order over the course of the year.

As she reads each book, the student will add a page to each of the remaining three sections of the notebook.

Book Contexts

For each book on this personalized list, the student should follow this pattern:

1. Check the birth and death dates of the author, and the date of the book's composition.
2. Look up the year, decade, or century of the book's publication in a history atlas or encyclopedia (see Resources for recommendations).

For more modern books, a decade will give you plenty of context; older books may require that you look at an entire century (or even two or three hundred years, in the case of the most ancient texts) to place the work in its times.

3. Write a one-page summary of this historical information, setting the book in historical perspective. Draw on the history encyclopedia, the texts you're using for foundational history knowledge, and any other resources that you find helpful. Give basic information about the author, major historical events taking place during the author's life-span, the author's country, and the author's purposes in writing; summarize great events going on in the rest of the world. File this page in the Contexts section of the notebook. As you progress through the lists in chronological order, this section will begin to resemble a one-volume world chronology in its own right.[2]

Book Notes

Now the student should prepare to read the first Great Book on the list.

1. Determine the book's genre. Is it a novel, an autobiography, a work of history, philosophy, a play, a poem? The first time each genre is encountered, in each year of study, take the time to read the history of this genre and the instructions on how to read it in one of the "Reading Helps" listed at the end of the chapter.
2. Take notes on this reading about genre and keep the notes in the Book Notes section of the notebook. The yearly repetition of this foundational research into each genre is important; it will help the student gain a deeper and deeper understanding of how literature works.
3. Read through the text, pencil in hand. Note down the major events in the book. Mark any passages that seem significant, troubling, or puzzling. (You'll want to consult the "Reading Helps" for additional

---

[2] Create a Context page only for the Great Books themselves, not for the history books we've included on the list. The ninth grader should make a Book Context page for Cicero's *De republica*, written around 54 B.C., but not for William Davis's history book *A Day in Old Rome*.

direction in how to take notes on each type of book.) These notes should be *brief*; even for longer works, two to three pages of notes is plenty. Use the skills developed in summarizing and outlining over the past eight years to choose central and important events, rather than writing down long lists of less important points.

Compositions

1. Discuss the text. Talk about its purposes, its strengths, its weaknesses. Have a conversation about the ideas and whether or not they are valid. If you need assistance coming up with questions and answers, make use of the "How to Talk About the Great Books" section later in this chapter, as well as the "Discussion Helps" listed in the Resources at the end of this chapter.
2. Write about the text. This is a flexible assignment; the student can write a book report, an evaluation, an argumentative essay proving some point about the book, or an analysis of the book's ideas. All of these forms have been taught in the writing programs recommended in Chapters 18 and 26. Put the finished composition (at least two pages) in the Compositions section of the notebook.

We offer the following lists of Great Books as general guides for the high-school student. Although she isn't obliged to read everything on this list, what she does read should be read in chronological order, and the lists below are therefore also in chronological order.

Ninth Grade (5000 B.C.–A.D. 400)

Bible: Genesis—Book of Job
Epic of Gilgamesh (c. 2500 B.C.)
Homer, *Iliad* and *Odyssey* (c. 850 B.C.)
Sophocles, *Oedipus the King* (490 B.C.)
Aeschylus, *Agamemnon* (c. 458 B.C.)
Herodotus, *The Histories* (c. 441 B.C.)
Euripides, *Medea* (c. 431 B.C.)
Aristophanes, *The Birds* (c. 400 B.C.)
Thucydides, *The History of the Peloponnesian War* (c. 400 B.C.)

Plato, *The Republic* (c. 375 B.C.)

Aristotle, *On Poetics* (350 B.C.)

Aristotle, *Rhetoric* (c. 350 B.C.)

Bible: Book of Daniel (c. 165 B.C.)

Horace, *Odes* (c. 65 B.C.)

Lucretius, *On the Nature of Things* (c. 60 B.C.)

Cicero, *De republica* (54 B.C.)

Virgil, *Aeneid* (c. 30 B.C.)

Ovid, *Metamorphoses* (c. A.D. 5)

Bible: Corinthians 1 and 2 (c. A.D. 58)

Josephus, *Wars of the Jews* (c. A.D. 68)

Plutarch, *The Lives of the Noble Greeks and Romans* (c. A.D. 100)

Tacitus, *Annals* (c. A.D. 117)

Athanasius, *On the Incarnation* (c. A.D. 300)

Tenth Grade (Medieval–Early Renaissance)

Augustine, *Confessions* (c. 411)

Augustine, *City of God*, Book 8 (c. 426)

Boethius, *The Consolation of Philosophy* (524)

Koran (selections) (c. 650)

Bede, *The Ecclesiastical History of the English People* (731)

Beowulf (c. 1000)

Mabinogion (c. 1050)

Anselm, *Cur Deus Homo* (c. 1090)

Aquinas: Selected Writings (Robert Goodwin, ed.) (c. 1273)

Dante, *The Inferno* (1320)

Everyman (14th century)

Sir Gawain and the Green Knight (c. 1400)

Chaucer, *The Canterbury Tales* (selections) (c. 1400)

Margery Kempe, *The Book of Margery Kempe* (1430)

Malory, *Le Morte d'Arthur* (selections) (c. 1470)

Erasmus, *Education of a Christian Prince* (selections) (1510)

Machiavelli, *The Prince* (1513)

Thomas More, *Utopia* (1516)

Martin Luther, *Commentary on Galatians* (c. 1520)

John Calvin, *Institutes of the Christian Religion* (selections) (1536)

Christopher Marlowe, *Faustus* (1588)

Teresa of Avila, *The Life of Saint Teresa of Avila by Herself* (1588)

Edmund Spenser, *The Faerie Queene* (1590)

William Shakespeare, *Julius Caesar* (1599)

William Shakespeare, *Hamlet* (1600)

William Shakespeare, any other plays (c. 1592–1611)

Eleventh Grade (Late Renaissance–Early Modern, 1600–1850)

Miguel de Cervantes, *Don Quixote* (abridged) (1605)

King James Bible, *Psalms* (1611)

John Donne, *Divine Meditations* (c. 1635)

Rene Descartes, *Meditations* (1641)

John Milton, *Paradise Lost* (selections) (1644)

Molière, *Tartuffe* (1669)

Blaise Pascal, *Pensées* (1670)

John Bunyan, *The Pilgrim's Progress* (1679)

John Locke, "An Essay Concerning Human Understanding" or "On the True End of Civil Government" (1690)

Jonathan Swift, *Gulliver's Travels* (1726)

Jean-Jacques Rousseau, "The Social Contract" (1762)

Edmund Burke, "On American Taxation" (1774)

The Declaration of Independence (1776)

Thomas Paine, *Common Sense* (1776)

Immanuel Kant, "Critique of Pure Reason" (1781)

Alexander Hamilton et al., *The Federalist Papers* (1787–1788)

Constitution of the United States (ratified 1788)

William Blake, *Songs of Innocence and Experience* (1789)

Benjamin Franklin, *The Autobiography* (1791)

Thomas Paine, "The Rights of Man" (1792)

Mary Wollstonecraft, *A Vindication of the Rights of Woman* (1792)

William Wordsworth and Samuel Taylor Coleridge, *Lyrical Ballads* (1798)

Jane Austen, *Pride and Prejudice* (1815)

Mary Shelley, *Frankenstein* (1818)

John Keats, "Ode to a Nightingale" and other poems (1820s)

James Fenimore Cooper, *The Last of the Mohicans* (1826)

Alfred, Lord Tennyson, "The Lady of Shalott" and other poems (1832)

Charles Dickens, *Oliver Twist* (1838)

Edgar Allan Poe, "The Fall of the House of Usher" and other stories (1839)

Ralph Waldo Emerson, "Self-Reliance" (1844)

Charlotte Brontë, *Jane Eyre* (1847)

Nathaniel Hawthorne, *The Scarlet Letter* (1850)

Herman Melville, *Moby-Dick* (1851)

Twelfth Grade (1850–Present)

Emily Dickinson, *Final Harvest* (1830–1886)

Alexis de Tocqueville, *Democracy in America* (1835)

Karl Marx and Friedrich Engels, *Communist Manifesto* (1848)

Harriet Beecher Stowe, *Uncle Tom's Cabin* (1851)

Henry David Thoreau, *Walden* (1854)

Walt Whitman, *Leaves of Grass* (1855)

Fyodor Dostoyevsky, *Crime and Punishment* (1856)

Charles Darwin, *On the Origin of Species* (1859)

Charles Dickens, *Great Expectations* (1861)

Harriet Jacobs, *Incidents in the Life of a Slave Girl, Written By Herself* (1861)

Abraham Lincoln, Gettysburg Address (1863)

Leo Tolstoy, *Anna Karenina* (1877)

Thomas Hardy, *The Return of the Native* (1878)

Henrik Ibsen, *A Doll's House* (1879)

Frederick Douglass, *The Life and Times of Frederick Douglass* (1881)

Friedrich Nietzsche, *Thus Spake Zarathustra* (1883)

Mark Twain, *Huckleberry Finn* (1884)

W. B. Yeats, *Selected Poems* (1895)

Stephen Crane, *The Red Badge of Courage* (1895)

Oscar Wilde, *The Importance of Being Earnest* (1899)

Sigmund Freud, *The Interpretation of Dreams* (1900)

Booker T. Washington, *Up From Slavery* (1901)

Joseph Conrad, *Heart of Darkness* (1902)

W. E. B. Du Bois, *The Souls of Black Folk* (1903)

Edith Wharton, *The House of Mirth* (1905)

G. K. Chesterton, "The Innocence of Father Brown" (1911)

Wilfrid Owen, *Selected Poems* (1918)

Lytton Strachey, *Queen Victoria* (1921)

Robert Frost, "A Poem with Notes and Grace Notes" (Pulitzer, 1924)

Franz Kafka, *The Trial* (1925)

F. Scott Fitzgerald, *The Great Gatsby* (1925)

T. S. Eliot, *Murder in the Cathedral* (1935)

Zora Neale Hurston, *Their Eyes Were Watching God* (c. 1937)

George Orwell, *The Road to Wigan Pier* (1937)

Thornton Wilder, *Our Town* (1938)

John Steinbeck, *The Grapes of Wrath* (1939)

Adolf Hitler, *Mein Kampf* (1939)

George Orwell, *Animal Farm* (1945)

Tennessee Williams, *A Streetcar Named Desire* (1947)

Ralph Ellison, *Invisible Man* (1952)

C. S. Lewis, *Mere Christianity* (1952)

Arthur Miller, *The Crucible* (1953)

Saul Bellow, *Seize the Day* (1956)

Robert Bolt, *A Man for All Seasons* (1962)

Martin Luther King, Jr., "Why We Can't Wait" (1964)

Tom Stoppard, *Rosencrantz and Guildenstern Are Dead* (1967)

Aleksandr Solzhenitsyn, *The Gulag Archipelago* (1974)

Toni Morrison, *Beloved* (1988)

Philip Larkin, *Collected Poems* (1991)

Elie Wiesel, *All Rivers Run to the Sea: Memoirs* (1995)

An Example

A ninth grader, for example, would prepare to read Aristophanes' *The Birds* by first identifying the historical period under study: 450–387 B.C., the lifespan of Aristophanes. She'll then look up 450–387 B.C. in her history encyclopedia, where she might discover (for example) that during this period, several important law systems (the Torah and the Twelve Tables of the Roman law) were codified; Greek architecture flourished (the Acropolis was rebuilt along with several other important Greek buildings); the plague swept through Athens; Greece fought its way through a series of important battles, including the Peloponnesian War; and Ezra and Nehemiah rebuilt the wall of Jerusalem. Darius of Persia rose to power as well; the Paracus culture flourished in Peru; and in Ohio, the Adena people reached the peak of their civilization. Using this information plus knowledge gathered from her history reading, the student would go on to create a Context page—one or two pages summarizing the most significant historical events between 450 and 387 B.C. Since *The Birds* is a Greek work, the summary should begin by focusing on events in Greece— the Peloponnesian War, the renaissance in architecture, Greece's form of government—and should then go on to explain events in other countries. (Don't worry about having a "topic sentence" in this composition, or about putting it into essay format; although they should be grammatically correct and spelled properly, these Context pages are likely to sound list-like. "Meanwhile, over in Asia . . .")

This summary page is not meant to be an exhaustive study of ancient history between 450 and 387 B.C. Rather, the student should choose to focus on one series of events during this time. She'll write more than one summary about this period, after all; as she reads Herodotus or Sophocles or Plato, she'll come back to these years again and write yet another Context page, focusing on a different series of events. But even if she doesn't return to this period of history, don't worry. As in every part of the classical education, you're not aiming for a total mastery of history. You're teaching methods of learning—in this case, how to read historical documents and put them into context. The student who masters this process will go on "doing history" for the rest of her life. When this summary page is done, the student should file it in the Book Contexts section of the notebook.

The Birds is a play, so the student should now read about the development of drama from one of the recommended "Reading Helps" resources. She'll take notes, paying special attention to the development of Greek drama. She could also choose to read a brief summary of the plot of *The Birds*, which will make her initial reading of the play a little easier. Finally, she'll crack open her volume of Aristophanes and read *The Birds* for herself, taking notes as she goes. When she's finished, she'll head these notes "*The Birds* by Aristophanes" and put them in the Book Notes section of the History and the Great Books notebook.

Once this is done, she'll sit down with you (or a tutor; see pages 766– 767) and talk about the play. Why was it written? What's Aristophanes' main point? Does it succeed as a drama? Which parts were interesting? Which were boring? Why? What is the play's structure? How might it be staged? (See the following section for guidance in what questions to ask.)

When the conversation is over, the student is ready to write. She can do a standard "book report," summarizing the plot of *The Birds* and giving a brief evaluation of the play. She can answer one of the discussion questions used during the conversation above in writing. She can explain what Aristophanes is saying about the nature of man and either agree or disagree. She can write about some technical aspect of Greek drama and how it applies to a scene in the play (this might require some additional research about the staging of Greek drama). This finished composition—which will give her a chance to exercise some of the skills taught in the writing and rhetoric programs recommended in Chapters 18 and 25—should be filed in the Compositions section of the notebook.

How much should you do?

Rather than holding rigidly to a schedule of how much to complete per week, you should instead devote two hours per day to reading and taking notes on history, and to reading, talking about, and writing about the Great Books. You can choose to spend the first hour of each day on history, the second on Great Books; or the first five hours of each week on history, the second five on Great Books; or one week on history, one on Great Books; or the first semester of each year on history, the second on Great Books. Don't worry about keeping history reading and Great Books reading somehow parallel; the two areas of study will fall within the same historical period, but the student will progress through them at different rates. And the time spent on any particular Great Book can vary widely. If the ninth grader isn't stirred by Greek drama, she'll probably finish the Aristophanes assignment in a week. If she decides to write about a technical aspect of staging Greek drama, though, she'll need to do extra reading and research, and the *Birds* assignment could easily cover two or three weeks.

As a parent and a teacher, it's your responsibility to make sure that those two hours are actually spent in reading and writing, rather than in daydreaming or creating doodles on notebook paper. Especially in the early years of high school, you should supervise this process, rather than allowing the student to disappear into the family room alone with her books. Great Books study in particular is demanding. It requires the student to work hard, to abandon simple question-and-answer learning in favor of a struggle with ideas. Often, the material isn't immediately appealing. The philosophies may be unfamiliar; the opinions are complex; the vocabulary is challenging. Put the student at the kitchen table (or wherever you're planning to be) so that you can encourage her to keep working.

The resurgence of interest in Great Books curricula has produced afford-able reprints of most of the books listed. Where we know of a particularly good edition, we've listed it, along with ordering information, at the end of this chapter.

The sets of Norton anthologies described in Resources at the end of the chapter are wonderful reference works. These contain many difficult-to-find texts (such as the *Epic of Gilgamesh*) and a nice sampling of poetry. However, we suggest that you find "real books" (stand-alone texts) when possible because anthologies are awkward to handle and the print is very small. Also, they're hard to read in bed and impossible to handle in the bathtub.

HOW TO TALK ABOUT THE GREAT BOOKS

Talking is a necessary part of learning; a student can't write well about the Great Books until she's had an opportunity to converse about them. But many parents feel intimidated by the thought of carrying on a conversation about Aristophanes or *Moby-Dick*.

If you can read some of these books along with your student, the Dis-cussion Helps listed in the Resources will give you plenty of material for conversation. (Remember, there aren't necessarily "right" answers to most of these questions; what's more important is the process of talking the ideas through.) If you can't read the books, don't hesitate to make use of the discussion helps we list, which supply not only plot summaries, but also biographical notes, cultural background, discussion questions, and bibliographies for further reading.

However, you don't have to shoulder the responsibility of this study alone. When you home-educate a high-school student, you organize his curriculum—but you can always outsource teaching responsibilities for those subjects for which you feel unprepared. The student still benefits from the personalized programs and individual attention that are so char-acteristic of home schooling when you use a tutor.

What options do you have for Great Books study? First, ask around your community: colleagues, home-schooling friends, religious commu-nity. You might find an ex–English major who wrote a thesis on *Pride and Prejudice,* or an ex-classics major who studied Plato at Harvard twenty-five years ago and would be *delighted* to discuss the *Republic* with your high-school student. Asking a friend to tutor your student for a year would be an imposition. Asking a friend to have a two-hour conversation about one book isn't. Remember: your student is working on a very basic level during this first introduction to the classics. He doesn't necessarily need a PhD candidate to discuss the book with him.

If you live near a university or community college, call the secretary of the appropriate department (English for British or American literature, classics for Greek or Latin, comparative literature for modern works in translation, drama or theater for all plays) and ask whether any member of the faculty is interested in meeting with your student. You can also use graduate students and responsible seniors for this sort of tutoring; a good prep school might also supply you with a tutor.

At the end of this chapter, we have provided a list of universities that offer varying types of Great Books curricula. These will prove especially valuable to those who live nearby. Most of the universities will also supply you with copies of their Great Books reading lists and curricula on request; some may even allow you to join in online discussion groups or e-mail lists.

Online tutorials and discussion groups not connected to universities may also help your high-school student begin his study of Great Books.

Online classes, offering high quality Great Books, literature, and history lectures and paper assignments, are available from a number of reputable online academies; we have listed them along with links at our website, welltrainedmind.com.

WRITING PROJECTS

The student should plan on writing a research paper in the spring of the ninth- and tenth-grade years. These research papers—six to eight pages in ninth grade, seven to ten pages in tenth grade—explore a historical topic. The ninth- and tenth-grade research papers should attempt to prove a theory about some historical event or series of events, using four to ten history resources, both primary (the works of Plato) and secondary (a critic's book *about* the works of Plato). These papers will put the techniques of rhetoric now being learned into use in writing and will prepare the student for the junior and senior projects described in Chapter 34.

Research-paper forms and procedures are covered in all of the grammar and composition texts we recommend. But because the very term *research paper* seems to terrify many parents (and students), we offer the following brief guide to preparing the first two research papers.

Preparation

Classically educated students don't need to suffer from "paper phobia," since the ongoing study of grammar and composition from early on and the continual writing of short papers have prepared them for the writing of longer papers. Along with mechanics, style, paragraph organization, and the development of arguments—all taught in the texts we recommend— the student must know how to outline.

In a proper outline, each subpoint supports the point that comes before:

I.
  A.
    1.
      a.

Correct outlining is taught in the grammar programs we suggest; if your student needs a refresher, see our recommendations in "Paper Helps" at the end of this chapter.

Inventio

Classical rhetoric divides writing into three stages: *inventio, dispositio,* and *elocutio. Inventio,* formulating an argument, involves picking the subject, deciding on a specific topic, and writing a thesis statement. Think of *inventio* as a three-step process.

1. Prereading. The student shouldn't begin by trying to write a thesis statement. Nor should she start making note cards immediately. Rather, she should begin by spending three or four weeks reading about the general topic she's decided to write on. Begin this process sometime in January. If, for example, the ninth grader decides to write about the Greek Empire after the death of Alexander the

Great, she shouldn't try to come up with an exact subject for her paper right away. If she does, she'll more than likely end up with an unworkable subject—one that's too broad or too vague. Instead, she should plan to skim through plenty of books, reading the sections that deal with the Greeks after Alexander. She shouldn't make notes yet, but should put bookmarks (strips of notebook paper are fine) on any pages she finds particularly interesting or informative. As she reads, she should brainstorm, jotting down on a pad of paper thoughts that come to mind, questions that her reading brings up, and comments on what she's finding out. These jottings don't need to be connected in any way. The student is simply exploring all the branches of her topic.

2. Settling on an exact subject. After the student has done plenty of pre-reading—covering ten books or more—she should gather together all her jottings and look for a particular theme that keeps popping up. If she finds, for example, that she has continually written "The Seleucids came after Alexander in Syria. Syria was important because of the trade routes. Antiochus the Great ruled Syria. Antiochus thought he was the sun god. The Seleucids took over Israel," this suggests that she should narrow her topic to "The Rulers of Syria after Alexander the Great."

   This is a narrower and more manageable topic, but the student still isn't ready to write. Now she needs to settle on a thesis statement.

3. Developing a thesis statement is tricky. Fortunately, all the curricula we recommend carefully develop this skill. As the parent/teacher, you should remember this simple definition: a thesis is a statement that requires proof. "Alexander's successors in Syria" or "Syria under Antiochus the Great" aren't thesis statements—they're simply phrases; neither needs to be proved. "Alexander's successors shared his megalomania" or "Antiochus the Great's insanity caused him to lose control of Syria" are thesis statements. Both require the student to explain, using examples from history to support these conclusions.

   Bad thesis statements tend to have two problems: either they're not specific enough, or they're so obvious that they don't require support. "Antiochus the Great was a bad ruler" is a bad thesis because it isn't specific—you could say this about any number of ancient potentates ("Nero was a bad ruler," "Akhenaton was a bad ruler"). "Alexander's empire was divided among his generals" doesn't work either. This is perfectly obvious. What's left to say?

"Antiochus's religious obsessions ruined his hold on his empire" is a good thesis statement because it leaves the student something to prove. She's suggesting a specific cause for the decline of the Seleucid Empire. Now she has to defend this conclusion, using historical evidence.

Dispositio

Once the student settles on a topic, she has to arrange supporting information in proper order for a persuasive argument—*dispositio.*

The student should begin by glancing back over the notes she's taken on her reading. From this information, she should make an outline covering the main points of her argument. These are the facts her reader will have to believe in order to be convinced. The outline should be very basic, only three or four points long, each point assigned a Roman numeral. The ninth grader's outline might look like this:

   I. Antiochus suffered from religious delusions.
  II. These delusions kept him from paying attention to his borders.
 III. These delusions caused him to treat his subjects with unnecessary cruelty.

The student should then write each major point at the top of a separate sheet of paper.

Now she's ready to start making note cards. The classic way of collecting information for a research paper is to write down quotes and general information on 3 × 5 cards, each card marked with the title of the book used and the author's last name. The student should go back through the books she used for prereading. In each place where she put a marker, she should evaluate whether or not the information supports one of her main points. If so, she should jot down on the note card either a paraphrase of the idea in the book or an exact quote. And she should indicate on each card where the information belongs by marking it with a Roman numeral that corresponds to a numeral on the outline.

There's no reason why the student shouldn't do this on a computer. Note cards have traditionally been used because the student can shuffle them around as she works on the flow of her argument. But since the cut-and-paste function on a word processor has the same effect, she can input her quotes and paraphrases instead.

Once the student has collected information (four to six sources for a ninth-grade paper, six to ten for a tenth-grade paper), she should put the cards for each Roman numeral into a pile and use this information to develop a more detailed outline:

I. Antiochus suffered from religious delusions.
   A. He thought he was the god Zeus.
      1. He retreated to his estate to practice being divine.
      2. He demanded that his courtiers worship him.

Each of these points is based on a fact discovered while reading and jotted onto a card.

Elocutio

When the outline is complete, the student is ready to write. *Elocutio,* the final stage of written rhetoric, involves the words, phrases, figures of speech, and writing techniques used in persuasive writing. The student should sit down with the outline and note cards, and write one well-structured paragraph about each point in the outline. The paper should always conclude with a summary paragraph, restating the student's thesis and main supporting points. Each book consulted must be placed on a bibliography page, arranged alphabetically by author. We highly recommend keeping a standard research-paper guide on hand throughout this process (see "Paper Helps").

WHAT ABOUT AMERICAN HISTORY AND GOVERNMENT?

A course in American government is a requirement for high-school graduation in most states, and most American college admissions offices will be looking for one year of American history on the high-school transcript. How does that square with our recommendations?

If your student progresses through all four years of history, using the resources we recommend at the end of this chapter, he will have covered all of the topics offered in a typical American history course—just integrated into the third and fourth years of world history rather than separated out. We think that this is, intellectually, the best way to approach American history; you can note it on the high-school transcript for the third and fourth years of study like this:

Course	Name of class on transcript	Credit
History 1600–1850	Early Modern History, first semester.	5
	American History, Part I, second semester.	5
History 1850–present	American History, Part II, first semester.	5
	Modern History, second semester.	5

(See "How to Put it on the Transcript" at the end of this chapter for a fuller explanation.)

However, if you'd prefer to have a more traditional American history course, here's what we would suggest:

Ninth grade	Ancient history, until c. 500 A.D.
Tenth grade	Medieval, Renaissance, and Enlightenment history, 500–1750
Eleventh grade	American history
Twelfth grade	Early modern and modern world history, 1750–present

During eleventh grade, use the American history resources we list for a full focused year of American history, and then return to our world history resources to study the rest of the world from 1750 on, glancing only briefly on American events already covered during eleventh grade. You can adjust the literature lists earlier in this chapter by date and country of origin, isolating the American literature recommendations and doing them in eleventh grade, and rearranging the remaining Great Books to match the dates above.

How about American government?

Traditionally, American government is offered as a separate .5 credit course or as a full-year 1 credit course combining government and economics. However, there's no reason to artificially separate the study of America's present government from its historical development. Whether you cover American history and literature along with world history in grades 11 and 12, or whether you choose to do a one-year course dedicated to the history and Great Books of the United States, you'll cover American history from its foundation to the present. The Great Books list includes the foundational texts of America's government: The Declaration of Independence, *The Federalist Papers,* and the Constitution of the United States (check to see that your copy includes the Bill of Rights and amendments). Make sure that these classics, along with Burke's "On American Taxation," Thomas Paine's "The Rights of Man," and Alexis de Tocqueville's *Democracy in America,* are on the student's final reading list. The student who reads and understands these books has grasped the core principles of American civics.

You'll want to add a guide to American government. We've suggested several standard texts and a few more nontraditional guides at the end of this chapter. Assign the student the task of reading, outlining, and summarizing one of these guides. As long as the student spends at least 60 hours over the course of one year or semester studying American government, you can award .5 credit in American government. If you'd prefer to do a full-year government and economics course, we have also listed resources for this.

STARTING IN THE MIDDLE

Although this chapter describes beginning the study of the ancients in ninth grade and moving through the medieval/early Renaissance, late Renaissance/early modern, and modern lists in grades 10, 11, and 12, this pattern can be adjusted to fit your own needs. A student who has begun the chronological study of history in middle school may begin ninth grade having just finished the ancients, or ready to move into the late Renaissance/early modern years. Whenever your student reaches ninth grade, move him to whichever Great Books list corresponds to the period he would naturally study next.

If you're just beginning this for the first time with a high-school student who only has a couple of years left, you have several choices:

1. Begin with whatever Great Books list corresponds to the student's grade year and move forward; don't worry too much about what you've skipped. High-school standards in the United States mandate the study of American literature and history, but are much less likely to insist on the study of ancient classics.

2. Condense the first two years of study into one list, attempting to pick half of the year's books from the ancients list and half from the medieval/early Renaissance list.

3. Use a standard high-school history textbook, but fold the reading and writing about Great Books into this textbook study at the appropriate points (the student will read the *Odyssey* when studying Greece, *Moby-Dick* when studying nineteenth-century America) and give the student a literature credit for this work.

UNIVERSITY SOURCES FOR GREAT BOOKS CURRICULA

Investigate these university websites for faculty contacts, reading lists, course descriptions, online helps, and possible student tutors.

Alabama
Auburn University, Auburn
Faulkner University, Montgomery

California
Seaver College, Pepperdine University, Malibu
Thomas Aquinas College, Santa Paula

Canada
Brock University, St. Catharines, Ontario
Carleton University, Ottawa, Ontario
Concordia University, Montreal, Quebec
Vancouver Island University, Nanaimo, British Columbia

Connecticut
Wesleyan University, Middletown

Georgia
Mercer University, Macon

Idaho
New St. Andrews College, Moscow

Illinois
Shimer College, Waukegan
The University of Chicago, Chicago
Wilbur Wright College, Chicago

Indiana
University of Notre Dame, South Bend

Louisiana
Northwestern State University of Louisiana, Natchitoches

Maryland
St. John's College, Annapolis

Massachusetts
Boston University, Boston

Minnesota
Saint Olaf College, Northfield

New Hampshire
Saint Anselm College, Manchester

New Mexico
St. John's College, Santa Fe

New York
Columbia College, Columbia University, New York City

Oregon
Gutenberg College, Eugene

Pennsylvania
Temple University, Philadelphia

Texas
College of Arts and Sciences, University of North Texas, Denton

Virginia
Emory & Henry College, Emory
Lynchburg College, Lynchburg

Washington
Central Washington University, Ellensburg
Whitman College, Walla Walla

Wisconsin
The University of Wisconsin–Milwaukee, Milwaukee

SUGGESTED SCHEDULES

Ninth through twelfth grade	2 hours per day	Read, discuss, write about history and Great Books.

HOW TO PUT IT ON THE TRANSCRIPT

Four-year world history scheme:

Course of study	Name of class(es) on transcript	Area	Credit
Ancient history and Great Books, 5,000 B.C. to A.D. 400 (2 hours per day/240 hours per year)	Ancient History	Social Sciences	1
	World Literature I	Language Arts	1

Medieval and early Renaissance history and Great Books, 400–1600 (2 hours per day/240 hours per year)	Medieval and Renaissance History	Social Sciences	1
	World Literature II	Language Arts	1
Early modern history and Great Books, 1600–1850 (2 hours per day/240 hours per year)	Early Modern World History, first semester	Social Sciences	.5
	European Literature I, first semester	Language Arts	.5
	American History, Part I, second semester	Social Sciences	.5
	Early American Literature, second semester	Language Arts	.5
Modern history and Great Books, 1850–present (2 hours per day/240 hours per year)	American History, Part II, first semester	Social Sciences	.5
	Modern American Literature, first semester	Language Arts	.5
	Modern World History, second semester	Social Sciences	.5
	European Literature II, second semester	Language Arts	.5
60 additional hours of American government study OR	American Government	Social Sciences	.5 OR
60 additional hours of American government and 60 additional hours of American economics	American Government & Economics	Social Sciences	1

Three-year world history and literature scheme with one year of focused American history and literature:

Course of study	Name of class(es) on transcript	Area	Credit
Ancient history and Great Books, 5,000 B.C. to A.D. 500 (2 hours per day/240 hours per year)	Ancient History World Literature I	Social Sciences Language Arts	1 1
Medieval, Renaissance, and Enlightenment history and Great Books, 400–1750 (2 hours per day/240 hours per year)	Early European History World Literature II	Social Sciences Language Arts	1 1
American history and literature (2 hours per day/ 240 hours per year)	American History American Literature	Social Sciences Language Arts	1 1
Early modern and modern history and Great Books, 1750–present (2 hours per day/240 hours per year)	Modern World History Modern Literature	Social Sciences Language Arts	1 1
60 additional hours of American government study OR	American Government	Social Sciences	.5 OR
60 additional hours of American government and 60 additional hours of American economics	American Government & Economics	Social Sciences	1

RESOURCES

Most books can be obtained from any bookseller or library; most curricula can be bought directly from the publisher or from a major home-school supplier such as Rainbow Resource Center. Contact information for publishers and suppliers can be found at www.welltrainedmind.com. If availability is limited, we have noted it. Remember that additional curricula choices and more can be found at www.well trainedmind.com. Prices change constantly, but we have included 2016 pricing to give an idea of affordability.

Basic texts for the four-year rhetoric stage are listed first. A Great Books section follows. The list for each year of study is in chronological order. Most of these books are available in standard editions, but where we think a specific edition is particularly good, we have recommended it.

Many of the resources recommended in Chapter 17 are still suitable for high-school students.

Basic Texts

There are many textbook world histories suitable for high-school study; the list below is a conscious attempt to steer away from textbooks and toward single-author works, but this approach inevitably leaves gaps and requires additional planning. You may use the methods outlined in this chapter with any decent world history survey, or with your own selection of single-author works focused on different parts of the world.

Choose from among the following:

Ancient History

Bauer, Susan Wise. *The History of the Ancient World: From the Earliest Accounts to the Fall of Rome.* New York: W. W. Norton, 2007.

$35. A narrative history covering the entire known world, from nomadic times through the rule of Constantine. A good basic spine for the year.

Beard, Mary. *SPQR: A History of Ancient Rome.* New York: Liveright, 2015.

$35. A valuable supplement to flesh out Roman history, for students who wish to pay a little more attention to the classical world. Beard is a renowned historian and an engaging writer.

Kaziewicz, Julia. *Study and Teaching Guide: The History of the Ancient World.* Charles City, VA: Well-Trained Mind Press, 2013.

$24.95. Comprehension questions, discussion questions, essay topics, grading rubrics, map exercises, and more to turn *The History of the Ancient World* into a full history study.

Medieval/Early Renaissance History

Bauer, Susan Wise. *The History of the Medieval World: From the Conversion of Constantine to the First Crusade.* New York: W. W. Norton, 2010.

$35. Accessible narrative history covering the world through the eleventh century.

———. *The History of the Renaissance World: From the Rediscovery of Aristotle to the Conquest of Constantinople.* New York: W. W. Norton, 2013.

$35. Accessible narrative history covering the world from the eleventh century through 1453.

Cantor, Norman F. *The Civilization of the Middle Ages: A Completely Revised and Expanded Edition of Medieval History.* New York: HarperPerennial, 1994.

$18.99. A classic text with a focus on Europe.

Kaziewicz, Julia. *Study and Teaching Guide: The History of the Medieval World.* Charles City, VA: Well-Trained Mind Press, 2016.

$44.95. Comprehension questions, discussion questions, essay topics grading rubrics, map exercises, and more.

———. *Study and Teaching Guide: The History of the Renaissance World.* Charles City, VA: Well-Trained Mind Press, 2016.

$44.95. Comprehension questions, discussion questions, essay topics, grading rubrics, map exercises, and more.

Late Renaissance/Early Modern History

Burger, Michael. *The Shaping of Western Civilization, Volume 1: From Antiquity to the Mid-Eighteenth Century.* Toronto: University of Toronto Press, 2013.

$44.95. A concise, no-frills account of the West through the Enlightenment. Use the second half for this year's study.

Cotterell, Arthur. *Asia: A Concise History.* New York: John Wiley, 2011.

$29.95. A readable and accessible history of Asia, from its Mesopotamian origins through the present day. Add to more Europe-centered resources for a more balanced study.

Johnson, Paul. *The Renaissance: A Short History*. New York: Modern Library, 2002.

$15. Excellent focus on the European Renaissance.

Tindall, George, and David Shi. *America: A Narrative History, Brief Tenth Edition*, Vol. 1 (Single Volume). New York: W. W. Norton, 2016.

$60. This book comes in various volumes and editions; look for this particular one. Covers American history to the Civil War and Reconstruction (1877).

Modern History

Cotterell, Arthur. *Asia: A Concise History*. New York: John Wiley, 2011.

$29.95. A readable and accessible history of Asia, from its Mesopotamian origins through the present day. Add to more Europe-centered resources for a more balanced study.

Davies, Norman. *Europe: A History. A Glorious Chronicle of Europe, From Kings to Peasants, From the Urals to the Faroes*. New York: Harper Perennial, 1998.

$25.99. A broad-picture history of Europe from ancient times; a good comprehensive guide to major events.

Johnson, Paul. *Modern Times: The World from the Twenties to the Nineties*, rev. ed. New York: HarperPerennial, 2001.

$21.99.

Tindall, George, and David Shi. *America: A Narrative History, Brief Tenth Edition*, Vol. 2. New York: W. W. Norton, 2016.

$60. This book comes in various volumes and editions; look for this particular one. Covers American history from 1860 to the present.

History Atlases and Encyclopedias

The history encyclopedias recommended as spines in Chapter 17 can also be used for high-school reference.

Grun, Bernard, and Eva Simpson. *The Timetables of History*, 4th rev. ed. New York: Touchstone, 2005.

$35.

Hart-Davis, Adam. *History: From the Dawn of Civilization to the Present Day.* New York: Dorling Kindersley, 2012.

$32.95. An excellent survey with detailed sidebars.

Kagan, Neil. *National Geographic Concise History of the World: An Illustrated Time Line,* rev. ed. Washington, DC: National Geographic, 2013.

$40. A nicely illustrated atlas with plenty of detail.

Reading Helps

Bauer, Susan Wise. *The Well-Educated Mind: A Guide to the Classical Education You Never Had,* updated and expanded ed. New York: W. W. Norton, 2016.

$35. Brief histories of six different genres (novel, autobiography, history, poetry, drama, science) and lists of Great Books in each, with annotations that summarize content, suggest discussion questions, and give context. Also includes suggestions for how to read each genre.

Sutherland, John. *A Little History of Literature.* New Haven, CT: Yale University Press, 2014.

$15. A readable, entertaining survey of Great Books and their genres, from *Beowulf* and Chaucer through mystery plays and Shakespeare, the rise of the novel, nineteenth- and twentieth-century poets, and modern bestsellers.

Discussion Helps

Barrons Book Notes/Pink Monkey Notes. pinkmonkeynotes.com

Barrons Book Notes cover 109 different classic texts: criticism, discussion, author biography, historical context, analysis of plot, and literary devices. All can be found at the Pink Monkey Notes website, along with more than 350 additional titles covered by Pink Monkey Notes, which are comparable to Cliffs Notes but downloadable only.

Bauer, Susan Wise. *The Well-Educated Mind: A Guide to the Classical Education You Never Had,* updated and expanded ed. New York: W. W. Norton, 2016.

$35. See above.

Cliffs Notes Study Guides. Boston: Houghton Mifflin Harcourt.

Plot summaries, discussion questions, survey of critical issues, character lists, literature techniques utilized—you'll find them all here, for hundreds of classic books. Buy from the publisher or from any bookstore; full listing on the publisher's website.

Foster, Thomas C. *How to Read Literature Like a Professor: A Lively and Entertaining Guide to Reading Between the Lines,* rev. ed. New York: Harper Perennial, 2014.

$15.99. Fantastic jump-start to thinking critically about literature.

Paper Helps

Armstrong, William H. *Study Is Hard Work: The Most Accessible and Lucid Text Available on Acquiring and Keeping Study Skills Through a Lifetime,* 2nd ed. Boston: David R. Godine, 2010.

$12.95. An excellent guide to study skills. Chapter Six, "Putting Ideas in Order," covers outlining skills, but the entire guide is valuable.

Graff, Gerald, and Cathy Birkenstein. *They Say, I Say: The Moves That Matter in Academic Writing,* 3rd ed. New York: W. W. Norton, 2014.

$23.91. An invaluable guide to citing authorities and sources: summarizing, quoting, responding, and more. Very valuable for the budding rhetorician.

Rozakis, Laurie. *Schaum's Quick Guide to Writing Great Research Papers,* 2nd ed. New York: McGraw-Hill, 2007.

$16. A straightforward manual covering research, documentation, and all the technical aspects of putting together a summary of information.

American Government and Economics

Bauman, Yoram. *The Cartoon Introduction to Economics,* illus. Grady Klein. New York: Hill & Wang.

$17.95 for each volume. An economist and illustrator team up to make economics a little clearer. It's still pretty thick, but the cartoons help a lot.

Volume One: Microeconomics. 2010.

Volume Two: Macroeconomics. 2013.

Bundy, George. *You Decide: Applying the Bill of Rights to Real Cases.* Pacific Grove, CA: Critical Thinking Press, 1992.

$26.99 ($14.99 additional for the teacher's guide, which is necessary because it contains the Supreme Court decisions). Presents the student with clear retellings of seventy-five Supreme Court cases and invites her to judge them, using the Bill of Rights as a guide. Good to fill out those necessary hours after going through the basic guide to government.

Kishtainy, Niall, et al. *The Economics Book: Big Ideas Simply Explained.* New York: DK Publishing, 2012.

$25. An unusually clear and engaging guide to economics, taking a historical perspective (from Plato and Aristotle to the present), making use of a time line and plenty of visuals.

Ragone, Nick. *The Everything American Government Book: From the Constitution to Present-Day Elections, All You Need to Understand Our Democratic System.* Avon, MA: Adams Media, 2004.

$15.95. Like the *Complete Idiot's Guide* that follows, this "non-textbook" guide contains everything covered in a standard American government one-semester course.

Scardino, Franco. *The Complete Idiot's Guide to U.S. Government and Politics.* New York: Alpha Books, 2009.

$19.95. An engaging and sometimes irreverent "text" that nevertheless covers all the government required for standard exams such as the AP or CLEP.

Wilson, James Q., John J. Dilulio, Jr., and Meena Rose. *American Government,* 11th ed. Boston: Wadsworth/Cengage Learning, 2013.

$160.95. For those who prefer a traditional textbook approach, this is a standard high-school text (and priced like one). Can be rented, bought used, or bought in a previous edition for less. Enough material for an entire year of study, particularly if supplemented with economics materials.

For Additional History Reading

Daugherty, James. *The Magna Carta.* Sandwich, MA: Beautiful Feet Books, 1998.
$13.95. A classic guide.

Davis, William S. *A Day in Old Athens.* Minneapolis: University of Minnesota Press, 1960.
$18. Davis, a wonderful writer and respected historian, brings past cultures to life.

——. *A Day in Old Rome.* New York: Biblo & Tannen, 1963.
$25.

——. *Life in a Medieval Barony.* New York: Biblo & Tannen, 1990.
$25.

——. *Life in Elizabethan Days.* New York: Biblo & Tannen, 1994.
$25.

Fairbank, John King, and Merle Goldman. *China: A New History,* 2nd enlarged ed. New York: Belknap Press, 2006.
$29.

Howarth, David. *1066: The Year of the Conquest.* New York: Penguin, 1981.
$15.

Johnson, Paul. *A History of the American People.* New York: HarperPerennial, 1999.
$22.99.

Keay, John. *India: A History,* rev. and updated ed. New York: Grove Press, 2011.
$20.

Lee, Ki-Baik. *A New History of Korea.* Trans. Edward W. Wagner. Boston: Harvard University Press, 1984.
$27.50.

Marrin, Albert. *America and Vietnam: The Elephant and the Tiger.* Sandwich, MA: Beautiful Feet Books, 2002.

$13.95. Marrin's history books are excellent for beginning historians; they offer readable overviews of complex events, driven by a strong narrative style.

————. *Empires Lost and Won: The Spanish Heritage in the Southwest*. New York: Simon & Schuster, 1997.

$19. Order from any bookstore.

————. *George Washington and the Founding of a Nation*. New York: Dutton, 2003.

$14.99.

————. *Stalin: Russia's Man of Steel*. Sandwich, MA: Beautiful Feet Books, 2002.

$13.95.

Meyer, Milton W. *Japan: A Concise History*, 4th ed. Lanham, MD: Rowman & Littlefield, 2012.

$35.

Morgan, Kenneth O., ed. *The Oxford Illustrated History of Britain*, rev. ed. Oxford: Oxford University Press, 2010.

$34.95.

Reader, John. *Africa: A Biography of the Continent*. New York: Vintage Books, 1999.

$20. Good guide to African history, from prehistoric times through the present.

Roberts, John Morris, and Odd Arne Westad. *The New Penguin History of the World*, 6th rev. ed. London: Penguin Books, 2014.

$25.

Great Books

Any titles listed without mentioning a specific edition can be easily located in standard editions. Texts can be bought through bookstores or online book services. In addition, public libraries should carry almost all of these titles.

The easiest way to read the Great Books is to buy a Norton anthology— the standard collection of classic works between two covers, all properly annotated. These are great reference works, but, like all reference works, they are unwieldy and have very small print. Your student won't read these in bed or in the car, only at a desk or table. We think you should use individual texts where possible because they're easier to read and more fun. Also, some works that you'll want to read in full are only excerpted in the anthologies. But consider investing in the Norton anthologies to fill in the gaps. You can also buy instructor's manuals with discussion questions and guides—an extremely valuable resource.

Baym, Nina, gen. ed., et al. *The Norton Anthology of American Literature*, 8th ed. New York: W. W. Norton.

This anthology is divided into five volumes (A–E) but ships in two packages, each of which has its own ISBN.

Package 1 (Volumes A, B): *Literature to 1865*. 2011. $61. From the explorers and settlers through Whitman; includes the American Founding Fathers.

Package 2 (Volumes C, D, E): *1865 to Present*. 2012. $57. From Samuel Clemens through the modern poets.

Greenblatt, Stephen, gen. ed. *The Norton Anthology of English Literature*, 9th ed. New York: W. W. Norton.

Package 1 (Volumes A, B, C): *The Middle Ages through the Restoration and the Eighteenth Century*. 2012. $62.33.

Package 2 (Volumes D, E, F): *The Romantic Period through the Twentieth Century*. 2012. $60.

Puchner, Martin, et al. *The Norton Anthology of Western Literature*, 9th ed. New York: W. W. Norton, 2014.

$81.25 for each volume.

Previous editions, called *The Norton Anthology of World Masterpieces*, can be bought used.

Volume 1.

Volume 2.

Ancients, 5000 B.C.–A.D. 400 (Ninth Grade)

Bible: Genesis—Book of Job.

Use a modern version for clarity. The New International Version is colloquial and clear; the New American Standard Bible is more stilted and also more literal.

Epic of Gilgamesh (c. 2500 B.C.).
Gilgamesh: A New English Version. Trans. Stephen Mitchell. New York: Atria Books, 2013.

Homer, *Iliad* and *Odyssey* (c. 850 B.C.).
Homer. *The Iliad*. Trans. Robert Fagles. New York: Penguin Books, 1999.
Homer. *The Odyssey*. Trans. Robert Fagles. New York: Penguin Books, 1999.

Sophocles, *Oedipus the King* (490 B.C.).
Sophocles. *The Oedipus Cycle*. Trans. Robert Fitzgerald and Dudley Fitts. San Diego: Mariner, 2002.

Aeschylus, *Agamemnon* (c. 458 B.C.).
Aeschylus. *Aeschylus I: The Oresteia*. Trans. David R. Slavitt. Philadelphia: University of Pennsylvania Press, 1997.

Herodotus, *The Histories* (c. 441 B.C.).
Trans. Robin Waterfield. Oxford: Oxford University Press, 2008.

Euripides, *Medea* (c. 431 B.C.).
Euripides. *Euripides: Medea, Hippolytus, Electra, Helen*. Trans. James Morwood. Oxford: Oxford University Press, 1998.

Aristophanes, *The Birds* (c. 400 B.C.).
Aristophanes. *Aristophanes I: Clouds, Wasps, Birds*. Trans. Peter Meineck. Indianapolis: Hackett, 1998.

Thucydides, *The History of the Peloponnesian War* (c. 400 B.C.).
The Landmark Thucydides. Trans. Richard Crawley. New York: Free Press, 1998.

Plato, *The Republic* (c. 375 B.C.).
Trans. G. M. A. Grube, rev. C. D. C. Reeve, 2nd ed. New York: Hackett Publishing, 1992.

Aristotle, *On Poetics* (350 B.C.).
Aristotle. *Aristotle on Poetics*. Trans. Seth Benardete. South Bend, IN: St. Augustine Press, 2002.
Aristotle, *Rhetoric* (c. 350 B.C.).

Bible: Book of Daniel (c. 165 B.C.).

Horace, *Odes* (c. 65 B.C.).

New Translations by Contemporary Poets. Ed. J. D. McClatchy. Princeton, NJ: Princeton University Press, 2005.

Lucretius, *On the Nature of Things* (c. 60 B.C.).
   On the Nature of the Universe. Trans. Ronald Melville. Oxford: Oxford University Press, 2009.

Cicero, *De republica* (54 B.C.).
Virgil, *Aeneid* (c. 30 B.C.).
Ovid, *Metamorphoses* (c. A.D. 5).
Bible: Corinthians 1 and 2 (c. A.D. 58).
Josephus, *Wars of the Jews* (c. A.D. 68).

Plutarch, *The Lives of the Noble Greeks and Romans* (c. A.D. 100).
   Plutarch. *Roman Lives: A Selection of Eight Lives.* Trans. Robin Waterfield. Oxford: Oxford University Press, 2009.
   Plutarch. *Greek Lives: A Selection of Nine Lives.* Trans. Robin Waterfield. Oxford: Oxford University Press, 2009.

Tacitus, *Annals* (c. A.D. 117).
Athanasius, *On the Incarnation* (c. A.D. 300).

Medieval/Early Renaissance, 400–1600 (Tenth Grade)
Augustine, *Confessions* (c. 411).
   Trans. Henry Chadwick. Oxford: Oxford University Press, 2009.

Augustine, *City of God,* Book 8 (c. 426).
   Abridged ed. Trans. Marcus Dods. New York: Modern Library, 2000.

Boethius, *The Consolation of Philosophy* (524).

Koran (selections) (c. 650).

Bede, *The Ecclesiastical History of the English People* (731).
   Ed. Judith McClure and Roger Collins. Oxford: Oxford University Press, 2009.

Beowulf (c. 1000).
   Beowulf: A New Verse Translation. Trans. Seamus Heaney. New York: W. W. Norton, 2001.

Mabinogion (c. 1050).

Anselm, *Cur Deus Homo* (c. 1090).

Thomas Aquinas, *Selected Writings* (c. 1273).
Thomas Aquinas. *Selected Writings of St. Thomas Aquinas.* Trans. Ralph McInerny. New York: Penguin, 1999.

Dante, *The Inferno* (1320).
Trans. Robert Pinsky. New York: Farrar, Straus and Giroux, 1996.

Everyman (14th century).

Sir Gawain and the Green Knight (c. 1400).
Sir Gawain and the Green Knight, Patience, Pearl: Verse Translations. Trans. Marie Boroff. New York: W. W. Norton, 2009.

Chaucer, *The Canterbury Tales* (selections) (c. 1400).
Trans. Nevill Coghill. New York: Penguin Books, 2003 (rev. ed.).

Margery Kempe, *The Book of Margery Kempe* (1430).
Margery Kempe. *The Book of Margery Kempe: A New Translation, Contexts, Criticism.* Trans. and ed. Lynn Staley. New York: W. W. Norton, 2001.

Malory, *Le Morte d'Arthur* (selections) (c. 1470).

Erasmus, *Education of a Christian Prince* (selections) (1510).

Machiavelli, *The Prince* (1513).
2nd ed. Trans. Harvey C. Mansfield. Chicago: University of Chicago Press, 1998.

Thomas More, *Utopia* (1516).
Trans. Robert M. Adams. New York: W. W. Norton, 1991.

Martin Luther, *Commentary on Galatians* (c. 1520).

John Calvin, *Institutes of the Christian Religion* (selections) (1536).

Christopher Marlowe, *Faustus* (1588).

Teresa of Avila, *The Life of Saint Teresa of Avila by Herself* (1588).
Trans. J. M. Cohen. New York: Penguin, 1988.

Edmund Spenser, *The Faerie Queene*, selections (1590).

William Shakespeare, *Julius Caesar* (1599).

William Shakespeare. *Julius Caesar: Oxford School Shakespeare*. 3rd ed. Ed. Roma Gill. Oxford: Oxford University Press, 2010.

William Shakespeare, *Hamlet* (1600).
William Shakespeare. *Hamlet: Oxford School Shakespeare*. Rev. ed. Ed. Roma Gill. Oxford: Oxford University Press, 2009.

William Shakespeare, any other plays (c. 1592–1611).

Late Renaissance/Early Modern, 1600–1850 (Eleventh Grade)
Miguel de Cervantes, *Don Quixote* (1605).
Abridged. Trans. Walter Starkie. New York: Signet, 2013.

King James Bible, *Psalms* (1611).
John Donne, *Divine Meditations* (c. 1635).
Rene Descartes, *Meditations* (1641).
John Milton, *Paradise Lost* (selections) (1644).
Molière, *Tartuffe* (1669).

Blaise Pascal, *Pensées* (1670).
The *Pensées* are lengthy. If you'd prefer an edited version, try Peter Kreeft's *Christianity for Modern Pagans: Pascal's Pensées Edited, Outlined, and Explained* (Fort Collins, CO: Ignatius Press, 1993). This picks out the most relevant of the *Pensées* for today's student and provides discussion.

John Bunyan, *The Pilgrim's Progress* (1679).

John Locke, "An Essay Concerning Human Understanding" or "On the True End of Civil Government" (1690).
Jonathan Swift, *Gulliver's Travels* (1726).
Edmund Burke, "On American Taxation" (1774).

Jean-Jacques Rousseau, "The Social Contract" (1762).
Trans. Maurice Cranston. New York: Penguin, 1968.

The Declaration of Independence (1776).
Thomas Paine, *Common Sense* (1776).
Immanuel Kant, "Critique of Pure Reason" (1781).
Alexander Hamilton et al., *The Federalist Papers* (1787–1788).
Constitution of the United States (ratified 1788).

William Blake, *Songs of Innocence and Experience* (1789).

Benjamin Franklin, *The Autobiography* (1791).

Thomas Paine, "The Rights of Man" (1792).

Mary Wollstonecraft, *A Vindication of the Rights of Woman* (1792).

William Wordsworth and Samuel Taylor Coleridge, *Lyrical Ballads* (1798).

Jane Austen, *Pride and Prejudice* (1815).

Mary Shelley, *Frankenstein* (1818).

John Keats, "Ode to a Nightingale" and other poems (1820s).

James Fenimore Cooper, *The Last of the Mohicans* (1826).

Alfred, Lord Tennyson, "The Lady of Shalott" and other poems (1832).

Charles Dickens, *Oliver Twist* (1838).

Edgar Allan Poe, "The Fall of the House of Usher" and other stories (1839).

Ralph Waldo Emerson, "Self-Reliance" and other essays (1844).

Charlotte Brontë, *Jane Eyre* (1847).

Nathaniel Hawthorne, *The Scarlet Letter* (1850).

Herman Melville, *Moby-Dick* (1851).

Modern, 1850–Present Day (Twelfth Grade)

Alexis de Tocqueville, *Democracy in America* (1835).
    Trans. Harvey Manfield and Delba Winthrop. Ed. and abridged by Richard D. Heffner. Chicago: University of Chicago Press, 2002.

Karl Marx and Friedrich Engels, *Communist Manifesto* (1848).

Harriet Beecher Stowe, *Uncle Tom's Cabin* (1851).

Henry David Thoreau, *Walden* (1854).

Walt Whitman, *Leaves of Grass* (1855).

Emily Dickinson, *Final Harvest* (1830–1886).
    Ed. T. H. Johnson. Boston: Back Bay Books, 1997.

Charles Darwin, *On the Origin of Species* (1859).

Charles Dickens, *Great Expectations* (1861).

Harriet Jacobs, *Incidents in the Life of a Slave Girl, Written By Herself* (1861).

Abraham Lincoln, Gettysburg Address (1863).

Fyodor Dostoyevsky, *Crime and Punishment* (1866).
    Trans. Richard Pevear and Larissa Volokhonsky (New York: Random House, 2008) or Constance Garnett (New York: Dover, 2001).

Leo Tolstoy, *Anna Karenina* (1877).
> Trans. Constance Garnett, rev. Leonard J. Kent and Nina Berberova. New York: Modern Library, 2000.

Thomas Hardy, *The Return of the Native* (1878).

Henrik Ibsen, *A Doll's House* (1879).
> Trans. Frank McGuinness. New York: Dramatists Play Service, 1998.

Frederick Douglass, *The Life and Times of Frederick Douglass* (1881).
Friedrich Nietzsche, *Thus Spake Zarathustra* (1883).
Mark Twain, *Huckleberry Finn* (1884).

W. B. Yeats, *Selected Poems* (1895).
> W. B. Yeats. *The Collected Poems of W. B. Yeats,* 2nd rev. ed.. Ed. Richard J. Finneran. New York: Scribner's, 1996.

Stephen Crane, *The Red Badge of Courage* (1895).
Oscar Wilde, *The Importance of Being Earnest* (1899).
Sigmund Freud, *The Interpretation of Dreams* (1900).
Booker T. Washington, *Up From Slavery* (1901).
Joseph Conrad, *Heart of Darkness* (1902).
W. E. B. Du Bois, *The Souls of Black Folk* (1903).
Edith Wharton, *The House of Mirth* (1905).
G. K. Chesterton, "The Innocence of Father Brown" (1911).
Wilfrid Owen, *Selected Poems* (1918).
Lytton Strachey, *Queen Victoria* (1921).
Robert Frost, "A Poem with Notes and Grace Notes" (Pulitzer, 1924).

Franz Kafka, *The Trial* (1925).
> Trans. Breon Mitchell. New York: Schocken Books, 1999.

F. Scott Fitzgerald, *The Great Gatsby* (1925).
T. S. Eliot, *Murder in the Cathedral* (1935).
Zora Neale Hurston, *Their Eyes Were Watching God* (c. 1937).
George Orwell, *The Road to Wigan Pier* (1937).
Thornton Wilder, *Our Town* (1938).
John Steinbeck, *The Grapes of Wrath* (1939).

Adolf Hitler, *Mein Kampf* (1939).
> Trans. Ralph Manheim. Boston: Houghton Mifflin, 1998.

George Orwell, *Animal Farm* (1945).

Tennessee Williams, *A Streetcar Named Desire* (1947).

Ralph Ellison, *Invisible Man* (1952).

C. S. Lewis, *Mere Christianity* (1952).

Arthur Miller, *The Crucible* (1953).

Saul Bellow, *Seize the Day* (1956).

Robert Bolt, *A Man for All Seasons* (1962).

Martin Luther King, Jr., "Why We Can't Wait" (1964).

Tom Stoppard, *Rosencrantz and Guildenstern Are Dead* (1967).

Aleksandr Solzhenitsyn, *The Gulag Archipelago* (1974).
   Aleksandr Solzhenitsyn. *The Gulag Archipelago: An Authorized Abridgement.*
   Ed. Edward E. Ericson, Jr. New York: Harper Perennial, 2007.

Toni Morrison, *Beloved* (1988).

Philip Larkin, *Collected Poems* (1991).
   Ed. Anthony Thwaite. New York: Farrar, Straus and Giroux, 2004.

Elie Wiesel, *All Rivers Run to the Sea: Memoirs* (1995).

28

COMFORT WITH NUMBERS:

MATH

The cumulative and coherent study of mathematics is, in fact, a microcosm of the entire curriculum and reflects in its expanding field the workings of the scholarly mind in a manner analogous to that which we examined in the field of arts and letters.

—David Hicks, *Norms and Nobility*

SUBJECT: **Higher mathematics**

TIME REQUIRED: **5 hours per week for each year of study**

A classical education considers competency in higher-level math skills (algebra, plane geometry, and geometrical proofs) and comfort with mathematical thinking to be part of basic literacy. The classically educated student will complete courses in geometry, first-year algebra, and second-year algebra (this coincides with the bare minimum demanded by most colleges for admission) and move on to at least one year of advanced mathematics: trigonometry, pre-calculus and calculus, statistics and probability.

By high school, STEM-focused students, headed for further study in science, technology, engineering, or mathematics, should already be well on the way to completing this basic sequence:

Grade	Course
Ninth	Algebra I
Tenth	Geometry
Eleventh	Algebra II
Twelfth	Trigonometry/Pre-calculus

or one of the following sequences:

Grade	Course	Grade	Course
Seventh	Pre-algebra	Seventh	Algebra I
Eighth	Algebra I	Eighth	Geometry
Ninth	Geometry	Ninth	Algebra II
Tenth	Algebra II	Tenth	Trigonometry/Pre-calculus
Eleventh	Trigonometry/Pre-calculus	Eleventh	Calculus
Twelfth	Calculus	Twelfth	Statistics & probability

both of which demonstrate a very high level of mathematical achievement.

We suggest, however, that if possible all students aim to complete at least one advanced mathematics course in twelfth grade. An understanding of statistics and probability (the study of how data is collected, analyzed, and interpreted) is vital to anyone who wants to understand what poll results really mean, how to make a decision based on a collection of facts, what the likelihood of an asteroid hitting the earth might actually be. Trigonometry is geometry put to use, the study of how to use geometrical formulas to solve real problems: the exact borders of a piece of land, a better digital recording, the strength of a bridge.

Too often, humanities-focused students come away from algebra (let alone the higher levels of math) convinced that the purpose of mathematics is to solve abstract puzzles for no particular reason. Most of the time, this is a teaching problem, not a learning problem. So as a home-educating parent, you have one of two challenges: either to share your own love of math, or (if you're not a maths person yourself) to find good teaching and bring it to your student.

The curricula described in the Resources at the end of this chapter can all be used by a skilled and enthusiastic teacher. Your task: become or locate that teacher.

Online learning can become particularly valuable for upper-level math. Visit welltrainedmind.com for an ongoing list of excellent online math options.

We would also suggest that, particularly in eleventh and twelfth grades, you return to the list of math books for general readers listed in Chapter 6 and assign at least one book per year to your student. We've listed a few more titles in the Resources at the end of this chapter; choose from these as well. Advanced math courses require a great deal of technical work, and it's very easy for students to lose sight of *why* they're working so hard. When you're laboring in a thicket of equations, the whole forest often disappears.

A WORD ABOUT STUDENTS WHO STRUGGLE

If your ninth grader is still battling with algebra and making little progress, *change your approach*. Whatever program you're using, try another one. Whatever tutor, co-op, or online class you've invested in, switch. Do not keep pushing forward, hoping that things will get better. Students who are perplexed by algebra will not be able to advance without frustration; algebraic skills are absolutely foundational to further math study.

However, students who battle hard just to reach algebra II should probably be allowed to "rest on their oars." Rather than requiring additional upper-level math, consider a yearlong "math reading" program during which the student will read additional books about math from the Chapter 6 list and the Additional Reading list at the end of this chapter. This will work to build general math literacy and may also give the student the motivation to return to math, either in college or later in life, and tackle it with added maturity.

SUGGESTED SCHEDULES

High-school math requires at least an hour per day, four or five times per week. The fifth day could also be used for general math reading.

HOW TO PUT IT ON THE TRANSCRIPT

Entering mathematics classes on the transcript is simple: the name of the class is simply Algebra I, Geometry, Algebra II, etc., and each class is 1 credit when completed.

You cannot give high-school credit for pre-algebra even if it is taken in ninth grade. You can give high-school credit for algebra 1, even if taken in seventh or eighth grade, but the student is probably better served by going on to take additional upper-level math classes in the junior and senior year and receiving high-school credit for those.

You need a minimum of 3 high-school credits in mathematics; four is ideal.

RESOURCES

Most books can be obtained from any bookseller or library; most curricula can be bought directly from the publisher or from a major home-school supplier such as Rainbow Resource Center. Contact information for publishers and suppliers can be found at www.welltrainedmind.com. If availability is limited, we have noted it. Remember that additional curricula choices and more can be found at www.well trainedmind.com. Prices change constantly, but we have included 2016 pricing to give an idea of affordability.

Math Curricula

Note: There are many programs available to home educators; explore more advanced mathematics options and read user reviews at www.well trainedmind.com.

Art of Problem Solving

The Art of Problem Solving math program is a highly conceptual, discovery-oriented program. Rather than learning concepts and then practicing skills to reinforce them, students are challenged to solve problems in order to find their way to mastery; puzzlement is an important part of the program. Students work their way through sets of problems that slowly increase in difficulty in order to uncover a concept, and are then given an explanation of the concept itself *afterward.*

This will suit students who enjoy a challenge and who prefer to find their way independently, but frustrate those who need a little more specific guidance and leading from a teacher. For those whose learning style suits the program, AOPS can lead to high achievement.

Diagnostic tests and samples are available at the publisher's website; online classes using the books, and online versions of the texts, are also offered.

Art of Problem Solving mathematics curriculum. Alpine, CA: AOPS Press.

Prealgebra. Richard Rusczyk, David Patrick, and Ravi Boppana. Text and solutions, $54.

Introduction to Algebra. Richard Rusczyk. Text and solutions, $59.

A complete Algebra I course with some Algebra II material included.

Introduction to Geometry. Richard Ruscyzk. Text and solutions, $57.

Basic geometry course.

Intermediate Algebra. Richard Ruscyzk and Matthew Crawford. Text and solutions, $64.

Algebra II with some pre-calculus topics.

Precalculus. Richard Ruscyzk. Text and solutions, $53.

Covers both pre-calculus and trigonometry; a one-year course. Give credit for Trigonometry & Pre-Calculus.

Calculus. David Patrick. Text and solutions, $49.

Covers all material needed for a 1-credit course in calculus.

Additional elective:

Introduction to Counting & Probability. David Patrick. Text and solutions, $42.

Intermediate Counting & Probability. David Patrick. Text and solutions, $47.

Complete both books to award 1 credit. The course is called "Counting and Probability" and falls under advanced mathematics.

Math-U-See

In the upper levels, Math-U-See continues on with the workbook/video/manipulative combination previously used. The algebra sequence follows the standard progression of pre-algebra, first-year algebra, geometry, second-year algebra, and trigonometry.

Each Universal Set is $151 and includes all manipulatives as well as instructional DVD, solution manual, student workbook, and tests. Students who have used previous levels of Math-U-See may already have the manipulatives and can simply order the Base Set for pre-algebra and algebra I for $79.

Placement tests, online samples, and more ordering options can be found at the publisher's website.

> Math-U-See. Lancaster, PA: Math-U-See, Inc.
> *Pre-Algebra Universal Set* ($151) or *Base Set* ($79).
> *Algebra I Universal Set* ($151) or *Base Set* ($79).
> *Geometry Universal Set.* $81.
> *Algebra II Universal Set.* $110.
> *Pre-Calculus Universal Set.* $110.
> Includes trigonometry.
> *Calculus.*
> *Calculus Student Pack.* $35.
> *Calculus Instruction Pack.* $72.

Saxon

The upper levels of Saxon continue with the same careful procedural approach as the elementary and middle grades. Placement tests can be downloaded from the publisher's website. Supplement with conceptual resources as necessary.

Previous editions of Saxon math had "integrated geometry"; rather than being divided into the traditional American sequence of algebra I, geometry, and algebra II, the three books (Algebra I, Algebra II, and Advanced Mathematics) spread algebraic and geometric topics out over three years. The current edition follows the standard American pattern instead. If you are using an older version, be aware that all geometry topics will not be covered until the end of the third year, which may affect testing results (since most American standardized tests assume all geometry has been covered in the second year).

Make sure you choose the kit *with* Solutions Manual; the regular "Homeschool Kit" without Solutions Manual specified contains student materials only.

Saxon Homeschool Mathematics. Boston: Houghton Mifflin Harcourt.

Saxon Algebra 1/2 Kit with Solutions Manual, 3rd ed.. $120.60.

 Pre-algebra.

Saxon Algebra I Homeschool Kit with Solutions Manual, 3rd ed. $129.20.

Saxon Homeschool Geometry Kit with Solutions Manual, 1st ed. $135.80.

Saxon Algebra 2 Homeschool Kit with Solutions Manual, 3rd. ed. $130.50.

Saxon Advanced Math Homeschool Kit with Solutions Manual, 2nd ed. $136.85.

 This is Saxon's trigonometry and pre-calculus course.

Saxon Calculus Homeschool Kit with Solutions Manual, 2nd ed. $146.90.

VideoText

Developed by mathematics teacher Tom Clark, VideoText takes a different approach to algebra. The first course, *Algebra: A Complete Course,* covers pre-algebra, algebra I, and algebra II in a single course that stretches over 176 lessons (and can take up to three years to complete), while *Geometry: A Complete Course* is 176 lessons covering geometry, trigonometry, and pre-calculus. Since the geometry course follows the algebra course, students will not complete geometry topics normally taught after algebra I until later years of study; this is a perfectly reasonable strategy but may affect test results (particularly SAT scores) for students who begin the sequence late.

You will need to use another resource for calculus if the student wishes to continue on.

VideoText, recommended by the developer of RightStart as a good follow-up to the RightStart elementary course, is mastery-oriented (not spiral), and nicely blends conceptual teaching with procedural practice. Students watch a DVD lesson, pausing when instructed to answer questions or complete assignments, and then work through practice problems.

The program is particularly well suited to students who are ready to begin pre-algebra relatively early, giving them a good chance of getting through both courses before SAT testing begins. Students who do not wish to go on to trigonometry may want to substitute a separate geometry course.

Scope and sequence and further explanations of the method are available at the publisher's website. Instructional materials include DVDs, workbook, print version of DVD instruction, solutions manual, progress tests, and instructor's guides; the publisher also offers an online version of the program with varied pricing depending on the number of students taking part.

Algebra: A Complete Course.
Algebra Modules A-B-C. $279.
Algebra Modules D-E-F. $279.
Geometry: A Complete Course with Trigonometry. $529.

Supplementary Resources

Khan Academy.

Founded by Salman Khan as a nonprofit educational organization, Khan Academy offers "microlectures" in all elementary mathematical concepts, along with online exercises and practice problems. Use to learn or review specific topics, or design a personalized instructional plan. Highly recommended as a supplement to any math program. www .khanacademy.org.

Life of Fred. Reno, NV: Polka Dot Publishing. Order from the publisher. Entertaining math surveys that encourage critical thinking.

Beginning Algebra Expanded Edition. $39.
Advanced Algebra Expanded Edition. $39.
Geometry Expanded Edition. $39.
Trigonometry Expanded Edition. $39.
Calculus. $39.
Calculus Answer Key. $6.
Statistics $39.
Statistics Answer Key. $6.

Mathematics Enhancement Program

A British version of a mathematics program developed in Hungary, MEP offers free online practice sheets, answers, and some teacher helps, along with number lines and number and shape cards. When followed sequentially, the lessons are spiral in approach. Download at the Centre for Innovation in Mathematics Teaching. www.cimt.plymouth.ac.uk. Excellent resources for statistics, further calculus, and other advanced math topics.

The Practice of Statistics: For the AP Exam, 5th ed. New York: W. H. Freeman, 2014.

$133.32. Can be rented or bought used (or in an earlier edition) for much less. Standard statistics and data analysis textbook.

Serra, Michael. *Patty Paper Geometry*. San Francisco, CA: Playing It Smart, 2011.

A discovery-oriented, hands on, completely different approach to geometry.

Additional Reading

Also see the list of recommended general math books in Chapter 6, pages 120–121.

Harris, Michael. *Mathematics Without Apologies: Portrait of a Problematic Vocation*. Princeton, NJ: Princeton University Press, 2015.

For mature readers; a pure mathematician muses about his research and the place it occupies in the real world.

Huff, Darrell. *How to Lie With Statistics*, illus. Irving Geis. New York: W. W. Norton, 1993.

Breezy exploration of how numbers can mislead.

Stewart, Ian. *In Pursuit of the Unknown: 17 Equations That Changed the World*. New York: Basic Books, 2013.

Great discoveries in mathematics.

———. *Professor Stewart's Cabinet of Mathematical Curiosities*. New York: Basic Books, 2009.

Puzzles and oddities.

———. *Professor Stewart's Casebook of Mathematical Mysteries*. New York: Basic Books, 2014.

Curiosities and conundrums.

———. *Professor Stewart's Hoard of Mathematical Treasures*. New York: Basic Books, 2010.

Games, riddles, paradoxes, and more.

Zaccaro, Edward. *The 10 Things All Future Mathematicians and Scientists Must Know (But Are Rarely Taught)*. Bellevue, IA: Hickory Grove Press, 2003.

An exploration of the connections between maths and real-world problems.

Zaccaro, Edward, and Daniel E. Zaccaro. *Scammed By Statistics*. Bellevue, IA: Hickory Grove Press, 2010.
How data can be manipulated, and how to spot the scam.

29

PRINCIPLES AND LAWS:
SCIENCE

Science without conscience is the death of the soul.

—François Rabelais

SUBJECT: High-school science (biology, astronomy, chemistry, physics)

TIME REQUIRED: 4 or more hours per week

How does the classical approach to the study of science differ from science taught in schools across the country?

Two distinctive characteristics set rhetoric-stage science apart. First, science studies are rigorous and intellectually demanding, like all classical subjects. The student is encouraged to study science for all four years of high school, passing again through such fields as biology, astronomy,[1] chemistry, and physics. She'll study the principles and laws of each science, finishing high school with a sound grasp of foundational scientific

---

[1] In high school, earth science gives way to a more intensive study of astronomy.

ideas. As in all stages of classical education, she will read and write about science as well as performing hands-on work and experiments. And she'll be encouraged to explore science resources, rather than filling in workbooks and answering comprehension questions.

But rigorous science education can be found in any number of nonclassical curricula. "Classical" science is further distinguished by its demand that the student do science *self-consciously*—not simply learn about the world, but ask what the implications of each discovery might be. What does this theory say about my existence? What does that principle imply about human beings and their place in the universe? What are the implications for the human race?

As a whole, then, rhetoric-stage science is taught in the context of the student's broader study of ideas. The student isn't merely learning abstract principles; she's seeing how they fit into the Great Conversation she's having with the great books of the classical curriculum.

AN OVERVIEW OF RHETORIC-STAGE SCIENCE

Rhetoric-stage science study falls into three parts.

1. **The study of principles.** Using texts and experiment books, the student will learn the basic laws and principles of each scientific field.
2. **Source readings.** Each year, the student will also investigate the development of a given scientific field and will read from primary scientific sources—the reflections of contemporary scientists on the work being done in their own day. This gives historical perspective to the study of science and its ongoing debates.
3. **Joining the Great Conversation.** Each year, the science student will complete a project and/or write a paper illuminating the history and development of some new technology or knowledge. This paper should be centered around the field being studied. The biology student, for example, could write on the changing ideas about origins, investigate the problems of extinction or the rise of new diseases or the development of antibiotic-resistant pathogens. The astronomy student could write about the changing paradigms of the universe—

the earth's move from the center of the universe to its edge—and the effect this shift had on our view of ourselves. The chemistry student could research the development of various types of fuels and how they have changed the landscape of work and daily life. Physics students could choose any twentieth-century technology, from the splitting of the atom to the development of the Internet, and write about both its past history and its possible future.

WHAT TO STUDY, AND WHEN

In previous editions of *The Well-Trained Mind*, we suggested studying the sciences in relationship to history: biology along with ancient history, astronomy during medieval and early Renaissance history, chemistry and physics with early modern and modern history respectively.

This pairs each science with the era during which its greatest technical advances were made. However, the link isn't strong enough to rule out other schemes: a year spent on technology and engineering, for example, or two (or more) years spent on one field of science in order to gain a deeper expertise. You should feel free to evolve your own scheme of study, using these parameters:

1. Award at least 3 high-school science credits; 4 is better.
2. At least two of your sciences should have a lab component; three is better (and you should check both your standards, and the expectations of any university that your student might be contemplating; state universities can be inflexible in their prerequisites).
3. At least two different fields of science should be studied (so, for example, a student might choose to do Introduction to Biology one year, followed by an advanced biology course the following year, but the third year should choose chemistry, physics, astronomy, or a technological field instead).
4. Remember that physical science (as opposed to physics) and earth science are not considered high-school courses; these will be questioned if you include them on the transcript. Geology and technology courses are less common, but still acceptable if pursued at a high-

school level. Computer science (oddly enough) is only accepted as a legitimate science elective in about half of the United States; as of this writing, it's safest to use it as your fourth science credit rather than as one of the core three.

5. Delay physics until last so that the student has enough advanced math to do the necessary calculations.

HOW TO DO IT

As in the previous two stages, we suggest using a notebook to organize the student's work. Each notebook should have three sections: Principles, Source Readings, and Project Notes.

The Study of Principles

By "Principles," we simply mean: the organized content of each scientific field.

Unlike history and literature, high-school sciences need to be studied in a particular order: in chemistry, you've got to learn the makeup of an atom before you learn about atomic bonding; in biology, you have to understand the structure of a cell before you can investigate how particular cells function. In other words, science combines aspects of *skill mastery* with *content learning* (see the distinction we draw in Chapter 2. So we recommend working through a well-done textbook, with accompanying exercises, assignments, and experiments, as the spine of high-school science.

In the Resources at the end of this chapter, we've recommended a number of highly regarded science textbooks that home educating parents have used with success. Also consider online classes (see our updated list at welltrainedmind.com). Don't forget that some public school systems will open their science classes to home educators; and junior and senior high-school students may also be able to make use of local community college classes (see Chapter 45 for more).

Depending on the textbook, course, and subject, the student's work will vary. But keep all important assignments and completed work filed in the Principles section of the science notebook.

Source Readings

The student should begin to explore the development of scientific thought by spending some time investigating the historical development of life science, astronomy, chemistry, physics, and technology and by reading selected original works of science (or excerpts from them). This study promotes critical thought; the student learns to view science not as an unerring oracle, but as a human endeavor, limited by time and culture. The reading of source works each year makes science human.

Suggested source readings might include

Biology
Hippocrates, *On Airs, Waters, and Places* (c. 420 B.C.)
Aristotle, *History of Animals* (c. 330 B.C.)
William Harvey, *De Motu Cordis* (1628)
Comte de Buffon, *Natural History: General and Particular* (1749–1788)
Jean-Baptiste Lamarck, *Zoological Philosophy* (1809)
Charles Darwin, *On the Origin of Species* (1859)
Gregor Mendel, *Experiments in Plant Hybridization* (1865)
Rachel Carson, *Silent Spring* (1962)
Desmond Morris, *The Naked Ape* (1967)
James D. Watson, *The Double Helix* (1968)
Richard Dawkins, *The Selfish Gene* (1976)
E. O. Wilson, *On Human Nature* (1978)
James Lovelock, *Gaia* (1979)
Stephen Jay Gould, *The Mismeasure of Man* (1981)
Erwin Schrödinger, *What Is Life?* (1944)
Walter Alvarez, *T. Rex and the Crater of Doom* (1997)
Ray Kurzweil, *The Singularity Is Near: When Humans Transcend Biology* (2005)

Chemistry
Robert Boyle, *The Sceptical Chemist* (1661)
Robert Hooke, *Micrographia* (1665)
Dmitri Mendeleev, "The Periodic Table" (first draft, 1869)
Erwin Schrödinger, *What Is Life?* (1944)

Astronomy
Ptolemy, *Almagest* (c. A.D. 150)
Nicolaus Copernicus, *Commentariolus* (1514)
Galileo Galilei, *Dialogue Concerning the Two Chief World Systems*
(1632)
Edwin Hubble, *The Realms of the Nebulae* (1937)
Fred Hoyle, *The Nature of the Universe* (1950)
Steven Weinberg, *The First Three Minutes: A Modern View of the Origin of
the Universe* (1977)
Robert Jastrow, *Red Giants and White Dwarfs* (1980)
Stephen Hawking, *A Brief History of Time* (1988)

Geology
James Hutton, *Theory of the Earth* (1785)
Georges Cuvier, "Preliminary Discourse" (1812)
Charles Lyell, *Principles of Geology* (1830)
Arthur Holmes, *The Age of the Earth* (1913)
Alfred Wegener, *The Origin of Continents and Oceans* (1915)
Walter Alvarez, *T. Rex and the Crater of Doom* (1997)

Physics
Aristotle, *Physics* (c. 330 B.C.)
Lucretius, *On the Nature of Things* (c. 60 B.C.)
Isaac Newton, "Rules" and "General Scholium" from *Philosophiae
Naturalis Principia Mathematica* (1687/1713/1726)
Albert Einstein, *Relativity: The Special and General Theory* (1916)
Max Planck, "The Origin and Development of the Quantum Theory"
(1922)
Erwin Schrödinger, *What Is Life?* (1944)
Edwin Hubble, *The Realms of the Nebulae* (1937)
Fred Hoyle, *The Nature of the Universe* (1950)
Steven Weinberg, *The First Three Minutes: A Modern View of the Origin of
the Universe* (1977)
James Gleick, *Chaos* (1987)
Stephen Hawking, *A Brief History of Time* (1988)
Paul Davies, *The New Physics* (1989)

Technology and computer science are young sciences, not yet mature enough to have spawned classics written by practicing scientists, but the following titles would certainly widen and deepen study. Some are college level, but certainly accessible to good readers; some are written by scientists, others by cultural critics; some are utopian, others deeply pessimistic. This list will certainly seem dated before the next edition of *The Well-Trained Mind*, but may point you in the direction of other titles.

Jacques Ellul, *The Technological Society* (1964)

Lewis Mumford, *Technics and Human Development: The Myth of the Machine, Volume One* (1967)

Neil Postman, *Technopoly* (1992)

Kirkpatrick Sale, *Rebels Against the Future: The Luddites and Their War on the Industrial Revolution: Lessons for the Computer Age* (1995)

Mark Slouka, *War of the Worlds: Cyberspace and the High-Tech Assault on Reality* (1995)

Ray Kurzweil, *The Age of Spiritual Machines: When Computers Exceed Human Intelligence* (1999)

Neil Postman, *Amusing Ourselves to Death: Discourse in the Age of Show Business* (2005)

Freeman Dyson, *The Scientist as Rebel* (2006)

Nicholas Carr, *The Shallows: What the Internet Is Doing to Our Brains* (2010)

Clive Thompson, *Smarter Than You Think: How Technology Is Changing Our Minds for the Better* (2013)

Steven Kotler and Peter H. Diamandis, *Abundance: The Future Is Better Than You Think* (2014)

Martin Ford, *Rise of the Robots: Technology and the Threat of a Jobless Future* (2015)

How should these books be used?

First: before beginning each year's Primary Source reading, the student should read a brief history of the field of study (biology, physics, etc.). Short, accessible resources are recommended at the end of this chapter.

Second, while reading each text, the student should keep notes (as in the Great Books readings) of the major points; when finished, he should write a brief (two-page) summary of the content or argument in the text (or at least the excerpt he read).

Third, this brief summary should be placed in the Primary Sources section of the science notebook.

The Great Conversation

Each year, the student should undertake a project that investigates some scientific discovery, natural phenomenon and human response, or technological innovation. This project should examine the present form of the topic, but also trace its historical development and mention any ethical issues raised. A biology paper on infectious disease, for example, might begin with the Black Death and progress through the 1917 influenza epidemic, the discovery of antibiotics, and the development of antibiotic-resistant "superbugs." The student should then conclude by asking: What overall effect has the use of antibiotics had on the war against disease? What defenses against the superbugs remain? Don't expect the student to solve these dilemmas; do encourage him to consider them.

In *The End of Education,* Neil Postman suggests that any student who has truly studied science and technology will consider certain questions, including:

1. Any technology offers both advantages and disadvantages. What are they?
2. These advantages and disadvantages aren't evenly spread throughout the population; some will benefit, others will be injured. Who are they?
3. All technologies come complete with a philosophy about what is important about human life and what is unimportant. What parts of life does the technology exalt? What parts does it ignore?
4. Every technology competes with an old technology for time, money, and attention. What technology is being replaced or squeezed out?
5. Every technology favors a certain type of intellectual expression, a

certain type of emotional expression, a certain type of political system, a certain type of sensory experience. What are these?[2]

These questions will serve as thought starters for the student as he considers topics. Postman further proposes the following assignment:

Choose one pre-twentieth century technology—for example, the alphabet, the printing press, the telegraph, the factory—and indicate what were the main intellectual, social, political, and economic advantages of the technology, and why. Then indicate what were the main intellectual, social, political, and economic disadvantages of the technology, and why.[3]

The same question could be asked of any twentieth or twenty-first century scientific advance.

This project should conclude with a written component; it could range from four to fifteen pages, depending on the student's interests, writing style, and topic. (See the writing resources recommended in Chapters 25 and 26 for guides to this sort of written report.)

SUGGESTED SCHEDULES

How much time should the student spend on investigating source readings and working on the yearly project?

You have a great deal of flexibility to plan out the year. A humanities-oriented student might choose to spend six to eight weeks of the year reading four or five primary sources and another three weeks researching the year's project; as long as she also completes the science textbook, this is fine. A more STEM-oriented student might only read one or two pri-

---

[2] Neil Postman, *The End of Education: Redefining the Value of School* (New York: Knopf, 1995), pp. 192–93. For a full explanation that will help both you and the student think through these issues, we highly recommend reading Postman's essay on the necessity of "technological education."

[3] Ibid., p. 193.

mary sources, but might do a much more extensive project with a complex experimental element to it; this could mean two to three total weeks spent on primary sources, but as much as six to eight weeks on the project. A student who is working hard to master the basic principles of a scientific field might need to spend almost all of her time on the textbook and assignments, perhaps only devoting a week or two each to primary sources and the project.

By the rhetoric stage, flexibility becomes vital; students differ so widely in their interests and strengths that it's impossible to lay down a hard and fast rule. Just keep in mind those three elements of the classical approach to science: principles and laws; primary source readings; and original investigation into some scientific or technological advance. Try to plan out the year to involve all three.

At the beginning of each year, make a tentative plan: How many of the primary source readings will the student plan to tackle? Will she read excerpts (usually best for the longer and more detailed works) or entire books? When will she do this reading? Will you integrate the reading and writing into her history and Great Books study or will it stand alone? Be willing to revise this plan as the year goes on.

Then, encourage the student to keep a running list of (1) questions that pop into her mind as she works through her science textbook, and (2) discoveries or inventions that she finds particularly fascinating. In January, go through this list together. Does anything on the list bear further investigation as a possible science project? Her logic-stage science study and her work in rhetoric should have equipped her to begin to carry out research; also see the Resources at the end of this chapter for further suggestions. The project and experiment resources we suggest may help spur your student's imagination.

Mark out three to four weeks at the end of the year for her to finish and document her research project.

Grades 9–12   Spend 5 or more hours per week on science. Over the course of the year, incorporate two or more primary source readings and one research project (with a written component of four or more pages) into science study.

HOW TO PUT IT ON THE TRANSCRIPT

Course	Name of class on transcript	Area	Credit
First year of science [e.g., Biology]	[Name of science, e.g., biology]	Natural science	1
First year of science [e.g., Biology with Lab]	[Name of science plus lab, e.g., biology plus lab component]	Natural science	1
Second year of same science [e.g., Advanced Biology]	[Name of science plus advanced, e.g., Advanced Biology]	Natural science	1
Second year of same science [e.g., Biology with Lab]	[Name of science plus advanced, e.g., Advanced Biology plus lab component]	Natural science	1

RESOURCES

Most books can be obtained from any bookseller or library; most curricula can be bought directly from the publisher or from a major home-school supplier such as Rainbow Resource Center. Contact information for publishers and suppliers can be found at www.welltrainedmind.com. If availability is limited, we have noted it. Remember that additional curricula choices and more can be found at www.well trainedmind.com. Prices change constantly, but we have included 2016 pricing to give an idea of affordability.

Note: The basic texts listed below are just a few of the available standard guides to each field of science. For additional texts, online classes, and more options, visit welltrainedmind.com.

Science texts produced for classrooms are excruciatingly expensive. You can rent, buy used, or look for previous editions of any recommended science texts; the changes between editions are generally minor, although you will not have access to the most current online supplements.

For links to the most recent versions of the text/online support packages listed below, visit our website.

Reference Materials for All Four Years

Bauer, Susan Wise. *The Story of Western Science: From the Writings of Aristotle to the Big Bang Theory.* New York: W. W. Norton, 2015.

$26.95. Brief, readable histories of the development of life sciences, chemistry, physics, and geology from ancient times until the present, along with helpful summaries of most of the Great Books on the list in this chapter, recommended translations and editions, and links to the most important excerpts of the longer works. Will greatly simplify the student's work in source readings.

Brock Magiscope. Maitland, FL: Brock Optical, Inc.

$179 and up. Order from Brock. To view more options and links to additional lab equipment visit welltrainedmind.com.

Bynum, William. *A Little History of Science.* New Haven, CT: Yale University Press, 2013.

$15. A very entertaining and accessible guide to the development of science, from the earliest mathematicians until today.

Gribbin, John. *The Scientists: A History of Science Told Through the Lives of Its Greatest Inventors.* New York: Random House, 2004.

$17.95. A biographical history of science, with plenty of additional detail; look up each author of a science source to learn more about the scientist, the book itself, and the inventions or discoveries chronicled.

Harland, Darci J. *STEM Student Research Handbook.* Arlington, VA: NSTA Press, 2011.

$30.95. A valuable guide for finding and focusing research topics, researching and testing, and writing up results. Particularly useful for STEM-focused students; helpful for research topics that are more experiment-based.

Lightman, Alan. *The Discoveries: Great Breakthroughs in 20th Century Science (including the original papers).* New York: Vintage, 2006.

$21. A wonderful resource chronicling twenty-five "breakthroughs" in science (for example, the discovery of hormones, the formulation of the theory of special relativity, the first uses of antibiotics, nuclear fission) and including original letters, articles, and writings from the scientists involved. Excellent for generating project research ideas.

Science: The Definitive Visual Guide. New York: DK Publishing, 2011. $24.95. A general science encyclopedia organized chronologically; useful to place and understand discoveries, inventions, and scientists.

Biology

Basic Texts

Miller & Levine Biology Curriculum. Boston: Pearson Education.
This widely used biology textbook has an engaging narrative style and covers the full range of high-school topics: cells, evolution, plants, chordates, ecology, genetics, microorganisms, invertebrates, and the human body. Copies can be purchased used, but if you buy new from Pearson Education you can also gain access to online helps. You will need:
   On-level Student Edition with Digital Courseware Student License. $93.47.
   On-level Teacher's Edition. $109.97.
   Study Workbook A Student Edition. $11.47.
   Study Workbook A Teacher Edition. $27.97.
   Laboratory Manual A Student Edition. $14.47.
   Laboratory Manual A Teacher Edition. $27.97.

   There are also "B" levels listed, but this is the same material simplified.

   Lab materials may be purchased from Carolina Biological Supply or Home Science Tools. Completing the Laboratory Manual allows you to award a laboratory science credit.

Campbell Essential Biology. San Francisco, CA: Benjamin Cummings.
This biology text pays more attention to biochemistry and genetics, little attention to the animal and plant kingdoms. Benjamin Cummings is an imprint of Pearson Education, and *Essential Biology* can be purchased from Pearson. You will need:
   Campbell Essential Biology, 6th ed., packaged with *Mastering Biology Virtual Lab Full Suite.* $205.53.

   This provides the student text and full online access to assessments, lab assignments, and more.

Campbell Biology: Concepts & Connections. San Francisco, CA: Benjamin Cummings.

Concepts & Connections has a lighter emphasis on biochemistry and much more focus on the plant and animal kingdoms (almost half the text is on "Animals: Form and Function" and "Plants: Form and Function"). You will need:

Campbell Biology: Concepts & Connections Plus Mastering Biology with eText: Access Card Package, 8th ed. $226.13.

This includes access to the virtual lab and online resources.

Holt McDougal Biology. Orlando, FL: Holt McDougal, 2012.

This is a standard and very user-friendly biology text, widely available secondhand. Because it is published by Houghton Mifflin Harcourt, which has the most user-hostile website of any major publisher, it is almost impossible to find the correct edition. Look for secondhand copies of the student and teacher edition; you will need to devise your own labs and experiments in order to give a lab credit.

Holt McDougal Biology Student Edition. $97.85.

Holt McDougal Biology Teacher Edition. $135.95.

Supplementary Resources

Eyewitness Books. New York: Dorling Kindersley.

$16.99 each. Designed by Dorling Kindersley, these are museums in a book—photos, reference text, definitions, all beautifully done.

Burnie, David, and Peter Chadwick. *Bird* (2000).

———. *Tree* (2015).

Parker, Steve, and Philip Dowell. *Pond and River* (2011).

———. *Skeleton* (2004).

Whalley, Paul, et al. *Butterfly and Moth* (2000).

Gardner, Robert. *Genetics and Evolution Science Fair Projects.* Berkeley Heights, NJ: Enslow, 2013.

$10.95 for the Kindle version.

Hershey, David R. *Plant Biology Science Projects.* New York: John Wiley, 1995.

$21.

Kapit, Wynn, and Lawrence M. Elson. *Anatomy Coloring Book.* 4th ed. Paramus, NJ: Pearson Education, 2013.

$21.80. Even more detailed than the *Gray's Anatomy* coloring book (see below). Covers, in 400 pages, all major body systems. Revised to include information on AIDS.

Pollock, Steve. *Eyewitness: Ecology.* New York: Dorling Kindersley, 2005.
$15.99. This is a particularly good guide for students trying to come up with paper topics. Examines cause and effect in the natural world.

Rainis, Kenneth G. *Cell and Microbe Science Fair Projects.* Berkeley Heights, NJ: Enslow, 2013.
$10.95 for the Kindle version.

Stark, Fred. *Start Exploring Gray's Anatomy: A Fact-Filled Coloring Book.* Philadelphia, PA: Running Press, 2011.
$12.95. Detailed drawings to color, with descriptions from the classic anatomy text.

VanCleave, Janice. *Janice VanCleave's A+ Projects in Biology.* New York: John Wiley, 1993.
$12.95.

Walker, Pam, and Elaine Wood. *Ecosystem Science Fair Projects.* Berkeley Heights, NJ: Enslow, 2005.
$26.60.

Astronomy

Basic Text

Chaisson, Eric, and Steve McMillan. *Astronomy: The Universe at a Glance.* Boston: Pearson, 2016.
Excellent standard astronomy text. Astronomy changes quickly; the current edition is the 7th edition, but look for the most recent. You can buy the stand-alone text,
Astronomy: The Universe at a Glance. $84.20.
but we suggest adding:
Astronomy: The Universe at a Glance Plus Mastering Astronomy with eText— Access Card Package. $91.53.

Supplementary Resources

Lippincott, Kristen. *Eyewitness: Astronomy*. New York: Dorling Kindersley, 2013.

$16.99. Reviews the history of astronomy along with recent discoveries.

Moche, Dinah L. *Astronomy: A Self-Teaching Guide*. New York: Wiley, 2014.

$21.95. Order through a bookstore or online bookseller.

Ridpath, Ian, and Wil Tirion. *Stars and Planets: Princeton Field Guides*. Princeton, NJ: Princeton University Press, 2008.

$19.95. Photos, diagrams, and lots of information.

VanCleave, Janice. *Janice VanCleave's A+ Projects in Astronomy*. New York: John Wiley, 2001.

$12.95.

Geology

Basic Texts

Glencoe Earth Science: Geology, the Environment, and the Universe. New York: McGraw Hill Education.

Accessible geology text, slightly lower level than the Prentice Hall text below.

Student Edition (2013). $84.

Lab Manual, Student Edition (2013). $8.13.

Teacher Edition (2013). $113.97.

Lab Manual, Teacher Edition (2013). $28.59.

Earth: An Introduction to Physical Geology. Upper Saddle River, NJ: Prentice-Hall.

Colorful, well-written text covering all major geology topics. Buy from Pearson Learning in order to access online tools.

Earth: An Introduction to Physical Geology Plus Mastering Geology with eText: Access Card Package, 11th ed. $176.33.

Supplementary Resources

Gardner, Robert. *Planet Earth Science Fair Projects*. Berkeley Heights, NJ: Enslow, 2005.

$27.94.

Wilkerson, M. Scott, M. Beth Wilkerson, and Stephen Marshak. *Geotours Workbook: A Guide for Exploring Geology and Creating Projects Using Google Earth.* New York: W. W. Norton, 2011.

$26.75. Nineteen virtual field trips exploring geology, along with instructions for students to create their own virtual tours.

Chemistry

Basic Texts

Chemistry: Concepts and Applications. New York: McGraw Hill Education.

Accessible conceptual chemistry text, slightly lower level than the Prentice Hall text below.

Student Edition (2014). $90.

Lab Manual, Student Edition (2009). $8.13.

Teacher Edition (2014). $111.99.

Lab Manual, Teacher Edition (2009). $28.59.

Suchocki, John A. *Conceptual Chemistry.* Upper Saddle River, NJ: Prentice-Hall.

Excellent introduction to chemistry, originally designed for non-chemistry-major college students. Purchase from Amazon (as of this writing, Pearson, Prentice-Hall's parent company, will not sell this book to individuals). Can be rented or purchased used for less.

Conceptual Chemistry, 5th ed. (2013). $156.32.

Laboratory Manual for Conceptual Chemistry (2013). $39.38.

Supplementary Resources

CHEM C3000 Chemistry Kit. Portsmouth, RI: Thames & Kosmos.

$249.95. Order from Thames & Kosmos; the company makes two lower-priced sets as well, but this one contains all necessary high-school materials.

ElementO.

$34.95. Order from Rainbow Resource Center. In this Monopoly-type game, players collect elements and pay each other with proton and neutron certificates. Keep track with the Periodic Table of Elements in the middle of the board. A great way to memorize the basic properties of chemistry.

Gardner, Robert, and Barbara Gardner Conklin. *Organic Chemistry Science Fair Projects, Revised and Expanded Using the Scientific Method.* Berkeley Heights, NJ: Enslow, 2013.
$9.49 for the Kindle version.

Goodstein, Madeleine P. *Plastics and Polymers Science Fair Projects.* Berkeley Heights, NJ: Enslow, 2010.
$10.95 for the Kindle version.

Herr, Norman, and James Cunningham. *Hands-On Chemistry Activities with Real Life Applications.* New York: Jossey-Bass, 1999.
$32.95.

Houk, Clifford C., and Richard Post. *Chemistry: Concepts and Problems—A Self-Teaching Guide.* 2nd ed, New York: Wiley, 1996.
$21.95.

Periodic Table of Elements Chartlet.
$2.49. Order from Rainbow Resource Center. A 17 × 22-inch reference chart of the table of elements.

Trombley, Linda, and Thomas G. Cohn. *Mastering the Periodic Table: Exercises on the Elements.* Portland, ME: J. Weston Walch, 2000.
$24. Order from J. Weston Walch or from Rainbow Resource Center.

VanCleave, Janice. *Janice VanCleave's A+ Projects in Chemistry.* New York: John Wiley, 1993.
$14.95.

Physics

Basic Texts

Saxon Physics Homeschool Kit with Solutions Manual, 1st ed.
$131.10. Includes student textbook, solutions manual, tests, worksheets. Math-intensive approach to physics.

Hewitt, Paul. *Conceptual Physics.* Reading, MA: Addison Wesley.
A well-regarded physics text that requires less technical mathematical knowledge. Purchase from Amazon (as of this writing, Pearson, Addi-

son Wesley's parent company, will not sell this book to individuals). Can be rented or purchased used for less.

Conceptual Physics, 12th ed. (2014). $156.32.

Laboratory Manual: Activities, Experiments, Tech Labs: Conceptual Physics, 12th ed. (2013). $51.95.

Problem Solving for Conceptual Physics, 12th ed. (2013). $53.78.

Supplementary Resources

Cunningham, James, and Norman Herr. *Hands-On Physics Activities with Real-Life Applications: Easy-to-Use Labs and Demonstrations for Grades 8–12.* New York: Jossey-Bass, 1994.

$34.95. Order from any bookstore.

Gardner, Robert. *Electricity and Magnetism Science Fair Projects.* Berkeley Heights, NJ: Enslow, 2010.

$35.94. Order from any bookstore.

———. *Forces and Motion Science Fair Projects.* Berkeley Heights, NJ: Enslow, 2010.

$35.94. Order from any bookstore.

———. *Light, Sound, and Waves Science Fair Projects.* Berkeley Heights, NJ: Enslow, 2010.

$35.94. Order from any bookstore.

———. *Science Fair Projects About the Properties of Matter.* Berkeley Heights, NJ: Enslow, 2004.

$27.94. Order from any bookstore.

Kuhn, Karl F. *Basic Physics: A Self-Teaching Guide,* 2nd ed. New York: Wiley, 1996.

$22.95. Order through any bookstore or online bookseller.

Physics Projects Kits. Riverside, NY: Educational Designs.

$11–$12 each. Order from Rainbow Resource Center. Each kit is complete with all materials.

Crystal Radio.

A working crystal radio.

Electric Bell.

Build a bell-buzzer-telegraph.

Electric Motor.
Electro-Magnetix.
　Electromagnetic motor to build.

Technology and Computer Science

Because these fields are evolving so quickly, you can find both basic texts and supplementary resources at welltrainedmind.com.

30

LEARNING OTHER WORLDS:
FOREIGN LANGUAGES

We are greatly helped to develop objectivity of taste if we can appreciate the work of foreign authors, living in the same world as ourselves, and expressing their vision of it in another great language.

—T. S. Eliot

SUBJECT: **Classical and modern languages**
TIME REQUIRED: **3 to 6 hours per week**

When it comes to rhetoric-stage foreign-language study, you have two goals. One is to fulfill the standard college-prep high-school requirement—at least two consecutive years of a foreign language, studied during the high-school years (grades 9–12).[1] Students who have followed our suggested middle-grade program will be in good shape. Two additional years of high-school language study should lead to at least basic conversational fluency, as well as the ability to read popular-level foreign-language literature.

This two-year requirement is a minimum. The classically educated

---

[1] Languages studied before ninth grade generally don't count in the eyes of college admissions officers; they assume that this study was on a lower level.

student has other purposes in mind: ideally, the mastery of one foreign language (the equivalent of four years of study, resulting in the ability to read literature fluently), and the beginning study at the high-school level (two years) of another. One of these languages should be ancient Greek or Latin, while the other should be a modern spoken language.

Why this more ambitious program?

During the rhetoric stage, the student is continually dealing with words—how they should be put together, how they express emotions and ideas, how they can be arranged for greatest effect. Study of two foreign languages teaches the student how writers from other cultures, thinking in different ways, deal with words. This expands the student's grasp of language, raising questions about the relationship between language and thought.

In his 1892 essay "The Present Requirements for Admission to Harvard College," James Jay Greenough pointed out that reading in a foreign language forces the student to look at each thought from two points of view: that of the original language and that of the English translation he is producing. This gives the student "a clearer conception of the thought than he could possibly get by looking at it from the English side only. . . . He grows accustomed to clear thinking, and therefore expresses his own thoughts more clearly both in speech and in writing." Language study, in other words, is central to the skills of expression being worked on during the rhetoric stage.

Let's be realistic: most STEM students won't manage to study two foreign languages during high school, since so much time and energy is going into advanced maths study. But mathematics is its own sort of foreign language—a mode of expression that uses its own particular vocabulary and syntax to describe and talk about the world. Adding at least one more foreign language (ideally, to the point of fluency) to high-level mathematics achievement accomplishes the same goal: clear expression of thought in more than one language.

WHICH LANGUAGES?

For the four-year language requirement, we suggest that most students keep studying Latin, completing the equivalent of Latin IV during the high-school years. The student who truly loathes Latin could be permitted to drop it after completing Latin II, but he should plan on studying a modern foreign language through the fourth-year level. The modern language resources listed in Chapter 19 only take you through second-year studies. As you continue, you should choose a tutor, a community college, a beginning university course, or an online course for the third and fourth levels of study.

The student with a strong interest in the classics could substitute Greek I and Greek II for a modern foreign language, while continuing with the study of Latin through Latin IV.

Since the study of modern languages was begun in the middle grades, the rhetoric-stage student who applies himself for an additional two years of high-school study will progress much further than students who come into high school unprepared. As mentioned before, we strongly recommend the study of Spanish for the modern foreign-language requirement; French, Italian, German, Russian, Japanese, Chinese, and Hebrew are also possibilities. T. S. Eliot, in his essay "The Man of Letters," suggests that scholars with "very exceptional linguistic ability" will benefit from studying a language that is "more remote" from our own. He mentions Hebrew and Chinese, but Japanese, Korean, or Arabic (and, to a lesser degree, Russian) would have the same effect.

Ancient Languages

Students who have not yet begun Latin can start now with Latin I; students who have been studying since the grammar or logic stage should continue into the higher levels of reading Latin literature. You should not give high-school credit for language study before ninth grade. Fairly or not, it's assumed that languages done in middle school were studied at a lower level, unless you can demonstrate through an outside evaluation (an AP, SAT II, or CLEP exam, for example) that the achievement was at high-school level. But putting Latin III or Latin IV on the transcript will point out the student's advanced knowledge.

Greek (either classical or Koine) or biblical Hebrew can be added as a second language, but at least two years of a modern foreign language are strongly recommended.

Modern Languages

If you haven't yet begun a modern foreign language, consider one of the courses described in Chapter 19. If the student has already finished both levels of a modern language course in the middle grades, she has two options: learn a second modern language in high school (she will need to have those two high-school years for the sake of college admissions) or she can continue to study the language she has been learning for two additional years.

For the latter option, you'll need to "outsource"—find a teacher or class. Modern foreign-language literature should be read with a teacher who's enthusiastic and knowledgeable about both the culture and the language. You may be able to locate a tutor who would be willing to do a two-year reading course with a student who's already had the language basics—try the language department of your local college or call a good private school and ask for options. Or you can enroll your high-school student in a class at your local university or community college (see Chapter 45 for concurrent enrollment). We suggest that you and your child talk to the instructor, who will want to evaluate the student's readiness. In most cases, two years of high-school study is considered the equivalent of one year of college study, so a student who has finished two years of French or Spanish will probably be placed in a second-year class. After this two-semester class, the student will advance to a literature class. These two years of college study (French II and French literature, Spanish II and Spanish literature, and so forth) are the equivalent of four high-school years of study (French I–IV, Spanish I–IV, and so on).

PLANNING THE PROGRESSION

The basic goal of language study in grades 9 through 12 is

- two years of study in one language (which completes the learning of basic grammar and conversational vocabulary)

The advanced goal is

two years of study in one language
four years of study in another language (grammar, vocabulary, plus
    two years of developing reading competency)

Ideally, one of these languages should be modern, the other, ancient.

SUGGESTED SCHEDULES

Plan on studying at least one foreign language for at least four or five hours per week. You may also choose to study more than one language.

HOW TO PUT IT ON THE TRANSCRIPT

Course	Name of class on transcript	Area	Credit
Third or fourth year of study continuing from middle grades.	[Language] III [Language] IV	Foreign language	1
Beginning or second year of study.	[Language] I [Language] II	Foreign language	1

RESOURCES

Most books can be obtained from any bookseller or library; most curricula can be bought directly from the publisher or from a major home-school supplier such as Rainbow Resource Center. Contact information for publishers and suppliers can be found at www.welltrainedmind.com. If availability is limited, we have noted it. Books in series are listed together. Remember that additional curricula choices and more can be found at www.welltrainedmind.com. Prices change constantly, but we have included 2016 pricing to give an idea of affordability.

See Chapter 19 for additional foreign-language resources.

Latin

Progression from Logic-Stage Programs

Students who are working in *Latin Alive!* should continue on through the reader level of the program. After completing the final levels, they should be qualified to take the Latin AP Exam or the National Latin Exam to document their progress.

Students who are working in *Latina Christiana* should continue on to *First Form Latin* and complete the program.

Students who are working in the *Form Latin* series should complete the program and then continue on to *Henle Latin II*.

Students who are working in the *Latin Road to English Grammar* should complete all three levels; this is the equivalent of two years of high-school Latin. They may then continue on to Latin reading; we suggest *Henle Latin II* and the following levels.

Basic Texts

The following are appropriate for high-school beginners.

Beers, Barbara. *The Latin Road to English Grammar,* Redding, CA: Schola Publications, 1997.

This course assumes no prior Latin knowledge on the part of either parent or student. Completion of all three levels is the equivalent of two years of high-school Latin. Order from the publisher. Additional helps and worksheets are available at the publisher's website.

Volume I.
Teacher Curriculum Set. $199.
Teacher Training DVDs. $129.
Latin Road Complete Student Package. $63.95.
Volume II.
Teacher Curriculum Set. $199.
Teacher Training DVDs. $129.
Latin Road Complete Student Package. $63.95.
Volume III.
`Teacher Curriculum Set. $219.
Latin Road Complete Student Package. $59.95.

Henle, Robert J., S.J. *Latin.* Chicago: Loyola Press, 1958.

Order this classic Latin text and helps from Memoria Press. Almost all of the grammar is in Latin I, which may take more than one year to work through; the remaining levels focus on reading.

  Latin I

    Latin 1 Text. $16.95.

    Latin 1 Key. $5.

    Henle Grammar. $9.50.

    Units 1–2 Study Guide. $14.95.

    Units 1–2 Test/Quiz Package. $9.95.

    Units 3–5 Study Guide. $14.95.

    Units 3–5 Test/Quiz Package. $9.95.

    Units 6–14 Study Guide. $14.95.

    Units 6–14 Test/Quiz Package. $9.95.

  Latin II Text & Key. $17.95.

  Latin III Text & Key. $17.95.

  Latin IV Text & Key. $17.95.

Supplementary Resources

Hammond, Mason, and Anne R. Amory. *Aeneas to Augustus: A Beginning Latin Reader for College Students.* Cambridge, MA: Harvard University Press, 1967.

$42. A standard introduction to great Latin writers.

Lenard, Alexander, and A. A. Milne. *Winnie Ille Pu: A Latin Version of A. A. Milne's Winnie-the-Pooh.* New York: Penguin, 1991.

$15.

Rowling, J. K. *Harrius Potter et Philosophi Lapis.* New York: Bloomsbury USA, 2003.

$29.99.

Russell, D. A. *An Anthology of Latin Prose.* Oxford: Oxford University Press, 1990.

$73. A standard reader that may be simpler than the Hammond/Amory reader for home use, since it doesn't include poetry (which is extremely difficult).

Greek

Basic Texts

Lawall, Gilbert, Maurice G. Balme, and James Morwood. *Athenaze: An Introduction to Ancient Greek.* 3rd ed. Oxford: Oxford University Press, 2014.
Book 1. $44.95.
Workbook to Accompany Athenaze, Book 1. $27.95. *Book 2.* $44.95.
A Little Greek Reader. $19.95.

Supplementary Resources

Betts, Gavin, and Alan Henry. *Complete Ancient Greek: A Teach Yourself Guide.* New York: McGraw-Hill, 2011.
$32. If *Athenaze* proves too challenging, you can use this mass-market self-teaching guide as a supplement or even a substitute. It isn't as complete, but you may find it easier to use.

Gatchell, Christine. *Elementary Greek: Koine for Beginners.* Louisville, KY: Memoria Press, 2015.
Order from the publisher. Koine (New Testament Greek) is a vernacular descendent of classical Greek and operates under slightly different rules.
Year One Kit. $57.80.
Year Two Kit. $60.80,
Year Three Kit. $62.80.

Pharr, Clyde, John Henry Wright, and Paula Debnar. *Homeric Greek: A Book for Beginners,* 4th ed. Norman: University of Oklahoma Press, 2012.
$29.95. A good complement to *Athenaze.* This book, designed for students who know no Greek, plunges them into the reading of Homer almost straightaway. A good motivator for the first-year Greek student.

Modern Languages

Basic Texts

Most reasonably effective modern language programs are now web-based, giving students better access to conversational resources, drills, interactive exercises, etc. Visit welltrainedmind.com for links to the following programs and additional interactive live instruction options.

Duolingo. Pittsburgh, PA: Duolingo.

Thirteen different languages, including Esperanto and Irish, taught through interactive online modules. At the moment, a free program; most grammar and writing instruction is done through quick "tip sheets" that will be hard for middle-grade students to absorb, but the aural and oral instruction is very well done.

Visit the Duolingo website, www.duolingo.com, for online tutorials and language options.

Fluenz. Miami Beach, FL: Fluenz, Inc.

A full program that can be downloaded, with a substantial online component. Grammar, pronunciation, online taught sessions. Currently six languages available. Visit the website, www.fluenz.com, for pricing and options.

Rosetta Stone Homeschool. Harrisonburg, VA: Rosetta Stone.

An interactive computer-based language-learning program that uses photos, graphics, and interactive lessons to encourage students to think in a foreign language. The home-school editions include both student materials and parent resources, including lesson plans, multiple paths emphasizing different skills (grammar, speech, reading, etc.), tests, and the ability to generate reports. Visit the Rosetta Stone website, www.RosettaStone .com, for pricing options and the twenty-five available language programs. (Actually, twenty-three for English speakers, since Rosetta Stone classifies American English and British English as two different languages.)

Supplementary Resources

Calvez, Daniel J. *French Grammar: A Complete Reference Guide*. 2nd ed. New York: McGraw-Hill, 2004.

$20. A useful grammatical supplement to the spoken-language courses recommended above, which tend to be light on grammar.

Parish, Peggy, et al. *Amelia Bedelia (Ya Se Leer)*. New York: Lectorum, 2000.

$7.99. A children's standard, for fun Spanish reading; see how the puns work in another language.

Saint-Exupery, Antoine de. *Le Petit Prince*. French ed. Boston: Harcourt, 2001.

$11. A good first excursion into French literature.

Viorst, Judith, and Alma F. Ada. *Alexander y el Dia Terrible, Horrible, Espantoso, Horrorosa,* illus. Ray Cruz. Boston: Modern Curriculum Press, 1989. $7.99. Another children's favorite in Spanish, just for fun.

Wiley Self-Teaching Guides. New York: John Wiley Publishers. $18.95–$21.95 each. These paperbacks, designed for independent study, will fill in the grammar "holes" that may be left by conversation-focused programs. Good to have on hand for reference.

> Hershfield-Haims, Suzanne A. *French: A Self-Teaching Guide.* 2nd ed. 2000.
>
> Lebano, Edoardo A. *Italian: A Self-Teaching Guide.* 2nd ed. 2000.
>
> Prado, Marcial. *Practical Spanish Grammar: A Self-Teaching Guide.* 2007.
>
> Taylor, Heimy, and Werner Haas. *German: A Self-Teaching Guide.* 1997.

31

LOOKING BEHIND THE CURTAIN: TECHNOLOGY SKILLS

The Internet is the first thing that humanity has built that humanity doesn't understand.

—Eric Schmidt

SUBJECT: **Basic computer programming**

TIME REQUIRED: **3 to 5 hours per week (or as interest dictates)**

Computer technology has changed the way we live—and so quickly that our chapters on technology in earlier editions of this book sound embarrassingly dated. This chapter will probably age badly as well. So we'll keep it short and just say two things.

THE OBLIGATORY WARNINGS ABOUT THE INTERNET, SOCIAL MEDIA, ETC.

The truth is that nobody knows exactly what computer technology is doing to our brains. In some ways, it doesn't matter. We're already into the digital age, and, barring the arrival of the zombie apocalypse (in which case we'll all have other things to worry about), we won't be leaving it anytime soon.

But remember that growing children are physical beings, and keep in mind that the Internet and social media channels are body-neutral. Physical sensations—touch, smell, taste, balance—are irrelevant.

What are the implications of that? At least two stand out.

First, because we're physical beings, our intellectual pursuits affect our bodies. Numerous studies have been done on how different experiences change the physical makeup of the brain. Specifically, the brain of the student who spends eight hours per day in front of the computer looks different than the brain of the student who spends an hour in front of the computer, four hours in front of books, and the other three hours doing outside activities. Any constantly repeated activity develops some neural pathways at the expense of others. In other words, balance computer use with paper-and-pencil work and active learning. Otherwise, you'll be developing certain parts of the brain while ignoring others. Don't let this form of modern technology dominate your child's spare time; time spent online is time that isn't spent building models, reading Plato, playing a musical instrument, cutting the grass, drawing, keeping a journal, eating, sleeping, or staring into space and thinking about what life means.

A second implication is especially important for high-school students. Any normal adolescent—by which we mean one who is insecure, struggling to face others with both grace and confidence, self-conscious about skin and hair and weight—prefers to communicate via chat. Electronic friends are much safer than flesh-and-blood companions; don't allow them to take the place of real live give-and-take between people who are physically present.

For high school, we're not laying down hard-and-fast rules. We are encouraging you to realize that computers, like all technologies, put priorities on some types of experience and relegate others to the background.

BASIC PROGRAMMING IS IMPORTANT

"Software engineering," says programmer Mel Klimushyn, "is the closest I could come to fulfilling my lifelong dream of becoming a wizard."

All technology looks like magic to the uninitiated. (Arthur C. Clarke said it first.) But classical education, although it has great respect for myth and legend, doesn't really have room in it for magic. So we think that all rhetoric-stage students, even the humanities-focused ones, should learn some basic programming. This is the most straightforward way to take the mystery out of computers and put them in their place—as powerful tools, not as dictators of culture.

We suggest that during eleventh or twelfth grade, you schedule at least a year of beginning computer programming into the student's curriculum (see Chapter 31). Whatever language and resources we recommend will be outdated by the time you read this, so visit welltrainedmind.com for links to online tools and the most recent wisdom about languages for beginning students.

SUGGESTED SCHEDULES

Grade 11 or 12: a one-year course in beginning computer programming for three to five hours per week.

32

APOLOGIZING FOR FAITH:
RELIGION AND ETHICS

Educating the mind without educating the heart is not education
at all.

—Aristotle (attributed)

One goal of rhetoric is the *apologia*, the articulate and well-reasoned
defense of belief. During the rhetoric stage, the student should
certainly learn to defend his own faith without resorting to rhetorical
abuses—ad hominem attacks, abusive fallacies, black-and-white fallacies,
or any of the other illegitimate arguments forbidden by both logic and
rhetoric. And the study of rhetoric should protect the student from abuse
of his own beliefs by others.

Religion and rhetoric have an even deeper relationship, though. Classical rhetoric cannot be pursued apart from the considerations of faith. In
Rhetoric, Aristotle writes that the man who wishes to master rhetoric must
be able (1) to reason logically, (2) to understand human character and
goodness in their various forms, and (3) to understand the emotions—

that is, to name them and describe them, to know their causes and the ways in which they are excited.[1]

The ability to reason logically is learned during the logic stage; rhetoric itself aims to name and describe human emotions. But an understanding of human character and goodness in its various forms cannot be separated from our belief about who human beings are, where they came from, and what they are essentially like. Goodness itself cannot be defined without making serious faith decisions: either goodness resides in a Being or it exists as a social construct.

This is the foundation of ethics.

Nor can ethics be discussed in some sort of "neutral" fashion. If you are a theist, you believe that human character comes from a Creator and reflects some of the Creator's qualities. If you are a materialist, you believe that human character is primarily the result of biological factors, some of which can be controlled, some of which can't. If you are a Christian, you believe that moral absolutes are binding upon every human being. If you are an agnostic, you believe that moral absolutes are unknowable and that making pronouncements about moral absolutes thus reaches the height of arrogance.

What sort of neutral ground can these views meet on?

None. Rhetoric involves an intensive discussion of social ethics, the nature of good and evil, individual responsibility, and the extent to which the manipulation of emotions is morally acceptable. None of these issues can be tackled without a grasp of ethics. And ethics is, itself, inseparable from our view of God, our belief about the nature of humankind, and our expectations of society.

The rhetoric exercises we recommend—evaluating the ideas and philosophies of the Great Books, writing about the moral and ethical implications of technology—have to be done in the context of faith. Tolerance for the faith of others doesn't mean that the student simply throws open his arms and says, "We're *all* right"; that makes nonsense of five thousand years of deeply held and contradictory beliefs. The tolerance taught by rhetoric involves the student's holding on to his own deep, well-reasoned convictions, while simultaneously treating others with respect. Respect doesn't mean admitting that someone else is right. It does mean refraining

---

[1] Aristotle, *Rhetoric* I.2.

from resorting to abusive fallacies and the rhetoric of propaganda so that those of different faiths can seriously and peacefully argue about ideas.

We think that every rhetoric-stage student should make at least a preliminary study of ethics. Since ethics is related to belief, we can't (obviously) recommend an ethics text that will satisfy all home schoolers. We encourage you, as you work through the rhetoric stage with your high-school student, to formulate your own beliefs. Use logic and rhetoric to extract what you really believe from the cloudy ideas that may be swirling around you. And then base your own discussions of ethics—right and wrong—self-consciously on those beliefs.

RESOURCES

These are good starting places; consult your own religious or intellectual community for additional resources.

Blackburn, Simon. *Ethics: A Very Short Introduction.* Oxford: Oxford University Press, 2009.
$11.95. An excellent starting point.

Marino, Gordon, ed. *Ethics: The Essential Writings.* New York: Modern Library, 2010.
$18. A valuable collection of excerpts from philosophers and ethicists ranging from ancient times to the present; multiple topics and points of view.

33

APPRECIATING THE ARTS:
ART AND MUSIC

Art is the imposing of a pattern on experience, and our aesthetic enjoyment is recognition of the pattern.

—A. N. Whitehead

SUBJECT: Art and music

TIME REQUIRED: 2 hours, twice per week

The rhetoric student recognizes both art and music as types of expression that are as valid as words. Just as words, spoken and written, are governed by the rules of rhetoric, so art and music are governed by conventions. The study of art and music during the final four years of classical education will center on those conventions—how they are used, how they are altered, how and when they are discarded.

Logic-stage study of art and music was tied chronologically to the study of history. The student was attempting to establish logical connections between artists and musicians and their times. Rhetoric-stage art and music study doesn't need to be connected quite so closely to the historical periods under study. Rather, the study focuses on art and music as the means by which ideas are expressed, just as the study of Great Books centers on writing as the expression of ideas in words. Pablo Picasso was a philosopher; Cubism embraced an ethical system; Ludwig van Beethoven and John Cage subscribed to widely different worldviews, and their compositions express this difference. Gothic cathedrals were built to demonstrate God's place at the center of existence; fifteen hundred years later, London artist Francis Bacon painted a screaming pope surrounded by sides of beef to show that "we are all carcasses."

Art *is* rhetoric.

Keep roughly to the same schedule you've been using all along— one one- to two-hour period per week for music study, another for art study. The student will keep two notebooks, one for art and the other for music. These notebooks should last for the entire four years of the rhetoric stage.

ART

The high-school student should continue to study both art skills and art appreciation. As in middle school, the student can alternate art projects one week with art appreciation the next. Or she can choose to study drawing, painting, and modeling one semester and art appreciation the following semester.

Art Skills

The high-school student can continue to divide art-project days among drawing, painting, and modeling (as in the middle grades). Or she can focus on one of these skills, developing a real mastery. For an artistically gifted student, you may want to consider "outsourcing"—hiring a tutor for her (most artists are accustomed to teaching for bread-and-butter money) or enrolling her in a college or adult-education art class. Call your local art association and ask for a recommendation. Art museums and galleries often offer art classes, taught by professionals, that are appropriate for students who've already mastered basic skills.

Use any of the drawing and painting resources listed at the end of Chapter 21. We have listed a few additional resources at the end of this chapter.

Art Appreciation

The high-school student is ready for a full art-history course, one that covers techniques, the philosophies of individual artists, and the rise of the various schools.

Use an art survey as a basic text (see the Resources at the end of this chapter) to learn about schools, periods, artists, and techniques in architecture, painting, and sculpture, from prehistoric times through postmodernism. In a thirty-six-week school year, the student should spend eighteen weeks studying art history. In each of these eighteen weeks, she should read from her base text and use additional resources to study the artists and works of art discussed. She should then record something she's learned, either writing briefly about it or using the distinctive characteristics of the artist or school under discussion to sketch something in that style. These notebook pages and sketches can be kept in the art notebook or filed in the history notebook.

If the ninth grader, for example, is studying the Italian Renaissance, she'll read through the appropriate pages in the textbook and pick one of the subjects discussed (the life of Leonardo da Vinci, the composition of the *Mona Lisa* or *The Last Supper*, Michelangelo's accomplishments, Raphael as a representative of the High Renaissance, Titian's methods of painting textures, or the four Rs of Renaissance architecture (Rome, rules, reason, and 'rithmetic). Whatever subject she chooses, she'll look at any relevant paintings and read any relevant background material. Then she'll write, briefly (three-quarters of a page to a full page is fine) summarizing the information. If suitable, she could also sketch her report; if she were studying the composition of the *Mona Lisa* or *The Last Supper*, for example, she could simply draw the layout, adding annotations that contain the information she's learned (the diagonal lines all converge on Christ's head; Mona Lisa sits in an innovative, three-quarter pose). Creativity in reflection should be encouraged during the rhetoric stage of art-historical study.

MUSIC

Music Skills

By high school, those students who are not interested in playing an instrument will have dropped lessons, while those who are interested will have developed some proficiency and will know whether they want to keep on.

Music Appreciation

Whether or not the student is taking music lessons, he should continue to spend one and a half to two hours every week doing music appreciation.

We have recommended several possible base texts at the end of this chapter. Rather than charging through these books at a set number of pages per week, the student should progress through them in a relaxed manner, taking plenty of time to find and listen to recordings of the pieces mentioned. It's fine to take all four years to cover these resources. Follow these guidelines:

1. Write a short biographical sketch (one to two pages long) for each composer encountered. Try to focus not just on facts (birth and death dates, training, posts held), but on the development of each composer as an artist. Did he ever express his purpose for composing? What were his musical models? What did he consider to be his greatest work? Why? Did he hold to his early training or break away from it?

2. Whenever a certain school of composition is mentioned, write a couple of paragraphs discussing the school's characteristics and its major followers. Then make a brief list of important world events and philosophical movements going on at the same time.

3. For each composer studied, keep a list of works that you've listened to. Before you move on to another composer, write a couple of paragraphs describing the quality of this composer's work (this is a creative assignment). What effect does the music have on you? Do you like it? dislike it? Are you excited by it? bored? Be sure to give specific reasons.

The student encountering Chopin, for example, could linger on this section until he's listened to several weeks' worth of Chopin's music. When he's ready to move on, he should (1) write a biographical sketch of Chopin, (2) briefly describe the Romantic movement and list major world events and philosophical shifts (for example, the Romantic movement in literature), and (3) list the works of Chopin listened to and write a couple of paragraphs about the effects of Chopin's music on him. He can file all these papers in a music notebook or in the history notebook.

SUGGESTED SCHEDULES

| Grades 9–12 | Mondays, 2 hrs. | Alternate art projects with studying art history. |
| | Thursdays, 2 hrs. | Work through music appreciation text. Listen to music, write biographies, descriptions of musical schools, and reactions to compositions. |

HOW TO PUT IT ON THE TRANSCRIPT

Course	Name of class on transcript	Area	Credit
	Art and Art and Music History appreciation	Fine Arts music	.5 for 60 hours 1 for 120 hours

RESOURCES

Most books can be obtained from any bookseller or library; most curricula can be bought directly from the publisher or from a major home-school supplier such as Rainbow Resource Center. Contact information for publishers and suppliers can be found at www.welltrainedmind.com. Remember that additional curricula choices and more can be found at www.welltrainedmind.com. Prices change constantly, but we have included 2016 pricing to give an idea of affordability.

These resources are divided into three lists: art skills, art appreciation, and music appreciation (at this stage, music skills should be studied with a professional teacher). For each list, we have given basic texts first, followed by supplementary resources (you can pick and choose among these). You can also use many of the resources listed in Chapter 21, particularly the art-skills books and materials.

Art Skills

Basic Techniques series. Cincinnati, OH: North Light Books.
$19.99–$22.99 each. Order from North Light Books.
Albert, Greg. *Basic Figure Drawing Techniques.* 1994.
Reid, Jack. *Watercolor Basics: Let's Get Started.* 1998.
Wolf, Rachel. *Basic Flower Painting Techniques in Watercolor.* 1996.

Brown, Claire Waite, ed. *The Sculpting Techniques Bible: An Essential Illustrated Reference for Both Beginners and Experienced Sculptors.* Edison, NJ: Chartwell Books, 2006.
$14.99.

Creevy, Bill. *The Pastel Book.* New York: Watson Guptill, 1999.
$24.99.

Lucchesi, Bruno, and Margit Malmstrom. *Modeling the Figure in Clay.* New York: Watson-Guptill, 1996.
$21.99.

———. *Modeling the Head in Clay.* New York: Watson-Guptill, 1996.
$21.95.

Willenbrink, Mark, and Mary Willenbrink. The Art for the Absolute Beginner series. Cincinnati, OH: North Lights Books, 2006.
$22.99 each.
Drawing for the Absolute Beginner. 2006.
Drawing Nature for the Absolute Beginner. 2013.
Drawing Portraits for the Absolute Beginner. 2012.
Oil Painting for the Absolute Beginner. 2010.
Watercolor for the Absolute Beginner. 2009.

Art Appreciation

Strickland, Carol. *The Annotated Mona Lisa: A Crash Course in Art History from Prehistoric to Postmodern*, 2nd ed. Kansas City, MO: Andrews McMeel, 2007. $22.99. This survey walks the beginner through art history in a brisk, nontechnical manner. We suggest dividing it as follows:

Ninth grade	"The Birth of Art" through "The Renaissance: The Beginning of Modern Painting"
Tenth grade	"Baroque: The Ornate Age" through "Birth of Photography"
Eleventh grade	"Impressionism: Let There Be Color and Light" through "Expressionism"
Twelfth grade	"Mondrian: Harmony of Opposites" through "The New Breed: Post-Modern Art"

Music Appreciation

Copland, Aaron. *What to Listen for in Music*. New York: Signet, 2002. $7.95. Order from any bookstore; a reprint of the classic jargon-free guide by composer Aaron Copland.

Hoffman, Miles. *The NPR Classical Music Companion: An Essential Guide for Enlightened Listening*. New York: Mariner Books, 2005. $18.95.

Jacobson, Julius H., II. *The Classical Music Experience: Discover the Music of the World's Greatest Composers*. Naperville, IL: Sourcebooks, 2002. $39.95.

34

THE SPECIALIST

Any child who already shows a disposition to specialize should be given his head: for, when the use of the tools has been well and truly learned, it is available for any study whatever. It would be well, I think, that each pupil should learn to do one, or two, subjects really well, while taking a few classes in subsidiary subjects so as to keep his mind open to the inter-relations of all knowledge.

—Dorothy Sayers, "The Lost Tools of Learning"

SUBJECT: Junior and senior project
TIME REQUIRED: 2 to 3 hours or more per week in grades 11 and 12

In the preceding chapters, you will have noticed that the number of subjects studied is reduced in the junior and senior years of high school. For example, math and language study can be completed in tenth or eleventh grade; the formal study of writing ends. By the junior year in high school, the typical student of rhetoric is spending two hours per day studying Great Books, an additional hour and a half two days per week studying science, and a couple of hours twice a week dealing with art and music. He's also pursuing an elective—computer programming, advanced language, or Advanced Placement math. This schedule leaves time for the junior and senior writing projects. Eleventh and twelfth graders should choose a major research project in a field that interests them and carry this project out. This is the equivalent of a high-school "honors" program.

During the high-school years, most students begin to develop a "specialty," a skill or branch of learning in which they have a particular talent and interest. Computer programming, Victorian novels, ancient Britain, Renaissance art, French poetry, piano performance, gymnastics, baseball, writing fiction—whatever the student chooses to spend his time doing can become a specialty.

The junior and senior projects give the student an opportunity to exercise all his hard-learned skills in writing and reasoning on a subject that excites him. The opportunity to do in-depth reading and writing on these subjects may steer him toward (or away from) a college major.

GENERAL GUIDELINES

The junior and senior projects are wider in scope than the ninth- and tenth-grade research papers. Research papers focus on a topic that can be summarized in a thesis statement; they tend to deal with a single time and place (that is, they are *synchronic*—they examine a particular point in time). The junior and senior projects should be more complex—they should be *diachronic* (moving through history, examining the origins and historical development of the topic under study).

Any subject, Neil Postman observes, can be given scholarly value if the student traces its historical development, reflects on its origins, and theorizes about its future.[1] Every topic treated in this way sheds light on human endeavor—the way we live. Baseball, for example, becomes a fascinating and fruitful study if the student follows it back to its beginnings and traces it from there. Bat-and-ball games were played as far back as the Aztecs; baseball became a popular child's game in the nineteenth century; the mutation of baseball into a professional sport parallels the general shift in American culture from rural-centered to urban-centered; baseball clubs, first formed in the 1870s, were plagued by corruption; in the

---

[1] Neil Postman, *The End of Education: Redefining the Value of School* (New York: Knopf, 1995), p. 112.

twentieth century, baseball heroes were carefully shielded by the media, which felt it had a duty to protect the hero status of baseball players by not reporting on their misdeeds; baseball players evolved into "celebrities"; and so forth. This study pinpoints a number of cultural shifts in American life—amateur to professional, rural to urban, hero to celebrity. Any student who completes this project will have a better understanding not only of baseball, but of his own culture and history.

The student should keep these questions in mind while developing his topic of study:

- When did this begin? What was its original form? What cultural purpose did it serve?
- Who performed this activity? What cultural place did they occupy? How were they regarded by others?
- What prior historical events did this event/activity resemble? Is this coincidental? Did this event/activity model itself on something that came before? What philosophy does this reveal? (The Olympics, for example, obviously owe a great deal to the ancient Greeks and their ideas about what makes an ideal human being.)
- What ideal picture of human beings does this activity/event hold up?
- How did this activity develop from its beginnings to the present day?
- What effects did this event have on its surroundings? On the generation directly after? Five hundred years later? The present day?
- How did this activity/event change the way people viewed nature? How did it change the way they thought about God?
- What current cultural trends are reflected in this activity? What cultural trends resulted from this event?

Not all of these questions will be applicable to every topic. But if the student can address these queries in some form, his paper will begin to take shape.

For example, suppose the high-school junior loves the novels of Jane Austen. If he decides to do a project on Austen's novels, he needs to think widely about the origins of the novel, its development, Austen's use of it, and the effects of Austen's work on present-day readers. His questions, then, might take the following form:

- When were the first novels written? What were the first novels? (*Don Quixote* is widely regarded as the first European novel.) What cultural shifts around the time of Cervantes led him to create this new form?

- Who originally wrote novels? (Men.) What cultural place did they occupy? (They were thinkers and philosophers.) How were they regarded by others?

- What is the relationship between the historical forms that came before the novel (the epic poem, the fable) and the novel itself? How do novels differ from epic poems and fables? How are they the same? What can a novel do that a poem or fable can't?

- How did novel reading develop from Cervantes to Austen? (This is an immensely fruitful area—novels were viewed with suspicion by the Church; novel reading became a silly, "female" activity and thus was considered trivial and a waste of time; the "lady novelist" was a figure of fun.)

- How did novel reading develop from Austen to the present? (Novels slowly gained their position as serious reflections on the human condition, paralleling in some ways the rise in status of women in society.)

- What effects did Austen's novels have on novel writing in general? (The "novel of manners"—a new genre—was created.) What is the twentieth-century equivalent of the novel of manners?

- What is the relationship of "women's fiction" in the twentieth century to Austen's novels? Have certain types of novel become (once more) the province of "lady novelists"?

- What does the current popularity of Austen's novels say about our own culture? (Quite a bit has been written about the postmodern longing for a return to proper etiquette and manners.)

As in preparation for writing the research papers for ninth and tenth grades, the student should plan on doing a great deal of prereading (the entire fall semester can be spent prereading). Extensive reading in criticism, history, and theory can clarify which of the questions can be answered and which don't apply.

After prereading, the student can follow the general guidelines for preparing the research paper, given in Chapter 26.

The junior paper should be fifteen to twenty pages long; the senior paper, twenty or more pages long.

FLEXIBILITY

Allow some room for creativity. At least one of the projects (ideally, the junior project) should be in standard research-paper form. But permit the second to vary. A student with an interest in creative writing could research the novel in the junior year and write part of a novel for the senior project. The junior with an interest in physics can write a historical study of some development in physics during the junior year; in the senior year, she could perform a complex experiment and document it. The musical student could write a music-history paper in the junior year and give a recital (or compose a piece) for the senior project. The gymnast can write a history of gymnastics in the junior year and prepare for a serious competition to take place the year after.

Just keep the following guideline in mind: whatever creative project is undertaken for the senior year must be documented—it must involve *writing*. The high-school scientist can perform experiments, but she must then write an article about her findings—just as practicing scientists do. The gymnast must write an account of his preparation and competition. The musician must write an essay explaining her choice of recital pieces or analyzing the form of her composition. If the senior writing project is combined with some other activity, it can be shorter (ten pages is a good rule of thumb), but it can't disappear entirely. These writing projects force the student to evaluate what he's doing. They also serve as documentation of the senior project for school boards and college admissions officers.

SPECIFIC GUIDELINES

During the rhetoric stage, knowledge is interrelated. The student writing a history paper will find himself discussing scientific developments; the physicist will have to deal with the religious implications of discoveries in physics (something that occupied Einstein); the musician will find herself studying philosophy. However, projects in each area of knowledge should follow specific guidelines.

History

The student who chooses to research a historical event or era should be careful not to get "stuck in the past." He should deal with the event's relationship to similar prior events, its effect on the surrounding cultures, and any effects that stretch to the present day. The student working on a historical topic should always conclude his paper by answering the question: What does this tell me about my own day and culture?

Research on the lost continent of Atlantis, for example, should deal with early stories of lost civilizations, early volcanic eruptions and other natural disasters that wiped out entire groups of people, the specific events surrounding the loss of Atlantis, the stories of the lost continent told by different cultures (each one varies slightly, depending on the culture that tells it), and the theme of a lost country in twentieth-century American science fiction, fantasy, and folklore. You might answer the question "What does Atlantis tell me about my own day and culture?" by saying: "We have a constant longing to find an 'unspoiled' country, free from the problems we see around us."

For a shining example of this sort of history, read Thomas Cahill's *How the Irish Saved Civilization*, in which the author relates the manuscript copying activities of a group of Irish monks to both ancient culture and the preservation of Western civilization in our own day. (He also points out eerie parallels between the descent of darkness in the Middle Ages and the "new barbarism" of our own times.)

Literature

The student working on literature should always treat the development of the genre under study, from its roots to the present day. This will yield a number of insights, as is illustrated by the Jane Austen example above. Why was novel reading considered a female activity? Why has the epic poem fallen out of favor? Why was philosophy first written in verse and then in prose? These sorts of questions will widen the study of literature.

Mathematics

Mathematics projects can take two forms: the historical development of a type of mathematics (from Pythagoras and Euclid to the present) and the application of mathematics to specific scientific problems. Generally, the junior mathematics project should trace historical development. The senior project can involve the solving of problems, as long as the student writes up her findings as though for publication.

Science

Scientific projects should follow the same guidelines as those given for mathematics. A historical survey in the junior year can be followed by experimentation or projects in the senior year, providing everything is properly documented.

Foreign Languages

The language student can write a paper on the literature of another country, following the literature guidelines above. For a more challenging project, he can write a literature, history, or creative paper *in* the foreign language of his choice. Like the science student, the language student can do a project for the senior year (teaching a language class to other home-schooled students; going abroad to the country where that language is spoken). This project should be summarized in a ten-page essay.

Computer Programming

Any student planning to specialize in computers *must* write a junior or senior paper following Neil Postman's guidelines:

Indicate, first, what you believe are or will be the main advantages of computer technology, and why; second, indicate what are or will be the main disadvantages of computer technology, and why.[2]

[2] Ibid., p. 93.

The second project can be a programming one, which must be properly documented. A manual to accompany the project could fulfill this requirement.

Religion and Ethics

A paper on religion will resemble a history paper in that it will trace the development of a certain aspect of faith and practice and will reflect on present-day effects and applications. Ethics papers should follow the same general guidelines. Any paper treating the ethical aspect of some behavior (assisted suicide or cloning, for example) must examine the history of the issue as well as evaluating present guidelines.

The Arts: Painting, Sculpture, Theater, Music

As in science and math, the junior project should be a historical survey (of a painting or sculptural style or school, the development of a particular theatrical convention, the performance history of one of Shakespeare's plays, the development over time of a particular musical form or style, the development of an instrument). The senior project can be a recital, an art exhibit, or a theatrical performance. A ten-page essay should document and explain this project.

Sports

As demonstrated in the discussion of baseball, sports can provide great cultural insight if studied historically. Sports are a type of performance, and, as with the performing arts, the student should write one historical study. The senior year can be devoted to a sports performance, properly documented with a ten-page essay.

EVALUATION

We strongly suggest that you find someone to guide and evaluate the junior and senior projects. Enlist local college faculty members or experts in the student's field. You can also write to authors, musicians, and scholars, asking them to evaluate the junior and senior papers and projects. If you can afford it, you should offer to pay for these evaluations. (If you can't, the student has the chance to write a persuasive essay, explaining why he's worthy of the scholar's time and energy.)

If the expert agrees, the student should follow this pattern:

1. Preread.
2. Make an appointment to discuss the topic with the expert, either in writing or by phone, on the Internet or in person. The expert will have additional suggestions, clarifying questions, and resources for the student to investigate.
3. Write or perform the project.
4. Submit the project for evaluation. Ask the expert to comment on and evaluate it.
5. Rewrite the project according to suggestions made by the expert.
6. Resubmit the completed, revised project.

Since this will take a fair amount of time and effort on the part of the expert, you should offer him or her a one-hundred-dollar honorarium, a small but acceptable token of good faith (it shows that you are appreciative of the time he or she is spending helping your student).

This outside evaluation has two purposes. (1) The student is submitting his work to an expert who can help him to sharpen and improve his knowledge in the specific area. (2) The expert is now in a position to write letters of reference for the student when the student applies to colleges.

SUGGESTED SCHEDULES

Eleventh grade	Allow 2 to 3 hours or more per week in the fall for prereading, 2 to 3 hours or more per week in the spring for writing.
Twelfth grade	Allow 2 to 3 hours or more per week in the fall for pre-reading or preparation, 2 to 3 hours or more per week for writing or performance.

HOW TO PUT IT ON THE TRANSCRIPT

If the project is undertaken as part of the student's study in one of the subject areas, it does not earn a separate credit. If the student puts in at least 60 additional hours, you may issue a half credit:

Course	Name of class on transcript	Area	Credit
Junior project	Junior Thesis	Elective	.5
Senior project	Senior Thesis	Elective	.5

35

SOME PEOPLE HATE HOMER

Tomorrow's economy will be volatile and dependent on flexible workers with a high level of intellectual skills. Thus, the best vocational
education will be . . . in the use of one's mind.

—Theodore R. Sizer, *Horace's Compromise*

Classical education's fine for the college-bound. Homer and Plato might
be fun for intellectuals. But what about the student who isn't interested in college? What about the student who doesn't really care about
scholarship? What about the student who wants to finish high school, get
out, and work?

A classical education is valuable even for people who hate Homer.

At a recent conference on education in Richmond, Virginia, a top executive from a car manufacturer let fly in frustration: Why are you asking me
how to prepare students for the job market? Most of the high-school graduates who apply for jobs with us can't write, don't read well, can't think
through a problem. We spend an unbelievable amount of money retraining
these graduates in basic academic skills *before* we can teach them how to
do their jobs. Don't bring more vocational training into the high-school

curriculum. Teach them how to read, to write, to do math, and to think. *We'll* train them in the specific job skills they need.

A well-trained mind is a necessity for any job—from car repair person to university teacher. The mechanic with a classical education will be more successful than her untrained counterparts; she'll know how to plan her business, how to relate to her customers, how to organize her responsibilities, how to *think*. A classical education is the best possible preparation for the job market.

Throughout this book, we've maintained that the classical education is not intended to teach all subjects comprehensively—history, science, math, language. The classical education *is* designed to teach the student how to learn. In its constant demand that the student read and then analyze and write about what she's read, the classical education trains the mind to gather, organize, and use information. And the student who knows how to learn—and has had practice in independent learning—can successfully do any job.

In their book *Teaching the New Basic Skills: Principles for Educating Children to Thrive in a Changing Economy*, authors Richard J. Murnane and Frank Levy analyze the hiring practices of several large companies. They conclude that while employers look for certain basic skills—the ability to do math, to read well, to communicate effectively in writing and in speech, to use computers for simple tasks—the primary quality that makes students employable is the ability to "raise performance continually" by learning on the job.[1] Such ability follows the Platonic definition of *knowledge*—an activity, a continual process of learning, not some sort of static body of information. Gene Edward Veith points out that the Greeks would have viewed with suspicion education that trains the student for a highly specific job. Such training creates "a slave mentality, making the learner an obedient worker utterly dependent upon his masters."[2] In an economy where the average

[1] Richard J. Murnane and Frank Levy, *Teaching the New Basic Skills: Principles for Educating Children to Thrive in a Changing Economy* (New York: Free Press, 1996), p. 32.

[2] Gene Edward Veith, "Renaissance, Not Reform," an essay posted at the Philanthropy, Culture and Society website, August 1996; www.capitalresearch.org. See also Gene Edward Veith, Jr., and Andrew Kern, *Classical Education: Towards the Revival of American Schooling* (Washington, DC: Capital Research Center, 1997), p. 78.

worker has held five different jobs over the space of a career, only the flexible can survive (and be free).

A classical education is useful.

But to a certain extent, to ask "What's the use?" is itself antithetical
to the goals of the classical education. "The practical life," writes David
Hicks, in a paraphrase of Plato, "falls short of completeness. The wealth
one acquires in business is a useful thing, but as such, it exists for the sake
of something else."[3] The classically educated student aims for more than
a life of comfort; she aims for a "life that knows and reveres, speculates
and acts upon the Good, that loves and re-produces the Beautiful, and that
pursues excellence and moderation in all things."

The classical education, with its emphasis on the life of the mind, on
reading and writing about ideas, is aimed at producing a student who
pursues excellence and moderation in all things. This is Plato's "virtuous
man" (who, parenthetically, is generally highly employable—a side effect).

There's yet another reason for classical education, which has to do with
the nature of a democracy. From ancient times through recent centuries,
only a small, elite segment of the population received the kind of education
we've outlined in these chapters. Because only a fraction of society was
equipped to think through ideas and their consequences, only that fraction
was qualified to govern—an act that demands that the governing members
of society look past the immediate, the popular, and the simplistic in order
to evaluate long-range consequences and complex cause and effect.

But in a democracy, all citizens have a part in government. They should
be able to look past immediate gratification, rhetorical flourishes, and simplistic solutions in order to understand which course of action is the right
one to take. In a healthy democracy, the casting of a vote is the act of a
well-trained mind.

Every citizen in a democracy takes on the responsibilities that were
once reserved for the well-educated aristocratic segment of society. And so
every citizen, college-bound or not, should receive the type of education
that will develop the life of the mind.

What happens if this is neglected?

"The average citizen," David Hicks writes, "will begin to doubt the

---

[3] David Hicks, *Norms and Nobility: A Treatise on Education* (New York: Praeger, 1981),
p. 20.

soundness of his own judgments. He will surrender his fundamental democratic right to ideas and to decision making to a few experts. . . . [He will] grow lazy in his demand for a high quality of public thought and information. He will doubt his ability to decide the issues shaping his life, and he will take another step beyond representative government in relinquishing the privilege of self-government by putting himself at the mercy of a few experts. At last, abandoning his Western classical heritage, he will resign himself and his children to . . . a democracy in name only."[4]

It's a chilling scenario, but already these tendencies are visible in America in the beginning of the twenty-first century. The classical education—for all students, not just for some college-bound "elite"—is the best preventive.

And you don't have to wait for your local school to come to this conclusion. You can train your child's mind yourself.

[4] Ibid., p. 83.

PART III

EPILOGUE

The Rhetoric Stage at a Glance

Rhetoric	3 hours per week
Grammar & writing skills	3 hours per week
History & literature	8–10 hours per week
Mathematics	5+ hours per week
Science	4+ hours per week
Latin/foreign language	3–6 hours per week
Art & music	4 hours per week

Because high-school curricula options vary so much, we have not provided checklists for the upper grades. Instead, use the "Planning Ahead" form in Chapter 24 to plot the high-school years.

PART IV

COMING
HOME

How to Educate Your Child at Home

36

※

THE KITCHEN-TABLE SCHOOL:
WHY HOME-EDUCATE?

Home schooling, once dismissed as a fringe activity practiced by head-in-the-sand reactionaries and off-the-grid hippies, is now widely considered an integral part of the mainstream education system.

—*Education Week*

The perfect school is a myth. Rather than trying to do the impossible by attempting to duplicate the perfect (and imaginary) school experience, be realistic and diligent about what you can do well. Offer personal, individual tutoring; use your time efficiently; control the child's social and moral environment until she's mature enough to make wise decisions. Your aim is education, not the duplication of an institution.

Remember, you aren't alone. Home-schooling is now legal in all fifty states for one reason—parent activism. The beginning of the modern home-school movement can be traced to the alternative schools founded in the 1960s and 1970s by parents who defended their right to choose from among educational alternatives.

These alternative schools tended to be politically liberal and activist.[1] Parents without access to these schools or who saw themselves as more conservative followed the trend of parent involvement by choosing instead to home-school their children quietly. By the 1980s, increasing numbers of Christian Protestants were taking their children out of the public school system, which they saw as culturally and spiritually alien to their values. Catholic families had done this years before, as had Orthodox Jewish families; now there are Jewish, Muslim, Mormon, and secularist home-school support organizations as more and more parents decide to exercise their option to choose an alternative to the public school system.

The reasons for making this choice are varied: unhappiness with academic standards, a wish to avoid negative social pressures, frustration with oversized classes, disagreement with the philosophy of education held by local schools. What all these parents have in common is a single belief: the right of all parents to choose how to educate their children. And all of them are actively, not passively, involved in helping their children learn.

WHY SHOULD YOU HOME-SCHOOL?

Over the years, we've heard a number of reasons why parents choose to take their children out of school. They include

- Boredom.
- Fatigue caused by long bus rides or unreasonable schedules.
- Frustration and academic failure.
- Lack of academic challenge.
- Constant family travel that requires missing school.
- Health problems that prevent the child from taking part in a regular school-day program.
- School pressure for conformity, rather than flexible programs that enable children to develop their own strengths and solve their own problems.

[1] Shawn Callaway, "Home Education, College Admission, and Financial Aid," *Journal of College Admission* (Spring 1997): p. 8.

- The need for one-on-one instruction, individual attention, time, and encouragement to develop special talents or strengths.
- Negative peer pressure. The child starts to adopt the standards of her peer group and reject those of her family.
- The need for quiet. The child doesn't mentally operate well where there is confusion and noise.
- Learning problems that aren't being solved. The child isn't being challenged to overcome weaknesses.
- Peer or faculty intimidation. The child is being intimidated, teased, or abused verbally or physically by classmates or teachers.
- The need for more or less time per subject. The rate of instruction (too fast, too slow) doesn't match the child's rate of learning.
- Too much emphasis on nonacademic activities. Extracurricular activities usurp time necessary to achieve academic excellence.
- The waste of a gifted student's time. The gifted child is used by the teacher to tutor slower students, rather than being challenged to press forward.
- An emphasis on popularity rather than on academic achievement. The child becomes popular, but not productive and literate.
- The "pariah" status of the gifted student. The quick student feels discriminated against because of giftedness—often jealousy and resentment from classmates, sometimes even from teachers.
- The ostracization of the student who is different. The child with a mild problem or difference (lisp, shyness, or even slowness in doing work because she's unusually careful) often gets placed in a special-education class and is then negatively labeled by both classmates and teachers for the rest of her school career.[2]
- Conflicting family schedules. The parent may have a work situation that doesn't allow him to spend time with the child except during school hours.

---

[2] Students with mild speech impediments are often placed in special-education classes. According to an article in the *New York Times,* financial incentives encourage schools to keep these children in special education, a situation that often yields "isolation and failure." These children often never return to mainstream classes and many do not graduate with a regular diploma. ("Fresh Thinking on Special Education," *New York Times,* November 26, 1996, sec. A, p. 20.)

- Loss of academic self-esteem. The child is losing confidence in her ability to learn. (Jessie once worked with a sixteen-year-old girl who was unresponsive and discouraged. Jessie kept on with one-on-one instruction, basic phonics, remedial math and writing, and lots of encouragement. Eventually the girl returned to regular school, graduated, and completed nursing school. She came back for a visit after she had worked as a nurse for several years. "Thank you," she said, "for making me believe that I *could* learn.")
- The parent is shut out of the educational system and wants back in. A December 8, 1996, article in the *New York Times* tells of a peer intervention program in the New York City public schools. Instead of being dismissed, incompetent teachers are allowed to enroll in a remedial program for poor teachers "in which a teaching coach works one-on-one in the classroom for as long as a year. . . . Parents who ask," the article continues, "are generally given the impression that the extra adult in class is a teacher's assistant."[3] In other words, these parents aren't told the truth. The article goes on to describe a first-grade teacher who yells at the children and humiliates them. The teaching coach corrects him privately, but the parents are never told what's going on in the classroom.

These are reasons to home-educate.

ENCOURAGEMENT FOR PARENTS

Don't be intimidated because you can't reproduce a classroom environment or school activity. Remember, programs, multiple aids, and group activities are designed for groups. Tutoring is probably the most efficient method of education since the teaching is tailored to the individual child's needs and rate of learning. You can supply this.

And as teaching progresses, parents can teach not only academic subjects, but life experiences as well. Home schooling allows time and space for the teaching of practical skills; older students especially have the flex-

---

[3] Pam Belluck, "Poor Teachers Get Coaching, Not Dismissal," *New York Times,* December 8, 1996, sec. A, pp. 1 and 46.

ibility to learn painting, papering, carpentry, woodworking, electrical and plumbing repair, food preparation, car repair, gardening, yard care, and so on. We've listed a few high-school electives to help you teach these practical skills at the end of this chapter.

Parents also serve as models and guides for acceptable, productive behavior. When you teach your child at home, you're training her to work hard and to be disciplined. Help her set goals with a plan for reaching those goals—this gives a reason for the hard work. Teach her how to manage time and schedule tasks. Work on gradual improvement, keeping records of progress and planning rewards for increments of achievement. Don't spend time only on the tasks you like, but form a plan to improve weaknesses. Take rest and recreation breaks when your student becomes nonproductive. All of these are principles for success in any endeavor, not just in home education.

In classical education, the teacher isn't a never-ceasing fount of information from which students continually drink up answers. Instead, the model of the classical teacher and students is that of leader and "disciples," meaning that the teacher and students are united together in the same task, learning an inherited body of knowledge together. "The teacher's true competence," writes classical headmaster David Hicks, "is not in his mastery of a subject, but in his ability to provoke the right questions and . . . [in his] peculiar eagerness to explore new subjects and new ideas with his students."[4]

Given the time and the resources we suggest, any dedicated parent can do this.

Plan ahead, of course, but don't panic, when your child is in first grade, that you won't be able to do eighth-grade algebra. Take one year at a time. You'll study and grow and learn with your child. Jessie says that she learned more when she was home-educating her children than she did in college.

The home-school environment prepares children for the "real world" better than identification with age-segregated peer groups. After all, the typical workplace contains a number of different ages and abilities, not a single peer group. The home, with its mixed-age, mixed-ability environment, is much more like this workplace than the single-grade classroom.

---

[4] David Hicks, *Norms and Nobility: A Treatise on Education* (New York: Praeger, 1981), p. 129.

A special encouragement to the parents of high-school students: you don't have to teach everything. If your child were enrolled in a large, well-equipped high school that offered many courses, time would still allow only so many selections. Jessie has observed that in larger schools with more courses, students often end up with less-than-desirable schedules—courses fill up, guidance counselors are overworked, students are given too much freedom to take easy courses. We know of one student at a big, prosperous high school who was allowed to sign up for four art courses—not because he was interested, but because he thought they would be easy. By the time his mother saw his schedule, he wasn't able to sign up for a better-balanced year because the other classes were full.

FIRST STEPS

If you have decided to home-school, start by contacting your state home-schooling organization. It can give you information about the laws in your state. (Different states require different types of notification: some want you to submit a general plan of study; some require a photocopied college diploma.) We've provided a list of home-schooling organizations at the end of this chapter. They'll also give you advice on the best way to remove your child from public or private school, if she's already enrolled there.

Look at all the material out there. Visit home-schooling forums (ours, forums.welltrainedmind.com, is one of the largest and most active; pay us a visit). Examine the websites of some of the publishers we've listed. Read a few home-school blogs.

Gather together what you'll need to start the year. Plan schedules for your family. (See Chapter 40 for suggestions.)

Visit a home-school support group. Your state organization will give you a list of local groups.

Two cautions. Jessie has found that when you choose a group for ongoing support and as a social outlet for yourself and your children, it may not be the one closest to you. Local support groups, of necessity, take on the personality and philosophy of the leadership. Some are inclusive; some are exclusive and make those who don't agree uncomfortable. You have to find the one that best suits you.

Also, you may find that your local home-school group is populated mostly by "unschoolers." Classical education is not easily compatible with pure "unschooling," which is popular among many home schoolers. "Unschooling" is child-centered. It assumes that the child will learn all that he needs to know by following his natural impulses and that any learning that is "imposed" on the child by an authority figure will prove unproductive.

Classical education is knowledge-focused, not child-focused. It attempts to teach knowledge in a way that awakens the child's interest, but the child's interest is not the sole determining factor in whether or not a subject should be taught. How does a child know whether something will interest and excite him unless he works at unfamiliar (and perhaps intimidating) material to find out what it's all about?

Unschoolers may also tend to denigrate "book" learning in favor of "real" learning. Many unschoolers claim that the day-to-day realities of family life provide plenty of opportunities for learning. For these unschoolers, taking care of the house, grocery shopping, cooking, car repair, working in the family business, writing thank-you notes, and so on provide enough opportunity for children to learn real-life skills without "doing school" in a formal way.

While this may be true, a child's education shouldn't be limited to "real-life skills." Classically educated children should be able to cook, write thank-you notes, and tie their shoes. They also know where their country came from, how to construct a logical argument, and what *puella* means.

Unschoolers sometimes claim that students who aren't forced to learn the mathematics tables in third grade can pick them up in a day once they hit sixth or seventh grade and get interested on their own. In our experience, the student who doesn't learn the math tables in third grade will never be comfortable enough with math to get interested in sixth or seventh grade.

If you end up in a local group of unschoolers and you want to follow the curriculum we've outlined in this book, you may need to switch groups.

TAKING YOUR CHILD OUT OF SCHOOL

If your child has been in a bad situation—destructive peer relationships, discouraging classroom experiences—and you've brought her home to rescue her, expect a period of adjustment. Be understanding but firm in your decision. Fully explain what you are doing and why. Your confidence in the decision that what you are doing is best for her will be communicated. So will indecision, which will make her resist the change even more.

Any radical change can cause "culture shock." Children generally prefer a known situation, no matter how flawed, to an unknown one—structure and routine are always comforting. Expect a period of adjustment. But use common sense. If you see depression and anger that doesn't adjust in six weeks or so, take your child to a trusted counselor so that you can both talk out the problems.

THE REALITIES OF HOME SCHOOLING

While we think home education is wonderful—we've seen children and parents thrive at home, we've heard hundreds of success stories—you must go into it with your eyes open.

- Home schooling is time-consuming hard work.
- Housework suffers. Books and science experiments and papers are all over the house.
- Everyone wants to quit at some point during the school year.
- The kids aren't always perfect, and you can't blame it on school or on their friends.
- Academic schedules are frequently interrupted by sickness, family needs, and life in general.
- Children often "just don't get it"—that is, they may experience plateaus or have difficulty with a new concept.
- Grandparents may think you're ruining your children.
- The neighbors will probably tell you that you're crazy.

A PERSONAL WORD FROM JESSIE

I was often tired and sometimes felt overwhelmed by what I had undertaken—that is, home-educating my children. And if I'd had a perfect school available, I would have enrolled my children in it. But I looked at the academic and social options, and concluded that, in spite of my failures, my children were doing better under my tutoring than they would have done in a group situation.

Personally, I decided to put on hold some of my goals. But I held on to the wise counsel given me when my children were toddlers: "Live your life in chapters. You don't have to do everything you want to do in life during this chapter of rearing children." This advice provided the cornerstone of my plans for personal goals.

I wanted to write. I wanted to make a hand-braided early American–style rug. When my three children were toddlers, I had a whole stash of wool, all stripped in preparation for braiding. Since toddlerhood wasn't the right time to start such a large project, I stored it in boxes "until the children are in school." Instead of sending them off each morning while I quietly braided the rug, I was even more busy with home schooling than I had been with three preschoolers.

I have time to write now. My rug-in-waiting is still in boxes, although I can almost see the time approaching to start it—thirty years later! But my children are the most creative project I have been involved in. I can't compare the relationship I have with them to a relationship with a rug, no matter how beautifully hand-crafted. And my crafting of their education has been life-enriching to all of us.

There were times when I longed for a magazine-beautiful house instead of a house with "projects" all over it. Housework wasn't always done on time. Every October and March, I wanted to quit. (I learned to take a week off when that feeling came over me. Rest and change of pace renewed my focus.) When my children needed correction, I had to take the responsibility and not blame it on bad friends. Academic schedules were sometimes interrupted by life. My father had a brain tumor. My son had allergies. But looking back, I can see that even when we took off from school for the necessities of family life, we had a long-range goal in mind. We were able to get back on track and continue with our plan, taking up where we left off.

The most discouraging thing I encountered was the lack of support from family and neighbors. When I started home-schooling, I worried a lot. I worried I wouldn't be able to keep up with my children's grade levels. I worried that their social development would suffer. The neighbors said, "They'll never get into college." The grandparents cried.

But as I look back, none of the worries materialized. My children did get into college. They have careers and relationships. And even the grand-parents, seeing the academic progress and the better-than-normal social development, eventually admitted that they had been mistaken.

RESOURCES

For a list of home-education organizations and links to state laws regulating home education, visit welltrainedmind.com.

37

WHEN LEARNING
DOESN'T IMPROVE: DIFFICULTIES
AND CHALLENGES

When in doubt, go and get your child assessed.
—Experienced home-schooling parent

The plan for classical education that we describe in this book is a *pattern* for home schooling. *Pattern: the regular and repeated way in which something happens or is done.* (Thanks, *Merriam-Webster.*)

But there are thousands of children who don't learn in a regular way. Everything that we suggest is within the capabilities of learners who are "neurotypical"—a newly invented word that originally was used for anyone who wasn't on the autism spectrum, but which is now widely used by many home educators to mean (more or less) that you're cognitively, intellectually, and developmentally "normal."

So what's "non-neurotypical"?

The child who just can't figure out reading.

The child who seems to have no grasp of spelling.

The child who at nine, ten, eleven is still staring at addition problems as though he's never seen them before.

The preteen whose handwriting is still so poor that you can barely read it.

The teenager who has given up.

No matter how good your teaching is, or what curriculum you use, if your child is not processing information in a "neurotypical" way, you might strike out. There are many non-neurotypical students out there: dyslexic, dysgraphic, dyscalculic (unable to process numeric information normally), twice-exceptional (gifted in one area and struggling hard in another), dealing with processing difficulties, seizure disorders, autism, and other difficulties. In fact, as one home-schooling parent remarked to us, the home-education population may have more non-neurotypical kids in it than the general school population, because the frustrations of dealing with these problems in a classroom situation causes many parents to turn to home schooling.

And we've heard one message over and over again: I wish I'd had my child evaluated sooner.

Here's just one of the many stories we've heard, shared with the permission of this mother.

The first point in time which I realized that my son (now nineteen) was not just "learning differently," but needed intervention in order to cope was when he was in kindergarten. I found out that the teachers were regularly sending my son for time outs—some of them lasting for forty-five minutes, because he would not do his printing work properly.

The behaviors he showed were: scribbling hard on the workpage with a look of frustration and anger when asked to keep trying. He would sometimes scrunch up and throw his paper and pencil on the floor.

I started home schooling my son at the end of grade one. I thought that if I taught him at home and used some strategies given to me by an occupational therapist for his fine motor skills everything would go along smoothly and he would then catch up. His printing improved. However, new areas of weakness kept popping up that needed to be addressed. I was using the curriculum suggested in The Well-Trained Mind and I kept hoping that all my son needed was good curriculum and an understanding teacher (me).

Fast forward a couple of years: I started to see signs that there was something else going on with my son. He would take a long time to do his work and I would have to keep telling him to focus, as he would drift off. He would get frustrated if the worksheet I gave him seemed to have too much work on it. He would give up easily and say things like, "I just can't do it." And he would sometimes resort to his old behavior of scribbling on his worksheet when he was frustrated. Coming up with a sentence to write seemed extremely difficult. He just couldn't seem to find the words, for verbal or written work. I kept having to go back and repeat lessons already taught because the next level up seemed too hard. He seemed to tire easily.

Looking back, the clues and behaviors that my son was not just "learning differently" but needed intervention in order to cope were all there.

I wish I had gotten my son assessed earlier. I wish I hadn't pushed my son through the lessons—doing too much and moving too fast.

I would suggest that other parents look for signs of their child's not being able to keep up, not understanding what is being asked of him or her, not being able to focus, having to have instructions repeated over and over again. And look at your child's behaviors (like my son's scribbling, pushing, throwing, scrunching his worksheets) *and* whether he or she displays feelings of anger and frustration and wanting to give up.

When my son was assessed by an occupational therapist, it helped me to understand that he had fine motor challenges; the therapist gave me strategies to help him cope and learn to print. When my son had trouble understanding instructions and couldn't manage expressive language, I had a speech and language assessment done. This helped me understand where his delays and strengths were and gave me strategies to help him.

Unfortunately, the cognitive delays took longer for me to see; it wasn't until my son was a teenager that I got him a psychoeducational assessment.

But now that I know where his weaknesses and strengths are, I understand more and have more strategies to help my son learn better, at a pace that works for him. The good news is that, after twelve years of home schooling, my son is still learning and progressing academically. He gets tested—academic screening—every year by his doctor. He is now working at a high-school level for all of the main subjects. It took us a lot longer to move up through the grade levels, but with lots of patience we are getting there.

There may be a very clear physical cause for learning difficulties: we've heard from parents who discovered, well into their child's teenage years, that the child was actually suffering from a degree of mild cerebral palsy, deafness, or difficult-to-diagnose vision problems. But *all* learning difficulties can be better dealt with once they're labeled. "It is the fact that we finally got a label," another mother wrote to us, "combined with the specifics of testing, that makes me now able to help my child. I know when to ease up on him, when to accommodate and when it is okay to push. Without the label I was always pushing him beyond his capabilities. I am sure he felt helpless and inadequate and he didn't even know why. His 'label' has made him a happier kid and given him parents who are better informed and therefore better teachers and advocates. Labels can be beautiful."

So don't delay for years if you sense that your child is not progressing normally. "My biggest regret," one parent told us, "is that I listened to the 'he's just a late bloomer' voices instead of listening to my intuition. We lost a few years of remedial academics because of the wait-and-see approach."

Adapting classical education to the varied needs of non-neurotypical students is beyond the scope of this chapter (and this book is already big enough), but we encourage you to visit our forums at forums.welltrained mind.com and join the ongoing conversation at our Learning Challenges board, where hundreds of parents have shared their strategies and stories. And investigate the many additional curricula suggestions at welltrained mind.com.

38

THE CONFIDENT CHILD:
SOCIALIZATION

The Smithsonian Institution's recipe for genius and leadership: (1) children should spend a great deal of time with loving, educationally minded parents; (2) children should be allowed a lot of free exploration; and (3) children should have little to no association with peers outside of family and relatives.

—H. McCurdy, "The Childhood Pattern of Genius"

"**B**ut what about socialization?" If you haven't asked this question already, a neighbor or grandparent certainly will.

The most convincing proof that home-educated children develop normally is a conversation with a home-educated child who's bright, engaged, polite, interesting, and outgoing. Home-school graduates get into college and do fine; they get jobs and excel.

But it's important to understand what socialization means. According to the dictionary, *socialization* is "the process by which a human being, beginning in infancy, acquires the habits, beliefs, and accumulated knowledge of his society." In other words, you're being socialized when you learn habits, acquire beliefs, learn about the society around you, develop character traits, and become competent in the skills you need to function properly in society.

Who teaches all of this? Agents of socialization include the family (both immediate and extended), the religious community, neighborhoods, tutors and mentors, the media (TV, radio, films, books, magazines all tell the child what's expected of him, for better or worse), clubs (social or academic), the arts (both in observation and participation), travel, jobs, civic participation. And formal schooling in an institution.

Taking the child out of school doesn't mean that you're going to remove him from the other "agents of socialization" that surround him. Furthermore, think about the type of socialization that takes place in school. The child learns how to function in a specific environment, one where he's surrounded by forty-five children his own age. This is a very specific type of socialization, one that may not prove particularly useful. When, during the course of his life, will he find himself in this kind of context? Not in work or in family life or in his hobbies. The classroom places the child in a peer-dominated situation that he'll probably not experience again.

And this type of socialization may be damaging. Thirty years ago, Cornell University professor of child development Urie Bronfenbrenner warned that the "socially-isolated, age-graded peer group" created a damaging dependency in which middle-school students relied on their classmates for approval, direction, and affection. He warned that if parents, other adults, and older children continued to be absent from the active daily life of younger children, we could expect "alienation, indifference, antagonism, and violence on the part of the younger generation." [1]

Peer dependence is dangerous. When a child is desperate to fit in—to receive acceptance from those who surround him all day, every day—he may defy your rules, go against his own conscience, or even break the law.

We live in an age in which people think a great deal about peers, talk about them constantly, and act as if a child's existence will be meaningless if he isn't accepted by his peer group. But the socialization that best prepares a child for the real world can't take place when a child is closed up in a classroom or always with his peer group. It happens when

---

[1] Urie Bronfenbrenner, *Two Worlds of Childhood* (London: George Allen & Unwin, 1971), p. 105.

the child is living with people who vary widely in age, personality, background, and circumstance.

The antidote for peer-centered socialization is to make the family the basic unit for socialization—the center of the child's experience. The family should be the place where real things happen, where there is a true interest in each other, acceptance, patience, and peace, as far as is possible. Socialization in the family starts when very young children learn that they can trust adults to give them answers, to read books to them, to talk to them, to listen to music with them. Socialization continues as the child learns to fit into the lives of his parents and siblings, to be considerate and thoughtful of other people, to be unselfish instead of self-centered. A two-year-old can learn to play alone for a few minutes while the parent teaches a ten-year-old; an eight-year-old can learn not to practice the piano during the baby's nap time. It's the *real* world when a child learns to play quietly because Daddy is working on his income taxes. (We still talk about "the year we couldn't go into the living room" because Dad was being audited and his tax papers were spread throughout the living room for weeks.)

In our society, children, taught by their peer groups, learn to survive, not to live with kindness and grace. Exclusive peer groups—cliques—start forming around age five. Even in kindergarten, children are accepted or rejected on the basis of what they wear, what toys they own, what TV programs they watch. Even when adults are supervising, these cliques survive—and strengthen—as children grow. And only the strongest flourish.

The trend in our culture is to devalue—even bypass—the family as a basic unit of socialization. But it's within the family that children learn to love by seeing love demonstrated; learn unselfishness both through teaching and through example (choosing to teach a child at home is unselfishness at work); learn conflict resolution by figuring out how to get along with parents and with each other.

The family unit—this basic agent of socialization—is itself a place to communicate with people of different ages. But socialization doesn't stop there. As a family, you should make a wide range of friends of various ages. Home-school parent and lawyer Christopher Klicka points out that home-educated children are continually socialized through community activities, Little League, Scouts, band, music lessons, art classes, field trips, and the numerous events sponsored by local home-school support groups.[2]

By means of these activities, parents teach children how to live in society and how to relate to others. In contrast, peer groups teach a child either to take direction from the most popular kid in school or to transform himself into the most popular kid at school, often sacrificing intelligence and character in the process.

What about high school?

High-school students demonstrate what sociologist Charles Horton Cooley describes as "the looking-glass self"—they evaluate their worth by looking at themselves in the mirror held up by their peers.[3] Unfortunately, the qualities that lead to high-school success—such as peer popularity and athletic prowess—are precisely those that may be of least use during later life. In contrast, the home-style classical education develops and rewards skills (perseverance, dedication, patience) that will be useful in later life. Is it more important that the high-school years be ones of dizzying social success followed by a lifetime of nostalgia or a time of preparation for a successful life?

Of course, high school isn't a "dizzying social success" for most people.

At a reception for students at Cornell University, a ring of young women closes around Jane [Goodall], who is describing how adolescent chimp females often leave their community to join another. Kimberly Phillips, a graduate student in genetics, asks what kind of welcome a female can expect from the new community.

"Well, the males are delighted," Jane says. "But the females beat her up. They don't want the competition. One strategy the newcomer can use, however, is to attach herself to a high-ranking female, even if she is treated badly by that female. The others will eventually accept her."

"God, it sounds just like high school," Kimberly says.[4]

---

[2] Christopher Klicka, *The Case for Home Schooling*, 4th rev. ed. (Gresham, OR: Noble, 1995), p. 13.

[3] Charles Horton Cooley, *Human Nature and the Social Order* (New York: Scribner's, 1902), pp. 184–85.

[4] Peter Miller, "Jane Goodall," *National Geographic*, December 1995, p. 121.

By the time the student reaches high school, he's looking at a future that will probably be spent in family life, work, and community involvement. Doesn't it make sense to spend your training time with these emerging young adults preparing them for the real life they're getting ready to enter? There is life after high school. (There is even life after college and graduate school.)

In this day of endemic family breakup, teaching your high schooler to live peacefully in a family is probably the most important feat of socialization you can accomplish. Teach skills of resolving conflict, habits of doing for others instead of self, truthfulness, loyalty, sensitivity.

What about dating?

We'll brave the collective wrath of American high-school students by suggesting that exclusive dating in high school is a waste of time. After all, what are you going to do if you fall deeply in love at seventeen? Get married? Break up? Have sex? We believe that sex without commitment is damaging at any age (we're pro-marriage). But it's even worse for teens, who are uncertain, vulnerable, and unsure of their own attraction. Sex can be a powerful, manipulative tool even for supposedly mature adults. It's even more devastating when wielded by the unready. We have yet to find an adult who remembers high-school dating as rewarding and life-enriching.

Not that you should ignore the opposite sex (a practical impossibility). Lots of family-oriented socializing—parties that include not just teens, but people of all ages—give teens plenty of practice in relating to the opposite sex in an atmosphere that isn't fraught with sexual tension, the pain of uncertainty, and the possibility of rejection. Look at the general state of peace, joy, and sexual fulfillment at the average high school and ask: Is this what I want my teen to be socialized to?

Positive socialization is all about living in your world responsibly, fulfilling your potential, taking advantage of opportunity, making the lives of others around you better. You don't need the institutional school to teach these values to your child.

Practically speaking, you provide positive socialization through family-based and interest-based activities. The Red Cross offers CPR and baby-sitting instruction. Museums offer special classes. Church and community teams offer sports participation. Clubs for every hobby from photography to stamp collecting meet regularly. Science fairs, debate clubs, swimming lessons—all of these provide opportunities for social interaction.

Nor should you be afraid of being alone. A measure of solitude can develop creativity, self-reliance, and the habit of reflective thought. Socialize, but don't crowd the schedule so full that the child has no time to think, to sit and stare at the walls, to lie in the backyard and watch ants crawl by.

39

THE CHARACTER ISSUE:
PARENTS AS TEACHERS

Becoming a responsible human being is a path filled with potholes
and visited constantly by temptations. Children need guidance and
moral road maps, and they benefit immensely with the examples of
adults who speak truthfully and act from moral strength.

—Vigen Guroian, *Tending the Heart of Virtue*

Schools have tried to implement "character training," an enterprise
that's bound to fail because it's been taught in a theological and philosophical vacuum. Moral issues are discussed, but no one moral standard
can be settled on since someone might disagree and the beliefs of all
must be respected. Right and wrong can't be asserted with too much
vigor because "we want our children to be tolerant, and we sometimes
seem to think that a too sure sense of right and wrong only produces
fanatics."[1]

Character training isn't some sort of subject, like algebra or spelling,
that can be packaged into a curriculum and taught to everyone, regardless of belief. The definition of character is tied to standards of right and

---

[1] Vigen Guroian, *Tending the Heart of Virtue: How Classic Stories Awaken a Child's Moral
Imagination* (New York: Oxford University Press, 1998), p. 3.

wrong, which in turn are tied to religious belief; the training of character is done through example and teaching—not in a classroom, but in daily life.

What is character? Character is the possession of moral qualities that have become habits of life. As a partial list, we offer:

Boldness	Honesty
Compassion	Humility
Creativity	Initiative
Dependability	Patience
Determination	Perseverance
Diligence	Responsibility
Endurance	Self-control
Enthusiasm	Sincerity
Fairness	Thoroughness
Forgiveness	Tolerance
Gratefulness	Truthfulness

While we can't imagine anyone arguing about the components of this list, we also can't figure out how to teach them in the abstract without some sort of philosophical, theological underpinning (taboo in public schools).

Be diligent, the teacher of the character curriculum says.

The student yawns: I'm bored with the subject. I don't see what good it's doing me. So why be diligent?

As parents, we answer: Because we believe that this subject *will* do you good down the road, and that's what we're aiming you toward. (Schools don't really have the right—or the authority—to make career plans for students. Parents do.) And even if you don't see this, we have the responsibility of planning for your future and the authority to tell you how to prepare for it.

This is our approach—yours might be different. The point is that the parent and child share a context—a worldview—within which certain qualities of character can be explained in a way that makes sense. Without this shared context, character training becomes a matter of following pointless rules. And this sort of character building lasts only until the student reaches the age of independence.

When it comes to the more demanding virtues—tolerance, forgiveness, humility—that shared context is even more vital. The Christian believes in a forgiveness that is modeled after God's—it doesn't expire after a certain number of offenses. A secular, Muslim, Buddhist, or Scientologist definition of forgiveness might be expressed differently. The unfortunate teacher, honor-bound not to step on anyone's toes, has to allow the class to evolve a lowest-common-denominator definition of *forgiveness* from the students' shared consciousness. By the time this is done, the moral quality under discussion—supposedly a yardstick for the students to measure themselves against—has become a loosely worded definition of what everyone is prepared to accept.

To define *character* properly may be nearly impossible for schools, but to build character is even further out of the realm of possibility. These moral qualities have to become habits, and habits are often achieved by going against the immediate short-term desire of the child. This is a parent's job, not a teacher's.

If these moral qualities are to become habits of life, they must be reinforced by both observation and practice. As you supervise your child's education, you can encourage him to read books and watch movies that demonstrate admirable character. Be careful of the character content of teen or young-adult books. Some are excellent, some aren't. Jessie remembers her sixth-grade son picking up a book full of sexual obsession with no encouragement of positive morality. The author of that book has said in interviews that any experience children have is a valid theme for literature. But the whole enterprise of teaching character assumes that some experiences are worth dwelling on and striving for, while others aren't.

You must also be a model of these qualities every day. When you forgo your own wants to tutor your child through fifth-grade math, you're demonstrating self-control. When you patiently go through a lesson several times until the child figures it out, you're showing perseverance. When you introduce a history lesson, complete with coloring books, paper models, and interesting books that you've collected, you're showing enthusiasm. When you turn off the TV because a program you want to watch wouldn't be good for your child, you're showing self-discipline. These qualities have to be internalized by the child, and this will only happen if she continually sees them being practiced by you.

As you work with her every day, you're helping her to put good character into practice. To develop character, a child has to learn obedience. Obviously, strict obedience changes as the child grows older and shows herself to be responsible. But it is impossible to teach a child over whom you have no control (ask any public-school teacher). Currently, obedience is a virtue that isn't popular since it's at odds with the autonomy now touted as being essential to proper development. But total autonomy—what *I* want supersedes any consideration for family, community, or government—can ultimately turn into disregard for laws or restrictions.

It's an expression of intelligent, loving care to teach a child that disregarding certain rules brings unpleasant consequences. You can't live in the real world without structure and authority: every day, we stop at stop signs, drive on the right side of the road, refrain from stealing food at the grocery store. The child with character has learned to thrive within structure.

Requiring a child to work and study hard in the early years develops the moral qualities of industry and perseverance. This doesn't mean that the child has a cheerless education. Many of the subjects studied *are* enjoyable, fascinating, immediately engrossing. But others won't be instantly fun. Some will require hard work so that the student can acquire skills she'll need in the future. The reality of life is that disciplined people usually accomplish more and can achieve their goals.

Powerful models of character are found in stories. Read them together. Talk about them. The joy of home education is that all of this learning takes place in the context of the family. You're not just teaching hard principles. You're also living them out. Thus, education becomes entwined with the living of life—together.

RESOURCES

Guroian, Vigen. *Tending the Heart of Virtue: How Classic Stories Awaken a Child's Moral Imagination.* New York: Oxford University Press, 2002.
    A fantastic book about good, evil, friendship, redemption, faith, and courage. Read it together, and read the books Guroian discusses. Available at bookstores and online.

Kilpatrick, William, Gregory Wolfe, and Suzanne M. Wolfe. *Books That Build Character: A Guide to Teaching Your Child Moral Values through Stories.* New York: Touchstone, 1994.
    An introduction to morality, along with descriptions of dozens of stories for families to read together. Available at bookstores and online.

40

๛

AND JUST WHEN DO I DO
ALL THIS? SCHEDULES FOR
HOME SCHOOLERS

> To choose time is to save time.
> —Francis Bacon

H ome education is a family commitment. We've noticed that in many families the entire responsibility for teaching the kids is shifted to one overworked parent. If one parent works full-time while the other teaches, that's a fine arrangement. But the job of planning lessons, investigating curricula, taking trips, reviewing progress, going to conventions, and generally talking about what goes on in home school needs to be shared by both parents.

Life is made up of hard but rewarding choices. It isn't possible for both parents to pursue demanding full-time careers while home-educating. Flex-time, part-time, or semester-oriented jobs (like teaching) can be worked around home schooling. A full-time criminal lawyer and a practicing obstetrician, married to each other, won't be able to manage.

We know of families that home-educate almost entirely in the evenings because of job schedules; we know of families that do school in the summer because the parents teach during the school year; we know families with home businesses and telecommuting jobs who set up school right in the home office and do it, on and off, throughout the day; we know single parents who home-school when they're not working. Although it takes organization, energy, and determination, combining home school with work can be done. And if you're able to do this, your child will be involved in a great part of your life—and you in his.

When Susan's children were young, she and her husband, Peter, both worked at home, and Susan also taught at the university during the school year. In the mornings, Peter worked while Susan did grammar, writing and spelling, and history or science with the boys. At 2 P.M., they swapped shifts, Susan went to work, and Peter did math with the boys and took them to appointments (swimming, doctor's visits, grocery store). Art and music fit into the evenings and weekends. Sundays and Mondays were family days, for housework, museums, zoo visits, worship, and doing nothing.

An important, sanity-preserving part of every home-school day ought to be the "afternoon nap." Jessie scheduled an afternoon nap for all three of her children up until the time they finished high school. For two hours, everyone went to his or her room and pursued a quiet activity alone, while Jessie put her feet up. Bedtime was also strictly enforced—no one went wandering through the house after the lights were off.

Susan, following the same principles, had her preschoolers go from taking naps to a two-hour rest period, even though they stopped sleeping. The boys had toys, coloring books, other books, and tape recorders with good books on tape to listen to. If they got out of bed (except to go to the bathroom, of course), they lost a privilege (like the tape recorder). They never got accustomed to skipping the nap; it was a regular part of every day. Susan kept certain books, tapes, and craft supplies just for naptime use. This middle-of-the-day break period is necessary for everyone. The children need it after studying hard all morning; the baby needs it; and parents certainly need the chance to sit down, rest, have a cup of coffee, and catch up on business.

Home-educating parents like their children's company. They don't want to send the kids off for most of every day. But they need a break in the middle of the day, someone to share the job of teaching, and quiet evenings. And in terms of parental sanity, the younger the children, the more important these rest times and early bedtimes.

HOW MUCH TIME DOES IT TAKE?

After having taught in a classroom, Jessie found that she could accomplish as much instructing—and a great deal more one-on-one interacting—in less time at home. The children didn't spend time on a bus or in lines. And with immediate detection of errors and on-the-spot correction, instruction time is more efficient and progress is faster.

For kindergarten, intensive instruction in reading, writing, and math can be done in about an hour, gradually increasing to five to six hours per day in high school. If the foundations are properly laid in basic reading, writing, spelling, and math, the student becomes more independent and less in need of direct instruction.

Jessie found that by high school, her role became one of "chief of accountability" and encourager. She helped her high-school children keep in mind their long-range goals (college) as well as their daily and weekly goals. Education took place continually, not just in a "sit at the desk" format. Discussion occurred around the table, during snacks and meals. We listened to tapes and had conversations in the car, going to the library or to music lessons or on field trips. We played classical music while cleaning. Books were everywhere in the house (we took the TV out). The children read all the time—while waiting, in the car, at bedtime, during rest periods. And while she polished shoes, Susan even read the newspaper that was under them.

As the children got older, Jessie taught them how to prepare meals. In the beginning, this was time-consuming; but when Susan was thirteen, she asked, and was permitted, to prepare a full-course dinner for an extended family birthday celebration (Jessie has pictures of a very tired but accomplished cook). In his teens, Susan's brother, Bob, hand-kneaded and made all the family bread. Her sister, Deborah, became the expert pie baker and did much of the general cooking. These are not only time-savers for the parent-teacher, but life skills that have been mastered by the children.

Jessie still remembers her surprise when a group of Susan's college friends came to her home for the weekend. One girl didn't even know how to tear lettuce and make a salad. She was a good student, with a traditional institutional education, but had never been allowed in the kitchen.

Read through time-management books for hints, both corporate (how to handle paperwork) and domestic (freedom from unnecessary house-work). We've listed Jessie's favorites on page 739.

The home-schooling parent must make time for reading. Read at night, at lunch, in the bathroom, while waiting, and whenever else you can squeeze in the time. Turn off the TV, and reclaim those hours.

YEARLY PLANNING

There's no particular reason why you should home-school every day for nine months and then take the summer off. The children burn out during the year and get bored (and forget all their math) over the long summer break. We advise going year-round and taking vacations throughout the year. Here are plans that are time-equivalent to the traditional nine-month school year. You can adjust your time off for family vacations, company, illness, a new baby, or whatever else you have planned.

Option 1

School	September, October, November
Break	December
School	January, February, March
Break	April
School	May, June, July
Break	August

Option 2

School for three weeks and break for one week, year-round.

Option 3

Adjust breaks around holidays and times when everyone is growing tired of school.

School	September through mid-October
Break	Week off
School	Late October until Thanksgiving
Break	Week off
School	Early December
Break	Three weeks off for Christmas and New Year's
School	Mid-January until late February or early March
Break	Two weeks (Everyone gets tired of school by late February!)
School	March, April
Break	Two weeks off
School	Late April, May, on through summer
Breaks	Anytime during the summer, whenever you're vacationing, visiting, entertaining, etc.

For each year, set goals ("Finish the whole math book," "Read through the Renaissance in history," "Teach my five-year-old to read"). Then, as you divide your year into monthly, weekly, and daily segments, ask: What am I doing to achieve this goal? Be specific. The math book is divided into daily lessons; you need to do 140 days of math to finish the book. Your school year is nine months long, and you have 200 history pages to cover; that's around 22 pages per month or 6 pages per week. In ten minutes per day of phonics, the five-year-old can learn to read.

Set goals for each subject, and chart out the pace you would like to keep. If you're using a textbook, you can divide the number of pages by the number of days or weeks you plan to study. Write down the master plan. You can accelerate or slow down as you progress, but you have this general guide to keep you on target. You may want to have a master-plan notebook to record goals for each subject; checking periodically will give you a feeling for the progress you've made. Also, there are courses that have daily plans for you. Try to follow whatever plan you choose, but be flexible. If the child needs to work more slowly or wants to work faster, accommodate him.

With the older child who is studying more independently, check on his progress weekly. When Susan was in eighth grade, she was generally responsible and studied hard, so Jessie didn't check on her progress in accounting for several months. By the time Jessie did check, Susan was far behind; since she was doing the course by correspondence, she had a huge amount of work to do to catch up.

In spring—preferably by June—read through the next year's suggested work, write and call for information, and try to place orders. The earlier you order books, the quicker they'll arrive. Remember that since by mid-summer everyone's buying books, you can expect a six- to eight-week delay in the processing of your order.

In his book *How to Get Control of Your Time and Your Life*, Alan Lakein suggests setting A, B, and C priorities. Do the A's first, the B's next, and let the C's fall off your schedule if you don't have time for them.[1]

WEEKLY PLANNING

Many home schoolers are able to accomplish in four days what would normally take five days in a classroom setting. The fifth day can be used for library trips, tutoring, lessons, field trips, or other "off-campus" learning. Jessie did four-day school weeks and was still able to take off three months every year; she also took a week off in October and February, when everyone was feeling stressed. If she could do it over again, she would follow Option 3, above, but she says, "I wasn't courageous enough to completely break out of the school mold!"

We sometimes found it less crowded and more convenient to take "Saturday trips" during the week, when most other children are in school, and to use Saturday as a school day.

Start the year with a disciplined approach, following a preplanned, written schedule. If the plan is too strenuous, you can adjust and ease up, which is much easier than starting out with a relaxed approach and then finding that you are not accomplishing your goals or that your child is becoming lazy.

Don't panic about illness or doctors' appointments. The child would miss those days from school anyway. And Jessie found that a bored, mildly

[1] Alan Lakein, *How to Get Control of Your Time and Your Life* (New York: Signet, 1974), pp. 28–29.

sick, or recovering child welcomed "something to do." If there was no TV allowed, he continued to do some schoolwork.

Don't be upset over unavoidable interruptions. Remember, schools have interruptions, too: the teacher is sick and the substitute doesn't follow her lesson plan; weather or mechanical problems close down the school; violence or lack of discipline sometimes disrupts teaching; strikes or political demonstrations interfere with instruction. In the midst of interruptions, teach children to be flexible. And don't worry about your child lagging behind the rest of the class. Simply take up where you left off.

Jessie's Weekly Schedule

4 days	"In-house" teaching
1 day	"Off-campus" learning—library, tutoring, lessons, short trips
1 day	Major projects (household, yard, shopping) or family trips
1 day	Rest, worship, relaxation

DAILY PLANNING

Plan a schedule for daily life, and stick to it. If you can, go to bed early and get up early—mind and body are fresher in the morning. Get up at the same time every day.

Plan how much time you'll spend on each lesson. Always leave some wiggle room by scheduling in a little more time than you think you'll need. Schedules reduce indecision and arguing because everyone knows what to do and is able to get on with the job at hand.

Have a specific time each day for each class, and try to keep to this. Math, spelling, and writing are skills that need daily practice and feedback in a predictable routine.

Be flexible. Schedules will change as children grow. And a new baby or suddenly mobile toddler can wreck the most carefully put together schedule. You have the freedom to change activities around. If a small child becomes interested in earthworms, you'd still do basic skills—phonics, reading, writing, math—every day, but you might not do history for a week while he learns about earthworms. A high-school student might suddenly develop an interest in some research project. You should keep up with the daily lesson in math because it's an incremental skill. But he can spend a week on just history or just science and catch up on his other work later. The key is the *intentional* use of flexibility for an educational goal, rather than allowing students to do what they "feel like" doing.

Write down all family activities on a chart. Once a week, we filled out a wall chart that had a column for each member of the family. On it were the unchangeables: outside work, appointments, deadlines for lessons or hobbies, meetings. If Mom and Dad were taking a child to a recital, that went on all three columns (Mom's, Dad's, and the child's). Then we scheduled school lessons, meals, naps, practices, chores, housework, and free time. This way, Jessie could assign subjects with an eye to her availability: Susan didn't need help practicing the piano, but Bob needed help with grammar, so Mom put Bob's grammar lesson on her schedule at the same time Susan practiced.

JESSIE'S METHOD OF ORGANIZING: A PERSONAL ACCOUNT

I started with a 3 × 5-inch notebook to carry in my purse, but soon I needed more space. I went to the 5 × 8-inch size, which is the size of many daily business organizers available at office-supply stores. Calendars, paper, and plastic zip cases are easy to find for this size.

I put a plastic zip case containing a 2 ½ × 4-inch pocket calculator in the front of this notebook (handy for figuring shopping bargains).

I kept a Month At-A-Glance tabbed yearly planning calendar just behind the plastic zip case. All appointments, meetings, birthdays, deadlines, holiday celebrations, and so forth were kept in it, colored with highlighters.

I bought a set of blank 5 × 8-inch notebook dividers and made the following personal divisions in the notebook:

Daily Plan Here I put in blank sheets of paper, each one dated at the top, and outlined the family activities for that day. I kept a week ahead and threw sheets away as I transferred unfinished items to the next page. I kept one page separate and wrote a list of large projects to plan for.

Shop In this division, I kept current shopping lists (except the grocery list, which I kept on the refrigerator until grocery day). Clothes, hardware, office supplies—all this was available whenever we shopped or had the chance to run into a store.

Household Information Here I kept all the notes useful for running the household: printer and typewriter model numbers, sizes of household items (like the dining-room table's dimensions for tablecloth shopping), paint shades, appliance model numbers.

Clothes I kept current sizes of all family members here and their current needs in case I saw a sale.

Business Here I kept Social Security numbers of family members, contents of the safety deposit boxes, frequently used phone numbers, account numbers, and so forth.

Books I kept a running list of books, videos, tapes, and music to look for at libraries, stores, and sales.

Directions Because we live out in the country, I kept a typed-up set of directions to the house so that service companies could find us. (You might not want to do this for security reasons. And in the days of smartphones it might not be necessary—although GPS services *still* often can't find our house.)

Gifts Here I jotted down ideas for gifts for all family members.

Miscellaneous Notes Just what it sounds like—recipes I read in magazines at the doctor's office, notes about people I met, addresses, things to think about.

Make your own personal dividers according to the information you need at your fingertips. I was never able to buy a preprinted plan book that could satisfy my needs.

GOOD USE OF TIME

Read in the evenings, instead of watching TV.

For once-a-week family entertainment, go to the public library together instead of to the mall or movies. Read books together; go to evening storytime with younger children; check out CDs and books. Get all the books for the next week's study.

Take control of the telephone. Take it off the hook, turn off the ringer—but don't answer it when you're home-schooling. And tell family and frequent callers not to call when you're teaching. Jessie's father had a long and serious illness at one point when the children were still studying; she put in a second line and gave that number only to family.

Limit outside commitments. You don't have to meet all personal goals while you are home-educating your children. As a family, discuss, decide, and keep in mind your long-term goals. Balance other responsibilities with these goals.

Simplify life. Jessie's lifestyle while home-educating didn't require formal entertainment. So she put away silver that needed polishing, chose not to buy clothes that required special care, put time-consuming hobbies on hold. Instead of entertaining, the family shared meals with friends.

Try to set aside a place for learning, not playing. If you don't have a separate room, the kitchen table is fine. When you get ready to do school, clear off the table. Don't allow toys or other distracting objects to coexist with the books and papers.

Remember that everything costs either money, time, or energy, all of which are in limited supply. If you have more money than time or energy, buy your teaching aids. If you have more time and energy, make them.

HOME SCHOOLING WITH BABIES AND TODDLERS

Try these ideas to keep babies and toddlers occupied:

- Do something with the youngest children first. Then give them independent activities or toys that are only brought out at "schooltime."
- Make a "job" chart for toddlers, with pictures of activities.
- Don't ask, "What do you want to do?" or "Do you want to color?" Children always choose to do something else. State what the toddler can do, leaving no options. (Unless, of course, he's ill or fatigued and needs special attention.)
- Let a baby or toddler sit on your lap during some of the instruction. Children can be taught to sit still in a lap if it is made a habit. (Jessie's two-year-olds learned to sit through hour-long religious services because the small church didn't have a nursery. They slept, listened, or looked at picture books.)

- Hire an older sibling (or use a grandparent) to babysit. Be careful not to use older children as unpaid labor; however, a seven-year-old can earn extra pocket money by baby-sitting (and can get in some good job practice).
- Start actual instruction with toddlers—simple repetition, with no pressure. Susan's eighteen-month-old learned to say his letters when Daddy held up the wooden blocks, and her toddlers drew frantically with a pencil when the older children were doing writing. Jessie's oldest, Bob, learned his alphabet by playing with refrigerator magnets. *B* was on the refrigerator until he learned it; then Jessie added other letters one at a time.
- Don't let the baby's morning nap disappear. (A home-schooling friend of Susan's told her to keep putting the baby in his crib with plenty of toys, even when he gave up sleeping. She did, and he took a "crib break" for half an hour every midmorning, during which time Susan did intensive, one-on-one instruction in math with her older children.)
- Don't worry if toys and books get spread all over the house. Schedule a daily fifteen-minute pickup before lunch and dinner, and put everything back in its place.

Susan used to put her toddler at the sink and let him play with water, even though some got on the floor; she also hid Cheerios around the house for the baby to find; made suds in the tub with Ivory soap; turned the living room into a set of connected forts made with blankets; and generally allowed her younger son to make a mess so that she could tutor the older two.

SCHEDULES FOR HOME SCHOOLERS

At the beginning of every school year, we make out a schedule. We adhere slavishly to it for about two weeks—and then we loosen up.

You must have a schedule to start with. You need some idea of how much time each subject should take, how often to take breaks, when to start, when to stop. But once you've worked with your child for several weeks, you'll know how to adjust the schedule to suit yourself. You'll find that math may take less time and grammar more time than scheduled (or vice versa). You'll discover that your child can do certain tasks on her own, allowing you to rearrange the schedule so that these tasks coincide with putting the baby to bed or making phone calls. Or, if you're a working parent, you'll change the schedule so that the child is schooled when you're there.

Make sure that evenings are free to do some schoolwork and reading since the student doesn't have "homework" in addition to her regular study.

One Family's Schedule

Susan and her family had a master "week plan" that told everyone where they needed to be on what day (Susan and Peter made a new one at the beginning of every week). They found it easier not to have set times for each subject, since all days are subject to interruption. The children always got up at the same time every day, did chores before school, had a naptime/rest time/play alone period from 1 to 3 P.M., and went to bed on a regular schedule (7:30 for the toddler, 8 for the younger children, 8:30 for the almost-teen). Since Peter did a good portion of the home schooling, their lists were divided into two columns; Peter supervised the left-hand side of each page, while Susan did the right-hand subjects. Saturday was a workday, but the family took Mondays off for recreation.

This schedule from the fall of 2002 reflects the assignments for Christopher (eleven), Benjamin (nine), and Daniel (just turned six, doing some first grade and some kindergarten work):

Tuesday

Christopher	Trumpet	_____	Grammar	_____
	Math	_____	History	_____
	Latin Cards	_____	Writing	_____
	Geography	_____	Reading	_____
	Science	_____	Latin	_____
	Experiment	_____	Logic	_____
Benjamin	Drum	_____	Grammar	_____
	Latin Cards	_____	History	_____
	Spelling	_____	Writing	_____

	Geography	_____	Reading	_____
	Science	_____	Latin	_____
	Experiment	_____	Piano	_____

Daniel	Math	_____	Spelling	_____
	Reading	_____	First Language	_____
	Lessons	_____	Piano	_____
	Geography	_____		

Wednesday

Christopher	Trumpet	_____	Writing	_____
	Math	_____	Latin	_____
	Latin Cards	_____	Music Theory	_____
	Spelling	_____	Library	_____
	Geography	_____	Handwriting	_____

Benjamin	Drum	_____	Handwriting	_____
	Math	_____	Music Theory	_____
	Latin Cards	_____	Reading	_____
	Spelling	_____	Piano	_____
	Geography	_____	Library	_____

Daniel	Math	_____	Spelling	_____
	Reading	_____	Piano	_____
	Geography	_____	Library	_____

Thursday

Christopher	Trumpet	_____	Grammar	_____
	Spelling	_____	History	_____
	Latin Cards	_____	Writing	_____
	Choir	_____	Reading	_____
	Handwriting	_____	Logic	_____
	Piano	_____		

Benjamin	Drum	_____	Grammar	_____
	Math	_____	History	_____
	Choir	_____	Writing	_____

| | Handwriting | _____ | Piano | _____ |
| | Spanish | _____ | Reading | _____ |

Daniel	Math	_____	Spanish	_____
	Choir	_____	Spelling	_____
	Lessons	_____	First Language	_____

Friday

Christopher	Trumpet	_____	Grammar	_____
	Math	_____	History	_____
	Latin Cards	_____	Writing	_____
	Piano	_____	Reading	_____
	Science Reading	_____	Latin	_____
	Logic	_____		

Benjamin	Drum	_____	Grammar	_____
	Math	_____	History	_____
	Latin Cards	_____	Writing	_____
	Spelling	_____	Reading	_____
	Science Reading	_____	Latin	_____
	Piano	_____		

Daniel	Math	_____	Piano	_____
	Science Reading	_____	Spelling	_____
	Lessons	_____	First Language	_____

Saturday

Christopher	Trumpet	_____	Piano	_____
	Math	_____	Science Report	_____
	Spelling	_____	Reading	_____
	Handwriting	_____	Latin	_____
	Music Theory	_____		

Benjamin	Drum	_____	Grammar	_____
	Math	_____	Science Report	_____
	Handwriting	_____	Writing	_____

	Spelling	_____	Spanish	_____
	Music Theory	_____		

Daniel	Reading	_____	Science Report _____	
	Spelling	_____	Spanish	_____
	Piano	_____		

JESSIE'S FAVORITE RESOURCES

Bauer, Susan Wise.
> *Homeschooling the Real Child*
> *Teaching Students to Work Independently*
> *Burning Out: Why It Happens and What to Do About It*
> Susan's audio conference workshops reflect nearly two decades of home-schooling experience. You can download these recordings from Well-Trained Mind Press; you will find the handouts at welltrained mind.com. Other workshops are also available.

Lakein, Alan. *How to Get Control of Your Time and Your Life.* New York: Signet, 1989.
> A guide to setting priorities for work and home jobs.

McCullough, Bonnie. *Bonnie's Household Organizer: The Essential Guide for Getting Control of Your Home.* 2nd rev. ed. New York: St. Martin's, 1983.
> Strategies for spending a minimum amount of time on household jobs.

McCullough, Bonnie, and Susan Monson. *401 Ways to Get Your Kids to Work at Home.* New York: St. Martin's, 2003.
> Tips for training children to work.

41

PAPER PROOF:
GRADES AND
RECORD KEEPING

The purpose . . . is to communicate his nontraditional education in the
traditional terms outsiders will understand.

—Debra Bell

Ironically, a classical education is now considered "nontraditional"
because it doesn't fit into the neat credits-per-subject pattern of the
average high school. Home education is nontraditional as well. Your task
is to record what your student is doing in a way that makes sense to school
administrators and college admissions officers.

Fortunately, many people have walked this road before you. Your state
home-school organization can send you a packet of information covering
state requirements for home schoolers, the awarding of grades and diplomas, and the keeping of an appropriate transcript. As a home-educating
parent, you'll be doing paperwork in three areas: notification, portfolio
keeping for elementary-school and middle-school students, and transcript
preparation for high-school students.

NOTIFICATION

When you begin home-schooling, you'll need to notify your local school system. Contact your state organization for the exact way to do this. In some states, if you have a college diploma, you simply fill out an "Intent to Home School" form and send a copy of your diploma. If you don't have a diploma, the state may require you to submit an outline of study, which is simply a list of the books you plan to cover each year in each subject. Only basic texts need be listed.

ELEMENTARY SCHOOL
AND MIDDLE SCHOOL: PORTFOLIOS

In elementary school and middle school, you must keep track of each subject taught each year. Since no one but you and the local school district will ever see the grades for school years K–8, you should check with your school administrators. Most schools will happily accept portfolios of work as proof that you're doing what you're supposed to do; the notebooks you create for each subject fulfill this requirement. Keep these notebooks filed where you can get to them, and offer them when you need to document your child's work at home.

The only reason for you to issue the child a letter or number grade for K–8 is (1) if the school district demands it (very rare) or (2) if you think the child might want to transfer into a school that requires transcripts. In most cases, schools are content with portfolios—which, in any case, offer a much better picture of the child's achievements. If you do want to issue a grade, you can keep a K–8 transcript like the one we've suggested you use for high school (see below). But in most situations, this is unnecessary.

A word about testing. We don't think there's much point in administering tests in grades 1 through 4. During those years, you should be evaluating rather than testing. Watch the child's work to see what errors she makes again and again. Then reteach those concepts.

In middle grades, you should start giving tests in the "skills" areas—

math, grammar, spelling—just to accustom the student to the testing process. You can do this with the tests supplied in the teacher's editions and test booklets that accompany your texts. But in history, science, and reading—the "content" areas—the child is continually reading, writing, and talking about what she's learning. There's no need to create some kind of test for this material.

HIGH SCHOOL: TRANSCRIPTS

For grades 9 through 12, issuing grades and filling out a transcript form is necessary. The transcript records subjects studied, years of study, units of credit, and final grades. Transcripts ought to be kept on permanent file. Although some colleges are happy to accept portfolios for home-school applications (see Chapter 44), others insist on a regular transcript. Employers and educational institutions will often request a high-school transcript. (Occasionally, a potential employer will still call Jessie and ask for the high-school transcript of a student she tutored ten years ago.) That piece of paper is important!

At a minimum, you should record each subject studied, the traditional end-of-semester grades—A, B, C, and so forth—and achievement test scores. Having taught in traditional schools, Jessie knows that many factors influence a final course grade, among them attendance, participation, application, attitude, projects, and activities. We also know of some classrooms where an A equals 95 to 100, and other classrooms where an A equals 90 to 100. Failing scores are always determined by the teacher and can range from 60 to 75. The home-school teacher is allowed to exercise the same flexibility of judgment as the traditional schoolteacher. Taking all of the above factors into account, Jessie awarded an A for excellent work and application, a B for above-average work that could have been a little better, a C for meeting-the-grade work, and a D for performance that was much less than the child was capable of doing.

Because, in a home situation, Jessie continually evaluated and tested for mastery before testing to award a grade, the grades were usually high. She also tried to match the grades to achievement scores (see Chapter

40 for more on testing). A transcript with all A's and low standardized test scores won't appear credible (although a standardized test doesn't necessarily test the material taught and shouldn't be used to determine a course grade).

Even if your school system allows a portfolio assessment instead of traditional grades, you must keep this official transcript for high school. You might be asked for it at the most unexpected times.

The student needs to fulfill a minimum number of credits in order to graduate from high school. Traditionally, 1 credit in high school equals 120 hours of classwork, or 160 45-minute periods. Labs and projects, field trips, and independent reading can all count as classwork.

Check with your support group, state home-school organization, or local school-board office on graduation requirements. Remember, they do change from time to time and from state to state. (See Chapter 24.)

The student who follows the classical curriculum outlined in Part III and holds to a basic 36-week school year will spend, on average, the following hours in study every year (this is adjusted to allow for illness, field trips, and other skipped days of school):

Ninth Grade

Grammar	120 hours
Rhetoric	90 hours
Great Books	320 hours
Math	120 hours
Science	108 hours
Foreign language	108–216 hours
Art and music appreciation	108 hours

Tenth Grade

Grammar	120 hours
Rhetoric	90 hours
Great Books	320 hours
Math	120 hours
Science	108 hours
Foreign language	108–216 hours
Art and music appreciation	108 hours

Eleventh Grade

Grammar	120 hours
Great Books	320 hours
Math	120 hours
Science	108 hours
Foreign language	108–216 hours
Art and music appreciation	108 hours
Junior thesis	100–150 hours
(Computer programming)	(150 hours)

Twelfth Grade

Grammar	120 hours
Great Books	320 hours
Math	120 hours
Science	108 hours (more like 180 hours, if physics is elected)
Foreign language	108–216 hours
Art and music appreciation	108 hours
Senior thesis	100–150 hours
(Computer programming)	(150 hours)

How does this fit into a transcript? If you keep to this schedule, you award 1 English credit per year for the study of grammar (that's the language arts requirement). You also award 1 math credit each year that a math course is completed. After the ninth- and tenth-grade years, math courses can be counted toward the eight required electives.

Science courses are slightly below the normal class hours, but don't forget that home study tends to be more concentrated than classroom work. Also, the 108 hours of science is supplemented by the works on science read in the Great Books course and by extra time spent on science-fair projects and outside reading. If the junior and senior projects are science-oriented, the number of hours climbs even more. So it's perfectly legitimate for you to award 1 science credit for each year of study. And if, by the end of the year, you don't feel that the child has done the equivalent of a year's study, simply continue into the summer until those extra 12 hours are completed (it's only four extra weeks—less if you do more than 3 hours per week). Use common sense and look at what the student has completed when deciding to award the credit.

We suggest you award 1 fine arts elective credit for every year's work in art and music appreciation combined. Award 1 foreign-language credit for each one-year course in foreign language completed. For physical education, award the student 1 credit for a full year's involvement in organized physical activity—aerobics classes, tennis lessons, karate lessons, community softball or basketball leagues. Alternately, the student can just keep a yearlong log of the time spent in regular physical activities such as walking, jogging, and bike riding. When she reaches 120 hours, award her 1 physical-education credit (everyone who does the exercise gets A's in physical education). This will encourage the child to exercise regularly, which will help her overall health.

The Great Books study is the equivalent of considerably more than two high-school courses. Add the study of rhetoric in ninth and tenth grades, and the junior and senior theses in eleventh and twelfth grades, and you've got more credits than needed for graduation. The study of Great Books encompasses world history, world literature (although the study of grammar provides the necessary language arts credit, you can give elective credit in world literature for every year of Great Books study), American history, and American government (it includes source readings from all the texts required in a government course plus the background readings in ancient political theory that most high-school courses simply can't cover). If you do debate, count rhetoric and debate club together as 1 speech elective. Computer programming is another elective. Furthermore, in the junior and senior years, the senior thesis requirement can be counted as an honors elective course in independent research.

The transcript is not the place to explain that you've done rhetoric and Great Books instead of traditional textbook courses. The transcript will show that your student has met and exceeded the minimum state requirements; the portfolio, that those requirements have been met in a challenging, creative way—it accompanies your transcript when your student applies to college (see Chapter 44).

We've given suggestions throughout Part III about how to put courses on the transcript. Here's yet another overview of how a transcript might look:

High-School Credits

Curriculum		What you put on transcript	
Course	**Hours**	**Course**	**Units**
Ninth grade			
Grammar	120	English 1	1 language arts
Rhetoric	90	Speech 1	1 elective
Great Books	320	World lit. 1	1 elective
		World hist. 1	1 history
Math	120	Algebra	1 math
Science	108	Biology	1 science
Foreign lang.	108–216	Latin/modern	1–2 foreign lang.
Art and music	108	Fine arts 1	1 elective
Tenth grade			
Grammar	120	English 2	1 language arts
Rhetoric	90	Speech 2	1 elective
Great Books	320	World lit. 2	1 elective
		World hist. 2	1 history
Math	120	Algebra	1 math
Science	108	Earth science	1 science
Foreign lang.	108–216	Latin/modern	1–2 foreign lang.
Art and music	108	Fine arts 2	1 elective
Eleventh grade			
Grammar	120	English 3	1 language arts
Great Books	320	Victorian lit.	1 elective
		American hist.	1 history
Math	120	Advanced math	1 math
Science	108	Chemistry	1 science
Foreign lang.	108–216	Latin/modern	1–2 foreign lang.
Art and music	108	Fine arts 3	1 elective
Junior thesis	100–150	Junior honors	1 elective
(Computer prog.)	(150)	(Computer prog.)	(1 elective)

Twelfth grade

Grammar	120	English 4	1 language arts
Great books	320	Modern lit.	1 elective
		American gov.	1 government
(Math, elective)	(120)	(Elective)	(1 math)
Science	108	Physics	1 science
Foreign lang.	108–216	Latin/modern	1–2 foreign lang.
Art and music	108	Fine arts 4	1 elective
Senior thesis	100–150	Senior honors	1 elective
(Computer prog.)	(150)	(Computer prog.)	(1 elective)

The student who follows this curriculum ends up with these credits:

Language Arts	4
Mathematics	3–4
Foreign language	4–8
World History	2
American History	1
American government	1
Science	4
Electives	10–14

Add 2 credits in physical education, and this goes far beyond the average high-school college-prep track.

As can be seen, it's acceptable (especially for the student who isn't college bound) to simplify the high-school curriculum. The fine arts electives aren't necessary either for graduation or for the college track. One to two years of science could be eliminated as well as several years of foreign language and at least one year of mathematics.

But a rigorous high-school program prepares the student for the unexpected—a future change in employment, a sudden desire to go to college or graduate school, a growing home business that requires a high level of intellectual competency. We recommend as vigorous a curriculum as the child's mental ability allows. Jessie also feels that every student, even those who don't plan on college, ought to take the PSAT and SAT (see Chapter 40). If, two or three years later, the high-school graduate decides to go to college, the standardized scores already exist; she doesn't have to take tests on material that's been partially forgotten.

Any courses taken through a community college or a concurrent program at a local university should be listed on the high-school transcript along with the grade earned. These courses also count toward high-school graduation credits.

The high-school transcript also includes space for extracurricular activities. Record all the student's nonacademic activities (teams, hobbies that she puts significant time into, athletic pursuits, music lessons, competitions, volunteer work, jobs, all memberships in any kind of organization, any leadership positions at church or in community groups, all participation in regular community activities). You'll probably have to list these on a separate sheet of paper or fit them into a margin on the transcript since most transcripts have a preset list of extracurricular activities ("Offices Held" or "Band"). Just make sure these activities appear with the transcript wherever it is submitted.

DIPLOMA

If your state home-school association has a graduation ceremony that awards high-school diplomas (as Virginia does), you can take advantage of it. And if your state allows your home school to operate as a private school, you can design and present your own diploma with the name you have selected for your institution. Home-school diplomas can be designed and purchased at homeschooldiploma.com. (There is so much flexibility because it is the transcript form, not the diploma, that proves that your student has completed the necessary work for graduation.)

Many home-schooling organizations suggest that students take the GED. We're not sure this is a good idea, especially for classically educated students. The GED really only requires a mastery of tenth-grade material and taking it tends to lump highly accomplished, academically oriented students together with those who couldn't or wouldn't finish eleventh grade.

We suggest calling the admissions offices of colleges your student might be interested in and asking them how they view a home-schooled transcript and whether they require a diploma. Most colleges now have specific application processes for home-educated students.

If the student is thinking about joining the military, talk to a local recruiter about the high-school graduation requirement and how you can best document graduation.

Your transcript (and portfolio) plus achievement scores are much more valuable than a diploma. Schools all across the United States vary so widely in the skills required to gain a diploma that the piece of paper itself has lost much of its meaning. Again, the most important thing you can do is *call* any of the institutions requiring a diploma and ask what they prefer for home schoolers.

RESOURCES

Instructor Daily Planner. New York: Scholastic, 2003.
$4.95. Order from Rainbow Resource. This basic record book supplies space to keep track of dates, assignments, field trips, and grades in K–12.

Diploma.
$30–$50, depending on features. Order from HomeschoolDiploma .com.

Edu-Track Home School Software.
$59. Order from ConTech Solutions. Generates lesson plans, progress reports, transcripts, report cards, certificates, diplomas, and other forms.

Home School Cumulative Record.
$2.95. Order from Rainbow Resource. Cardstock folder for keeping important papers has a transcript draft form on the back and on the inside.

Homeschooler's High School Journal.
$10.95. Order from Rainbow Resource Center. Highly recommended, this spiral-bound journal gives the student sections for recording test scores, daily logs for recording time spent on each subject and time spent on field trips or research, library list forms to keep track of what has been read, a chart to keep track of weekly hours spent on each subject, and a grade record.

Make your own transcript form at https://www.teascript.com.

42

THE YARDSTICK:
STANDARDIZED TESTING

> In some ways, parents who educate at home are in better shape
> because of the sanctity of modern testing. It's not that hard to teach a
> child to do well on a standardized test, and since the tests are sacred,
> good results command respect.
>
> —Mary Pride, *The New Big Book of Home Learning*

Standardized tests are necessary evils. On the negative side, they don't necessarily measure the child's knowledge or skill; they may not coincide with what you've been working on; and they require specific test-taking skills that your child will have to practice when he could be doing something else. On the positive side, standardized tests are a great equalizer. Because grading standards vary so much from school to school, standardized test scores have become the ultimate proof that you're doing a good job educating your child. High Scholastic Aptitude Test (SAT) scores will open dozens of doors for high-school seniors. Advanced Placement (AP) tests give college credit to the well prepared. Students with a good grounding in the foundational skills of reading, writing, and mathematics generally test well; students who read widely almost always score high.

YEARLY TESTING

If you're home-educating, you may need to have your child tested every year. Although this is a pain in the neck, look on the bright side: children who are accustomed to taking timed standardized tests inevitably score well on college admissions exams. Jessie, paranoid about academic achievement back when no one else she knew was home-schooling, had her children tested every year. As a result, when they took their PSATs and SATs, they were relaxed and confident, and came out with high scores.

There are a slew of standardized skills tests for grades K–12. The only way to negotiate the maze is to follow these steps:

1. Call your state home-school organization and ask what your state's regulations are. When does the child need to be tested? What tests are acceptable? (In Virginia, home-schooled students are allowed to use any nationally standardized achievement test, not only the test that happens to be used by the local school district.)
2. Decide how you want the test to be administered. You have several options:

   - If you want to, and if you have a well-ordered, friendly private school nearby, call and ask whether your children can take the standardized test on test day.[1] You will have to register ahead of time and pay a nominal fee, show up with the children on test day for the test, and take them home. This is especially good for older children (seventh grade and up) since it exposes them to the conditions that will surround SAT testing. Younger home schoolers are better off taking the test in a familiar setting, preferably from

---

[1] Jessie doesn't recommend that elementary-age home schoolers take tests with public-school students unless the state requires this. The confusion and unfamiliar chaos of a big class sometimes prevents the child from concentrating on the test. We have also heard of an occasional case where hostility to home schoolers has made a child uncomfortable.

an administrator they know. At the very least, go to the test site before the test date and wander around.

- Administer the test yourself. A number of the standardized basic tests—including the California Achievement Test and the Comprehensive Test of Basic Skills (information about these two tests can be found at the end of this chapter)—can be given by the parent and sent back for grading. This is the best option for K–4 students. Jessie thinks that at this stage the parent should give the test and then teach the child what he needs to know about taking tests.

- Take your children to a professional testing site for private test administration. Your state organization can tell you where to find a local test site. The education department of a local college or university should also have this information.

- Prepare for the test using a basic guide to standardized test taking. Jessie spent time prior to standardized testing teaching each child how to take the tests. They practiced taking sample tests so that the techniques of test taking became familiar and they could focus on content.

- The best way to reduce anxiety, though, is for you to accept the status of the test as "no big deal." If you're agitated because you feel that your success as a parent and teacher is resting on this standardized test, your child will pick up on your urgency.

- Take sample tests. You can often find these online, or order sample tests from the testing centers.

- Make sure you tell the child, before he takes the test, that it will contain material beyond his grade level. For example, a test for grades 1 through 3 typically contains material from the fourth, fifth, and sixth grade in order to identify highly gifted or advanced third graders. But if the student doesn't know that some of the material is purposely designed to be too hard, he might panic and stop thinking clearly.

What if the child doesn't do well? Perhaps the child was sick or was upset about an unrelated matter or was suffering from text anxiety. Or perhaps you didn't cover the material emphasized on the test.

In most cases, you're given a second year to show substantial progress—something you'll need for a child who's doing remedial work. Spend extra time before the next test working on test skills.

A great advantage to administering the test yourself or having it done privately is that you can schedule the test three to four months before the deadline your state requires. Then, if the child doesn't score well, you can prepare again and retest.

You can also appeal for a different form of testing: an individual, portfolio-based assessment of the student's progress. Your state organization can help you with the appeal and steer you toward a professional assessment service. Portfolios are made up of samples of the child's work, arranged chronologically to demonstrate achievement in different areas. They include information that can't be tested—art talent, engineering projects, community-service award. These are valuable for showing reasonable progress for a child who's testing below grade level. Contact your portfolio evaluator (recommended by your home-school state organization) at the beginning of each year to see what materials you should include.

Even if you use portfolios to satisfy the school system, you should keep on taking standardized tests. Tests are a reality of educational and professional life (you even have to take a test to get a driver's license), and constant practice will eventually dull test anxiety. You can give these tests privately, without forwarding the results to school officials.

Use the test results to target weak areas that need more study, as well as to praise the child when scores show that he has made progress. If the child consistently tests poorly in a particular skill, you might want to consult a professional evaluator to see whether the child has a learning problem or simply needs more time in that area. At its best, standardized testing is a tool for evaluating instruction. It should be used to plan the next step in the educational process. *Never make an important educational decision on the basis of one test.*

Note that a fairly new development on the scene are tests such as Performance Assessment in Mathematics (PAM) and Performance Assessment in Language (PAL). These require the student to explain in writing why he chose the answer he did. Because these answers are open to wide interpretation by the test scorer, Jessie recommends avoiding this type of testing.

AP AND CLEP EXAMS

High-school students who take advanced electives can earn college credit through the Advanced Placement and College Level Examination Program exams administered by the College Board. High scores on these exams don't mean that you'll actually get credit on a college transcript. (This depends on the college to which you apply—some will give you credit, others simply allow you to skip low-level classes and go into more advanced work.) But high scores from home schoolers demonstrate that you have, indeed, mastered the material on your transcript. AP and CLEP scores, according to the College Board, improve the admission appeal of home schoolers "by demonstrating college-level knowledge."[2]

The College Board offers thirty-four CLEP exams as well as AP exams in twenty areas of study. For online information on both types of exams, visit the College Board website at www.collegeboard.org. The website offers online test reviews and an evaluation service as well as information about all the exams. Ideally, you should get this information in ninth grade to help you plan your high-school electives.

AP exams are given at local high schools. As long as they have studied the subject in depth, home-school students can take AP exams without enrolling in the school-offered AP course. You can obtain practice AP exams from the College Board.

CLEP exams determine placement in a number of subjects—most notably foreign languages—and measure achievement. Visit the CLEP section of the College Board website.

If your student will be taking an AP or CLEP exam, get a review book from Barron's, the College Board, or Princeton Review. During the semester before the exam, spend several hours per week preparing for the test.

---

[2] "Getting College Credit before College," College Board Online, www.collegeboard.com/parents/csearch/know-the-options/21298.html.

PSAT, SAT, AND ACT

The PSAT, the SAT, and the ACT (American College Test) are all standardized high-school achievement/skill-evaluation tests used by colleges to sort through and rank applicants. If your student is planning to attend college, take these tests seriously. Finish as much math as possible before the junior year. The Latin and vocabulary programs as well as *The Well-Educated Mind* will thoroughly prepare your student for the vocabulary and reading-comprehension sections of the test. Logic will help with the analytical sections.

However, you should also study directly for the tests. Beginning in tenth grade, spend at least an hour a day working through one of the review guides published by Barron's, the College Board, or the Princeton Review. All tests have their peculiarities, and the types of problems may not be familiar to your student if you don't prepare him. Study regularly, and administer at least three practice tests under test conditions—timed, sitting in one place without getting up for water or cookies. Susan scored above the 90th percentile in all college admissions tests by studying Latin, finishing Algebra II and geometry, and working through review books every day for over a year before taking the tests. The effort paid off in scholarship money and admission to every program she applied to.

Find out what format the test will be in. Currently, standardized tests are in the middle of a shift from paper-and-pencil administration to computerized administration, but as of this writing the SATs are still taken with paper and pencil. If your student will be taking a traditional exam, use a book to prepare for it instead of the review software sold by the College Board or Princeton Review. There's enough of a difference in the way the problems are presented via computer to throw the student off when he sits down with the test booklet.

The PSAT/NMSQT (Preliminary SAT/National Merit Scholarship Qualifying Test) is administered by the College Board. It not only offers practice for the SATs, but serves as a qualifying exam for scholarships offered by the National Merit Scholarship Corporation. The PSAT is generally taken during the sophomore or junior year of high school. Students who take it in the fall of the junior year generally score higher and have a better chance of qualifying for National Merit scholarships. Questions about National Merit scholarships should be directed to the National Merit Scholarship Corporation at 847-866-5100. Home-school students register for the PSAT/NMSQT through the local high school. Note that, unlike the SAT, the PSAT is given *only* in October—and if you miss it, it's gone. Call your local public or private high school in the spring of the freshman or sophomore year and arrange to take the test the following October. Ask to speak to the PSAT administrator. Find out the day and time the test is being given. Ask about the fee (if you can't afford it, ask how you can apply for a fee waiver) and how to register. Home-school students use a College Board home-school code when filling out the registration forms.

The College Board suggests that, if the school seems resistant, you contact another public high school or try a private school. PSAT scores for home schoolers are sent directly to your home.

The SAT, the standard college admissions test, has two faces. SAT I is the test everyone takes. SAT II, or subject, tests are optional, but home schoolers should strongly consider taking as many of them as they feel prepared for. The tests are one-hour multiple-choice exams that measure knowledge in specific areas. Good scores on the SAT II tests will validate the high-school transcript.

The SAT should be taken no later than January of the senior year (if you think your student might want to take it more than once, take it in the spring of the junior year or the fall of the senior year). Register online at collegeboard.org. Home-schooled students will be given instructions about what code to use during registration. The College Board recommends that you ask for their free publications, which have test-taking tips and practice test questions. As with the PSAT, you can request a fee waiver if the SAT test fees are too much for your budget.

When you fill out the form, you'll choose three test centers close to you. When your registration is confirmed, you'll be informed about where and when to take the test.

The ACT is widely, although not universally, accepted for college admissions—check with the college your student wants to attend. However, if you have to choose between the SAT and the ACT, pick the SAT.

The four ACT tests cover English, mathematics, reading, and science reasoning. The test is three and a half hours long and is given five times—in October, December, February, April, and June. For information about the ACT, visit their website, www.act.org. The student should take the ACT in the spring of his junior year. For registration and location information, visit www.actstudent.org.

RESOURCES

Test Ordering Information

Check with your state home-education organization to find out which of these is accepted by your state. The following tests can be administered by parents under certain conditions:

California Achievement Test.
Order through the Independent Test Service of Christian Liberty Academy. This national test can be given by the parent. The test has to be mailed back to CLA, where it will be scored and returned. http://www .shopchristianliberty.com/special-service/

Comprehensive Test of Basic Skills.
Order from Seton School, and mail back to Seton for scoring and evaluation. Adds science, social science, and reference skills to the material tested by the other exams. http://www.setontesting.com/

43

※

WHERE'S THE TEAM?
ATHLETICS AT HOME

Serious sport has nothing to do with fair play. It is bound up with
hatred, jealousy, boastfulness, disregard of all rules . . . it is war minus
the shooting.

—George Orwell, "The Sporting Spirit"

Can home schoolers play team sports? It depends on what you mean.
If your teenager has a good chance of becoming a professional basketball or football player, home schooling probably isn't a good option.
There's simply no foolproof way to plug a home-schooled student into the
pro-sports assembly line that starts in high school.

But student athletes who are serious contenders for a professional team
sports career make up a very small segment of the total high-school population. For the average, academically inclined teenager, we think the question of organized team sports has gotten too much emphasis. How many
students will find that team sports make up an important part of life after
high school? And even in a regular school, very few students are actually
able to play regularly on official teams.

However, home schoolers can make arrangements to take part in team
sports. Church and community leagues often welcome home schoolers—

call your local Parks and Recreation office for information on community leagues. Check the bulletin boards at local sports stores to find out about special-interest sports groups and small clubs; many of these are family-oriented and welcome all ages. Youth groups such as Little League, 4-H, Scouts, Camp Fire, and Civil Air Patrol sponsor sports teams.

Home-school support groups, particularly in areas where home schooling is popular, sponsor teams especially for home schoolers. Call several local support groups (your state home-schooling organization can give you names and numbers), and find out whether any of them has put a basketball, baseball, or soccer team together. (If no one has, you can always start your own.) Your state organization may also know of home-school teams; some states have organized statewide home-school leagues.

Private schools, especially smaller ones, are often willing to allow home schoolers to play on school teams. If no one's ever asked to do this before, suggest that your child try it for a few weeks on a trial basis.

As in other high-school subjects, use your community-college resources for older students. A teenaged home schooler can enroll for physical-education (or kinesiology) classes. This can lead to team participation once the student becomes familiar with the coaches and sports staff.

Some states make specific provisions for home-schooled students to participate in public-school sports. Call your state organization and ask what the existing policy is. In many states, there's no official policy—you'll simply need to approach your school district and ask whether your child can participate. However, if you've taken your child out of school to avoid a destructive social environment, this obviously is not a good choice. A more relaxed approach to physical education is simply making sure that your children exercise every day, from kindergarten through twelfth grade. In elementary and middle school, play games together at least twice a week (we've suggested three good books on children's games in the Resources at the end of this chapter). Jessie concentrated on general physical fitness and on sports skills that could be honed either individually or without a large team of people: running (Susan ran a half marathon at thirteen), cycling (her brother trained alone or with Mom "drafting" him in the station wagon), horseback riding, tennis, golf, handball, swimming. All are suitable for individual recreation as well as for competition, if the student enjoys the challenge.

Walking is free (except for good shoes) and can be done alone or with a friend or sibling. Aerobics can be done in a regular class or with a home video. Pickup games of basketball, softball, and soccer with family and friends teach basic games-playing skills. Activities such as hiking, karate, skating, skiing, swimming, dancing (folk, ethnic, ballroom, classical, modern), and weight training can be learned privately. Investigate classes at your local community recreation center; generally, these are offered for a wide range of ages and levels. Clubs and gyms offer instruction in martial arts, gymnastics, fencing, and other sports or skills.

As described in Chapter 39, the high-school student should, for at least two years, keep a log of hours spent doing physical activity, including in the log brief descriptions of the activity itself and the skills practiced and mastered. These logs can serve as the basis for credits awarded for physical education. The student must devote 120 hours per year to doing physical activity in order to earn 1 unit of credit; 2 units are required for high-school graduation.

Another kind of physical activity that is often overlooked is physical work, which builds muscles as well as character. Jessie's home schoolers cut grass, gardened, took care of animals (carrying feed and water in freezing weather as well as cleaning their living quarters), and hired themselves out to trusted friends and neighbors for housework and yardwork.

RESOURCES

Bailey, Guy. *The Ultimate Homeschool Physical Education Game Book*. Columbus, OH: Educator's Press, 2003.
$19.95.

Maguire, Jack. *Hopscotch, Hangman, Hot Potato, and Ha, Ha, Ha: A Rulebook of Children's Games*. New York: Touchstone, 1990.
$15. A classic with rules for all the active kids' games your child would play in elementary and middle-school PE.

Wise, Debra. *Great Big Book of Children's Games*. New York: McGraw-Hill, 2003.
$17. Dozens more games.

44

THE LOCAL SCHOOL:
DEALING WITH YOUR
SCHOOL SYSTEM

Out of sight, out of mind.
—Proverb

Most home schoolers find that the easiest way to deal with their local school system is simply to stay out of sight once the legal formalities have been completed. Many local schools are cooperative and friendly to home schoolers. But we've also heard of a few instances where local school systems, in cooperation with social-services personnel, have interfered in family life, taken away parental authority, and sometimes even removed children from homes even though no abuse has occurred—only differences in philosophy or opinion over how a child should be educated.

For this reason, many home-schooling parents are wary of using public-school facilities and programs. When a home-schooled child becomes part of a public-school class or activity, she's placed under the jurisdiction of public-school authorities, who may take the opportunity to investigate the home-based part of the child's education.

Be careful, but don't assume the worst about your local schools. Assume what is most frequently the truth—that your local school officials want to make sure that you're providing a quality education at home. The best way to avoid any trouble is to comply fully with all state laws about notification, testing, and record keeping. Although some states offer a "religious exemption" clause for home schoolers—this excuses you from any accountability to the state on the ground that such accountability will violate your conscience—we do not encourage you to take this option. It is possible that you may have to prove in court that your definition of "religious exemption" is the same as that of your school authorities.

Don't draw attention to yourself or encourage retaliation by openly attacking and criticizing your local schools. If you want to change your school, you need to keep your child enrolled and bring about change from the inside. But if you've decided to invest your own time in educating your child, make the transition from public school to home school as quietly as possible. Be polite and respectful. Realize that public schools provide a valuable service to the community and to those who can't home-school. Your energies should now go toward creating an excellent education at home and not toward establishing an adversarial relationship with your school system. School systems in areas where home schooling is common will be well acquainted with the law. In other places, schools may simply be unaware of the legal right to home-school. If your officials protest that you can't home-school, or if they tell you that public-school authority extends to all children of school age whether they're enrolled or not, they may be operating from a position of ignorance. Get a copy of your state law from your state home-school organization, and bring it to all meetings.

School officials need to see that you're using a good curriculum, that you're having your child properly tested, that the child is involved in outside activities, and that you're keeping decent academic records. You'll save yourself trouble if you create a "founding document" for your home school—a brief paper with the following sections:

1. Your educational background and any teaching experience or professional capabilities that support your ability to tutor your child at home.
2. Your philosophy of education—in other words, an explanation of

why you're teaching at home. If you're convinced that your child needs a religious education that outside schools can't provide, say so. If you're working toward academic excellence in a one-on-one, tutorial-based environment, put that down, too. You can use our explanation of the three stages of the trivium in Chapter 2 as part of your educational-philosophy statement.

3. The legal requirements of the state—notification, record keeping, testing—and how you plan to meet them.

Every year, write up a summary of your educational plans, complete with titles of texts. (You may not need this, but if you're questioned, having it on hand will add to your credibility.) You can use the "At a Glance" sections we've provided in the epilogue to each part, which summarize the program of study and the time spent on each subject. Add specific basic text titles, and you have a summary that should satisfy any school system. Be faithful about keeping the notebooks we describe. These prove that your child is doing good, continual work in every subject.

Some school systems happily allow parents to home-school, even encouraging home schoolers to take part in the system's programs, labs, and sports. If you want to participate in selected school activities, approach the local school. If no home schooler has ever made such a request, the school might not have a policy in place. Suggest participation on a trial basis. If the arrangement works out, the school will probably create a policy favorable to home schoolers. Be aware, though, that using your public-school system for anything invariably opens the rest of your home program to closer scrutiny.

It's an unfortunate truth that some school systems attempt to exclude parents from the educational process because they view education as the sole responsibility of the state. Other schools may be afflicted by a single zealous social worker out to prove that home-schooled kids are socially deprived. Join your state home-school organization for support and good advice. Parents experienced in home schooling unanimously agree that you should not allow social workers or school officials to tour your home even if they show up at the door. Sometimes, one phone call from a neighbor who notices your kids in the backyard will trigger a social-services visit. Even in states where legal restrictions on home schoolers are relaxed, a home visit from a social worker can land you in a morass of legal problems. You're not legally required to let anyone into your home who doesn't have a search warrant. Furthermore, denying access won't prejudice any legal system against you.

But these situations are rare. In most cases, diplomacy and good record keeping will resolve any difficulties. Collect any favorable newspaper and magazine reports about home schooling and use them for PR when you talk to your local officials. If you can, get to know your school-board members. And always ask for access as though you're requesting a privilege, not demanding a right.

45

YELLING FOR HELP:
TUTORS, ONLINE RESOURCES, DISTANCE
LEARNING, COOPERATIVE CLASSES, AND
COLLEGES AND UNIVERSITIES

Two heads are better than one.
—Proverb

In the early grades, parents serve as the child's primary teacher. Any literate parent can master the basics of an academic subject well enough to teach it to an elementary or middle-school child.

Parents are accustomed to using private teachers for music, gymnastics, or any other subject that requires a high degree of accomplishment. Upper-level academic subjects are no different. When your home-schooled student develops proficiency in a field of study, you may want to enlist help for further work.

"Outsourcing" is one of the secrets of success for high school at home. Tutors, online services, and distance learning courses all preserve the strengths of home schooling—flexibility, one-on-one attention, expertise above and beyond that permitted by a normal high-school curriculum—

while eliminating its one weakness—parental ignorance of the subject at hand. Cooperative and college classes give the student a chance to get used to the classroom environment, while still following a home-based program. And the student also gets a needed break from working with Mom and Dad.

TUTORS

Throughout Parts I through III, we've mentioned the use of a private tutor for certain subjects. You can employ a tutor for one-on-one work in a subject you're not comfortable teaching or simply to give yourself (and the student) a change of pace. Jessie used tutors for high-school math, foreign language, art, and music. She suggests the following for finding tutors and for supervising the work:

- Local colleges are a good source of help. Don't advertise for a tutor. Instead, call the department of the subject you want tutored and ask for recommendations. Make sure that the person you speak to (the chairman of the department or the departmental secretary) knows the age of the student you want tutored. Accomplished scholars aren't always good teachers, and you want someone who's patient and comfortable with your child's skill level. Also, ask what the going rate for private tutoring is. Expect to pay an hourly rate of $10 for a student to $20 or more for a professor. Schedule sessions for once a week, and make sure the tutor gives the child assignments to complete before the next session.
- If you use a college student, make sure your tutor is the same gender as the child. This eliminates the embarrassment factor between child and tutor (especially as the child moves into adolescence).
- Supervise tutorials. Any time a child is in an intimate, one-on-one setting with an older person who has a measure of authority, the potential for abuse exists. Jessie always made sure that tutorials took place in a public setting (the university student center), and she stayed in sight (sitting on the side of the room and catching up on paperwork or reading while the tutorial took place). Don't leave a child at the

tutor's house; wait in an adjoining room instead. This provides protection for the student as well as the tutor.

- Private schools are another good source for tutors. Private-school teachers are often happy to supplement their income by tutoring home schoolers. Expect to pay a little more than you would for a college student.
- Junior- and senior-high-school students (recommended by their teachers) are quite capable of tutoring elementary and middle-grade students.
- If you're in an active home-school community, older home schoolers may also be willing to work with younger students. Our advice about supervision still applies.
- Continue to keep an eye on the child's work. You're still responsible for issuing a grade (for high-school students) or for proving to your local school superintendent that reasonable progress has been made in the subject being studied.

ONLINE RESOURCES

Live, online classes with highly qualified instructors who lecture, grade, and evaluate are widely available. For an updated list of recommended online academies with links to course offerings and sample lectures, visit welltrainedmind.com.

CORRESPONDENCE SCHOOLS

A number of universities and private schools offer correspondence courses in dozens of subjects. The advantage of correspondence is that your student gets a detailed outline, course information, step-by-step instruction, and an official grade. The disadvantage is that correspondence courses lock you into inflexible schedules and particular texts. The best way to decide whether you want to use correspondence courses is to visit each college's website and examine its offerings. See welltrainedmind.com for a directory.

COOPERATIVE CLASSES

In many areas, home-school groups have set up cooperative classes taught by parents with particular knowledge or skills. Parents of home schoolers include doctors, lawyers, aerospace engineers, diplomats, and university teachers, and these parents often organize cooperative classes in their areas of expertise. In larger cities, home schoolers have even set up "academies," where students can enroll for one, two, or three courses in exchange for a time donation from student and parent. Contact your local and state home-school organizations, and ask what resources are already in place.

Even if you don't find a formal group, don't overlook the possibility of swapping with another home-school parent. If you were a math major in college but hated grammar, you can probably find a parent with a degree in English but few math skills and teach each other's children in your respective areas of expertise. This works best when the children are of similar age and ability. And if you can make this arrangement with another home-school family you trust, you can reduce the workload for both sets of parents since you will each only have to prepare for one class rather than two.

COMMUNITY COLLEGES AND LOCAL UNIVERSITIES

Community colleges and university classes are usually open to home schoolers. Community colleges are the easiest to deal with. Just call the Office of the Registrar, and ask about enrolling your high-school student in one or two classes. Universities often offer a "concurrent" program, which allows high-school students to take a class or two per semester for high-school credit. The registrar will be able to steer you toward the proper contact.

Do remember, though, that high-school students on a college campus are vulnerable—they're younger than the other students and more uncertain. Supervise attendance. You don't have to sit in on the class, but it's probably not a good idea to leave a high-school student on campus for hours alone. Also, try to make an appointment with the professor before classes start so that the student can meet the instructor face-to-face. This will reduce nervousness and give the instructor a chance to evaluate your student's readiness for college work.

46

GOING TO COLLEGE:
APPLICATIONS FOR
HOME SCHOOLERS

We favor well-prepared students wherever they attend school.
—Stanford Admissions Office

The education we describe in Parts I through III is college-preparatory. College isn't for everyone, but a student who plans on a white-collar or intellectual job should go to college. The possession of a college degree has risen in importance over the last decades as the value of a high-school diploma has dropped.

According to the National Center for Home Education, 93 percent of colleges polled in a recent study were willing to accept course descriptions or portfolios instead of a high-school diploma.[1] Some universities will always look at nontraditional work with suspicion; state universities will occasionally take an inflexible stand. But as the home-schooling wave

---

[1] Christopher J. Klicka, *Home Students Excel in College*, rev. ed. (Washington, DC: National Center for Home Education, 1998), p. 1.

continues to swell, more and more colleges are growing accustomed to home-school applications.

Generally, we favor smaller schools; we've noticed that home schoolers do better in a more intimate environment in their first two years away from home. Small schools also may be more likely than large schools to extend a welcome to home schoolers, with their nontraditional preparation and nonstandardized transcripts. But home education is now so widely accepted that home-school students should feel free to apply anywhere. (Susan has, so far, graduated three sons from home school, and all three were admitted to different, well-regarded Virginia public universities.)

PLANNING FOR COLLEGE

Many parents and students don't think about a high-school program until eighth grade. But if college is a goal for your child, you should begin preparation for a college-track program in middle school (grades 5 and 6). Critical-thinking courses, research projects, elementary Latin, and modern foreign language—all of these are college-readiness courses. Ideally, the college-bound student will begin Algebra I no later than eighth grade in preparation for the SAT and ACT. The minimum math requirement for a college-prep program is Algebra I, completed in ninth grade, and a course in geometry, completed before the PSATs given in the fall of the eleventh-grade year. Latin increases vocabulary scores and general reading and grammar skills. Since students who do well on the SATs have read widely for the previous ten years, the middle-grade student should develop the habit of reading, rather than constantly watching TV or playing computer games.

Although the program outlined in Part III should be more than adequate for any set of college admission requirements, you should still get a catalog from prospective colleges before ninth grade in order to find out their requirements and to make sure that your high-school program includes these courses.

Jessie suggests the following timetable for parents and students thinking of college:

Grades 5–6	Plan a math sequence that will finish up Algebra II and geometry by PSAT time. Also plan to complete the Vocabulary from Classical Roots series, the courses in logic, and at least two years of Latin before taking the PSAT.
Grades 7–8	Start requesting college catalogs to find out what high-school requirements you must fulfill in grades 9–12. (See "Choosing a College," pages 773–774.)
Grade 9	Ask prospective colleges what form they prefer home-school admissions to take—a transcript, a portfolio, and so forth. That way, you can start to keep your high-school records in an orderly manner. If you're not sure, just keep good records so that you can be flexible when application time comes. *Keep a transcript, even if your colleges don't require it.* You never know when you might need one.
Grade 10	Find out from a local public- or private-school guidance counselor when the PSAT will be given (in the fall of the eleventh-grade year) and how to preregister. The PSAT can be taken any time from eighth grade on and as many times as you wish. But if you're interested in a National Merit scholarship, take it only once—in the eleventh-grade year. Start working daily through an SAT preparation guide as though you were teaching an extra course.
Grade 11	Register for the SAT, which will be taken in the fall of the twelfth-grade year. Continue working daily through the SAT preparation guide. Visit colleges, and zero in on choices. Call admissions offices; find out when they start taking applications for early decision and regular admissions and how to apply for financial aid. Early applications produce better aid packages than last-minute submissions.

Investigate taking classes for college credit. Some colleges allow students who take college courses during their senior year to apply these credits to the freshman year.

These classes also prove that your student is capable of doing college work.

Grade 12   Take the SATs. Complete the college application forms. Submit these forms and the financial-aid forms as soon as possible. If the college conducts interviews, practice role-play interviews. Use a guide to job interviews to check on basic skills (dress nicely, make eye contact, shake hands).

CHOOSING A COLLEGE

After sending her own children to college—and after years of counseling other home schoolers—Jessie strongly advises parents to exercise their judgment (and economic leverage) to steer high-school students away from making college decisions that might sabotage their mental, physical, social, or spiritual health. Your shy eleventh grader may think that he wants to live in a freshman dorm at a twenty-thousand-student state university. But if you believe he should spend two years at a smaller school and then transfer, limit his options to those that are acceptable to you. One of the saddest statements we ever heard was from a mother who told Jessie, "I spent forty thousand dollars to ruin my daughter's life." She had let her daughter make all the choices about college, despite her own serious misgivings.

Over the last fifteen years, Jessie has observed that home-schooled students who flourish both academically and personally keep close ties with family, make dear and valuable friends, and adjust well to the demands of college. These students invariably attend small colleges that have a moral and religious climate similar to that found at home. Many large universities have big, unrestricted dormitories, where bedlam reigns and there is no check on adolescent behavior. Your student may be both mature and responsible. But if he's forced to live on a floor filled with noisy, immature students who stay up until 2 A.M. dropping firecrackers down the toilets or having all-night concerts in the hall (as in the freshman dorm that Susan's brother lived in), he probably won't flourish.

Don't let financial need scare you off. Private universities often have better financial-aid packages than large state universities. Small religious schools can dig up funds for worthy students from unexpected places. And the student who cannot complete a desired major at a small school can always transfer after sophomore year. If you think this might be the way to go, call the college that the student is thinking of transferring to and find out which courses will transfer.

Start the college search by talking to friends, relatives, and other home schoolers about college experiences, both positive and negative. Consult the most recent guides to colleges to narrow your search to the colleges with the academic specialties, geographic location, and campus climate that you're looking for.

THE APPLICATION PROCESS

Find out what colleges need to see from home-schooled students by visiting the admissions web page; if you can't find the information, call and ask for it. Some want transcripts; others ask for a listing of courses, projects, and books read; still others will examine a complete portfolio. Find out whether financial aid requires a diploma (financial-aid forms and admissions applications generally go to two different offices).

It's always good to take at least two subject tests in addition to the SAT, especially if the student tests well.

According to the College Board, a transcript isn't necessary for college admissions. Nevertheless, many of the college admissions officers we spoke to were overworked and didn't want to plow through portfolios. "Send us a standard transcript form," one admissions office told us. So take that transcript seriously. A good transcript plus standardized scores will serve as the foundation of your college application.

An application will give your student room to describe areas of interest, extracurricular activities, and any special research projects she's done. Maximize the application by using the lines set aside for interests, activities, and clubs to emphasize language accomplishments and Great Books studies. Make sure to describe the junior and senior thesis projects, which will set your student apart from most high-school students. List all community-service projects—anything she has volunteered for that benefits others.

Many colleges have an "early decision" process where the student agrees to enroll in that college if accepted. Then the senior year of high school can be finished with an assured fall acceptance. If you're interested in early decision, make sure to ask about the application deadline (it differs from the regular deadline).

If your student is interested in college sports, call the Home School Legal Defense Association, and ask for the packet that assists home schoolers in validating their completion of all initial eligibility requirements for the National Collegiate Athletic Association.

THE PORTFOLIO

If the college agrees to look at a portfolio (and many do), this will be your most persuasive tool.

What should be included in your student's portfolio?

1. A narrative description of the student's high-school studies. This is the place to explain the Great Books program.
2. A list of all significant books read (from about seventh grade on).
3. At least one writing sample.
4. A description of any academic contests and honors.
5. Descriptions of any apprenticeships, interesting work experiences, and internships.
6. A brief description of any special area of expertise.

ONE SUCCESSFUL APPLICATION

Home schooler Peggy Ahern's daughter was admitted to an Ivy League college. As well as the standard application, admissions essay, and SAT scores (including four SAT II subject-area tests), Peggy and her daughter submitted a thirty-two-page portfolio with the following eight sections:

1. *School Philosophy* A one-page statement written by Peggy about why she taught her daughter at home, including her summary of their use of the trivium.

2. *Character Profile* A brief assessment written by Peggy, using comments from teachers, friends, relatives, and siblings.

3. *Student Assessment of Home Schooling* A one-page critique written by Peggy's daughter of her home-school experience, including both positives and negatives.

4. *Curriculum Description* A narrative description of each course done in high school, written by Peggy. According to Peggy, this turned out to be thirteen pages long—much longer than necessary for most home schoolers.

5. *Teacher Evaluations* Copies of evaluations written by some of Peggy's daughter's other tutors.

6. *Sample Papers* Three papers written by Peggy's daughter. One is sufficient for most portfolios.

7. *Reading List* All the books read by Peggy's daughter since eighth grade.

8. *Music Achievement* Details of competitions, master classes, recitals, and a tape. Any major achievement could be similarly documented here.

Although Peggy and her daughter were successful in their Ivy League applications, Peggy isn't sure that a portfolio of this length will continue to be read by admissions officers—particularly if home-school applications continue to rise. We suggest that you follow Peggy's pattern, but make each section as brief as possible. And always call first to make sure that a portfolio submission is acceptable and what length is preferred.

Peggy adds these words on college preparation:

I realized that outside substantiation of her work was going to be particularly helpful when it came time to put together that transcript, and that good teacher recommendations would be invaluable. So for all four years, I actively sought out teachers for at least one or two subjects each year. I never found any locally, but did find some through correspondence and then later on through the Internet, all of whom developed enough of a relationship with her that they could have written recommendations. I think it is very wise for home schoolers to actively seek out and cultivate relationships with a few teachers. Further, if possible, I would recommend seeking out college-level teachers and courses for the student, even if it is not-for-credit, for several reasons:

1. A teacher who can vouch for the student's ability to handle college level work and to contribute in a meaningful way to class discussion will go a long way toward allaying certain admissions concerns.

2. A teacher who has been a part of the collegiate community will hopefully have a good idea of what sort of issues are typically addressed in these recommendations, how they're written and so forth, and therefore will do an effective job of it.

By the end of her four years, my daughter had a number of choices as to from whom she would seek her two recommendations. She and I really strategized at this point. We knew that any of these teachers would highly recommend her. But several of them had stand-out writing skills as well as long-term experience in higher education, and we knew that their high recommendations would likely be far more effective than those of her other options. I think it is a fair conclusion that these two recommendations played a very major role in her acceptance.

A WORD ABOUT EARLY ADMISSIONS

Many home schoolers finish their high-school studies early. It's been our experience that students are better off spending the extra time before college by studying and reading while working at an internship, apprenticeship, or other meaningful job. Maturity can't be forced—students who go to college early are more likely to founder socially, academically, or spiritually. There's no rush. So stay at home. Read, work, write, study, enjoy life. And go to college with everyone else your age. You'll be that much better prepared.

RESOURCES

Guides to Application Procedures

Creating Your High School Portfolio, 3rd ed. Indianapolis, IN: Jist Works, 2009. $19.95. A useful workbook that leads students through many of the steps involved in writing essays, choosing a major, and making up a resume.

Gelb, Alan. *Conquering the College Admissions Essay in 10 Steps: Crafting a Winning Personal Statement,* 2nd ed. Berkeley, CA: Ten Speed Press, 2013.
$11.99

Metcalfe, Linda. *How to Say It to Get into the College of Your Choice: Application, Essay, and Interview Strategies to Get You the Big Envelope.* Upper Saddle River, NJ: Prentice Hall, 2007.
$15.95. The problem with most books about college applications—including this one—is that they cultivate an unnecessary sense of panic; getting into any particular college is partly (sometimes almost entirely) a matter of luck, and it is a huge mistake to spend too much time fretting and planning instead of learning. However, there are good tips in this book. Just don't get sucked into the panic.

47

WORKING: APPRENTICESHIPS
AND OTHER JOBS

Employment is nature's physician, and is essential to
human happiness.

—Galen

Because of their flexibility of schedule, home-educated students have
more opportunity to work at meaningful jobs. They're not limited to
the typical after-school and summer routine of fast-food and retail service.
We encourage you to think of high-school employment not as jobs, but
as apprenticeships—preparation for a career. If financial pressures allow,
it's always better for a student to take a low-paying or nonpaying apprenticeship or internship that gives her training and experience in important
job skills than for her to make more money waiting tables. The classical
approach to education emphasizes long-range goals over short-term satis-
factions. The student who is so busy making money that she can't prepare
for worthwhile work as an adult is substituting quick pleasure for long-
term gain.

Of course, many students need to make money for college. But if you
can involve your child in training and apprenticeship work early, you can

improve the money-making skills she'll need for college summers. The student who takes an unpaid position at a computer firm, learning consulting, will make much more money in the summer after her freshman year than the student who works a paying retail job in high school.

Be creative when looking for job opportunities. Network with friends and relatives. Do you know a computer consultant, a newspaper editor, or an electrician? Ask whether your teen can do a six-week internship to learn about the business. When the internship is over, if the student has an interest, ask whether she can stay for three more months. If she becomes substantially more skilled and begins to contribute to the business, that's the time to broach the subject of pay.

Even before beginning this process, encourage your young teen to ask questions about the jobs that relatives and neighbors have. What do you like about your work? What do you dislike? What's the most important skill you have? What skills do you wish you had? How did you get this job? What preparation would I need to get it? What's your daily schedule like? These questions will help the thirteen- or fourteen-year-old begin to think of her own interests and skills in terms of employment.

Also assign the fourteen- or fifteen-year-old regular reading in the career and employment books written for young people. Ask your local librarian to guide you toward age-appropriate career books. Reading through these books now, before work has become a pressing issue for the student, makes career planning a fun exercise in thinking through possibilities.

For older teens, look for series such as Careers in Focus and Career Opportunities. Most teens don't have any idea of the variety of jobs that are available. The classic job-hunter's manual *What Color Is Your Parachute? A Practical Manual for Job Hunters and Career Changers,* by Richard Bolles, has sections on developing interests, looking for specific jobs, interviews, and more. Your library will also have the most recent guides to internships for junior- and senior-high-school students.

Every high-school student should also spend some time reading through newspaper and magazine want ads. These provide a valuable look at the sorts of jobs that are available and the qualifications needed to land them.

A crucial part of skill development is learning to do home chores responsibly. Prepare your student for successful internships and apprenticeships by assigning regular work at home and allowing her to work for neighbors and friends as soon as you feel that she's mature enough to do a good job.

Volunteer work is also important. It develops skills and experience, and often opens the door to paid jobs later on.

If your high-school senior has no particular interest in a field of study and no burning career plans, don't push her straight into college. Let her take a year or two off to work. College will still be there when she's ready to go. And she may discover, through an apprenticeship or internship, a career that doesn't require a college degree.

RESOURCES

Bolles, Richard. *What Color Is Your Parachute? 2015: A Practical Manual for Job Hunters and Career Changers*. Berkeley, CA: Ten Speed Press, 2014.
Directed at adults and older teens. One of the most popular resources for job-seekers.

———. *What Color Is Your Parachute for Teens: Discovering Yourself, Defining Your Future*, 3rd ed. Berkeley, CA: Ten Speed Press, 2015.

Career Opportunities in . . . series. New York: McGraw-Hill.
Each book describes a number of career paths open to students who have particular skills.

Ferguson's Careers in Focus series. Chicago: Ferguson Publishing.
A whole range of books, each describing the aspects of a single career.

Sher, Barbara. *I Could Do Anything If I Only Knew What It Was: How to Discover What You Really Want and How to Get It*. New York: Dell, 1995.
Written for adults, but helpful for older teens who are beginning to think through their options.

48

THE FINAL WORD:
STARTING IN THE MIDDLE

Finally, what if you're starting to home-educate a third grader or fifth grader or tenth grader? Generally speaking, it's better to go quickly through foundational materials (such as basic grammar, pre-algebra, or beginning logic) than to start using material that will frustrate a student. The following are some general guidelines to help you find your child's place in the classical curriculum. Check the Resources section of the appropriate chapters for information on the teaching/learning apparatuses mentioned here. Throughout this book, we have given suggestions for how to start history, science, languages, and other subjects "in the middle." Refer to each chapter for these detailed directions. In addition, keep the following principles in mind:

Reading	If a student is having difficulty reading, *start at the beginning*. Use a beginning primer to review basic phonetic

reading. When it comes to reading, many children stumble because they've never been taught the principles of phonics. As a matter of fact, phonics is often used remedially even by those school systems that take a whole-language approach in the classroom. Jessie has done beginning phonics with eighth graders; the earlier pages are easy and build confidence, while the later pages improve both reading and spelling skills.

Grammar Most grammar programs can be begun on grade level; the texts we recommend all start with a detailed review of material that should have been learned in previous years.

Writing Students who struggle with writing should begin with the dictation and narration exercises described in Chapter 5, and progress from that point—no matter how old they are.

Math If you know your child's grade level, the chapters on mathematics should give you the information you need to select a text. If you're not sure what level your child is working on, most programs offer a diagnostic test.

Logic Always begin with the lowest level of logic and move forward.

Languages Unless a student has a particular interest in a modern language, we recommend doing at least a year of Latin as the first foreign language. It greatly simplifies the learning of other languages.

History Begin history with whichever year you please. Use whichever resources are age-appropriate and continue forward chronologically from that point. See Chapters 7 and 17 for more details.

Science You can choose whichever science fits into your curriculum.

Great Books As with history, begin the Great Books curriculum in any year and progress up to the present. See Chapter 27.

Research paper Do *not* begin a research paper with a student who isn't ready. Before doing the research paper, the student should complete at least a year of systematic grammar and short writing assignments; he should also be comfortable with the outlining process. It's fine to wait until eleventh (or even twelfth) grade for the research paper, if you have catch-up work to do.

What if you're home-schooling two children or more? We suggest that you keep each child doing individual, grade-level work in mathematics, grammar, writing, spelling, and vocabulary. The content areas—history, science, reading—can be done simultaneously with children of different ages. If you have a fifth grader and an eighth grader, don't drive yourself insane by doing ancient history, ancient readings, modern history, modern readings, biology, and physics. Synchronize their schedules so that both students are doing ancient history, ancient readings, and biology. You'll still have to get two sets of books, differing in complexity and reading level, but at least you'll be covering the same basic material with each child. The same is true of a first grader and a third grader, or a seventh grader and a ninth grader. Require more writing, a higher level of difficulty in reading and experimentation, and more complex outlines from the older student. If one student goes through the four-year history cycle two and a quarter times, while the other goes through it three times, it will affect neither their academic achievement nor the quality of their lives.

APPENDIX

TAKING AN ORAL HISTORY

This is a simplified version of the "Oral History Interview Outline" developed by Judith Ledbetter for the Charles City County Historical Society. Thanks to them for their help.

Record the name of the interviewer, the date, the time, and the place of the interview.

Record the name and a general description of the interview subject.

1. When and where were you born?
   a. Names of parents, parents' occupations.
   b. Siblings?
   c. Birth assisted by doctor or midwife?
2. What are your earliest memories about food and meals?
3. What do you remember about school?
   a. Transportation to school.

b. School buildings.

c. Subjects taught.

d. Teachers.

e. Discipline, sports, extracurricular activities.

4. How did you spend time outside of school? What kinds of games did you play? What chores did you do?

5. Were you sick in childhood? What illnesses did you have? Who was your doctor, and what was he or she like?

6. How did you travel (foot, horse, wagon, auto, bus, train, boat)?

7. Tell me about holidays when you were small—birthdays, religious holidays, Thanksgiving. Did your family have any special days?

8. What religion did your family observe? How did you observe it?

9. Do you remember going fishing/hunting, farming, gardening, or getting food in other ways?

10. What stores were near you? What were post offices like? How about banks? Where did people go for entertainment?

11. What stories do you remember your parents, grandparents, or other older people telling?

    a. Slavery, Civil War, Reconstruction.

    b. Bootleggers, stills, illegal activities, Prohibition.

    c. Woman's suffrage.

    d. World War I.

    e. The flu epidemic of 1917–1918.

    f. Ghosts or other paranormal happenings.

    g. Sensational crimes (lynchings, murders, fires, etc.).

    h. Racial relations—white/black, white/Indian, black/Indian, etc.

12. What do you remember about the Great Depression?

13. What do you remember about segregation in schools and other public places? How about other kinds of discrimination?

14. Do you remember when electricity/telephone service first came to your house?

15. What do you remember about World War II?

    a. Service in the armed forces.

    b. Friends or relatives who lost lives.

    c. Rationing.

    d. Precautions (e.g., blackout curtains, school drills, bomb shelters, etc.).

e. News stories about the war.

f. Letters to and from home.

16. When did you get married? What was your courtship like? How was it different from current traditions?

17. When were your children born? Where? Were they born in a hospital or at home?

18. What do you remember about the Korean conflict? Were you affected by it?

19. What do you remember about the Civil Rights movement?

    a. *Brown v. Board of Education.*

    b. Passage of the Voting Rights Act.

    c. Passage of the Fair Housing Act.

    d. The death of Martin Luther King, Jr.

20. What do you remember about the assassination of President Kennedy? Of Robert Kennedy's assassination?

21. What do you remember about the Vietnam War? Did it have an effect on your hometown?

22. Could you describe the jobs you've held during your lifetime—your responsibilities, skills, the working conditions, the pay and benefits?

23. How has life changed the most since you were a child?

INDEX